Advances in Distributed and Parallel Knowledge Discovery

Advances in Distributed and Parallel Knowledge Discovery

Edited by

Hillol Kargupta and Philip Chan

AAAI Press / The MIT Press
Menlo Park, California • Cambridge, Massachusetts • London, England

Copublished and distributed by The MIT Press,
Massachusetts Institute of Technology,
Cambridge, Massachusetts, and London, England.

ISBN 0-262-61155-4

Library of Congress Cataloging-in-Publication Data

Kargupta, Hillol, 1967–
Advances in distributed and parallel knowledge discovery / edited by Hillol Kargupta and Philip Chan.
p. cm.
Includes bibliographical references and index.
ISBN 0-262-61155-4
1. Electronic data processing – Distributed processing. 2. Parallel processing (Electronic computers). 3. Database searching. I. Chan, Philip, 1964– II.Title.
QA76.9.D5 K348 2000
004′.35–dc21 00–026879
CIP

This book was set in Times Roman
by The AAAI Press and manufactured in Canada

10 9 8 7 6 5 4 3 2 1

To Mom, Dad, Disha, Rinku, and Angar
– Hillol Kargupta

To my parents
– Philip Chan

Contents

Part II: Distributed Data Mining Techniques

Part III: Architectural, Security, and Data Issues in Distributed Data Mining

Contributors

Rakesh Agrawal, *IBM Almaden Research Center* (ragrawal@almaden.ibm.com)
Khaled AlSabti, *King Saud University* (alsabti@ccis.ksu.edu.sa)
Stuart Bailey, *University of Illinois at Chicago* (sbailey@uic.edu)
Philip K. Chan, *Florida Institute of Technology* (pkc@cs.fit.edu)
David Cheung, *University of Hong Kong* (dcheung@csis.hku.hk)
Vincent Cho, *Hong Kong Polytechnic University* (msvcho@polyu.edu.hk)
Joydeep Ghosh, *University of Texas, Austin* (ghosh@ece.utexas.edu)
Robert Grossman, *University of Illinois at Chicago and Magnify, Inc.* (rlg@magnify.com)
Yi-ke Guo, *Imperial College* (y.guo@ic.ac.uk)
Srinath Gutti, *University of Illinois at Chicago* (sgutti2@uic.edu)
John Hale, *University of Tulsa* (john-hale@utulsa.edu)
John Hall, *Hewlett Packard Company* (john_hall2@am.exch.hp.com)
Daryl Hershberger, *Washington State University* (darylh@andrew.cmu.edu)
Ching-Tien Ho, *IBM Almaden Research Center* (ho@almaden.ibm.com)
Erik L. Johnson, *Washington State University* (erikj@wsunix.wsu.edu)
Chris Jones, *Washington State University* (cjones@eecs.wsu.edu)
Chandrika Kamath, *Lawrence Livermore National Laboratory* (kamath2@llnl.gov)
Hillol Kargupta, *Washington State University* (hillol@eecs.wsu.edu)
Vipin Kumar, *University of Minnesota* (kumar@cs.umn.edu)
Charles Lo, *Hong Kong Polytechnic University* (cschamlo@comp.polyu.edu.hk)
Balinder Malhi, *University of Illinois at Chicago*
Ron Musick, *Lawrence Livermore National Laboratory* (musick2@llnl.gov)
Vincent Ng, *Hong Kong Polytechnic University* (cstyng@comp.polyu.edu.hk)
Byung-Hoon Park, *Washington State University* (bhpark@eecs.wsu.edu)
Srinivasan Parthasarathy, *University of Rochester* (srini@cs.rochester.edu)
Andreas L. Prodromidis, *Columbia University* (andreas@cs.columbia.edu)
Foster Provost, *New York University* (fprovost@stern.nyu.edu)
Joshua Pun, *Hong Kong University of Science and Technology* (punjcc@cs.ust.hk)
Ashok Ramu, *University of Illinois at Chicago*
Sanjay Ranka, *University of Florida* (ranka@cise.ufl.edu)
Mahesh K. Sreenivas, *Microsoft Corporation* (maheshs@microsoft.com)
Salvatore J. Stolfo, *Columbia University* (sal@cs.columbia.edu)
Ramesh Subramonian, *Intel Corporation* (subramon@gomez.sc.intel.com)
Janjao Sutiwaraphun, *Imperial College* (j.sutiwaraphun@ic.ac.uk)
Kagan Tumer, *NASA Ames Research Center* (kagan@ptolemy.arc.nasa.gov)
Andrei Turinsky, *University of Illinois at Chicago*
Beat Wüthrich, *Hong Kong University of Science and Technology* (beat@cs.ust.hk)
Mohammed J. Zaki, *Rensselaer Polytechnic Institute* (zaki@cs.rpi.edu)
Jian Zhang, *Hong Kong University of Science and Technology* (jzhang@cs.ust.hk)

Foreword

Explosive growth in the availability of various kinds of data has resulted in an unprecedented opportunity to develop automated data-driven techniques for discovering knowledge. The field of knowledge discovery builds upon the ideas from diverse fields such as machine learning, pattern recognition, statistics, database systems, and data visualization. But, techniques developed in these traditional disciplines are often unsuitable due to some unique characteristics of today's data-sets. Often times, the data is naturally distributed, and cannot be made available in a centralized location due to bandwidth limitations or security/privacy considerations. In such cases, knowledge discovery techniques need to be developed that can work with distributed data. The huge size of the available data-sets and their high-dimensionality in many emerging applications can make knowledge discovery computationally very demanding, to an extent that parallel computing can become an essential component of the solution.

This book is an outstanding resource for anyone interested in learning about the state-of-the-art in parallel or distributed knowledge discovery. Chapters are written by experts in the field, and include both introductory tutorial-style chapters as well as those that contain in-depth descriptions of state-of-the-art techniques, algorithms, and systems. Chapters on distributed knowledge discovery discuss a variety of methods for aggregating multiple data models, actual systems, as well as results on real, large and distributed data sets. Chapters on parallel knowledge discovery cover techniques for reduction in I/O time for accessing disk-resident data as well as parallel formulations of association mining and classification algorithms. Topics covered range from discussion of issues such as scalability, privacy, security, and data quality, to actual practical applications such as credit card fraud detection and analysis of stock market data.

I greatly enjoyed reading this book, and recommend it highly.

– *Vipin Kumar,* University of Minnesota

Preface

Efficient technology for extracting useful and interesting knowledge from data is a necessity for managing the overwhelming amount of information available today. Knowledge discovery in databases (KDD) deals with this issue. It primarily relies on different statistical and machine learning techniques for identifying the trends, associative dependencies, clusters, classifiers, and other kinds of patterns. Unfortunately, most of these techniques for data analysis and modeling were developed in an era when computing was quite different from what it is today. At least two important aspects of computing emerged in the last couple of decades. First of all, communication has become an integral part of computation. Second, the amount of available information is becoming increasingly overwhelming.

Modern KDD needs to address these developments. Most of the existing KDD systems still use statistical and machine learning algorithms that were primarily designed for monolithic sequential computing architectures. Development of knowledge discovery techniques for distributed environments is very important for the future of KDD. Distributed knowledge discovery (DKD) addresses this issue. Scaling up the speed of a KDD process is also important for managing large, voluminous data within a short period of time. Parallel knowledge discovery (PKD) addresses this aspect of KDD. In the near future, a successful KDD system will have to deliver scalable performance in a large, distributed computing environment with voluminous data. Therefore, both DKD and PKD are likely to play an extremely important role in the future.

The need for this book emerged after the first one-day workshop on distributed data mining, held during the Fourth International Conference on KDD,

1998 in New York City. The workshop brought together the critical group of researchers and practitioners who helped crystallizing the field of DKD. This book contains extended versions of the selected papers from the workshop and several other contributions.

This book compiles the recent advances in distributed and parallel knowledge discovery (DPKD). To help interested researchers and practitioners who are not familiar with the field, we begin with an introductory article and a part on articles surveying the research area of DPKD. Two separate parts are devoted to distributed and parallel data mining techniques. Another part focus on architectural, security, and data issues, which are important in complementing the data mining techniques for the entire knowledge discovery process. We conclude the book with an article on additional resources that are useful for further exploration and some thoughts on interesting problems DPKD may face in the near future.

Before concluding this prologue we would like to point out the synonymous use of the terms *knowledge discovery* and *data mining* in this book. While we understand some researchers promote the subtle differences between these two terms, we also note the growing use of the term data mining for the complete knowledge discovery process by many authors, including the contributors in this volume. Our choice of knowledge discovery instead of data mining for part of the title of this book reflects this observation and the historical precedence that we discuss in the introduction of this book.

We are grateful to the reviewers for making the several rounds of reviews possible. We would also like to thank the American Association for Artificial Intelligence and the MIT Press for actively engaging in the publication of this book, and Intel Corporation and Magnify Inc. for supporting the 1998 workshop. Additional thanks goes to Kakali Sarkar, Susan Wallen, and the School of EECS, Washington State University. Philip Chan acknowledges the support from Florida Institute of Technology.

– Hillol Kargupta and Philip Chan

Distributed and Parallel Data Mining: A Brief Introduction

Hillol Kargupta and Philip Chan

Introduction

The field of knowledge discovery and data mining emerged in the recent past as a result of the dramatic evolution of the technology for information storage, access, and analysis. The philosophical motivation behind this development can be better appreciated by noting other similar developments in modern civilization. For example, consider the problem of documenting thoughts and events. It is a classical problem that existed even during the prehistoric days. Early civilizations developed techniques such as cave paintings and hieroglyphs for this purpose. The fundamental problem is still very relevant. However, now it has a different shape with many new dimensions. Today we deal with a lot more information; events are more complex; thoughts are supposedly more involved. These developments call for new perspectives and techniques. As a result, we had to abandon the cave painting approach and start developing the practice of desktop publishing, multi-media publishing for the Internet, and so forth. There exist many such domains like transportation, farming and others where we needed new technology for dealing with the new facets of problems that challenged human civilization from its inception.

Data mining also shares a similar flavor. It deals with the problem of discovering unknown patterns from data. Discovery of unknown knowledge from data of course requires an existing perception of what is known. It also calls for exploration of knowledge, and its comparison with the existing perception for identifying new discovery. Statistics, information theory, and machine learning are a few examples of many different fields that address this problem. In general all these fields rely on data analysis and modeling techniques for capturing new and existing knowledge. However, the data analysis and modeling problem itself is evolving fast. For example, data analysis algorithms are no longer independent of the characteristics of the data storage, computing environment, and the human-computer interaction issues. The choice of a data analysis algorithm depends on whether or not the data set can be completely loaded in the memory. On the other hand algorithms that scale poorly to multiprocessors may be of little use in a high performance parallel computing environment. The data may be inherently distributed and difficult to aggregate to a single site. This requires algorithms that can correctly perform distributed data analysis. The human factor also plays an important role in modern data analysis. For example, data mining requires ratification of new knowledge as a useful, truly new discovery. To this day, this process depends heavily on the human intervention and this is likely to be so in the near future. As a result, interactive presentation of the explored knowledge and the user-feedback—in general the human-computer-interaction issues—play an important role in data analysis. The issue of data security is also extremely important and it imposes constraints on the architecture of the data analysis system. Data mining addresses these new emerging dimensions of data analysis and modeling. It still faces the core problem of data analysis and modeling, but in a new context.

Data mining is sometimes viewed as data analysis from large data sets. However, large data set issue should be viewed as only one aspect of the several emerging new dimensions of this field. This book adopts the bigger picture of data mining that considers dimensions like heterogeneous computing, large databases, security, and human-computer interaction in a common context—distributed data.

Some researchers view data mining (application of pattern learning algorithms to data) as a component of the overall knowledge discovery from data (KDD) process which includes pre and post-processing of data in addition to data mining. However, there also exists a large body of literature where this distinction is smeared and the term *data mining* is used for representing the complete KDD process. Almost synonymous use of the terms *data mining* and *knowledge discovery* appears to be gaining popularity. Therefore, whenever appropriate we shall also use the terms distributed and parallel data min-

Account number	Amount	Location	Previous record	Unusual transaction
11992346	99.84	Seattle	Good	No
12993339	29.33	Seattle	Good	Yes
45633341	34.89	Portland	Okay	No
55564999	980.00	Spokane	Good	Yes

Table 1: Homogeneous case: Site A with a table for credit card transaction records.

Account number	Amount	Location	Previous record	Unusual transaction
87992364	20.00	Chicago	Good	No
67845921	447.34	Urbana	Good	Yes
85621341	19.78	Chicago	Okay	No
95345998	800.00	Peoria	bad	Yes

Table 2: Homogeneous case: Site B with a table for credit card transaction records.

ing to imply the full KDD process in the distributed and parallel environment respectively.

On a nostalgic note, before the term *data mining* was coined, the field has been using the term *knowledge discovery*. Knowledge discovery in databases (KDD) was the title of a series of workshops, which evolved into the current series of conferences. Though the full title of the conference is now "Knowledge Discovery and Data Mining," the conference's acronym is still KDD. Our choice of the term *knowledge discovery* instead of *data mining* as part of the title of this book reflects this historical anecdote.

Distributed and Parallel Data Mining

Distributed data mining (DDM) is a result of further evolution of the data mining technology. DDM embraces the growing trend of merging computation with communication. It considers all the new dimensions of the data mining process in the context of the emerging distributed computing environments. DDM accepts the fact that data may be inherently distributed among different loosely coupled sites connected by a network and the sites may have heterogeneous data. It offers techniques to discover new knowledge through distributed data analysis and modeling using minimal communication of data.

DDM must deal with different possibilities of data distribution. Different sites may contain data for a common set of features of the problem domain. In case of relational data this would mean consistent database schemas across all the sites. This is the homogeneous case. Tables 1 and 2 illustrate this case

City	Temp.	Humidity	Wind Chill
Lewiston	37	64%	35
Spokane	38	55%	37
Seattle	48	93%	46
Portland	47	89%	44
Vancouver	46	94%	35

City	State	Size	Average earning	Teen population
Lewiston	ID	Small	Low	5K
Spokane	WA	Medium	Medium	30K
Seattle	WA	Large	High	250K
Portland	OR	Large	High	200K
Vancouver	BC	Medium	Medium	199K

Table 3: Heterogeneous case: Site X with two tables, one for weather and the other for demography.

State	Movie	Rating	Current ticket Sale (In millions)
WA	Hyper Space	A+	6
OR	Yes I Do	A+	5
ID	Once Upon A Time	B-	2
BC	The King And The Liar	B+	8
CA	The Shepard	A-	10

Table 4: Heterogeneous case: Site Y with one table for box office statistics.

using an example from credit card transaction domain.[1] There are two data sites A and B, connected by a network. The data mining objective is to find patterns of fraudulent transactions. Note that both the tables have the same schema. Even if the data sites share a common schema they may not have data with the same underlying distribution. This may offer more challenges to the homogeneous DDM technology.

The data sites may also be heterogeneous. In other words, sites may contain data for different features. Let us illustrate this case again with relational data. Table 3 shows two data-tables at site X. The table on the left contains weather-related data and the one on the right contains demographic data. Table 4 shows the content of site Y that contains box office data. The objective of the data mining process is to detect relations between the ticket sales and the demographic and weather related features.

Consider the large databases available in the Internet. There already exist

[1] Please note that the credit card domain may not always have consistent schema. The domain is used just for illustration.

sites for weather, city demography, and box office sales information in the world wide web. If the databases are large it will become nearly impractical to download everything from each site and then to build the global data model. In the case of credit card problem such transfer of data in large amount may cause security problems. In general such a centralized approach may not scale up in a loosely coupled distributed environment. Instead it will be very nice if we can still build a correct global model by simply downloading partial data models and possibly a small fraction of the actual data from each site.

DDM promises to offer exactly that. It notes that communication of large amount of data over the network and the centralized architecture is primarily responsible for the bottleneck. So it performs partial analysis of data at individual sites and sends out the outcome to other sites. Typically a small fraction of data is also moved. This subset of data is sometimes required to correctly aggregate the partial results together and to validate the resulting global outcome. DDM replaces communication of large amount of distributed data by that of tuples (*partial model, data subset*). This saves communication overhead, offers better scalability, requires minimal communication of possibly secured data, and sometimes offers the only feasible way to mine distributed data sets.

Public data sets in the Internet, corporate databases in an intranet, mobile computing environments, and distributed collection of sensor data for situation monitoring are only a few of many possible applications of DDM. In short, if a data analysis application deals with a distributed computing environment then DDM may offer better scalability, increased data security, and improved response time compared to its centralized counterpart. The field is new and there are many issues that need to be explored before DDM is ready for practice. Most of the existing statistical and machine learning-based data analysis algorithms were originally developed for centralized data. These techniques need to be modified for handling the distributed case. Particularly more algorithm development work is needed for the general case when the sites are heterogeneous. Architectural issues and communication protocols need to be further explored. The human-computer interaction issues become more complex in DDM. In a distributed environment evaluation of the discovered knowledge and the feedback may also take place in a distributed fashion. This requires development of collaborative problem-solving technology for DDM applications. Data preprocessing in DDM is also an important issue. We need further development of problem decomposition techniques, feature selection algorithms, and data quality evaluation techniques for DDM.

DDM becomes a necessity when the large data sets are inherently distributed over a network with a limited bandwidth. However, when the network is very fast and the host computers are tightly coupled DDM can be approached from the traditional perspective of parallel computing. This approach is particularly useful when the data sets are large and data analysis is computationally intensive. Large data sets are common in many business and scientific applications. Satellite images, transaction records, and simulation results are some common sources of large data sets. High performance parallel computing environments are often used for quick access and manipulation of such data sets. Therefore, it makes sense to exploit such computing environments for scaling up the data mining process. Parallel data mining (PDM) does that. PDM can be practiced using either a coarse-grained or a fine-grained approach. The former approach discovers knowledge from distributed data using a collection of loosely coupled algorithms. This approach significantly overlaps with the field of DDM. The fine-grained approach is suitable for tightly coupled system. In this book we present PDM from the latter perspective since the former will be covered by the chapters on DDM.

There are two dominant approaches for utilizing multiple processors: *distributed memory* machine (DMM), in which each processor has a private memory and communication takes place via message-passing; and *shared memory* (SMP), in which all processors access common memory and communication takes place via shared variables. A shared memory architecture offers programming simplicity, but the finite bandwidth of a common bus can limit scalability. A distributed memory, message-passing architecture cures the scalability problem by eliminating the bus, but at the cost of programming simplicity. A third paradigm, combining the best of both the distributed and shared memory approaches is becoming increasingly popular. Clusters of SMP workstations fall in this mixed paradigm.

The objectives of parallel data mining change depending on the underlying architecture. In distributed-memory systems synchronization is implicit in message passing, so the goal becomes communication optimization. For shared-memory systems, synchronization happens via locks and barriers, and the goal is to minimize these points. Data decomposition is very important for distributed memory, but not for shared memory. While parallel I/O is relatively free in DMM, it can be problematic for SMP machines, which typically serialize I/O. The main challenge for obtaining good performance on DMM is to find a good data decomposition among the nodes, and to minimize communication. For SMP the objectives are to achieve good *data locality*, i.e., maximize accesses to local cache, and to avoid/reduce *false sharing*, i.e., minimize the ping-pong effect where multiple processors may be trying to modify different variables which coincidentally reside on the same cache line. A common objective is to achieve a good load balance, i.e., each processor should have an equal amount of work.

There are two main paradigms for exploiting algorithm parallelism: Data and Task Parallelism. For data mining, data parallelism corresponds to the case where the database is partitioned among different processors. Each processor works on its local partition of the database, but performs the same computation such as constructing a global decision tree in classification, or counting the same candidate sets in association mining. Task parallelism corresponds to the case where the processors perform different computations independently, such as counting a disjoint set of candidates or constructing separate subtrees, but have/need access to the entire database.

PDM using either of these two or the hybrid approach needs extensive development. Development of data analysis algorithms that offer minimal disk I/O and easy parallelization is of critical interest. Dynamic switching from task to data parallel approach, data preprocessing, and evaluation techniques for parallel data mining environments also need more attention.

Fine-grained PDM may offer scalable performance through task or data parallelism or a combination of both. Task parallel data mining involves parallelization of the procedures for data preprocessing, analysis, and postprocessing. This approach solves different components of the data mining technique independently and coordinates them as needed for putting together the final solution. On the other hand, the data parallel approach requires partitioning data among different nodes and contributing each node to share the execution of the data mining process for the partitioned data sets.

Both of these fields are growing rapidly. The advances in these fields have already started influencing the practice of data mining. Several KDD businesses are starting to adopt this emerging technology. This book puts together a collection of chapters that represents the state-of-the-art in DDM and PDM in many ways.

Content of this Book

This book introduces the reader to the field of distributed and parallel data mining, presents extensive reviews of the field, and offers in depth perspectives on the state-of-the-art techniques. The contributing chapters of the book are discussed in the following. The Overview of Distributed and Parallel Data Mining section introduces the reader to the existing literature on DDM and PDM. The Distributed Data Mining Techniques section presents different DDM techniques for homogeneous and heterogeneous environments. The Systems and Data Issues section discusses different architectural and data preprocessing issues in DDM. The Parallel Data Mining section presents several state-of-the-art PDM techniques.

Overview of Distributed and Parallel Data Mining

Foster Provost presents an overview of the field of DDM in chapter 1, with a focus on distributed data mining (DDM) techniques. His presentation first approaches DDM from the scalability point of view. He argues that DDM may play a key role in scaling up data mining algorithms for large applications. He reviews the existing literature from this perspective. Next he extends the case for DDM beyond the scalability issue. He points out that DDM offers a more natural way to view data mining in many real-life computing environment where coalescing distributed databases offer a major challenge.

Preprocessing and subsequent mining of large data sets are often time consuming. Since parallel databases are typically used for storing large business and scientific data sets, development of high performance algorithms using both fine and coarse-grained parallelism is important. This is a rapidly growing research area with strong interests from the practitioners. In chapter 2, Chandrika Kamath and Ron Musick present an overview of this field. They mainly focus on fine-grained parallelism. The chapter offers an extensive review of the different techniques for both data preparation and data analysis in tightly-coupled multiprocessors machines.

Distributed Data Mining Techniques

Andreas Prodromidis, Philip Chan, and Salvatore Stolfo overview, in chapter 3, the issues and techniques addressed by the Java agents for metalearning (JAM) research project. The JAM system allows data at distributed hosts to be mined by diverse learning algorithms and the resulting models be combined by learning ("metalearning") from the learned models' behavior. Issues and techniques discussed include scaling to large amounts of data by distributing subsets to different host, resolving incompatibility in data schemata by "bridging" attributes, adapting to concept drift by selecting temporally relevant models, preventing performance degradation due to data skewness by adjusting their distributions, and increasing execution efficiency by pruning redundant models. They evaluated these techniques on detecting fraudulent behavior in a large number of credit card transactions at two banks.

Yi-ke Guo and Janjao Sutiwaraphun present in chapter 4 the knowledge probing approach that deals with DDM from homogeneous data sites. This technique is similar to metalearning. However, this approach is particularly designed for inducing descriptive data model from the predictions of black box classifiers learned in a distributed environment.

In chapter 5, Hillol Kargupta, Byung-Hoon Park, Daryl Hershberger, and Erik Johnson introduce the collective data mining (CDM) framework for addressing data mining from distributed, heterogeneous sites. Most of the existing techniques for multiple model aggregation are applicable only when the data sites are homogeneous. However, there exist many real life application domains where sites are heterogeneous. They show that naive application of existing data mining techniques for local data analysis may result in incorrect and ambiguous outcome. The CDM framework guarantees correct local analysis and correct aggregation of local data models with minimal data communication. It blends theory of communication with statistics and machine learning. They discuss extension of CDM for wavelet-based polynomial regression and Fourier representation-based decision tree construction. They also report the ongoing work on the BODHI system for distributed knowledge discovery.

Kagan Tumer and Joydeep Ghosh propose, in chapter 6, a new order statistics-based approach for aggregating multiple data models. This approach is particularly useful for DDM from heterogeneous data sites. As shown in the chapter by Kargupta et al., local analysis of data in a heterogeneous environment may produce models that are far from perfect. This is likely to introduce high variance in the performance of different models. Aggregation of such models calls for robust statistical techniques. Order statistics offers a useful technique to do so. This chapter analytically shows that in general the ith order statistics improves the classification performance. It also introduces the trim and spread combiners that are based on linear combinations of the ordered classified outputs.

Vincent Ng, David Cheung, and Charles Lo address, in chapter 7, the problem of efficiently mining association rules constrained by numeric inequalities in a parallel and distributed environment. The proposed FDM technique reduces the communication overhead of exchanging statistics on candidate sets by generating fewer candidate sets and pruning candidate sets locally and globally. Three methods were introduced to generate candidate sets according to certain inequality constraints. The Incremental algorithm is a simple extension of FDM. The DCDM algorithm allows more asynchronous processing among the host. The DMI algorithm uses the inequality constraints to reduce the number of generated candidate sets. Experiments were performed to compare the developed methods in two different networked computing environments.

Systems and Data Issues in Distributed Data Mining

In chapter 8 Srinivasan Parthasarathy and Ramesh Subramonian present a SIMD DOALL primitive that was implemented on a network of workstations. This primitive can reduce the complexity of parallel programming in a distributed environment. They also introduce resource-aware (or affinity) scheduling algorithms for assigning tasks to processors to improve load balancing. In resource-aware scheduling, the scheduler considers resources (e.g., content of local caches) available at each processor in assigning tasks. Scheduling algorithms that make decisions based on only local information and global status were proposed and analyzed. They empirically evaluated their DOALL primitive and scheduling algorithms on two-dimensional discretization and clustering tasks.

Robert Grossman, Stuart Bailey, Ashok Ramu, Balinder Malhi, and Andrei Turinsky took a "macro" view of distributed data mining and implemented preliminary versions of a wide-area DDM system called *Papyrus* in chapter 9. Clusters of data and compute hosts form the whole system that is distributed across different sites (some sites are in different countries). Performance characteristics for inter and intracluster communication are considered in determining whether data, models, or results are transferred to achieve high efficiency. On top of the clustered hosts, the three functional layers: data warehouse, data mining, and predictive modeling are constructed. Various tools like a persistent object manager called PTool, a modeling language called Predictive Model Markup Language (PMML), a model manager called Anubis, and an object transportation layer named Bast were devised to facilitate the local data mining and wide-area combining processes.

In chapter 10, Chris Jones, John Hall and John Hale review existing security techniques and proposed general guidelines for distributed data mining. Their guidelines include identifying risks that are acceptable and unacceptable, being "paranoid" in setting security policies, stating explicitly the assumptions about the security of the computing environment, understanding which security measures are practical, and utilizing existing security technologies. Issues in authentication, authorization, nonrepudiation of mining agents to protect the hosts are discussed. In addition, issues in secure communication and safeguarding agent state and code to protect the agents are described.

Beat Wüthrich, Vincent Cho, Joshua Pun, and Jian Zhang attempt in chapter 11 to tackle the problem of selecting data sources that are relevant to the mining task from a pool of distributed repositories. For each data source, their approach first estimates the conditional probabilities of all possible classes given an instance. Correct classification and large differences in the posteriors indicate the corresponding data source is of high quality. They use a k-cluster approach (similar to a weighted k-nearest-neighbor algorithm) to combine the posterior estimates of multiple data sources. Choosing a subset of relevant data sources is achieved by a greedy method of iteratively adding a data source that maximizes the gain in performance to the selected set until performance does not improve. A final mining step uses the selected data sources to build the overall model using a rule-based algorithm. The researchers evaluated their approach on finding relevant sources of financial news that are used to mine stock market models.

Parallel Data Mining

Mahesh Sreenivas, Khaled AlSabti and Sanjay Ranka present, in chapter 12, parallel I/O techniques that reduce I/O time for accessing large amounts of disk-resident data in binary tree classification algorithms. They explored mixed parallelism by considering data parallelism for constructing large nodes and task parallelism for small nodes where each node is assigned to a processor. A threshold is used to switch from data parallelism to task parallelism. For determining a splitting point for numeric attributes, a replicated method and a distributed method were introduced for the communication of statistics among processors in large nodes. Then a subset of "alive" intervals are identified at each processor. Local splitting points with the lowest GINI are located and the globally best splitting point is found via min-reduction. Systematic experiments were performed to observe the effects of different thresholds on parallel runtime and the influence of different configurations on the amount of I/O needed.

Mohammed Zaki explores hierarchical parallel techniques for finding frequent itemsets in mining association rules in chapter 13. He uses a lattice-theoretic approach to represent the space of frequent itemsets and partitions it into smaller subspaces (sublattices) for parallel processing. Each node in the lattice represents one of the possible itemsets. Prefix-based and maximal-clique-based schemes are proposed to partition the lattice space of frequent itemsets. Search direction for enumerating frequent itemsets in each subspace can be bottom-up, top-down, or hybrid. His techniques require only two database scans. This chapter presents and evaluates four parallel algorithms based on the different combinations of partitioning schemes and search directions. It experimentally compares the four algorithms with the existing Count Distribution algorithm on different configurations and amounts of data.

In chapter 14, Mohammed Zaki, Ching-Tien Ho, and Rakesh Agrawal introduce parallel techniques for binary tree classification algorithms on shared-memory multiprocessor systems. An attribute list is built for each attribute and it provides an index of attribute values to records in the data set. Based on the attribute lists, count matrices are generated, which are then used in functions for splitting nodes. After the winning split attribute is determined, the data as well as the attribute lists are partitioned. They propose two general approaches to explore parallelism: data (intratree-node) and task (intertree-node) parallelism. In intratree-node parallelism they investigate concurrently evaluating the different attributes at each node. Scheduling algorithms for assigning attribute evaluations to processors and management schemes for disk-resident attribute lists are examined. In intertree-node parallelism they explore building subtrees in parallel. A queue-based scheduling algorithm for assigning subtree construction is investigated. They systematically evaluate their techniques on different number of processors, number of records, and configurations.

In the final chapter, Hillol Kargupta, Chandrika Kamath, and Philip Chan take a closer look at the roots and the developments of the distributed and parallel data mining technology. They note the growing interest in these areas and sketch some of the exciting applications that we may see in the near future. At the end, they also provide a list of web sites that may be useful for readers.

These chapters present several important dimensions of the field of distributed and parallel data mining. We hope that this book will consolidate the field and advance it by attracting creative minds to this emerging area.

Acknowledgments

We are grateful to Mohammed Zaki for his insightful comments and contribution to the portion of this article on parallel knowledge discovery. Hillol Kargupta would like to acknowledge support from the National Science Foundation Grant IIS-9803360 and the American Cancer Society. Philip Chan would like to acknowledge support from DARPA (F30602-96-1-0311).

Part I

Overviews

Chapter 1

Distributed Data Mining: Scaling Up and Beyond

Foster Provost

1.1 Introduction

Until recently, research on distributed data mining (DDM) has been motivated primarily by the desire to mine very large databases. Questioning how often it is necessary to mine huge databases, as opposed to mining a sample of the data, fuels an interesting debate—to which DDM researchers should pay heed. Nevertheless, it is clear that faster data mining sometimes is necessary. Its easy decomposability makes data mining an ideal candidate for parallel processing, and several lessons emerge from existing work.

Although scaling up is an important issue, it also is important for DDM research to look beyond scaling up, where many important research problems lie, relatively unaddressed. Thus, to counterbalance the existing body of work using DDM for scaling up, I argue that in many situations DDM is preferable to monolithic data mining. Databases *are* distributed. They are heterogeneous. They have privacy restrictions. There often are myriad databases, electronic documents, websites, etc., that might contain information relevant to a particular data mining problem. Building a monolithic database, in order to perform nondistributed data mining, may be infeasible or simply impossible. Hopefully this argument will give additional impetus to research in potentially fruitful areas: mining multitable databases, mining the web, mining with background knowledge, etc.

Viewing knowledge discovery as an inherently distributed activity makes existing data mining technology seem only narrowly applicable. Should not data mining algorithms be able to take advantage of all the data, information, and knowledge that is available only a mouse click away? Even a little of it? Currently, researchers are designing meta-data that will facilitate machine access to the vast universe of digital information. We should prepare for automated knowledge discovery.

1.1.1 Lessons from Scaling Up with DDM

The most common motivation for research on distributed data mining is the need to scale up to massive data sets. Because the run-time complexity of data mining typically is linear or worse in the total number of instances, massive data sets can be prohibitively expensive to mine unless attention is paid to scaling up. Besides simply having a massive data set, other motivations for fast data mining include: interactive induction (Buntine 1992), in which an inductive program and a human analyst interact in real time; mining multiple models and combining their predictions (Dietterich 1997); and wrapper approaches, which for a particular problem and algorithm iteratively search for feature subsets or good parameter settings (Kohavi and Sommerfield 1995),(Kohavi 1996), (Provost and Buchanan 1995), (Provost 1992). In addition to making many runs of a data mining program, experimenting with many machine-learning biases requires a large data set to avoid overfitting due to bias selection (DesJardins and Gordon 1995). Furthermore, in a wrapper approach, each evaluation may involve multiple runs to produce performance statistics (e.g., with cross-validation).

Venkat Kolluri and I recently (1999) surveyed the state of the art of scaling up decision-tree/rule induction. Four main ideas that emerge from existing work on distributed data mining are as follows.

Distributing the search space can be problematic. Doing so does not address directly the problem of massive data, and load balancing is difficult and costly. Shared-memory systems can alleviate the problems, because massive data transfers can be avoided.

Operating on distributed instances can be effective and very efficient, if centralized control is possible. The gathering of the statistics needed to evaluate a particular pattern (e.g., a rule) can be parallelized all the way down to the individual instances, providing tremendous speedups.

Using a distributed database management system (DBMS) to control the process is not completely straightforward. There are several ways of implementing data mining routines within a DBMS, each with its own tradeoff. Until flexible and effective DBMS mining routines are commonly available, mining within a DBMS will require specialized programming. Also, it has been observed that even with a fast database machine, mining database-resident data directly is often considerably slower than flat-file mining (Musick 1998).

Cooperation among distributed processes allows effective mining even without centralized control. Two main techniques for cooperation have been particularly effective. Processors can operate independently on subsets of the data, and then combine their models. A processor also can share potential knowledge as it is discovered, in order to get the opinions of the other processors (e.g., their statistical assessments).

In section 1.2 I will discuss and provide references to some instances of work based on these ideas.

1.1.2 Why Scale Up to Massive Data Sets?

Databases of customer, operations, scientific, and other sorts of data continue to grow rapidly (Fayyad, Piatetsky-Shapiro, and Smyth 1996). Both manual data mining and the direct application of today's mining techniques can be problematic when data sets exceed 100 megabytes (Provost and Kolluri 1997, Huber 1997). Huber (1997, p. 306) observes that "somewhere around data sizes of 100 megabytes or so, qualitatively new, very serious scaling problems begin to arise, both on the human and on the algorithmic side."

Scaling up is desirable, because increasing the size of the training set often increases the accuracy of induced classification models (Catlett 1991). In many cases, the degradation in accuracy when mining smaller samples stems from overfitting due to the need to allow the program to find *small disjuncts* (Holte, Acker, and Porter 1989), elements of a class description that cover few data items. In some domains, small disjuncts account for a large portion of the class description (Danyluk and Provost 1993). Overfitting from small data sets also may be due to the existence of a large number of features describing the data. Large feature sets increase the size of the space of models. Searching through and evaluating more candidate models increases the likelihood that, by chance, the program will find a model that fits the data well (Jensen and Cohen 1999), and thereby increases the need for larger data sets (Haussler 1988). Things get particularly difficult when there are many features *and* there is the need to find small disjuncts. Specifically, because large feature sets lead to large and often sparsely populated model spaces, a program biased to search for models covering special cases can be inundated with small disjuncts from among which it cannot choose.

Some data mining applications are concerned not with predictive modeling, but with the discovery of interesting knowledge from large databases. In such cases, increasing accuracy may not be a primary concern. However, scaling up nonetheless may be an issue. For example, finding small disjuncts often is of interest to scientists and business analysts, because small disjuncts may capture special cases that were unknown previously (the analysts often know the common cases). As with classifier induction, in order not to be swamped with spurious small disjuncts it is essential for a data set to be large enough to contain enough instances of each special case from which to generalize with confidence (Provost and Aronis 1996).

For all its theoretical considerations, the issue of scaling up is inherently pragmatic. For scaling up induction algorithms, the issue is not as much one of speeding up a slow algorithm as one of turning an impracticable algorithm into a practicable one. The crucial issue is seldom "how fast" you can run on a certain problem, but instead "how large" a problem can you feasibly deal with. Both time and space considerations are critical. Time- and space-complexity analyses should address asymptotic complexity as the numbers of instances and features grow. Also important, the absolute size of the main memory with which the computing platform is equipped should be considered. Almost all existing implementations of induction algorithms operate with the training set entirely in main memory; no matter what the computational complexity of the algorithm, if exceeding the main memory limitation leads to virtual memory thrashing, the algorithm will not scale well.

Finally, the goal of the data mining must be considered. Evaluating the effectiveness of a scaling technique becomes complicated if a degradation in the quality of induction is permitted. The vast majority of work on induction algorithms uses classification accuracy as the metric by which different algorithms are compared. In such cases, we are most interested in methods that scale up without a substantial decrease in accuracy. For problems that require mining regularities from the data for purposes other than classification, metrics should be chosen by which effectiveness can be measured (and compared) as the system scales up.

1.1.3 Is Subsampling Sufficient?

Before moving on discuss existing work more specifically, let me tarry a while on a point that often is not treated thoroughly enough in papers on scaling up to massive data sets.

Data sampling is well accepted by the statistics community, who observe that "a powerful computationally intense procedure operating on a subsample of the data may in fact provide superior accuracy than a less sophisticated one using the entire data base." (Friedman 1997). The question of scalability asks whether the algorithm can process large data sets efficiently, while building from them the best possible models. Thus, for anyone wanting to mine a large data set, an important question is: must I process the whole thing? Or will sampling be effective? The answer is: it depends on the data set and the algorithm. Just because a massive database exists does not imply necessarily that you have to mine it all. In practice, as the amount of data grows, the rate of increase in accuracy slows (Frey and Fisher 1999). Whether sampling will be effective depends on how dramatically the rate of increase slows. Also, different algorithms benefit from additional data to different degrees. For example, Harris-Jones and Haines (1997) observe that the learning curves of classic statistical algorithms tend to level off after relatively few data, in contrast to the learning curves of algorithms considered more typically by machine learning researchers.

Determining how much data to use is difficult, in general, because the smallest sufficient amount depends on factors not known a priori. For example, it depends on the minimum size of the special cases that must be discovered in order to model the phenomenon effectively. However, if one is willing to bias an algorithm (explicitly or implicitly) against finding very small special cases, then recent work on determining sufficient sample sizes for similar data mining problems provides relevant results. For example, Toivonen (1996) and Zaki, Parthasarathy, Li, and Ogihara (1997) discuss the determination of sufficient sample sizes for finding association rules that are no smaller than a predefined size, based on tolerances on the probability of error and the size of the error. A different view of sufficient sample size, that of *sample complexity*, is provided by Valiant's theoretical framework (Valiant 1984, Haussler 1988), which for a given hypothesis space allows the calculation of the number of instances sufficient for inducing with high probability a good approximation to the "true concept," if one exists in the hypothesis space. It should be noted that determining the sample size sufficient for induction may say little about how many examples are necessary in practice. Recent work has investigated systems that can determine empirically how many examples are necessary, by starting small and progressively sampling larger subsets until model performance no longer improves (John and Langley 1996; Provost, Jensen, and Oates 1999).

Published work provides differing views of how often real-world classifier learning curves level off before massive data sets are needed. Catlett's work shows that induction from subsets of data decreases accuracy. Despite the advantages of certain sampling strategies, viz., improving run times and improving the accuracy of the classifier over random sampling in noise-free domains, Catlett (1991) concludes that they are not a solution to the general problem of scaling up to very large data sets. However, it should be noted that at the time of Catlett's study, massive data sets were much smaller than they are today, and processing times much longer.

Oates and Jensen (1997) study inducing decision trees for nineteen data sets, and look specifically at the number of instances necessary before the learning curves reach a plateau. They regard a plateau to have been reached when an accuracy estimate is within a certain tolerance of the maximum (specifically, one percent, in their experiments). Surprisingly, for these nineteen data sets, an accuracy plateau is reached after relatively few training instances. The three data sets for which the most instances were needed were (from the UCI repository of Machine Learning Databases (Blake, Keogh, and Merz):[1] letter-recognition (17,000 instances), led-24 (4,500 instances), and census-income (9,768 instances).

In another recent study, Harris-Jones and Haines (1997) analyze the relationship between data-set size and accuracy for two large business data sets (up to 300,000 instances), by estimating learning curves empirically. They found that while some algorithms level off quite early, in some cases algorithms (decision-tree inducer C4.5 and its successor C5, in particular) continue to show accuracy increases across the entire range of data-set sizes. However, the improvements in accuracy at the upper size limit have become quite small, and it is difficult to conclude that they would continue with another order of magnitude increase in data-set size. Even if they would, it is important to question whether the benefit of further, diminishing improvements is worth the associated cost.[2]

Neither these results nor Catlett's provide ample justification for using DDM to scale up. Every data set in both studies would fit in the main memory of a modern desktop PC, and, given the existence of fast algorithms for mining monolithic data sets (Provost and Kolluri 1999) and the increasing speed of desktop computers, only under very tight time constraints would DDM be necessary.[3] Distributed data mining, as a field of study, would benefit from a few prominent examples of the need to scale up beyond reasonable main memory limits.

---

[1] http://www.ics.uci.edu/ mlearn/MLRepository.html

[2] Personal 1998 communication with T. L. Haines.

[3] In fact, the experiments of Harris-Jones and Haines were conducted on a dual-processor 133MHz Compaq computer with 256M RAM running Windows NT. The run time for C5 on 283,649 instances was fifty minutes (fifteen minutes for 99,303 instances).

1.2 Existing Methods for Scaling Up with Parallel Processing

Questions of necessity aside, data mining is an ideal application for parallel processing. The problem can be decomposed along many dimensions, often to a very fine granularity. The rich decomposability is illustrated by the variety of approaches that have seen success. Tight, fine-grained parallelization has succeeded for massively parallel machines. Coarser, looser coupling has succeeded for collections of stand-alone computers. With some approaches, the distributed processors act independently, only sharing their final results. With other approaches, they cooperate so that individual processors can obtain a global perspective.

1.2.1 Fine-Grained Parallelization

Fine-grained parallelization can take advantage of two types of decomposability: *search-space parallelization* and *parallel matching*. Data mining can be framed as the search of a very large space of patterns. In search-space parallelization, the space of patterns is decomposed and different processors search different portions in parallel (Cook and Holder 1990), similar to the parallelization of other forms of heuristic search (Kumar and Rao 1987, Rao and Kumar 1987). Load balancing and interprocess communication add additional complexity and overhead. Search-space parallelization should be particularly useful for data mining algorithms that perform massive search, such as the MetaDENDRAL-style, systematic-search rule learners (Buchanan and Mitchell 1978; Clearwater and Provost 1990; Smyth and Goodman 1992; Segal and Etzioni 1994; Webb 1995; Oates, Schmill, and Cohen 1997), and the experiments of Oates, Schmill and Cohen (1997) show that, indeed, speedups of nearly n can be obtained with n processors (they report results with $n = 2$ and $n = 3$). Mining Bayesian networks from data (Cooper and Herskovits 1992) also requires massive amounts of search, and Lam and Segre (1997) show that search-space parallelization can allow much larger networks to be found than with traditional, serial approaches.

In general, search-space parallelization does not address the problem of very large data sets, because each processor will have to deal with all the data or will have to subsample. However, recently Zaki, Ho, and Agrawal (1999b) have had success with search-space parallelization of a decision-tree learner; by taking advantage of a shared-memory multiprocessor, they are able to avoid replicating or communicating the entire data set among the processors. Using shared memory also allows the development of effective load-balancing techniques. Galal, Cook, and Holder (1998) recently have had success using search-space parallelism to scale up a scientific discovery system, dealing ef-

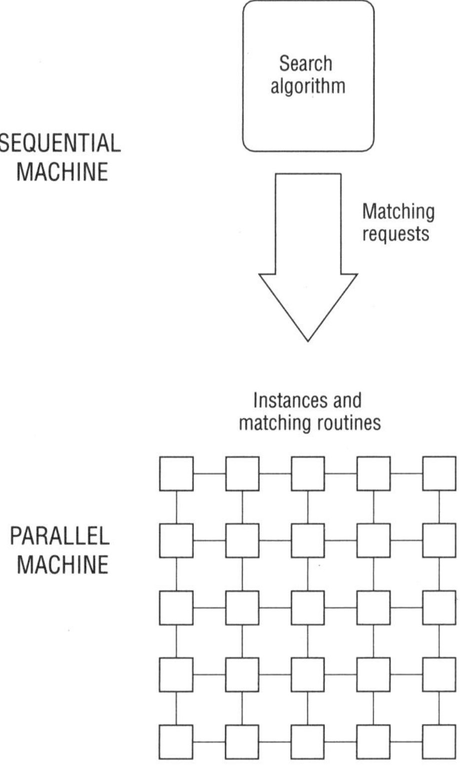

Figure 1.1: Parallel matching.

fectively with load balancing by having a master manage a priority queue of search nodes, serving them to the slaves as needed.

Massively parallel induction has been more successful when a finer-grained decomposition is used. Parallel matching is based on the observation that search for data mining is different from most other AI searches. In data mining the cost of evaluating a node in the search space is very high, but also is highly decomposable. Nodes (e.g., partial rules or decision tree branches) are hypothesized and each is matched against many instances to gather statistics. With parallel matching, depicted in figure 1.1, this compute-intensive matching process is parallelized by migrating the instance set and matching routines to a parallel machine, while the main induction algorithm (the *master*) may run on a sequential front end.

Parallel matching has been used by Lathrop, Webster, Smith, and Winston (1990), by Provost and Aronis (1996), and in the parallelization of the SPRINT algorithm (Shafer, Agrawal, and Mehta 1996). The former two efforts use a straightforward parallelization of the matching routines. SPRINT builds data structures called attribute lists, vertical partitions of the data set, used to facilitate efficient construction of decision trees. In the parallel implementation, each processor builds a sublist of each attribute list, and for each decision-tree node sends the master a portion of the statistics needed to determine the best split.

Impressive speedups are reported for parallel matching: less than a minute to mine one million instances on a CM-2 Connection Machine with 8192 bit-slice processors (Provost and Aronis 1996); 400 seconds to mine 1.6 million instances on an IBM SP2 with 16 processors (Shafer, Agrawal, and Mehta 1996).[4] Kufrin (1997) uses parallelization to speed up C4.5's transformation of decision trees to rules (C4.5rules), using parallel matching for two phases of rule-set postprocessing, and dividing up the rule set itself for a third. He also reports impressive speedups (efficiencies averaging more than 0.9 for four induction tasks and up to eight processors).

Zaki (1998) points out that shared-memory multiprocessor (SMP) systems are much more common than massively parallel machines. Motivated by this observation, he presents a parallel matching approach to the design of an SMP version of SPRINT. Instead of distributing the instances, vertical partitions corresponding to SPRINT's attribute lists are distributed and processed in parallel. The attribute lists are divided equally among the processors, which return the matching statistics to the master.

If the data already are resident in a data warehouse with a parallel infrastructure, parallel matching can be done by the existing database server (Freitas and Lavington 1996). This approach is fundamentally similar to that shown in figure 1.1, except the implementation-specific parallel data representation is replaced by an existing parallel database system. Also, for communication between the front- and back-end, implementation-specific matching requests are replaced with SQL queries. Parallel data mining is treated in more detail by Freitas and Lavington (1997) and by Provost and Kolluri (1999). Provost and Kolluri also discuss in more detail the use of database systems and SQL queries for scaling up.

1.2.2 Loosely Coupled Distributed Data Mining

The previous section addressed fine-grained decompositions, where parallelism is used to speed up existing data mining algorithms so that they feasibly can be run on massive data sets. Alternatively, the data can be partitioned, and mined by a loosely coupled collection of inductive algorithms. Data partition-

[4]These run times are given for illustration only. No comparison should be inferred.

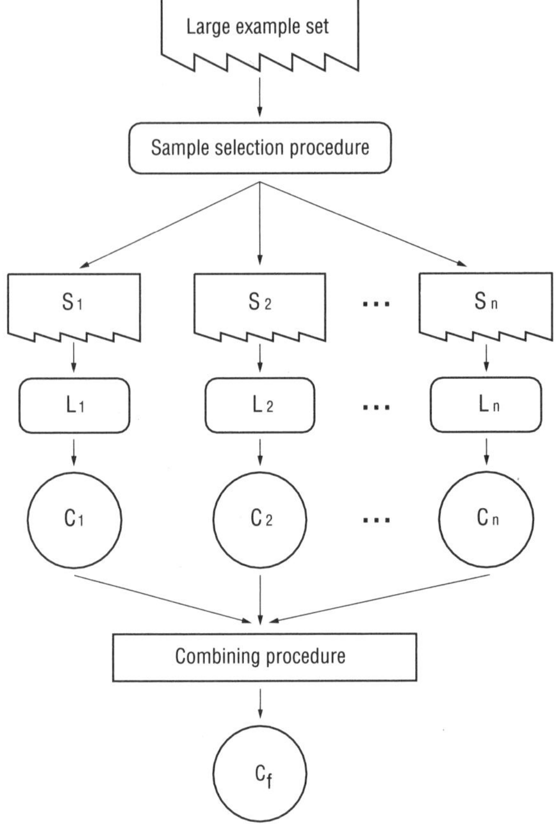

Figure 1.2: Mining partitioned data.

ing techniques separate subsets of instances or subsets of features; viewing the data set as a table, this corresponds to selecting rows versus selecting columns.

Figure 1.2 depicts a general model showing the similarities among partitioned data approaches. Systems using these approaches select subsets S_1, ..., S_n of the data based on a *selection procedure*. Data mining algorithms $L_1, \ldots, L_n$ are run on the corresponding subsets, producing concept descriptions $C_1, \ldots, C_n$. Then the concept descriptions are processed by a *combining procedure*, which either selects from among $C_1, \ldots, C_n$ or combines them to produce a final concept description (c_f)—the distributed data mining result. Loosely coupled systems differ in the particular procedures used for selection and combining. They also differ in the amount and style of interaction among the mining algorithms.

More precisely, figure 1.2 shows a model of *independent multi-sample mining*, because no interaction is depicted between the n mining runs; the C_i are formed independently, and then combined. Fayyad, Weir, and Djorgovski (1993) use a sequential version of independent multi-sample approach in which the L_i are decision-tree inducers; the C_i are rule sets extracted from the decision trees, and the combination procedure is a greedy covering algorithm.

Independent multi-sample mining can be distributed easily. Power is obtained through the combining procedure, which can take place as a sequential post-process, or can be parallelized (as by Kufrin 1997). Sikora and Shaw (1996) mine multiple rule sets in this manner; their combining procedure is a genetic algorithm. Hall, Chawla, and Bowyer (1998) discuss this approach for building decision trees. Similar to a distributed version of the approach of Fayyad and others, their system builds trees independently from partitioned data, and the trees are converted to rules. The rule sets are merged following the method described by Williams (1990), which resolves conflicts among similar rules.

D. Shasha and his research group[5] have implemented PC4.5, a parallel version of C4.5 (Quinlan 1993), which uses a simpler instantiation of the framework of figure 1.2. Specifically, each C_i is a decision tree built from a different subset of instances. The combining procedure evaluates each C_i on a subset of instances (disjoint from S_i), and chooses the one with the best accuracy as the final concept description.

Chan and Stolfo (1993c, 1996) take an independent multi-sample approach in which the L_i can be different induction algorithms, as well as separate instantiations of the same algorithm. Notably, their method forms C_f as a hybrid of the C_i. Instead of constructing C_f by combining selected pieces of the C_i, their approach combines the C_i whole, and makes predictions using a multiple-model, or *ensemble*, approach (Ali and Pazzani 1996). Domingos (1996a) also experiments with ensemble combining, finding it superior to taking a simple union of the C_i. The independent multi-sample approach also has been studied from the perspective of learning theory (Kearns and Seung 1995, Yamanishi 1997).

A potential problem with creating a multiple-model hybrid is the resulting loss of comprehensibility. Prodromidis and Stolfo (1998b) study several methods for evaluating, composing and pruning hybrid classifiers that reduce size while preserving or even improving predictive performance. A quite different approach to creating comprehensible classifiers from ensembles is taken by Craven (1996), by Domingos (1997b), and by Guo and Sutiwaraphun (1998). These authors take advantage of the ability to use machine-learning algorithms to induce understandable models of complex classification systems (Craven

[5] http://merv.cs.nyu.edu:8001/~binli/plinda

1996) (cf. Danyluk and Provost 1993). Specifically, they use the predictions of the ensemble as training labels, and induce from them a decision tree that models the hybrid's performance (with comparable accuracy). The resultant single tree is more understandable than the multiple-model hybrid.

Kargupta and others (Kargupta, Johnson, Sanseverino, Park, Silvestre, and Hershberger 1998b; Hersberger and Kargupta 1999; and chapter 5 in this book) consider distributed processing of vertically partitioned data (each processor has a subset of the features, rather than of the instances). Key to the approach is their use of an orthonormal basis-function representation; the coefficients for most of the basis functions can be determined from the partitions independently. If there are critical dependencies among variables that do not reside on the same processor, some communication is required. However, for many data sets the independently learned basis functions may comprise the majority of the function to be learned, and the communication needs will be small. To instantiate their method, they describe how to use various basis functions to build linear discriminant functions, linear regression models, and decision trees. This work relates to the suggestive prior work of Provost and Buchanan, who show that if the description language is modular, such that useful modules (in their case, rules) can be learned from many different feature subsets, then accurate class descriptions can be built without ever processing a single, suitable subset of features (Provost and Buchanan 1995).

Different from the fine-grained parallel approaches described in section 1.2.1, accuracy may be degraded with these partitioned-data techniques, as compared to running a single induction algorithm with all the data (if that were feasible).

1.2.3 Cooperative Distributed Data Mining

When multiple samples are being processed sequentially, it is possible to take advantage of knowledge mined in one iteration to guide mining in the next. Examples of sequential multi-sample mining techniques include windowing (Quinlan 1983, Fürnkranz 1998), incremental batch learning (Clearwate, Cheng, Hirsh, and Buchanan 1989, Provost and Buchanan 1995, Domingos 1996a, Wu and Lo 1998) and some wrapper-based methods for feature selection (Kohavi and John 1997, Kohavi 1996, Provost and Buchanan 1995, Provost 1992), all of which are described in more detail by Provost and Kolluri (1999). Figure 1.3 shows two approaches to *sequential multi-sample mining*. In *model-guided instance selection*, shown in figure 1.3(a), class description C_i is used in the selection of S_{i+1}. In *incremental batch learning*, shown in figure 1.3(b), class description C_i is taken as input to the data mining program and is used in building C_{i+1}.

Concurrency precludes the straightforward parallelization of partitioned

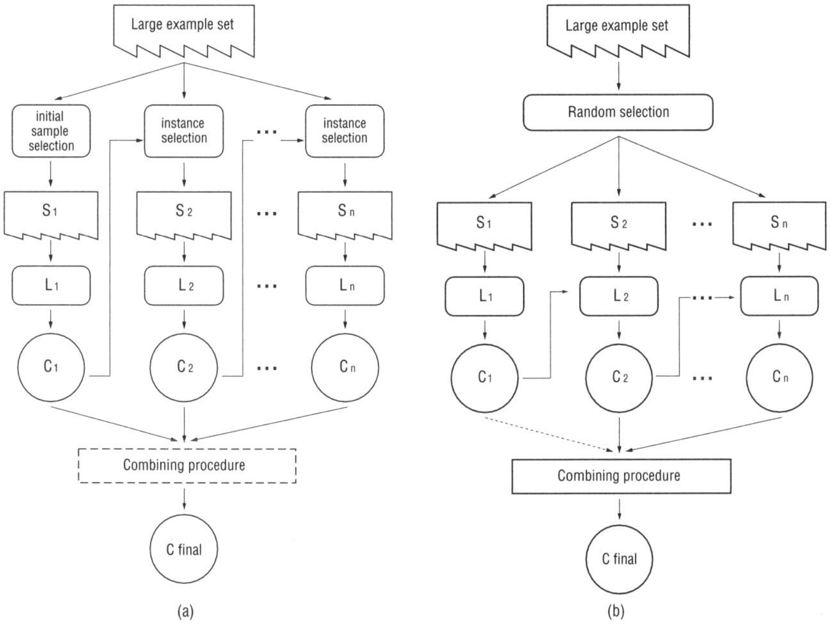

Figure 1.3: Sequential multisample mining (a) model-guided instance selection, and (b) incremental batch learning.

data approaches for which the results from one stage are required as input to the next. Therefore, partitioned-DDM must take a slightly different tack. Rather than assume that results are available before a stage begins, distributed algorithms can cooperate by sharing results as they become available (as depicted in figure 1.4). Since many mining algorithms operate naturally as anytime algorithms, producing some results very quickly and then more as time progresses, early in the DDM process there likely will be results that can act similarly to those passed from stage to stage in the sequential mode.

For distributed mining of rules and similar patterns, a useful observation is that certain evaluation metrics obey an *invariant-partitioning property* (Provost and Hennessy 1994, 1996). That is, every rule that is acceptable globally (using the entire data set) according to the metric, will be acceptable on at least one partition. This invariant-partitioning property holds, for example, for many variants of support and confidence (Provost and Hennessy 1994, 1996, Cheung, Han, Ng, Fu, and Fu 1996). By taking advantage of this property, a superset of the rules that satisfy the metric will be generated when all partitions are considered independently. The problem of finding the acceptable rules thus is reduced to selecting from this superset only those rules that are

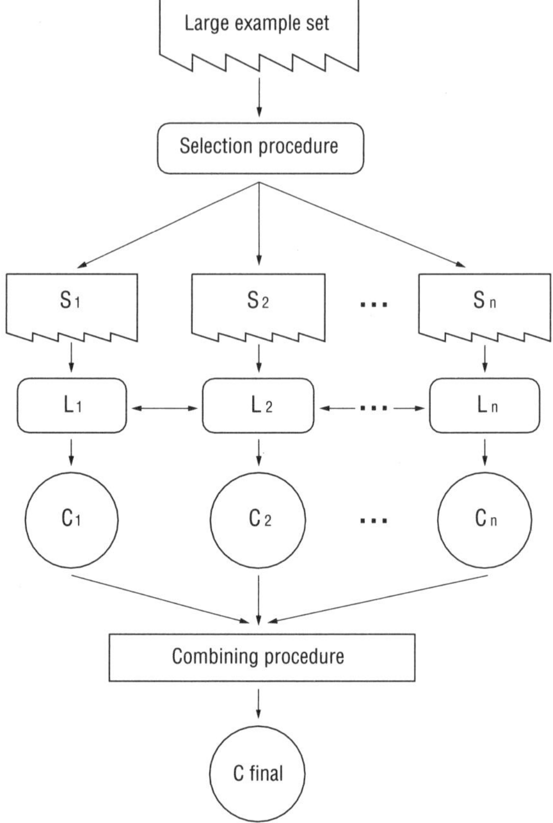

Figure 1.4: Cooperating DDM.

acceptable globally.

Provost and Hennessy (1994, 1996) allow individual processes to cooperate, in order to select all and only the globally acceptable rules. The cooperation takes the form of requests (from the other induction processes or from a server with the entire database) for verification of statistics regarding the best discovered rules. The combining procedure takes the union of the C_i. Interprocess communication is minimal, because cooperation requests are limited to rules that appear acceptable to at least one induction process, and each cooperation request requires simply that the rule be passed to each processor (which uses very few messages, especially if a logical ring network topology exists within the physical network topology). Provost and Henessy observe speedups linear in the number of distributed processors. The system is effective for very large data sets, up to the point where the individual processors run out of core memory and page thrashing begins (for the data considered, with 64M of main memory, thrashing sets in at several hundred thousand records per processor). Other forms of cooperation, such as sharing pruning information, also are presented.

A similar method is employed by Cheung, Ng, Fu, and Fu (1996) and Cheung, Han, Ng, Fu, and Fu (1996) to learn association rules. Essential to most association rule learning algorithms is finding rules with support greater than a prespecified level. Since support satisfies the invariant-partitioning property, the search can be distributed, as discussed above. Cheung and colleagues also discuss efficient cooperation by sharing statistics and by sharing pruning information.

A sequential, but easily distributable, version of this approach is the basis for the algorithm Partition (Savasere, Omiecinski, and Navathe 1995), which has been called one of the most efficient association-rule algorithms in terms of database operations (Toivonen 1996). Similarly, for scaling up a scientific discovery system, Galal, Cook and Holder (1998) found the concurrent–cooperative approach to be the best (among the various techniques they studied). They also partition the problem and then share the best discoveries, which are evaluated by all the processors to obtain a global perspective.

1.3 Beyond Scaling Up to Networked, Cooperating Knowledge Services

The generic model described in the previous section included a sample selection procedure that partitioned a large instance set into several subsets. However, in some cases such an explicit procedure is superfluous, because the data are partitioned and distributed naturally. This is true for traditional databases in corporate environments, many types of public data, and what are becoming known as digital libraries (Fox, Akscyn, Furuta, and Legsett 1995). Indeed, distributed data *defines* the most easily accessible data repository of all, the Internet.

Coalescing already-distributed data at best is a time-consuming, partially manual task. In a traditional corporate environment, for example, a product database typically is stored separately from a customer database—often in a different department, in a different building, or even in a different city. The recent trend toward "data warehouses" promises to collect all the relevant data in one, huge, monolithic repository. The promise is encouraging for well-scoped, predefined analyses, such as those typical of OLAP. However, it rings hollow for the purposes of data mining. Experienced data-mining practitioners know that which data are relevant only becomes clear as the knowledge-discovery cycle iterates. Exploration continually provides new prospects for augmenting the data, to improve the chances of making a useful discovery the next time around. Thus, crafting the data set for monolithic data mining often is a substantial part of a data miner's effort. Coalescing data sets consumes much more hands-on time than actually running the mining algorithms.

1.3.1 An Example: Credit Card Fraud Detection

Consider a simple, concrete example: a company that issues credit cards wants to mine its customer data for patterns that indicate fraudulent activity (so that it can detect fraud better). What data are relevant for this mining task? Interpreting "data" broadly, this question itself is the crux of knowledge discovery and data mining. Once just-the-right data are described by just-the-right attributes in just-the-right representation language, standard statistical or machine-learning algorithms will compress them into patterns that predict fraud.

Why is this particularly relevant to distributed data mining? Consider some of the steps a fraud-detection data miner would take to build just-the-right data set. First, historical customer transactions would be obtained from the billing department. These include customer id, transaction id, transaction date, transaction amount, transaction type, transaction location, etc. What they do *not* include is an indication as to whether the transaction had been fraudulent. There is a separate database detailing which transactions had been fraudulent.[6]

To craft his data set, our data miner must cross-reference this secondary table in order to label transactions as fraudulent or legitimate. Further complications arise during the cross-referencing. For example, the data miner notices that the fraud database contains transactions that do not appear in his transaction table! Investigation reveals that there is yet another table of "fraudulent transactions that were never billed to the customer," including those transactions occurring between the date fraud was detected (recall that this is historical data) and the date the previous customer bill had been printed. In order to have a complete picture of the fraud, these data must now be incorporated.

Thus the initial data set is built. Soon our hero realizes that he wants more than just transaction data. For example, it seems useful to add information on the customers themselves: a customer's address may help to decide whether or not transactions were made locally; a customer's credit history may help to decide whether a particular balance is unusual.

Good database design insists that these factors be stored in tables separate from the transaction data, and, in fact, for organizational reasons they are

[6]Or, more precisely, which transactions had been credited to the customer as being fraudulent, only some of which were actually fraudulent.

likely to reside in separate databases. Furthermore, the data miner may want to create his own auxiliary databases, for example, customers' favorite transactions, locations, and merchants, or bandits' favorite transactions, locations, and merchants.

In current data mining practice, much of the "art" of data mining is to craft a single, monolithic table from this inherently distributed information. Unfortunately, producing monolithic tables from multiple, real-world, multitable, relational databases is fraught with problems. The flattening-out process can be quite time consuming; substantial storage space is needed, and keeping the monolithic tables around leads to the problems that relational databases are designed to avoid (e.g., update and delete anomalies). Indeed, flattening may create, from otherwise manageable databases, monolithic tables that can no longer fit in main memory.

As an example, consider a database with only three tables: a customer table containing one million customers with twenty fields including address and product preference; a state table containing fifty states with eighty fields of information on each state; and a product field containing ten products with four hundred fields of information on each product. Furthermore, assume that the average size of a field is five bytes. Even in this vastly oversimplified example, flattening out a 100 megabyte database results in a 2.5 gigabyte flat file. Also notice that coalescing heterogeneous databases usually forces choices regarding which data to use and which data to exclude, choices that may restrict the discoveries that later data mining can make. Consider the realization that additional geographic information may be helpful to our fraud miner. Transaction locations may be very specific, say at the zipcode level. Based only on this fine-grained information, a data mining program may notice few regularities. However, useful high-level regularities might become apparent if transaction locations were grouped into neighborhoods, or cities, or states, or regions, or countries.

Should every transaction be annotated not only with the specific location, but also with the neighborhood, city, county, state, region, country, and continent? If not, how should one decide which safely can be ignored without affecting data mining?

1.3.2 A Distributed Data Mining View of the Example

Practitioners will agree that shifting perspectives by incorporating new information from additional databases (or other information sources) is one of the common features of the KDD process. It does not occur more frequently at the beginning of the process, only to taper off, and it is not an indication of incompetent design. Rather, it is a defining feature of exploration, the process leading to discovery. A distributed data mining approach would alleviate many of the problems sketched in the previous example. A data mining program should be told, "the data in database X on system Y is related to the current data in such-and-such a way," and the system(s) should be able to take care of the details. Indeed, a proposal for true "knowledge discovery" from databases would be short-sighted if it did not at least suggest that systems be given the opportunity to frame for themselves such relations.

Of course, viewing data mining as distributed demands that the other databases be easily accessible. It also suggests that the other databases be set up for distributed data mining. Whether or not all databases need special data-mining interfaces depends on the DDM design. Consider as a simple example a DDM design wherein, except for the primary system, all data mining is implemented as SQL queries. Such a system only requires that the other databases have an accessible SQL server.

Thus, with a DDM approach, the problems vanish from our example of data mining for fraud detection. The DDM system starts with a database of historical transactions. In order to get class labels, it queries the database of fraud credits. In order to include the additional transactions, it links to the database of unbilled transactions. While mining, it accesses the databases of customer information and geographic information, in order to find relationships or patterns of similarity. If the data miner creates auxiliary databases of bad locations, or bad merchants, or users' favorites, the DDM system simply can be told of their existence, their relevance, and their location. Never does the data miner face the issue of coalescing databases into a single table, or even a single, multitable database. Excluding relevant information is no longer a worry. The data miner may instead be concerned that existing relevant databases may be overlooked (which, of course, also is a problem for standard, monolithic data mining, but usually is buried far beneath the concerns already discussed).

1.3.3 Privacy Restrictions May Make Monolithic Mining Impossible

Sometimes databases have privacy restrictions. You may think the answer then is simple: these can not be mined. However, not all restrictions are completely exclusive. They vary in scope and sometimes have complicated rules. Herein lies perhaps the most convincing argument against monolithic data mining: building a monolithic data set may be prohibited. For example, an organization may choose not to, or may not be allowed to, provide access to individuals' data. However, organizations owning data may be interested in participating in a data mining effort, and may be willing to provide answers to queries for aggregate statistics, even if they are unwilling to share the lower-level data.

In fact, although data mining has raised fearful concern regarding loss of privacy (e.g., consider the KDD-98 panel on Privacy and Data Mining), we should argue that, if done right, data mining should *increase* privacy. As mentioned already, data mining programs need not examine individual records; rather, they need aggregate information. Individual information can be protected on a secure server that only answers certain requests from trusted clients. An individual customer still might ask, why take the chance? Why not just disallow data mining altogether? However, data mining also has potential to enhance privacy. Fraud detection is an obvious example, but consider also junk mail (and junk email, and junk phone calls, etc.), an often-cited privacy concern. If target-marketing data mining were to work perfectly, there would be no "junk." Only consumers who would be interested in a product would be targeted. Of course data mining is unlikely to be perfect, but consider the alternative: relatively blind mass marketing.

Distributed data mining is essential to reconcile these opposing privacy concerns, namely, protecting individual data and reducing unwanted privacy intrusions. Let's continue with our concrete example of credit-card fraud detection, which provides a clear illustration of the conflict. Customers prefer to have their transaction data examined as little as possible, and when it becomes necessary, examination by a computer system (with no ulterior motives) is probably universally preferable—a standard billing system going through our records causes no concern. On the other hand, customers tend to prefer that banks take action to verify usage that appears to be fraudulent. Presumably, customers would prefer that a computer examine their transaction histories (looking for indications of fraud, and nothing else), rather than a bank employee.

At Columbia University, Salvatore Stolfo and his students, in collaboration with several large banks, have been studying data mining for fraud detection (Stolfo, Fan, Lee, Prodromidis, and Chan 1997). Indeed banks would like to collaborate, effectively pooling their data, to produce more powerful fraud-detection models. However, they are in fact prohibited by law from sharing individual customers' data. Stolfo and his students report that by taking a distributed approach, the data both can be mined effectively and can be kept secure. As described in section 1.2.2, models of fraud are mined independently by the individual banks, each bank needing to see only its own customers' data. The models of fraud then are shared and combined. To understand why combining models from different banks can lead to more effective fraud detection, consider two banks whose customers are concentrated in different areas, say New York City and Los Angeles. Mining the New York data, one would discover subtle, local fraud patterns that would not be sufficiently concentrated in the Los Angeles data. However, when Los Angeles customers (or their credit-card numbers) travel to New York, their home bank can use these subtle New York patterns for more effective fraud detection.

This example illustrates distributed data mining across relatively homogeneous data sets. Although the structure and content of the banks' records will differ to some degree, the distributed data sets all represent the same basic information: historical credit-card transactions. Privacy also is a concern for distributed, heterogeneous data. Different databases, containing different information, will have different levels of required security. Some may be too sensitive for any data mining, but others may allow limited querying for aggregate information. In some cases, privacy concerns may stem from a desire to profit from collected data. A company that has a lot of data may decide to issue subscriptions to a data-mining server, which provides aggregate information mined from their data. By allowing only limited querying, and by stipulating query restrictions in the subscription contract, companies may be able to profit from the massive volume of data they collect routinely, while protecting individuals' privacy.

1.3.4 Is this View of Distributed Data Mining Realistic or Far-Fetched?

These arguments notwithstanding, our current discussion would be incomplete if we did not address whether this view of DDM is realistic or far-fetched. With respect to mining relatively homogeneous databases for purposes of classification, the answer is easy. It is not far-fetched, and in fact Stolfo's group provides web-accessible software for distributed data mining[7].

With respect to mining heterogeneous databases (containing completely different, but related, tables), there also is evidence that it is not far-fetched. At its most simple, heterogeneous DDM could involve SQL queries to auxiliary databases for what to this point I vaguely have called "aggregate statistics." Is this realistic? In other words, is it technically feasible for data mining to be performed through SQL queries for statistics, without access to the underlying data? The answer, of course, is "yes." Several authors discuss how to do just this. The main insight is that matching hypotheses against the data is not necessary: for most of the processing, all that is needed is a set of sufficient statistics from which the results of matching can be computed (Fayyad 1997). Separating the generation of the sufficient statistics from their use in the evaluation of hypotheses allows each to be treated separately—first using the data to populate the statistics data structure and then operating only on the data structure—which affords both optimized use of memory and improved run-time complexity (Aronis and Provost 1997). More specifically, consider mining classification models. For most of the critical data mining operations, such as choosing nodes when constructing decision trees, one must tally for

[7] See http://www.cs.columbia.edu/~sal/JAM/PROJECT

all the instances (at a particular point in the search) the class labels associated with the different values of each attribute. A straightforward data structure to store such statistics is a contingency table of instance counts for each attribute, indexed by attribute-value and class. This data structure can be populated by SQL requests for statistics (Agrawal and Shim 1996a, 1996b, John and Lent 1997, Graefe, Fayyad, and Chaudhuri 1998).

Sarawagi, Thomas, and Agrawal (1998) provide perhaps the most comprehensive discussion of integrating data mining with database management systems. Their focus is on mining association rules, but they illustrate principles that apply more generally. They point to several efforts to extend SQL to support mining operations, and discuss expressing mining algorithms in SQL.

In particular, Sarawagi and others discuss pushing into the database system parts of the application program that perform intensive computations on the individual records, instead of bringing the records of the database into the application program. One method is to encapsulate the statistics gathering as a stored procedure, which is executed on the database machine.

A somewhat different approach is to represent the individual data mining operations as user-defined functions placed in SQL data scan queries (which also will run on the database machine) (Agrawal and Shim 1996a, b). Sarawagi, Thomas, and Agrawal also consider the more general case where a preprocessor translates data mining operations into the appropriate form for a particular environment.

There also has been work demonstrating the feasibility of distributed mining of heterogeneous data. Aronis and colleagues (1997) describe the WoRLD (Worldwide Relational Learning Daemon) system, that mines multiple, multitable databases distributed across networks. The key to the WoRLD's ability to treat distributed databases transparently is its use of spreading activation (Quillian 1968), instead of item-by-item matching, as the basic operation of the inductive engine. Each instance is labeled with a marker, and the WoRLD propagates these markers through databases looking for features where markers of one class accumulate. This process can span several databases, possibly on different machines, with markers transmitted across network links. As with the WWW, there is no need for a master map of the entire structure—each database can have its own links to other related databases, which the WoRLD can follow as it encounters them.

1.4 Discussion

Besides being tedious, being prohibited by privacy restrictions, and potentially losing information, the process of coalescing already-distributed databases introduces other problems. The content of many databases is dynamic: it changes in response to changes in the world. Once data miners create their own mining database that incorporates information from auxiliary databases, the mining database quickly can become obsolete. Data miners do not want to, and often are not equipped to, duplicate the management of the auxiliary data. Neither do they want to rebuild their mining database repeatedly. A DDM system that can query the existing auxiliary databases as needed, leaving their management to their managers, would obviate this problem—also created by the awkward, non-distributed view.[8]

At this point, you may feel that I have glossed over a lot of very hard problems—and you would be right. As an example of a particularly telling problem, how is ontological mismatch to be resolved? Different databases may use the same term to mean different things, and may use different terms to refer to the same thing. A DDM system would have to either (partially) solve this problem, or would have to make very strong assumptions. I would counter this (correct) observation by pointing out that this is not a problem specific to distributed data mining; it just comes to the fore when it has to be automated. This is a hard, basic research problem for data mining, that current data mining research is glossing over.

1.4.1 The Distributed Data Mining View Opens New Avenues for Research

Lots of other fundamental KDD research problems, that go beyond designing new or faster induction algorithms, also rear their attractive heads. Solutions to some technical DDM problems are beginning to be addressed (Grossman and Bailey 1998). For example, how can heterogeneous processors and network links best be used (Grossman, Bailey, Kasif, Mon, Ramu, and Malhi 1998)? However, consider a different type of problem. While building their monolithic database, data miners often notice that "database X is relevant in such-and-such a way," and work to incorporate X. Few authors address the fundamental issue: How and from where do such insights come? Taking a DDM view (and assuming the existence of database maps or metadata, other relevant research areas), systems themselves should be able to notice that "database X is relevant in such-and-such a way," and query it. Once again, the attempt to automate this part of the process brings it into the research spotlight.

[8]At first it may seem that in such cases, managing the data in a distributed database management system (DDBMS), with incorporated mining routines, would be sufficient. However, although mining DDBMSs is one very interesting method for DDM, this view is incomplete. For organizational reasons, many auxiliary databases are not, and will not be, managed in a DDBMS; yet it still may be useful to use them when mining. Viewing DDM only as mining a DDBMS either (1) demands that a particular DDBMS incorporate all auxiliary data whenever they are deemed potentially relevant, or (2) restricts the use of some such data.

DDM as simply issuing SQL queries, while currently the most feasible approach, certainly is not the most ambitious vision. A DDM visionary might see distributed mining agents cooperating in a knowledge economy. Closer to feasibility are data mining servers, available on the network, that publish their capabilities for data mining clients to consider. These servers could sit atop data with varying degrees of privacy, and if necessary could serve only trusted clients or clients under contract. The emergence of a knowledge economy for data mining may not be all that far away. Once distributed data mining becomes a reality, it is not a stretch to foresee organizations developing that profit by providing knowledge services. They will store and manage large and potentially changing databases, and data miners will pay for access. For instance, fraud detectors and target marketers would be delighted if a demographic data provider were established, which for a small fee would provide just-the-right auxiliary knowledge for a particular problem.

1.4.2 Distributed Data Mining as Knowledge Discovery

Section 1.2 presented arguments for distributed data mining based on computational efficiencies due to parallelization of the distributed mining processes. I have tried to argue that although the effect of parallelization is important, it is less important than the effect of taking a distributed view of the problem. The question of whether the distributed mining processes must reside on separate processors, or whether they profitably could be simulated on a single processor, does not seem particularly important when juxtaposed with the conceptual neatness of the DDM problem formulation. Of all the examples heretofore presented, the most convincing in this respect may be DDM's potential to eliminate much of the manual effort needed to coalesce heterogeneous, multitable databases. It seems that, in light of the current state of the art, a data miner would value a reduction in the manual effort (of coalescence) more highly than the corresponding reduction in computational effort (by parallization).

There is another way in which a distributed view of data mining may lead to remarkable computational efficiencies. Data mining is one element of a larger process of discovery. Therefore, the correct direction and manner to proceed are inherently ill defined. A single explorer must try one thing, then another, then another, and so on, until either he finds something interesting or he runs out of resources. This describes the essential nature of the process of exploration, including not only what has been called "the knowledge discovery process," but also geographic exploration (e.g., in the fifteenth and sixteenth centuries) and the typical process of science. The length of a discovery's delay is related directly to the explorer's ability to prioritize possible paths of exploration.

On the other hand, a (distributed) group of explorers follows many paths simultaneously. Indeed, different explorers follow different paths almost by necessity. Herein lie two key insights. First, the speed of the group progresses at the speed of the fastest member of the group. Second, the entire group capitalizes on the discovery (once it is made known), and ratchets up its goals. Examples abound. In geographic discovery, once a shorter route was found to a desired destination, explorers used it to set their sights even higher for future discoveries. In science, once a (sub-)problem has been solved by one research group, the results are published and all research groups can now "stand on their shoulders" (paraphrasing Newton). Why is this relevant to distributed data mining? As with other explorations, by its very nature knowledge discovery is an ill-defined process. Thus we must try and try again to formulate just-the-right direction and manner of search. We may have many possibilities at the outset, but little reason to prefer one over another. If each is time consuming, discovery may be inefficient. However, every weather-worn data miner has experienced the phenomenon that once the right problem formulation is concocted, discoveries are made remarkably, sometimes embarassingly, quickly.

If many different starting points and directions are begun simultaneously, and the "right one" is among the group, then the discovery may be made very quickly in real time, and perhaps even with much less combined effort than in the sequential case. In a different context, this phenomenon has been called a "combinatorial implosion" (Kornfeld 1982), and has been studied in other areas of artificial intelligence (e.g., for constraint satisfaction (Clearwater, Huberman, and Hogg 1991, 1992).

1.5 Summary

Distributed data mining lately has been receiving increasing attention. Most work uses distributed processing to scale up to large databases, and the rich decomposability of data mining problems has led to successful techniques all along the spectrum from fine- to coarse-grained. The search space can be partitioned and different processors can search different parts, or the data can be partitioned. Nevertheless, scaling up is but one motivation for distributed data mining. Distributed data mining also eliminates the need to coalesce already distributed data. Coalescence is severly problematic, both in principle and in practice. Often, certain data are left out of a problem formulation not because they are deemed irrelevant, but because including them is too awkward. Distributed data mining avoids these problems, and also eliminates storage, time, and data management inefficiencies associated with coalescence. Finally, privacy concerns may prohibit coalescence altogether. Distributed data mining can allow access to a wide variety of data, while protecting data privacy.

Potential consumers of auxiliary knowledge already exist—consumers who are not shy about spending money on data mining. Potential suppliers await the development of infrastructure. Once DDM becomes a practical reality, implying not only solutions to the computational and network-related issues of distributed mining, but also the existence of published data maps and metadata, then data-mining-supported knowledge economies will develop.

Acknowledgements

I thank John Aronis, Lars Asker, Bruce Buchanan, Jason Catlett, Scott Clearwater, Pedro Domingos, Phil Chan, Doug Fisher, Dan Hennessy, David Jensen, Ronny Kohavi, Rich Segal, Sal Stolfo, and anonymous referees of previous papers, who have influenced my view of scaling up and of DDM. Thanks also to the authors of the work surveyed, to the many who have pointed to relevant work, and especially to Venkat Kolluri, who has contributed in many ways.

Chapter 2

Scalable Data Mining through Fine-Grained Parallelism

Chandrika Kamath and Ron Musick

2.1 Introduction

Many organizations, both scientific and commercial, are routinely gathering data at an ever increasing pace. As these data sets grow into the tera-byte range and beyond, it is no longer possible to manually extract the useful information from the data. A new generation of tools and techniques in the area of data mining or knowledge discovery is rapidly gaining acceptance for the automated analysis of large and complex data sets (Fayyad and Uthurusamy 1996; Fayyad, Piatetsky-Shapiro, Smyth, and Uthurusamy 1996; Kennedy 1998). As this technology is successfully applied to many different areas, it is becoming apparent that some of the terms, especially *data mining,* have come to mean very different things to different people. It therefore seems appropriate to start this chapter with our definition of data mining.

We view data mining as the process concerned with uncovering patterns, associations, anomalies, and statistically significant structures and events in data. One of the key steps in data mining is pattern recognition, or the discovery and characterization of patterns in data. A pattern is an arrangement or an ordering in which some organization of underlying structure can be said to exist. Patterns are identified using features, where a feature is any measurement or attribute that can be extracted from the data, such as a customer identification or a transaction amount in commercial data, and signal intensities or aspect ratios in scientific data.

Experienced practitioners are well aware that data mining is an interactive, iterative, multistep process, involving data preparation, search for patterns, knowledge evaluation, and possible refinement based on input from domain experts or feedback from one of the steps (Fayyad, Piatetsky-Shapiro, and Smyth 1996). Figure 2.1 describes how useful information, or "knowledge," can be extracted from raw data. First, we process the raw data to reduce its size through techniques such as sampling or multiresolution analysis. Next, we extract relevant features from this target data and apply dimension reduction techniques to identify the key features in order to make the search for patterns in a multidimensional search space tractable. This preprocessing of the raw data is followed by the identification of interesting patterns using classification or clustering algorithms. Finally, the patterns are presented to the user in an easy-to-understand manner. As the various steps in this process are refined iteratively, the model that is built from the data is validated (or invalidated).

The data preprocessing step is critically important in practice, but is rarely discussed in the data mining community as a research topic of interest. We have devoted part of this chapter to highlighting some of the more interesting challenges faced in parallelizing this step. Data preprocessing is important because raw data, whether commercial or scientific, is rarely in a form suitable for pattern recognition. For example, scientific data is frequently available as image data, from which appropriate features have to be extracted depending on the goal at hand. Both commercial and science data can be fraught with missing or erroneous values, as well as a great deal of *implicit* information, from which useful *explicit* features must be derived. Tools for "cleaning" data help somewhat, although the user may find that the ranges of most of the variables are inappropriate, or the resulting data is far from "clean." (Radcliffe and Flockhart 1996). Hence, additional work is often required prior to the application of the pattern recognition algorithms. Much of this work is problem dependent, and requires close collaboration with the domain specialists.

Data mining is a multidisciplinary field, combining ideas from diverse areas such as machine learning, statistics, high performance computing, math-

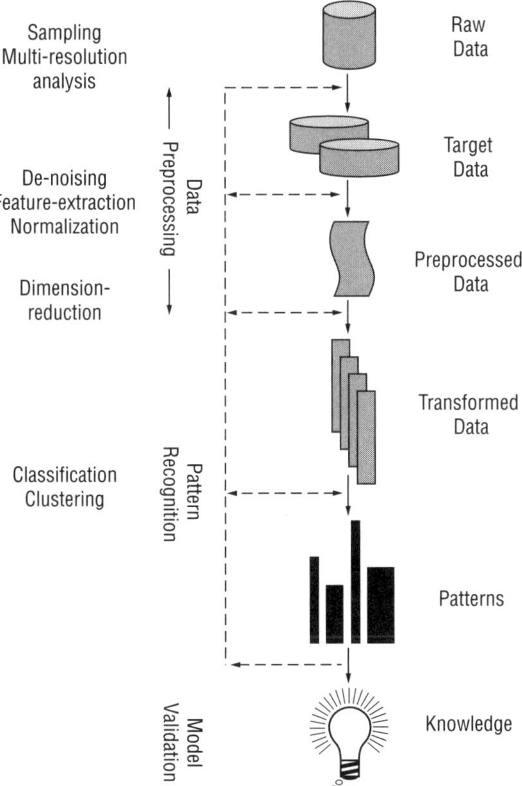

Figure 2.1: The data mining process.

ematical programming and optimization, soft computing, and visualization. Good software engineering practices, as well as sophisticated parallel programming techniques have become important as the need for scalable, domain independent data mining software has grown. Finally, domain knowledge will always play a very crucial role in the data mining process, as it is an invaluable component of feature extraction and model validation.

2.1.1 Need for Scalable Data Mining

As we mine increasingly larger and more complex data sets, both in commercial and scientific areas, it is becoming clear that we require a process that is scalable. In a parallel setting, by *scalable* we generally mean the ability to use additional computational resources, such as CPUs and memory, in an effective manner to solve increasingly larger problems. An excellent introduction to approaches to scaling pattern recognition can be found in Provost and Kolluri (1999).

The fundamental reason driving scalable data mining solutions is simple—we need to build accurate models quickly. This can be beneficial in several different ways. First, faster turnaround times tend to yield better models. The wall-clock time necessary to build a model is a major factor that can affect the ability of a user to explore many different solutions. Fast model production allows multiple models to be built quickly. Besides making operations like cross validation or boosting (which require multiple models) practical, it is important simply because a data miner will be able to explore a larger space of models, and thus be more likely to find a better model. Second, there can be great scientific or business value in being able to apply complex pattern recognition algorithms to data as it is being acquired. For example, for clustering to be effective in domains where the transient effects are the important ones (asteroids in astrophysics data, or fraud in business transactions), the processing must keep up with the rate of new data acquisition.

There are several key issues that must be considered in order to make data mining algorithms scalable.

The scalability of the algorithm itself. Here, scalability is a description of how the total computational work requirements grow with problem size, an issue which can be discussed independent of the computing platform. Ideally, we would like the computational requirements for an algorithm to grow slowly as the problem size increases. While this may not always be possible, the payoffs can be immense, even on a single processor. Therefore, techniques that enhance the scalability of an algorithm must not be neglected as we explore ways of parallelizing data mining algorithms.

Scalability of all steps in the data mining process. Frequently, practitioners focus on the scalability of only the pattern recognition algorithms. However, this task is one of many in the data mining process. For the *entire* data mining process to be scalable, each step in the process must be scalable as well.

Ease of data movement. Each step in the data mining process is performed many times over the course of one complete analysis. It is therefore important that we manage the data appropriately between the various steps. For example, the output of the feature extraction step should be in an appropriate format so that it can be directly input to the dimension reduction software. Another important concern arises if the data is being generated at a location different from where it is mined. Data sets are growing much faster than increases in network and disk I/O bandwidths. As the size to bandwidth mismatch continues to grow, the choice of where and when to process and mine the data will be crucial to the overall success of a project. Science data is already reaching the stage where data mining must be incorporated directly with the data collection or generation stage in order to output the feature vectors needed for clustering or classification algorithms.

Fast I/O to the data mining application. For the business community, parallel database management systems (DBMS) are the primary underlying data store. In such applications, it is important to create fast, parallel, specific access methods that *forgo* the access methods that are invoked by the query optimizer of a standard relational DBMS. In a typical DBMS, the overhead stemming from proper transaction semantics, locking, logging, and other features that are unnecessary for mining applications can slow the entire process down immensely.

The discussion above focuses on scalability issues related to data mining algorithms, independent of the computing platform. In section 2.2.4, we review the factors that affect the performance of an algorithm implemented on a fine-grained parallel machine. The overall scalability of the parallel data mining process is determined by both the scalability of the process and the parallel implementation.

2.1.2 Nature and Scope of this Survey

This chapter is a survey of techniques that use fine-grained parallelism as a means of achieving scalable data mining. We provide a coherent introduction to the techniques used in both data preprocessing and pattern recognition, describe how these techniques can be parallelized, and then focus on some of the key research issues in these areas. As with any endeavor that surveys the state of the art in a field, we realize that it is seldom possible to include all relevant papers, or mention all the ideas that have contributed to progress in the field. This is especially difficult in a rapidly evolving area such as data mining which draws from so many relevant disciplines. We therefore limit the scope of our survey as described in this section.

Parallel data mining can be broadly categorized into two approaches—fine-grained and coarse-grained. In the latter case, the data is partitioned and mined by a loosely coupled collection of algorithms, and the results combined in a suitable manner, usually through a voting scheme. This approach is most natural for the case where the data is globally distributed, and either for privacy reasons, or for efficiency, it is not practical to merge the data to perform monolithic data mining. Coarse-grained data mining is often referred to as distributed data mining, a term that should not be confused with data mining on distributed memory architectures.

Our focus is on fine-grained data mining, where all the data to be mined is typically at the same site, on the same machine. The fine granularity of the tasks to be parallelized implies that the processors used in parallel data mining be tightly coupled by a high bandwidth interconnection network. While our focus is on fine-grained algorithms, algorithms developed in the context of distributed data mining can be applied equally well in the case where the processors are tightly coupled. The reverse is however not true, as fine-grain data mining algorithms exploit the close coupling between processors, and therefore will be very inefficient on loosely coupled systems.

Fine-grained parallel algorithms are important for scalable data mining in situations where all the data required for mining is local. Examples include computational data from scientific simulations, observation data collected by astrophysicists, or warehoused business data, all of which is typically stored at the site where it is collected or generated. In such cases, distributing the data globally to exploit coarse-grained distributed data mining may not be a practical option. Furthermore, as multiprocessor personal computers with 2–8 CPUs become inexpensive and common-place, fine-grained approaches will be needed to better exploit the new capabilities provided by these systems.

A different driving force behind the use of tightly-coupled multiprocessor systems is the need for quick and accurate solutions. When accuracy is an issue, for example in a classification problem, a fine-grained approach on an entire data set will typically produce a more accurate model than sampling-based, or distributed data mining approaches. This argument must be used with care, however, since the net gain in accuracy drops off as the size of the data increases. When speed is an issue, tightly coupled processors on a high bandwidth network will generally be faster than a distributed cluster of single processors on a lower-bandwidth local area or wide area network.

In this chapter, we will consider fine-grained parallel algorithms for both the data preprocessing and the pattern recognition steps. While preprocessing the data is time consuming and would therefore benefit greatly from parallelism, the techniques used are frequently specific to the domain and the problem. To address a broad audience, we will therefore focus mainly on the pattern recognition algorithms which have more general applicability. We will, however, discuss some of the data preprocessing steps that are common to several applications, and briefly describe some techniques that are specific to scientific applications.

Science data poses unique problems at the preprocessing stage (Fayyad, Haussler, and Stolorz 1996; Fayyad and Smyth 1995). As mentioned earlier, the data is usually available in the raw form as images, and considerable effort has to be invested in extracting the features relevant to a problem. The data may also be available as time-series data, which can be difficult to handle if there are multiple variables being measured at different scales. On the positive side, science data is rarely kept in a database, and its availability as flat files implies that we do not have to take into account the overhead of database access. However, as these data sets are very large, much of the data will be disk resident, requiring good out-of-core algorithms that do not ignore the cost of disk access.

As the use of parallel processing in data mining is relatively recent, it is uncommon to find extensive studies on the topic of parallelizing data mining algorithms. However, several algorithms that are in use in the data mining community, such as principal component analysis, have been parallelized when they have been used in other fields, such as numerical analysis. Borrowing ideas from other technical domains can only enrich the practice of data mining. This is especially true for domains such as numerical optimization, high performance computing, and linear algebra, where parallel processing has had a long and illustrious history, and we can benefit from software that has not only been extensively tested, but is also highly optimized and parallelized. Wherever possible, we will refer to such work as it indicates how data mining techniques can be parallelized. In this chapter, we also refer to work done in other areas that is applicable to data mining, but has not yet been actively adopted by the data mining community.

2.1.3 Examples of Relevant Applications

There are several applications that can benefit from fine-grained parallelism, in both commercial and scientific domains. Prototypical business applications (Lewinson 1994) like direct mail, fraud detection, or market-basket related activities are all likely to benefit from scalable fine-grained algorithms. Historical data in such domains can lead to particularly rich applications. Since large-scale data mining has been discussed extensively in the context of business data, we provide a brief look at a few scientific domains that can benefit from these techniques. An important point to note about scientific domains is that we need to carefully examine the need for large-scale classification algorithms. Labeled data is often required as input to a classification algorithm, and can sometimes be difficult to obtain in large quantities. For example, for some scientific applications, the only labeled data available is that which the scientist constructs by hand. If this is the only source of labeled data, then algorithms focused on the parallel construction of classifiers are likely to be overkill. Historical outcomes are an exception, since the end result (or labels) of many types of prediction-oriented tasks naturally fall out over the passage of time, especially in business or financial applications. Large amounts of labeled data can also result from scientific tasks that are related to the comparison of experimentally- versus computationally-derived data.

As multiprocessor systems with thousands of processors are becoming easily accessible, scientists have started to simulate increasingly complex phenomena involving the interaction of many variables in three dimensions. The output resulting from such simulations can be immense, with conceivably a tera-byte of data being generated at each time step in the simulation (Baldwin, Kamath, and Musick 1999). This output is usually analyzed by means of visualization techniques, a mode of interaction which unfortunately does not scale well to very large data sets since the exploration is driven by a human. The space that a scientist has to explore is huge, since interesting interactions can involve any subset of the variables, and occur anywhere in the three-dimensional data. Despite the advances in visualization hardware and software, automated techniques, such as those provided by data mining, are required to make it possible to analyze these data sets effectively.

A research area with great promise is the intersection of data mining with visualization. Using this approach, the scientist would first identify the "interesting" regions in a data set, which can then be explored using sophisticated visualization techniques. In this case, the most practical time to mine the data may be soon after it is generated, while it still resides on the local disks on the parallel machine (before being moved off to a larger global disk farm, or tertiary storage). Given this scenario, fine-grained parallel approaches would provide the most appropriate solution.

A similar situation arises in astrophysics data, where scientists typically identify interesting regions by visually looking at the data. SKICAT and Jartool are two well known projects wherein data mining techniques were brought to bear on the exploration of scientific data sets (Fayyad, Smyth, Burl, and Perona 1996). Another similar project that is geared towards the exploitation of fine-grained parallel systems for mining science data is Sapphire.[1] This effort involves research in scalable algorithms for the interactive exploration of large, complex, multidimensional scientific data. The goal is to develop a new generation of computational tools and techniques that will be used to improve the way in which scientists extract useful information from data. The data sets being considered are obtained from simulations and observations in areas such as physics, climate modeling, and astronomy.

A slightly different situation arises in some scientific areas such as climate modeling. Here again, the scientists are making use of large parallel machines to implement highly sophisticated atmospheric, oceanic, and coupled models. In addition to output from these simulations, satellite observations are further increasing the amount of data available. These two types of data need to be considered together as scientists search for correlations and anomalies, modes of variability, and comparisons between observed and modeled data.

2.2 Parallel Architectures

A survey of parallel data mining techniques would be incomplete without a brief overview of parallel architectures and the issues to be considered in the

[1] http://www.llnl.gov/casc/sapphire

efficient implementation of parallel algorithms. Programming for a parallel machine is significantly more complex than programming for a serial machine and requires a good understanding of the underlying machine architecture.

Parallel computers have had a long history, mainly as research efforts in scientific computing. However, in the last two decades, as the need for compute power has increased, there has been a greater acceptance of parallel computers in both the commercial and the scientific domains. This has also been made possible through several commercially viable multiprocessor systems that are described in detail later in this section.

Traditionally, the distinction between parallel architectures was between "single instruction stream, multiple data stream" or SIMD machines and "multiple instruction stream, multiple data stream" or MIMD machines. In the former, thousands of relatively simple processing elements, with limited local memory, executed the same instruction on different data. MIMD systems on the other hand, had fewer, but more powerful processors, each executing potentially different programs. Several commercial systems were built, exploiting both SIMD and MIMD architectures (Fox, Williams, and Messina 1994). However, except for specialized applications such as image processing, MIMD architectures currently dominate the market; the distinction today is not between SIMD and MIMD systems, but between shared-memory and distributed memory architectures. An excellent survey of the advantages and disadvantages of some of the current architectures was written by Bell and Van Ingen (1999).

2.2.1 Shared-Memory Architectures

Shared memory machines, also known as symmetric multiprocessors (SMP), have multiple processors accessing the common memory through a single, shared bus, figure 2.2. Examples of such systems include various Cray X-MP and Y-MP vector/multiprocessor systems, the HP/Convex C-Series, and the SGI Power Challenge.

The programming model for SMP systems is based around a single address space. Data are shared by processes when they directly reference the address space. The programmer must properly identify when and what data are being shared, and synchronize the processes explicitly to ensure that shared variables are accessed in the proper order.

In practice, software is written for SMP systems using either Pthreads, which is an IEEE POSIX standard (Nichols, Buttlar, and Farrell 1996), or the new OpenMP standard for portable shared memory programs.[2] Both approaches require the programmer to parallelize the code. The Pthreads standard uses function calls, while OpenMP uses compiler directives.

[2] http://www.openmp. org

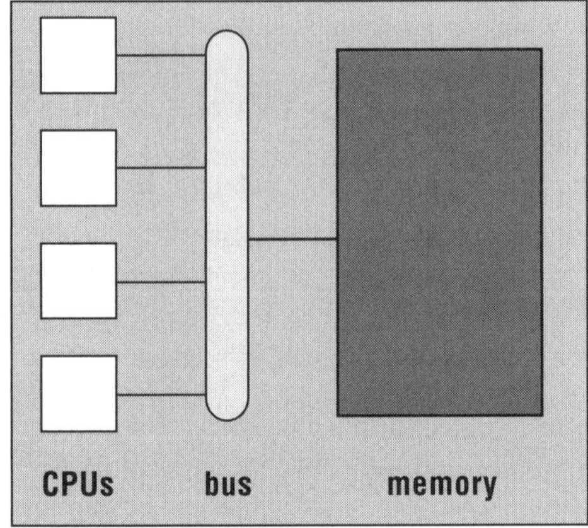

Figure 2.2: SMP architecture.

SMP systems typically consist of 2 to 16 processors. As the number of processors increases beyond 16 or so, they have to be connected by buses that are increasingly wider, with a higher bandwidth and lower latency. Unfortunately, as the number of processors sharing the bus increases, the bandwidth available per processor decreases, resulting in substantial performance degradation. This lack of scalability of bus-based architectures can be overcome either by using a different system interconnect such as crossbar interconnects, or by moving to distributed memory architectures.

2.2.2 Distributed-Memory Architectures

High-performance systems that can scale to large numbers of processors are designed from the start to avoid the bottlenecks of shared interconnects. Such systems, called distributed memory machines, "shared nothing" systems or massively parallel processors (MPP), consist of separate computing nodes with no shared structure other than the interconnect, which is usually a switched, or crossbar connection that scales with the number of processors, figure 2.3. As a result, the interconnect bandwidth available per processor remains relatively constant across configuration sizes. Examples of MPP systems include Cray T3D, Cray T3E, Intel iPSC/860, and the Intel Paragon.

Distributed memory systems use the message passing programming model to communicate data among processors. The memory of the entire system is partitioned into distinct address spaces, and a processor has direct access to only its local memory. The program on each processor must be aware of when and what data it needs to send to, or receive from, another processor, and

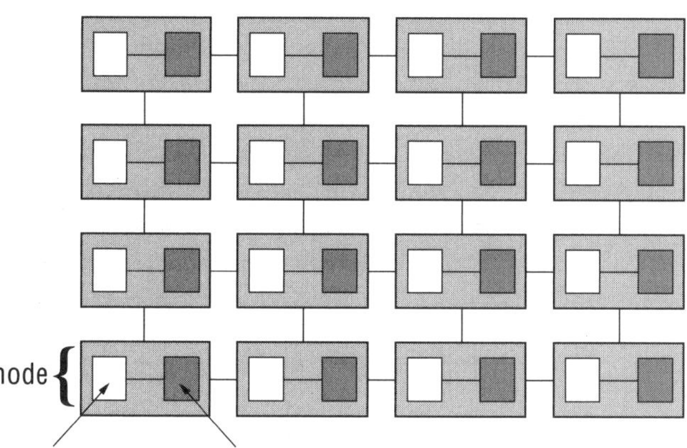

Figure 2.3: MPP architecture.

must include the code that handles this communication. As a result, MPP systems are typically harder to program than SMP systems. In addition, as communication is done through a software layer, the overhead costs can be sizable.

The two message passing software packages currently in use are MPI[3] and the parallel virtual machine.[4] While the two packages are very similar, a richer set of communication features and improved communication performance tend to make MPI the preferred choice for fine-grained data mining. The subtle differences between the two are summarized by Geist, Kohl, and Papadopoulos (1996).

2.2.3 Hybrid Architectures

As the need for processing power increases, an obvious solution is to use an SMP system as the basic node in an MPP system, figure 2.4. This approach, sometimes referred to as "clusters of SMPs," can provide a significant increase in the peak node performance at a cost that is not much higher than the cost of a uni-processor with the same amount of storage. Such hierarchical architecture machines include commercial machines such as the IBM SP-2, SGI Origin 2000, and the HP/Convex Exemplar systems.

A major, and as yet unsolved, problem with clusters of SMPs is that the programmer now has to manage two levels of parallelism, with big differences

[3]http://www.mpi-forum.org

[4]http://www.epm.ornl.gov/ pvm/

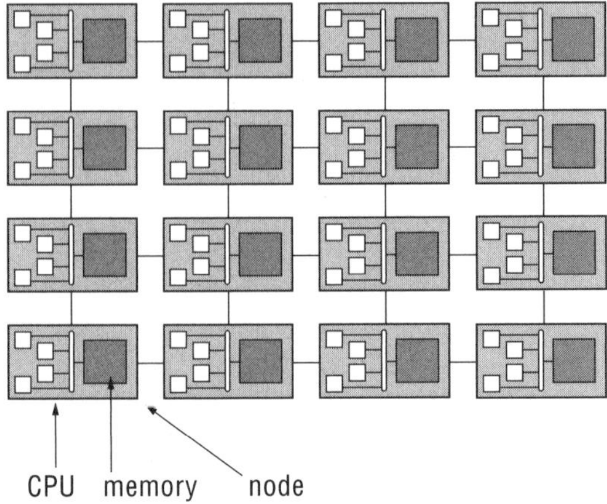

Figure 2.4: Clusters of SMPs.

in performance and function between the inter-node and intra-node communication. One approach, using software, is to use OpenMP within a node, and MPI across the nodes.

A somewhat different approach is used in the distributed shared memory (DSM) architectures, where the memory is physically distributed, but the system implements a single shared address space, thus retaining the shared memory model for communication and programming. Several DSM systems are available commercially; however, there are open issues that must still be addressed regarding scalability and efficient implementations (Bell and Van Ingen 1999).

The current fastest supercomputers in the Department of Energy's Accelerated Strategic Computing Initiative (ASCI), are all clusters of SMPs. The ASCI Blue Pacific is an IBM SP-2 system consisting of three 488-node sectors, where each node is a 4-way SMP system. The ASCI Blue Mountain system consists of 48 SGI Origin 2000 shared memory multiprocessor nodes with 128 processors on each node. The ASCI Red machine is a 4000 node MPP, where each node has two Pentium Pro Processors.

2.2.4 Programming Issues

Obtaining high performance from a data mining application using fine-grained parallelism is not a straightforward task. Broadly speaking, parallelizing code can follow *task parallel*, *data parallel*, or *hybrid* approaches. Task parallel approaches attempt to break the work down so that each processor is working on an independent piece of the problem space, with coordination at the end to form the global result. This can require data being replicated to all processors, or clever schemes for partitioning the data across processors without incurring large communication costs. Data parallel approaches involve partitioning the data across nodes, and having all nodes participate in expanding each part of the problem space by working together. This can involve large synchronization costs due to poor load balancing. Synchronization costs occur where processors idle-wait for others to catch up and pass relevant information on before proceeding.

There are several generally accepted metrics that can be used to measure the overall quality of a parallel solution. If T_s is the serial runtime of an algorithm, and T_p is the parallel runtime on P processors, the *speedup* is T_s / T_p. Ideally, this should increase linearly with the number of processors. The *efficiency* of an algorithm is defined as $T_s / P T_p$; this should be close to (or greater than) 1. Othcr pcrformancc mctrics, such as scaled speedup, absolute speedup, relative speedup and iso-efficiency, are described by Kumar, Grama, Gupta, and Karypis (1994).

Several factors can affect the performance of an application, as described by Kumar, Grama, Gupta, and Karypis (1994) and Dowd and Severance (1998). We discuss a few of them briefly.

Single Processor Performance. While much of the work in fine-grained parallel data mining focuses on the parallel performance, we must also ensure that the single processor implementation of the data mining algorithm has been fully optimized. This is especially true as the newer processors available commercially all have deep memory hierarchies, and care must be taken to exploit the differences in data transfer rates between different levels.

One of the most important factors that affects the performance on a single processor is the data locality in a program. Programs that have a high spatial and temporal locality make extensive use of instructions and data that are near to other instructions and data, both in space and time. Several ways of improving data locality, such as changing the order of loops or unrolling them are discussed by Dowd and Severance (1998). Such optimizations are frequently done automatically by the compiler. Others such as changing the data layout must be done by the programmer.

Data Layout. Data layout is an important issue that the programmer must address, especially for MPP systems. As a processor has access only to its local memory and disk, any data that is required by the processor, but is not in its local memory or disk, results in communication overhead. Therefore, it is important that a processor has most of the data it needs in its local memory. In addition, within each processor, the data should be arranged, and the algorithm written, in such a way that cache misses and page faults are minimized. This benefits not only the single processor performance, but also reduces the demand for bus bandwidth in SMP systems (Dowd and Severance 1998).

Load Balancing. Another problem that usually degrades performance in both SMP and MPP systems is load imbalance. This occurs when one or more processors has less work to do than the other processors, and is idle during part of the computation. In SMP systems, techniques such as guided self-scheduling can be used for load balancing. In MPP systems, initial load balancing is typically achieved by distributing the data equally across processors. However, the load may become unbalanced during the computation, requiring a re-distribution of data, resulting in communication and synchronization overhead. This problem occurs often in scientific computing, and efficient solution techniques have been studied extensively (Bader and Ja'Ja' 1995; Kumar, Grama, and Rao 1994; Ou and Ranka 1996; Mukherjee, Sharma, Hill, Larus, Rogers, and Saltz 1995; Fox, Williams, and Messina 1994).

Inter-processor communication. In MPP systems, communication costs add to the overhead of the data mining algorithm. They can adversely affect parallel performance to a great extent, and considerable effort may be required to achieve scalability on MPP systems. Techniques to reduce the time spent in communication include merging several short messages into a long one, using an appropriate data layout, trading communication for redundant computation, and overlapping communication with computation, if allowed by the system. Partitioning the problem so that the computation to communication ratio is high may require the complete rewrite of an implementation, or the development of new algorithms. To accomplish this, we can borrow ideas from distributed data mining algorithm research, where the global distribution of the data requires coarse-grained parallelism, and forces the algorithm designers to minimize communication costs.

I/O. Both memory and disk bandwidth continue to grow more slowly than capacity. For example, while disk capacities have been increasing at about 60% a year, the I/O bandwidth has increased only 40% a year. As the bandwidth to capacity ratio shrinks, it takes longer to read or write all the memory (or disk) available to a system. The practical definition of *large* in large-scale data mining tends to be set by the total size of memory and disk available to an application. This implies that the high cost of data movement, algorithm setup, data redistribution, and data scanning will only worsen with time. At the very least, this will increase the pressure on developing algorithms that require fewer passes over the data. Designing algorithms that can make accurate decisions with less data will be important as well.

2.3 Role of Parallel Databases

Along with parallel hardware architectures, parallel software infrastructures for data management are an important component of many data mining applications. There are a large number of special purpose, fast data management systems in use in the scientific community; however, such systems play a very small role when compared to commercial DBMSs. By far, the greatest intersection between the data management and data mining communities is with mining commercial data stored in DBMSs and parallel DBMSs.

In business applications, much of the available data resides in relational and object-oriented DBMSs. Access to data controlled by a DBMS can be rather slow compared to accessing the same data directly from the operating system. DBMSs add a significant layer of functionality between the algorithm and the data that often is not directly relevant to the data mining process. This includes transaction processing, locking, logging, page and tuple management, and more. This extra functionality can be quite costly, to the extent that, for typical scientific queries, the performance penalty of using a commercial DBMSs can be a 5 to 50 times reduction in throughput (Musick 1998). Techniques for improving access to the data are therefore of great interest. Interfacing data mining to parallel DBMS servers (Holsheimer 1996) is a starting point, but there is room for much improvement. For example, Freitas and Lavington (1996a) and Freitas (1997) have presented generalized primitives (SQL queries) for data mining operations. Turning these into specialized parallel access methods on the database back end would be a big step forward.

Doing basic work such as parallelizing operations on a DBMS that are common across many data mining algorithms such as proximity joins (Shafer and Agrawal 1997), or fast quantile estimation (Alsabti, Ranka, and Singh 1997), is another area of research that will eventually have a positive impact on the capabilities of current systems. A good introduction to some related work was given by Han (1998).

2.4 Data Preprocessing

Preprocessing the input data to simplify the pattern recognition problem, without throwing away important information, is a time consuming, but critical first step in data mining. The patterns that can be found in a data set are determined by the quality of the features used to describe the data. As these features represent the data item, any meaningful relationships between the data items must be preserved when the data item is represented as a feature vector.

Data preparation or preprocessing is a topic that is frequently overlooked in the data mining literature. Much of the actual work in mining raw data occurs in this extremely important, but difficult step. It is possibly one of the main reasons why data mining is an interactive and iterative process, and without it, the return on the resources spent in pattern recognition is likely to be disappointing.

The usefulness of different data preprocessing techniques is strongly dependent on the application. Therefore, a comprehensive treatment of the topic would be an immense task. In this section, we introduce the basic approaches that are used, focusing more on methods that are applicable across a wide range of problems, in both the scientific and commercial domains.

2.4.1 Data Size Reduction

One of the first options when faced when mining a large data set, is to reduce the size of the data to make it easier to handle. There are two basic approachcs—sampling and multiresolution analysis.

Sampling is a technique that has been studied extensively, and accepted as a viable approach in statistics. While some may question the use of sampling in data mining as it reduces the size of the data set being processed, it is important to examine the function the data mining algorithm is performing (Provost and Kolluri 1999). If the questions being asked of the data can be answered to sufficient accuracy while using less than the entire giga- or tera-byte data set, then sampling could be used profitably to improve accuracy while mitigating computational requirements. Friedman (1997) observes that "a powerful, computationally-intense procedure operating on a subsample of the data may in fact provide superior accuracy than a less sophisticated one using the entire data base."

While the effectiveness of sampling depends on the data set and the problem, several authors have discussed the issues that must be considered in the use of sampling. For example, Fayyad and Smyth (1995) indicate that random sampling should be avoided when searching for new classes using clustering, as members of a minority class could completely disappear from any small, or even not so small, sample. This could be an important issue in both science data, where the minority class is the one that scientists would like to study further, and in business data, where the incidents of fraud occur relatively infrequently, but are the class of interest to the data miner. Instead, an iterative sampling scheme is suggested that exploits the fact that using a constructed model to classify the data scales linearly with the number of data points to be classified.

A different approach to sampling is described by Musick, Catlett, and Russell (1993), where "active" sampling is done to reduce the computational cost as learning algorithms process large data sets. For example, the search for good split values in decision trees can be done using subsets of the examples at any node, rather than operating on the entire set.

A common thread that emerges from the work on sampling in data mining is that it is not a straightforward matter. In fact, Provost and Kolluri (1999), identify sampling as the one area which is most in need of additional research as there are very few guidelines that are available to guide data mining researchers and practitioners.

While sampling selects a subset of data items, a different approach to reducing the size of the data set is used in multiresolution analysis (MRA). MRA involves creating a series of hierarchical abstractions of the original data, referred to as the fine level data. This data is progressively coarsened and data analysis is done at the coarsest level on a much smaller data set. Whenever analysis requires exploration at a finer level, the appropriate transform is applied to the coarse level data to yield the fine level data.

Multiresolution analysis techniques, especially those based on wavelets, are rapidly gaining acceptance in the scientific visualization community, where they are used for interactive visualization of massive data sets (Stolinitz, Derose, and Salesin 1996). These techniques are also beginning to make inroads into the data mining community (Starck, Murtagh, and Bijaoui 1998). While wavelets lend themselves to parallelization (section 2.4.2), feature extraction and pattern recognition on data that has been transformed using multiresolution techniques remains an open research area.

A different approach is used by Wang, Yang, and Muntz (1997) for spatial data mining. Here the spatial area is divided into rectangular cells; several different levels of these rectangular cells form a hierarchical structure. Each cell at a high level is partitioned to form a number of cells at the lower level. Statistical information on each cell is calculated and stored beforehand, and used to answer queries. This approach can be trivially parallelized.

2.4.2 Feature Extraction

Extraction of relevant features from the raw data set is a very important step in data mining. If the features extracted from the data are not representative of the pattern that is to be recognized, it is impossible to detect the pattern. For commercial data, the very nature of the data makes feature extraction relatively simple. However, this task may be nontrivial for science data. We next describe briefly some of the problems encountered in parallelizing feature extraction from image data, a format often used for data in medicine and astrophysics.

There are several operations that may be used to extract features from images such as image segmentation, registration, enhancement, contour pixel detection, linear approximation, and so on (Jähne 1997). These operations are typically parallelized by partitioning an $n \times n$ array of pixels into P uniform subimages, where P is the number of processors and each subimage is of size $\frac{n}{\sqrt{P}} \times \frac{n}{\sqrt{P}}$. While the operations used in feature extraction from images are very dependent on the problem, there are several common underlying issues that affect performance on parallel machines:

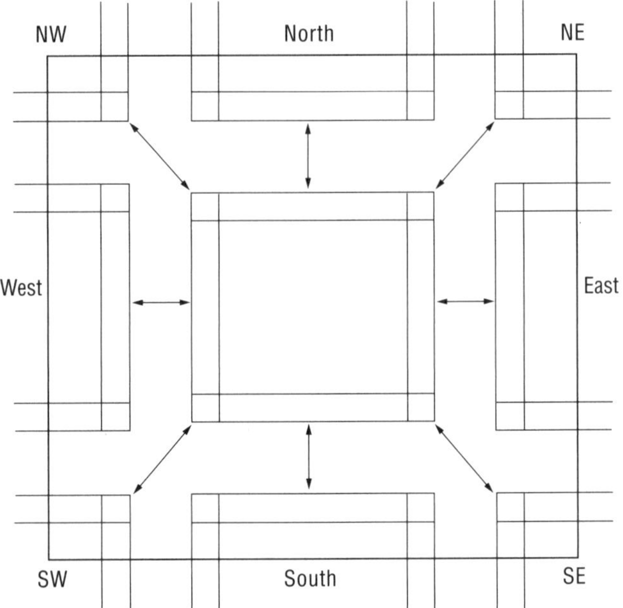

Figure 2.5: Data exchange with ghost cells.

Handling of "ghost cells." An image processing operation, when applied to a pixel, often requires the values of the pixels in the immediate neighborhood. On MIMD systems, this usually implies that for any pixel on the boundary of a subimage, we need the values of the pixels on the boundaries of the subimages in the neighboring processors, figure 2.5. In order to make programming easier, the data structure used for storing the subimage within a processor is padded on all sides with additional pixels that are referred to as "ghost cells." These contain the pixel values from the boundaries of the subimages on the neighboring processors.

The problem of keeping ghost cells updated during the computation has been extensively studied in the area of numerical methods (Kumar, Grama, Gupta, and Karypis 1994). Effective solutions include combining several short messages into a longer message and overlapping communication with computation.

A different problem arises when wavelets are used to process images. In this case, providing a layer of ghost cells is not a simple matter—as the number of levels of the wavelet transform grows, the amount of extra data (and thus the extra computations) needed grows as a power of two. This constraint may limit the number of steps of the wavelet transform that can be done on one processor using data only in the processors in its immediate neighborhood (Sullivan 1991).

Handling "global" features: In some tasks, the feature being extracted may be spread across more than one subimage. Care must be taken to extract such features correctly. Chung and Prasanna (1998) consider the case where line segments are extracted from a contour-pixel array using linear approximation. The case of a local contour, where the entire contour is within a subimage, is easy to handle. However, for a global contour, the processing of a contour segment within a subimage can start only when the processor that owns the preceding part of the contour has finished processing its segment. Since each processor on a MIMD system does not have global information that determines such inter-processor dependencies, parallelizing linear approximation can be difficult. After exploring several different alternatives, Chung and Prasanna found that an asynchronous algorithm, combined with a priority-based heuristic, enabled them to avoid problems due to load imbalance and obtain good speedup.

A similar problem with global feature extraction occurs in the process of finding connected components within an image. While each processor can determine the connected components within its subimage, it is more difficult to find connected components that span several subimages. Bader, Ja'Ja', Harwood, and Davis (1995) use a divide and conquer approach, where the algorithm iterates $log_2 P$ times, alternating between combining the subimages in horizontal merges of vertical borders, and vertical merges of horizontal borders.

Another parallel approach to finding connected components for image segmentation is described by Moga, Cramariuc, and Gabbouj (1998), using the watershed transformation. They describe two versions of the approach. In the first version, called "rain-falling simulation," at each pixel, one can "walk" downward following a steepest slope line toward a minimum pixel, and propagate the label of the latter backward along the whole path. The second version, called the "hill-climbing simulation" does the opposite, where water springs from regional minima and immerses higher neighborhoods that have not been already flooded. Using relatively simple communication across neighboring processors they demonstrate good speedup on up to 128 processors on the Cray T3D using MPI.

Communication Costs. A problem that arises in implementing multidimensional wavelet transforms is that expensive data transfers have to be done after the transform has been calculated in each dimension. Yang and Misra (1998) investigate various data distribution schemes that minimize this data movement. Their experiments on a cluster of SGI workstations using MPI indicate that alternative data distributions are worth investigating. A similar result was obtained by Uhl (1996) on tightly coupled parallel machines.

2.4.3 Dimension Reduction

Dimension reduction, or feature selection is the task of reducing the number of features used to represent a data mining application. As pattern recognition algorithms have to search through a combinatorial space whose dimension is equal to the number of features, it is important that we identify the minimal set of features that will allow us to obtain accurate results efficiently. Using a minimal number of features often leads to better generalizations and simpler models that can be more easily interpreted. In addition, by getting rid of the features that are not important to the task at hand, we make the job of the pattern recognition algorithm easier.

The simplest way to do feature selection is to use domain expertise to determine the relative importance of the features, as well as to identify which of the features are most important for discrimination, and which are acting primarily as "noise." Another approach is to use search techniques to find an optimal subset from a larger set of possible features. However, exhaustively trying all the subsets of feature combinations is computationally very expensive.

A machine learning solution to this problem is to use either the filter approach or the wrapper approach (Kohavi and John 1998). In the former, feature subset selection is done independent of the induction algorithm used in classification. As these methods do not take into account the biases of the induction algorithms, they may not perform well. In the wrapper approach, the feature subset selection is done using the induction algorithm as a black box to evaluate the subset. Starting with a training set for the classification problem, and an initial set of features, various subsets of these features are selected. For each subset, the inductive algorithm is used to generate a model based on the training data. The performance of a subset is measured by how well it classifies the test set. The best feature subset found is then used in the actual design of the classification system.

An example of this approach is described by Vafaie and De Jong (1998), where the C4.5 program is used for induction and genetic algorithms are used for feature subset construction. A similar technique using genetic algorithms and k-nearest-neighbors is described by Punch (1993). In both cases, the reduction in the number of features substantially reduced the execution time without adversely affecting accuracy. This approach to feature selection can be easily parallelized by using parallel implementations of genetic algorithms and induction algorithms as described in sections 2.5.5 and 2.5.1.

A different approach to feature selection is described by Bradley, Mangasarian, and Street (1998) where the authors combine feature selection with pattern recognition. They consider the binary classification problem of discriminating between two given sets in an n-dimensional feature space by using as few of the given features as possible. This problem is converted to a mathematical programming problem, with a parametric objective function that achieves the task by generating a separating plane in a feature space of as small a dimension as possible, while minimizing the average distance of misclassified points to the plane. Results on small data sets with many features are encouraging. While the test problems used for demonstrating this approach are quite small, and there is no need for parallelism, it does raise the interesting possibility that for much larger problems, we may be able to benefit from the current state of the art in parallel optimization software, as described in section 2.5.6.

A more traditional approach to feature selection or dimension reduction uses the Principal Component Analysis (PCA), also known as the Karhunen Loève transformation, or the Hotelling transform (Jackson 1991). PCA is a multivariate technique in which a number of related variables are transformed to a smaller set of uncorrelated variables with desirable properties. One way of implementing PCA is using a Singular Value Decomposition (SVD), which essentially calculates the eigenvectors and eigenvalues of the covariance matrix. This decomposition has been extensively studied in the numerical methods community (Golub and Van Loan 1989) and several parallel software packages are available.

If $\mathbf{A}$ is an $m \times n$ matrix of the centered feature vectors for the data sets under consideration, with $m \geq n$ and $rank(\mathbf{A}) = r$, the singular value decomposition of $\mathbf{A}$ is defined as

$$\mathbf{A} = \mathbf{U}\Sigma\mathbf{V}^T$$

where $\mathbf{U}^T\mathbf{U} = \mathbf{I}_m$, $\mathbf{V}^T\mathbf{V} = \mathbf{I}_n$, and $\Sigma = diag(\sigma_1, \sigma_2, \ldots, \sigma_n)$, $\sigma_i > 0$ for $1 \leq i \leq r$ and $\sigma_j = 0$ for $j > r$. Here, $\mathbf{I}_m$ is the identity matrix of order m. The first r columns of the orthogonal matrices $\mathbf{U}$ and $\mathbf{V}$ define the orthonormal eigenvectors associated with the r nonzero eigenvalues of $\mathbf{A}^T\mathbf{A}$ or $\mathbf{A}\mathbf{A}^T$, respectively. $\mathbf{U}$ and $\mathbf{V}$ are referred to as the left and the right singular vectors respectively, and the singular values of $\mathbf{A}$ are the diagonal elements of Σ, which are the nonnegative square-roots of the n eigenvalues of $\mathbf{A}\mathbf{A}^T$.

There are several public domain packages available to calculate the singular values and singular vectors, both for the case where the matrix $\mathbf{A}$ is sparse, that is, not every feature is present in a data set, as well as when $\mathbf{A}$ is dense, that is, all features are present in all data sets. In the dense case, the ScaLAPACK software package (Blackford et al. 1997) provides a well tested, state-of-the-art software package for calculating the singular values, and optionally, the left and right singular vectors, on distributed memory machines. ScaLAPACK is built on top of more fundamental matrix and vector operations called the PBLAS, which are parallel versions of the basic linear algebra subroutines (BLAS) (Lawson, Hanson, Kincaid, and Krogh 1979; Dongarral Dongarral, Du Croz, Hammarling, and Hanson 1988; Dongarral, Du Croz,

Duff, and Hammarling 1990). These operations are highly optimized for various parallel machines, and therefore result in high performance in the calculation of the SVD. Communication is through a layer called basic linear algebra communication subprograms (BLACS)[5], which supports various communication packages including PVM and MPI. As with the BLAS, several computer vendors have optimized BLACS, resulting in high performance. For shared memory machines, the precursor to ScaLAPACK, called LAPACK (Anderson et al. 1995), is available, providing the same functionality. Both packages are available in the public domain.[6]

When the matrix **A** is sparse, one way of calculating the SVD is by doing an eigen-decomposition of the matrix $\mathbf{A}^T\mathbf{A}$ or $\mathbf{A}\mathbf{A}^T$. As these matrices are symmetric, a method that is commonly used is the Lanczos method (Saad 1992), which requires the matrix only in a matrix-vector multiplication operation. Instead of forming the matrices $\mathbf{A}^T\mathbf{A}$ or $\mathbf{A}\mathbf{A}^T$, the matrix-vector multiplication is done by two separate matrix-vector multiplies using **A** and $\mathbf{A}^T$. This method is particularly useful when only a few eigenvalues and vectors are required, which is the case for data mining applications. P_ARPACK (Maschoff and Sorensen 1996) is a parallel software package that implements the Implicitly Restarted Lanczos method for symmetric matrices. As the Lanczos method requires an inordinate amount of storage, the re-started version was used to overcome memory requirements. P_ARPACK requires the user to provide the matrix-vector routine, which is convenient for our matrix under consideration, as this can be achieved using two matrix-vector multiplies. Both BLACS and MPI versions of P_ARPACK are available from the public domain at www.netlib.org.

2.5 Parallel Pattern Recognition Algorithms

Large scale data mining is very much in its infancy, and as such, the search for effective, scalable, serial algorithms is still a very active area of research in the machine learning community. Research in earnest into parallel versions of these algorithms has really only just begun, with much of the work occurring within the last five years.

While work in parallel data mining algorithms is very recent, extensive research has been done in parallel algorithms in the scientific and numerical analysis communities. There are excellent resources available for standard tools like parallel quick-sorts, hash tables (Kumar, Grama, Gupta, and Karypis 1994), parallel search trees (Steinberg and Solomon 1990), and parallelized mathematical libraries, which we refer to throughout the text. Such tools form

[5] http://www.netlib.org/blacs/

[6] http://www.netlib.org/

the core of many data mining approaches, and should be taken advantage of whenever possible.

We have briefly discussed parallel programming issues in general in section 2.2.4. In the rest of this section we focus attention on different approaches for parallelizing decision tree induction, association rule discovery, neural network classification, clustering, genetic algorithms, and mathematical optimization. Decision trees and association rules in particular have received much attention, with much of the impetus coming from the business sector. Our descriptions assume that the reader has some familiarity with the algorithms being discussed. We will focus on the salient issues, ignoring some of the details. Examining the work done in the areas mentioned above will help us understand the approaches used in the area of fine-grained, parallel pattern recognition algorithms. For descriptions of distributed data mining approaches, a good introduction is given by Chan and Stolfo[7]. For an in-depth look into scaling algorithms to larger problem sizes, Provost and Kolluri (1999) provide an excellent collection of ideas and work.

2.5.1 Decision Trees

Decision trees address the following problem: using a set of examples whose classification is known, automatically construct a set of rules, or equivalently a *decision tree*, that will be able to predict the classification of new examples that have not yet been seen. The process of constructing the tree is called *induction*, and the use of the tree as a classifier to classify new, unseen examples is the *prediction* phase. While the induction phase is expensive, the prediction phase is typically very fast, normally requiring just a few comparisons. Furthermore, once a tree (or equivalently, a set of rules) has been constructed, the classification of a large number of objects is embarrassingly parallel.

Terminology

More formally, using notation taken from Musick, Catlett, and Russell (1993), we are given a *training set* $\mathcal{S} = \{s_1 \dots s_N\}$ where each instance in $\mathcal{S}$ is described using attributes $\mathcal{A} = \{A_1 \dots A_M\}$, and further annotated with the instance's classification $\{c_1 \dots c_N\} \in \mathcal{C}$. The induction problem is to construct a set of rules using the information in $\mathcal{A}$ such that given a *test set* of instances which have not yet been classified (i.e. assigned $\{c_1 \dots c_N\} \in \mathcal{C}$), the rules will correctly predict the class of each member of the test set.

Induction is typically done in two steps—decision tree construction, followed by pruning. Pruning is fast, normally less than 1% of the overall cost

[7] Scalability of Hierarchical Meta-Learning on Partitioned Data, http://www.cs.columbia.edu/ sal/recent-papers.html

of tree induction. The traditional algorithm used to construct a decision tree (Quinlan 1986) is based on ID3 (and equivalently, C4.5 and C5). Working from the training set $\mathcal{S}$, the algorithm first selects an attribute A_i and an attribute value v to form the root of the tree, then splits $\mathcal{S}$ according to one of several simple tests ($<$, $>$, $=$, $\in$) comparing v to the value of attribute A_i for each instance in $\mathcal{S}$. The algorithm then applies itself recursively to each subset of $\mathcal{S}$ thus formed. For large training sets, the major costs arise in selecting an attribute for the root of the current subtree, and in choosing appropriate threshold values for numeric attributes. Attributes are selected using information gain criteria that will attempt to maximally distinguish the class distributions in a sample.

Initial Approaches to Parallelizing Decision Trees

C4.5 formed the basis for several early attempts to building parallel decision trees. Darlington, Guo, Sutiwaraphun, and To (1997) propose a straightforward task-parallel scheme for parallelizing C4.5. Their approach is based on a master-slave configuration, where the master distributes independent tasks to each slave processor. Initially, all data is replicated across all P processors. The master node expands the decision tree depth-first until the number of nodes in the tree equals the number of processors available in the slave pool, at which point the nodes are handed off to the slave processors, which can proceed with no further communication. This approach suffers two major problems—poor usage of the aggregate memory of the system, and poor load balancing. The first few expansions of the decision tree are always the most expensive, both in terms of computation and memory requirements. This approach requires the master node to do all the work at first, and only uses the local memory of one processor. Subsequent load balancing is an issue as well, since some processors may have received decision tree nodes with little or no work left, while other processors might be stuck with the majority of the remaining training samples.

Kufrin (1995) proposed a design for a data parallel approach for parallelizing C4.5 tree induction called PDT, and later proposed a method for speeding C4.5's rule construction process (Kufrin 1997). PDT partitions the data across the processors, so that each processor has $N/(P-1)$ training instances. The master processor is responsible for coordination and notification alone. Each processor locally sorts the numeric data for all attributes. Then, the sorted data as well as the related statistics are written asynchronously to the network, where the next processor that finishes can asynchronously read, update statistics, and write again to the network. There is a barrier synchronization here, where all processors wait for the rest of the processors to finish. At the end of this communication phase, the master node chooses a split point, and broadcasts that to the rest of the processors. The work continues in a similar way until the tree is finished. The total communication is $O(N)$, or $O(N/P)$, and so is scalable with the size of the data. The downside of this approach is load balancing. There is no way to tell a priori which data will end up in which part of the decision tree. Some processors can very quickly end up with all their partitioned data fully classified. Since the data is statically partitioned, these processors will contribute no further cycles (or local memory) to the problem's solution. Furthermore, this type of communication tends to be bursty, leading to large synchronization times while waiting for bandwidth. While PDT experimental results were not reported, it is likely that the overall scalability of the approach would be limited, and would drop off rapidly as the number of available processors grows.

A final example that we give in this section is an early parallel implementation by Cherkauer and Shavlik (1993) with the goal of using the decision tree to help with a constructive induction task. This example demonstrates the problem-dependent nature of this work. In this task, the goal was to use the decision tree to help evaluate as many new induced features (or attributes) as possible. The total size of the data set Cherkaur and Shavlik used was small, and replicating that across all nodes was feasible. The algorithm follows a task parallel approach, where the data is partitioned vertically, or by attribute, rather than horizontally by record. The master node holds an attribute pool. When determining a split, the master node sends an "active bit-vector" indicating which training set samples are part of the current node to be split. Every processor requests an attribute index from the pool, locally determines the best split for that attribute, sends the information back to the master and requests the next available attribute index. This approach does well distributing the load. When all attributes are processed, the master selects the global best feature, and updates the active training set bit-vectors. While this approach worked well for a small data set with a very large set of attributes, it would perform poorly for a large data set since communicating the feature and active example bit-vectors would be very costly.

Breaking through to Scalable Classifiers

None of the algorithms above scale to large data and massively parallel machines. In 1996, Shafer, Agrawal, and Mehta (1996) introduced an algorithm called SPRINT, which presented a radical departure from the above approaches. In previous algorithms, each attribute needed to be sorted at every split decision. SPRINT eliminates all but 1 sorting pass on the data, without any approximations. This was done by using a simple indexing strategy. In addition, they provided a parallel version of this algorithm that, while not perfectly linearly scalable, was a major improvement in the general case over any previous approach. SPRINT essentially helped researchers break out of a fairly rigid mold for thinking about parallelization of decision trees, and has lead to some excellent work.

SPRINT uses a data parallel approach, assuming MPPs with message passing. We next outline the main flow to help elucidate the strengths and the weaknesses of the approach. We do not address here the actual data structures used. Also, we do not discuss how categorical attributes are handled, since that is not as interesting as the differences in handling continuous attributes.

Initialization

1. Data is partitioned among the processors with each getting N/P training examples, where N is the total number of samples, and P the number of processors. Each processor creates a set of attribute lists, which basically break the training set into M arrays (an array per attribute). Each attribute list value has a training example identification number (TID) attached to it that identifies the training example it came from.

2. The next step in the initialization is to perform a parallel sort on each of the numeric attributes. After this redistribution, each attribute list for each processor contains a static, contiguous, sorted portion of the attribute. Note that in any processor, the values in an attribute list A_i may come from different training examples than the values in $A_{j \neq i}$. The last step is to build count-oriented statistics.

If all data does not fit in memory, it is all kept on disk. Note that without the identification information, we would be unable to re-construct a training set example from the newly ordered attribute vectors.

Main loop

1. Find the optimal split point:

    - Each processor evaluates each of the local attribute lists to find the best local split
    - Communicate local best splits and count statistics to all processors
    - Each processor determines the best global split (it will always be consistent)

2. Split the data:

    - Each processor splits the winning attribute, and sends the local TIDs of the new left and right nodes to all other processors

- Each processor builds a hash table containing all TIDs, and identification of which decision tree node the TIDs belong to
- Each processor, for each attribute, probes the hash table for each TID to determine how to split that attribute value

3. Carry out the same on the next unsolved decision tree node.

SPRINT's scale-up, speedup and size-up results are nearly linear for 16 nodes of an IBM SP-2, and much better than previous approaches. One would expect the deviation from linear to be more apparent as the number of processors were scaled up to hundreds or thousands of processors. Also, scalability seems to improve as the number of data elements per processor grows, since the relative communication to computation cost is actually shrinking.

The main source of overhead in this implementation is the hash table used to split other attributes. The hash table is of the same order of size as the training set size at the node of interest. Near the top of the tree, this is basically the entire training set. While attribute lists can be read in from disk, this hash table must remain memory resident. The hash table also incurs a communication overhead of $O(N)$ per processor to gather all the bookkeeping information. SPRINT's scalability limitations then are an overhead of $O(N)$ per processor in both memory and communication.

ScalParC (Joshi, Karypis, and Kumar 1998) is an extension of SPRINT which, in many ways, demonstrates the value of making use of existing optimized parallel tools. ScalParC follows the same basic algorithmic structure as outlined above. ScalParC makes two major adjustments, inspired by parallel sparse matrix multiplication algorithms. First, a distributed hash table (Kumar, Grama, Gupta, and Karypis 1994) is used, rather than a global hash table replicated at each processor. This cuts memory requirements to $O(N/P)$ per processor, making the algorithm scalable in this regard. The distributed hash table does not incur a major communication overhead. Group reduction is used for much of the communication, which is an $O(log(P))$ operation rather than $O(P)$. Second, the decision tree nodes are constructed breadth-first rather than depth-first, and processor synchronization is held off until all work is done for that level of the tree. This has two significant benefits. Synchronizing communication is limited, and load balancing is much better since processors finishing quickly with one node of the tree will be able to move directly on to the next.

ScalParC brings out an interesting issue regarding load balancing. If the attributes are dependent, or correlated, then some splits may unequally load the processors, even for the breadth-first tree expansion.

The algorithms above have all been embedded in either a task parallel, or a data parallel approach. The effectiveness of these approaches, however, depends on the size and shape of the decision tree, as well as the results of the splits at any node. For example, task parallel approaches will be most effective when the decision tree is bushy. In this case, data can be distributed to balance loads, after which there will be minimal communication costs. For small, thin trees, there will not be enough independent tasks for the processors (as seen in the Darlington approach described above), and there would be too much idle-waiting. In these situations, data parallel approaches tend to work better. Data parallel approaches start losing ground as the tree grows bushy, since the communication requirements grow. What is particularly challenging for decision tree induction is that trees will change their basic nature as computation progresses from a single root node (small and thin) to a large, bushy tree, which implies that no single approach is likely to perform well in the general case.

This problem is well described by Srivastava, Han, Kumar, and Singh (1999). They present a dynamic approach to this problem where they gradually migrate the algorithm from data parallel to task parallel as the shape of the tree changes. The switch for each processor is made when the expected communication cost of remaining in the data parallel mode exceeds the cost of redistributing data within and between the two new partitions. The resulting algorithm performs well, and it is likely that dynamic hybrid algorithms will become much more popular in the future.

Limitations and Open Questions

The tremendous progress in parallelizing decision trees made over the past few years seems to have increased the frontiers of what we do not understand. The need for further research in this area continues to grow. For example, there has been very little work to date on algorithms for parallel architectures other than MPP. Zaki, Ho, and Agrawal (1998, 1999b) have done some work exploring ways to take advantage of SMP and hybrid architectures. This will be described in much more depth in the next few chapters. There has been a good amount of work done on linear or sublinear techniques for choosing split points based on sampling and clustering (Musick, Catlett, and Russell 1993; Srivastava, Singh, Han, and Kumar 1997; Alsabti, Ranka, and Singh 1998). The tradeoff between the computational cost and the resulting accuracy, especially in the face of large data and parallel implementations, has not been explored in any depth. There has been very little work done on optimizing the use of cache, memory and disk hierarchies (Mehta, Agrawal, and Rissanen 1996). In fact, the reported usage in many of the algorithms described in this section is rather crude. There are many unrealistic assumptions in theoretical performance evaluations (such as equal communication costs, no bus contention, perfect synchronization, average costs assumed with little discussion of worst case costs, independent attributes), and many gaps in experimental evaluations (few data sets, few processors, few ties to domain dependent outcomes). We are just coming to grips with the difficult issues of load balancing for decision trees. Even the basic underlying data structures, order of tree expansion, and which serial algorithms to parallelize are all unclear at this point. Finally, boosting scalability and performance is still an important goal, and there is yet a lot of room for improvement.

2.5.2 Association Rule Discovery

Associations are rules of the form {Beer, Milk} $\Rightarrow$ {Diapers}, that is, the presence of beer and milk in a transaction implies the presence of diapers. These rules typically are not functional (guaranteed) dependencies, but more likely to be probabilistic in nature. The problem of association rule discovery is, given a set of transactions, find all associations that have a certain minimal level of support in the data, and have a certain level of confidence. The notion of transactions here is quite general. In a business setting, a set of transactions could be a handful of grocery receipts, of which each receipt contains a set of items (like milk or beer). In a scientific setting, a transaction could be a handful of zones from a computational mesh, of which each zone contains a set of mixed materials (like oxygen and hydrogen). The task of finding associations is a computationally challenging, but important one for the data mining community. There are several closely related problems that have seen some parallel work that we do not cover here, including functional dependencies (Parikh, Ganesh, and Srivastava 1996), association rules with is-a hierarchies (Srikand and Agrawal 1995; Shintani and Kitsuregawa 1998a), and sequential association rules (Shintani and Kitsuregawa 1998b).

Terminology

More formally, using notation taken from Han, Karypis, and Kumar (1999), let $\mathcal{T}$ be a set of transactions, where each transaction is made up of a subset of allowed items $\mathcal{I}$. Let C be a specific set of items in $\mathcal{I}$. Then the support $\sigma(C)$ of C in the set of transactions $\mathcal{T}$ is a count of the number of transactions in $\mathcal{T}$ that contain C.

An association rule is an expression of the form $X \Rightarrow Y$ with minimal support s and minimum confidence α, where $X \subset \mathcal{I}$ and $Y \subset \mathcal{I}$. The minimum support s is $s = \sigma(X \cup Y)/|\mathcal{T}|$, and the minimum confidence α is $\alpha = \sigma(X \cup Y)/\sigma(X)$. The minimum confidence measures how often X and Y occur together in the same transaction in $\mathcal{T}$ as a fraction of the total transactions in which X occurs.

The Progenitor

The standard algorithm for finding association rules stems from work by Agrawal, Imielinski, and Swami (1993) and Agrawal and Srikant (1994) on Apriori. The first step is to find the set of candidate item sets, or subsets of $\mathcal{I}$ that could occur in the transactions $\mathcal{T}$. This step can be very expensive, and can require multiple passes over the data. The next step is to use the candidate sets to create rules that have the minimum required support and confidence. This step is easy, details for solving it can be found in Agrawal, Imielinski, and Swami (1993b).

Apriori is a serial algorithm from which has sprung a long line of data-parallel adaptations. Apriori approaches candidate set generation by pruning the possible candidates before generating them. This generate, test, and prune approach turns what was an intractable problem (evaluating the power-set of items in $\mathcal{I}$ is a super-exponential proposition) into something manageable. Apriori also takes advantage of the fact that the support of X will always be greater or equal to the support of $X \cup Y$. The core Apriori algorithm for generating the candidate set is as follows:

1. Initialize the set C_1 of candidate sets of size $k = 1$ as $\mathcal{I}$.
2. Prune C_k by eliminating those elements that do not have minimum support.
    - Scan the set of transactions.
    - For each transaction, increase the count of any element in C_k that is covered by the transaction.
    - When done, eliminate those elements in C_k whose count is not greater or equal to the minimum support.
3. If C_k is empty, stop.
4. Create the set of elements C_{k+1} by extending C_k.
5. Increment k, and go to step 2.

To speed the process, the candidate elements are kept in a specialized hash tree, which is a clever mechanism for carrying out the comparisons with transactions in step 2 reasonably quickly. This algorithm can be expensive. A total of k passes are required over the data, and step 2, even with the hash tree, consumes most of the time for the algorithm. There are several other interesting characteristics about this iterative approach to generating C_k. The size of the problem in this case is controlled not just by the number and complexity of the transactions, but also by the minimum required support and confidence. Also, the shape of the candidate elements tends to grow like a pear, with C_1 being small, C_2—C_{2+j} (for small j) being large, and C_i for i near k being small again. In fact, the structure of the candidate sets is a version space (Mitchell 1981). Research in this area has produced compact ways to represent the most specific and most general boundaries of the space, and search techniques for reducing the size of the space optimally fast.

It is interesting to note that in the same papers, Agrawal and colleagues presented several other algorithms. While they performed better than Apriori in general, Apriori was used as the core later simply because it was easier to parallelize.

Trading Communication for Redundant Computation

One common way to parallelize the above algorithm is to partition the data horizontally across P processors, and to have each processor generate the full set of candidate elements step by step as laid out in Apriori. Since generation of C_k requires counts from all transactions, counting the support occurs in two steps. First, each processor creates local counts from its local N/P transactions. Second, there is a global reduction to add all the local counts, followed by a broadcast to provide the global count information back to the processors. Each processor then proceeds to prune according to the counts, and generate C_{k+1}. At a high level, this is the basic underlying algorithm used for CD (Agrawal and Schafer 1996), PDM (Park, Chen, and Yu 1995a, 1995b), and NPA (Shintani and Kitsuregawa 1995).

In this approach, there are k barrier synchronizations for each of the k levels, and approximately k passes over the data. Each processor builds and stores the exact same candidate hash tree. On the positive side, the load is very well balanced here. On the negative side, not only is there a large amount of redundant computation taking place, but the aggregate memory utilization is very poor. The candidate set must fit entirely in $1/P$th the total memory of the system. What is interesting in this approach, is that when the problem fits in memory, this simple algorithm scales as well as, or better than, the more complex approaches described below. This demonstrates how costly communication in such systems can actually be.

Memory Efficient Approaches

The other common method for parallelizing Apriori is similar to what was just described, but with modifications needed to make full use of all the system memory. This is done by distributing both the transactions (horizontally), and the candidate set across the P processors. Each processor P_i starts with its local portion C_k^i of C_k. Pruning C_k by dropping elements without minimum support requires counting all transactions. In this case, processors $P_{j \neq i}$ can not evaluate C_k^i. To generate full counts, processors redistribute local transactions to processors with relevant subsets of C_k. Each processor ends up seeing all the data needed to prune their local C_k^i. Once the pruning stage is done, the pruned C_k^i are communicated globally. The final step at any level is for each processor P_i to use the full, pruned candidate set at level k to generate C_{k+1}, and C_{k+1}^i.

This is the core algorithm followed by CanD and DD (Agrawal and Schafer 1996), HPA and HPA-ELD (Shintani and Kitsuregawa 1995), and IDD (Han, Karypis, and Kumar 1999). Each of these algorithms vary in how the assignment of C_k^i is generated, in how the transaction communication or redistribution is carried out, and in ways of short-circuiting the amount of data that needs to be sent. For example, IDD does not do an all-to-all communication of the local transactions, but rather communicates the data asynchronously in a round robin style. This reduces overall communication costs, and also helps overlap communication with computation, that is, a barrier synchronization is not required. HPA-ELD is interesting in that it makes use of any left-over memory at the processors by keeping more of the candidate hash tree at each processor. This makes the algorithm act more like CD when memory is available, but transitions gracefully to a DD-like algorithm with memory runs down.

All these algorithms share the same general characteristics. First, the better the C_k^i distribution, the closer the algorithm can come to a task parallel approach, which would eliminate much of the communication cost. While main memory is utilized effectively, the communication cost has significantly increased. There can still be a good deal of redundant computation, since each transaction may need to be processed for several different subsets C_k^i. Also, the communication can tend to be bursty, leading to contention on the bus, and idle-waiting processors.

New Directions and Open Questions

A different style of a hybrid approach is given by Han, Karypis, and Kumar (1999) in an algorithm called HD. Recall the pear-shaped look of the size of the C_k elements as k varies from 1 to the max. At levels where the number of candidate elements is large, the DD-related approaches above tend to perform well, since the relative size of the communication overhead is small and the load can be easily balanced. At the start of the task, and for large k, the candidate sets will be small and CD-like algorithms are a much better choice. HD takes advantage of this by arranging the processors in a set of groups (or equivalently, as a 2D grid). Internally, each group is doing IDD, but between groups the processors are communicating with a CD-style approach. The size of the groups is dynamic, and is a function of the size of the candidate set at any particular level. This approach scales much better than the individual DD or CD oriented algorithms.

A very different way of looking at this problem was initiated by Savasere, Omiecinski, and Navathe (1995) with the Partition algorithm. Partition is a serial approach that introduces a means of working with vertically partitioned transaction data. Partition also introduced the notion of essentially *bounding* the total set of candidate items C_k in one pass of the transaction data, then correcting this initial estimate with a second pass. As a result, in two passes over the data, and with similar computational requirements as other serial approaches, Partition achieves identical results. Zaki, Parthasarathy, Ogihara, and Li (1998) extend concepts in Partition in several important ways. First, they provide four parallel algorithms for a hierarchical SMP architecture. They lay out the version space for C_k much more clearly, and demonstrate methods for quickly generating a very accurate minimum-support boundary within that space. Finally, they provide a means of partitioning the candidate elements within that boundary (and the respective transaction data) in such a way that the algorithm proceeds in a task parallel fashion. Again, the result is that only two passes are required over the transaction data. The serial performance is an order of magnitude faster than previous approaches. Unfortunately, the scalability experiments of the approach were inconclusive, as speedup on a 4 node, 8 processor per node machine rapidly drops off to CD-like algorithms. These algorithms are explored in detail in later chapters in this book.

There has been tremendous progress in parallel algorithms for association rule discovery over the past few years, and again, there are a great many unanswered questions. There has been little work to date on optimizing memory access patterns (Zaki, Ho, and Agrawal 1998) although there is a large body of literature available on the topic[8]. There has been little work on architectures beyond generic MPPs. Load balancing is a difficult problem-dependent issue here as well, since for example, the cost of traversing a candidate hash tree depends on the complexity of the transaction involved. Recent work in hybrid algorithms includes techniques that intermix data and task parallel approaches (Zaki, Parthasarathy, Ogihara, and Li 1998), or modify basic behaviors depending on the shape characteristics of the particular problem (Han, Karypis, and Kumar 1999), or of the state of machine use (Shintani and Kitsuregawa 1995). It seems likely that dynamic, hybrid approaches will be a very active area of research for the next several years. As with decision trees, the basic underlying data structures, and choice of which serial algorithms to parallelize are all unclear at this point, making it very likely that impressive gains in performance can still be obtained.

---

[8]See the 1999 paper by J. S. Vitter, "External Memory Algorithms and Data Structures," http://www.cs.duke.edu/ jsv

2.5.3 Neural Networks

There has been a resurgence of interest in neural networks in the last few years for use in both supervised and unsupervised learning. Since ANN theory is based on massive parallelism, it is evident that parallel machines can be used to exploit this inherent parallelism. Such parallel implementations are especially necessary in light of the fact that neural networks have a high computational complexity as training instances are often presented many times and network performance is achieved only after gradual modification of the network weights. As a result, many researchers have actively explored the use of parallel machines to reduce the time for learning. While several of these systems are special purpose machines, we will focus on implementations on the more general parallel architectures which are available commercially.

Terminology

Neural networks are patterned after the biological ganglia and synapses of the nervous system. The essential element of the neural network is the neuron. A typical neuron j receives a set of input signals from the other connected neurons x_i, each of which is multiplied by a synaptic weight of w_{ij}. The resulting activation weights are then summed to produce the activation level for the neuron j. Learning is carried out by adjusting the weights in a neural network. Neurons that contribute to the correct answer have their weights strengthened, while other neurons have their weights reduced. Several architectures and error correction algorithms have been developed for neural networks (Haykin 1999).

The classic algorithm used to train neural networks is back-propagation. This has two phases. In the forward phase, the input pattern is fed to the network, and propagated through the layers to compute the activations of the nodes in each layer. The difference between the desired output, and the output of the nodes in the final layer defines the error in the final layer. In the backward phase, this error from the final or output layer is propagated backward to the lower layers, and the errors for each node in various layers is computed. The resulting weight changes reduce the total error at the nodes in the output layer.

Parallelization of Neural Networks

While parallelism is implicit in neural networks, the parallel implementation of neural models is not trivial, and requires sophisticated algorithm design to efficiently map the implementation onto a chosen parallel computer. There are a variety of approaches to this problem (Sundararajan and Saratchandran 1998).

One approach to parallelizing neural networks exploits the fact that the computational requirements of a neural network can be expressed as matrix-vector computations (Petrowski, Personnaz, Dreyfus, and Girault 1989). Techniques from the field of parallel matrix computations can then be applied to solve the problem (Kumar, Grama, Gupta, and Karypis 1994). Many neural networks are fully connected, such that each neuron in a layer is connected to all neurons in the preceding and succeeding layers. As we try to solve more complex problems that require networks with a large number of nodes, it is very likely that we will need to move towards a sparsely connected network instead of a fully connected one. Again, parallel techniques from sparse matrix computations can help provide a solution to this problem.

In a 1997 survey paper Misra describes various parallel environments for the implementation of neural networks and prescribes desired characteristics to look for in parallel implementations. Noting that turnover in the world of parallel computers is very high, which makes code developed for a machine obsolete in a few years, the author suggests developing neural network software in a modular fashion. In this approach, the description of the network would be maintained in a machine independent format, and translation modules written for each parallel machine.

Another good survey of the parallel formulation of the back-propagation algorithm is given by Kumar, Shekhar, and Amin (1994), wherein the authors categorize parallel implementations as follows:

Network partitioned: In this case, the nodes and the weights are partitioned among different processors, and the computations of the node activations, node errors, and weight changes are parallelized. One might think of this approach as parallelism being exploited at the fine grain level.

The nodes can be partitioned in several ways. Complete partitioning assigns one node per processor, while vertical sectioning divides the nodes in a layer among the processors and each processor gets some nodes from a layer.

Similarly, the weights can be partitioned in various ways. In complete partitioning each processor gets one weight in the network. While this approach maximizes concurrency, it also requires communication to accumulate the terms. Two other schemes, inset and outset grouping, are often used in conjunction with vertical sectioning. Inset grouping schemes form sets representing the collection of weights at the incoming edge of a node. The inset of a node is assigned to the processor that owns the node. This reduces the need for communication in computing node activations during forward propagation. Similarly, outset grouping groups weights in the outgoing edges from a node, and eliminates the need for communication to compute the error vectors in the backward phase. Both inset and outset schemes can be used together, though it results in a duplication of each weight on two processors. A different partitioning, the check-board approach, partitions the weights by grouping the rows and the columns of the weight matrix. With enough processors, this reduces to complete partitioning.

Pattern partitioned: Here, the network nodes and weights are replicated on each processor. The pattern set is divided equally among processors, each of which carries out the forward and backward phases for its local set of patterns, and accumulates the corresponding weight changes. Then the processors communicate to accumulate the weight changes to update the network. This scheme is preferred when there are a large number of patterns, and the machine architecture supports an efficient broadcast operation. It can be considered as a coarse-grained form of parallelism. In pattern partitioning, it is also possible to exploit medium-level parallelism by pipelining the computation across the different layers, with each layer working on a different input pattern at any time.

Hybrid partitioning: The two techniques described above can also be combined for hybrid schemes, for example, pipelining can be combined with vertical sectioning.

Kumar, Shekhar, and Amin (1994) describe a check-board partitioning scheme that allows them to replace the all-to-all broadcast required in vertical partitioning by concurrent, noninterfering, single-source broadcasts. They demonstrate that their approach performs well on hypercube connected machines. It can also be combined with pattern partitioning to provide very high overall performance on commercial parallel machines.

Neural Networks and Mathematical Optimization

Several authors have observed, and exploited, the role that mathematical programming or optimization can play in improving the time it takes to train a neural network (Fox, Williams, and Messina 1994; Mangasarian 1992). This observation enables us to benefit from the extensive work done in fine-grained, parallel mathematical programming techniques.

Supervised learning through neural networks can be viewed as the process of learning an association between input and output patterns from a set of examples. A multilayer perceptron, initialized with random weights, would give a random output pattern. During learning, we progressively modify the values of the connection strengths to make the outputs of the network closer to the prescribed values. If we define the "energy" as the sum of the squared errors between the desired output and the obtained output, we can view the learning task as an optimization problem, namely the minimization of the energy function.

A common technique used to minimize the "energy" is the steepest descent method, wherein the negative gradient of the energy with respect to the weights is calculated, and a step is taken in that direction. If the step is small enough, energy reduction is assured. However, if it is too small, convergence to the minima will be slow; if it is too large, oscillations may result. Further, even with the optimal step size, steepest descent can be arbitrarily slow. To overcome this slow convergence, the conjugate gradient technique is sometimes used instead of the steepest descent. Fox, Williams, and Messina (1994) describe the use of the Broyden-Fletcher-Goldfarb-Shanno (BFGS) one-step, memory-less, quasi-Newton method as another good candidate, one that performed very efficiently on different problems. Both the conjugate gradient and the BFGS method are used extensively in the numerical methods community, and can be implemented efficiently on MIMD parallel computers.

A very different approach to using optimization in neural networks is used in support vector machines, wherein an algorithm more general than backpropagation is used in learning. This approach is described in detail in section 2.5.6.

Neural Networks and Genetic Algorithms

The fact that learning in neural networks can be viewed as an optimization problem, implies that other techniques such as genetic algorithms, which essentially solve an optimization problem, can also be used in learning. Once again, we can benefit from the work that has been done in parallelizing genetic algorithms. There are several ways in which genetic algorithms can be used in conjunction with neural networks (Whitley 1995).

First, they can be used to set the weights in fixed architectures. In this task, they compete with the highly effective gradient based methods discussed in the previous section. In addition, genetic algorithms that rely on recombination may not inherently be a good match for training neural networks. The source of this problem is that there can be several equivalent symmetric solutions to a neural network weight optimization problem, each solution obtained by rearranging the order of the hidden units. While this has no affect on the functionality of the network, it creates a problem for the population based search of genetic algorithms since several different strings in the population may not map functionality to the different hidden units in the same way. One solution to this is to use genetic algorithms to find an initial set of good weights, and then change to a gradient based search to refine the solution.

Second, genetic algorithms can be used to learn network topologies, by using selection and mutation to search the space of possible architectures. In this case, both the weights and the topology would be learned at the same time. A third application of genetic algorithms to neural nets would be in the selection of the training data and the interpretation of the output behavior by identifying the inputs that resulted in a particular classification. This use of genetic algorithms to improve the performance and understandability of neural nets allows us to borrow from the work done in the area of parallel genetic algorithms (section 2.5.5).

Kohonen Self-Organizing Maps

Our discussion of parallel implementations of neural networks in data mining has focussed on supervised learning, or classification. We would be remiss if we did not include the use of neural networks for clustering as well as dimension reduction. The best example of this use of neural networks in unsupervised learning is the Kohonen self-organizing map (Kohonen 1997). These methods can be parallelized on MIMD machines using the techniques that have been discussed in the sections above.

These networks are based on competitive learning, which is an adaptive process in which the neurons in a network gradually become sensitive to different input categories or sets of samples in a specific domain of the input space. This specialization occurs when the neuron that is best able to describe the input pattern, wins the competition, and is allowed to learn the pattern even better. In a self-organizing map, the neurons are placed at the nodes of a lattice, which is usually one or two dimensional. In order to generalize the competitive learning algorithm, the neurons that are neighbors of the winning neuron, are allowed to learn as well, and, in the process, gradually specialize to represent similar input patterns. A self-organizing map is therefore characterized by the formation of a topographic map of the input patterns in which the spatial locations of the neurons in the lattice are indicative of intrinsic statistical features contained in the input patterns.

The self-organizing map is an inherently nonlinear process, and as it maps the high dimensional input space into a lower-dimensional display, it can also be used as a nonlinear generalization of principal component analysis. In addition, the adaptive-subspace SOM (ASSOM) (Kohonen 1997), can be used as a first step towards a general purpose feature extractor; it extracts invariant features from its input, features that are invariant to the particular transformation that operated on the input data.

2.5.4 Clustering

Clustering is a descriptive task that seeks to identify homogeneous groups of objects based on the values of their attributes. Clustering can be used in several applications, including image segmentation, separating regions of graphics and text in documents, satellite image processing, image registration, and so on. Techniques used for clustering can be broadly classified into two. The problem of partitional clustering can be stated as follows—given n feature vectors in a $d-$dimensional space, determine a partition of the vectors into K

groups, or clusters, such that the vectors in a cluster are more similar to each other than to vectors in different clusters. The value of K may or may not be specified. The second category, hierarchical clustering, looks at generating a nested sequence of partitions. In the agglomerative version, clustering starts by placing each object in its own cluster, and then merges these clusters into larger and larger clusters until all objects are in one cluster. The divisive approach reverses the process by starting with all objects in one cluster and subdividing into smaller clusters (Jain and Dubes 1988).

One of the most popular groups of clustering algorithms is that based on the least squared error criterion. Stated formally, the set of n vectors is to be partitioned into the clusters, $C_1, C_2, \ldots, C_K$, with cluster C_k containing n_k vectors. Each vector is assigned to a unique cluster.The centroid of the cluster C_k is defined as

$$m^k = \frac{1}{n_k} \sum_{k=1}^{n_k} x_i^k$$

where x_i^k is the $i-$th vector belonging to cluster C_k. The square error e_k^2 for each cluster C_k is the sum of the squared Euclidean distances between each vector in C_k and its centroid, and the square error for the entire K cluster partition is

$$E_k^2 = \sum_{k=1}^{K} e_k^2.$$

A problem with squared-error and other partitional clustering methodologies is that there is no computationally feasible method for guaranteeing that a given clustering minimizes the total square error. The number of possible assignments, even for small number of vectors and clusters, can be extremely large. Therefore many clustering algorithms use iterative hill climbing techniques that terminate when:

- no improvement can be made in the clustering
- when the change in the total error drops below a threshold, or
- when a predetermined number of iterations has been completed.

Clustering algorithms tend to be very compute intensive, especially for large data sets. Parallel implementations therefore provide a means of making this task manageable. Several authors have experimented with parallel implementations of clustering algorithms (Olson 1995; Ranka and Sahni 1991; Rivera, Ismail, and Zapata 1990) on SIMD systems. Others (Copty 1995) have considered hierarchical clustering on distributed memory machines, using High Performance Fortran, a set of extensions to Fortran 90[9]. In this approach, clustering is done using multigraphs, which is a graph in which a pair

[9]http://www.crpc. rice.edu/HPFF/home.html

of vertices can be connected by more than one edge. This allows different clustering criteria to be used for different features in a feature vector, an option that may be useful when the scale levels of the features vary widely, and a single metric measuring the similarity or dissimilarity between two feature vectors is insufficient.

We next describe in some detail, the approach used by Judd, McKinley, and Jain (1998) to parallelize large-scale data clustering. They use a client-server model to determine the best clustering containing $1, 2, \ldots, KMAX$ clusters, for a specified value of $KMAX$, where the starting point for the kth clustering is based on the result of the $(k-1)$st clustering. Next, a forcing pass is used to create another set of clusters by merging existing clusters, two at a time, to determine if a better clustering can be achieved. The tasks performed by the server and the clients are as follows:

1. Server: The server reads the input information, including $KMAX$, and the feature vectors, and divides the feature vectors into n blocks, where n is the number of clients. It then distributes the blocks to the clients and also calculates the mean and standard deviation of the data.

2. Server: For a given k clustering, the server calculates the initial set of cluster centroids based on the centroids of the $(k-1)$ clustering, by splitting the centroid of the cluster with the largest total variance. The new centroids are obtained by adding, and subtracting, the standard deviation of each feature of the cluster to, and from, each feature vector. The remaining new centroids are identical to the remaining centroids from the $(k-1)$ clustering. Next, the server broadcasts the new centroids to the clients.

3. Client: Each client does clustering on its subset of feature vectors by assigning each vector to the cluster that has the minimum distance from vector to cluster centroid. For each cluster, the sum of all the feature vectors assigned to the cluster is computed on a feature by feature basis. The client then sends the number of vectors in each cluster and the partial sum to the server.

4. Server: The server adds the information from each client. If any of the clusters are empty, the centroids are recalculated, broadcast to the clients and the process returns to Step 3. If no feature vectors have changed clusters, or a maximum number of iterations has been reached, the process for the kth clustering is stopped, and the process for the $(k+1)$st clustering begun at Step 2. Otherwise, the server recomputes the new centroids, broadcasts them to the clients, and goes to step 3.

5. Server: For a given k clustering, the server finds the cluster pair that when merged, causes the least increase in total error. These two clusters are merged and the resulting centroid, along with the other $(k - 2)$ centroids are used as the new centroids for a $(k - 1)$ clustering. These new centroids are broadcast to the clients and the steps 3 through 4 are repeated to determine if the new clustering reduces the total error. If so, the results are saved.

6. Server: Repeat step 5 for all clusters from $(KMAX - 1)$ clusters, down to three clusters.

7. Server: Repeat steps 2 through 6 until no clustering is improved.

Judd, McKinley, and Jain (1998) report good performance on a 16 node IBM SP-2, as well as a cluster of 16 Sun workstations for their algorithm using MPI. In addition to scalability studies, they also experimented with various techniques to speed up the performance of the clustering algorithm itself. This was done by exploiting the fact that after a small number of passes through the data, relatively few feature vectors changed their cluster assignments. They noted that 70-80 percent of the changes in cluster assignment occurred in the first two iterations, even though the clustering pass may require over 100 iterations to complete. A very interesting observation made was that the original algorithm, with improvements, on the slow system (the cluster of Sun workstations), outperformed the original algorithm, without improvements on the fast system (IBM SP-2). This underscores the need for additional research in parallel clustering algorithms.

A very different approach to clustering is used in Kohonen Self Organizing Maps (section 2.5.3). While this technique is closely related to k-means, in SOM, the distance of each feature vector from all of the reference vectors is taken into account, not just the closest one. Despite the similarity, the two techniques are used in different contexts in data mining. In k-means, the number of clusters is chosen according to the number of clusters in the data, while in the SOM, the number of reference vectors can be chosen to be much larger, irrespective of the number of clusters in the data (Kaski 1997).

2.5.5 Genetic Algorithms

Genetic algorithms (GAs) are stochastic search algorithms based on the principle of natural selection and recombination. They try to find an optimal solution to the problem by manipulating a population of candidate solutions. At each iteration, the members of the population are evaluated according to their fitness function. A new population is generated by probabilistically selecting the most fit individuals in a population, some of whom are carried forward into the next generation intact, while others are used as the basis for creating new individuals through operations such as cross-over or mutation.

There are four fundamental differences between genetic algorithms and the traditional optimization and search procedures mentioned in section 2.5.6 (Goldberg 1989): (1) GAs work with a coding of the parameter set, not the parameters themselves. (2) GAs search from a population of points, not from a single point. (3) GAs use objective function information, not derivatives or other auxiliary knowledge. (4) GAs use probabilistic transition rules, not deterministic rules.

GAs can be used in data mining in several different ways. In section 2.4.3 we discussed how GAs can be used in feature construction and feature selection. In section 2.5.3, we described the use of GAs in conjunction with neural networks. In addition, they can be used directly for learning as described by Flockhart and Radcliffe (1996). Work in this area of genetic learning systems has been traditionally grouped into two approaches. In the Pittsburgh approach (Smith 1980), each entity in the population is a set of rules representing a complete solution to the learning problem. In the Michigan approach (Holland 1986), the population consists of individual rules, each of which represents a partial solution to the overall learning task. An example of the former approach is the GA_MINER system (Flockhart and Radcliffe 1995), which has been parallelized for both SMP and MPP systems. Another data mining system based on the Pittsburgh approach is the GA/RULE systems described by Pei, Goodman, and Punch (1997) for the production of rules. While this system is not parallel, the techniques described in this section can be applied to improve the performance of the software.

Parallel Genetic Algorithms

The very nature of GAs, with their embarrassing parallelism, makes them very suitable for implementation on parallel machines. While this was recognized in the early work of Holland (1962), it is surprising that not much attention was given to parallel implementations until relatively recently. An issue that makes parallel GAs rather interesting is that many parallel implementations are very different from the traditional genetic algorithms, especially with regards to population structure and selection mechanisms. It is therefore reasonable to assume that this effects the problem solving ability of the underlying algorithm. While some implementations, such as the synchronous master-slave prototype of Grefenstette (1981), do not alter the search behavior of the serial genetic algorithm, many other parallel implementations do. If the parallel implementation of a genetic algorithm slows down the problem solving ability, we may need extra processors to compensate. On the other hand, if the problem solving ability improves, one may use the parallel implementation even on a serial machine.

Gordon and Whitley (1993) compare several parallel GAs across a wide range of optimization functions to determine whether these changes have a positive or negative effect on the problem solving capabilities. They concluded that performance benefits due to parallelism are not offset by declines in problem solving abilities. In fact, when some form of restricted selection and mating based on locality was used in a serial implementation, they often obtained better performance than single populations with global "panmictic" mating. This observation is also made by Chipperfield and Fleming (1995).

A good survey of parallel genetic algorithms can be found in Cantu-Paz (1998) wherein the author describes various categories of parallel GAs based on the ways in which a population is distributed, the ways in which the individuals migrate between populations, and the effects these choices have on the overall quality of the solution obtained. Other studies on parallel GAs are described by Zomaya and Olaiu (1997).

Coarse and Fine-Grained Parallel Genetic Algorithms

Genetic algorithms can be broadly classified into two categories depending on the granularity of the population—coarse grained and fine grained. Note that this usage of terms is slightly different from the usage in the rest of this chapter.

In coarse grained GAs, each processor runs its own GA with its own subpopulation, each trying to optimize the same function. By viewing the individual subpopulations as isolated island communities, and introducing migration as a way to move individuals between subpopulations, the genetic diversity of different subpopulations can be exploited. However, migrating a large number of individuals too often may drive out any local differences between islands, destroying global diversity. On the other hand, if migration does not happen often enough, we may have premature convergence. Various issues to be considered in a coarse-grained model as described by Pit (1995) include: (1) the processors with whom each processor exchanges individuals, (2) migration frequency, or how often a processor exchanges individuals; (3) migration rate, or the number of individuals exchanged between processors; (4) the individuals that are exchanged; and (5) the individuals deleted after an exchange has occurred.

Fine-grained GAs (Manderick and Spiessens 1989), also known as cellular GAs, typically have one individual on each processor, and individuals select mates and recombine with other individuals in their immediate neighborhood. Such algorithms are best suited for SIMD machines, where the interconnect allows efficient communication with only the nearest neighbor. Various issues to be considered in a fine-grained model as described by Pit (1995) include: (1)

the neighborhood structure (2) the selection scheme; and (3) the replacement scheme

It is difficult to say whether fine or coarse grained parallelism in GAs give better performance. As mentioned in Cantu-Paz (1998), there are examples in which each is observed to be better, and care must be taken to identify the criterion on which comparison is made—minimization of wall clock time or maximization of solution quality. It must also be noted that coarse-grained GAs can be implemented on fine-grained parallel machines including both SMP and MPP systems, and are therefore suitable for discussion in this chapter. However, with SIMD machines no longer being manufactured commercially, fine-grained GAs will need to be "simulated" on MIMD systems.

Of particular interest for implementation on hierarchical architectures such as clusters of SMPs, are the hierarchical parallel GAs, described by Cantu-Paz (1998). At the higher level, corresponding to the nodes in the clusters of SMPs architectures, we have coarse-grained GAs, while at the lower level, corresponding to the processors within a node, we can have either fine-grained, coarse-grained, or master-slave GAs.

Parallel GAs are very complex, and there are still several unsolved issues such as the determination of the migration rate, the communications topology that will allow mixing of good solutions, but will not result in excessive communication costs, and the optimal number of subpopulations that would maximize reliability.

Two software packages that implement parallel GAs are the Genetic Algorithms Optimized for Portability and Parallelism System (GALOPPS) (Goodman 1996), which includes a threaded SMP version as well as a distributed memory version using PVM, and PGAPACK, (Levine 1996) which is based on MPI.

2.5.6 Optimization

An area that has the potential of making substantial contributions to data mining is optimization or mathematical programming. Several problems in data mining and pattern recognition can be reformulated as mathematical programming problems (Bradley, Fayyad, and Mangasarian 1998). For example, classification can be considered as a partitioning of the feature space into decision regions. In the case of two regions, this reduces to a linear programming problem which obtains an approximate separating plane that minimizes a weighted sum of the distances of misclassified points to the plane. Similarly, given the number of clusters, a clustering algorithm determines the cluster centers such that the sum of the distances of each point to the nearest cluster center is minimized. This allows us to reformulate clustering as a constrained minimization problem.

A different application of mathematical programming to data mining problems is used in support vector machines (SVM) (Burges 1999). SVMs, instead of minimizing the error in separating the given data, incorporate structured risk minimization, which minimizes an upper bound on the generalization error. For the simple case of finding a single hyperplane separating two classes, the idea is to determine, among the infinite number of planes correctly separating the two classes, the one which will have the smallest generalization error. SVMs choose the plane that maximizes the margin separating the two classes, where the margin is defined as the sum of the distances of the separating hyperplane to the nearest point in each of the classes. As explained by Burges (1999), the solution to support vector learning is really a constrained optimization problem. They suggest solving the problem using either one step of the Newton's method, or the conjugate gradient iterative technique, or a combination of gradient and conjugate gradient ascent.

It is interesting to note that unlike most other techniques that employ dimension reduction to project a multidimensional data into lower dimensional subspace, SVMs employ a reverse technique where dimensionality is purposefully increased to render the classification problem linear. This mathematical programming formulation of SVMs can be used to train neural networks and construct decision trees.

A major benefit of viewing data mining problems as variants of optimization techniques is that it provides easy access to algorithms and software that have been optimized and parallelized for high performance on parallel machines (Bertsekas and Tsitsiklis 1989; Censor and Zenios 1997; Migdalas, Pardalos, and Storoy 1997). The Optimization Subroutine Library (OSL) from IBM is a parallel optimization package that has been optimized for IBM parallel systems. Another commercially available parallel optimization package that is supported on a variety of parallel systems is CPLEX[10].

2.6 Future Directions and Challenges

The disciplines that contribute to data mining have been in existence for many decades. In the last few years, as data mining has been applied to increasingly larger and more complex data sets, techniques from these disciplines have been used together to provide a viable solution to the task of (partially) automating data analysis. As data mining gains acceptance in both the business and scientific communities, many shortcomings in the current state-of-the-art in this field are becoming apparent. These have been discussed at length in several excellent surveys (Fayyad and Smyth 1995; Fayyad, Haussler, and Stolorz 1996; Bradley, Fayyad, and Mangasarian 1998; Provost and Kolluri 1999). In this

[10]http://www.cplex.com/

section, we will focus on the challenges that arise from the use of fine-grained, parallel algorithms in data mining.

Parallel algorithms research has been an active area for more than 20 years, but its adoption in the mainstream data mining and pattern recognition communities is much more recent. Many of the standard algorithms that work well on serial machines are difficult to parallelize. While inroads have been made in this area in the last few years, much still needs to be done and the field is wide open in terms of research potential. We next discuss some of the important research challenges that will dominate the field of fine-grained, parallel data mining for the next decade or two. Some of these issues are from areas not tradititionally part of data mining, such as computer science, or not very specific to data mining, such as efficient parallel implementations. However, they must be addressed in the context of data mining applications if we want to provide a practical, efficient, high-quality solution to the mining of massive data sets using fine-grained parallelism.

Algorithms that are scalable and perform well on parallel machines are critical. There is much that remains to be done in this area. We are at an early stage where we have just begun experimenting with different basic underlying parallel data structures and algorithms (Joshi, Karypis, and Kumar 1998), and understanding how best to achieve load balance in the extraction of global features (Chung and Prasanna 1998). In fact, we are still developing algorithms that show an order of magnitude serial performance increases (Zaki, Parthasarathy, Ogihara, and Li 1998). As Intel-based SMP systems with two to eight processors become common-place today, scalability to a large number of processors will become an issue in the next few decades. Many of the current pattern recognition algorithms show a rapid decline in parallel efficiency with 16 processors; the more scalable methods do not show a noticeable drop until 64 or 128 processors. How will current algorithms scale when implemented on thousands of processors?

With raw data sizes growing faster than available I/O bandwidth, algorithms that require multiple passes over the data will become more and more impractical. Even a single pass over the data may not be practical. For example, as scientific simulations running on MPP systems generate a tera-byte or more of data at each time step, it will no longer be feasible to move this data off the machine and mine it elsewhere. More flexible approaches to feature set generation and data preprocessing will have to be considered. For example, we may need to consider the option of doing sampling, multiresolution transformations, and feature extraction on the data while it is being generated. This would call for continued research into fine-grained approaches to data preparation, especially in the areas of load balancing during feature extraction, identification of global features that are spread out over more than one processor, extraction of features from data that has undergone multiresolution transformations, and the effects of parallel sampling techniques. This research may require that some of the paths that identify data flow in the basic data mining process, figure 2.1, need to be re-examined.

Hybrid parallel algorithms that dynamically modify their behavior on the fly (i.e. shifting from a task parallel to a data parallel approach) as the computation progresses are an important area of research. Many standard pattern recognition algorithms change characteristics over the course of run substantially enough so that a fixed approach with a rigid pattern of computation and communication will not perform well. This is also true in feature extraction from image data, where an initial step that operates on all pixels uniformly is load balanced, but a subsequent step, where features are extracted from each subimage, is not. In addition, dynamic approaches can also help to tailor a pattern recognition algorithm to a specific problem by exploiting the differences in the number of attributes, their complexity, and the existence of any correlations in the attributes.

As we parallelize data mining algorithms to enable real-time search for patterns in tera-byte data sets, there are several issues pertaining to the parallel hardware that must be considered for efficient implementation. With MIMD architectures rapidly replacing SIMD architectures commercially, it makes sense to focus on MIMD systems and understand how one can extract the most from such systems. The shared memory programming model is rapidly gaining acceptance, not only with the easy availability of multiprocessor Intel-based systems, but also with the introduction of commercial distributed shared memory systems. And, as ever larger systems are put together in the form of clusters of SMPs, a new area of research is opened up as we try to investigate ways of implementing data mining techniques efficiently on such systems. But, we need to pay attention to not just the parallel system architecture, but to the implementation of the architecture itself. Algorithms that obtain the best from a system with fast processors connected by a relatively slow network may be radically different from algorithms that work well on a system that is balanced. The problems of load balancing, as well as techniques for minimizing the communication remain to be solved, especially in the context of data mining algorithms. Another issue that is often overlooked is the performance of the algorithms on a single processor. With current processors being designed with deep memory hierarchies, we can no longer ignore techniques that exploit such hierarchies. The work done in the area of high performance computing can be invaluable in helping us take advantage of modern architectures.

As data mining continues to gain acceptance in the commercial and scientific communities, it is becoming increasingly apparent that there is a need for robust software tools built using modern software engineering practices such as object-oriented programming and software component technology. A well tested, portable suite of tools that also enables easy plug and play of different techniques will be of immense use not only to data mining practitioners but also to data mining researchers. This is another area where data mining could benefit from the work done in the numerical methods and high performance computing communities, especially in their tradition of making high quality parallel software easily accessible to the public (Dongarral, Du Croz, Hammarling, and Hanson 1988; Dongarral, Du Croz, Duff, and Hammarling 1990; Lawson, Hanson, Kincaid, and Krogh 1979; Anderson et al. 1995, Blackford et al. 1997).

Another issue that is becoming important as data mining techniques are increasingly being applied to a wide variety of applications in parallel environments is the robustness of the algorithms themselves. It is well understood that not all algorithms work equally efficiently on all problems. As data sets enter the tera-byte range, will algorithms that worked well on smaller data sets continue to be the ones that work well on very large data sets? And, what happens as we move from SIMD machines to MIMD machines—which algorithms will work well on the new architectures? More importantly, are we in a position to provide users of data mining software guidelines which would help them select an algorithm that is well suited to the task at hand?

We need to improve current methods for evaluating the performance of parallel pattern recognition algorithms. There is still a limited availability of massively parallel machines in academia, which explains why scalability studies are usually done on few processors. Beyond this, however, many experimental results are on the same synthetic data set. Real data may see very different performance characteristics, and multiple tests from multiple domains (as is done in the broader machine learning community) may show an even greater variance. Theoretical performance models also have much progress to make before being accurate in the face of hardware and domain-dependent complexities.

A challenging question that has not been addressed by the community is the interaction between parallel processing, large data availability, computational requirements, and desired accuracy. Under what conditions does it make sense to expend a great deal of computational power for a potentially modest increase in accuracy? Sampling is an effective way of reducing computational requirements by limiting the amount of data that is used—what is the cost in terms of accuracy of the resulting model of not using all the data? For example, decision tree algorithms repeatedly decide how to split the examples at a node. Methods for speeding this up can achieve very strong approximations of any splitting criteria (such as information gain, or the gini index), without sorting, or without using all the available data (Musick, Catlett, and Russell 1993; Srivastava, Singh, Han, and Kumar 1997; Alsabti, Ranka, and Singh 1998). Since the splitting criteria are heuristic in nature to begin with, approximations of the criteria may lead to models that are as good as, or better than the more computationally expensive approaches in the first place. If a parallel approach has been chosen for its potential to provide more accurate models, then what level of approximation would be acceptable internally in the algorithm? Can this be quantified well enough so that intelligent choices can be made about when and how to compute in a parallel environment?

As parallel processing becomes accepted in the data mining community, and parallelism is exploited at each step in the data mining process, it is also important to take advantage of the extensive work done in the area of parallel visualization. This is especially true in light of the fact that the patterns obtained during data mining will have to be presented to the end user visually, and the user may want to browse through the results interactively. How data mining and visualization can interact in a parallel environment remains an open research question.

Acknowledgements

We would like to thank the members of the Sapphire project for the many discussions regarding parallelization of data mining and pattern recognition algorithms on fine-grained multiprocessor systems. We would also like to thank the authors of the papers surveyed—it is, after all, they who made this chapter possible. This work was performed under the auspices of the U.S. Department of Energy by Lawrence Livermore National Laboratory under contract no. W-7405-Eng-48, UCRL-JC-133694.

Part II

Distributed Data Mining Techniques

Chapter 3

Meta-Learning in Distributed Data Mining Systems: Issues and Approaches

Andreas L. Prodromidis, Philip K. Chan, and Salvatore J. Stolfo

3.1 Introduction

During the last decade, our ability to collect and store data have significantly outpaced our ability to analyze, summarize and extract "knowledge" from this continuous stream of input. A short list of examples is probably enough to place the current situation into perspective:

- NASA's earth observing system of orbiting satellites and other space-borne instruments send one terabyte of data to receiving stations every day (Way and Smith 1991).

- The world wide web is estimated to have at least 6 terabytes of text data in 3 million servers and as many as 800 million HTML pages (as of June 1999), and is still growing exponentially — as recently as 1993, there were a mere 50 servers (Lawrence and Giles 1999).

- Today, a typical Fortune 500 company is estimated to possess more than 400 trillion characters in their electronic databases requiring 400 terabytes of mass storage.

Traditional data analysis methods that require humans to process large data sets are completely inadequate and to quote John Naisbett, "We are drowning in information but starving for knowledge!"

The relatively new field of knowledge discovery and data mining (KDD) has emerged to compensate for these deficiencies. Knowledge discovery in databases denotes the complex process of identifying valid, novel, potentially useful and ultimately understandable patterns in data (Fayyad, Piatetsky-Shapiro, Smyth, and Uthurusamy 1996). *Data mining* refers to a particular step in the KDD process. According to the most recent and broad definition (Fayyad, Piatetsky-Shapiro, Smyth, and Uthurusamy 1996), "data mining consists of particular algorithms (methods) that, under acceptable computational efficiency limitations, produce a particular enumeration of patterns (models) over the data."

In a relational database context, a typical data mining task is to explain and predict the value of some attribute given a collection of tuples with known attribute values. One means of performing such a task is to employ various machine learning algorithms. An existing relation, drawn from some domain, is thus treated as training data for a learning algorithm that computes a logical expression, a concept description, a descriptive model, or a *classifier*, that can later be used to predict (for a variety of strategic and tactical purposes) a value of the desired or target attribute for some record whose desired attribute value is unknown.

The field of machine learning has made substantial progress over the last few decades and numerous algorithms, ranging from those based on stochastic models to those based on purely symbolic representations like rules and decision trees, have already been developed and applied to many problems in diverse areas. Over the past decade, machine learning has evolved from a field of laboratory demonstrations to a field of significant commercial value (Mitchell 1997a). Machine-learning algorithms have been deployed in heart disease diagnosis (Detrano, Janosi, Steinbrunn, Pfisterer, Schmid, Sandhu, Guppy, Lee, and Froelicher 1989), in predicting glucose levels for diabetic patients (Carson and Fischer 1990), in detecting credit card fraud (Prodromidis and Stolfo 1999), in steering vehicles driving autonomously on public highways at 70 miles an hour (Pomerleau 1992), in predicting stock option pricing (Malliaris and Salchenberger 1993) and in computing customized electronic newspapers (Lang 1995), to name a few applications. Many large business institutions and market analysis firms attempt to distinguish the low-risk (high profit) potential customers by learning simple categorical classifications of their potential customer base. Similarly, defense and intelligence operations utilize similar methodologies on vast information sources to predict a wide range of conditions in various contexts. Recently, for example, data mining techniques have been successfully applied to intrusion detection in network-based systems (Mok, Lee, and Stolfo 1998).

One of the main challenges in machine learning and data mining is the development of inductive learning techniques that scale up to large and possibly physically distributed data sets. Many organizations seeking added value from their data are already dealing with overwhelming amounts of information. The number and size of their databases and data warehouses grows at phenomenal rates, faster than the corresponding improvements in machine resources and inductive learning techniques. Most of the current generation of learning algorithms are computationally complex and require all data to be resident in main memory which is clearly untenable for many realistic problems and databases. Notable exceptions include IBM's SPRINT (Shafer, Agrawal, and Metha 1996) and SLIQ (Mehta, Agrawal, and Rissanen 1996) decision tree-based algorithms and Provost's and Hennessy's DRL rule-based algorithm for multi-processor learning.

Furthermore, in certain cases, data may be inherently distributed and cannot be localized on any one machine (even by a trusted third party) for a variety of practical reasons including security and fault tolerant distribution of data and services, competitive (business) reasons, statutory constraints imposed by law as well as physically dispersed databases or mobile platforms like an armada of ships. In such situations, it may not be possible, nor feasible, to inspect all of the data at one processing site to compute one primary "global" classifier.

Meta-learning is a technique recently developed that deals with the problem of computing a "global" classifier from large and inherently distributed databases. Meta-learning aims to compute a number of independent classifiers (concepts or models) by applying learning programs to a collection of independent and inherently distributed databases in parallel. The "base classifiers" computed are then collected and combined by another learning process. Here meta-learning seeks to compute a "meta-classifier" that integrates in some principled fashion the separately learned classifiers to boost overall predictive accuracy.

Our primary objective is to take advantage of the inherent parallelism and distributed nature of meta-learning and design and implement a powerful and practical distributed data mining system. Assuming that a system consists of several databases interconnected through an intranet or internet, the goal is to provide the means for each data site to utilize its own local data and, at the same time, benefit from the data that is available at other data sites without transferring or directly accessing that data. In this context, this can be materialized by learning agents that execute at remote data sites and generate classifier agents that can subsequently be transfered among the sites. We have achieved this goal through the implementation and demonstration of a system we call Java agents for meta-learning (JAM). To our knowledge, JAM is the first system to date that employs meta-learning as a means to mine distributed databases. (A commercial system based upon JAM has recently appeared [Grossman, Baily, Kasif, Man, and Ramu 1998].)

JAM, however, is more than an implementation of a distributed meta-learning system. It is a distributed data mining system addressing many practical problems for which centralized or host-based systems are not appropriate. Distributed systems have increased complexity. Their practical value depends on the scalability of the distributed protocols as the number of the data sites and the size of the databases increases, and on the efficiency of their methods to use the system resources effectively. Furthermore, distributed systems may need to run across heterogenous platforms (portability) or operate over databases that may (possibly) have different schemas (compatibility). There are other important problems, intrinsic within data mining systems that should not be ignored. Data mining systems should be adaptive to environment changes (e.g. when data and objectives change over time), extensible to support new and more advanced data mining technologies and last but not least, highly effective. The intent of this study is to identify and describe each of these issues separately and to present an overview of existing approaches—detailed discussions of techniques and findings appear in publications cited throughout this study.

JAM has been used in several experiments dealing with real-world learning tasks, such as solving crucial problems in fraud detection in financial information systems. The objective is to employ pattern-directed inference systems using models of anomalous or errant transaction behaviors to forewarn of impeding threats. This approach requires analysis of large and inherently (e.g. from distinct banks) distributed databases of information about transaction behaviors to produce models of "probably fraudulent" transactions.

The remainder of this chapter describes the JAM system, views the scalability, efficiency, portability, compatibility, adaptivity, extensibility and effectiveness desiderata as an integral part of the design and implementation of JAM, and presents the efficacy of our approaches in predicting fraudulent credit card transactions as a case study. In section 3.2 we introduce the meta-learning process. Section 3.3 presents the distributed architecture of JAM, together with our proposed approaches to scalability and efficiency. Section 3.4

addresses the portability issues, and section 3.5 describes our methods for overcoming the obstacles posed by databases with schema differences. In sections 3.6 and 3.7, we detail our techniques for incorporating newly computed models and for extending JAM with new machine learning technologies and in section 3.8 we elaborate on the effectiveness of data mining systems. Section 3.9 presents our results in the credit card fraud detection task and finally, section 3.10, concludes the chapter.

3.2 Inductive Learning and Meta Learning

Inductive learning (or *learning from examples* [Michalski 1983]) is the task of identifying regularities in some given set of training examples with little or no knowledge about the domain from which the examples are drawn. Given a set of training examples, i.e. $\{(\mathbf{x_1}, y_1), ..., (\mathbf{x_n}, y_n)\}$, for some unknown function $y = f(\mathbf{x})$, with each $\mathbf{x_i}$ interpreted as a set of attribute (feature) vectors x_i of the form $\{x_{i1}, x_{i2}, ..., x_{ik}\}$ and with each y_i representing the class label associated with each vector ($y_i \in \{y_1, y_2, ..., y_m\}$), the task is to compute a classifier or model $\hat{f}$ that approximates f and correctly labels any feature vector drawn from the same source as the training set. It is common to call the body of knowledge that classifies data with the label y as the *concept* of *class* y.

Some of the common representations used for the generated classifiers are decision trees, rules, version spaces, neural networks, distance functions, and probability distributions. In general, these representations are associated with different types of algorithms that extract different types of information from the database and provide alternative capabilities besides the common ability to classify unseen exemplars drawn from some domain. For example, decision trees are declarative and thus more comprehensible to humans than weights computed within a neural network architecture. However, both are able to compute concept y and classify unseen records (examples). Decision trees are used in ID3 (Quinlan 1986), where each concept is represented as a conjunction of terms on a path from the root of a tree to a leaf. Rules in CN2 (Clark and Niblett 1989) are if-then expressions, where the antecedent is a pattern expression and the consequent is a class label. Each version space learned in VS (Mitchell 1982) defines the most general and specific description boundaries of a concept using a restricted version of first order formulae. Neural networks compute separating hyperplanes in n-dimensional feature space to classify data (Lippmann 1987). The learned distance functions in exemplar-based learning algorithms (or nearest neighbor algorithms) define a similarity or "closeness" measure between two instances (Stanfill and Waltz 1986). In genetic algorithms, hypotheses are usually represented by application-specific bit strings. These algorithms search for the most appropriate hypotheses (Hol-

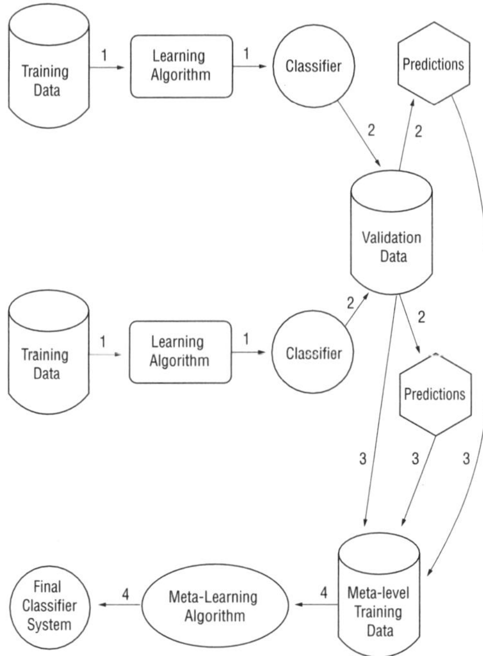

Figure 3.1: Meta-learning.

land 1986; DeJong 1988) by simulating evolution, i.e. they generate successor hypotheses by repeatedly mutating and recombining (crossover) parts of the best currently known hypothesis (Holland 1975; DeJong, Spears, and Gordon 1993). Conditional probability distributions used by Bayesian classifiers are derived from the frequency distributions of attribute values and reflect the likelihood of a certain instance belonging to a particular classification (Cheeseman, Kelly, Self, Stutz, Taylor, and Freeman 1988). Implicit decision rules classify according to maximal probabilities.

Meta-learning (Chan and Stolfo 1993b) is loosely defined as learning from learned knowledge. In this case, we concentrate on learning from the output of concept learning systems. This is achieved by learning from the predictions of these classifiers on a common validation data set. Thus, we are interested in the output of the classifiers, not the internal structure and strategies of the learning algorithms themselves. Moreover, in some of the schemes defined, the data presented to the learning algorithms may also be available to the *meta-learner*.

Figure 3.1 depicts the different stages in a simplified meta-learning scenario:

1. The classifiers (base classifiers) are trained from the initial (base-level) training sets.

2. Predictions are generated by the learned classifiers on a separate validation set.

3. A meta-level training set is composed from the validation set and the predictions generated by the classifiers on the validation set.

4. The final classifier (*meta-classifier*) is trained from the meta-level training set.

In meta-learning a learning algorithm is used to learn how to integrate the learned classifiers. That is, rather than having a predetermined and fixed integration rule, the integration rule is learned based on the behavior of the trained classifiers. In the following sections we present some of the different strategies used in our meta-learning study.

3.2.1 Voting, Arbitrating, and Combining

We distinguish three distinct strategies for combining multiple predictions from separately learned classifiers. *Voting* generally is understood to mean that each classifier gets one vote, and the majority (or plurality) wins. *Weighted voting* provides preferential treatment to some voting classifiers, as may be predicted by observing performance on some common validation set. The outcome of voting is simply to choose one of the predictions from one or more of the classifiers. The second major strategy is *arbitration*, which entails the use of an "objective" judge whose own prediction is selected if the participating classifiers cannot reach a consensus decision. Thus, the arbiter is itself a classifier, and may choose a final outcome based upon its own prediction but cognizant of the other classifiers' predictions. Finally, *combining* refers to the use of knowledge about how classifiers behave with respect to each other. Hence, if we learn, for example, that when two classifiers predict the same class they are always correct (relative to some validation set), this simple fact may lead to a powerful predictive tool. Indeed, we may wish to ignore all other classifiers when they predict a common outcome.

We distinguish between *base classifiers* and *combiners/arbiters* as follows. A base classifier is the outcome of applying a learning algorithm directly to "raw" training data. The base classifier is a program that given a test datum provides a prediction of its unknown class. A *combiner* or *arbiter*, is a program generated by a learning algorithm that is trained on the predictions produced

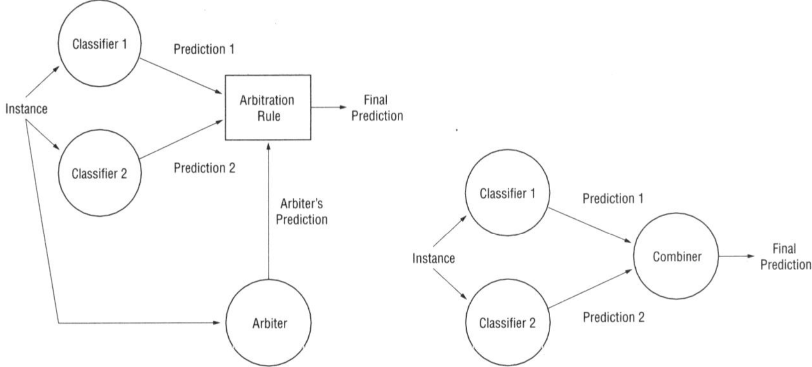

Figure 3.2: An arbiter with two classifiers (left). A combiner with two classifiers (right).

by a set of base classifiers on raw data. The arbiter/combiner is also a classifier, and hence other arbiters or combiners can be computed from the set of predictions of other combiners/arbiters in a hierarchical manner.

Briefly, an arbiter (Chan and Stolfo 1993c) is the result of a learning algorithm that learns to arbitrate among predictions generated by different base classifiers. This arbiter, together with an *arbitration rule*, decides a final classification outcome based upon the base predictions. The left diagram of figure 3.2, depicts how the final prediction is made with input predictions from two base classifiers and a single arbiter. The rest of this chapter, concentrates on the combiner strategy.

Before we detail the combiner strategy, for concreteness, we define the following notation. Let **x** be an instance whose classification we seek, and $C_1(\mathbf{x})$, $C_2(\mathbf{x})$,..., $C_k(\mathbf{x})$ be the predicted classifications of **x** from the k base classifiers, C_i, $i = 1, 2, ..., k$. $class(\mathbf{x})$ and $attrvec(\mathbf{x})$ denote the correct classification and attribute vector of example **x**, respectively.

3.2.2 Combiner Strategy

In the combiner strategy the predictions of the learned base classifiers on the validation set form the basis of the meta-learner's training set. A *composition rule*, which varies in different schemes, determines the content of training examples for the meta-learner. From these examples, the meta-learner generates a meta-classifier, that we call a *combiner*. In classifying an instance, the base classifiers first generate their predictions. Based on the same composition rule, a new instance is generated from the predictions, which is then classified by the combiner (see right diagram of figure 3.2). The aim of this strategy is to

Example	Class	Attribute vector	Base classifiers' predictions	
x	$class(x)$	$attrvec(x)$	$C_1(x)$	$C_2(x)$
x_1	*table*	$attrvec_1$	*table*	*table*
x_2	*chair*	$attrvec_2$	*table*	*chair*
x_3	*table*	$attrvec_3$	*chair*	*chair*

Training set from the class-combiner scheme		
Example	Class	Attribute vector
1	*table*	(*table, table*)
2	*chair*	(*table, chair*)
3	*table*	(*chair, chair*)

Training set from the class-attribute-combiner scheme		
Example	Class	Attribute vector
1	*table*	(*table, table*, $attrvec_1$)
2	*chair*	(*table, chair*, $attrvec_2$)
3	*table*	(*chair, chair*, $attrvec_3$)

Figure 3.3: Sample training sets generated by the class-combiner and class-attribute-combiner schemes with two base classifiers.

"coalesce" the predictions from the base classifiers by learning the relationship or correlation between these predictions and the correct prediction. A combiner computes a prediction that may be entirely different from any proposed by a base classifier, whereas an arbiter chooses one of the predictions from the base classifiers and the arbiter itself.

We experimented with three schemes for the composition rule (more details are in Chan and Stolfo (1993a). First, the predictions, $C_1(\mathbf{x})$, $C_2(\mathbf{x})$, ... $C_k(\mathbf{x})$, for each example $\mathbf{x}$ in the validation set of examples, E, are generated by the k base classifiers. These predicted classifications are used to form a new set of "meta-level training instances," T, which is used as input to a learning algorithm that computes a combiner. The manner in which T is computed varies as defined below:

Class-combiner. The meta-level training instances consist of the correct classification and the predictions; i.e., $T = \{(class(\mathbf{x}), C_1(\mathbf{x}), C_2(\mathbf{x}), \ldots C_k(\mathbf{x})) \mid \mathbf{x} \in E\}$. This "stacking" scheme was also proposed by Wolpert (1992). See figure 3.3 for a sample training set.

Class-attribute-combiner. The meta-level training instances are formed as in class-combiner with the addition of the attribute vectors; i.e., $T = \{(class(\mathbf{x}), C_1(\mathbf{x}), C_2(\mathbf{x}), \ldots . C_k(\mathbf{x}), attrvec(\mathbf{x})) \mid \mathbf{x} \in E\}$. See figure 3.3 for a sample training set.

binary-class-combiner. The meta-level training instances are composed in a manner similar to that in the class-combiner scheme except that each prediction, $C_i(\mathbf{x})$, has l binary predictions, $C_{i_1}(\mathbf{x}), \ldots, C_{i_l}(\mathbf{x})$, where l is the number of classes. Each prediction, $C_{i_j}(\mathbf{x})$, is produced from a binary classifier, which is trained on examples that are labeled with classes j and $\neg j$. In other words, we are using more specialized base classifiers and attempting to learn the correlation between the binary predictions and the correct prediction. For

Example	Class	Attribute vector	Base classifier1's predictions		Base classifier2's predictions	
x	$class(x)$	$attrvec(x)$	$C1_{table}(x)$	$C1_{chair}(x)$	$C2_{table}(x)$	$C2_{chair}(x)$
x_1	*table*	$attrvec_1$	yes	no	yes	no
x_2	*chair*	$attrvec_2$	yes	yes	no	yes
x_3	*table*	$attrvec_3$	no	yes	no	yes

Training set from the binary-class-combiner scheme

Instance	Class	Attribute vector
1	*table*	(yes, no, yes, no)
2	*chair*	(yes, yes, no, yes)
3	*table*	(no, yes, no, yes)

Figure 3.4: Sample training set generated by the binary-class-combiner scheme with two base classifiers.

concreteness, $T = \{(class(\mathbf{x}), C_{1_1}(\mathbf{x}), \ldots, C_{1_l}(\mathbf{x}), C_{2_1}(\mathbf{x}), \ldots, C_{2_l}(\mathbf{x}), \ldots C_{k_1}(\mathbf{x}), \ldots, C_{k_l}(\mathbf{x})) \mid \mathbf{x} \in E\}$. See figure 3.4 for a sample training set.

These three schemes for the composition rule are defined in the context of forming a training set for the combiner. These composition rules are also used in a similar manner during classification after a combiner has been computed. Given an instance whose classification is sought, we first compute the classifications predicted by each of the base classifiers. The composition rule is then applied to generate a single meta-level test instance, which is then classified by the combiner to produce the final predicted class of the original test datum.

3.2.3 Benefits of Meta-Learning

Meta-learning improves efficiency by executing in parallel the base-learning processes (each implemented as a distinct serial program) on (possibly disjoint) subsets of the training data set (*a data reduction technique*). This approach has the advantage, first, of using the same serial code without the time-consuming process of parallelizing it, and second, of learning from small subsets of data that fit in main memory.

Meta-learning improves predictive performance by combining different learning systems each having different *inductive bias* (for example, representation, search heuristics, search space) (Mitchell 1982). By combining separately learned concepts, meta-learning is expected to derive a higher level learned model that explains a large database more accurately than any of the individual learners. Furthermore, meta-learning constitutes a scalable machine learning method since it can be generalized to hierarchical multi-level meta-learning.

Most of the methods reported in the machine learning and KDD literature that compute, evaluate and combine ensembles of classifiers (Dietterich 1997) can be considered as weighted voting among hypothesis (models). Furthermore, most of these algorithms, generate their classifiers by applying the same learning algorithms on variants of the same data set (Breiman 1994; Freund and Schapire 1995; Jacobs, Jordan, Nowlan, and Hinton 1991; Jordan and Jacobs 1994; Krogh and Vedelsby 1995; Opitz and Shavlik 1996; Perrone and Copper 1993; Schapire 1990; Tresp and Taniguchi 1995). Breiman (1996b) and LeBlanc and Tibshirani (1993), for example, acknowledge the value of using multiple predictive models to increase accuracy, but they rely on cross-validation data and analytical methods, (e.g. least squares regression), to compute the best linear combination of the available hypothesis. Instead, the combiner methods apply arbitrary learning algorithms to discover the correlations among the available models and compute non-linear relations among the classifiers (at the expense, perhaps, of generating less intuitive representations).

Other methods for combining multiple models, include Merz and Pazzani's PCR^* (Merz and Pazzani 1998) and Merz's SCANN (Merz 1998) algorithms. The first integrates ensembles of regression models for improving regression estimates while the latter for improving classification performance. Both rely on methods similar to principal components analysis to map the estimates of the models into a new representation space upon which they compute a higher level model. PCR^* and SCANN are sophisticated and effective combining algorithms, but too computationally expensive to combine models within domains with many models and large data sets. SCANN, in fact, is cubic in the number of available models.

Meta-learning is particularly suitable for distributed data mining applications, such as fraud detection in financial information systems. Financial institutions today typically develop custom fraud detection systems targeted to their own asset bases. Recently though, banks have come to search for unified and global approaches that would also involve the periodic sharing with each other of information about attacks.

The key difficulties in this approach are: financial companies avoid sharing their data for a number of (competitive and legal) reasons; the databases that companies maintain on transaction behavior are huge and growing rapidly; real-time analysis is highly desirable to update models when new events are detected and easy distribution of models in a networked environment is essential to maintain up to date detection capability. Meta-learning is a general strategy that provides the means of learning how to combine and integrate a number of classifiers or models learned separately at different financial institutions. JAM allows financial institutions to share their models of fraudulent transactions that each computes separately, while not disclosing their own proprietary data.

Next, we describe how meta-learning is incorporated in JAM. We detail the fundamental issues of scalability, efficiency, portability, compatibility, adaptivity, extensibility and effectiveness of distributed data mining systems. We overview our solutions to these issues within the JAM framework, and provide empirical evidence that JAM constitutes an effective system as exemplified by the credit card fraud detection domain.

3.3 Scalability and Efficiency

The *scalability* of a data mining system refers to the ability of the system to operate as the number of data sites increases without a substantial or discernable reduction in performance. *Efficiency*, on the other hand, refers to the effective use of the available system resources. The former depends on the protocols that transfer and manage the intelligent agents to support the collaboration of the data sites while the latter depends upon the appropriate evaluation and filtering of the available agents to minimize redundancy. Combining scalability and efficiency without sacrificing predictive performance is, however, an intricate problem. To understand the issues and better tackle the complexity of the problem, we examine scalability and efficiency at two levels, the system architecture level and the data site (meta-learning) level.

3.3.1 System Architecture Level

First we focus on the components of the system and the overall architecture. Assuming that the data mining system comprises of several data sites, each with its own resources, databases, machine learning agents and meta-learning capabilities, we designed a protocol that allows the data sites to collaborate efficiently without hindering their progress. JAM is architected as a distributed computing construct that supports the launching of learning and meta-learning agents to distributed database sites.

First, local or imported *learning agents* execute on the local database to compute the data site's local classifiers. Then, each data site may import (remote) classifiers from its peer data sites and combine these with its own local classifier using meta-learning agents. Again, the meta-learning agents can be either local or imported from other data sites. Finally, once the base and meta-classifiers are computed, the JAM system manages the execution of these modules to classify data sets of interest. These actions may take place at all data sites simultaneously and independently. The JAM system can thus be viewed as a coarse-grain parallel application where the constituent sites function autonomously and (occasionally) exchange classifiers with each other.

The configuration of the distributed system is maintained by the Configuration Manager (CM), an independent server, much like a simple name server,

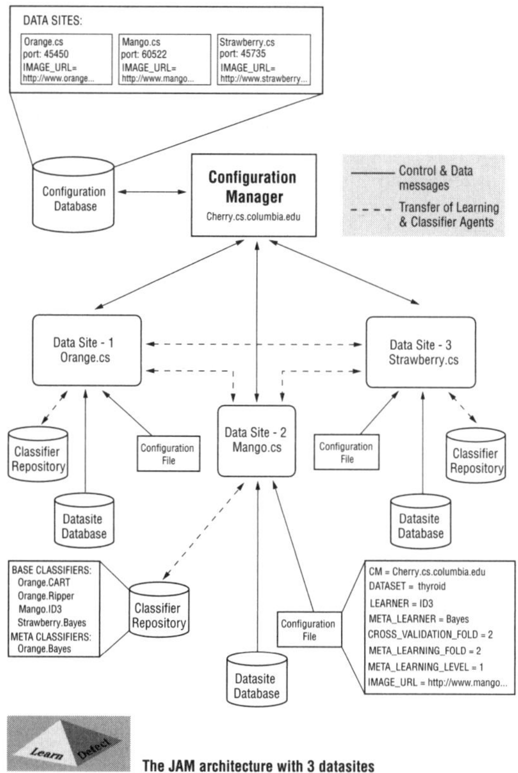

Figure 3.5: The architecture of the meta-learning system.

that is responsible for keeping the state of the system up-to-date. The logical architecture of the JAM meta-learning system is presented in figure 3.5. In this example, three JAM sites Orange, Mango and Strawberry exchange their base classifiers to share their local view of the learning task. The user of the data site controls the learning task by setting the parameters of the user configuration file, e.g. the algorithms to be used, the database to learn, the images to be used by the animation facility, the folding parameters, etc. In figure 3.5, for example, the CM runs on Cherry and the Mango JAM site ends up with four base classifiers (one local plus the three imported classifiers) and a single Bayesian meta-classifier (imported from Orange).

JAM is designed with asynchronous, distributed communication protocols that enable the participating database sites to operate independently and collaborate with other peer sites as necessary, thus eliminating centralized control and synchronization points. Each JAM site is organized as a layered collec-

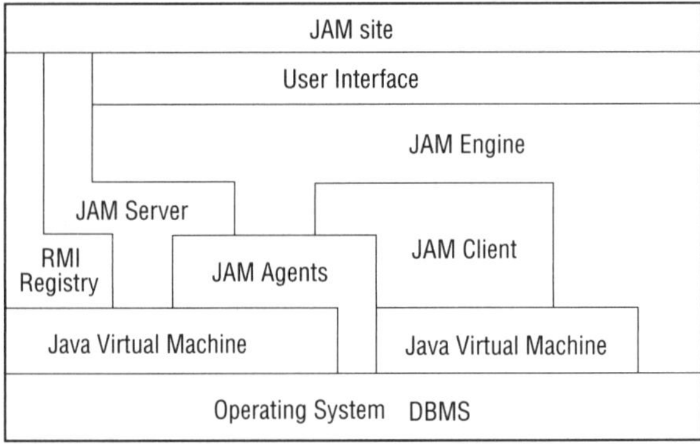

Figure 3.6: JAM site layered model.

tion of software components shown in figure 3.6. In general, the system can be decomposed into four separate subsystems, the User Interface, the JAM Engine and the Client and Server subsystems. The User Interface (upper tier) materializes the front end of the system, through which the owner can define the data mining task and drive the JAM Engine. The JAM Engine constitutes the heart of each JAM site by managing and evaluating the local agents, by preparing/processing the local data sets and by interacting with the Database Management System (DBMS), if one exists. Finally, the Client and Server subsystems compose the network component of JAM and are responsible for interfacing with other JAM sites to coordinate the transport of their agents. Each site is developed on top of the JVM (Java Virtual Machine), with the possible exception of some agents that may be used in a native form and/or depend on an underlying DBMS. A Java agent, for instance, may be able to access a DBMS though JDBC (Java Database Connectivity). The RMI registry component displayed in figure 3.6 corresponds to an independent Java process that is used indirectly by the JAM server component. For the interested reader, the JAM system is described in detail by Stolfo, Prodromidis, Tselepis, Lee, Fan, and Chan[1] (1997) and Prodromidis (1999).

3.3.2 Meta-Learning Level

Employing efficient distributed protocols, however, addresses the scalability problem only partially. The scalability of the system depends greatly on the efficiency of its components (data sites). The analysis of the dependencies among the classifiers, the management of the agents and the efficiency of the

[1] Their paper, "Agent-Based Fraud and Intrusion Detection in Financial Information Systems," is available from http://www.cs.columbia.edu/~sal/JAM/PROJECT

meta-classifiers within the data sites constitutes the other half (meta-learning level) of the scalability problem.

Meta-classifiers can be defined recursively as collections of classifiers structured in multi-level trees (Chan and Stolfo 1996). Such structures, however, can be unnecessarily complex, meaning that many classifiers may be redundant, wasting resources and reducing system throughput. (Throughput here denotes the rate at which a stream of data items can be piped through and labeled by a meta-classifier.) We study the efficiency of meta-classifiers by investigating the effects of pruning (discarding certain base classifiers) on their performance. Determining the optimal set of classifiers for meta-learning is a combinatorial problem. Hence, the objective of pruning is to utilize heuristic methods to search for partially grown meta-classifiers (meta-classifiers with pruned subtrees) that are more efficient and scalable and at the same time achieve comparable or better predictive performance results than fully grown (unpruned) meta-classifiers. To this end, we introduced two stages for pruning meta-classifiers, the a priori pruning or pre-training pruning and the a posteriori pruning or post-training pruning stages. Both levels are essential and complementary to each other with respect to the improvement of accuracy and efficiency of the system.

A priori pruning or pre-training pruning refers to the filtering of the classifiers before they are combined. Instead of combining classifiers in a brute force manner, with pre-training pruning we introduce a preliminary stage for analyzing the available classifiers and qualifying them for inclusion in a combined meta-classifier. Only those classifiers that appear (according to one or more predefined metrics) to be most promising participate in the final meta-classifier. Here, we adopt a black-box approach which evaluates the set of classifiers based only on their input and output behavior, not their internal structure. Conversely, a posteriori pruning or post-training pruning, denotes the evaluation and pruning of constituent base classifiers after a complete meta-classifier has been constructed.

We have implemented and experimented with three pre-training pruning and two post-training pruning algorithms each with different search heuristics. The first pre-training pruning algorithm is a metric-based algorithm, i.e. it ranks and selects the best k classifiers based on their individual performance on a separate validation set or via cross-validation. The second algorithm is a diversity-based algorithm that has preference towards classifiers with diverse predictive behavior.[2] Finally, the third pre-training pruning algorithm concentrates on sets of specialized classifiers (i.e. classifiers that are good in predicting specific classes) that achieve high coverage. [3] The pre-training pruning

[2]In general, the more diverse a set of classifiers is, the more room for improvement the meta-learning method has.

[3]Coverage denotes the fraction of instances of a validation set where at least one classifier

algorithms are described in detail in Prodromidis and Stolfo (1998b). The post-training pruning algorithms are based, the first on the mapping of the unpruned meta-classifiers as decision trees and their subsequent pruning (the nodes of such a decision tree represent base classifiers; pruning a node corresponds to the pruning of a base classifier), and the second on the removal of the base classifiers that are least correlated (and hence the least trusted) to the unpruned meta-classifier. Both post-training pruning algorithms are detailed in Prodromidis, Stolfo, and Chan (1999).

There are two primary objectives for the pruning techniques: (1) to acquire and combine information from multiple databases in a timely manner; and (2) to generate effective and efficient meta-classifiers. The pre-training pruning techniques preceed the meta-learning phase and, as such, can be used in conjunction with most of the combining techniques examined in section 3.2 (e.g. SCANN). Other methods for evaluating and pruning ensembles of classifiers have been studied by Provost and Fawcett and by Margineantu and Dietterich. Provost and Fawcett (1997, 1998) introduced the ROC convex hull method for its intuitiveness and flexibility. The method evaluates and selects classification models by mapping them onto a True Positive/False Positive plane and by allowing comparisons under different metrics (TP/FP rates, accuracy, cost, etc.). The intent of these algorithms, however, is to select the best classifier (not a group of classifiers) under a specific performance criterion (which could be adjusted in the ROC space). In this work, the focus is on methods with the potential to form effective ensembles of classifiers (Dietterich 1997; Hansen and Salamon 1990). In fact, the performance of sub-optimal yet diverse models can be substantially improved when combined together and even surpass that of the best single model.

Margineantu and Dietterich (1997) studied the problem of pruning the ensemble of classifiers (i.e. the set of hypothesis (classifiers)) obtained by the boosting algorithm ADABOOST (Freund and Schapire 1996). According to their findings, by examining the diversity and accuracy of the available classifiers, it is possible for a subset of classifiers to achieve similar levels of performance as the entire set. Their research however, was restricted to computing all classifiers by applying the same learning algorithm on many different subsets of the same training set. In JAM we consider the more general setting where ensembles of classifiers can be obtained by applying, possibly, different learning algorithms over (possibly) distinct databases. Furthermore, instead of voting (ADABOOST) over the predictions of classifiers for the final classification, we adopt meta-learning as a more general framework for combining predictions of the individual classifiers.

Our pre-training and post-training pruning methods have been tested in the

---

makes a correct prediction.

credit card fraud detection domain. The results are presented in section 3.9.

3.4 Portability

A distributed data mining system should be capable of operating across multiple environments with different hardware and software configurations (e.g across the internet), and be able to combine multiple models with (possibly) different representations.

The JAM system presented in this chapter, is a distributed computing construct designed to extend the OS environments to accommodate such requirements. As implied by its name (Java Agents for Meta-learning), portability is inherent within JAM. The "Java" part denotes that we have used Java technology to build the composing parts of the system including the underlying infrastructure, the specific operators that generate and spawn agents, the graphical user interface, the animation facilities to monitor agent exchanges and the meta-learning process and the learning and classifier agents. The "meta-learning" term refers to the system's methods for combining classifier agents. It constitutes a unifying machine learning approach that can be applied to large amounts of data in wide area computing networks for a range of different applications. It has the advantage of being algorithm and representation independent, i.e. it does not examine the internal structure and strategies of the learning algorithms themselves, but only the outputs (predictions) of the individual classifiers.

The learning agents are the basic components for searching for patterns within the data and the classifier agents are the units that capture the computed models and can be shared among the data sites. The platform independence of Java makes it easy for each JAM site to delegate its agents to any participating site. As a result, JAM has been successfully tested on the most popular platforms including Solaris, Windows and Linux simultaneously, i.e. JAM sites imported and utilized classifiers that were computed over different platforms.

In cases where Java's computational speed is of concern, JAM is designed to also support the use of native learning algorithms to substitute slower Java implementations. Native learning programs can be embedded within appropriate Java wrappers to interface with the JAM system and can subsequently be transfered and executed at a different site, provided, of course, that both the receiving site and the native program are compatible.

3.5 Compatibility

Combining multiple models has been receiving increased attention in the literature (Dietterich 1997). In much of the prior work on combining multiple models, it is assumed that all models originate from different subsets (not necessarily distinct) of a single data set as a means to increase accuracy, (e.g. by imposing probability distributions over the instances of the training set, or by stratified sampling, sub-sampling, etc.) and not as a means to integrate distributed information. Although the JAM system, as described in section 3.3 addresses the later by employing meta-learning techniques, integrating classification models derived from distinct and distributed databases may not always be feasible.

In all cases considered so far, all classification models are assumed to originate from databases of identical schemas. Since classifiers depend directly on the format of the underlying data, minor differences in the schemas between databases derive incompatible classifiers, i.e. a classifier cannot be applied on data of different formats. Yet these classifiers may target the same concept. We seek to bridge these disparate classifiers in some principled fashion.

Assume, for instance, we acquire two data sets of credit card transactions (labeled fraud or legitimate) from two different financial institutions (i.e. banks). The learning problem is to distinguish legitimate from fraudulent use of a credit card. Both institutions seek to be able to exchange their classifiers and hence incorporate in their system useful information that would otherwise be inaccessible to both. Indeed, for each credit card transaction, both institutions record similar information, however, they also include specific fields containing important information that each has acquired separately and which provides predictive value in determining fraudulent transaction patterns. In a different scenario where databases and schemas evolve over time, it may be desirable for a single institution to be able to combine classifiers from both past accumulated data with newly acquired data. To facilitate the exchange of knowledge and take advantage of incompatible and otherwise useless classifiers, we need to devise methods that "bridge" the differences imposed by the different schemas.

Integrating the information captured by such classifiers is a non-trivial problem that we have come to call, *"the incompatible schema"* problem. (The reader is advised not to confuse this with Schema Integration over Federated/Mediated Databases.)

3.5.1 Database Compatibility

The "incompatible schema" problem impedes JAM from taking advantage of all available databases. Lets consider two data sites A and B with databases DB_A and DB_B, respectively, with similar but not identical schemas. Without loss of generality, we assume that:

$$Schema(DB_A) = \{A_1, A_2, ..., A_n, A_{n+1}, C\} \tag{3.1}$$

$$Schema(DB_B) = \{B_1, B_2, ..., B_n, B_{n+1}, C\} \quad (3.2)$$

where, A_i, B_i denote the $i-th$ attribute of DB_A and DB_B, respectively, and C the class label (e.g. the fraud/legitimate label in the credit card fraud example) of each instance. Without loss of generality, we further assume that $A_i = B_i$, $1 \leq i \leq n$. As for the A_{n+1} and B_{n+1} attributes, there are two possibilities:

1. $A_{n+1} \neq B_{n+1}$: The two attributes are of entirely different types drawn from distinct domains. The problem can then be reduced to two dual problems where one database has one more attribute than the other, i.e.:

$$Schema(DB_A) = \{A_1, A_2, ..., A_n, A_{n+1}, C\} \quad (3.3)$$

$$Schema(DB_B) = \{B_1, B_2, ..., B_n, C\} \quad (3.4)$$

   where we assume that attribute B_{n+1} is not present in DB_B.[4]

2. $A_{n+1} \approx B_{n+1}$: The two attributes are of similar type but slightly different semantics that is, there may be a map from the domain of one type to the domain of the other. For example, A_{n+1} and B_{n+1} are fields with time dependent information but of different duration (i.e. A_{n+1} may denote the number of times an event occurred within a window of half an hour and B_{n+1} may denote the number of times the same event occurred but within ten minutes).

In both cases (attribute A_{n+1} is either not present in DB_B or semantically different from the corresponding B_{n+1}) the classifiers C_{Aj} derived from DB_A are not compatible with DB_B's data and hence cannot be directly used in DB_B's site, and vice versa. But the purpose of using a distributed data mining system and deploying learning agents and meta-learning their classifier agents is to be able to combine information from different sources. In the next section we investigate ways, called *bridging* methods, that overcome this incompatibility problem and integrate classifiers originating from databases with different schemas.

3.5.2 Bridging Methods

There are several approaches to address the problem depending upon the learning task and the characteristics of the different or missing attribute A_{n+1} of DB_B. The details of these approaches can be found in Prodromidis and Stolfo (1998a).

A_{n+1} *is missing, but can be predicted:* It may be possible to create an auxiliary classifier, which we call a *bridging agent*, from DB_A that can predict

[4]The dual problem has DB_B composed with B_{n+1} but A_{n+1} is not available to A.

the value of the A_{n+1} attribute. To be more specific, by deploying regression methods (e.g. CART (Breiman, Friedman, Olshen, and Stone 1984), locally weighted regression (Atkeson, Schaal, and Moore 2000), linear regression fit (Myers 1986), MARS (Friedman 1991) for continuous attributes and machine learning algorithms for categorical attributes, data site A can compute one or more auxiliary classifier agents C_{Aj}' that predict the value of attribute A_{n+1} based on the common attributes $A_1, ..., A_n$. Then it can send all its local (base and bridging) classifiers to data site B. At the other side, data site B can deploy the auxiliary classifiers C_{Aj}' to estimate the values of the missing attribute A_{n+1} and present to classifiers C_{Aj} a new database DB_B' with schema $\{A_1, ..., A_n, \hat{A}_{n+1}\}$. From this point on, meta-learning and meta-classifying proceeds normally.

A_{n+1} is missing and cannot be predicted: Computing a model for a missing attribute assumes a correlation between that attribute and the rest. Nevertheless, such a hypothesis may be unwarranted in which case we adopt one of the following strategies:

- *Classifier agent C_{Aj} supports missing values:* If the classifier agent C_{Aj} originating from DB_A can handle attributes with missing values, data site B can simply include null values in a fictitious A_{n+1} attribute added to DB_B. The resulting DB_B' database is a database compatible with the C_{Aj} classifiers. Different classifier agents treat missing values in different ways. Some machine learning algorithms, for instance, treat them as a separate category, others replace them with the average or most frequent value, while more sophisticated algorithms treat them as "wild cards" and predict the most likely class of all possible, based on the other attribute-value pairs that are known.

- *Learning agents at data site B can not handle missing values:* If, on the other hand, the classifier agent C_{Aj} cannot deal with missing values, data site A can learn two separate classifiers, one over the original database DB_A and one over DB_A', where DB_A' is the DB_A database but without the A_{n+1} attribute:

$$DB_A' = PROJECT\ (A_1, ..., A_n)\ FROM\ DB_A \tag{3.5}$$

  The first classifier can be stored locally for later use by the local meta-learning agents, while the later can be sent to data site B. Learning a second classifier without the A_{n+1} attribute, or in general with attributes that belong to the intersection of the attributes of the databases of the two data sites, implies that the second classifier makes use of only the attributes that are common among the participating data sites. Even though the rest of the attributes may have high predictive value for the data site that uses them, they are of no value for the other data site. After all, the other data site (data site B) did not include them in its database, and presumably other attributes, including the common ones, do have predictive value.

A_{n+1} is present, but semantically different: It may be possible to integrate human expert knowledge and introduce bridging agents either from data site A, or data site B that can preprocess the A_{n+1} values and translate them according to the A_{n+1} semantics. In the context of the example described earlier where the A_{n+1} and B_{n+1} fields capture time dependent information, the bridging agent may be able to map the B_{n+1} values into A_{n+1} semantics and present these new values to the C_{Aj} classifier. For example, the agent may estimate the number of times the event would occur in thirty minutes by tripling the B_{n+1} values or by employing more sophisticated approximation formulas using non uniformly distributed probabilities (e.g. Poisson).

These approaches address the "incompatible schema" problem and meta-learning over these models should proceed in a straightforward manner. The idea of requesting missing definitions from remote sites (i.e. missing attributes) first appeared in Maitan, Ras, and Zemankova (1989). In that paper, Maitan, Raś and Zemankova define a query language and describe a scheme for handling and processing global queries (queries that need to access multiple databases at more than one site) within distributed information systems. According to this scheme, each site compiles into rules some facts describing the data that belong to other neighboring sites which can subsequently by used to interpret and correctly resolve any non-standard queries posed (i.e. queries with unknown attributes).

More recently Zbigniew Raś(1998) further elaborated this scheme and developed an algebraic theory to formally describe a query answering system for solving non-standard DNF queries in a distributed knowledge based system (DKBS). Given a non-standard query on a relational database with categorical or partially ordered set of attributes, his aim is to compute rules consistent with the distributed data to resolve unknown attributes and retrieve all the records of the database that satisfy it. Our approach, however, is more general, in that, it supports both categorical and continuous attributes, and it is not limited to a specific syntactic case or the consistency of the generated rules. Instead, it employs machine learning techniques to compute models for the missing values.

3.6 Adaptivity

Most data mining systems operate in environments that are almost certainly bound to change, a phenomenon known as *concept drift*. For example, medical science evolves, and with it the types of medication, the dosages and treatments, and of course the data included in the various medical database; lifestyles change over time and so do the profiles of customers included in credit card data; new security systems are introduced and new ways to commit fraud or to break into systems are devised. Most traditional data mining systems are static.

The classifiers deployed in the traditional classification systems are obtained by applying machine learning programs over historical databases DB_i. The problem is to design a classification system that can evolve in case a new database DB_j becomes available.

One way to address this problem is to merge the old and new databases into a larger database DB and reapply the machine learning programs to generate new classifiers. This, however, cannot constitute a viable solution. First, learning programs do not scale very well with large databases and second, the main memory requirement by the majority of learning programs poses a physical limitation to the size of the training databases.

A second alternative would be to employ *incremental* machine learning programs, (e.g. ID5 (Utgoff 1988, 1989, 1994), an incremental version of ID3) or nearest neighbor algorithms. Incremental machine learning programs denote machine learning programs that are not constrained to retain all training examples in main memory; instead they examine one instance at a time and tune the model accordingly. Hence, the classifiers initially trained over DB_i can be updated later by resuming their training on the new database DB_j once it becomes available. On the other hand, these algorithms do not provide a means for removing irrelevant knowledge gathered in the past. Furthermore, updating a model on every instance may not be accurate in a noisy domain. This shortcoming can be avoided by employing incremental batch learning methods (Clearwater, Cheng, Hirsh, and Buchanan 1989; Domingos 1996a; Wu and Lo 1998), i.e. methods that update models using subsets of data. The problem with these approaches is that they are not general enough; instead they rely on specific algorithms, model representation and implementations.

We describe a new possibility, a mechanism that takes advantage of the capabilities and architecture of the JAM system to integrate new information. New information is treated in a fashion similar to the information imported from remote data sites in JAM. Instead of combining classifiers from remote data sites (integration over space), adaptive learning systems combine classifiers acquired over different time periods (integration over time). We employ meta-learning techniques to design learning systems capable of incorporating into their accumulated knowledge (existing classifiers) the new classifiers that capture emerging patterns learned over new data sources.

Let C_{new} be the set of classifiers generated from the latest batch of data and $C_{current}$ be the set of classifiers currently in use. The union of the $C_{current}$ and the C_{new} classifiers constitutes the new set of candidate classifiers. After the pruning process over the validation set, a new meta-classifier is computed via meta-learning. The classifiers from $C_{current}$ that survived the pruning stage represent the existing knowledge, while the remaining classifiers from C_{new} denote the newly acquired information. A key point in this process is the selection of the validation set that is used during the pruning and meta-learning stages. A straight-forward approach is to include in the validation set both old and new data and in proportions that reflect the speed of pattern changes (which can be approximated by monitoring the performance of $C_{current}$ over time). A more sophisticated approach would also weight data according to recency—weights decay over time.

In addition to solving the problem of how to make a learning system evolve and adjust according to its changing environment, this meta-learning-based solution has other advantages that make it even more desirable:

(1) It is simple. Different classifiers capture the characteristics and patterns that surfaced over different period of times and meta-learning combines them in a straight-forward manner.

(2) It integrates uniformly with the existing approaches of combining classifiers and information acquired over remote sources.

(3) It is easy to implement and test. In fact, all the necessary components for building classifiers and combining them with older classifiers are similar or identical to the components used in standard meta-learning and can be reused without modification.

(4) It is module-oriented and efficient. The meta-learning based system need not repeat the entire training process in order to create models that integrate new information. Instead it can build independent models that can plug-in to the meta-learning hierarchy. In other words, we only need to train base classifiers from the new data and employ meta-learning techniques to combine them with other existing classifiers. In this way, the overhead for incremental learning is limited to the meta-learning phase.

(5) It can be used in conjunction with existing pruning techniques. Normally, incorporating new classifiers in a meta-classifier hierarchy continuously would eventually result in large and inefficient tree-based hierarchies. But since the new classifiers are not different in nature from the "traditional" classifiers, it is possible that the meta-learning based system can analyze and compare them (pre- and post-training pruning) and keep only those that contribute to the overall accuracy and not over-burden the meta-classification process. For example, it can decide to collapse or substitute a sub-tree of the meta-classifier hierarchy with newly obtained classifier(s) that capture the same or new patterns.

This strategy opens a new research direction that is compatible with the JAM system and at the same time is scalable and generic, meaning that it can deal with many large databases that become available over time, and can support different machine learning algorithms respectively. The strategy allows JAM to extend and incorporate new information without discarding or depreciating the knowledge it has accumulated over time from previous data mining. We have not treated the issue of what to do about previously computed and unused (pruned) classifiers or models. Retaining and managing older unused classifiers or models is an interesting open question that has not been adequately addressed in our work.

3.7 Extensibility

It is not only data and patterns that change over time. Advances in machine learning and data mining are bound to give rise to algorithms and tools that are not available at the present time as well. Unless the data mining system is flexible to accommodate existing as well as future data mining technology it will rapidly be rendered inadequate and obsolete. To ensure extensibility, JAM is designed using object-oriented methods and is implemented independently of any particular machine learning program or any meta-learning or classifier combining technique.

The learning and meta-learning agents are designed as objects. JAM provides the definition of the parent agent class and every instance agent (i.e. a program that implements any of your favorite learning algorithms ID3 (Quinlan 1986), Ripper (Cohen 1995), CART (Breiman, Friedman, Olshen, and Stone 1984), Bayes (Duda and Hart 1973), WPEBLS (Cost and Salzberg 1993), CN2 (Clark and Niblett 1989), etc.) are then defined as a subclass of this parent class. Among other definitions which are inherited by all agent subclasses, the parent agent class provides a very simple and minimal interface that all subclasses have to comply with. As long as a learning or meta-learning agent conforms to this interface, it can be introduced and used immediately in the JAM system.

To be more specific, a JAM agent needs to have the following methods implemented:

(1) A *constructor* with no arguments. JAM can then instantiate the agent, provided it knows its name (which can be supplied by the owner of the data site through either the local user configuration file or the GUI).

(2) An *initialize()* method. In most of the cases, if not all, the agent subclasses inherit this method from the parent agent class. Through this method, JAM can supply the necessary arguments to the agent. Arguments include the names of the training and test datasets, the name of the dictionary file, and the filename of the output classifier.

(3) A *buildClassifier()* method. JAM calls this method to trigger the agent

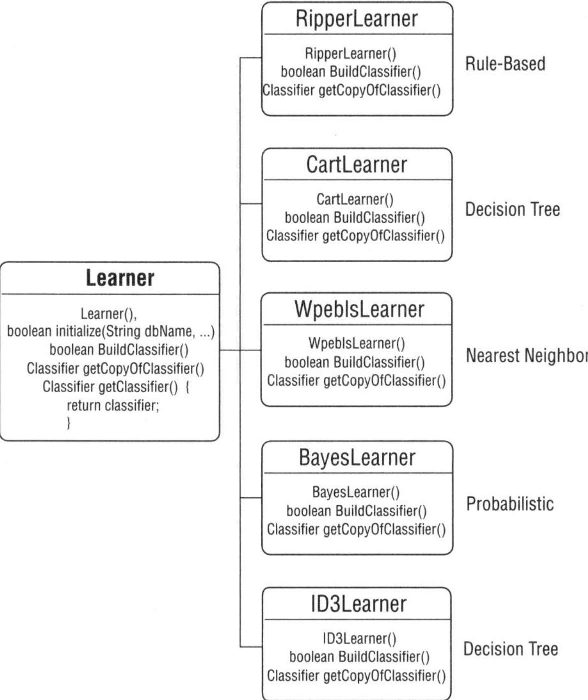

Figure 3.7: The class hierarchy of learning agents.

to learn (or meta-learn) from the training dataset.

(4) A *getClassifier()* and *getCopyOfClassifier()* methods. These methods are used by JAM to obtain the newly built classifiers which are then encapsulated and can be "snapped-in" at any participating data site! Hence, remote agent dispatch is easily accomplished.

The class hierarchy (only methods are shown) for five different learning agents is presented in figure 3.7. ID3, Bayes, WPEBLS, CART and Ripper inherit the methods *initialize()* and *getClassifier()* from their parent learning agent class. The MetaLearning, Classifier and MetaClassifier classes are defined in similar class hierarchies.

JAM's infrastructure is independent of the machine learning programs of interest. As long as a machine learning program is defined and encapsulated as an object conforming to the minimal interface requirements (most existing algorithms have similar interfaces already) it can be imported and used directly. This plug-and-play characteristic makes JAM a powerful and extensible data mining facility. In the latest version of JAM, for example, ID3 and CART are full Java agents, whereas Bayes, WPEBLS and Ripper are stored locally as native applications. It is exactly this feature that allows users to employ native programs within the Java agents if computational speed is crucial (see also section 3.4).

3.8 Effectiveness

We seek effective measures to evaluate the predictive accuracy of classification systems. Contrary to most studies on comparing different learning algorithms and classification models, predictive accuracy does not mean only overall accuracy (or minimal error rate). Instead, we must consider alternative and more realistic "optimality criteria." Other measures of interest include True Positive (TP) and False Positive (FP) rates for (binary) classification problems, ROC analysis and problem specific cost models are all different criteria relevant to different problems and learning tasks. A detailed study against the use of accuracy estimation for comparing induction algorithms can be found in Provost, Fawcett, and Kohavi (1998). In the credit card fraud domain, for example, overall predictive accuracy is inappropriate as the single measure of predictive performance. If 1% of the transactions are fraudulent, then a model that always predicts "non-fraud" will be 99% accurate. Hence, TP rate is more important. Of the 1% fraudulent transactions, we wish to compute models that predict 100% of these, yet produce no false alarms (i.e. predict no legitimate transactions to be fraudulent). Hence, maximizing the TP-FP spread may be the right measure of a successful model. Yet, one may find a model with TP rate of 90%, i.e. it correctly predicts 90% of the fraudulent transactions, but here it may correctly predict the lowest cost transactions, being entirely wrong about the top 10% most expensive frauds. Therefore, a cost model criterion may be the best judge of success, i.e a classifier whose TP rate is 10% may be the best cost performer.

Furthermore, using the natural class distribution of a data set might not yield the most effective classifiers (particularly when the distribution is highly skewed). Given a skewed distribution, we would like to generate the desired distribution without removing any data. Our approach is to create data subsets with the desired distribution, generate classifiers from these subsets, and integrate them by meta-learning their classification behavior. If, for example, we aim to change a naturally skewed 20:80 distribution of a binary classification problem into a 50:50 distribution, we can randomly divide the majority instances into four partitions and form four data subsets by merging the minority instances with each of the four partitions containing majority instances. That is, the minority instances are replicated across four data subsets to generate the desired 50:50 distribution. Figure 3.8 depicts this process. Our empirical

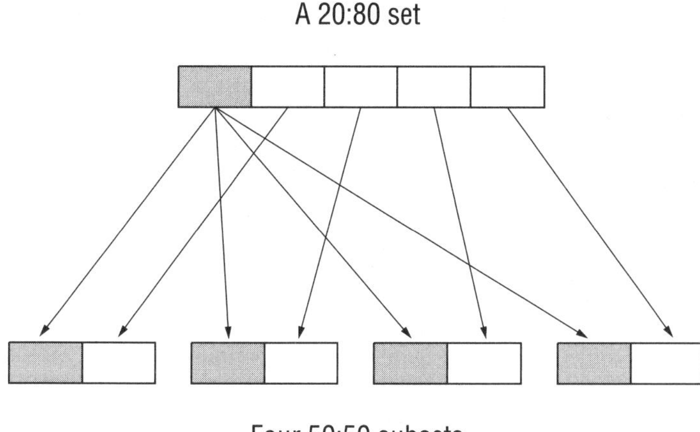

Figure 3.8: Generating four 50:50 data subsets from a 20:80 data set.

results indicate that our multi-classifier meta-learning approach using a 50:50 distribution in the data subsets for training can significantly reduce the amount of dollar loss due to illegitimate transactions. Details of our techniques and results are in Chan and Stolfo (1998).

Formally, let n be the size of the data set with a distribution of $x : y$ (x is the percentage of the minority class) and $u : v$ be the desired distribution. The number of minority instances is $n \times x$ and the desired number of majority instances in a subset is $nx \times \frac{v}{u}$. The number of subsets is the number of majority instances ($n \times y$) divided by the number of desired majority instances in each subset, which is $\frac{ny}{\frac{nxv}{u}}$ or $\frac{y}{x} \times \frac{u}{v}$. (When it is not a whole number, we take the ceiling ($\lceil \frac{y}{x} \times \frac{u}{v} \rceil$) and replicate some majority instances to ensure all of thc majority instanccs arc in thc subscts.) That is, wc havc $\frac{y}{x} \times \frac{u}{v}$ subscts, each of which has nx minority instances and $\frac{nxv}{u}$ majority instances.

The next step is to apply a learning algorithm(s) to each of the subsets. Since the subsets are independent, the learning process for each subset can be run in parallel on different processors. For massive amounts of data, substantial improvement in speed can be achieved for super-linear-time learning algorithms. The generated classifiers are combined by learning (meta-learning) from their classification behavior.

At this stage, pruning can be used as additional means to improve the predictive performance of the final classification model (meta-classifier). In general, learning algorithms are designed to compute classification models with as small error rate as possible. However, when the models are evaluated with respect to different metrics (e.g. TP, cost model), their results are bound to be sub-optimal, except perhaps by chance. In such cases, pruning can help discard from the ensemble the base classifiers that do not exhibit the desired property with positive impact on the predictive performance of the final meta-classifier.

3.9 Empirical Evaluation

JAM has been used to compute classifier and meta-classifier agents to forewarn of possibly fraudulent credit card transactions. This section describes our experimental setting, reports the results and compares the performance of the different approaches.

3.9.1 Experimental Setting

Learning algorithms Five inductive learning algorithms are used in our experiments, Bayes, C4.5, ID3, CART and Ripper. ID3, its successor C4.5 (Quinlan 1993), and CART are decision tree based algorithms, Bayes, described in Minsky and Papert (1969), is a naive Bayesian classifier, and Ripper (Cohen 1995) is a rule induction algorithm.

Learning tasks Two data sets of real credit card transactions were used in our experiments. The credit card data sets were provided by the Chase and First Union Banks, members of FSTC (Financial Services Technology Consortium).

The two data sets contained credit card transactions labeled as fraudulent or legitimate. Each bank supplied half a million records spanning one year with 20% fraud and 80% non-fraud distribution for Chase bank and 15% versus 85% for First Union bank. The schemas of the databases were developed over years of experience and continuous analysis by bank personnel to capture important information for fraud detection. We cannot reveal the details of the schema beyond what is described in Stolfo, Fan, Prodromidis, Lee, Tselepis, and Chan (1998). The records have a fixed length of 137 bytes each and about thirty numeric attributes including the binary class label (fraudulent/legitimate transaction). Some of the fields are numeric and the rest categorical, i.e. numbers were used to represent a few discrete categories.

To evaluate and compare the meta-classifiers constructed, we adopted three metrics: the overall accuracy, the TP-FP spread and a cost model fit to the credit card fraud detection problem. Overall accuracy expresses the ability of a classifier to provide correct predictions, TP-FP[5] denotes the ability of a

[5]The TP-FP spread is an ad-hoc, yet informative and simple metric characterizing the perfor-

classifier to catch fraudulent transactions while minimizing false alarms, and finally, the cost model captures the performance of a classifier with respect to the goal of the target application (stop dollar loss due to fraud).

Credit card companies have a fixed overhead that serves as a threshold value for challenging the legitimacy of a credit card transaction. If the transaction amount *amt*, is below this threshold, they choose to authorize the transaction automatically. Each transaction predicted as fraudulent requires an overhead referral fee for authorization personnel to decide the final disposition. This overhead cost is typically a fixed fee that we call $\$Y$. Therefore, even if we could accurately predict and identify all fraudulent transactions, those whose *amt* is less than $\$Y$ would produce $\$(Y - amt)$ in losses anyway. To calculate the savings each fraud detector contributes due to stopping fraudulent transactions, we use the following cost model for each transaction:

- If prediction is "legitimate" or $(amt \leq Y)$, authorize the transaction $(savings = 0)$;
- Otherwise investigate the transaction:
  - If transaction is "fraudulent," $savings = amt - Y$;
  - otherwise $savings = -Y$;

First we distribute the data sets across six different data sites (each site storing two months of data) and we prepared the set of candidate base classifiers, i.e. the original set of base classifiers the pruning algorithm is called to evaluate. We computed these classifiers by applying the five learning algorithms to each month of data, therefore creating sixty base classifiers (ten classifiers per data site). Next, we had each data site import the "remote" base classifiers (fifty in total) that were subsequently used in the pruning and meta-learning phases, thus ensuring that each classifier would not be tested unfairly on known data. Specifically, we had each site use half of its local data (one month) to test, prune and meta-learn the base-classifiers and the other half to evaluate the overall performance of the pruned or unpruned meta-classifier (more details can be found in Prodromidis and Stolfo [1998b] and Prodromidis, Stolfo, and Chan [1999]). In essence, the setting of this experiment corresponds to a parallel six-fold cross validation.

Finally, we had the two banks exchange their classifier agents as well. In addition to its ten local and fifty "internal" classifiers (those imported from their peer data sites), each site also imported sixty external classifiers (from the other bank). Thus, each Chase data site was populated with sixty (ten local

mance of the classifiers. In comparing the classifiers, one can replace the TP-FP spread, which defines a certain family of curves in the ROC plot, with a different metric or even with a complete analysis (Provost and Fawcett 1997) in the ROC space.

Type of Classification Model	*Size*	*Accuracy*	*TP - FP*	*Savings*
COTS scoring system from Chase	-	85.7%	0.523	$ 682K
Best base classifier over single subset	1	88.7%	0.557	$ 843K
Best base classifier over largest subset	1	88.5%	0.553	$ 812K
Meta-classifier over Chase base classifiers	50	89.74%	0.621	$ 818K
Meta-classifier over Chase base classifiers	46	**89.76%**	0.574	$ 604K
Meta-classifier over Chase base classifiers	27	88.93%	0.632	$ 832K
Meta-classifier over Chase base classifiers	4	88.89%	0.551	**$ 905K**
Meta-classifier over Chase and First Union base classifiers (without bridging)	110	89.7%	0.621	$ 797K
Meta-classifier over Chase and First Union base classifiers (without bridging)	65	89.75%	0.571	$ 621K
Meta-classifier over Chase and First Union basc classificrs (without bridging)	43	88.34%	**0.633**	$ 810K
Meta-classifier over Chase and First Union base classifiers (without bridging)	52	87.71%	0.625	$ 877K

Table 3.1: Performance results for the Chase credit card data set.

and fifty remote) Chase classifiers and sixty First Union classifiers and each First Union site was populated with sixty (ten local and fifty remote) First Union classifiers and sixty Chase classifiers. Again, the sites used half of their local data (one month) to test, prune and meta-learn the base-classifiers and the other half to evaluate the overall performance of the pruned or unpruned meta-classifier. To ensure fairness, the ten local classifiers were not used in meta-learning. The two databases, however, had the following schema differences: (1) Chase and First Union defined a (nearly identical) feature with different semantics; (2) Chase includes two (continuous) features not present in the First Union data

For the first incompatibility, we had the values of the First Union data mapped to the semantics of the Chase data. For the second incompatibility, we deployed bridging agents to compute the missing values (for a detailed discussion, see Prodromidis and Stolfo [1998a]). When predicting, the First Union classifiers simply disregarded the real values provided at the Chase data sites, while the Chase classifiers relied on both the common attributes and the predictions of the bridging agents to deliver a prediction at the First Union data sites.

Tables 3.1 and 3.2 summarize our results for the Chase and First Union banks respectively. Table 3.1 reports the performance results of the best classification models on Chase data, while table 3.2 presents the performance results of the best performers on the First Union data. Both tables display the accuracy, the TP-FP spread and savings for each of the fraud predictors examined and the best result in every category is depicted in bold. The maximum achievable savings for the "ideal" classifier, with respect to our cost model, is

Type of Classification Model	*Size*	*Accuracy*	*TP - FP*	*Savings*
Best base classifier over single subset	1	95.2%	0.749	$ 800K
Best base classifier over largest subset	1	95.5%	0.790	$ 803K
Meta-classifier over First Union base classifiers	50	96.53%	0.831	$ 935K
Meta-classifier over First Union base classifiers	14	96.59%	0.797	$ 891K
Meta-classifier over First Union base classifiers	12	96.53%	0.848	$ 944K
Meta-classifier over First Union base classifiers	26	96.50%	0.838	$ 945K
Meta-classifier over Chase and First Union base classifiers (without bridging)	110	96.6%	0.843	$ 942K
Meta-classifier over Chase and First Union base classifiers (with bridging)	110	**98.05%**	0.897	**$ 963K**
Meta-classifier over Chase and First Union base classifiers (with bridging)	56	98.02%	0.890	$ 953K
Meta-classifier over Chase and First Union base classifiers (with bridging)	61	98.01%	**0.899**	$ 950K
Meta-classifier over Chase and First Union base classifiers (with bridging)	53	98.00%	0.894	$ 962K

Table 3.2: Performance results for the First Union credit card data set.

$1470K for the Chase and $1085K for the First Union data sets. The column denoted as "size" indicates the number of base-classifiers used in the classification system.

The first row of table 3.1 shows the best possible performance of Chase's own COTS authorization/detection system on this data set. The next two rows present the performance of the best base classifiers over a single subset and over the largest possible [6] data subset, while the next four rows detail the performance of the unpruned (size of 50) and best pruned meta-classifiers for each of the evaluation metrics (size of 46 for accuracy, 27 for the TP-FP spread, and 4 for the cost model). Finally, the last four rows report on the performance of the unpruned (size of 110) and best pruned meta-classifiers (sizes of 65, 43, 52) according to accuracy, the TP-FP spread and the cost model respectively. The first four meta-classifiers combine only "internal" (from Chase) base classifiers, while the last four combine both internal and external (from Chase and First Union) base classifiers. Bridging agents were not used in these experiments, since all attributes needed by First Union agents, were already defined in the Chase data.

Similar data is recorded in table 3.2 for the First Union set, with the exception of First Union's COTS authorization/detection performance (it was not made available to us), and the additional results obtained when employing special bridging agents from Chase to compute the values of First Union's missing attributes. (In table 3.1 we do not report results using bridging agents.

[6]Determined by the available system resources.

First Union classifiers do not require predictive bridging agents to estimate any additional values; instead they ignore the two extra attributes of the Chase data.)

The most apparent outcome of these experiments is the superior performance of meta-learning over the single model approaches and over the traditional authorization/detection systems (at least for the given data sets). The meta-classifiers outperformed the single base classifiers (local or global) in every category. Moreover, by bridging the two databases, we managed to further improve the performance of the meta-learning system. Notice, however, that combining classifiers agents from the two banks directly (without bridging) is not very effective. This phenomenon can be easily explained from the fact that the attribute missing from the First Union data set is significant in modeling the Chase data set. Hence, the First Union classifiers are not as effective as the Chase classifiers on the Chase data, and the Chase classifiers cannot perform at full strength at the First Union sites without the bridging agents.

An additional result, evident from these tables, is the invaluable contribution of pruning. In all cases, pruning succeeded in computing meta-classifiers with similar or better fraud detection capabilities, while reducing their size and thus improving their efficiency. A comparative study between predictive performance and meta-classifier throughput can be found in Prodromidis, Stolfo, and Chan (1999).

3.10 Conclusions

Distributed data mining systems aim to discover and combine useful information that is distributed across multiple databases. A widely accepted approach to this objective is to apply to these databases various machine learning programs that discover patterns that may be exhibited in the data and compute descriptive representations of the data, called classification models or classifiers. In this study, we concentrated on the problem of acquiring useful information, efficiently and accurately, from large and distributed databases. In this respect, we described the JAM system, a powerful, distributed agent-based meta-learning system for large scale data mining applications. Meta-learning is a general method that facilitates the combining of models computed independently by the various machine learning programs and supports the scaling of large data mining applications.

In the course of the design and implementation of JAM we identified several issues related to the scalability, efficiency, portability, compatibility, adaptivity, extensibility and effectiveness of distributed data mining systems. We addressed the efficiency and scalability problems first by employing distributed and asynchronous protocols at the architectural level of JAM for managing the learning agents across the data sites of the system, and second by introducing special pruning algorithms at the data site level (meta-learning level) to evaluate and combine only the most essential classifiers. To preserve portability across heterogenous platforms we built JAM upon existing agent infrastructure available over the internet and to achieve compatibility we employed special bridging agents to resolve any differences in the schemata among the distributed databases. Adaptivity is attained by extending the meta-learning techniques to combine both existing and new classifiers while extensibility is ensured by decoupling JAM from the learning algorithms and by introducing plug-and-play capabilities through objects. Finally, to evaluate and improve the effectiveness of our data mining system, we investigated more appropriate metrics (some of which are task specific) and applied meta-learning and distribution manipulation techniques to tasks with skewed distributions.

The design and implementation of useful and practical distributed data mining systems requires extensive research on all these issues. The intent of this chapter is not to provide a detailed exposition of techniques but to overview the important issues and our proposed approaches (detailed discussions of our techniques and findings appear in publications cited throughout this study). This area is open and active and these problems have not been fully explored. The proposed methods were empirically evaluated against real credit card transaction data provided by two separate financial institutions where the target data mining application was to compute predictive models that detect fraudulent transactions. Our experiments suggest that meta-learning, together with distributed protocols, the pruning methods and bridging techniques constitute a highly effective and scalable approach for mining distributed data sets with the potential to contribute useful systems with broad applicability.

Acknowledgements

This research is supported by the Intrusion Detection Program (BAA9603) from DARPA (F30602-96-1-0311), NSF (IRI-96-32225 and CDA-96-25374) and NYSSTF (423115-445). We wish to thank Adam Banckenroth of Chase Bank and Tom French of First Union Bank for their support of this work.

Chapter 4

Distributed Classification with Knowledge Probing

Yi-ke Guo and Janjao Sutiwaraphun

4.1 Introduction

Distributed learning concerns the problem of knowledge discovery from distributed data sets. The key word *distributed* can be understood in two different ways: *Distributed by partitioning:* In this sense, the original data set exists as one large piece. It is divided into small subsets by applying data partitioning techniques. *Distributed by nature:* Data to be learned is physically distributed at different sites and sometimes data sharing is not permitted (due to confidentiality or cost of data migration).

In the scenario of distribution by partitioning, distributed learning constitutes a scaling mechanism for learning from large data sets. Since the execution time of a learning process can be prohibitive when data size is too large, data partitioning techniques can be applied to break down a large data set into small subsets to speed up the learning process or to avoid the limitation on memory size. These subsets are regarded as distributed data sets which can be learned concurrently with a distributed or parallel computing system. The learned results can be combined into a unified model which represents the knowledge learned from the entire data set.

In the second scenario, distributed learning is a mechanism of distributed information comprehension. That is, we are learning some global knowledge from distributed data. This learning procedure involves integrating models which are locally learned at different locations in a pragmatical and statistically sound fashion.

This difference in understanding distributed learning results in the diversity of research issues in this area. However, there are two main characteristics which both scenarios have in common: (1) Gaining partial knowledge from parts of the data; and (2) approximating a global model by integrating the partial knowledge. The major challenge in distributed inductive learning is to learn a high quality unified model from partial models which are learned from subsets of data.

Recently, distributed learning or, more precisely, distributed classification, which involves learning classification models from partitioned or distributed data sets, has become an active research area (Chan and Stolfo 1993c; Provost and Hennessy 1996; Chan and Stolfo 1998). Many works in this area have been influenced by multiple model learning or committee learning research, which is an active research field in machine learning. Committee learning concerns learning from multiple models which are generated by means of variations in either the learning algorithm or the data set. These multiple models are then combined to make joint predictions. It has been widely accepted that committee learning provides an effective way of improving classification accuracy as well as stability of predictions by averaging base models to overcome the bias and variance introduced by data and learning methods (Breiman 1996a; Ali and Pazzani 1996a; Domingos 1997b; Bauer and Kohavi 1998).

The close relationship of distributed classification data mining and committee learning is rather obvious; both paradigms deal with learning from multiple models. Although sharing the same nature, the semantics of their base models are different. In multiple model learning, base models are generated from the same data source by either varying the distribution of the data set or the deterministic procedure of the learning algorithm. Those base models, therefore, are about one whole source of data. In distributed data mining, local models are about the partial data in the case of data distributed by partitioning or about the different data in the case of data distributed by nature. This difference in the semantics of the base models has to be aware especially when multiple model methodologies are applied to solve problems in distributed data mining. In the case where base models are highly inconsistent or, in other words, the distribution of the local data is very different, special mechanisms, for example, data redistribution techniques, are required to adjust the distribution of the local data to enable the local models to become consistent to certain levels.

In the next section, the basic concepts of distributed inductive learning are discussed under the Bayesian learning framework. In section 4.3, we introduce knowledge probing as a technique for generating descriptive models from black box models. By viewing a set of distributed learned models as a black box and applying Knowledge Probing technique to such black box, we propose distributed learning with knowledge probing (DLKP) as a framework for generating a unified model in distributed data mining environments. An empirical study has shown that the effectiveness of DLKP varies from domain to domain. We show that the effectiveness of DLKP is related to the shape of margin distribution graph of the corresponding model committee. Margin distribution is introduced in section 4.4 together with the consistency of the local models which is another important issue of DLKP. Details of the empirical study and analysis of the use of DLKP are given in section 4.5. The conclusion is in section 4.6.

4.2 Distributed Inductive Learning

In this section, basic concepts of distributed inductive learning are discussed within the framework of Bayesian learning. Consider a training data set D generated according to an unknown parametric distribution $P(D|\theta)$. *Inductive learning* concerns the problem of learning this parametric distribution or target distribution, by estimating the parameter θ. The learned target distribution constitutes a model that can be used to predict the probability of an unseen data item. A classification problem is an inductive learning problem whose training data items are labelled with class values and the target distribution can be represented as a probabilistic function mapping an attribute vector v to a class value c (i.e. computing the conditional probability $P(c|v)$).

A distributed inductive learning system consists of a number of local learners (L-learners) and a meta learner (M-learner). Each L-learner independently observes a set of examples generated independently according to a local target distribution $P(D|\theta)$ and outputs a model which is able to estimate θ. Let θ_i be the estimation computed by the i-th L-learner. The M-learner takes $\theta_1, \ldots, \theta_n$ as input and outputs an estimation of θ as a function of $\theta_1, \ldots, \theta_n$. That is, the M-learner learns from the results of local learners to form a global model.

This formation of distributed inductive learning model reveals the basic features of distributed learning by introducing the concept of local learner and meta learner:

1. L-learner: gaining partial knowledge from a part of the data.

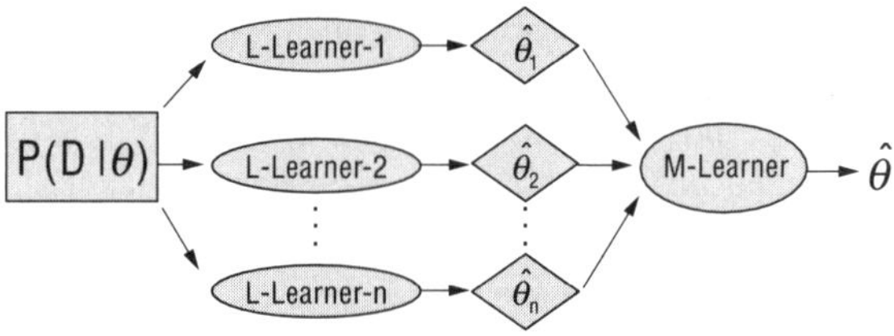

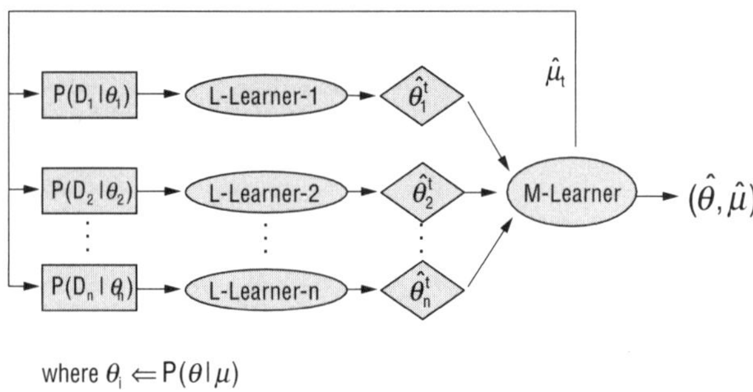

Figure 4.1: An abstraction of the distributed inductive learning from homogeneously and heterogeneously distributed data sets.

2. M-learner: approximating a global model by integrating partial knowledge.

We may assume that all the local target distributions $P(D_i|\theta_i)$ in a distributed inductive learning system are identical, $\theta_i = \theta_j$, $(i \neq j)$. That is, all the local training data share the same distribution. Each local learner estimates a common variable θ_i. The meta learner integrates the local models by averaging all the local θ_i. This corresponds to the notion of plain learning model of distributed Bayesian learning as proposed by Yamanishi (1997). An abstraction of this scenario is shown in the top diagram of figure 4.1. The multiple model learning is obviously a special case of the plain learning model.

A more complicated distributed learning approach is required when each local learner deals with different data distribution. For example, we may assume that all the local target distributions $P(D_i|\theta_i)$ in a distributed inductive learning system are not necessarily identical and each of the unknown parameters θ_i is independently generated from a prior distribution $P(\theta|\mu)$, where μ is an unknown meta-parameter. In this case, a distributed learning system should not only involve an induction of all θ_i which model local distributions, but also involve an induction of μ which models the interrelationship between distributions of all local data. Iterative process might be required to obtain optimal μ. That is, at a particular time step t, θ_i^t is learned by the i-th L-learner from the local data D_i with the parameter μ^{t-1}. μ^t will be induced by the M-learner from all θ_i^t $(i = 1, \ldots, n)$[1]. This corresponds to the notion of hierarchical learning model in Yamanishi (1997). An abstraction of this scenario is shown in the second diagram of figure 4.1. This learning model is the generalization of the notion of mixed models addressed in the EM algorithm (Dempster, Laird, and Rubin 1977).

One of the key points of this formulation of distributed learning is that, given a L-learner and a M-learner, a distributed learning system can be made by applying the L-learner to form local models and employing the meta learner to combine those local models. Moreover, in the learning process, the structure of the M-learner as well as the result (a global model) are determined by the assumption we made on the distribution of local data sets.

4.3 Distributed Learning with Knowledge Probing

In this section, we propose a framework for generating a unified classification model in distributed inductive learning environment based on the plain learning model. That is, the local training data sets are generated from the same parametric model.

Given a group of n data sets $S_1, S_2, \ldots, S_n$, the learning algorithms L_1, $L_2, \ldots, L_n$ are applied to the corresponding data sets and produce local models (local models) $M_1, M_2, \ldots, M_n$. The locally learned models are integrated by a combining procedure to produce a final model. This architecture is the same as the learning using data partitioning (LUDP) model described by Provost and Kolluri (1999) as a method of scaling up inductive learning algorithms. By applying this architecture to distributed inductive learning environments, the main issue emphasized in our framework is to integrate the models learned locally into a model which can be used as a representative of the entire knowledge in an understandable representation. In our framework, the integration is done by applying the knowledge probing technique.

Knowledge probing was proposed by Guo, Rueger, Sutiwaraphun, and Forbes-Millot (1997) as a technique to probe descriptive knowledge from a

---

[1] μ^0 is usually given based on the prior knowledge.

Input: A set S of n unseen data items,
a black box model B,
a learning algorithm D, which provides descriptive output.

Prediction phase: creating the class values of data items in S using B

$$C = B(\ \{s\_i \mid s\_i \in S, i = 1, \ldots, n\}\ )$$

Learning phase: learning from the new training set constructed from S and the predicted class values C

$$B^* = D(\ \{(s\_i, c\_i) \mid s\_i \in S, c\_i \in C, i = 1, \ldots, n\}\ )$$

Output: Descriptive model B^*

Figure 4.2: The basic principle of knowledge probing.

black box model, such as a neural network. The key idea underlying knowledge probing is to derive a descriptive model from a black box model B by learning from a new data set whose class values are assigned by B. The basic principle of knowledge probing can be described as in figure 4.2.

In distributed learning, a set of local models can be used collaboratively to make predictions by applying a prediction scheme to combine their predictions. A prediction scheme can be viewed as an approach to make a joint prediction from the output of the local models. Many approaches of making joint prediction have been proposed in the school of multiple model learning, for example, uniform voting, trained predictor (Chan and Stolfo 1993c), likelihood combination (Ali and Pazzani 1995a) and Bayesian combination (Buntine 1992; Ali and Pazzani 1995b). Several prediction schemes are summarized in Ali and Pazzani (1996a). A short description of each approach is reviewed as follows.

Uniform Voting: In this scheme, all base or local models are assigned the same reliability. Each local model first gives a prediction (or a class value) on an unseen data item. The class that is most frequently predicted becomes the final prediction. In the case of tie (more than one classes have the highest frequency count), an arbitration rule has to be adopted.

Trained Predictor: In this approach, a special model is learned to resolve the conflict among local models. It is either trained on confusing data items, i.e. the items which cause a disagreement among local models or on a set of predictions from local models and the correct predictions. This approach was proposed by Wolpert (1992) as model stacking and used in most of Chan and Stolfo's works (Chan and Stolfo 1993b, 1993c, 1995, 1996) for distributed classification.

Likelihood Combination: This method associates the degree of logical sufficiency (LS) (Duda, Gaschnig, and Hart 1979) with each rule. The LS of a rule of $class_i$ is defined as the ratio of the following probability

$$\frac{p(rule(x) = true \mid x \in Class_i)}{p(rule(x) = true \mid x \notin Class_i)}$$

where x is a random example. Each probability is estimated using the Laplace method. The LS of the representative rule (the most reliable one) of a class is multiplied by the prior odds of that class. The final prediction is the class that maximizes this product.

Bayesian Combination: In this approach, each model is weighted by its posterior probability given a training data (Buntine 1992). In general, the posterior probability of a model is higher if the model fits the training data better (Ali 1996). The combined prediction is the class having highest expected posterior probability.

Distributed Summation (Ali 1996): In this method, the training coverage of satisfied rules are summed up. Each rule is attached with a k-component vector. k is the number of classes. Each component represents a number of training examples of a particular class which are covered by that rule. A vector summation is formed over all rules that match a test example. The combined prediction is the highest component of the summed vector.

All of these methods can be used as a prediction scheme in distributed learning. By viewing a set of local models together with its prediction scheme as a black box model, the knowledge probing technique can be applied to derive a descriptive model from them. The DLKP framework is defined as shown in figure 4.3:

The key factor of the framework is how to prepare the probing data set (S). Ideally, this probing data set is expected to share the common distribution with all the local data sets. However, because we cannot expect all the local data sets to have a common distribution, we also cannot form a probing set which shares that property.

There are also several other works that share the same flavor as DKLP. The difference of the approaches lie in the ways of selecting data items for the second learning phase (the knowledge probing phase), the methods of deriving the new assigned class values and the problems to which the technique is applied. Craven (1996) studied an approach to extract comprehensible models from trained neural networks. He used trained neural networks as an oracle to assign the class values to the queries generated during the expansion of decision tree. Our framework is close to Domingos's 1997 work on knowledge acquisition via multiple models. Generally, the same technique is applied. The input of second learning phase is the data in which the class values are assigned by the model which is the output of the first learning phase (local model learning phase). Domingos used the probing set which was composed of the examples generated from the regions defined by each model and the original data set. In

Input: A set $\mathcal{M}$ of k local models,
a prediction scheme P,
a learning algorithm L, which provides descriptive output.

Probing set preparation phase: using a probing strategy to
select a set of unlabelled data

$$S = \{x\_1, \ldots, x\_n\}$$

Prediction phase: creating the class values of data
items in S using k local models and
the prediction scheme P

for $i = 1$ to n {
for $j = 1$ to k {
$\{c\_ij = M\_j(x\_i) \mid M\_j \in \mathcal{M}, x\_i \in S\}$
}
$C\_i = \mathcal{P}(c\_i1, \ldots, c\_ik)$
}
$C = \{C\_i \mid i = 1, \ldots, n\}$

Learning phase: learning from the new training set constructed
from S and the corresponding combined prediction
in C

$$B^* = \mathcal{L}(\ \{(s\_i, C\_i) \mid s\_i \in S, C\_i \in C, i = 1, \ldots, n\}\ )$$

Output: Descriptive model B^*

Figure 4.3: DLKP framework definition.

our work, the technique is applied to a distributed learning environment. Thus, selecting a small set of probing data is an important consideration. If all the data have to be used in the second learning phase, the computation and communication cost will be at least equal to a migration of data from all distributed sources to one single site to perform the learning, which is not the aim of our study. The aim of the DLKP framework is to integrate the knowledge from local models learned under distributed learning environment into one unified model. The classification error of that such model should, at worst, be the same as the average classification error of local models or, at best, lower than the error of the non-distributed learned model of the same domain.

Chan and Stolfo (1995) have also investigated different techniques for learning from partitions of data. The main differences between our approach and their approach are the second learning phases (the meta-learning phase) and forms of the final results. In Chan and Stolfo's study, one or more special classifiers were trained to arbitrate or combine the output of the base models. These models together with the base models were used to give predictions on unseen data items. In our work, the second learning phase was performed on the probing set whose class values were the combinations of predictions from base models. The result was one descriptive model at the base level rather than the meta level.

4.4 Key Issues of the DLKP Framework

In this section, two key issues of the formulation of DLKP are addressed. The first issue is about the consistency of the local models. The margin information and its distribution graphy, which are the tools used to indirectly observe such consistency, are addressed as the second issue.

4.4.1 The Consistency of the Local Models

To integrate the local models into one global model, we have to assume that all the local data sets are consistent to certain levels or generated from a common target distribution. In distributed learning, as mentioned in section 4.1, it is unrealistic to assume that all the data partitions initially satisfy this property. Thus, if base models which are learned from different data partitions are highly inconsistent, it is crucial to employ a procedure of *data redistribution* to dynamically change the distribution of local data sets based on the results of the current local learning processes. In our framework, data redistribution can be done by using an iterative learning procedure. Since a model learned from a data set S_i reflects the target distribution of S_i, thus, the consistency of locally learned models $M_1^t, M_2^t, \ldots, M_n^t$ (at the time step t) reflects the consistency of the distribution of local data sets. We can, therefore, use this information to change their distributions. That is, each local model will be tested with a data set, called a consistency test set, which is randomly selected from each local training set. The data item which causes the disagreement among local models will be added to all the local data sets. With this redistribution procedure, the data distribution in each local site is adaptively changed. In the next iteration (time step $t + 1$), the newly refined data sets will be re-learned to induce a new set of local models. By repeatedly sharing the redistributed information after the initial learning, the local models are expected to gradually become consistent. This iteration will continue until the local models are consistent to a certain level, i.e. the local models largely agree on the consistency test set. After the local models become consistent, DLKP can be applied to integrate those models into a single accurate, comprehensive and stable global model.

The effectiveness of data redistribution technique has been studied in our previous work (Guo and Sutiwaraphun 1998). The initial result suggested that the consistency of the local model can be improved by data redistribution technique. The technique was shown to continuously decrease number of conflicting data items as the iteration proceeds. The consistency curves of some

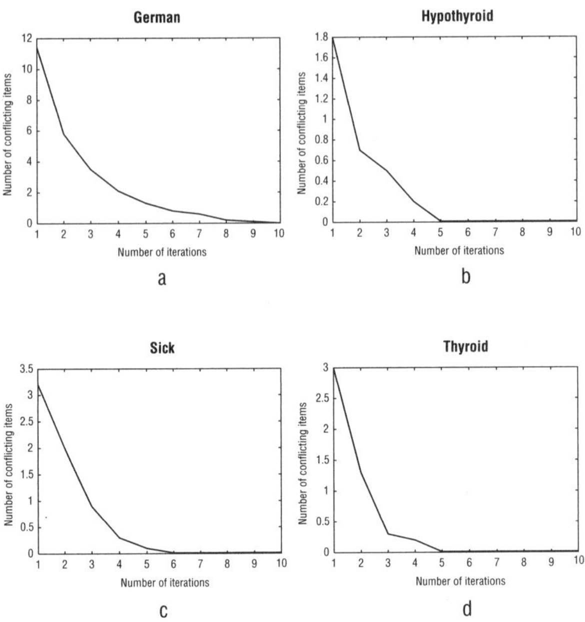

Figure 4.4: Some consistency curves from the iterative data redistribution procedure. (a) German. (b) Hypo. (c) Sick. (d) Thyroid.

data sets are shown in figure 4.4.

Although it is generally known that diversity among local models is useful in combining multiple models (Kwok and Carter 1990; Ali and Pazzani 1996a; Sollich and Krogh 1996), it is worth noting here that in those works, base models are deliberately generated from a single data source. Different techniques, e.g. stochastic hill-climbing (Ali and Pazzani 1996a), bagging (Breiman 1996a) and randomization (Dietterich 1998), are used to inject the stochastic effect into the base model generation process to increase a diversity among base models. In other words, those techniques stochastically expand the spaces[2] of the base models (especially in the border area). This means although diverse, these models are not completely different and still sharing a common part of the model space. An abstraction of these scenario is shown in diagram (b) in figure 4.5. Having better coverage, the combination of these models by a voting scheme is likely to yield higher accuracy. In this study, as we aim to apply DLKP to the environment where data is already distributed[3],

[2]By viewing concept learning as the task of searching through a large space of hypothesizes as defined in Mitchell (1982).

[3]In this study, the worst scenario of that such environment is simulated by data partitioning

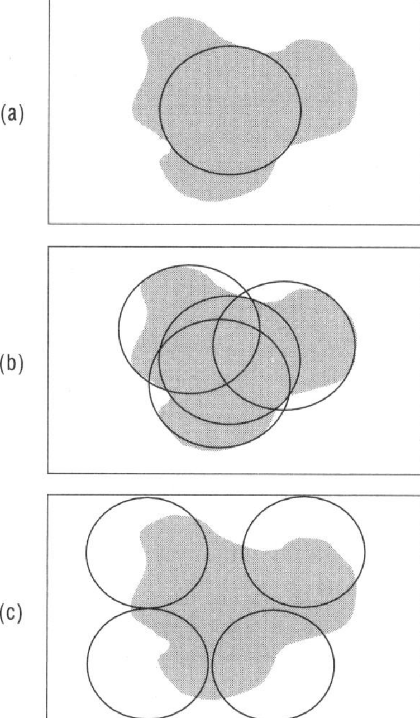

Figure 4.5: An abstraction of different scenarios of coverage of the model space on the target concept. (The gray area represents a target concept. A circle represents a model space.) Diagram (a) represents the coverage of a single model on the target concept space. Diagram (b) represents the coverage of multiple models which are sharing a common model space. Diagram (c) represents the coverage in the worst scenario where there is no overlap between each model space.

therefore, no assumption about any form of sharing can be made. In the worst scenario where each local data has nothing in common (diagram (c) in figure 4.5), no benefit can be expected by combining the models by any voting scheme. In such scenario, data redistribution technique can be used to improve the consistency of the base model to a predefined threshold.

4.4.2 Margin Information and Margin Distribution Graph

Margin can be considered as useful information obtained from voting. Margin information is used to explain the effectiveness of the boosting algorithm in

technique.

Schapire, Freund, Bartlett, and Lee (1998). In their work, weighted voting was used as a prediction scheme. A weight of a particular class (label) is referred to as a sum of the weights of all local models predicting that class. The *classification margin* is defined as the difference between the weight assigned to the correct class and the maximal weight assigned to any single incorrect class. The value of margin, thus, ranges between -1 and 1.

In this study, margin information is applied to the analysis in two different ways: (1) *An analysis of a single model.* Since C4.5 is used as the algorithm of study, by using the probability which C4.5 assigns to each class in the prediction as the class weight, we can calculate the margin information of the probed model (i.e. the model which is the result of knowledge probing phase.) and the non-distributed learned model (i.e. the model which is learned from the entire data set.) on the test set. (2) *An analysis of a model committee* (i.e. a set of local models together with a prediction scheme). Since the probabilistic prediction[4] is used as a prediction scheme, by using the summed probability as a class weight, the margin information of a model committee on the test set can be calculated.

Margin distribution graph is a tool which has been used to indicate how confident a model is in making a prediction on one particular data set. The high margin indicates high confidence in the prediction. The low margin indicates that the prediction is made with low confidence. An example of the margin distribution graph can be seen from figure 4.7. The X-axis represents the margin. The Y-axis represents the percentage of data items whose margin is less than or equals the corresponding margin (value of x). As the value of margin ranges between -1 and 1, the first half of the graph represents the misclassification behavior of the model. On the other hand, the second half represents its behavior of correct classification. The point where the graph crosses the vertical line (where margin is equal to zero) represents the generalization error of the model or the performance of the model on the unseen test set. In the ideal case where the model performs extremely well on the unseen test set, we expect to see the graph which is parallel to the X-axis and sloping up as x-value (or margin) is closed to 1, e.g. graph (j) in figure 4.7.

4.5 Empirical Studies

In our previous studies (Sutiwaraphun 1998; Guo and Sutiwaraphun 1998), the knowledge probing technique appears to produce the model (the probed model) which has a comparable or, sometimes, better accuracy than the non-

[4] In probabilistic prediction, each local model gives a prediction as a set of probabilities of each class. The probabilities which belong to the same class are summed and the final prediction is the class of the highest probability.

Data Set	Size	Attribute		Missing	#Class
		Discr.	Cont.	value(%)	
Real World Data Set					
ABALONE	4,177	1	7	0	29
GERMAN	1,000	13	7	0	2
HYPOTHYROID	3,163	18	7	6.74	2
CHESS	3,196	36	0	0	2
LETTER	20,000	0	16	0	26
NURSERY	12,960	8	0	0	5
SATELLITE	6,435	0	36	0	7
SEGMENT	2,310	0	19	0	7
SICK	3,162	18	7	6.74	2
THYROID	3,772	22	7	5.54	5
Artificial Data Set					
LED7	2,000	7	0	0	10
WAVEFORM	5,000	0	40	0	3

Table 4.1: Details of the data sets used in the experiments.

distributed learned model. In this section, we present our study of the influence of probing set size to the quality of the probed model learned under the DLKP framework. The behavior of the DLKP framework is studied by comparing it with the non-distributed learning approach.

The experiments are done on twelve data sets from the University of California, Irvine, Department of Computer Science's Repository of Machine Learning Databases[5]. We simulate distributed environment by partitioning a data set into subsets. A probing set consists of data randomly sampled from the training set. In order to provide a reasonable amount of data for the local model learning phase and the knowledge probing phase, we choose data sets which are relatively large in size (at least 1,000 instances). The details of all data sets are shown in table 4.1.

4.5.1 Experimental Design

Each experiment is separated into two phases: local model learning phase and knowledge probing phase. The data is prepared for ten-fold cross validation experiments and is done once for each data set. The same training and test sets are used in the later phases for both non-distributed and distributed experiments. In this study, C4.5 is used as a learning algorithm (L). The probabilistic prediction is used as a prediction scheme (P). The number of partitions is chosen to be four.

[5]www.ics.uci.edu/~mlearn/MLRepository.html

Local Model Learning: Each training set is divided into four roughly equal subsets by mutually exclusively partitioning. With a given learning algorithm L, we learn a local model from each subset. Also, the non-distributed learning is done by learning a single model from the entire training set by the learning algorithm L. This model is then evaluated on the test set. (For the rest of the chapter, we will refer to this model as a non-distributed learned model or an ND-model.)

Knowledge Probing: The probing set consists of data items randomly selected from the training set. In order to investigate the influence of the size of a probing set on the quality of the probed model, the experiments in this phase are repeated ten times. Each time, the size of the probing set is increased by ten percent. The experiments are done on probing sets whose sizes ranging from 10% to 100%.

The set of four local models from the first phase is used to give four sets of predictions on the probing set. A prediction scheme P is used to combine those sets of predictions into a set of combined predictions. A probing set whose class values are the combined predictions is used by L to generate a final model. The final model is evaluated on the test set. (For the rest of the chapter, we will refer to this model as a probed model or a P-model.)

4.5.2 The Comparison of the Classification Error and the Margin Distribution

The comparison of the classification error is shown in figure 4.6. All the comparisons are done between the probed model (P-model), the non-distributed learned model (ND-model) and the average of the corresponding local models. From figure 4.6, along different probing set sizes, in every data set, there are certain points where the P-model has lower classification error than the average classification error of the local models. In ABALONE, GERMAN, SICK, THYROID, LED7 and WAVEFORM data sets, the P-models even have lower error than their corresponding ND-models.

From this observation, we can conclude that the size of the probing set is a significant factor in DLKP framework. When the probing set is of certain size, the accuracy of the P-model is comparable to the corresponding local models and the ND-model. The optimum size of the probing set is domain dependent. From the experiments, we also observed that by using 30% of the training data to probe the knowledge in the knowledge probing phase, we can usually achieve a satisfying accuracy of the final model. It is of much interest to further study a technique for finding the optimal size of the probing set and its selection process.

Considering that an optimal size of the probing set is data dependent and the effectiveness of DLKP varies from domain to domain, we further investi-

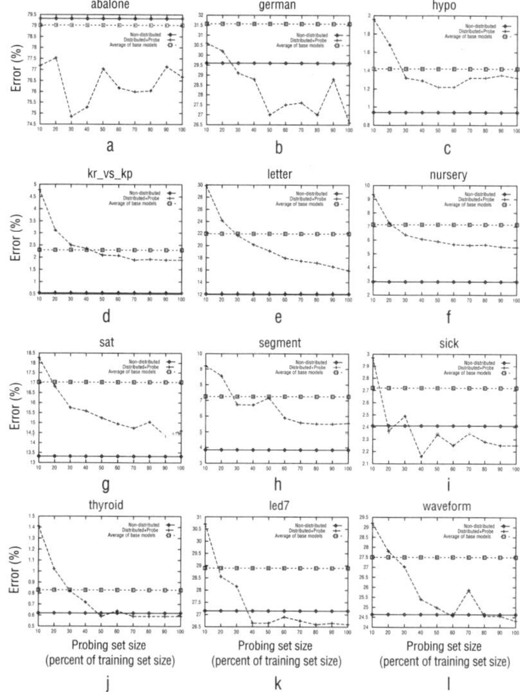

Figure 4.6: Classification error of the P-model, ND-model and the average error of the local models plotted against probing set sizes. (a) ABALONE. (b GERMAN. (c) HYPOTHYROID. (d) CHESS. (e)LETTER. (f) NURSERY. (g) SATELLITE. (h) SEGMENT. (i) SICK. (j) THYROID. (k) LED7. (l) WAVEFORM.

gate behavior of the DLKP framework by using margin distribution graph.

Each graph in figure 4.7 shows the margin distribution of a model committee's predictions on the test set. By correlating figure 4.6 and figure 4.7, we observe that the shape of the margin distribution graph is related to the performance of the models later probed from the corresponding model committee.

For the group of graph (c) HYPOTHYROID, (d) CHESS, (i) SICK and (j) THYROID, the shape of these graphs is close to the ideal shape, which means the conflict among the local models is very low. It can be seen from the corresponding classification error graphs of these data sets in figure 4.6 that the improvement that can be achieved by the P-model over either the ND-model or the average of the local models is very limited. It is in the range of 0.1 - 0.5 %.

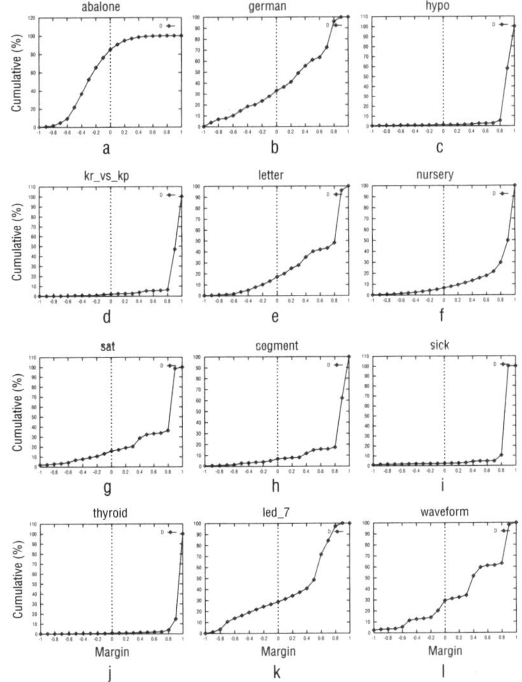

Figure 4.7: Margin distribution graphs of model committees' predictions on unseen test set. (a) ABALONE. (b) GERMAN. (c) HYPOTHYROID. (d) CHESS. (e) LETTER. (f) NURSERY. (g) SATELLITE. (h) SEGMENT. (i) SICK. (j) THYROID. (k) LED7. (l) WAVEFORM.

The other group consists of the rest of the data sets which are (a) ABALONE, (b) GERMAN, (e) LETTER, (f) NURSERY, (g) SATELLITE, (h) SEGMENT, (k) LED7 and (l) WAVEFORM. In this group, the margin distribution graphs show that their generalization performance on the unseen test sets is quite poor. Relating to the corresponding classification error graphs from figure 4.6, it is interesting to see that the improvements that can be achieved by the P-models is more significant than those in the first group.

Therefore, we can conclude that the margin distribution graph provides useful insight on the effectiveness of distributed classification. It may also help to determine the potential generalization performance of the final model learned under the DLKP. In the case where the margin distribution is close to ideal, the final model can be arbitrarily selected from local models because all the models rarely have conflict in the predictions which means they are generally the same. In the case where the margin distribution graph is poor, the local models are highly inconsistent and likely to have low confidence in making predictions. Thus, no local model can be used as a representative of the others. The results have shown that some improvement can be achieved by applying DLKP to those models.

The comparison is also made between the margin distribution graph of the non-distributed learned model (the ND-model) and the probed model (the P-model). figure 4.8 shows the margin distribution graph of the ND-model and the P-model of different probing set sizes (20%, 40%, 60%, 80% and 100%). From figure 4.8, it can be seen that in all data sets, except (l) LED7, the margin distribution graph of the ND-model is of the same shape as the one of the P-model. This means the model probed from local models has the same generalization behavior as the model which is learned from a complete data set. We also observe that when comparing the margin distribution graph of the P-model from figure 4.8 to the corresponding graph of the model committee in figure 4.7, the graphs of the P-models are improved more than those of the model committee.

4.6 Conclusion

In this chapter, we have presented DLKP as a framework of distributed classification. The aim of our framework is to generate a unified model which, at worst, has the comparable generalization error as the average error of the local models or, at best, has lower error than the non-distributed learned model of the same domain. To investigate this framework, the experiments are done on different probing set sizes. The results show that, with some proper sizes of the probing set, there is always a possibility that the probed model would result in a better generalization error than the average of the local models. In some data sets the generalization error of the probed model is even lower than the non-distributed learned model. We investigate this behavior of the framework and find that there is a relationship between the margin distribution graph of the model committee's predictions on the test set and the improvement which can be achieved by the DLKP framework. In the case where the margin distribution is closed to ideal, the improvement which can be achieved by knowledge probing technique is limited. The unified model can be arbitrarily selected from local models. The DLKP framework is beneficial to the case where the margin distribution graph of a model committee is relatively poor. Margin distribution graph, therefore, can be used as a tool to optimise the efficiency of the DLKP framework. The experimental results have also shown that the framework appears to be effective in converging the generalization performance of the distributed learning to the non-distributed learning.

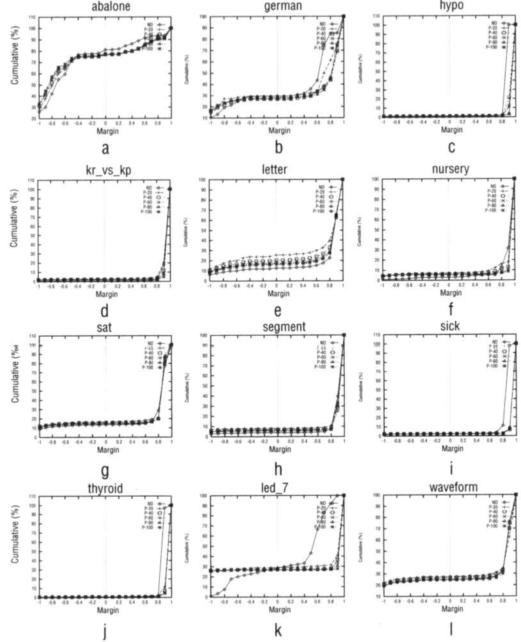

Figure 4.8: Margin distribution graphs of the predictions made by nondistributed learned model (ND) and the probed model (P) on unseen data sets. (a) ABALONE. (b) GERMAN. (c) HYPOTHYROID. (d) CHESS. (e) LETTER. (f) NURSERY. (g) SATELLITE. (h) EGMENT. (i) SICK. (j) THYROID. (k) LED7. (l) WAVEFORM.

Acknowledgements

We would like to thank two anonymous reviewers for their comments and suggestions on the earlier draft of this chapter. Janjao Sutiwaraphun gratefully acknowledge support from the Royal Thai Government.

Chapter 5

Collective Data Mining: A New Perspective Toward Distributed Data Analysis

Hillol Kargupta, Byung-Hoon Park, Daryl Hershberger, and Erik Johnson

5.1 Introduction

Distributed data mining (DDM) is a fast growing area that deals with the problem of finding data patterns in an environment with distributed data and computation. Although today most of the data analysis systems require centralized storage of data, the increasing merger of computation with communication is demanding data mining environments that can exploit the full benefit of distributed computation. For example, consider the following data analysis applications.

Example one: An epidemiologist is interested in finding out the dependency of the emergence of hepatitis-C in U.S. on the weather pattern. She has access to a large hepatitis-C database at the Center for Disease Control and an environmental database at the Environmental Protection Agency. However, they are at two different places and analyzing the data from both of them using a conventional data mining software requires combining the databases at a single location, which may be quite impractical.

Example two: Two major financial organizations want to cooperate for preventing fraudulent intrusion into their computing system. They need to share data patterns relevant to fraudulent intrusion. However, they do not want to share the data since it is sensitive. Therefore, combining the databases may not be feasible. Existing data mining systems cannot handle this situation.

Example three: A defense organization is monitoring a situation. Several sensor systems are monitoring the situation and collecting data. Fast analysis of incoming data and quick response is imperative. Collecting all the data to a central location and analyzing it there consumes time and this approach may not be scalable for modern situation monitoring systems with large number of different sensors.

Example four: A major multi-national corporation wants to analyze the customer transaction records for quickly developing successful business strategies. It has thousands of establishments through out the world and collecting all the data to a centralized data warehouse, followed by analysis using existing commercial data mining software, takes too long.

DDM offers a viable solution to many such practical problems. A good DDM algorithm analyzes data in a distributed fashion with modest data communication overhead. Typically DDM algorithms involve local data analysis followed by the generation of a global data model through the aggregation of the local results. Unfortunately, naive approaches to local analysis may produce ambiguous and incorrect global data model. Particularly in the general case, where different sites observe different sets of features, this problem becomes very critical. Therefore, developing a well-grounded methodology to address this general case is important. This chapter offers a viable approach to the analysis of distributed, heterogeneous data sets using the collective data mining (CDM) framework.

Section 5.2 describes the DDM problem considered here and some of the problems of naive data analysis algorithms in a DDM environment. In section 5.3, the foundation of CDM is presented followed by a discussion on construction of orthonormal representation from incomplete domains and the relation of such representation to mean square error minimization. Sections 5.4 and 5.5 present the development of CDM versions of two popular data analysis techniques, decision tree learning and regression. Section 5.6 presents an overview of a CDM based experimental system called "beseizing knowledge through distributed heterogeneous induction" (BODHI), that is currently under development. Section 5.7 discusses future research directions.

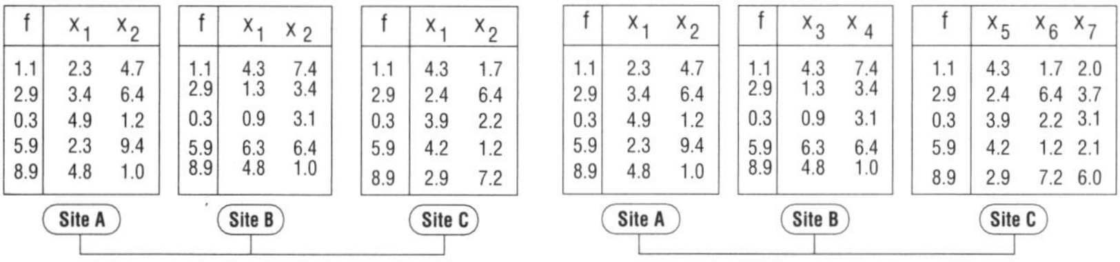

f	x_1	x_2
1.1	2.3	4.7
2.9	3.4	6.4
0.3	4.9	1.2
5.9	2.3	9.4
8.9	4.8	1.0

Site A

f	x_1	x_2
1.1	4.3	7.4
2.9	1.3	3.4
0.3	0.9	3.1
5.9	6.3	6.4
8.9	4.8	1.0

Site B

f	x_1	x_2
1.1	4.3	1.7
2.9	2.4	6.4
0.3	3.9	2.2
5.9	4.2	1.2
8.9	2.9	7.2

Site C

f	x_1	x_2
1.1	2.3	4.7
2.9	3.4	6.4
0.3	4.9	1.2
5.9	2.3	9.4
8.9	4.8	1.0

Site A

f	x_3	x_4
1.1	4.3	7.4
2.9	1.3	3.4
0.3	0.9	3.1
5.9	6.3	6.4
8.9	4.8	1.0

Site B

f	x_5	x_6	x_7
1.1	4.3	1.7	2.0
2.9	2.4	6.4	3.7
0.3	3.9	2.2	3.1
5.9	4.2	1.2	2.1
8.9	2.9	7.2	6.0

Site C

Figure 5.1: Distributed (left) homogeneous and (right) heterogeneous data sites.

5.2 Background

This section presents the background material for this chapter. It first explains the general model of distributed, heterogeneous data sites considered here. Next, a review of related research in DDM is presented. The section concludes by showing that naive approaches to DDM in a heterogeneous environment can be ambiguous or incorrect even for simple data modeling problems.

5.2.1 Problem Description

In a DDM environment data may be distributed among different sites because of various reasons. For example, the environment may have different databases. On the other hand data may be artificially partitioned among different sites for achieving better scalability. The data sites may be *homogeneous*, i.e. each site stores data for exactly the same set of features. In the general case, however the data sites may be *heterogeneous*, i.e. each site storing data for different sets of features, possibly with some common features among the sites. In this document we will consider only the relational model of data. Therefore, the data sets can be viewed as tables with rows and columns. Although in the general case a hierarchy of such relational tables may exist at each site, this chapter considers only one table per site in order to build a solid foundation starting from a simpler case. When there are only one table at each site the homogeneous and heterogeneous cases are also sometimes called *horizontally* and *vertically* partitioned. Figure 5.1 illustrates these two cases. In case of homogeneous sites, each row defines a unique observation. However, in the heterogeneous case different observed features of the same event are distributed among different locations. As a result, the heterogeneous case must come with some predefined way to define the correspondence between the different components of the same event. Row index key and common database schema features are some of the possibilities that may be used to identify the correspondence among different rows stored at different sites.

In this chapter we consider the problem of supervised learning/analysis for the heterogeneous case. Given a set of observed feature values, the task is to learn a function that computes the unknown value of a desired feature as a function of other observed features. The given set of observed feature values is sometimes called the training data set. In figure 5.1 (right) the column for f denotes the feature value to be predicted; $x_1, x_2, x_3, x_4, x_5, x_6$ and x_7 denote the features that are used to predict f. The data sets available at the different sites are used as the training data. If the f column is not observed everywhere then it is broadcasted to every site. There exists little work for this general case of DDM. The following section reviews related work in distributed data mining.

5.2.2 Related Work

Although distributed data mining is a fairly new field, it has been enjoying a growing amount of attention since inception. A large fraction of the DDM literature considers homogeneous data sites. Distributed data analysis from homogeneous data sites involves combining different models of data from different sites. There exist several techniques to combine multiple data models. A class of statistical techniques for aggregating multiple models generated from homogeneous data sets was proposed by Breiman (1996, 1999). The bagging approach (Breiman 1996) increases the accuracy of the model by generating multiple models from different data sets chosen uniformly with replacement and then averaging the outputs of the models. Although the bagging technique was initially developed for increasing the accuracy of "unstable" data analysis algorithms, this can be extended to multiple model aggregation in DDM from homogeneous data sets. This perspective is presented by Breiman (1999).

Like bagging, stacking offers an alternate technique to increase the accuracy of the data model by aggregating multiple data models. In stacking first multiple models are learned on different homogeneous data sets and their joint generalization behavior is observed on a different testing data set. Finally a new model learned using all the data sets and the knowledge about the joint generalization behavior are used for classification or target function prediction. Like bagging, stacking can also be extended for combining models in a distributed environment. An experimental investigation of such techniques for combining multiple models is reported elsewhere (Ting and Low 1997).

Meta-learning (Chan and Stolfo 1993a, 1993c, 1998) offers another class of techniques for mining homogeneous, distributed data. This approach shares a lot of similarities with bagging and stacking. In this approach, supervised learning techniques are first used to detect concepts at local data sites, then meta-level concepts are learned from a data set generated using the locally learned concepts, resulting in a meta-classifier. Different inductive learning algorithms may be employed to learn the local concepts, and the meta-level learning may be applied recursively, producing a hierarchy of meta-classifiers. The JAM system (Stolfo 1997) is a meta-learning based distributed data mining framework. It has been used for fraud detection in the banking domain (Lee, Stolfo, and Mok 1999). The knowledge probing approach is reported by Guo and Sutiwaraphun (chapter 4). This technique is similar to meta-learning. However this approach is particularly designed for inducing descriptive data model from the predictions of black box classifiers learned in a distributed environment.

The distributed cooperative Bayesian learning approach was developed by Yamanishi (1997). This technique considers homogeneous data sets. In this approach different Bayesian agents estimate the parameters of the target distribution and a population learner combines the outputs of those Bayesian models. The agents and the population learner are based on a probabilistic version of the Gibbs algorithm. The theoretical analysis of the algorithm shows that it performs almost as good as a centralized Bayesian learning algorithm. This chapter also proposes a Monte Carlo technique for addressing problems where the hypotheses space is hierarchically parameterized and there is a a feedback mechanism from the population learner to the agent learners.

The *fragmented approach* to mining classifiers from distributed data sources is suggested by Cho and Wüthrich (1998). In this method, a single, best, rule is generated in each distributed data source. These rules are then ranked using some criterion and some number of the top ranked rules are selected to form the rule set. Lam and Segre (1997) report a technique to automatically produce a Bayesian belief network from discovered knowledge using a distributed approach.

The PADMA system (Kargupta, Hamzaoglu, Stafford, Hanagandi, and Buescher 1996, Kargupta, Hamzaoglu, and Stafford 1997) also deals with the problem of distributed data mining from homogeneous data sites. This system implemented a distributed clustering algorithm that was aided by relevance feedback-based supervised learning techniques. The PADMA system has an agent based distributed architecture where the partial data cluster models are first computed in a distributed fashion at different sites; once the individual models are collected to a central site a second level clustering among the different models is performed to generate the overall cluster model. The second level clustering is performed among different clusters by exploiting their statistical representations. A k-means clustering algorithm for distributed environment was reported by Dhillon and Modha (1999). This algorithm notes the inherent data-parallelism in the *k*-means algorithm and asymptotically approaches near optimal performance.

The fast distributed mmning (FDM) algorithm (Cheung, Ng, Fu, and Fu 1996) can be used for mining association rules from distributed, homogeneous data sets. FDM notes that in a distributed environment, every globally large itemset must be locally large at one or more sites. It explores this relationship between locally and globally large itemsets in order to minimize the communication overhead. FDM requires $O(s)$ message communication (s is the number of data sites) for determining whether a candidate set is large.

The architecture of a distributed data mining system plays an important role in its performance. Architectural requirements for efficient data communication in a wide area network are explored by Grossman (chapter 9). This work also reports several tools like a persistent object manager called PTool, a modeling language called Predictive Model Markup Language (PMML), a model manager called Anubis, and an object transportation layer named Bast to facilitate the local data mining and wide-area combining processes.

A DOALL primitive is proposed by Subramonian (chapter 8) for reducing the complexity of parallel programming in a distributed environment. This work reports scheduling algorithms for assigning tasks to processors to improve load balancing. It also presents empirically evaluation of the DOALL primitive and scheduling algorithms on two-dimensional discretization and clustering problems.

A technique for problem decomposition and local model selection is proposed by Pokrajac, Fiez, Obradovic, Kwek, and Obradovic (1999). This approach first learns regression models at local data sites. Next it identifies the subset of the data for which the local model works fine. This information is used for partitions the data into different disjoint subsets. Next it learns the distribution functions in order to identify the appropriate local model for each data point. This approach is applied to analyze agricultural data and the authors report substantial improvement in performance compared to a single global model.

There exists very little literature for analyzing data from heterogeneous sites. Learning from heterogeneous data sites is discussed by Provost and Buchanan (1995) from the perspective of inductive bias. This work notes that such partitioning of the feature space can be addressed by decomposing the problem into smaller subproblems when the problem is site-wise decomposable. The WoRLD system (Aronis, Kolluri, Provost, and Buchanan 1997) addressed the problem of concept learning from heterogeneous sites by developing an "activation spreading" approach. This approach first computes the cardinal distribution of the feature values in the individual data sets. Next, this distribution information is propagated across different sites. Features with strong correlations to the concept space are identified based on this first order statistics of the cardinal distribution. The selected features are used for learning the appropriate concept. Since the technique is based on the first order statistical approximation of the underlying distribution, it may not be appropriate for general problems where concept learning requires higher. order statistics. The propagation of marker activation records from one site to another is accomplished through basic database operations. This makes the approach easily implementable in database systems. Nevertheless, a general methodology for learning functions from distributed, heterogeneous data sites with guaranteed control of accuracy and minimal communication overhead is still an open issue.

This chapter offers one possible solution to this problem. This chapter describes the Collective Data Mining methodology that can learn different popular data models such as regression, decision trees in a distributed environment. Interested readers may refer to Hershberger and Kargupta (1999) for additional experimental and theoretical analysis of this framework. The main motivation behind this framework is that direct application of existing machine learning and statistical algorithms to local data sites may produce partials models that are completely incorrect and possibly ambiguous. The following section illustrates this observation.

5.2.3 Naive Approach: May Be Ambiguous and Incorrect

Data modeling is a mature field that has many well-understood techniques in its arsenal. However, many of these traditional techniques cannot be directly used in a distributed environment with vertically partitioned feature space. In this section we shall see that even a simple, decomposable data modeling problem can be ambiguous and misleading in a distributed environment.

Let $f(x_1, x_2) = a_1x_1 + a_2x_2$. Consider the data set

$$D = \{(x_1, x_2, f(x_1, x_2)\} = \{(0, 0, 0), (1, 0, a_1), (0, 1, a_2), (1, 1, a_1 + a_2)\}$$

generated by $f(x_1, x_2)$. When both the variables and the corresponding $f(x_1, x_2)$ value are observed at the same site, fitting a linear model of the form $\hat{f}(x_1, x_2) = b_0 + b_1x_1 + b_2x_2$ to the data is quite straight forward.

Now consider a distributed environment with two sites, A and B. A observes $\{(x_1, f(x_1, x_2))\}$ and B observes $\{(x_2, f(x_1, x_2))\}$. Consider the dataset at A, $D_A = \{(0, 0), (1, a_1), (0, a_2), (1, a_1 + a_2)\}$. If site A now tries to fit a local linear model of the form $\hat{f}_A(x_1) = b_0' + b_1'x_1$ to the data, then it will get four different solutions of the coefficients, $\{(b_0', b_1')\} = \{(0, a_1), (0, a_1 + a_2), (a_2, a_1), (a_2, a_1 - a_2)\}$. A similar situation also arises at site B. Resolving these ambiguities requires communication between the two sites. The collective data mining approach offers a solution to this decomposable problem with no communication at all. However, before discussing the CDM let us investigate another possibility: generating local models that minimizes the error between the correct value of $f(x_1, x_2)$ and the models. Unfortunately, as shown in the following, this may also lead to misleading results. Consider the function, $g(x_1, x_2) = 5x_1 + 67.9x_2$, where x_1 and x_2 are real valued variables. Con-

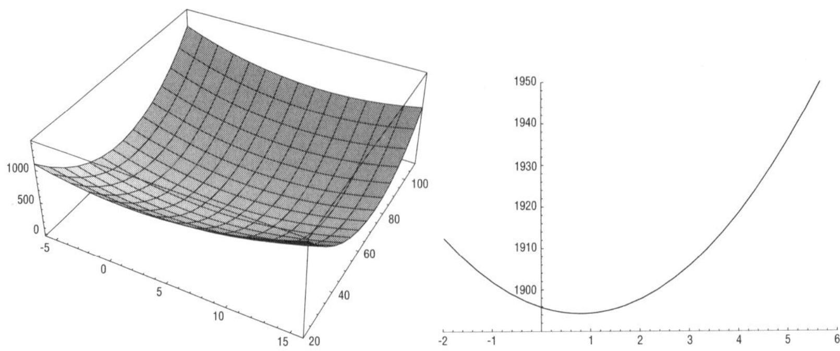

Figure 5.2: The global error function (left). The local error function at site A (right).

sider the sample data set $D = \{(1.1, 0.1, 12.29), (1.5, -1.0, -60.4), (-1.9, -0.5, -43.45)\}$, where each entry is of the form $(x_1, x_2, g(x_1, x_2))$. Let us try to fit a model, $\hat{g}(x_1, x_2) = b_1x_1 + b_2x_2$, to this data by minimizing the mean-square error. The overall mean square error computed over the data set D is, $\frac{1}{3}\sum_{x_1,x_2\in D}(g - \hat{g})^2 = 2.3567(5 - b_1)^2 + 0.42(67.9 - b_2)^2 - 0.1467(5 - b_1)(67.9 - b_2)$

Figure 5.2 (left) shows the error surface with a global minima at $b_1 = 5$ and $b_2 = 67.9$. It is a simple quadratic function and the finding the minima is quite straight forward.

Now let us consider the data set to be vertically partitioned; meaning, x_1 is observed at site A and x_2 is observed at a different site B. Let us choose a linear model, $\hat{g}(x_1) = b_1x_1$. The mean square error function for site A is, $\frac{1}{3}\sum_{x_1,x_2\in\Omega}(f - \hat{f})^2 = (2.3567(5 - b_1)^2 + 1936.3722 - 19.9173(5 - b_1)$. Figure 5.2 (right) shows this local error function. It clearly shows that the minima of this error function is not same as the globally optimal value of b_1, i.e. 5. This example demonstrates that even for simple linear data and model, naive approaches to minimize mean-square error may be misleading in a distributed environment. The CDM offers a correct, viable solution to this problem. The following section presents the foundation of CDM.

5.3 The Foundations of Collective Data Mining

Inducing a function structure from data is a common problem in statistics and machine learning. This chapter considers distributed function induction from data sets with known function values. In the machine learning literature this is called supervised learning.

In supervised inductive learning, the goal is to learn a function $\hat{f} : X^n \rightarrow Y$ from the data set $\Omega = \{(\mathbf{x}_{(1)}, y_{(1)}), (\mathbf{x}_{(2)}, y_{(2)}), \cdots (\mathbf{x}_{(k)}, y_{(k)})\}$ generated by underlying function $f : X^n \rightarrow Y$, such that the $\hat{f}$ approximates f. Any member of the domain $\mathbf{x} = x_1, x_2, \cdots x_n$ is an n-tuple and x_j-s correspond to individual features of the domain. In the heterogeneous case, this would mean learning a function in terms of the features observed at different sites. In most practical situations, distributed inductive learning requires the availability of the y-values, i.e. $y_{(1)}, y_{(2)}, \cdots y_{(k)}$ at all the sites. In some applications, the observed data for this particular feature (usually the feature to be predicted or the class label of the events) may be naturally available. If not, then this information may be broadcasted to all the sites. The CDM approaches supervised data analysis and modeling from this perspective of function learning.

5.3.1 Foundations: Blending Theory of Communications with Machine Learning and Statistics

A typical DDM algorithm works by (1) performing local data analysis for generating partial data models, and (2) combining the local data models from different data sites in order to develop the global model. As we saw in the previous section, conventional approaches for local analysis can be ambiguous and misleading. We need to make sure that the local analysis produces correct partial models that can be used as building blocks for the global model. Once the partial models are generated from the local data sites, the next step is to combine them for generating the global model. However, we need to keep in mind that nonlinear dependency among the features across the different data sites may exist. Therefore, locally generated partial models alone may not be sufficient to generate the global model. The CDM addresses both of these issues as described in the following.

The foundation of CDM is based on the fact that any function can be represented in a distributed fashion using an appropriate basis. Let Ξ be a basis set. Let us index the basis functions in Ξ and denote the k-th basis function in Ξ by Ψ_k. Let Ξ_I be the set of all such indices of the basis functions. A function $f(\mathbf{x})$ can be represented as,

$$f(\mathbf{x}) = \sum_{k \in \Xi_I} w_k \Psi_k(\mathbf{x}) \tag{5.1}$$

where $\Psi_k(\mathbf{x})$ denotes the k-th basis function and w_k denotes the corresponding coefficient. The objective of a learning algorithm can be viewed as the task to generate a function, $\hat{f}(\mathbf{x}) = \sum_{k \in \hat{\Xi}_I} \hat{w}_k \Psi_k(\mathbf{x})$, that approximates $f(\mathbf{x})$ from a given data set; $\hat{\Xi}_I$ denotes a subset of Ξ_I; $\hat{w}_k$ denotes the approximate estimation of the coefficients w_k. For a given basis representation, the underlying learning task is essentially to compute the nonzero, significant (not negligible) coefficients, $\hat{w}_k$-s. Any inductive data modeling algorithm like regression, decision trees and neural networks can be viewed from this perspective. The CDM notes that although direct application of these modeling algorithms may not produce correct results, the orthonormal spectrum of such models can be accurately learned in a distributed fashion and then finally the model can be constructed from the spectrum. The orthonormality property guarantees correct and independent local analysis that can be used as a building-block for the global model. The main steps of the CDM approach are as follows: (1) Choose an appropriate orthonormal representation for the type of data model to be built. For example, our preliminary investigation in this chapter and Hershberger and Kargupta (1999) noted the suitability of Fourier and wavelet representations for decision tree and multi-variate regression respectively. (2) Construct the orthonormal representation from the data in a distributed fashion. (3) Construct the model in its canonical representation (e.g. a tree in case of a decision tree) from the orthonormal representation

Both continuous and discrete functions can be learned in this fashion. However, in the following discussion we shall use only discrete functions for explaining the basic concepts. The following sections explain the basic mechanism of CDM using a simple example.

Generating Correct Partial Models Using Only Local Features

Consider a quadratic data modeling problem in which the data set is generated by the function $f(x_1, x_2) = a_1x_1 + a_2x_2 + a_3x_1x_2$, where x_1 and x_2 are Boolean variables. Note that the function is not site-wise decomposable. The data set is $D = \{(x_1, x_2, f(x_1, x_2)\} = \{(0, 0, 0), (1, 0, a_1), (0, 1, a_2), (1, 1, a_1 + a_2 + a_3)\}$. As before, sites A and B observe x_1 and x_2 respectively. Although the naive approach faces an ambiguous situation, no such problem exists if we use orthonormal basis functions for modeling the data. For example, let us consider discrete Fourier basis representation. In this case, $\Xi_k = \{00, 10, 01, 11\}$ (i.e., the set of all 2-bit strings). Any function $f(\mathbf{x})$ of Boolean variables can be written as $f(\mathbf{x}) = \sum_{\mathbf{j} \in \Xi_k} w_{\mathbf{j}} \Psi_j(\mathbf{x})$, where $\Psi_{\mathbf{j}}(\mathbf{x})$ denotes the $\mathbf{j}$-th Fourier basis function and $w_{\mathbf{j}}$ denotes the corresponding Fourier coefficient; for this case $\mathbf{x} \in \{00, 10, 01, 11\}$ and $\Psi_{\mathbf{j}}(\mathbf{x}) = (-1)^{\mathbf{j}\cdot\mathbf{x}}$. Fourier coefficients are defined as $w_{\mathbf{j}} = \frac{1}{N} \sum_{\mathbf{x}} f(x)\Psi_j(\mathbf{x})$, where $N = 4$ is the total number of members of the domain. There are four Fourier basis functions in a function of two variables: $\Psi_{00}(\mathbf{x}) = 1$, $\Psi_{10}(\mathbf{x}) = (-1)^{x_1}$, $\Psi_{01}(\mathbf{x}) = (-1)^{x_2}$ and $\Psi_{11} = (-1)^{x_1+x_2}$. Clearly, computation of w_{00} does not require either of x_1 and x_2; computation of w_{10}, w_{01}, w_{11} requires *only* information concerning x_1, x_2, or x_1, x_2 respectively. Using the above definitions, we get $w_{10} = -(2a_1 + a_3)/4$ from site A and $w_{01} = -(2a_2 + a_3)/4$ from site B; $w_{00} = (2a_1 + 2a_2 + a_3)/4$ can be computed at either site A or site B since computation of w_{00} does not require the feature values.

We can easily demonstrate that the locally generated Fourier coefficients represent partial models that can be finally put together for generating the correct global data model. In order to show that, let us use the locally generated model at site A, $\hat{f}_a(x_1) = w_{00} + w_{10}(-1)^{x_1}$, to generate a data set $D_a = \{x_1, \hat{f}_a(x_1)\} = \{(0, w_{00} + w_{10}), (1, w_{00} - w_{10})\}$. Similarly at site B we generate the dataset $D_b = \{x_2, f_b(x_2)\} = \{(0, w_{01}), (1, -w_{01})\}$ using the model $f_b(x_2) = w_{01}(-1)^{x_2}$. Solving a set of linear equations we generate the partial models in the canonical representation, $y = b_0 + b_1 x_1$ at site A. This results in the local model y_a an't site A, and a similarly generated model y_b at Site B, where:

$$
\begin{aligned}
y_a &= \frac{a_2}{2} + \frac{2a_1 + a_3}{2} x_1 \\
y_b &= -\frac{2a_2 + a_3}{4} + \frac{2a_2 + a_3}{2} x_2
\end{aligned}
$$

Before combining these partial models we need to generate the nonlinear term involving the features from both site A and B. The following section describes that process.

Generating Cross-Terms Involving Features from Different Sites

If the model is not completely decomposable among the data sites, cross-terms involving features from different sites will exist in the model. Determination of these cross-terms is essential for accurate modeling of the data. For the particular example at hand, there exists one coefficient w_{11} that corresponds to $\Psi_{11}(\mathbf{x})$, a basis function requiring both x_1 and x_2. The coefficient w_{11} can be computed using the feature values of a single a row from all the datasets. In general if there are m cross-terms involving features from different sites, for a well-posed problem solving the m terms requires exactly m rows from all the data sites. For large databases, m is typically a much smaller number compared to the total number of rows in the databases. For example, let us bring the $x_2 = 0$ information from the first data row to site A in order to have a complete row of data $\{x_1 = 0, x_2 = 0, f(x_1, x_2) = 0\}$. After combining the locally generated partial models we get the following expression, $\hat{f}(\mathbf{x}) = 0 = w_{00} + w_{10} + w_{01} + w_{11}$. Since, we already know all the coefficients except w_{11}, it can be easily solved to get $w_{11} = a_3/4$. As we see, the Fourier representation of a nonlinear model can be generated by moving only a small fraction of data. If the cost of moving a data row from one site to the common site computing the cross-terms is c, then the cost of the communication is $O(c\ m)$. Since many of the real-life interesting problems exhibit bounded nonlinearity, i.e. at most some κ variables nonlinearly interact with each other, m is expected to be a small number compared to the typical number of rows in a large database.

Now the partial model involving the cross-term w_{11} can be used to generate the remaining part of the global model in the canonical representation. Since this term involves both x_1 and x_2, the general model for this part takes the form $y = b_0 + b_1x_1 + b_2x_2 + b_3x_1x_2$. We can generate the dataset $D_c = \{x_1, x_2, f_c(x_1, x_2)\} = \{(0, 0, \frac{a_3}{4}), (1, 0, -\frac{a_3}{4}), (0, 1, -\frac{a_3}{4}), (1, 1, \frac{a_3}{4})\}$ using the function $y_c = w_{11}(-1)^{x_1x_2}$. The resulting model in the canonical representation turns out to be:

$$y_c = \frac{a_3}{4} - \frac{a_3}{2}x_1 - \frac{a_3}{2}x_2 + a_3x_1x_2$$

Now we can combine all the locally generated models in the canonical representation, resulting in:

$$y = y_a + y_b + y_c = a_1x_1 + a_2x_2 + a_3x_1x_2.$$

This illustrates that locally generated Fourier coefficients and the cross-terms computed using only $O(c\ m)$ communication cost can be effectively used for distributed data modeling. However, there is one final issue that we need to address. So far, our discussion considered a data set that is exactly the complete domain. Typically, learning and data analysis is performed on a sample of the domain, not the complete domain. This would require efficient estimation of the coefficients from incomplete knowledge about the domain. The following section addresses this issue.

5.3.2 Orthonormal Representation Construction from Incomplete Domain

Construction of an orthonormal representation requires computation of the basis coefficients. The exact procedure for computing these coefficients depends upon the specific set of chosen basis functions. Different specialized "fast" techniques exist for computing different orthonormal representations. However, regardless of the specific choice, a function with a large number of significant basis coefficients will require significant time for computing the orthonormal representation. Polynomial time computation of the coefficients requires two things: (1) a sparse representation, where most of the coefficients are zero or negligible, and (2) approximate evaluation of the significant coefficients. Fortunately, this requirements has deep connection to the foundation of search, machine learning, and optimization. For most practical data mining applications these conditions can be satisfied without sacrificing the quality of the process.

Typically, one of the main objectives of a data mining application is to capture a salient data pattern in a simple, easy-to-understand representation. For example, in a classification problem we want not too complex rules that are fairly accurate and covers a reasonable portion of the event space. If we are trying to build a predictive model using polynomial regression techniques, then for all practical purposes we would like to have a model with the degree of polynomial bounded by some constant. Even for black-box learning techniques such as neural networks, specialized, restricted representations are often required for efficient polynomial-time learning. A simple decision tree learning algorithm like the ID3 (Quinlan 1986) may engage in an exponential-time tree-construction in the worst case unless we impose a restriction on the depth of the tree. For most practical applications of a decision tree, we want a tree of short depth since they give rise to simple rules. If the performance of the short tree is not good then we may conclude that the decision tree may not be a good representation for the given learning problem. Such restriction of representation is certainly a trade-off. It imposes an algorithmic bias and therefore it restricts the scope of the algorithm. However, it is also often necessary from the perspective of efficiency and efficacy.

Fortunately such restriction on the data model is also reflected in its orthonormal representation. For example, a bounded depth decision tree has a very sparse Fourier representation with only a polynomial number of nonzero coefficients (Kushilevitz and Mansour 1991). Moreover, as we will see later in this chapter, some of these coefficients are exponentially larger than the rest of the coefficients. This essentially means that the Fourier representation of a decision tree can be approximated by a very small number of nonzero coefficients. Similar properties show up for decision rules involving only a bounded number of features. If the dependency among the different features is bounded, i.e. if only a constant number of features may depend on a particular feature then the orthonormal representation is going to be sparse.

Estimation of orthonormal coefficients is something that is done on a regular basis in many daily appliances that require signal-processing. If our sample size is reasonable (which is typically the case in data mining) this can be adequately addressed.

Let us illustrate the rationale behind this observation using our Fourier basis example. Consider what happens when we multiply both sides of equation 5.1 by $\Psi_{\mathbf{j}}(\mathbf{x})$; we get $f(\mathbf{x})\Psi_{\mathbf{j}}(\mathbf{x}) = \sum_{k\in\Xi_I} w_k\Psi_k(\mathbf{x})\Psi_{\mathbf{j}}(\mathbf{x})$. If we denote our sample data set by Γ, then by summing both side over all members of Γ we get:

$$\sum_{\mathbf{x}\in\Gamma} f(\mathbf{x})\Psi_{\mathbf{j}}(\mathbf{x}) = \sum_{\mathbf{x}\in\Gamma}\sum_{\mathbf{k}\in\Xi_I} w_{\mathbf{k}}\Psi_{\mathbf{k}}(\mathbf{x})\Psi_{\mathbf{j}}(\mathbf{x}) \tag{5.2}$$

Now note that since $\Psi_{\mathbf{j}}(\mathbf{x})\Psi_{\mathbf{j}}(\mathbf{x}) = 1$, we get: $\sum_{\mathbf{x}\in\Gamma}\Psi_{\mathbf{j}}(\mathbf{x})\Psi_{\mathbf{j}}(\mathbf{x}) = |\Gamma|$, where $|\Gamma|$ is the sample size. Now we can write,

$$\frac{1}{|\Gamma|}\sum_{\mathbf{x}\in\Gamma} f(\mathbf{x})\Psi_{\mathbf{j}}(\mathbf{x}) = w_{\mathbf{j}} + \sum_{\mathbf{k}\in\Xi_I,\mathbf{k}\neq\mathbf{j}} w_{\mathbf{k}}\frac{\sum_{\mathbf{x}\in\Gamma}\Psi_{\mathbf{k}}(\mathbf{x})\Psi_{\mathbf{j}}(\mathbf{x})}{|\Gamma|}$$

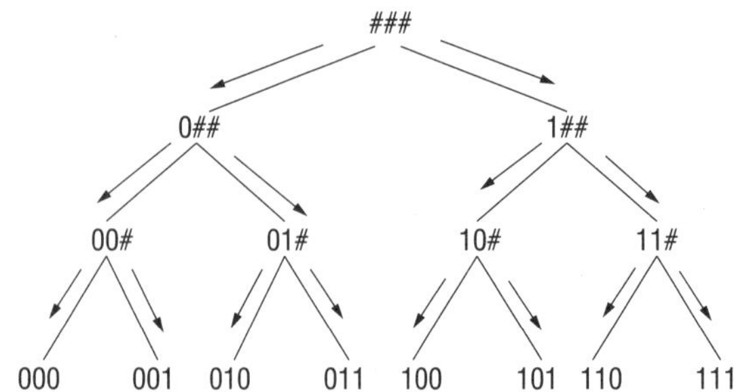

Figure 5.3: Flow of the S_α computation for different α values.

Since $\sum_{\mathbf{x}\in\Gamma} \Psi_{\mathbf{k}}(\mathbf{x})\Psi_{\mathbf{j}}(\mathbf{x})/|\Gamma|$ is the sample mean, and the population mean over the complete domain is zero, the sample mean must approach zero as the sample size increases. Therefore, for a large sample size, which is typically the case for data mining problems, the last term should approach zero. As a result, Fourier coefficients computed over large enough samples should approximate the exact coefficients well.

Approximate computation of basis coefficients can be made further efficient using different techniques. One possibility is to group the coefficients into different equivalence classes over the space of all indices and then estimating this individual groups. Consider the classes, $w_{0\#} = \{w_{00}, w_{01}\}$, $w_{1\#} = \{w_{10}, w_{11}\}$; the # character represents a wild card. Define, $S_\alpha = \sum_\beta w_{\alpha\beta}^2$; where α and β denote similarity based equivalence classes defined over the first $|\alpha|$ and the last $|\beta|$ values of the index respectively; 0# and #1 are examples of α and β respectively. $\alpha\beta$ denotes the intersection of classes α and β. For example, $S_{0\#} = w_{00}^2 + w_{01}^2$. Now note that if any of the individual $w_{\alpha\beta}$-s has a magnitude greater than some threshold value θ, then S_α must have a value greater than θ^2. Therefore, if $S_\alpha < \theta^2$, then none of the Fourier coefficients with an index string starting with α has a significant magnitude. Figure 5.3 schematically illustrates the flow of the algorithm. At every node of the tree we approximately compute S_α, and if S_α at the i-th node is less than θ^2 then none of its children can have an S_α value greater then θ^2 and therefore the subtree can be discarded. If the number of nonzero Fourier coefficients is bounded by a polynomial (recall our assumption of bounded nonlinearity), we should be able to discard many such subtrees just by checking the S_α at the root of the subtree. Using this idea, a polynomial time algorithm has been developed elsewhere (Kushilevitz and Mansour 1991) for learning Boolean functions with sparse Fourier representation. Also, note that the intersection of all the locally detected significant α-s defines a superset of all the indices corresponding to significant cross-terms. This can be used for efficiently approximating the orthonormal representation. In the recent past Kargupta and Sarkar (1999) and Kargupta and Park proposed several randomized and deterministic algorithm for efficiently constructing the Fourier representation.

When the underlying data sampling process is biased and the available data set is not large, alternate techniques may be used to estimate the coefficients. One may use the appropriate orthonormal representation and use standard error minimization algorithm such as least-square minimization technique for fitting the orthonormal coefficients to the available data. This approach will be illustrated in a later section for detecting decision rules.

Earlier, in section 5.2, we saw that minimizing the mean-square error of the local model can lead toward incorrect results. The following section shows that the orthonormal basis function based representation does not suffer from this problem.

5.3.3 Orthonormal Representation and Mean Square Error

The search for an appropriate data model can be posed as a model-error minimization problem. In this section we show that minimization of the error of a local model leads toward a correct partial model that can be used as a building-block of the correct global data model. Consider:

$$\begin{aligned} f - \hat{f} &= \sum_k (w_k - \hat{w}_k)\Psi_k(\mathbf{x}) \\ (f - \hat{f})^2 &= \sum_{j,k} (w_j - \hat{w}_j)(w_k - \hat{w}_k)\Psi_j(\mathbf{x})\Psi_k(\mathbf{x}) \end{aligned}$$

Now summing it over all the data points in the training set Γ:

$$\sum_{\mathbf{x}\in\Gamma} (f - \hat{f})^2 = \sum_{j,k} (w_j - \hat{w}_j)(w_k - \hat{w}_k) \sum_{\mathbf{x}\in\Gamma} \Psi_j\Psi_k$$

Where, Ψ_j is the abbreviated representation of $\Psi_j(\mathbf{x_i})$. Note that the basis functions are assumed to be orthonormal. Therefore, $\sum_{\mathbf{x}} \Psi_j(\mathbf{x})\Psi_k(\mathbf{x}) = 0$, when the sum is over all x-s in the space under consideration and $j \neq k$. On the other hand $\sum_{\mathbf{x}} \Psi_j(\mathbf{x})\Psi_j(\mathbf{x}) = 1$. Let us define a random variable $Z_i = \Psi_j(\mathbf{x_i})\Psi_k(\mathbf{x_i})$. Now $E[Z_i] = \sum_{\mathbf{x}_i} \Psi_j(\mathbf{x_i})\Psi_k(\mathbf{x_i}) = 0$, when $j \neq k$. By the law of large numbers $\frac{\sum_{\mathbf{x}_i \in S} Z_i}{n}$ approaches $E[Z_i] = 0$ as n increases. Therefore for large n, we can write,

$$\sum_{\mathbf{x}\in\Gamma} (f - \hat{f})^2 = \sum_j (w_j - \hat{w}_j)^2 \tag{5.3}$$

Clearly, the overall sum of square error is minimized when $\hat{w}_j = w_j$ for all j. This derivation assumes that all the feature variables are observed and available for model building at the same time. Let us now investigate if the situation changes when feature space is vertically partitioned. Let us assume that the feature space is divided into two sets A and B with feature spaces S_a and S_b respectively. Ξ_a and Ξ_b be the set of all basis functions defined by feature variables in S_a and S_b respectively; Ξ_{ab} be the set of those basis functions in Ξ that use feature variables from both S_a and S_b. Therefore $\Xi = \Xi_a \cup \Xi_b \cup \Xi_{ab}$. We write $j \in \Xi_a$ to denote a basis function $\Psi_j(\mathbf{x}) \in \Xi_a$; we also write $j \notin \Xi_a$ to denote a basis function $\Psi_j(\mathbf{x}) \in \Xi_b \cup \Xi_{ab}$. Now let us explore what happens when one of these sites try to learn $f(\mathbf{x})$ using only its local features. Let us define:

$$\hat{f}_a(\mathbf{x}) = \sum_{j \in \Xi_a} \hat{w}_j \Psi_j(\mathbf{x}) \tag{5.4}$$

From equations 5.1 and 5.4 we can write:

$$f(\mathbf{x}) - \hat{f}_a(\mathbf{x}) = \sum_{j \in \Xi_a} (w_j - \hat{w}_j)\Psi_j(\mathbf{x}) + \sum_{j \notin \Xi_a} w_j \Psi_j(\mathbf{x})$$

Using the above equation we can write:

$$\begin{aligned} (f(\mathbf{x}) - \hat{f}_a(\mathbf{x}))^2 \quad = \quad & \sum_{i,j \in \Xi_a} (w_i - \hat{w}_i)(w_j - \hat{w}_j)\Psi_i \Psi_j + \\ & \sum_{i \notin \Xi_a, j \in \Xi_a} w_i (w_j - \hat{w}_j)\Psi_i \Psi_j + \\ & \sum_{i \in \Xi_a, j \notin \Xi_a} w_j (w_i - \hat{w}_i)\Psi_i \Psi_j + \\ & \sum_{i \notin \Xi_a, j \notin \Xi_a} w_i w_j \Psi_i \Psi_j \end{aligned}$$

Now again using the law of large number we can write:

$$\sum_{\mathbf{x} \in \Gamma} (f - \hat{f}_a)^2 \quad = \quad \sum_{i \in \Xi_a} (w_i - \hat{w}_i)^2 + \sum_{j \notin \Xi_a} w_j^2 \tag{5.5}$$

Equation 5.5 tells us that $\sum_{\mathbf{x} \in \Gamma} (f - \hat{f}_a)^2$ takes the minimum value of $\sum_{j \notin \Xi_a} w_j^2$ when $\hat{w}_j = w_j$.

Although the minimum value of the error is nonzero, this optimal solution value of w_i, $\forall i \in \Xi_a$ remains correct in the global context, even when all the features are considered together. The only difference between the global learning and local learning process is the error term $\sum_{j \notin \Xi_a} w_j^2$ introduced by the basis functions defined by the feature variables not observed at site A.

Although our discussion so far considered only Boolean features, the CDM is certainly not restricted to such cases. The following section briefly discusses this issue.

5.3.4 Nonbinary Features and Collective Data Mining

Orthonormal representations for both nonbinary discrete and continuous valued features can also be computed for extending CDM to these domains. There exists many choices of orthonormal basis functions that can handle these cases. For example, discrete Fourier functions can be easily extended to λ-ary features (a feature can take λ different values).

$$\psi_{\mathbf{j}}^{(\lambda)}(\mathbf{x}) \quad = \quad \exp^{\frac{2\pi i(\mathbf{x}.\mathbf{j})}{\lambda}} \tag{5.6}$$

Where $\mathbf{j}$ and $\mathbf{x}$ are λ-ary strings of length ℓ. In other words $\mathbf{j} = j_1, j_2, \cdots j_\ell$ and $\mathbf{x} = x_1, x_2, \cdots x_\ell$. The set of all $\psi_j(\mathbf{x})$ for all possible λ-ary strings $\mathbf{j}$ defines a basis.

Wavelet representation (Wickerhauser 1994) is a possible choice of orthonormal basis functions for dealing with continuous valued features. We shall discuss these possibilities in detail in later sections. The following section identifies the overall CDM algorithm.

5.3.5 The Collective Data Mining Framework

The CDM is a framework that offers a methodology to develop distributed data analysis algorithms from heterogeneous sites. The main steps of this approach may be summarized as follows: (1) choose an orthonormal representation that is appropriate for the type of data model to be constructed; (2) generate approximate orthonormal basis coefficients at each local site; (3) if necessary, move an appropriately chosen sample of the datasets from each site to a single site and generate the approximate basis coefficients corresponding to nonlinear cross terms; and (4) combine the local models, transform the model into the user described canonical representation, and output the model.

Development of specific instances of CDM for different data mining techniques is currently on-going. The coming sections will present a flavor of that for two popular data mining techniques. The following section presents the CDM versions of rule-learning using decision tree .

5.4 Decision Tree Learning In Collective Data Mining

Decision trees (Quinlan 1986) are popular techniques for learning classifiers. In this section we describe the ongoing research on a CDM-based approach to construct both numeric and symbolic decision trees from heterogeneous data sites. First let us review a simple ID3 (Quinlan, 1986) like approach to construct decision trees

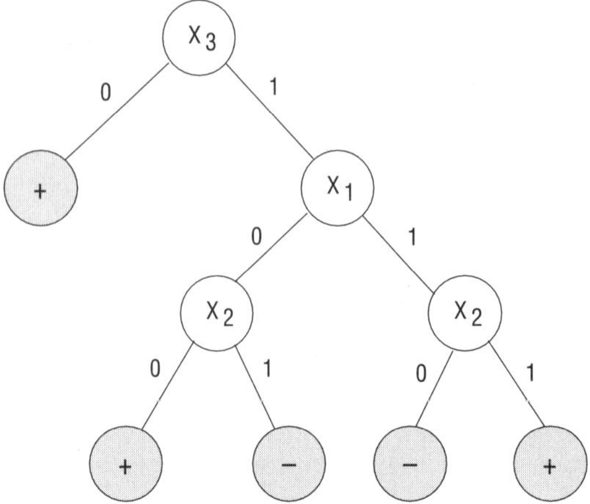

Figure 5.4: Boolean decision tree.

5.4.1 An Overview of the ID3 Algorithm

The ID3 algorithm builds a decision tree from a given labeled data set. For the sake of simplicity, let us consider a Boolean decision tree as depicted in figure 5.4. The Boolean class labels correspond to positive and negative instances of the concept class. We can express Boolean decision tree as a function $f : X^\ell \rightarrow \{0, 1\}$. The function f maps positive and negative instances to one and zero respectively. A node in a tree is labeled with a feature x_i. A downward link from the node x_i is labeled with an attribute value of i-th feature. A path from the root node to a successor node represents the subset of data that satisfies the different feature values labeled along the path. These data subsets are essentially similarity based equivalence classes and we shall call them schemata (schema in singular form). If $\mathbf{h}$ is a schema, then $\mathbf{h} \in \{0, 1, *\}^\ell$, where $*$ denotes a wild-card that matches any value of the corresponding feature. For example, the path $\{(x_3 \stackrel{1}{\rightarrow} x_1, x_1 \stackrel{0}{\rightarrow} x_2\}$ in figure 5.4 represents the schema $0 * 1$, since all members of the data subset at the final node of this path take feature values 0 and 1 for x_1 and x_3 respectively.

The ID3 algorithm builds the tree by first constructing the root node using the following scheme. It computes the information-gain for each variable and assigns the variable to the root that maximizes the expected information-gain. Given the schema $\mathbf{h}$ for the path to a node from the root, the information gained by replacing the wild card value of some feature x_i in $\mathbf{h}$ can be defined as,

$$Gain(\mathbf{h}, x_i) = Entropy(\mathbf{h}) - \sum_{v \in Values(x_i)} \frac{|\mathbf{h}_v|}{|\mathbf{h}|} Entropy(\mathbf{h}_v)$$

where $Values(x_i)$ is the set of all possible values for attribute x_i, and $|\mathbf{h}_v|$ is the set of those members of **h** that have a value v for attribute x_i; if p and q are the proportions of the positive and negative instances in some **h**, then $Entropy(\mathbf{h}) = -p \log p - q \log q$. Once a variable is assigned to the root, the ID3 algorithm computes information gain for its children and continues to add new nodes if the information gain is significant. As we see, computation of entropy for a given schema is what we need for a decision tree construction. Computation of the entropy at each node requires the knowledge of the distribution of class labels for the data set. In a heterogeneous environment, comparing the information gain requires exchange of distribution information among the different sites. The following section points out that the naive approach to do this by synchronous message exchange may not be scalable.

5.4.2 Naive Approach May Not Scale-up

First let us note that it is not obvious that decision trees constructed in an independent and asynchronous fashion at different heterogeneous data sites may not be combined to generate the correct tree that a centralized construction would produce. An alternate approach to guarantee correctness is synchronous construction where all the sites contribute in selecting a feature at every node of the globally maintained tree. However, the latter approach may not be scalable when the number of sites grows. Since at every node of the tree ID3 computes the information gain for every choice of feature, all the sites need to be informed regarding the particular subset of data subsumed at a particular node. Since the complete data set is distributed among all the nodes at a particular level, at each level the communication cost will be $O(n*s)$, where n is the number of data rows and s is the number of different data sites. If the tree has a depth bounded by some constant k then the overall communication cost will be $O(n*s*k)$. If the table has c columns and n rows then the cost of moving the complete data sets to a single site is $O(n*c)$. When $s*k > c$ distributed decision tree construction using the naive approach is computationally worse than the centralized approach. For distributed environments with large number of data sites this may be a major bottle-neck.

5.4.3 Fourier Spectrum of a Decision Tree

The CDM approach for distributed decision tree learning is based on a new perspective of decision tree construction. It notes that a decision tree defines a function over the domain under consideration. Even if the features are symbolic, the tree still defines a function. If we define a table that replaces the symbolic values of a feature by some numeric value then we can transform the symbolic function to a numeric function. Therefore we can always compute the Fourier spectrum of a decision tree. In this section, we shall first consider Boolean decision trees and then we shall gradually introduce the CDM approach toward non-Boolean decision tree. For almost all practical purposes, decision trees should have a bounded depth. It turns out that the Fourier representation of a decision tree with bounded depth has some very interesting properties (Kushilevitz and Mansour 1991) that can be quite useful for its distributed construction. These observations are discussed in the following: (1) Decision trees with bounded depth are normally useful for data mining purposes. (2) The Fourier representation of a bounded depth (say k) Boolean decision tree only has a polynomial number of nonzero coefficients; all coefficients corresponding to partitions involving more than k feature variables are zero. (3) If the order of a partition be its number of defining features then the magnitude of the Fourier coefficients decay exponentially with the order of the corresponding partition; in other words low order coefficients are exponentially more significant than the higher order coefficients.

The above two theorems rigorously prove that the spectrum of the decision tree can be approximated by computing only a small number of low-order[1]. The proposed CDM-based approach exploits this observation. In stead of moving all the data to a single data, this approach simply computes the low-order Fourier coefficients from the distributed sites, collects them to a single site, and use them to generate the decision rules. The main strength of this approach is fundamentally based on the suitability of the Fourier basis in representing a decision tree of bounded depth.

Although, the Fourier spectrum of a decision tree is sparse and it can be approximated by only the low-order coefficients, computation of these coefficients from the data set is slightly tricky. This is simply because the training data set is often only a small subset of the complete domain. Naive computation of the Fourier coefficients using only the sample data set may not give us the Fourier spectrum of the tree. Accurate computation of the spectrum from the sample data set will require appropriate estimation. However, before describing such a technique let us discuss the big picture that captures the course from data to the tree through Fourier analysis. The following section does that.

5.4.4 From Data to Decision Tree: One Goal but Different Roads

The CDM approach constructs the decision tree from the data set through Fourier analysis. Figure 5.5 presents a schematic diagram of the different possible ways to do this. First of all note that the computation of the Fourier

[1] Order of a coefficient $w_{\mathbf{j}}$ is the number of features defining the corresponding partition $\mathbf{j}$. For Boolean features, the order is essentially the number of 1-s in the partition. Low-order coefficients are the ones for which the orders of the partitions are relatively small

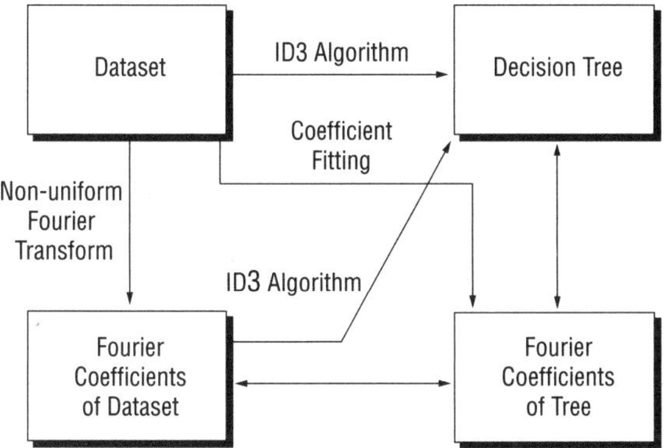

Figure 5.5: From data to decision tree through Fourier analysis.

coefficients require all the members of the domain (refer to section 3.1.1). However, the learning data set typically does not have that. It turns out that if we assume the class label ($f(\mathbf{x})$) to be 0 for all the members of the domain that are not in the learning data set then the Fourier spectrum exactly represents the data. This is called the nonuniform Fourier transformation (NFT) of the data (Bridges and Goldberg 1991). This will be explained in details in the coming sections. NFT faithfully represents the data; in other words for any member of the learning data set, it can correctly predict the corresponding class label. Fortunately construction of the decision tree using ID3 requires only this much information. We shall prove that one can exactly construct the decision tree from the NFT of the data. The link connecting the blocks at the lower-left corner of figure 5.5 and the upper-right corner represent this route.

The direct link connecting the blocks corresponding to the "dataset" and the "decision tree" represents the approach that a traditional ID3 algorithm takes. The NFT and the Fourier spectrum of the tree are also related. They share the same outcome for every member that is in the learning data set. We may be able convert either of them into the other; In fact, this may offer a viable way to construct the tree in a distributed fashion. This will be further explored in a later section. We may also be able to estimate the Fourier spectrum of the tree directly from the learning data. Although the Fourier spectrum of the tree is functionally equivalent to the tree itself, construction of the tree representation from the estimated Fourier coefficients is yet to be explored. The link between the two upper-right and the lower-right blocks represents this possible route.

Note that the NFT is not as same as the Fourier spectrum of the decision tree that an algorithm like ID3 may produce from the data. This is simply because the tree makes an inductive leap and it generalizes to the complete

$\mathbf{x}$	$f(\mathbf{x})$	$\overline{f}(\mathbf{x})$
0 0 0	1	0
0 0 1	1	0
0 1 1	0	1
1 0 1	0	1
1 1 0	1	0
1 1 1	1	0

Table 5.1: Data vectors with their original and complemented function values.

j	w_j	w'_j
000	$0.\dot{6}$	$0.\dot{3}$
001	0.0	$-0.\dot{3}$
010	0.0	0.0
011	0.0	0.0
100	0.0	0.0
101	0.0	0.0
110	$0.\dot{6}$	$-0.\dot{3}$
111	0.0	$0.\dot{3}$

$\mathbf{h}$	$\phi(\mathbf{h})$	$\overline{\phi}(\mathbf{h})$	(+/-)
$0 * *$	$0.\dot{6}$	$0.\dot{3}$	2/1
$1 * *$	$0.\dot{6}$	$0.\dot{3}$	2/1
$* 0 *$	$0.\dot{6}$	$0.\dot{3}$	2/1
$* 1 *$	$0.\dot{6}$	$0.\dot{3}$	2/1
$* * 0$	$0.\dot{6}$	0.0	2/0
$* * 1$	$0.\dot{6}$	$0.\dot{6}$	2/2

Table 5.2: Two sets of Fourier coefficients obtained from normal and complemented function values (left). Schemata of order one with their proportion-weighted fitness averages computed from normal/complemented function values (right).

domain by assigning the class labels based on the information from the learning data set. This has very interesting implications that will be discussed later. This chapter explores two of the possible approaches toward distributed construction of the tree through Fourier analysis. First, the route through construction of the NFT of the data is explored. This discussion is primarily of theoretical interest and it will help us understanding the subsequent practical approaches. Next, an alternate and possibly more practical approach through direct estimation of the Fourier spectrum of the tree is discussed.

5.4.5 From Nonuniform Fourier Coefficients to Entropy

As noted in an earlier section, construction of the decision tree using the ID3 algorithm requires computation of the entropy of different equivalence classes that we choose to call schema. This section shows that the schema entropies can be computed directly from the NFT. This section considers first the case where all the features are Boolean. Following Bridges and Goldberg (1991) let us define NFT in a rigorous fashion.

Let the proportion function $\mathbf{P(x)}$ be the number of instances of $\mathbf{x}$ divided by the size of the data set. Let us also define the proportion-weighted class label, $\phi(\mathbf{x})$ and its Fourier transformation as follows,

$$\phi(\mathbf{x}) = f(\mathbf{x})\mathbf{P}(\mathbf{x})2^l \tag{5.7}$$

$$w_j = \frac{1}{2^l}\sum_{\mathbf{x}=0}^{2^{l-1}} \phi(\mathbf{x})\psi_j(\mathbf{x}) \tag{5.8}$$

where $\psi_j(\mathbf{x})$ is the j-th basis function for Fourier transform. After finding the Fourier coefficients from the $\phi(\mathbf{x})$ values, we calculate the proportion of positive instances (class label 1) in a schema $\mathbf{h}$ as follows,

$$\phi(\mathbf{h}) = \sum_{\mathbf{j}\in\mathbf{J}(\mathbf{h})} w_j\psi_j(\beta(\mathbf{h})) \tag{5.9}$$

where,

$$J_i(\mathbf{h}) = \begin{cases} 0 & \text{if } h_i = *; \\ * & \text{if } h_i = 0, 1; \end{cases}$$

$$\beta_i(\mathbf{h}) = \begin{cases} 0 & \text{if } h_i = 0, *; \\ 1 & \text{if } h_i = 1; \end{cases}$$

Further details about NFT for binary features can be found elsewhere (Bridges and Goldberg 1991). Let us illustrate these equations using an example. Consider table 5.2 (left) that shows the Fourier Coefficients for $\phi(x)$. For example, $\phi(1**) = \sum_{\mathbf{j}\in\{000,100\}} w_j\psi_j(100) = w_{000} - w_{100} = 0.\dot{6}$. Note that $\phi(\mathbf{h})$ is nothing but the average of $\phi(\mathbf{x})$ values for all the members of schema $\mathbf{h}$, i.e.

$$\phi(\mathbf{h}) = \frac{1}{|\mathbf{h}|}\sum_{\mathbf{x}\in\mathbf{h}} \phi(\mathbf{x}) \tag{5.10}$$

where $|\mathbf{h}| = 2^{l-o(\mathbf{h})}$. Now using equation 5.7 we get,

$$\sum_{\mathbf{x}\in\mathbf{h}} f(\mathbf{x}) = \frac{|\mathbf{h}|\phi(\mathbf{h})}{P(\mathbf{x})2^l} \tag{5.11}$$

Equation 5.11 represents the number of members in $\mathbf{h}$ with function value one (positive instance). Since we do not know the number of members of $\mathbf{h}$, in order to get the number of negative instances in $\mathbf{h}$, we need another set of nonuniform Fourier Coefficients that can be obtained from the same data set but with complemented $f(\mathbf{x})$ values. The rightmost column of table 5.2 (right) shows the number of positive and negative instance vectors in each schema of order one. As a check, let us use equation 5.11 to calculate the number of positive and negative instances of schemata $1**$ and $**0$. For the schema

$1**$, number of positive and negative instances are obtained as,

$$\sum_{\mathbf{x}\in\{1**\}} f(\mathbf{x}) = \frac{|\mathbf{1}**|\phi(\mathbf{1}**)}{P(\mathbf{x})2^3} = \frac{4\times 0.\dot{6}}{\frac{4}{3}} = 2$$

$$\sum_{\mathbf{x}\in\{1**\}} \bar{f}(\mathbf{x}) = \frac{|\mathbf{1}**|\bar{\phi}(\mathbf{1}**)}{P(\mathbf{x})2^3} = \frac{4\times 0.\dot{3}}{\frac{4}{3}} = 1$$

$\bar{f}$ and $\bar{\phi}$ denote the complemented version of the functions f and ϕ respectively. Now, for the schema **0 we can write,

$$\sum_{\mathbf{x}\in\{**0\}} f(\mathbf{x}) = \frac{|**\mathbf{0}|\phi(**\mathbf{0})}{P(\mathbf{x})2^3} = \frac{4\times 0.\dot{6}}{\frac{4}{3}} = 2$$

$$\sum_{\mathbf{x}\in\{**0\}} \bar{f}(\mathbf{x}) = \frac{|**\mathbf{0}|\bar{\phi}(**\mathbf{0})}{P(\mathbf{x})2^3} = \frac{4\times 0.0}{\frac{4}{3}} = 0$$

We get the exactly the same numbers as in table 5.2 (right).

Since we can easily calculate the number of positive and negative instances of each schema, measuring information gain achieved by choosing an attribute is straightforward. We only need to give weights by dividing the number of instances in each schema by total number of instances in all schemata under consideration. For example, the weights assigned to $**0$ and $**1$ are 2/6 = 1/3 and 4/6 = 2/3 respectively. The resulting decision tree from the Fourier coefficients is identical to the one constructed by a regular ID3 approach and it is shown in figure 5.4. The following section considers the general case of building decision trees for nonbinary features.

5.4.6 Decision Trees with Nonbinary Features

In data mining, we generally deal with data sets with nonbinary features. Like *Outlook* in figure 5.6, a feature may have 4cardinality(the number of attribute values) of three or more. With the same Fourier basis functions, the decision tree building algorithm developed in the previous section fails to work in these nonbinary feature set. In this section, we extend the analysis by applying generalized nonuniform Fourier Transform in order to build a decision tree with nonbinary features. The following analysis can handle $\bar{\lambda}$-ary features with different cardinality values.

Recall λ-ary Fourier basis functions over the set of features of the same cardinality λ is defined as

$$\psi_{\mathbf{j}}^{(\lambda)}(\mathbf{x}) = \exp^{\frac{2\pi i}{\lambda}(\mathbf{x}\cdot\mathbf{j})} \tag{5.12}$$

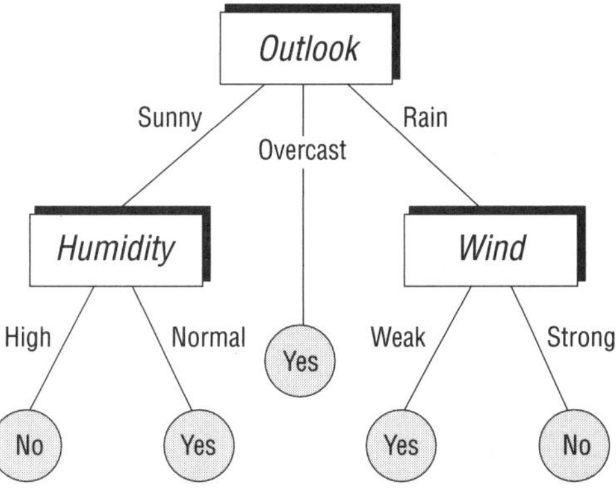

Figure 5.6: Nonbinary feature decision tree.

The generalized $\overline{\lambda}$-ary Fourier function over data vector of length l is defined as

$$\psi_{\mathbf{j}}^{\overline{\lambda}}(\mathbf{x}) = \Pi_{m=1}^{l} \exp^{\frac{2\pi i}{\lambda_m} x_m j_m} \tag{5.13}$$

where $\overline{\lambda} = \lambda_1, \lambda_2, \ldots\lambda_l$ and λ_j denotes the cardinality of j-th feature(x_j).

Similarly, we redefine proportion-weighted class label $\phi(\mathbf{x})$ and its $\overline{\lambda}$-ary Fourier transform as

$$\phi(\mathbf{x}) = f(\mathbf{x})\mathbf{P}(\mathbf{x})\Pi_{i=1}^{l}\lambda_i \tag{5.14}$$

$$w_{\mathbf{j}} = \Pi_{i=1}^{l}\frac{1}{\lambda_i}\sum_{\mathbf{x}}\overline{\psi_{\mathbf{j}}^{\overline{\lambda}}}(\mathbf{x})\phi(\mathbf{x}) \tag{5.15}$$

where $\overline{\psi_{\mathbf{j}}^{\overline{\lambda}}}(\mathbf{x})$ is the complex conjugate of $\psi_{\mathbf{j}}^{\overline{\lambda}}(\mathbf{x})$.

Using the redefined $\phi(\mathbf{x})$, we can compute the average of *proportion-weighted class label*($\phi(\mathbf{h})$) as follows.

$$\phi(\mathbf{h}) = \sum_{l_1}\sum_{l_2}\ldots\sum_{l_m} \exp^{2\pi i(\frac{l_1 b_1}{\lambda_{j_1}} + \frac{l_2 b_2}{\lambda_{j_2}} + \ldots + \frac{l_m b_m}{\lambda_{j_m}})} w_{(0,\ldots,l_1,0,\ldots,l_2,0,\ldots,l_m,\ldots 0)}$$

where $\mathbf{h}$ has m fixed bits b_i at positions j_i and l_i has the cardinality of λ_i.

Table 5.4 (left) shows the proportion-weighted class label averages of three order one schemata and table 5.4 (right) shows Fourier coefficients appeared in these average computations.

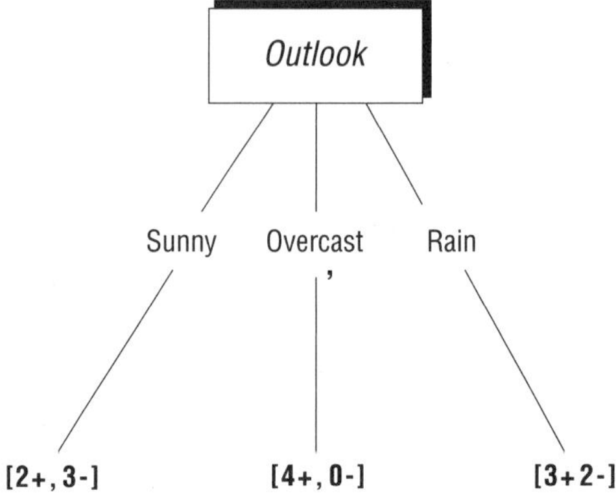

Figure 5.7: Positive/negative instances split by choosing *Outlook*.

For example, schema 0*** has average of 0.64286, which is obtained as,

$$\begin{aligned}
\phi(0***) &= \exp^{2\pi i \times \frac{0 \cdot 0}{3}} w_{0000} \\
&\quad + \exp^{2\pi i \times \frac{0 \cdot 1}{3}} w_{1000} + \exp^{2\pi i \times \frac{0 \cdot 2}{3}} w_{2000} \\
&= w_{0000} + w_{1000} + w_{2000} \\
&= 0.64286 - 0.12372\mathbf{i} + 0.12372\mathbf{i} \\
&= 0.64286
\end{aligned}$$

To illustrate how we calculate the information gain using generalized($\overline{\lambda}$) discrete Fourier transform, consider the data set in table 5.3 (Mitchell 1997b). Notice that both attribute values and class labels are mapped to integers for $\overline{\lambda}$-ary Fourier transform. In figure 5.6, *Outlook* of cardinality three is chosen as the root. The number of positive and negative instances split by choosing *Outlook* are shown in figure 5.7. The schema representations of the paths along *Sunny*, *Overcast* and *Rain* links are 2***,1*** and 0*** respectively. The proportion-weighted class label averages of these schemata are found in table 5.4. As we did in the previous section, we apply equation 5.11 to check the number of positive and negative instances along each schema. Notice that $\mathbf{P}(\mathbf{x})$ = 1/14 and $\Pi_{i=0}^{l}\lambda_i = 3 \times 3 \times 2 \times 2 = 36$. For the schema 2***,

$$\sum_{\mathbf{x} \in \{2***\}} f(\mathbf{x}) = \frac{|\mathbf{2}***|\phi(\mathbf{2}***)}{P(\mathbf{x})\Pi_l \lambda_l} = \frac{12 * 0.42587}{\frac{36}{14}} \doteq 2$$

$$\sum_{\mathbf{x} \in \{2***\}} \overline{f}(\mathbf{x}) = \frac{|\mathbf{2}***|\overline{\phi}(\mathbf{2}***)}{P(\mathbf{x})\Pi_l \lambda_l} = \frac{12 * 0.64286}{\frac{36}{14}} \doteq 3$$

Outlook	*Temperature*	*Humidity*	*Wind*	*PlayTennis*	x	$f(\mathbf{x})$	$\overline{f}(\mathbf{x})$
Sunny	Hot	High	Weak	No	2 2 1 0	0	1
Sunny	Hot	High	Strong	No	2 2 1 1	0	1
Overcast	Hot	High	Weak	Yes	1 2 1 0	1	0
Rain	Mild	High	Weak	Yes	0 1 0 0	1	0
Rain	Cool	Normal	Weak	Yes	0 0 0 0	1	0
Rain	Cool	Normal	Strong	No	0 0 0 1	0	1
Overcast	Cool	Normal	Strong	Yes	1 0 0 1	1	0
Sunny	Mild	High	Weak	No	2 1 1 0	0	1
Sunny	Cool	Normal	Weak	Yes	2 0 0 0	1	0
Rain	Mild	Normal	Weak	Yes	0 1 0 0	1	0
Sunny	Mild	Normal	Strong	Yes	2 1 0 1	1	0
Overcast	Mild	High	Strong	Yes	1 1 1 1	1	0
Overcast	Hot	Normal	Weak	Yes	1 2 0 0	1	0
Rain	Mild	High	Strong	No	0 1 1 1	0	1

Table 5.3: Data examples and their vector representations.

h	$\phi(\mathbf{h})$	$\overline{\phi}(\mathbf{h})$	j	w_j	w'_j
0 * * *	0.64286	0.42857	0000	0.64286	0.35714
1 * * *	0.85714	0.0	1000	-0.12372**i**	0.03572 + 0.18557**i**
2 * * *	0.42857	0.64286	2000	0.12372**i**	0.03572 - 0.18557**i**

Table 5.4: Proportion-weighted class label averages of the first bit fixed schemata and some Fourier coefficients generated from data in table 5.3.

For the schema 1***,

$$\sum_{\mathbf{x}\in\{1***\}} f(\mathbf{x}) = \frac{|\mathbf{1}***|\phi(\mathbf{1}***)}{P(\mathbf{x})\Pi_l\lambda_l} = \frac{12*0.85714}{\frac{36}{14}} \doteq 4$$

$$\sum_{\mathbf{x}\in\{1***\}} \overline{f}(\mathbf{x}) = \frac{|\mathbf{1}***|\overline{\phi}(\mathbf{1}***)}{P(\mathbf{x})\Pi_l\lambda_l} = \frac{12*0.0}{\frac{36}{14}} = 0$$

And for the schema 0***,

$$\sum_{\mathbf{x}\in\{0***\}} f(\mathbf{x}) = \frac{|\mathbf{0}***|\phi(\mathbf{0}***)}{P(\mathbf{x})\Pi_l\lambda_l} = \frac{12*0.64286}{\frac{36}{14}} \doteq 3$$

$$\sum_{\mathbf{x}\in\{0***\}} \overline{f}(\mathbf{x}) = \frac{|\mathbf{0}***|\overline{\phi}(\mathbf{0}***)}{P(\mathbf{x})\Pi_l\lambda_l} = \frac{12*0.42857}{\frac{36}{14}} \doteq 2$$

Once again, we get the exactly same numbers as in figure 5.7. As we see, a decision tree with nonbinary features can also be constructed directly from the NFT spectrum of the data. However, the NFT of the data does not guarantee the nice properties like polynomial description and exponentially decaying magnitude (listed in section 4.3). The communication of the NFT of the data is not guaranteed to have low overhead. Therefore, we may need a technique to estimate the spectrum of the tree.

One possibility is to estimate the Fourier spectrum of the tree (not the NFT of the data) directly from the data. This approach has some strong advantages. Recall that the Fourier spectrum of a bounded-depth tree has some very favorable properties (refer to section 4.3). It has only a polynomial number of nonzero coefficients and moreover it can be approximated by only a small number of low-order coefficients. Therefore, the distributed computation of the tree can be very efficient using this approach. The following section presents this.

5.4.7 Building Decision Trees Through Direct Estimation of Its Fourier Spectrum

The Fourier representation of a bounded-depth decision tree is sparse and it can be approximated using only a small number of coefficients since the coefficients exponentially decay as the orders of the corresponding partitions increase. Therefore, if we can find a direct way to estimate these coefficients from data then construction of the global tree will require minimal communication. This section describes one approach to do that.

Note that the construction of a globally accurate tree requires only the low order coefficients of the spectrum. So we only need to estimate the coefficients for which the order is bounded by some small constant. Let Ξ be the set of all coefficient-indices and Ξ_k be the set of those indices with order value less than equal to k. Let us divide the indices in Ξ_k into two groups. Let $\Xi_k^{(l)}$ be the indices that can be computed at a data site using only the local feature values. Let $\Xi_k^{(c)}$ be the rest of the indices for whom we need features values from different sites. $\Xi_k = \Xi_k^{(l)} \cup \Xi_k^{(c)}$. Now we can write,

$$f(\mathbf{x}) = \sum_{i \in \Xi_k} w_i \psi_i(\mathbf{x}) + \sum_{j \in \Xi - \Xi_k} w_j \psi_j(\mathbf{x})$$

The error in approximating $f(\mathbf{x})$ using only the coefficients in Ξ_k is,

$$\delta^{(t)}(\mathbf{x}) = \sum_{j \in \Xi - \Xi_k} w_j \psi_j(\mathbf{x}) = f(\mathbf{x}) - \sum_{i \in \Xi_k} w_i \psi_i(\mathbf{x})$$

This error term can be iteratively modeled using different sets of coefficients until the error converges. Let S be the training data set and $|S|$ be the cardinality of this set. The proposed algorithm works in the following manner.

Local Site:
Initialize:

- Set $\delta^{(t)}(\mathbf{x}) = f(\mathbf{x}), \forall x \in S; \delta^{(t)}(\mathbf{x}) = 0$ otherwise.
- Set the coefficients $w_j^{(0)} = 0$ for all $j \in \Xi_k^{(l)}$.

Iterate over t until $\delta^{(t)}(\mathbf{x})$ continues to decrease toward the acceptable level of the approximation error:

- Compute $w_j^{(t)} = \frac{1}{|S|} \sum_{\mathbf{x}} \delta^{(t)}(\mathbf{x}) \psi_j(\mathbf{x})$, such that $j \in \Xi_k^{(l)}$.
- Set $\delta^{(t+1)}(\mathbf{x}) = \delta^{(t)}(\mathbf{x}) - \sum_{i \in \Xi_k} w_i^{(t)} \psi_i(\mathbf{x})$.
- Update the estimate of the coefficients, $w_j^{(t+1)} = w_j^{(t-1)} + w_j^{(t)}$ for all $j \in \Xi_k^{(l)}$.

Global Site:
Collect all the locally computed coefficients and a small representative sample of the data from each sites.
Set $\delta^{(t)}(\mathbf{x}) = f(\mathbf{x}) - \sum_{j \in \Xi_k^{(l)}, \forall l} w_j^{(t)} \psi_j(\mathbf{x})$.

Iterate for all the coefficients corresponding to the cross-terms in $\Xi_k^{(c)}$. The iterative algorithm is exactly same as the one used for computing the local terms. The only difference is that $\Xi_k^{(l)}$ is replaced by $\Xi_k^{(c)}$. At each stage of the iteration, the error is computed over the sampled data set.

Note that the above calculation implicitly asserts $\delta^{(t)}(\mathbf{x}) = 0$ for all domain members that are not in the training data set while computing the Fourier representation of the error. This makes the computation of the coefficients possible by only considering the training data set. This approach to estimate the Fourier spectrum assumes that the tree has a bounded depth and therefore only the low order coefficients are required to approximate the tree. The algorithm then tries to approximate the function to be learned using only the low order coefficients defined by local features. The NFT assumes a function value of zero for every domain member that is not in the training data set. However, a decision tree constructed from the data does not do that. Instead the tree takes the inductive leap by assigning different function values to the member not in the training set based on the training data. The iterative process also does the same. It continues to approximate the contribution of the higher order coefficients using the partitions in Ξ_k by inducing different and possibly nonzero function values for the domain members that are not in the training data set. Once the error stops decreasing, the local partitions cannot help any more.

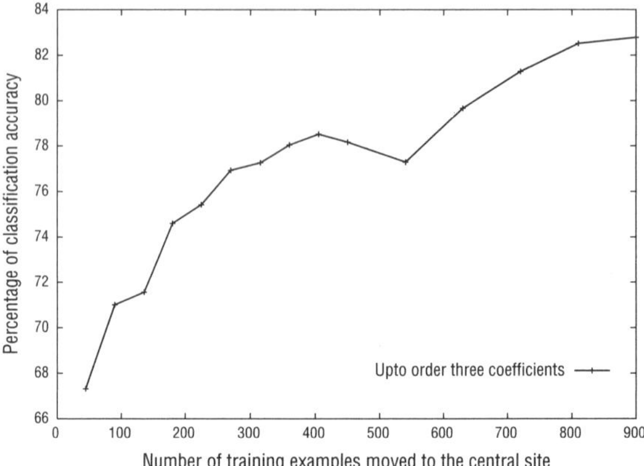

Figure 5.8: Variation of the classification accuracy with respect to the number of data points transferred to the central site for computing the cross-terms.

If the approximation error is significant then we need to compute the cross-terms. Since a bounded depth decision tree contains only a bounded number of cross-terms, estimation of the cross-terms from a relatively small sample set is feasible. As noted earlier in this chapter, this estimation of the cross-terms will require $O(|\Xi_k^c|)$ data row communication from each of the sites.

In order to show how the estimation accuracy varies with the size of the data sent to the central site, let us consider the experimental result presented in figure 5.8. The set up considers a dataset of 20 Boolean features, divided vertically and placed in two sites. Each site stores 104,857 training instances, which is about 10% of the complete domain. The classification problem is designed using a decision tree of bounded depth of seven, generated manually. Figure 5.8 shows the variation of the classification accuracy over a testing data set (similar in size to the training data set) with respect to the number of data points transferred to the central site for learning the cross-terms. As the experimental result shows, even with a small fraction of data instances, we could approximate the spectrum of the decision tree with good accuracy.

The portion of the work presented here is preliminary. The experiment considered all the coefficients up to order three. Since decision tree is a greedy search, a fair comparison will require incorporation of greedy search in the Fourier spectrum space. A hill-climbing technique is expected to reduce the number of higher order cross-terms considered in the central site. If the pruning is accurate then the cross-terms can be learned using even smaller number of examples. This will result in further reduction of communication overhead. An extended study of this technique is presented elsewhere (Kargupta and Park

$f(x_1, x_2)$	x_1	x_2
$b_0 + b_1 + b_2 + b_3$	1	1
$b_0 + b_1 - b_2 - b_3$	1	-1
$b_0 - b_1 + b_2 - b_3$	-1	1
$b_0 - b_1 - b_2 + b_3$	-1	-1

Table 5.5: Sample data for sparse representation example.

1999a). The following section discusses the extension of the CDM for polynomial regression that has already been applied to large problems (Hershberger and Kargupta 1999).

5.5 Collective Data Mining and Regression

Regression (Mosteller and Tukey 1977), like decision tree learning, is a popular data modeling technique. As we noted earlier in section 5.3, naive application of standard regression techniques may produce misleading and ambiguous results in heterogeneous, distributed environments. Earlier, we also saw a simple CDM regression example for a toy problem with discrete binary-valued feature variables. In this section, we address the issue in detail and present a method for distributed, polynomial-regression to the continuous-valued feature domain.

The CDM exploits the strength of a representation to describe a data model in a sparse and concise fashion. We saw that Fourier representation is good for representing decision trees. However Fourier or any such representation is unlikely to be good for every type of data model. Since there is no known technique to construct an appropriate representation in a domain independent fashion, the CDM research explores the suitability of such representations in a domain-specific fashion. In this section we choose wavelet representation (Hubbard 1998; Mulcahy 1997; Mulcahy 1996; Stolinitz, DeRose, and Salesis 1995; Wickerhauser 1994) since wavelets are widely acknowledged to have sparser representation in continuous domains with periodic patterns. Wavelets have already found many applications in signal processing, image compression, and data analysis. A detailed description of these applications can be found elsewhere (Wickerhauser 1994).

In order to further motivate the choice of wavelet over Fourier consider the function $f(x_1, x_2) = b_0 + b_1x_1 + b_2x_2 + b_3x_1x_2$, and the associated data samples shown in table 5.5.

If we apply a discrete Fourier transform and a wavelet-packet (to be described in the coming section) transform to the data, we obtain the results presented in table 5.6. The wavelet transform is seen to provide a sparser

Fourier Transform				
1	x_2	x_1	x_1x_2	$f(x_1, x_2)$
2	0	0	0	$2b_0$
0	0	$1+i$	$1-i$	$(b_1+b_3)+(b_1-b_3)i$
0	2	0	0	$2b_2$
0	0	$1-i$	$1+i$	$(b_1+b_3)-(b_1-b_3)i$

Wavelet-packet Transform				
1	x_2	x_1	x_1x_2	$f(x_1, x_2)$
1	0	0	0	b_0
0	0	-1	0	$-b_1$
0	-1	0	0	$-b_2$
0	0	0	1	b_3

Table 5.6: Discrete Fourier transform vs. wavelet-packet transform for spare representation example.

representation of the feature variables, reflecting the orthogonal basis in the feature space. For this particular example, the wavelet transform produces an orthogonal representation that is superior to that of the Fourier transform.

5.5.1 Wavelet Basis and Wavelet-Packet Analysis

A wavelet basis consists of two sets of functions, scaling basis functions, ϕ_i and wavelet basis functions, ψ_i, where the wavelet functions are dilated and translated versions of the scaling functions (Stolinitz, DeRose, and Salesis 1995). To understand the relation between the scaling and wavelet functions, consider a vector space S^j with 2^j dimensions defined on the interval [0, 1). S^j contains all functions defined on [0, 1) that are piece-wise constant on 2^j equal subintervals. If S^{j+1} is also defined on [0, 1) then every function in S^j is also in S^{j+1} since each interval in S^j may be considered to correspond to two contiguous intervals in S^{j+1}. Let $S^{j+1} = S^j + W^j$, where the subspace W^j is the orthogonal complement of S^j in S^{j+1}. If we assert that the basis functions for S^j are the scaling functions, ϕ_i^j, then the basis functions for W^j will be the wavelet functions, ψ_i^j. Note that since S^j and W^j are complementary orthogonal spaces, the ϕ_i^j and ψ_i^j will be orthogonal to each other in S^{j+1}. If, in addition, the ϕ_i^j form an orthogonal basis for S^j and the ψ_i^j form and orthogonal basis for W^j, then combined the ϕ_i^j and ψ_i^j form an orthogonal basis for S^{j+1}.

A simple set of scaling functions for S^j are the scaled and translated "box" functions (Stolinitz, DeRose, and Salesis 1995), defined on the interval [0, 1) by:

$$\phi_i^j(x) = \phi(2^j x - i), i = 0, \ldots, 2^j - 1,$$

where

$$\phi(x) = \begin{cases} 1 & \text{for } 0 \le x < 1 \\ 0 & \text{otherwise} \end{cases}$$

The wavelet functions corresponding to the box basis functions are the Haar wavelets:

$$\psi_i^j(x) = \psi(2^j x - i), i = 0, \ldots, 2^j - 1,$$

where

$$\psi(x) = \begin{cases} 1 & \text{for } 0 \le x < \frac{1}{2} \\ -1 & \text{for } \frac{1}{2} \le x < 1 \\ 0 & \text{otherwise} \end{cases}$$

Any function in S^j may be represented in terms of these basis functions as

$$f(\mathbf{x}) = s_0^j \phi_0^j + s_1^j \phi_1^j + \ldots + s_{2^j-1}^j \phi_{2^j-1}^j = \mathbf{S}^j$$

or also as

$$\begin{aligned} f(\mathbf{x}) &= s_0^{j-1} \phi_0^{j-1} \\ &+ \ldots + s_{2^{j-1}-1}^{j-1} \phi_{2^{j-1}-1}^{j-1} + d_0^{j-1} \psi_0^{j-1} \\ &+ \ldots + d_{2^{j-1}-1}^{j-1} \psi_{2^{j-1}-1}^{j-1} \end{aligned}$$

The coefficients, s_i^{j-1} and d_i^{j-1} are generated by convolution of the s_i^j with a set of orthogonal quadrature filters, H and G. For the Haar wavelets, $H = \{\frac{1}{\sqrt{2}}, \frac{1}{\sqrt{2}}\}$ and $G = \{\frac{1}{\sqrt{2}}, \frac{-1}{\sqrt{2}}\}$.

The wavelet-packet transform of a function in S^j is calculated by recursively applying the quadrature filters to the s and d coefficients of the next lower dimension scale space and wavelet space as if each represented a separate scale space. In this way, subspace coefficients are calculated for both the scale space and wavelet space representing the next higher dimension scale and wavelet spaces. Figure 5.9 shows how the quadrature filters are recursively applied to the scale and wavelet subspaces in generating the wavelet-packet transform. If the original function is in S^j then j recursive applications of H and G will result in 2^j orthogonal subspaces, $S_i^0, i = 0, \ldots, 2^j - 1$. At the top level, only a scale space exists and the 2^j function values are the coefficients for the "box" function basis for that space. Selecting the Haar wavelets as the basis functions results in the coefficients of the 2^j orthogonal subspaces, S_i^0, representing a Walsh transform of the original function.

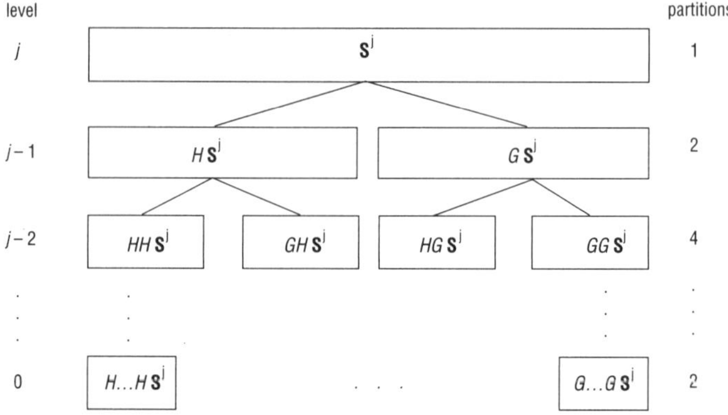

Figure 5.9: Application of quadrature filters in wavelet-packet decomposition.

5.5.2 Polynomial Regression

One technique for implementing polynomial regression using wavelet-based CDM is to first estimate locally the regression coefficients for terms that are based on feature subsets found in a single partition. Once these local coefficients are determined, they and a small subset of the sample data, are communicated to a central site to facilitate estimation of the coefficients for terms based on feature subsets that represent multiple partitions.

Given a partitioned set of real-valued features, $\mathbf{x}$, and a k-term polynomial function of those features, let Ξ_A be the set of indices of terms that are functions only of features found in partition A. In partition A, we can form the terms $T_k(\mathbf{x}), k \in \Xi_A$ of the polynomial for each sample and apply the wavelet-packet transform to the samples representing each term and to the samples of $f(\mathbf{x})$. Estimates of the local model coefficients, $a_k, k \in \Xi_A$, may be generated using standard regression techniques (Mosteller and Tukey 1977) directly on the wavelet-packet transforms since $\mathbf{S}^0_{f(\mathbf{x})} \approx \sum_{k \in \Xi_A} a_k \mathbf{S}_{T_k}$ and the $\mathbf{S}_{T_k}$ are sparse, making them a nearly orthogonal basis for $\mathbf{S}_{f(\mathbf{x})}$. Once the coefficients of the local terms have been estimated, the coefficients of the terms containing cross-partition feature variables may be determined by communicating $O(m)$ samples, as described previously, and using standard system of linear equations or multiple regression techniques, depending on the sample data characteristics.

To demonstrate the CDM regression algorithm using this technique, we consider only the estimation of local model coefficients since it is through these coefficients that a majority of the information contained in the partitioned data set is communicated to the aggregate model. For this example, we consider a quadratic polynomial in 15 real-variables with six nonlinear terms:

$$\begin{aligned} f(\mathbf{x}) = & \; 20x_0 + 5x_0^2 + 18x_1 - 8x_1^2 + 16x_2 + 13x_2^2 + \\ & 14x_3 + 11x_3^2 + 12x_4 - 14x_4^2 + 10x_5 - 8x_5^2 + \\ & 8x_6 + 11x_6^2 + 6x_7 + 13x_7^2 - 7x_8 - 12x_8^2 - \\ & 9x_9 + 15x_9^2 - 11x_{10} + 9x_{10}^2 - 13x_{11} - 10x_{11}^2 - \\ & 15x_{12} - 16x_{12}^2 - 17x_{13} - 10x_{13}^2 - 19x_{14} + 7x_{14}^2 + \\ & 5x_0x_1 - 3x_6x_{10} + 12x_4x_{11} - 8x_{12}x_{14} - 2x_{13}x_2^2 + 4x_4^2x_8^2 \end{aligned}$$

To observe the effect of sample set size, the CDM regression algorithm is applied to a series of data sample sets of increasing size. Each data sample set in the series contains 2^j data samples to allow for a simplified implementation of the wavelet-packet transform algorithm. The data sample set series contains sets for $j = 6, \ldots, 15$. Wickerhauser (1994) provides guidance on implementing the wavelet-packet transform algorithm to handle the general case of sample size $\neq 2^j$. A single data sample consisted of 15 randomly generated values of $x_i, i = 0, \ldots, 14$, and the associated value of $f(\mathbf{x})$ determined by applying those x_is to the polynomial. The random x_i values were generated using the subtractive method given by Knuth (1968). The evaluation results are summarized in figure 5.10 through figure 5.14. Each plot shows the ratio of estimated to actual local term coefficient on the vertical axis and log_2 of the sample set size on the horizontal axis. The plots show that for each local term, as the sample set size increases from 2^6 to 2^{15} the ratio of estimated to actual coefficient value converges toward 1.0. The results demonstrate that the wavelet-packet transform based CDM regression algorithm produces accurate estimates of the model coefficients.

Another technique for implementing polynomial regression using wavelet-based CDM is presented by Hershberger and Kargupta (1999). This second technique differs from the method presented here in that instead of estimating local regression coefficients and communicating these and a sample data subset to a central site, the significant wavelet coefficients for each feature are communicated to a central site. The coefficients of the terms in the polynominal may be estimated by performing the regression directly on the set of significant wavelet coefficients representing those terms. Either technique may provide superior performance relative to the other in terms of higher accuracy and lower communication cost depending on the characteristics of the feature set to which it is applied.

The technique presented by Hershberger and Kargupta (1999) was evaluated using the same polynomial used here. Like the technique presented here, the second technique becomes more accurate as the number of samples in the data set increases. The accuracy of the second technique was also show to inversely depend on the number of terms in the polynomial based on feature subsets that represent multiple partitions and to depend on the compatablilty of the wavelet basis selected with the data characteristics. Moreover, as the obtainable wavelet representation of the data set becomes relatively more sparse, and the wavelet coefficient values less uniform, the technique presented by Hershberger and Kargupta (1999) exhibits relatively better performance, all other factor being equal. In particular, time series data appears to exhibit the characteristics that result in better performance being realized using the second technique. Likewise, in cases where the wavelet representation in relatively less spares with more uniform wavelet coefficient values, the technique presented here performs relatively better.

Finally, Hershberger and Kargupta (1999) presents the results of an application of CDM regression to the problem of classification of the widely bench-marked Iris data (Fisher 1936). Under the assumption that each of the four iris features resided in a separate partition, a three-fold cross validation test produced 90.3% accurate classification using a single wavelet coefficient from each partition to build the aggregate classifier.

The following section describes an experimental system called BODHI for CDM-based distributed knowledge discovery.

5.6 BODHI: A Collective Data Mining Based Experimental System

Application of the CDM to practical problems requires development of a system that employs CDM for distributed knowledge discovery. A successful DDM system should have the following characteristics:

Communication facilities: The system must be able to communicate effectively between the various sites within the context of the system. Furthermore, the system should be built using existing protocols, and not concern itself with the underlying transport protocol (e.g., TCP/IP). The communication facilities of such a system must be able to handle the transfer of raw data, extracted knowledge, commands and command parameters to the learning algorithms, and even the learning algorithms themselves.

Expandibility: There are far too many different approaches and algorithms for machine learning to incorporate them all into a single system, and more are constantly being developed. Therefore, a CDM system must be able to incorporate new algorithms and methods as needed.

Flexibility: The system must be flexible enough to be adapted to different problems, while maintaining the expandibility capabilities noted previously, without significant changes to the core of the system.

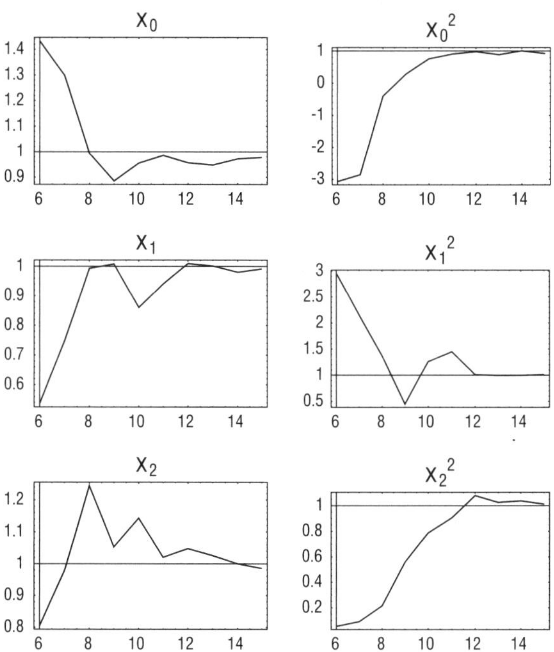

Figure 5.10: Ratio of estimated to actual coefficient value for terms $x_0, x_0^2, x_1, x_1^2, x_2, x_2^2$ converges toward 1.0 as sample size increases.

Mobility: It is important that when portions of the mining process must be performed in a sequential manner, as opposed to a parallel manner, that the CDM system be capable of allowing an algorithm to start at one location and then continue at another location.

Application independent representation of data models: An effective CDM system must be able to convey information regarding the partial data models among the various sites in the environment. This representation should not be system-specific. In other words, various sites must be able to communicate their knowledge in an agreed upon format regardless of the learning algorithm being applied to the problem.

Platform independence: For such a system to function well within the context of a heterogeneous mixture of platforms and operating systems, the system should be made as platform independent as possible.

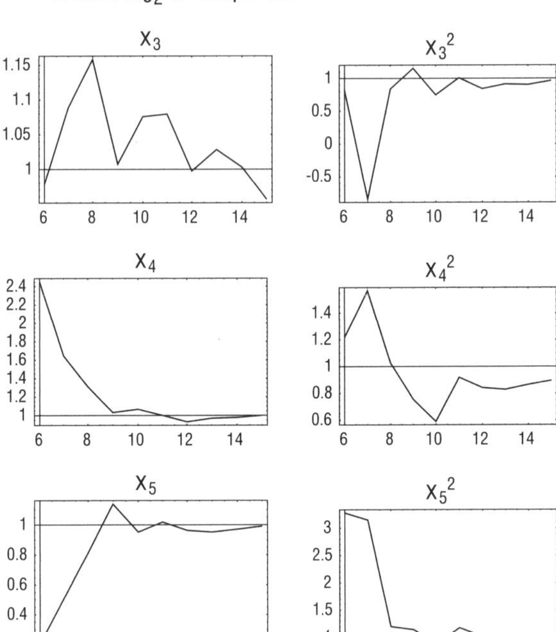

Figure 5.11: Ratio of estimated to actual coefficient value for terms $x_3, x_3^2, x_4, x_4^2, x_5, x_5^2$ converges toward 1.0 as sample size increases.

Security: The issue of security should be addressed. There are three primary areas that need to be addressed: authentication, encryption, and access permissions for the system.

Centralized and distributed control: The system should be able to handle both centralized and distributed control. Implementing centralized control is relatively straight-forward. This mode will be useful when the users of the system are centrally located. On the other hand, a distributed control mechanism will be needed to support collaborative, distributed user-interaction.

The BODHI system, currently under development, addresses all of the above issues. Although additional facets of DDM systems are likely to emerge in the future, we believe the characteristics, listed above, offer a good starting point for developing a DDM system. For example, the BODHI system was first reported in Kargupta, Johnson, Sanseverino, Park, Silvestre, and Hershberger (1998b), and since that point in time it has undergone significant design

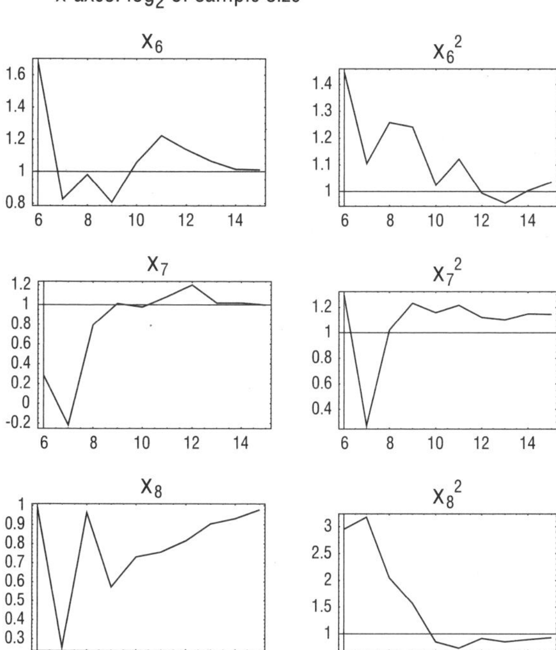

Figure 5.12: Ratio of estimated to actual coefficient value for terms $x_6, x_6^2, x_7, x_7^2, x_8, x_8^2$ converges toward 1.0 as sample size increases.

changes. Some of these changes came from practical issues that arose during the implementation process, and others out of further study and reflection upon the problems being addressed.

5.6.1 Design Principles

The BODHI system is an agent-based, distributed knowledge discovery system, that offers a transparent running environment and message exchange system, capable of handling mobile agents. The primary design goal of the BODHI system was to create a communication system and run time environment for use in collective data mining that was not bound to any specific platform, learning algorithm, or representation of knowledge. It was considered critical not to put limitations upon the system that would prevent its use in a variety of contexts and with a variety of distributed learning applications.

y-axes: Ratio of estimated to actual coefficient value
x-axes: $\log_2$ of sample size

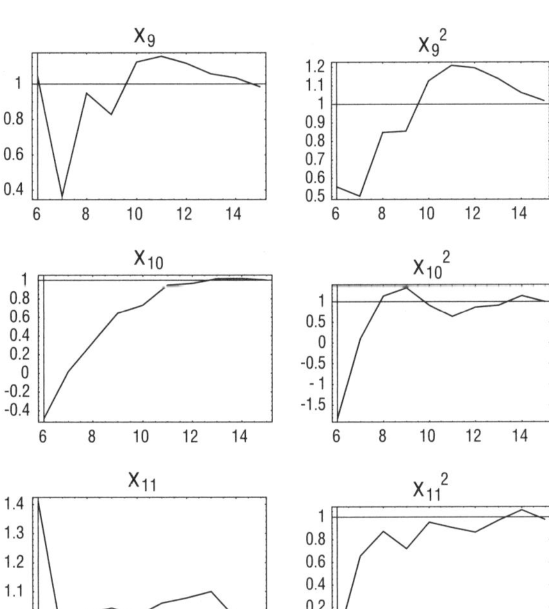

Figure 5.13: Ratio of estimated to actual coefficient value for terms $x_9, x_9^2, x_{10}, x_{10}^2, x_{11}, x_{11}^2$ converges toward 1.0 as sample size increases.

Therefore, the BODHI system was built as an extensible system, providing a framework for communication between, and control of, distributed agents within the system, but without being bound to any specific platform, knowledge representation or machine learning algorithms. To prevent the limitation of the platforms upon which the system could be used, the core of the system was developed using Java. In order to prevent limitations being placed upon the use of the system concerning the learning algorithms utilized or the knowledge and data format, the system provides a generic, extensible framework that is easily adapted to any number of learning algorithms and knowledge and data formats. It should be noted that the BODHI system operates independently of the learning algorithms implemented in the machine learning agents that operate under its control.

The BODHI system is a modularized system, designed using object oriented principles. There is a precise division of responsibility for various tasks

y-axes: Ratio of estimated to actual coefficient value
x-axes: $\log_2$ of sample size

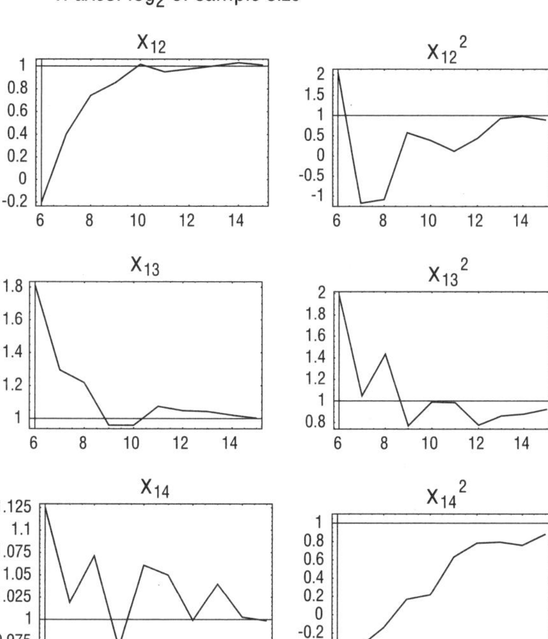

Figure 5.14: Ratio of estimated to actual coefficient value for terms $x_{12}, x_{12}^2, x_{13}, x_{13}^2, x_{14}, x_{14}^2$ converges toward 1.0 as sample size increases.

between the various components of the system. The primary component of the system is the *facilitator module*, which is responsible for directing data and control flow between the various distributed sites and the interfaces. Each local site has a communication module, known as the *agent station,* which is responsible for providing communication between the given local site and other sites, in addition to providing the runtime environment for the agents. Furthermore, the agent stations are responsible for communication security. The agent object within the BODHI framework is an extensible Java object that is used as the interface between the user implemented learning algorithm. This learning algorithm may be implemented either as an extended agent using Java only or as native code on the local machine. The individual agents and their learning algorithms are intended to be autonomous, and to this end, are not provided as a portion of the BODHI system. In the following discussion, the extensible agent class will be referred to simply as the agent class, or simply as an agent, and an agent class that has been extended to perform a specific learning task will be referred to as a learning agent. Finally, the *user interface* forms the final component of this system, and allows the user of the system to control the individual agents and schedule the events occurring within the context of the system as necessary.

The BODHI system is designed as an extensible hierarchy. Forming the base of the hierarchy are the individual agents. These agents are the components within the system that, when extended to specific learning algorithms, perform the actual machine learning for the given task. There may be any number of agents operating on a given site within the system, or no agents, on a given site within the system. Agents within the system are autonomous, with minimal restraints placed upon their implementation. These restrictions and criteria are discussed below, but in general, there are two restrictions: (1) that the agents within a given instantiation of the system be able to communicate using a user defined data and knowledge format, and (2) that certain control functions be implemented in each extended learning agent.

The agent station forms the second layer of the hierarchy. Each distributed site within the system is required to have a single agent station. The agent station on a given site is responsible for starting and stopping the agents operating on its site, in addition to keeping track of the capabilities of the agents upon that site. Furthermore, the agent station is responsible for providing the run time environment for all agents operating under its control, in addition to routing all incoming and outgoing communication from and to agents operating on that site.

The third layer of the hierarchy consists of the facilitator. The facilitator itself, for purposes of ease of communication, is actually an extended agent; however, it should be noted that from a design perspective, the facilitator is higher in the hierarchy than any agent that has been extended to perform a specific machine learning task. The facilitator is responsible, in conjunction with the agent stations, for coordination of communication security. Furthermore, the facilitator is responsible for tracking of access permissions for the individual agents and agent types.

All communication between the individual agents is accomplished using a message subsystem built into the BODHI system. This generic messaging system allows communication between the individual agents, agent stations, the facilitator, and the user interface. This messaging system is based upon a generic message class, which was loosely based upon the KQML format (Finin, Labrou, and Mayfield 1997), and is intended to allow new types and formats of messages to be added into the system as necessary. A message may carry either data or a command, or some combination thereof.

The message structure within the BODHI system was designed to be as generic as possible, so as not to constrain future expansions of the system, or limit the capabilities of the system through unnecessary constraints being placed upon the representation of the knowledge or data. Therefore, it is the responsibility of the individual agent to be aware of any message types that the given agent may encounter. Furthermore, when a new agent is added to the system, the knowledge and data formats understood by the new agent are registered in the facilitator.

Two types of security issues arose during the design process for the BODHI system: security of transmissions and access control of the various individual agents. Security of transmissions between two different sites was considered to be a critical point in the design of the system. In particular, two concerns arose: (1) that outsiders might be able to insert commands or data into the flow of messages within the system, and (2) that outsiders might be able to intercept data when it was transmitted from one site to another. These issues are being addressed through the current ongoing implementation of an RSA (Rivest, Shamir, and Adleman 1978) based encryption scheme. The issue of access control for the individual agents is currently being addressed through the development of a system of permissions, based both upon permissions for an individual agent and permissions based upon types of agents and the "domain" within which they are operating.

The BODHI system was designed to perform certain specific tasks, including control related tasks, such as initialization, shutdown, and movement of agents, and data flow related tasks, such as the transfer of raw data and extracted knowledge between the individual agents and the end user. The minimal set of basic functionality provided within the BODHI system is listed below:

Initialization and shutdown: One of the primary tasks of the system is to initialize and shut down the system on trusted remote sites.

Agent control: The BODHI system provides the basic framework for passing of control sequences to and between the agents and agent stations within the system. While it is required that a set of basic commands be incorporated into all agent types that are to be incorporated into the system, the specific implementation of these commands is left to the user of the system. Of course, additional commands may be added to individual agent implementations as needed.

Agent mobility: In many cases, it is necessary for an agent to act as a mobile agent. As all agents are extensions of a basic agent object, the BODHI system is easily capable of transferring an agent from one site to another, along with the agent's environment, configuration, current state, and learned knowledge.

Transmission of information: The BODHI system provides the basic functionality for the agents to communicate information, both knowledge and data, to other agents within the system. As with the control flow capabilities pro-

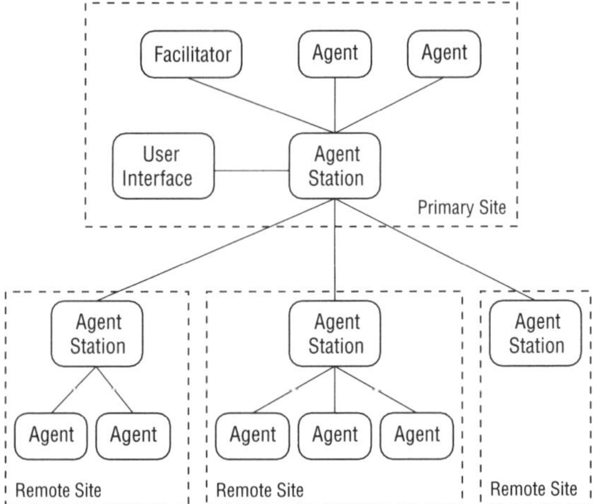

Figure 5.15: Overall systems diagram for the BODHI system.

vided by the BODHI system, many of the specifics of the type and format of the information and data are left to the end user. To wit, the framework for passing data is provided by the message subsystem, but the type and content are fields within the messages themselves that may be defined by the end user.

User interface: The BODHI system is designed to allow the distributed mining process to be controlled through a user interface that resides upon the primary, initializing node within the system. Therefore, the BODHI system provides the framework for the user interface to monitor and control the agents within the system. While the specific interfaces for specific agents are not provided, when an agent is extended to perform a specific machine learning task, the user interface must be likewise extended.

5.6.2 System Components

The BODHI system consists of five primary component types: (1) the individual agents, which are autonomous entities that perform specific learning tasks; (2) the agent stations, which are responsible for providing the run time environment and for communication between the agents and other sites within the system; (3) the facilitator, which is responsible for coordinating communication between the various agent stations; (4) the user interface, by which the user of the system is able to configure and control the system, and (5) the individual messages, which are passed through the system. Each of these is described below.

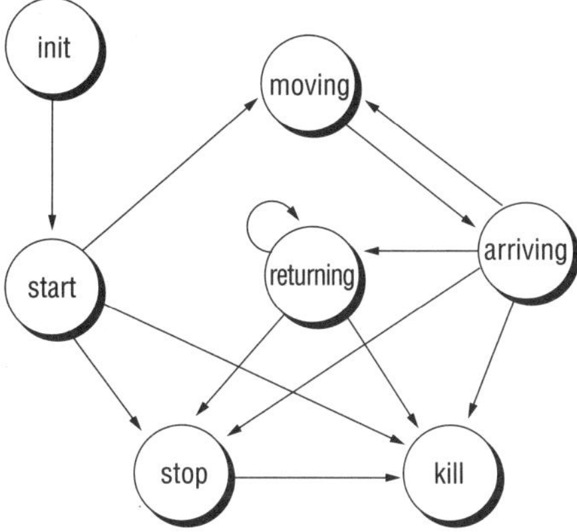

Figure 5.16: Life cycle state diagram for an agent within the BODHI system.

Agents

Agent is the extensible base class for any specific learning algorithm to be incorporated into the BODHI system. The BODHI system does not provide any specific learning algorithms bound to the agent class. Rather, the basis for using the agent class as the interface between the actual learning agent and the rest of the BODHI system is provided. It should be noted that the actual machine learning algorithm may be implemented as a Java extension to the agent class, or by extending the agent class in such a manner as to cause it to call native code on the host machine for the agent.

Agents in the BODHI system are mobile entities; that is, they are capable of being transferred from one site to another. When an agent moves from one site to another, all necessary information for the agent, including its current state, store of acquired knowledge, environment, and configuration, is moved with the agent.

There are seven methods that reflect the various states of the life cycle of an agent. These methods must be extended for each particular type of learning agent to be used within the system. While this is not intended to be a manual on the use of the BODHI system, it is informative to examine the basis for these seven methods that reflect the life cycle of the agents:

(1) The *init* method initializes the agent. All necessary initializations for the configuration of the agent are performed using this method.

(2) The *start* method initiates the actual main learning algorithm that the agent is to perform.

(3) The *moving* method is used to prepare the agent to be moved from one site to another. When an agent is to be moved, all configuration information,

acquired knowledge, environment information and current state must be bundled with the agent. Once this has been accomplished, the agent's agent station transmits the agent as a message. It is necessary once the agent has moved to another site to call the *arriving* method. The agent is required to maintain a list of sites that have been visited.

(4) The *arriving* method is the method used to restore an agent after it has been moved from one site to another. This method will restore the state of the agent at the new site, and will then cause the agent to continue in its learning process from where it left off at the point that the moving call was made.

(5) The *returning* method is similar to the moving method; however, in this case, the agent is prepared to return to the site from whence it originally came.

(6) The *stop* method stops the execution of the learning algorithm, and finalizes the results of the learning process. Once the any necessary cleanup has been performed, the kill method is called.

(7) The *kill* method halts the execution of the agent, and removes the agent from the system without any finalization processes being called.

Each agent is also associated with its own message queue. It is the responsibility of the individual agent to check the status of the queue periodically, and to respond to the messages within the queue as is appropriate. Certain control messages arriving at an agent's site (via the agent station) concerning that agent may be trapped and acted upon by the agent station (see below). It is the responsibility of the agent station to check if the arriving message is of this type (e.g., a kill message). If the arriving message does not fall into this category, it is simply placed in the agent's message queue, and becomes the agents responsibility to act on as needed.

Each individual agent and agent type is associated with certain permissions that control which sites, and in which domains, an agent may be instantiated, and what sort of movement is allowed. Furthermore, agents and agent types are associated with certain file system privileges. For more information, see the following section concerning security.

Agent Stations

Each node within the system contains a single instance of an agent station. The agent station is a daemon process responsible for providing the runtime environment for the agents, and passing messages between the individual agents, other agent stations, and facilitator. In addition, all encryption and decryption of all messages is performed by the agent station. The individual agents are never permitted direct access to any of the encryption and decryption routines.

The agent station at a given node is responsible for a number of specific tasks. It is the responsibility of the agent station to receive messages passed from other nodes within the system, and either take action upon them imme-

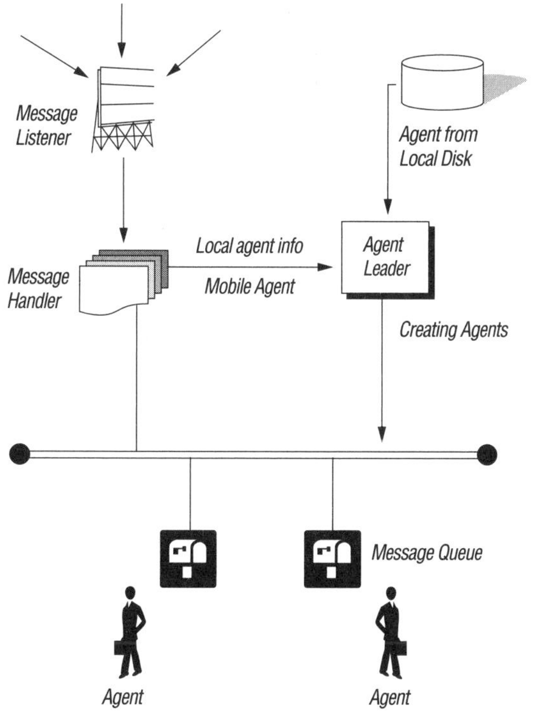

Figure 5.17: Communication flow within a BODHI agent station.

diately or to pass them to the appropriate agent under the control of the agent station via that agent's message queue. It is also the responsibility of the agent station to initialize the individual agents when they are called into existence, and to clean up after the agents.

When a message is received at a given agent station, through a special message listener, that message is passed to the message handler. If the received message is an instruction to create a new instance of an agent, the message handler passes the message to an agent loader, which is then responsible for creating the new instance of the agent from either the network or from the local file system. Otherwise, the message is passed to the message queue of the individual agent, and it becomes the responsibility of the agent to act upon it.

Prior to loading a new agent, the agent loader will verify that the request for the generation of the new instance of an agent is permissible and possible. A special configuration class associated with the agent is used for this verification that lists all of the necessary components of the agent to be generated, such as necessary classes and other external files. Furthermore, the representation and knowledge type is verified to be the same as the other agents operating under the system to ensure compatibility between the instantiated agents.

The Facilitator

The facilitator for the system is itself a special purpose agent. However, it is not intended to perform a machine learning task; rather, the job of the facilitator is to coordinate the communication and control flow between the individual agents. The facilitator is also responsible routing messages between the agents, and tracking the location of the individual agents.

The facilitator, like any other derived agent, operates under an agent station. Therefore, as with any other agent type, the facilitator never is to be allowed direct access to the encryption and decryption routines. However, unlike any other agent type, the facilitator is not permitted to move from one site to another; it must remain at the site where it originated.

The primary task of the facilitator is to coordinate communication between the agents. To this end, the facilitator is able to respond appropriately to several calls similar to the KQML scheme: ask one, ask all, tell one, and tell all. These functions allow a message routed through the facilitator to be sent to the appropriate destination or destinations.

The facilitator is responsible for resolution of the type and content of the knowledge represented in the messages passed between agents. When such resolution is necessary, the request will be passed up from the agent through the agent station and to the facilitator, which will then pass the response back to the agent.

Finally, the facilitator is responsible for pre-scheduled coordination of tasks within the overall system by the various agents and agent stations. To this end, when such a scheduling is necessary, the facilitator class is extended to include this functionality. As with much of the other adaptive functionality within this system, the framework for the functionality is provided, but it is left to the end user to implement the specific algorithms.

User Interface

The user interface for the BODHI system is designed, as are the other components of the system, to be expandable and adaptable to the types of agents that the user may incorporate into the system. Therefore, the base user interface is not intended to be the final user interface, but rather, a general basis for controlling the system.

The user interface of the BODHI system runs on the same machine as the facilitator, and communicates through the facilitator to the other components within the system. The user interface process cannot move from the machine that it was started upon.

Messages

Messages are the final component of the BODHI system. All communication between the various components, including all agents, the user interface and the facilitator, of the BODHI system is accomplished using messages. Once the security subsystem is implemented, all messages are to be encrypted by the agent station at the sending machine, and are to be decrypted by the receiving machine's agent station. Furthermore, every message will be signed so as to allow verification of the origin of the message.

In order to preserve the ability for the system to handle any data, knowledge or control strings needed for a given use of the system, the message format is defined in such a manner as to allow it to carry virtually any kind of content. The message consists of four primary sections: the envelope, the message type, the content description, and the message content.

The envelope portion of the message is the addressing portion of the message. This allows the sender and receiver, in addition to the node (agent station) where the sender and receiver are operating, to be identified. The envelope portion of the message contains four primary entries: the sender, the receiver, the sending agent station, and the receiving agent station. It should be noted that it is the responsibility of the facilitator to route the message; when the sender sends the message, it does not need to know the actual, real location (i.e., IP address) of the recipient; it need only know the system-assigned name of the recipient.

The message type determines what the purpose of the message is. The message type can be divided into three types, which are further divided into subparts. These three primary types are command, ask, and tell. The command type of message passes a command to either an agent station, telling that station to perform some action, such as creating an agent, or to an individual agent. The ask type is a request for information from a specific agent, and may be either a unicast or broadcast request for information. The tell type is an agent's way of sending data, and also can be of a unicast or broadcast type.

The content description of a message is a code signifying what the content of the message contains, and allows the recipient to parse the content of the message. It is the responsibility of the facilitator to maintain the table of types of messages, and it is further the responsibility of the specific agent to be able to respond to the message in an appropriate manner.

Finally, the content portion of the message is the main body of the message. Its encoding is determined by the content description field of the message. It is the responsibility of the individual agent to be able to understand this section based upon what the content description of the message indicates the format of the content section to be.

5.6.3 Security Issues

There are two types of security issues relating to the BODHI system. The first is message security, and involves outsiders being able to impersonate or intercept transmissions. The second issue involves user (or agent) privileges in terms of locations upon which an agent may operate, and what data it is able to access as it moves from one site to another.

Message Security

There were two primary concerns relating to message security during the design. The first concern was that outsiders might be able to insert a command or data message into the system. The second concern was that an outsider might be able to intercept data when it was transmitted from one node to another. It should be noted that at a given site, the BODHI portion of the system operates as a single threaded process, and therefore, there is no danger of interception of messages between an agent and its agent station.

The description of the security portion of the BODHI system is based upon the design performed. The actual implementation of the security system is still underway.

The approach to message security to be taken within the BODHI system involves two phases. First, the initial transmission that creates a new agent station on a remote machine is to be encrypted using an RSA public key encryption scheme. This requires that the remote machine have a private key associated with it, and that the initial node have the public key for the remote machine.

Included as an argument to the (encrypted) initialization command to the agent station process at the remote machine will be a private key. The associated public key will be broadcast to the other agent stations within the system. All future transmissions to the new agent station will be signed by the sender, and encrypted using the public key. This will ensure that false messages cannot be inserted into the system, and, furthermore, that the messages cannot be intercepted by an outside party.

Access Control

The second security issue relating to this sort of system involves access control, and control permissions. It is necessary that the data available to a given agent be controlled, especially when an agent may move from site to site. Furthermore, it is necessary that, as agents are allowed to send control commands to one another, that there be a method for controlling permissions for agents issuing commands to one another.

Access control is performed by associating a list of permissions with each individual agent and agent type. The facilitator is responsible for keeping track of these permissions. These permissions include the listing of the sites an agent is allowed to operate upon, what sort of agent movement is permissible, and what files are available upon the local file systems to the specific agent and type of agent. There is a global configuration for each type of agent, listing these parameters. When instance of an agent is instantiated, these permissions may be modified. It should be noted that this modification may include a further limitation of the permissions, but never an increase in the available permissions.

5.7 Conclusions and Future Work

Heterogeneous data sites are common in business, government, defense, and scientific information processing environments. The field of DDM must develop a well-grounded approach to deal with this general situation. Without that DDM is unlikely to be a viable alternative to current centralized data mining systems. The CDM technology offers one possible approach to this. The material presented in this chapter is a result of our preliminary investigation and the framework is currently further explored and extended (Hershberger and Kargupta 1999; Johnson and Kargupta 1999). However, the preliminary results demonstrate that CDM may offer a well grounded methodology for generating accurate global data models in a distributed fashion.

The CDM notes that almost all the practical data models have polynomial description. As a result it is often possible to find a polynomial description of a data model in some appropriate representation. If we can do that, we should also be able to build the model in a distributed fashion with only polynomially bounded amount of communication. As we see, the success of the CDM depends upon finding an appropriate representation and designing efficient algorithms to compute such representation. In this chapter we have seen that this may be possible for polynomial regression and decision trees. We need to investigate this approach for other types of data models like Bayesian, hidden Markov models, and neural networks. We are also extending the CDM work to the domain of unsupervised learning algorithms like hierarchical clustering (Johnson and Kargupta 1999). Additional work on efficient construction of orthonormal representations, BODHI system development, multi-media DDM, and various applications is ongoing.

Acknowledgements

The authors would like to acknowledge support from the National Science Foundation Grant IIS-9803360 and the American Cancer Society.

Chapter 6

Robust Order Statistics-based Ensembles for Distributed Data Mining

Kagan Tumer and Joydeep Ghosh

6.1 Mining of Distributed Data Sources

An implicit assumption in traditional statistical pattern recognition and machine learning algorithms is that the data to be used for model development is available as a single flat file. This assumption is valid for virtually all popular benchmark datasets such as those available from ELENA, Statlog or the UCI machine learning repository. Such datasets are small or medium sized, requiring a few megabytes at most. Thus the algorithms typically also assume that the entire data can fit in main memory, and do not address computational issues regarding scalability and "out-of-core" operations.

The tremendous explosion in the amount of data gathering and warehousing in the past few years has generated very large and complex databases.

Any effort in mining information from such databases has to address the fact that (1) data may be kept in several files as in interlinked relational databases, and information needed for decision making may be spread over more than one file. For example, the concept of "collective data mining" (see chapter 5) explicitly addresses "vertical partitioning" situations where the features or variables relevant to a classification decision are spread over multiple files, each accessible to only one classifier; (2) the files may be spread across several disks or even across different geographical locations, and (3) the statistical quality of data may vary widely. For example the percentage of cases involving financial or health-care fraud varies in different regions, and so does the amount of missing information.

One can argue that by transfering all data to a single warehouse and performing a series of merges and joins, one can get a single (albeit very large), flat file. A traditional algorithm can be used after randomizing and subsampling this file. But in real applications this approach may not be feasible because of the computational, bandwidth and storage costs. In certain cases, it may not even be possible for a variety of practical reasons including security, privacy, proprietary nature of data, need for fault tolerant distribution of data and services, real-time processing requirements, statutary constraints imposed by law, etc. (see chapter 3). Then there are two options. If the owners of the individual databases are willing to provide high level or summary information/decisions such as local classification estimates, and transmit this information to a central location, then a metalearner can be applied to the component decisions to come up with a final, composite decision. Note that such high level information not only has reduced storage and bandwidth requirements, but also maintains the privacy of individual records (DuMouchel 1999. Otherwise one has to resort to a distributed computing framework such as the emerging field of collective intelligence (COIN), wherein techniques are developed such that local and independent computations can still increase a desired global utility function (Wolpert and Tumer 1999).

The first option leads to several issues reminiscent of studies in decision fusion (Dasarathy 1994) applied largely to multi-sensor fusion and distributed control problems. It is also related to the theory of ensembles (Sharkey 1996) and integration of multiple learned models (Chan, Stolfo, and Wolpert 1996). But there are substantial new aspects that need to be addressed in a distributed data mining context.

This chapter is rooted in the ensemble framework and shows how order statistics can be used in the design of a "metalearner" that examines the outputs of multiple distributed classifers and provides a final decision. Order statistics is one of the key tools of robust statistics, tailored to handling data with outliers. In a distributed data mining scenario in which there is wide variability among the individual classifers because of the underlying quality of the local data that they examine, a metalearner should be able to tolerate a few outlier classifier results. The robust properties of order statistics based approaches such as median filtering and m-estimators (Arnold, Balakrishnan, and Nagaraja 1992), have been observed in many disciplines. Thus they are an obvious candidate for metalearning in such environments.

The next section provides a brief review of the metalearning framework for classification to put the proposed techniques in perspective. Section 6.3 summarizes the relationship between classifier errors and decision boundaries and provides the necessary background for mathematically analyzing order statistic combiners (Tumer and Ghosh 1996a). Section 6.4 introduces simple order statistic combiners. Based on these concepts, in section 6.5 we propose two powerful combiners, *trim* and *spread*, and derive the amount of error reduction associated with each. In section 6.6 we present the performance of order statistic combiners on several datasets. Section 6.7 discusses the implications of using linear combinations of order statistics as a strategy for pooling the outputs of individual classifiers.

6.2 A Brief History of Multi-Learner Systems

The idea of integrating multiple models for the *same* problem, has been examined for a long time. The main goal is to obtain a better composite global model, with more accurate and reliable estimates or decisions. Some notable early systems include Selfridge's Pandemonium (Selfridge 1958) where a head-deamon would select the deamon that "shouted the loudest," and Nilsson's committee machines. A strong motivation for such systems was voiced by Kanal in his classic 1974 paper (Kanal 1974):

> "It is now recognized that the key to pattern recognition problems does not lie wholly in learning machines, statistical approaches, spatial, filtering, ..., or in any other particular solution which has been vigorously advocated by one or another group during the last one and a half decades as the solution to the pattern recognition problem. No single model exists for all pattern recognition problems and no single technique is applicable to all problems. Rather what we have is a bag of tools and a bag of problems."

In the late 1970s, much work was done on combining linguistic and statistical models, and on combining heuristic search with statistical pattern recognition. Subsequently, similar sentiments on the importance of multiple approaches were also voiced in the AI community (Minsky 1991):

> "To solve really hard problems, we'll have to use several different representations. ... It is time to stop arguing over which type

> of pattern-classification technique is best. ... Instead we should work at a higher level of organization and discover how to build managerial systems to exploit the different virtues and evade the different limitations of each of these ways of comparing things."

Integration of multiple data sources and / or learned models can now be found in several disciplines, for example, the combining of estimators in econometrics (Granger 1989), evidences in rule-based systems (Barnett 1981) and multi-sensor data fusion (Dasarathy 1994). Of course, one can find numerous examples in the human central nervous system (Shepherd 1979), as well as in some large engineering systems such as those that demand fault tolerance or employing control mechanisms that may need to function in different operating regimes (Narendra, Balakrishnan, and Ciliz 1995). In particular, multiple models for nonlinear control has a long tradition.[1] Hybridization in a broader sense is seen in efforts to combine two or more of neural network, Bayesian, GA, fuzzy logic and knowledge-based systems (Aggarwal, Ghosh, Nair, and Taha 1996,Taha and Ghosh 1997). The goal is again to incorporate diverse sources and forms of information and to exploit the somewhat complementary nature of different methodologies.

Figure 6.1 shows a generic diagram of an *ensemble*, the simplest and most well understood type of multi-learner systems. Each component learner is a regressor or classifier, trying to solve the same task. While data ultimately originates from an underlying universal set X, each learner may receive somewhat different subsets of the data for "training" or parameter estimation (as in bagging [Breiman, 1996a] and boosting [Drucker, Cortes, Jackel, LeCun, and Vapnik 1994]), and may be using different feature extractors (fs) on the same raw data. For example, in our earlier work on sonar classification (Ghosh, Deuser, and Beck 1992), Fourier, wavelet and autoregressive coefficients extracted from the same preprocessed time series were used respectively for three different classifier types.

Along with selection of training samples and feature extractors, one needs to decide what types of learners to use and how many, and finally, how to design the metalearner. There are also larger issues of how to train the components given that they are part of a bigger system, and to estimate the overall gains achievable.

The simplest metalearner is the *combiner*, where the output y is determined solely from the outputs of the individual learners. In the past few years, a host of experimental results from both neural network and machine learning communities show that combining the outputs of multiple regressors or classifiers via (weighted) averaging, majority vote, product rule, entropy, etc., pro-

---

[1] See www.itk.ntnu.no/ansatte/Johansen_ Tor.Arne/mmamc/address.html for a detailed list of researchers in this area.

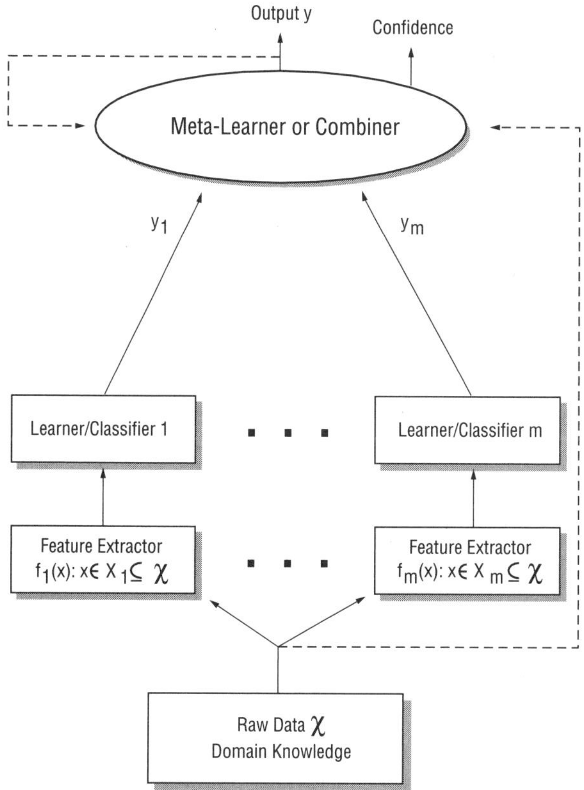

Figure 6.1: Generic architecture of a multi-learner system for regression or classification.

vides statistically significant improvement in performance along with tighter confidence intervals. Moreover, theoretical analysis has been developed for both regression (Perrone 1993, Hashem and Schmeiser 1993) and classification (Tumer and Ghosh 1996a, 1999), to estimate the gains achievable.

Beyond simple combiners are metalearning methods such as arbitration (Chan and Stolfo 1997) and stacking (Wolpert 1992). Also in this category are divide-and-conquer approaches, where relatively simple learners specialize in different parts of the input-output space, and the total model is a (possibly soft) union of such simpler models. Techniques of modular learning include "mixtures-of-experts," local linear regression, CART/MARS, adaptive subspace models, etc. (Jordan and Jacobs 1994; Ramamurti and Ghosh 1999; Holmstrom, Koistinen, Laaksonen, and Oja 1997). What distinguishes all these models from simple combiners is that the metalearner's actions now also depends on the current input and/or the target values, i.e. the dotted lines in figure 6.1 are also used.

The simple combining methods are best suited for problems where the individual classifiers perform the same task, and have comparable success. However, such combiners are more susceptible to outliers and to unevenly performing classifiers. On the other hand, the more general metalearners are conceptually more powerful but are vulnerable to all the problems associated with the added learning (e.g., overparameterizing, lengthy training time). They may also require access to the entire input database which may be impractical in a distributed data mining environment.

The performance of classifier ensembles has been spectacular. Brieman calls the combination of decision tree classifiers with boosting the most significant development in classifier design in this decade. Indeed, ensemble methods are even becoming available in commercial data mining tools such as SAS Enterprise Miner Version 3.0. To see intuitively why ensembles have been so effective, note that different types of classifiers have different "inductive biases" (Geman, Bienenstock, and Doursat 1992; Mitchell 1997b), and thus, in general, they do not generalize in identical ways even when they are trained on the same data set, and have comparable performance on a test set. Traditionally, the classifier perceived as the "best," as indicated by a suitable scoring function such as a cross-validation based estimation of the true generalization error, is selected. This means that the other classifiers that had been designed during the model exploration/development phase, get discarded. But this results in a potential loss of useful information and effort. An ensemble can effectively make use of such complementary information to reduce model variance (Perrone 1993, Tumer and Ghosh 1999) and in certain situations it also reduces bias as shown by the theory of large margin classifiers (Bartlett and Shawe-Taylor, 1998). It works best when each learner is well trained, but different learners generalize in different ways, i.e., there is diversity in the ensemble (Krogh and Vedelsby 1995). Diversity may be induced through different presentations of the input data, as in bagging, variations in learner design, or by adding a penalty to the ouputs to encourage diversity.

For large data sets, there is also a computational reason for using metalearners, namely, it can make certain inductive learners fairly scalable to large data sets (Chan and Stolfo 1997; Provost and Kolluri 1999; also see chapter 1 in this book). In Chan and Stolfo (1997) each component classifier uses a randomly chosen subset of the entire data set, and the decision tree classifiers can operate in parallel. This proves quite effective as overall computation can be greatly reduced with little loss in performance. A beneficial side-effect of using smaller datasets for decision tree classifiers is that the classifiers obtained are smaller in size (Oates and Jensen 1998). These two as well as other scalability techniques for decision tree based classifiers are covered in a nice recent survey (Provost and Kolluri 1999).

A fundamental assumption in all the multi-classifier approaches mentioned above is that the designer has access to the entire data set, which can be used in its entirety, resampled in a random (bagging) or weighted (boosting) way (Breiman 1999), or randomly partitioned and distributed. Thus, except for boosting situations, each classifier sees training data of comparable quality. If the individual classifiers are then appropriately chosen and trained properly, their performances will be (relatively) comparable in any region of the problem space. So gains from combining are derived from the diversity among classifiers rather that by compensating for weak members of the pool.

This assumption is clearly invalid for distributed data mining using heterogenous sites (see chapter 5). Such real-life conditions often result in a pool of classifiers that may have significant variations in their overall performance. Moreover, they may lead to conditions where individual classifiers have similar average performance, but substantially different performance over different parts of the input space. In such cases, combining is still desirable, but neither simple combiners nor metalearners are particularly well-suited for the type of problems that arise. For example, the simplicity of averaging the classifier outputs is appealing, but the prospect of one poor classifier corrupting the combiner makes this a risky choice. Weighted averaging of classifier outputs appears to provide some flexibility (Hashem and Schmeiser 1993, Merz and Pazzani 1997). Unfortunately, the weights are still assigned on a per classifier basis rather than a per sample or per class basis. If a classifier is accurate only in certain areas of the input space, this scheme fails to take advantage of the variable accuracy of the classifier in question. Using a metalearner that provides different weights for different patterns can potentially solve this problem, but at a considerable cost. Also, as explained earlier, the off-line training of a metalearner using substantial amount of data outputted by geographically distributed classifiers, may not be feasible or even allowable. In addition to providing robustness demanded in such situations, the order statistic combiners presented in this work also aim at bridging the gap between simplicity and generality by allowing the flexible selection of classifiers without the associated cost of training metaclassifiers.

6.3 Error Characterization in a Single Classifier

In this section we summarize the approach and results of Tumer and Ghosh (1996a, 1999),[2] that quantify the effect of inaccuracies in estimating a posterior class probabilities on the classification error for a single classifier. This

[2]This and other related papers can be downloaded from www.lans.ece.utexas.edu.

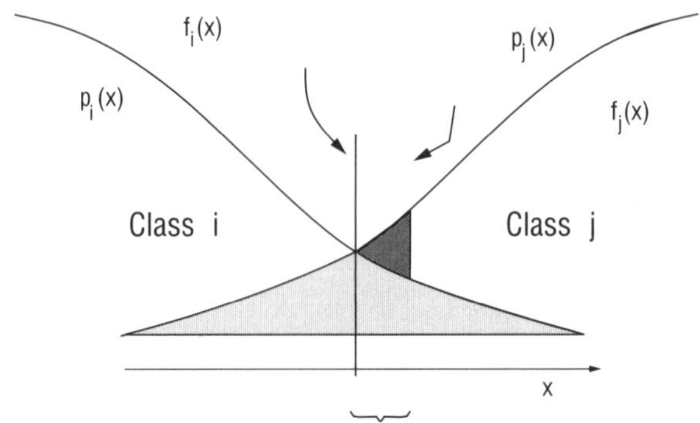

Figure 6.2: Error regions associated with approximating the a posteriori probabilities (Tugh 1996).

background is needed to characterize and understand the impact of order statistics combiners, as described in sections 6.3 and 6.4.

It is well known that, given *one-of-L* desired outputs and sufficient training samples reflecting the class priors, the outputs of certain classifiers trained to minimize a mean square or cross-entropy error criteria, approximate the a posteriori probability densities of the corresponding classes (Richard and Lippmann 1991; Ruck, Rogers, Kabrisky, Oxley, and Suter 1990). Based on this result, one can model the ith output of the mth such classifier as:

$$f_i^m(x) = p_i(x) + \epsilon_i^m(x), \tag{6.1}$$

where $p_i(x)$ is the true posterior for ith class on input x, and $\epsilon_i^m(x)$ is the error of the mth classifier in estimating that posterior.

Now, let us decompose the error into two parts: $\epsilon_i^m(x) = \beta_i^m + \eta_i^m(x)$. The first component does not vary with the input, and provides an offset, or systematic error for each class. The second component gives the variability from that systematic error, for each x in each class, and has zero mean and variance $\sigma^2_{\eta_i^m(x)}$. These two components of the error are similar to the bias and variance decomposition for a quadratic loss function given in Geman, Bienenstock, and Doursat (1992), although they are at the individual input level. We will therefore refer to classifiers as "biased" and "unbiased" implying $\beta_k^m \neq 0$ for some k, m, and $\beta_k^m = 0, \forall k, m$, respectively. Let b^m denote the offset between the ideal class boundary, x^* (based on $p_i(x) = p_j(x)$) and the realized boundary, x_b^m (based on $f_i^m(x) = f_j^m(x)$), as shown in figure 6.2 (Tumer and Ghosh 1996a). This boundary offset ($b^m = x_b^m - x^*$) has mean and variance given respectively by:

$$\beta^m = \frac{\beta_i^m - \beta_j^m}{s}, \tag{6.2}$$

and

$$\sigma_{b^m}^2 = \frac{\sigma_{\eta_i^m(x)}^2 + \sigma_{\eta_j^m(x)}^2}{s^2}, \tag{6.3}$$

where $s = p'_j(x^*) - p'_i(x^*)$ as introduced in Tumer and Ghosh (1996a).

Let us further denote the probability density function of this boundary offset by $f_b(x)$. The expected model error associated with the selection of a particular classifier m, can then be expressed as:

$$E_{model}^m = \int_{-\infty}^{\infty} A(b) f_b(b) db, \tag{6.4}$$

where $A(b) = \int_{x^*}^{x^*+b} \left(p_j(x) - p_i(x)\right) dx$ is the error due to the selection of a particular decision boundary. In general, it is not possible to obtain the density function for the boundary offset without making assumptions on the distributions of the errors. However, a first order approximation, derived in Tumer and Ghosh (1996a), leads to:

$$E_{model}^m = \int_{-\infty}^{\infty} \frac{1}{2} b^2 s f_b(b) db. \tag{6.5}$$

Let us define the first and second moments of the boundary offset as follows:

$$\mathcal{M}_1 = \int_{-\infty}^{\infty} x f_b(x) dx and \mathcal{M}_2 = \int_{-\infty}^{\infty} x^2 f_b(x) dx.$$

If the individual classifiers are unbiased, the offset b^m of a single classifier has $\mathcal{M}_1 = 0$ and $\mathcal{M}_2 = \sigma_{b^m}^2$, leading to:

$$E_{model}^m = \frac{s\mathcal{M}_2}{2} = \frac{s\sigma_{b^m}^2}{2}. \tag{6.6}$$

Now, if the classifiers are biased, the variance of b is left unchanged (given by Equation 6.3), but the mean becomes $\beta = \frac{\beta_i - \beta_j}{s}$. In other words, we have $\mathcal{M}_1 = \beta^m$ and $\sigma_{b^m}^2 = \mathcal{M}_2 - {\mathcal{M}_1}^2$, leading to the following model error:

$$E_{model}^m(\beta) = \frac{s\mathcal{M}_2}{2} = \frac{s}{2}(\sigma_{b^m}^2 + (\beta^m)^2). \tag{6.7}$$

To emphasize the distinction between biased and unbiased classifiers, the model error will be given as a function of β for biased classifiers. A more detailed derivation of class boundaries and error regions is presented in Tumer and Ghosh (1996a). For analyzing the error regions after combining and comparing them to the single classifier case, one needs to determine how the first and second moments of the boundary distributions are affected by combining. The following sections focus on obtaining those values for order statistics based combiners.

6.4 Combining Multiple Classifiers through Order Statistics

We start this section with a discussion of basic concepts, then turn our attention to order statistics combiners. We end the section with an analysis of the error regions for biased classifiers

6.4.1 Basic Concepts

In this section, we briefly discuss some basic concepts and properties of order statistics. Let X be a random variable with probability density function $f_X(\cdot)$, and cumulative distribution function $F_X(\cdot)$. Let $(X_1, X_2, \cdots, X_N)$ be a random sample drawn from this distribution. Now, let us arrange them in nondecreasing order, providing:

$$X_{1:N} \leq X_{2:N} \leq \cdots \leq X_{N:N}.$$

The ith order statistic denoted by $X_{i:N}$, is the ith value in this progression. The cumulative distribution function for the smallest and largest order statistic can be obtained by noting that:

$$F_{X_{N:N}}(x) = P(X_{N:N} \leq x) = \Pi_{i=1}^{N} P(X_{i:N} \leq x) = [F_X(x)]^N$$

and:

$$F_{X_{1:N}}(x) = P(X_{1:N} \leq x) = 1 - P(X_{1:N} \geq x)$$

$$= 1 - \Pi_{i=1}^{N} P(X_{i:N} \geq x)$$

$$= 1 - (1 - \Pi_{i=1}^{N} P(X_{i:N} \leq x) = 1 - [1 - F_X(x)]^N$$

The corresponding probability density functions can be obtained from these equations. In general, for the ith order statistic, the cumulative distribution function gives the probability that exactly i of the chosen X's are less than or equal to x. The probability density function of $X_{i:N}$ is then given by David (1970):

$$f_{X_{i:N}}(x) = \frac{N!}{(i-1)!(N-i)!} [F_X(x)]^{i-1} [1 - F_X(x)]^{N-i} f_X(x). \quad (6.8)$$

This general form however, cannot always be computed in closed form. Therefore, obtaining the expected value of a function of x using equation 6.8 is not always possible. However, the first two moments of the density function are widely available for a variety of distributions (Arnold, Balakrishnan, and Nagaraja 1992). These moments can be used to compute the expected values of certain specific functions, e.g., polynomials of order less than two.

6.4.2 Combining Unbiased Classifiers through Order Statistics

Now, let us turn our attention to order statistics (OS) combiners. For a given input x, let the network outputs of each of the N classifiers for each class i be ordered in the following manner:

$$f_i^{1:N}(x) \leq f_i^{2:N}(x) \leq \cdots \leq f_i^{N:N}(x).$$

Then one constructs the kth order statistic combiner, by selecting the kth ranked output for each class ($f_i^{k:N}(x)$), as representing its posterior.

In particular, *max*, *med* and *min* combiners are defined as follows:

$$f_i^{max}(x) = f_i^{N:N}(x), \quad (6.9)$$

$$f_i^{med}(x) = \begin{cases} \frac{f_i^{\frac{N}{2}:N}(x) + f_i^{\frac{N}{2}+1:N}(x)}{2} & \text{if } N \text{ is even} \\ f_i^{\frac{N+1}{2}:N}(x) & \text{if } N \text{ is odd,} \end{cases} \quad (6.10)$$

$$f_i^{min}(x) = f_i^{1:N}(x). \quad (6.11)$$

These three combiners are relevant because they represent important qualitative interpretations of the output space. Selecting the maximum combiner is equivalent to selecting the class with the highest posterior. Indeed, since the network outputs approximate the class a posteriori distributions, selecting the maximum reduces to selecting the classifier that is the most "certain" of its decision. The drawback of this method however is that it can be compromised by a single classifier that repeatedly provides high values. The selection of the minimum combiner follows a similar logic, but focuses on classes that are unlikely to be correct, rather than on the correct class. Thus, this combiner eliminates less likely classes by basing the decision on the lowest value for a given class. This combiner suffers from the same ills as the *max* combiner. However, it is less dependent on a single error, since it performs a min-max operation, rather than a max-max[3]. The median classifier on the other hand considers the most "typical" representation of each class. For highly noisy data, this combiner is more desirable than either the min or max combiners since the decision is not compromised as much by a single large error.

The analysis that follows does not depend on the particular order statistic chosen. Therefore, we will denote all OS combiners by $f_k^{os}(x)$ and derive the model error, E^{os}_{model}. The network output provided by $f_k^{os}(x)$ is given by:

$$f_k^{os}(x) = p_k(x) + \epsilon_k^{os}(x), \tag{6.12}$$

Let us first investigate the zero-bias case ($\beta_k = 0, \forall k$), where we get $\epsilon_k^{os}(x) = \eta_k^{os}(x)$. Proceeding as in section 6.3, the boundary b^{os} is shown to be:

$$b^{os} = \frac{\eta_i^{os}(x_b) - \eta_j^{os}(x_b)}{s}. \tag{6.13}$$

For *i.i.d.* η_k's, the first two moments will be identical for each class. Moreover, taking the order statistic will shift the mean of both η_i^{os} and η_j^{os} by the same amount, leaving the mean of the difference unaffected. Therefore, b^{os} will have zero mean, and variance:

$$\sigma^2_{b^{os}} = \frac{2\sigma^2_{\eta_k^{os}}}{s^2} = \frac{2\alpha\sigma^2_{\eta_k^m}}{s^2} = \alpha\sigma^2_{b^m}, \tag{6.14}$$

where α is a reduction factor that depends on the order statistic and on the distribution of b. For most distributions, α can be found in tabulated form (Arnold, Balakrishnan, and Nagaraja 1992). For example, table 6.1 provides α values for all order statistic combiners, up to 10 classifiers, for a Gaussian distribution (Arnold, Balakrishnan, and Nagaraja 1992, Sarhan and Greenberg 1956). (Because this distribution is symmetric, the α values of l and k where $l + k = N + 1$ are identical, and listed in parenthesis).

Returning to the error calculation, we have: $\mathcal{M}_1^{os} = 0$, and $\mathcal{M}_2^{os} = \sigma^2_{b^{os}}$, providing:

$$E^{os}_{model} = \frac{s\mathcal{M}_2^{os}}{2} = \frac{s\sigma^2_{b^{os}}}{2} = \frac{s\alpha\sigma^2_{b^m}}{2} = \alpha E^m_{model}. \tag{6.15}$$

Equation 6.15 shows that the reduction in the error due to using the OS combiner instead of the mth classifier is directly related to the reduction in the variance of the boundary offset b. Since the means and variances of order statistics for a variety of distributions are widely available in tabular form, the reductions can be readily quantified.

[3]Recall that the pattern is ultimately assigned to the class with the highest combined output.

N	k	α	N	k	α	N	k	α
1	1	1.00	6	2 (5)	.280		1 (9)	.357
2	1 (2)	.682		3 (4)	.246		2 (8)	.226
3	1 (3)	.560		1 (7)	.392	9	3 (7)	.186
	2	.449	7	2 (6)	.257		4 (6)	.171
4	1 (4)	.492		3 (5)	.220		5	.166
	2 (3)	.360		4	.210		1 (10)	.344
	1 (5)	.448		1 (8)	.373		2 (9)	.215
5	2 (4)	.312	8	2 (7)	.239	10	3 (8)	.175
	3	.287		3 (6)	.201		4 (7)	.158
6	1 (6)	.416		4 (5)	.187		5 (6)	.151

Table 6.1: Reduction factors α for the Gaussian distribution, based on Sarhan and Greenberg (1956).

6.4.3 Combining Biased Classifiers through Order Statistics

In this section, we analyze the error regions for biased classifiers. Let us return our attention to b^{os}. First, note that the error terms can no longer be studied separately, since in general $(a+b)^{os} \neq a^{os} + b^{os}$. We will therefore need to specify the mean and variance of the result of each operation[4]. Equation 6.13 becomes:

$$b^{os} = \frac{(\beta_i + \eta_i(x_b))^{os} - (\beta_j + \eta_j(x_b))^{os}}{s}. \tag{6.16}$$

Let $\bar{\beta}_k = \frac{1}{N}\sum_{m=1}^{N} \beta_k^m$ be the mean of classifier biases. Since η_k^m's have zero-mean, $\beta_k + \eta_k(x_b)$ has first moment $\bar{\beta}_k$ and variance $\sigma^2_{\eta_k^m} + \sigma^2_{\beta_k^m}$, with $\sigma^2_{\beta_k^m} = E[(\beta_k^m)^2] - \bar{\beta}_k^{\,2}$, where $[\cdot]$ denotes the expected value operator.

Taking a specific order statistic of this expression will modify both moments. The first moment is given by $\bar{\beta}_k + \mu^{os}$, where μ^{os} is a shift which depends on the order statistic chosen, but not on the class. Then, the first moment of b^{os} is given by:

$$\frac{(\bar{\beta}_i + \mu^{os}) - (\bar{\beta}_j + \mu^{os})}{s} = \frac{\bar{\beta}_i - \bar{\beta}_j}{s} = \bar{\beta}. \tag{6.17}$$

Note that the bias term represents an "average bias" since the contributions due to the order statistic are removed. Therefore, reductions in bias cannot be obtained from a table similar to table 6.1.

Now, let us turn our attention to the variance. Since $\beta_k^m + \eta_k^m(x_b)$ has variance $\sigma^2_{\eta_k^m} + \sigma^2_{\beta_k^m}$, it follows that $(\beta_k + \eta_k(x_b))^{os}$ has variance $\sigma^2_{\eta_k^{os}} = \alpha(\sigma^2_{\eta_k^m} +$

[4]Since the exact distribution parameters of b^{os} are not known, we use the sample mean and the sample variance.

$\sigma^2_{\beta^m_k}$), where α is the factor discussed in section 6.4.2. Therefore, the variance of b^{os} is given by:

$$\begin{aligned}\sigma^2_{b^{os}} &= \frac{\sigma^2_{\eta_i^{os}} + \sigma^2_{\eta_j^{os}}}{s^2} = \frac{2\alpha\sigma^2_{\eta_i^m}}{s^2} + \frac{\alpha(\sigma^2_{\beta_i^m} + \sigma^2_{\beta_j^m})}{s^2} \\ &= \alpha(\sigma^2_{b^m} + \sigma^2_{\beta^m}), \end{aligned} \tag{6.18}$$

where $\sigma^2_{\beta^m} = \frac{\sigma^2_{\beta_i^m} + \sigma^2_{\beta_j^m}}{s^2}$ is the variance introduced by the systematic errors of different classifiers.

We have now obtained the first and second moments of b^{os}, and can compute the model error. Namely, we have $\mathcal{M}_1^{os} = \bar{\beta}$ and $\sigma^2_{b^{os}} = \mathcal{M}_2^{os} - (\mathcal{M}_1^{os})^2$, leading to:

$$E^{os}_{model}(\beta) = \frac{s}{2}\mathcal{M}_2^{os} = \frac{s}{2}(\sigma^2_{b^{os}} + \bar{\beta}^2) \tag{6.19}$$

$$= \frac{s}{2}(\alpha(\sigma^2_{b^m} + \sigma^2_{\beta^m}) + \bar{\beta}^2). \tag{6.20}$$

The reduction in the error is more difficult to assess in this case. By writing the error as:

$$E^{os}_{model}(\beta) = \alpha\frac{s}{2}(\sigma^2_b + (\beta^m)^2) + \frac{s}{2}(\alpha\sigma^2_\beta + \bar{\beta}^2 - \alpha(\beta^m)^2),$$

we get:

$$E^{os}_{model}(\beta) = \alpha E^m_{model}(\beta) + \frac{s}{2}(\alpha\sigma^2_\beta + \bar{\beta}^2 - \alpha(\beta^m)^2). \tag{6.21}$$

Analyzing the error reduction in the general case requires knowledge about the bias introduced by each classifier. Unlike regression problems where the bias and variance contributions to the error are additive and well-understood, in classification problems their interaction is more complex.[5] Indeed it has been observed that ensemble methods do more than simply reduce the variance (Schapire, Freund, and Bartlett 1997).

Based on these observations and equation 6.21, let us analyze extreme cases. For example, if each classifier has the same bias, σ^2_β is reduced to zero and $\bar{\beta} = \beta^m$. In this case the error reduction can be expressed as:

$$E^{os}_{model}(\beta) = \frac{s}{2}(\alpha\sigma^2_b + (\beta^m)^2 = \alpha E^m_{model}(\beta) + \frac{s(1-\alpha)}{2}(\beta^m)^2,$$

where α balances the two contributions to the error. A small value for α will reduce the first component of the error (mainly variance), while leaving the

[5]See J. H. Friedman's 1997 paper, On Bias, Variance, 0/1-Loss, and the Curse-of-Dimensionality, available at www-stat.stanford.edu/ jhf/#reports.

second term untouched. The net effect will be very similar to results obtained for regression problems. In this case, it is important to reduce classifier bias before combining (e.g., by using an overparametrized model).

If on the other hand, the biases produce a zero mean variable, we obtain $\bar{\beta} = 0$. In this case, the model error becomes:

$$E^{os}_{model}(\beta) = \alpha E^{m}_{model}(\beta) + \frac{s\alpha}{2}(\sigma^2_{\beta^m} - (\beta^m)^2)$$

and the error reduction will be significant if the second term is small or negative. In fact, if the variation among the biases is small relative to their magnitude, the error will be reduced more than in the unbiased cases. If however, the variation is large compared to the magnitude, the error reduction will be minimal. Furthermore, if α is large and the biases are small and highly varied, it is possible for this combiner to do worse than the individual classifiers, which is a danger not present for regression problems. This observation very closely parallels results reported in Friedman (1997).

6.5 Linear Combining of Ordered Classifier Outputs

In the previous section, we derived error reductions when the class posteriors are directly estimated through the ordered classifier outputs. Since simple averaging has also been shown to provide benefits, in this section, we investigate the combinations of averaging and order statistics for pooling classifier outputs.

6.5.1 Spread Combiner

The first linear combination of ordered classifier outputs we study focuses on extrema. As discussed in section 6.4.2, the maximum and minimum of a set of classifier outputs carry specific meanings. Indeed, the maximum can be viewed as the class for which there is the most evidence. Similarly, the minimum deletes classes with little evidence. In order to avoid a single classifier from having too large of an impact on the eventual output, these two values can be averaged to yield the *spread* combiner. This combiner strikes a balance between the positive and negative evidence, leading to a more robust combiner than either of them.

Spread Combiner for Unbiased Classifiers:

For a classifier without bias, the spread combiner is formally defined as:

$$f_i^{spr}(x) = \frac{1}{2}(f_i^{1:N}(x) + f_i^{N:N}(x)) = p(c_i|x) + \eta_i^{spr}(x), \tag{6.22}$$

where:

$$\eta_i^{spr}(x) = \frac{1}{2}\left(\eta_i^{1:N}(x) + \eta_i^{N:N}(x)\right).$$

The variance of $\eta_i^{spr}(x)$ is given by:

$$\sigma^2_{\eta_i^{spr}} = \tfrac{1}{4}\sigma^2_{\eta_i^{1:N}(x)} + \tfrac{1}{4}\sigma^2_{\eta_i^{N:N}(x)} + \tfrac{1}{2}cov(\eta_i^{1:N}(x), \eta_i^{N:N}(x)). \tag{6.23}$$

where $cov(\cdot,\cdot)$ represents the covariance between two variables (even when the η_i's are independent, ordering introduces correlations). Note that because of the ordering, the variances in the first two terms of equation 6.23 can be expressed in terms of the individual classifier variances. Furthermore, the covariance between two order statistics can also be determined in tabulated form for given distributions. Table 6.2 provides these values for a Gaussian distribution based on Sarhan and Greenberg (1956). This expression can be further simplified for symmetric distributions where $\sigma^2_{\eta^{1:N}} = \sigma^2_{\eta^{N:N}}$ (e.g., Gaussian noise model) and leads to:

$$\sigma^2_{\eta_i^{spr}} = \frac{1}{2}\left(\alpha_{1:N} + B_{1,N:N}\right)\sigma^2_{\eta_i(x)}, \tag{6.24}$$

where $\alpha_{m:N}$ is the variance of the mth ordered sample and $B_{m,l:N}$ is the covariance between the mth and lth ordered samples, given that the initial samples had unit variance (Sarhan and Greenberg 1956). Because this is a symmetric distribution, the β values are also symmetric (e.g., $\beta_{1,2:5} = \beta_{4,5:5}$).

Then, using equation 6.3, the variance of the boundary offset b^{spr} can be calculated:

$$\begin{aligned}\sigma^2_{b^{spr}} &= \frac{\sigma^2_{\eta_i{}^{spr}} + \sigma^2_{\eta_j{}^{spr}}}{s^2} \\ &= \frac{1}{2}\left(\alpha_{1:N} + B_{1,N:N}\right)\sigma^2_b.\end{aligned} \tag{6.25}$$

Finally, through equation 6.6, we can obtain the reduction in the model error due to the spread combiner:

$$\frac{E^{spr}_{model}}{E_{model}} = \frac{\alpha_{1:N} + B_{1,N:N}}{2}. \tag{6.26}$$

N	k,l	B	N	k,l	B	N	k,l	B	N	k,l	B
2	1,2	.318		2,3	.189		1,4	.095		1,6	.059
3	1,2	.276	6	2,4	.140		1,5	.075		1,7	.049
	1,3	.165		2,5	.106		1,6	.060		1,8	.040
	1,2	.246		3,4	.183		1,7	.048		1,9	.031
4	1,3	.158		1,2	.196		1,8	.037		2,3	.154
	1,4	.105		1,3	.132		2,3	.163		2,4	.117
	2,3	.236		1,4	.099	8	2,4	.123		2,5	.093
	1,2	.224		1,5	.077		2,5	.098		2,6	.077
	1,3	.148		1,6	.060		2,6	.079	9	2,7	.063
5	1,4	.106	7	1,7	.045		2,7	.063		2,8	.052
	1,5	.074		2,3	.175		3,4	.152		3,4	.142
	2,3	.208		2,4	.131		3,5	.121		3,5	.114
	2,4	.150		2,5	.102		3,6	.098		3,6	.093
	1,2	.209		2,6	.080		4,5	.149		3,7	.077
	1,3	.139		3,4	.166		1,2	.178		4,5	.137
6	1,4	.102		3,5	.130		1,3	.121		4,6	.113
	1,5	.077		1,2	.186	9	1,4	.091			
	1,6	.056	8	1,3	.126		1,5	.073			

Table 6.2: Some Reduction Factors B for the Gaussian Distribution, based on Sarhan and Greenberg (1956).

Based on equation 6.26 and tables 6.1 and 6.2, table 6.3 displays the error reductions provided by the spread combiner for a Gaussian noise model (for comparison purposes, the error reduction for the min and max combiners is also provided. Note that for the Gaussian distribution, the error reduction of min is equal to that of max.).

Spread Combiner for Biased Classifiers:

Now, if the classifier biases are nonzero, the spread combiner's output is given by:

$$\begin{aligned} f_i^{spr}(x) &= \frac{1}{2}(f_i^{1:N}(x) + f_i^{N:N}(x)) \\ &= p(c_i|x) + (\eta_i(x) + \beta_i)^{spr}. \end{aligned} \tag{6.27}$$

In that case, the boundary offset is given by:

$$b^{spr} = \frac{(\beta_i + \eta_i(x_b))^{spr} - (\beta_j + \eta_j(x_b))^{spr}}{s}, \tag{6.28}$$

which after expanding each term and regrouping can be expressed as:

$$\begin{aligned} b^{spr} &= \frac{(\beta_i + \eta_i(x_b))^{1:N} - (\beta_j + \eta_j(x_b))^{1:N}}{2s} \\ &+ \frac{(\beta_i + \eta_i(x_b))^{N:N} - (\beta_j + \eta_j(x_b))^{N:N}}{2s}. \end{aligned} \tag{6.29}$$

N	$spread$	min or max
2	.500	.682
3	.362	.560
4	.299	.492
5	.261	.448
6	.236	.416
7	.219	.392
8	.205	.373
9	.194	.357
10	.186	.344

Table 6.3: Error reduction factors for the spread, min and max combiners with Gaussian noise model.

The first moment of b^{spr} can be obtained by analyzing each term of equation 6.29. In fact, the offset introduced by the first and nth order statistic for classes i and j will cancel each other out, leaving only the average bias between the min and max components of the error (as in equation 6.17), given by $\beta^{spr} = \frac{\beta_i^{1:N} - \beta_j^{1:N} + \beta_i^{N:N} - \beta_j^{N:N}}{s}$.

The variance of b^{spr} needs to be derived from equation 6.29. Proceeding as in equation 6.18, the variance of the spread combiner can be expressed as:

$$\sigma^2_{b^{spr}} = (\frac{1}{4}\alpha_{1:N} + \frac{1}{4}\alpha_{N:N} + \frac{1}{2}B_{1,N:N})(\sigma^2_{b^m} + \sigma^2_{\beta^m}). \tag{6.30}$$

For a symmetric distribution (where $\alpha_{1:N} = \alpha_{N:N}$), we obtain the following error:

$$\begin{aligned} E^{spr}_{model}(\beta) &= \frac{s}{2}\mathcal{M}_2 = \frac{s}{2}(\sigma^2_{b^{spr}} + \mathcal{M}_1{}^2) \\ &= \frac{s}{2}\left(\frac{1}{2}\alpha_{1:N} + \frac{1}{2}B_{1,N:N})(\sigma^2_{b^m} + \sigma^2_{\beta^m}) + (\beta^{spr})^2\right) \\ &= \frac{1}{2}(\alpha_{1:N} + B_{1,N:N})E_{model}(\beta) + \\ &\quad \frac{s}{4}(\alpha_{1:N} + B_{1,N:N})(\sigma^2_{\beta^m} - (\beta^m)^2) + \frac{s}{2}(\beta^{spr})^2, \end{aligned} \tag{6.31}$$

which is very similar to equation 6.21, where the value of α for a single order statistic is now replaced by $\frac{\alpha_{1:N} + B_{1,N:N}}{2}$, since the mean of the first and nth order statistic is used in the posterior estimate.

6.5.2 Trimmed Means

Instead of actively using the extreme values as was the case with the spread combiner, one can base the posterior estimate around the median values. However, instead of selecting one classifier output as was done for f^{med}, one can use multiple classifiers whose outputs are "typical." In this scheme, only a certain fraction of all available classifiers are used for a given pattern. The main advantage of this method over weighted averaging is that the set of classifiers which contribute to the combiner vary from pattern to pattern. Furthermore, they do not need to be determined externally, but are a function of the current pattern and the classifier responses to that pattern.

Trimmed Mean Combiner for Unbiased Classifiers:

Let us formally define the trimmed mean combiner ($\beta_k = 0, \forall k$) as follows:

$$\begin{aligned} f_i^{trim}(x) & \\ &= \frac{1}{N_2 - N_1 + 1} \sum_{m=N_1}^{N_2} f_i^{m:N}(x) \\ &= p(c_i|x) + \eta_i^{trim}(x), \end{aligned} \tag{6.32}$$

where:

$$\eta_i^{trim}(x) = \frac{1}{N_2 - N_1 + 1} \sum_{m=N_1}^{N_2} \eta_i^m(x).$$

The variance of $\eta_i^{trim}(x)$ is given by:

$$\begin{aligned} \sigma^2_{\eta_i^{trim}} & \\ = \frac{1}{(N_2 - N_1 + 1)^2} \sum_{l=N_1}^{N_2} \sum_{m=N_1}^{N_2} cov(\eta_i^{m:N}(x), \eta_i^{l:N}(x)) & \\ &= \frac{1}{(N_2 - N_1 + 1)^2} \\ \left(\sum_{m=N_1}^{N_2} \sigma^2_{\eta_i^{m:N}(x)} + \sum_{m=N_1}^{N_2} \sum_{l>m}^{N_2} 2cov(\eta_i^{m:N}(x), \eta_i^{l:N}(x)) \right). \end{aligned} \tag{6.33}$$

Again, using the factors in tables 6.1 and 6.2, equation 6.33 can be further simplified. Note that because the Gaussian distribution is symmetric, the covariance between the kth and lth ordered samples is the same as that between the $N + 1 - k$th and $N + 1 - l$th ordered samples. Therefore, equation 6.33 leads to:

$$\sigma^2_{\eta_i^{trim}} = \frac{1}{(N_2 - N_1 + 1)^2} \sum_{m=N_1}^{N_2} \alpha_{m:N} \sigma^2_{\eta_i(x)}$$

N	*ave* (for N)	*trim* (for $N_1 = 2$; $N_2 = N - 1$)	*ave* (for $N - 2$)
3	.333	.449	1.00
4	.250	.298	.500
5	.200	.227	.333
6	.167	.184	.250
7	.143	.155	.200
8	.125	.134	.167
9	.111	.113	.143

Table 6.4: Error Reduction factors for trim and two corresponding *ave* combiners with Gaussian noise model.

$$+ \quad \frac{2}{(N_2 - N_1 + 1)^2} \sum_{m=N_1}^{N_2} \sum_{l>m} B_{m,l:N} \sigma^2_{\eta_i(x)}, \tag{6.34}$$

where $\alpha_{m:N}$ is the variance of the mth ordered sample and $B_{m,l:N}$ is the covariance between the mth and lth ordered samples, given that the initial samples had unit variance (Sarhan and Greenberg 1956). Using the theory highlighted in section 6.3, and equation 6.34, we obtain the following model error reduction:

$$\frac{E^{trim}_{model}}{E_{model}} = \frac{1}{(N_2 - N_1 + 1)^2} \left(\sum_{m=N_1}^{N_2} \alpha_{m:N} + 2 \sum_{m=N_1}^{N_2} \sum_{l>m} B_{m,l:N} \right). \tag{6.35}$$

Based on equation 6.35 and tables 6.1 and 6.2, we have generated a sample *trim* combiner reduction table. Because there are many possibilities for N_1 and N_2, a table that exhaustively provides all reduction values is not practical. In this sample table we have selected $N_1 = 2$ and $N_2 = N - 1$, that is, averaging after the lowest and highest values have been removed. For comparison purposes the reduction factors of the averaging combiner for N and $N-2$ classifiers are also provided (for i.i.d. classifiers the reduction factors are 1/N as derived in Tumer and Ghosh [1996a]; similar results were obtained for regression problems [Perrone and Cooper 1993]). As these numbers demonstrate, although $N - 2$ classifiers are used in the trim combiner, selectively weeding out undesirable classifiers provides reduction factors significantly better than simply averaging $N - 2$ arbitrary classifiers. The *trim* combiner provides reduction factors comparable the the N classifier *ave* combiner without being susceptible to corruption by one particularly faulty classifier.

Trimmed mean Combiner for Biased Classifiers:

Now, if the classifier biases are nonzero, the trimmed mean combiner's output is given by:

$$\begin{aligned} f_i^{trim}(x) &= \frac{1}{N_2 - N_1 + 1} \sum_{m=N_1}^{N_2} f_i^{m:N}(x) \\ &= p(c_i|x) + (\eta_i(x) + \beta_i)^{trim}. \end{aligned} \tag{6.36}$$

In that case the boundary offset is given by:

$$b^{trim} = \frac{(\beta_i + \eta_i(x_b))^{trim} - (\beta_j + \eta_j(x_b))^{trim}}{s}. \tag{6.37}$$

The first moment of b^{trim} can be obtained from a manner similar to that of the spread combiner. Indeed, each mean offset introduced by a specific order statistic for class i will be offset by the one introduced for class j. Only the trimmed mean of the biases will remain, giving the first moment of b^{trim}:

$$\beta^{trim} = \frac{1}{N_2 - N_1 + 1} \sum_{m=N_1}^{N_2} \frac{\beta_i^{m:N} - \beta_j^{m:N}}{s}. \tag{6.38}$$

In deriving the variance of b^{trim}, we follow the same steps as in sections 6.4.3 and 6.5.1. The resulting boundary variance is similar to equation 6.18, but the since the reduction is due to the linear combination of multiple ordered outputs, α is replaced by $\mathcal{A}$, where:

$$\mathcal{A} = \frac{1}{(N_2 - N_1 + 1)^2} \left(\sum_{m=N_1}^{N_2} \alpha_{m:N} + 2 \sum_{m=N_1}^{N_2} \sum_{l>m} B_{m,l:N} \right). \tag{6.39}$$

The model error reduction in this case is given by:

$$\begin{aligned} E_{model}^{trim}(\beta) &= \frac{s}{2}\mathcal{M}_2 = \frac{s}{2}(\sigma_{b^{trim}}^2 + \mathcal{M}_1{}^2) \\ &= \frac{s}{2}\left(\mathcal{A}(\sigma_{b^m}^2 + \sigma_{\beta^m}^2) + (\beta^{spr})^2\right) \\ &= \mathcal{A}E_{model}(\beta) + \frac{s}{2}(\mathcal{A}(\sigma_{\beta^m}^2 - (\beta^m)^2) + (\beta^{spr})^2). \end{aligned} \tag{6.40}$$

Once again we need to look at the interaction between the two parts of the error reduction. The first term provides the error reduction compared to the model error of an individual classifier. The smaller $\mathcal{A}$ is, the more error reduction there will be. In the second term, on the other hand, a small value for $\mathcal{A}$ is only useful if the variability in the individual biases is higher than the biases themselves ($\sigma_{\beta^m}^2 > (\beta^m)^2$).

6.6 Experimental Results

The order statistics-based combining methods proposed in this article are tailored for situations where one or more of the following apply: (1) individual classifier performance is uneven and class dependent; (2) it is not possible (insufficient data, high amount of noise) to fine tune the individual classifiers without using computationally expensive methods; and (3) all the features may not be available to all the classifiers.

Such situations occur, for example, in electrical logging while drilling for oil, where data from certain well sites almost completely misses out on portions of the problem space, and in imaging from airborne platforms where the classifiers receive inputs from different satellites and/or different types of sensors (e.g., thermal, optical, SAR). In this article we restrict ourselves to public domain datasets and simulate such variability in two ways, namely, by (1) segmenting the feature set and allowing individual classifiers to have access to only a limited portion of the feature set; and (2) using "early stopping" i.e., prematurely terminating the training of the individual classifiers.[6]

For the experiments reported below, we used a multilayer perceptron (MLP) with a single hidden layer, whose weights were randomly initialized for each run. All classification results reported in this article are test set error rates averaged over 20 runs, along with the differences in the mean (standard deviation divided by square root of the number of runs). Several types of simple combiners such as averaging, weighted averaging, voting, median, products, weighted products (Bayesian), using Dempster-Schafer theory of evidence, and entropy-based averaging, have been proposed in the literature. However, on a wide variety of data sets, it has been observed that simple averaging usually provides results comparable to any of these techniques (and, surprisingly, often better than most of them) (Ghosh, Tumer, Beck, and Deuser 1992; Tumer and Ghosh 1996b). For this reason, in this study, we use the average combiner as a representative of simple combiners, for comparison purposes.

6.6.1 Variability through Segmentation

The first group of experiments focus on classifiers that because of circumstances (e.g., geography) have access to only a part of the full feature set. This situation fits the collective data mining framework wherein a globally distributed dataset is vertically partitioned (see chapter 5). Unfortunately, we are not aware of any public domain datasets for collective data mining, so we instead selected three data sets from the Proben1/UCI benchmarks (Prechelt 1994). Briefly these data sets, and the corresponding size of the MLP used,

[6]In all the experiments reported here, "high variability" means that classifiers in an ensemble were trained half as along as they would have been, had they been stand-alone classifiers.

Data	Number of Original Features	Number of Segments	Features per Segment	
			no Overlap	Overlap
Card	51	4	13-13-13-12	18-18-18-18
Gene	120	4	30-30-30-30	40-40-40-40
Sat	36	4	9-9-9-9	15-15-15-15

Table 6.5: Number of features in Proben1/UCI data sets.

are[7]: Card: a 51-dimensional, 2-class data set based on credit approval decision (Quinlan 1987b), with 690 patterns; an MLP with 10 hidden units; Gene: a 120-dimensional data set with two classes, based on the detection of splice junctions in DNA sequences (Noordewier, Towell, and Shavlik 1991), with 3175 patterns; an MLP with 10 hidden units; Satellite: a 36-dimensional, 6-class data set with 6435 examples of feature vectors extracted from satellite imagery; an MLP with 20 hidden units.

These three sets were chosen as they have relatively large number of features, somewhat large number of data points, and have been studied by several researchers. Also note that the Proben1 benchmarks are particular training, validation and test splits of the UCI data sets.[8] The results presented in this article are based on the first training, validation and test partition discussed in Prechelt (1994), where half the data is used for training, and a quarter each for validation and testing purposes.

We investigate two situations: one where the original features were randomly and disjointly partitioned among the different segments, and the second where there is some overlap among features in different segments. The exact segment count and number of features within each segment is specified in table 6.5.

For each data set, we present the original number of features, the number of new features sets that result when the feature set is segmented (for Gene we only have two new sets, because the low dimensionality prevents any further segmentation), and the resulting number of features in each segment with and without overlap among the features.

A classifier trains on data from one segment, and different classifiers operate on different segments. When the number of combiners were higher than the number of segments ($N = 8$) more than on classifier (starting from a different initialization) was trained on the same features.

Tables 6.6-6.7 present the results (with the best result for each case in bold font). The misclassification percentage for individual classifiers are reported in the first column. For the trimmed mean combiner, we also provide N_1 and N_2, the upper and lower cutting points in the ordered average used in

[7]The number of hidden units was determined experimentally.

[8]available from www.ics.uci.edu/~mlearn/MLRepository.html

Data	N	Ave	Max	Min	Spread	Trim (N_1-N_2)
Card	4	12.21 ± .00	**10.58 ± .06**	**10.61 ± .06**	**10.58 ± .00**	12.21 ± .00 (3-4)
30.30 ± 2.62	8	12.21 ± .00	**10.47 ± .00**	10.61 ± .06	**10.47 ± .00**	**10.47 ± .00** (7-8)
Gene	4	18.52 ± .10	**14.02 ± .13**	20.23 ± .31	14.72 ± .15	16.86 ± .15 (3-4)
34.80 ± 4.01	8	18.06 ± .06	**13.13 ± .06**	17.59 ± .17	13.69 ± .11	13.39 ± .08 (7-8)
Sat	4	14.16 ± .08	14.73 ± .18	14.64 ± .16	14.24 ± .12	**14.00 ± .07** (3-4)
16.40 ± 0.56	8	14.21 ± .05	15.27 ± .15	15.07 ± .15	14.49 ± .11	**14.01 ± .04** (3-5)

Table 6.6: Segmented features with overlap (% misclassified $\pm\sigma/\sqrt{n}$).

Data	N	Ave	Max	Min	Spread	Trim (N_1-N_2)
Card	4	12.21 ± .00	**10.49 ± .03**	**10.49 ± .03**	**10.49 ± .03**	12.21 ± .00 (3-4)
30.90 ± 2.66	8	12.21 ± .00	10.78 ± .07	10.78 ± .07	**10.52 ± .04**	11.05 ± .00 (7-8)
Gene	4	24.35 ± .13	15.82 ± .15	19.15 ± .22	**14.09 ± .11**	23.11 ± .15 (3-4)
36.87 ± 3.01	8	23.33 ± .19	14.99 ± .14	16.78 ± .24	**13.23 ± .15**	15.03 ± .17 (7-8)
Sat lap	4	14.39 ± .09	15.66 ± .15	15.46 ± .11	15.11 ± .11	**14.22 ± .07** (2-3)
17.13 ± 0.47	8	14.37 ± .05	15.93 ± .06	15.53 ± .06	15.18 ± .10	**14.04 ± .05** (3-5)

Table 6.7: Segmented features without overlap (% misclassified $\pm\sigma/\sqrt{n}$).

equation 6.32, obtained through the validation set.

In this case, for two of the three data sets (Gene and Card), there are striking gains due to using order statistics combiners. One cause for these gains is the high variability in performance among the component classifiers. In such cases, a small number of poor classifiers can corrupt the average combiner. By their very nature, though, combiners based on order statistics are immune to this type of corruption. The ave combiner performs well on the Sat data sets where the performance among the individual classifiers is much more homogeneous. In this case, the ave results are only marginally worse than those for the trimmed mean.

6.6.2 Variability through Early Stopping

For the second set of experiments we use two classes of acoustic underwater sonar signals[9]. From the original sonar signals of four different underwater objects (porpoise sound, cracking ice and two different whale sounds), two feature sets are extracted (Ghosh, Deuser, and Beck 1992): (1) WOC: a 25-dimensional feature set, consisting of Gabor wavelet coefficients, temporal descriptors and spectral measurements; and, (2) RDO: a 24-dimensional feature set, consisting of reflection coefficients based on both short and long time windows, and temporal descriptors. For both feature sets, an MLP with 50 hidden units was used.[10] Further details about this 4-class problem can be found in Ghosh, Deuser, and Beck (1992) and Tumer and Ghosh (1996b).

[9]Results on 6 Proben/UCI datasets were reported in Tumer and Ghosh (1999) and hence are not repeated here

[10]These data sets are available at www.lans.ece.utexas.edu.

Data	N	Ave	Max	Min	Spread	Trim (N_1-N_2)
RDO	4	11.57 ± .11	11.94 ± .12	11.52 ± .20	**11.04 ± .09**	11.34 ± .14 (3-4)
13.32 ± 0.83	8	11.64 ± .09	11.47 ± .11	**11.29 ± .13**	11.51 ± .09	12.30 ± .08 (4-5)
WOC	4	8.80 ± .09	**7.84 ± .10**	9.31 ± .12	8.54 ± .06	8.43 ± .13 (3-4)
12.07 ± 1.12	8	8.82 ± .08	**7.68 ± .12**	8.91 ± .06	8.24 ± .11	**7.81 ± .08** (7-8)

Table 6.8: Combining results in the presence of high variability in individual classifier performance for the sonar data (% misclassified $\pm\sigma/\sqrt{n}$).

Table 6.8 presents the combining results for the underwater acoustic data set when the individual classifier performance is highly variable. The results of table 6.8 as well as those given in Tumer and Ghosh (1999) indicate that when the individual classifier performance is highly variable, order statistics-based combiners (particularly the *spread* combiner) typically provide better classification results than other simple combiners. This performance improvement is obtained without sacrificing the simplicity of the combiner. One important thing to note, however, is that in all cases studied, the order statistics based combiners performed at least as well as the simple combiner, implying that no risk is taken by using this method.

A close inspection of these results reveals that using either the max or min combiner can provide better classification rates than *ave*, but it is difficult to determine which of the two will be more successful given a data set. A validation set may be used to select one over the other, but in that case, potentially precious training data is used solely for determining which combiner to use. The use of the spread combiner removes this dilemma by consistently providing results that are comparable to, or better than, the best of the max-min duo.

6.7 Concluding Remarks

In this article we present and analyze combiners based on order statistics. These combiners blend the simplicity of averaging with the generality of metalearners. They are particularly effective if there are significant variations among component classifiers in at least some parts of the joint input-output space. Variations can arise when the individual training sets cannot be considered as random samples from a common universal data set. Examples of such cases include real-time data acquisition and classification from geographically distributed sources or data mining problems with large and possibly heterogenous databases, where random subsampling is computationally expensive and practical methods lead to nonrandom subsamples (Bradley and Fayyad, 1998). The robustness of order statistics combiners is also helpful when certain individual classifiers experience catastrophic failures (e.g., due to faulty sensors).

The analytical framework provided in this chapter quantifies the reductions in error achieved when an order statistics based ensemble is used. It also shows that the two methods for linear combination of order statistics introduced in this chapter provide more reliable estimates of the true posteriors than any of the individual order statistic combiners.

The experimental results of section 6.5 indicate that when there is significant variability among the classifiers, the order statistics-based combiners substantially outperform simple combiners. Our previous results also showed that in the absence of such variability these combiners perform no worse. Thus the family of order statistic combiners are applicable over a wide range of situations. They are able to extract an appropriate amount of information from the individual classifier outputs without requiring tuning additional parameters as in metalearners, and without being substantially affected by outliers.

A future endeavor, which will be helpful for this work as well as for the study of collective data mining on very large datasets in general, is to obtain a suite of public domain datasets which are intrinsically partitioned into segments with varying quality. Though such situations sometimes occur in practice (for example in oil logging data[11]) and mortgage scoring[12]; both data sets proprietary), they are not represented in the standard, venerable databases such as UCI, ELENA and Statlog typically used by the academic community. Perhaps the recent CRoss-Industry Standard Process for Data Mining (CRISP-DM) initiative will provide a satisfactory solution to this problem in the near future.

Acknowledgments

This research was supported in part by ARO contracts DAAG55-98-1-0230 and DAAD19-99-1-0012, and NSF grant ECS-9900353.

---

[11] Private communication with S. Chakravarthy

[12] Private communication with C. J. Merz.

Chapter 7

Efficient Mining of Association Rules under Inequality Constraints in Distributed Databases

Vincent Ng, David Cheung, and Charles Lo

7.1 Introduction

Database mining has recently attracted tremendous amount of attention in the database research because of its wide applicability in many areas, including decision support, market strategy and financial forecast. Researchers and practitioners in industry, business, administration, engineering, and scientific research have collected huge amounts of data in their work and have been looking for automated tools to facilitate the utilization of their on-line or archived treasures. According to many studies on knowledge discovery in databases (Piatetsky-Shapiro and Frawley 1991; Fayyad, Piatetsky-Shapiro, Smyth, and

Uthurusamy 1998; Agrawal, Faloutsos, and Swami 1993b), mining knowledge from databases has two characteristics. (1) The size of the database is significantly large and distributed, it could scale up to gigabytes, terabytes, or even larger, in some applications. For example, the huge amount of transaction records of hundreds of Sears department stores are likely to be stored at the different sites. (2) The rules discovered is valid only in statistical terms. Users are looking for rules that hold for a significant amount of data, but not necessarily for all the data. Hence the scope of rule discovery is much wider than that covered in the classical database studies, such as functional dependency theory (Ullman 1989). Therefore, the number of rules returned from a mining activity could be large.

These observations indicate that the promise of database mining lies in the techniques to handle a large amount of data and to manage a substantial number of rules.

The problem of discovering association rules was first introduced by Agrawal and Srikant (1994). It is to find the possible associations between items when a user specifies a minimum support (s) and a minimum confidence (c). For example, one possible association rule can be "there are 10% of customers who made long distance calls to England last month and 80% of those customers also called USA." In this example, the support is 10% and the confidence is 80%. In performing the association mining, we believe that it would be difficult for a single processor system to provide reasonable response time because of the two characteristics mentioned.

Recently, there has been a lot of active work in extending the mining of association rules for parallel and distributed system. For parallel association mining, there can be two types of algorithms. The first type is involved with multi-processors that have distributed-memory, such as in Park, Chen, and Yu (1995a) or Cheung, Han, Ng, Fu, and Fu (1996). For these algorithms, computers are connected on a network, and each has its own private memory, processor and local disk storage. Communications are done via message passing. The other type of algorithms, such as in Cheung, Hu, and Xia (1998) or Agrawal and Shafer (1996), are developed for shared-memory multiprocessor systems (SMPs). In these systems, a single memory address space is available for all processors to access.

In mining the association rules, users often find that they are not only interested in the general associations. Rather, they always have a set of conditions for the possible rules to satisfy. Recently, Srikant, Vu, and Agrawal (1997) proposed the *multiplejoin* algorithm and the *direct* algorithm to discover association rules which satisfy a given boolean expression over the items of a database. The expression is used to indicate the existence or nonexistence of the items. Only association rules satisfying the expression are output. Consider a phone company with a large collection of items, and each item represents the monthly long distance charge of either peak time or nonpeak time that a client spends in calling a particular country. The company wants to find out if there are five different countries which are always called by a good number of customers but their total amount of long distance fees is less than $200. This would allow business analysts to focus on those countries with low calling activities and to decide if promotions in calling plans are needed. The work reported here can be viewed as a step towards enhancing the mining process in considering constraints rather than simple associations.

> Find four countries which are called by a good number of customers but the total monthly fees of the customers are less than $100." This query is a simple variation of the original association discovery. Quantitative values of the items in the associations are added and compared with the constant to determine the constraint is satisfied.
>
> Find three countries of calling region A and two countries of calling region B which are called by a good number of customers every month, and the differences of their monthly fees between 2 regions are greater than $300."

This query divides items into two groups. The intergroup operator is "-," and the intragroup operator is "+." Items are evaluated and the result is compared with the > operator to determine if the inequality is satisfied.

Instead of comparing the difference between two sums, it may be better to use a ratio (percentage). Therefore, we can rephrase the previous query as

> Find three countries of calling region A and two countries of calling region B which are called by a good number of customers every month, and the ratios of their monthly fees between 2 regions are greater than 2.

Note that the inter-group operator now becomes "/."

From the previous discussion, we observe that there are still two issues that may worth further investigations. (1) For most algorithms, messages are interchanged at the end of each mining iteration to perform the global counting and the pruning of candidate itemsets. In the case of a network of workstations, their individual performance may not be uniform and will likely depend on their processor speeds as well as the sizes of their local databases. Hence, some workstations (processors) may be idle when others are still working on the same mining iteration. (2) The current distributed and parallel algorithms are to discover binary association rules and the constraint information is not exploited in the mining process.

In the rest of this chapter, we first review the sequential mining of association rules and some recent work on parallel and distributed algorithms. In section 7.3, we then present a thorough discussion of the ideas in the fast distributed mining (FDM) algorithm. Following it will be a formal definition of our problem. In section 7.5 the three different approaches to solve the problem are proposed. Section 7.5.3 will have a detail discussion on the candidate set generation procedure in the DMI algorithm. We will then continue to present the experimental results of the three algorithms, and conclude our work in section 7.8.

7.2 Related Work

In this section, we review the sequential mining of association rules and some recent work on parallel and distributed algorithms.

7.2.1 Sequential Mining of Association Rules

In this section, we will formally defined what *association rules* are. Let $I = \{i_1, i_2, \ldots, i_M\}$ be a set of *items*. Let DB be a database of transactions, where each transaction T consists of a set of items such that $T \subseteq I$. Given an *itemset* $X \subseteq I$, a transaction T *contains* X if and only if $X \subseteq T$. An *association rule* is an implication of the form $X \Rightarrow Y$, where $X \subseteq I$, $Y \subseteq I$ and $X \cap Y = \emptyset$. The association rule $X \Rightarrow Y$ holds in DB with *confidence c* if $c\%$ of the transactions in DB that contain X also contain Y. The association rule $X \Rightarrow Y$ has *support s* in DB if $s\%$ of the transactions in DB contain both X and Y. The problem of mining association rules is to find all the association rules whose support is larger than a minimum support threshold and whose confidence is larger than a minimum confidence threshold.

For an itemset X, its *support* is the percentage of transactions in DB which contains X, and its *support count*, denoted by $X.sup$, is the number of transactions in DB containing X. An itemset X is *large* (or more precisely, *frequently occurring*) if its support is no less than the minimum support threshold. An itemset of size k is called a *k-itemset*. It has been shown that the problem of mining association rules can be reduced to two subproblems (Agrawal and Srikant 1994): (1) Find all itemsets whose supports are greater than the minimum support s and these itemsets are called *large itemsets*. (2) Generate the association rules. If {ABC} and {AB} are both in the large itemsets, we compute its confidence which is (the support of {ABC})/(the support of {AB}). If the ratio is higher than a present threshold c, the rule is established.

Since subproblem (1) dominates the overall cost of mining association rules, the research has been focused on how to develop efficient methods to solve the first problem. Among all the algorithms proposed, the Apriori (and its modifications) (Agrawal, Imielinski, and Swami 1993b) and the direct hashing and pruning (DHP) (Park, Chen, and Yu 1995a) algorithms are the two most successful. These two algorithms use the same framework. They both run a number of iterations and compute the large itemsets of the same size in each iteration, starting from the size-1 itemsets. In each iteration, they first construct a set of candidate itemsets and then scan the database to count the number of transactions that contain each candidate set. The key for optimization lies on the techniques used to create the candidate sets. The smaller the number of candidate sets is, the faster the algorithm would be. In general, the first few iterations have a dominant effect on the performance. In particular, the number of size-2 candidate sets created by Apriori in the second iteration is very large in comparison with those in the later iterations . The DHP algorithm improved this performance bottleneck by using a hashing technique in the first iteration which reduces significantly the number of the size-2 candidate sets. The experimental results reported by Park, Chen, and Yu (1995a) shows that DHP can improve the performance of Apriori significantly.

The Apriori and DHP algorithms are mainly dealing with items that are binary attributes and do not posses any quantitative values. It merely reveals the existence of different items in transactions but not the possible quantitative relationships between them. Different extensions on the binary association rules have been appeared in the past several years (Agrawal and Srikant 1995; Agrawal, Imielinski, and Swami 1993b; Cheung, Han, Ng, and Wong 1996; Klemettinen, Mannila, Ronkainen, Toivonen, and Verkamo 1994; Houstma and Swami 1993). Srikant and Agrawal (1996), proposed algorithm based on the *K-partial completeness* to discover quantitative association rules. Later in 1997, another algorithm utilizing the Birch algorithm (Zhang, Ramakrishnan, and Livny 1996) is developed to mine generalized quantitative association rules for interval data (Miller and Yang 1997).

7.2.2 Parallel and Distributed Algorithms for Mining of Association Rules

For the parallel environments, the PDM algorithm is one of the very first algorithms proposed to mine association rules (Park, Chen, and Yu 1995b). It is basically a parallelized version of the DHP algorithm. Each node (computer) computes the globally large itemsets by exchanging their support counts of the candidate sets. In order to apply the hashing technique, all nodes have to broadcast the hashing result, which causes a huge amount of communication. Park, Chen, and Yu (1995b) proposed a technique to decrease the number of messages. Amongst all the hash buckets, only those in which the total count are larger than a threshold are selected for bucket count exchange, so that not all buckets have to be broadcasted. After a node receives these partial count for the selected buckets, it polls the other sites to get the total counts. However, there are two unfavourable features. First, the reduction of candidate sets is only done in the second iteration. The number of candidate sets in some other iterations could also be quite large. Second, to find the large candidate sets, $O(n^2)$ messages are required for support count exchange for each candidate set, where n is the number of nodes.

Another algorithm proposed for parallel mining of association rules is the CD algorithm (Agrawal and Shafer 1996). It is an adaptation of the Apriori algorithm in the parallel case. At each iteration, it generates the candidate sets at every site by applying the Apriori-gen function on the set of large itemsets found at the previous iteration. Every site then computes the local support counts of all these candidate sets and broadcast them to all the other sites. Subsequently, all sites can find the globally large itemsets for that iteration, and then proceed to the next iteration. This algorithm utilizes a simple communication scheme for count exchange. However, it also has the similar problems of higher number of candidate sets and larger amount of communication overhead.

Four algorithms, NPA, SPA, HPA and HPA-ELD (Shintani and Kitsuregawa 1996), similar to those in Agrawal and Shafer (1996) are proposed for mining association rules on shared nothing parallel machines. In the NPA algorithm, candidate sets are copied among all processors, which may cause memory overflow for large databases. The other three algorithms partition the candidate sets amongst the processors. The SPA algorithm uses a simple method while the HPA algorithm uses a hash function to eliminate broadcasting. The last algorithm, HPA-ELD, has the best performance amongst all of them. It takes into the consideration of data skewness and fully utilizes the available memory space in replicating the most frequent candidate sets. Communication overhead is hence reduced and HPA-ELD attains a good linear speedup ratio.

The FDM algorithm (Cheung, Han, Ng, Fu, and Fu 1996) is developed for the mining of association rules in a distributed database environment. Its efficiency is attributed to three techniques: candidate sets generation, local pruning and messages optimization. Its performance depends on the distribution of the data across the partitions. The techniques of candidate sets generation and local pruning would be more powerful if the itemsets are distributed with a higher skewness among the partitions. More details of FDM will be covered in the next section.

The fast parallel mining (FPM) algorithm (Cheung and Xia 1998) adopts the count distribution approach and incorporated two pruning techniques: distributed pruning and global pruning. Under its communication scheme, only one round of message exchange is needed. In particular, its distributed pruning is very effective for highly skewed data. The experimental results reported by

Cheung and Xia (1998) also show that global pruning is more effective than distributed pruning even for the mild data skewness case.

7.3 The Fast Distributed Mining Algorithm

In developing the FDM algorithm, it has been assumed that the database to be studied is a transaction database although the method can be easily extended to distributed mining in relational databases as well. The database consists of a huge number of transaction records, each with a transaction identifier (TID) and a set of data items. Further, we assume that the database is *horizontally* partitioned (i.e., grouped by transactions) and allocated to the sites (computers) in a distributed system, and the sites communicate by message passing.

It has been well known (Agrawal, Imielinski, and Swami 1993a; Agrawal and Srikant 1994) that the major cost of mining association rules is the computation of the set of *large itemsets* in the database. Unfortunately, it is not so straightforward to compute such large items in a distributed environment. One may compute *locally large* itemsets easily, but a locally large itemset may not be *globally large*. Thus, one option is to broadcast all the counts of all the itemsets, no matter locally large or small, to other sites. Since a database may contain a large combinations of itemsets, it will involve passing a huge number of messages.

In viewing the problem, the FDM algorithm is developed with three distinct features in comparison with some straightforward distributed algorithm and some interesting parallel mining algorithms, such as PDM (Park, Chen, and Yu 1995b). (1) The generation of candidate sets is in the same spirit of Apriori. However, we observe some interesting relationships between locally large sets and the globally large ones and generate a smaller candidate set at each iteration. This also reduces the number of messages to be passed. (2) After the candidate sets have been generated, two pruning techniques, *local pruning* and *global pruning*, are developed to prune away some candidate sets at each individual sites. (3) In order to determine whether a candidate set is large, our algorithm requires only $O(N)$ messages for support count exchange, where N is the number of sites in the network. This is much less than a straight adaptation of Apriori, which requires $O(N^2)$ messages.

Before we describe the three techniques used in FDM, let us define the problem of mining of association rules in a distributed environment here. Let DB be a database with D transactions. Assume that there are n sites $S_1, S_2, \ldots, S_N$ in a distributed system and the database DB is partitioned over the N sites into $\{DB_1, DB_2, \ldots, DB_N\}$, respectively.

Let the size of the partitions DB_i be D_i, for $i = 1, \ldots, N$. Let $X.sup$ and $X.sup_i$ be the support counts of an itemset X in DB and DB_i, respectively.

$X.sup$ is called the *global support count*, and $X.sup_i$ the *local support count* of X at site S_i. For a given minimum support threshold s, X is *globally large* if $X.sup \geq s \times D$; correspondingly, X is *locally large* at site S_i, if $X.sup_i \geq s \times D_i$. In the following, L denotes the globally large itemsets in DB, and L_k the globally large k-itemsets in L. The essential task of a distributed association rule mining algorithm is to find the globally large itemsets L.

In the rest of this section, we will present the three distinct features of FDM in a better detail.

7.3.1 Generation of Candidate Sets

It is important to observe some interesting properties related to large itemsets in distributed environments since such properties may substantially reduce the number of messages to be passed across communication networks at mining association rules.

First, there is an important relationship between large itemsets and the sites in a distributed database: *every globally large itemsets must be locally large at* some *site(s)*. If an itemset X is both globally large and locally large at a site S_i, X is called *uniformly large*, or *gl-large* for short, at site S_i. The set of gl-large itemsets at a site will form a basis for the site to generate its own candidate sets.

Second, a gl-large itemset at a site has the following monotonic subset relationship property: *if an itemset is gl-large at a site S_i, all of its subsets are also gl-large at the site S_i.*

Based on these properties, an efficient algorithm can be worked out to generate a much smaller candidate sets at each site than those generated by applying Apriori-gen directly. This relationship can allow us to reduce the number of candidate itemsets as illustrated in example 1.

Example 1. Let *Apriori_gen* represents the candidate itemset generation procedure in Agrawal and Srikant (1994) and $L_{i(j)}$ represents the gl-large items at S_i during iteration j. Assuming there are 3 sites in a system which partitions the DB into DB_1, DB_2 and DB_3. In DB, the set of large 1-itemsets L_1 are {*A, B, C, D, E, F, G, H*} , in which *A, B* and *C* are locally large at site S_1, *B, C* and *D* are locally large at site S_2, and *E, F, G*, and *H* are locally large at site S_3. Therefore, $L_{1(1)} = \{A, B, C\}$, $L_{2(1)} = \{B, C, D\}$, $L_{3(1)} = \{E, F, G, H\}$. Based on the relationship, the set of size-2 candidate sets at site S_1 is $\{AB, BC, AC\}$. Similarly, at site S_2 and S_3, their candidate sets are $\{BC, CD, BD\}$ and $\{EF, EG, EH, FG, FH, GH\}$ respectively. Hence, the number of candidate sets for large 2-itemsets is 11 where it would be 28 if Apriori_gen is applied directly to L_1. Q.E.D.

7.3.2 Local Pruning of Candidate Sets

The previous subsection shows that one can generate usually a much smaller set of candidate sets than the Apriori algorithm in a distributed environment. We then examine how to generate gl-large sets and their associated counts efficiently.

When the set of candidate set C_k is generated, to find the globally large itemsets, the support counts of the candidate sets must be exchanged among all the sites. Another interesting observation is that some candidate sets in C_k can be pruned away by a *local pruning* technique before count exchange starts. The general idea is that at each site S_i, if a candidate set $X \in CG_{i(k)}$ is not locally large at site S_i, there is no need for S_i to find out its global support count to determine whether it is globally large. This is because in this case, either X is small (not globally large), or it will be locally large at some other site; and hence only a locally large site needs to be responsible to find its global support count.

In order to compute all the large k-itemsets, at each site S_i, the candidate sets can be confined to only the sets $X \in CG_{i(k)}$ which are locally large at site S_i. For convenience, we use $LL_{i(k)}$ to denote those candidate sets in $CG_{i(k)}$ which are locally large at site S_i.

Based on the above discussion, at every iteration (the kth-iteration), the gl-large k-itemsets can be computed at each site S_i according to the following procedure.

1. *Candidate Sets Generation:* Generate the candidate sets $CG_{i(k)} =$ Apriori_gen($L_{i(k-1)}$), based on the gl-large itemsets found at site S_i at the $(k-1)^{th}$-iteration. (That is, each site is responsible for generating its own set of candidate sets and hence computing its own set of large itemsets.)

2. *Local Pruning:* For each $X \in CG_{i(k)}$, scan the partition DB_i to compute the local support count $X.sup_i$. If X is not locally large at site S_i, it is excluded from the candidate sets $LL_{i(k)}$. (Note: This pruning only removes X from the candidate set at site S_i. X could still be a candidate set at some other site.)

3. *Support Count Exchange:* Broadcast the candidate sets in $LL_{i(k)}$ to other sites to collect support counts. Compute their global support counts and find all the gl-large k-itemsets in site S_i.

4. *Broadcast Mining Result:* Broadcast the gl-large k-itemsets found to all the other sites.

For clarity, the notations used so far are listed in table 7.1.

D	The number of transactions in database DB
s	The support threshold $minsup$
L_k	The set of globally large k-itemsets
C_k	The set of candidate sets generated from L_k
$X.sup$	The global support count of an itemset X
D_i	The number of transactions in the partition DB_i
$L_{i(k)}$	The set of gl-large k-itemsets at site S_i
$CG_{i(k)}$	The set of candidate sets generated from $L_{i(k-1)}$
$LL_{i(k)}$	The set of locally large k-itemsets in $CG_{i(k)}$
$X.sup_i$	The local support count of an itemset X at site S_i

Table 7.1: Notation table.

7.3.3 Message Optimization for Find Large Itemsets

To ensure that FDM requires only $O(n)$ messages for every candidate set in all cases, an optimization technique has been introduced. To achieve single broadcast, FDM uses some simple assignment functions, which could be a hash function, to determine a polling site for each candidate set.

For each candidate set X, its polling site is responsible for broadcasting the polling request, collecting the support counts, and determine whether X is large. Since there is one polling site for each candidate set X, the number of messages required for count exchange for X is $O(n)$.

In the kth-iteration, after the local pruning phase has been completed at a site S_i, FDM uses the following procedure to do the polling.

1. *Candidates send to Polling Sites:* S_i acts as a home site of its candidate sets; for every polling site S_j, S_j finds all the candidate sets in $LL_{i(k)}$ whose polling site are S_j and stores them in $LL^j_{i(k)}$, (i.e. candidates are being divided into groups according to their polling sites), the local support counts of the candidate sets are also stored in the corresponding set $LL^j_{i(k)}$; sends each $LL^j_{i(k)}$ to the corresponding polling site S_j.

2. *Polling Site send Polling Requests:* S_i acts as a polling site; S_i receives all $LL^j_{i(k)}$ sent to it from the other sites; fpr every candidate set X received, S_i finds the list of originating sites from which X is being sent; S_i then broadcasts the polling requests to the other sites not on the list to collect the support counts.

3. *Remote Site reply Polling Requests:* S_i acts as a remote site to reply polling requests sent to it; for every polling request $LL^p_{i(k)}$ from polling site S_p, S_i sends the local support counts of the candidates in $LL^p_{i(k)}$ back to S_p. (There is no need to scan the partition DB_i again to find the local support counts. It is found already during the local pruning.)

4. *Polling Site Compute Heavy Itemsets:* S_i acts as a polling site to compute the heavy itemsets; S_i receives the support counts from the other sites; computes the global support counts for its candidates in $LL_{i(k)}$ and finds the heavy itemsets; eventually, S_i broadcasts the heavy itemsets together with their global support counts to all the sites.

7.4 Mining Under Inequality Constraints

In section 2, we described a number of different algorithms for distributed and parallel mining of association rules. However, they are mainly dealing with items that are binary attributes and do not posses any quantitative values. As pointed out in the introduction, users are usually more interest in transactions that have quantitative items and the possible relationships and constraints among them. In this section, we formally define our quantitative mining problem here.

Let DB be a database with D transactions as defined before. Assume that there are N sites (workstations) $S_1, S_2, \ldots, S_N$ in a distributed system and the database DB is partitioned over the N sites into $\{DB_1, DB_2, \ldots, DB_N\}$, respectively. Here, we will use the same definitions of $X.sup$ and $X.sup_i$ as before. In DB, it has M quantitative items as $I = i_1, i_2, \ldots, i_M$. For each transaction t in DB, t[k] $>$ 0 means that t contains item i_k with the value t[k], and t[k]=0 means that i_k does not exist in t. In our work, we are interested in finding all quantitative association rules in DB that satisfy the following inequality IN:

$(i_{x1} \oplus i_{x2} \oplus \ldots \oplus i_{xm}) \ominus (i_{y1} \oplus i_{y2} \oplus \ldots \oplus i_{yn}) \nabla \ Cont$

where $\oplus$ is $+$ or $*$, $\ominus$ is $-$ or $/$, $\nabla \in \{<, >, =, \leq, \geq\}$, $Cont$ is a scalar value, $i_{x1}, i_{x2}, \ldots i_{xm}$ are the m items in X, and $i_{y1}, i_{y2}, \ldots i_{yn}$ are the n items in Y [1]. At the beginning of mining the association rules, the inequality IN is specified by 6 parameters as $(m, n, \oplus, \ominus, \nabla, Cont)$, and the size of IN is defined as the sum of m and n. Some examples of IN are

- $(3, 2, +, -, \geq, 10)$: $(X_1 + X_2 + X_3) - (Y_1 + Y_2) \geq 1000$
- $(4, 3, +, /, \leq, 2.5)$: $(X_1 + X_2 + X_3 + X_4)/(Y_1 + Y_2 + Y_3) \leq 2.5$

7.5 Three Approaches

In this section, we present three different approaches to discover the constrainted association rules. All three approaches will filter the correct rules in a post-processing step. Their main differences are the procedure of candidate

[1] Items in X and Y are disjoint and they are not fixed during the mining process.

Given the inequality IN, a threshold s, and $C_{i(k)}$.

1. For all tuples t in D_i do /* $C_{i(k)}$ counting */
   - if (t contains X in $C_{i(k)}$) and (items in X satisfied IN) then
     $X.sup_i := X.sup_i + 1$
2. For all itemsets X in $C_{i(k)}$ do /* $L_{i(k)}$ generation */
   - If ($X.sup_i \geq s \times D_i$) then
     $L_{i(k)} := L_{i(k)} + X$

Figure 7.1: Incremental algorithm: finding $L_{i(k)}$ at site S_i.

set generations and the support of asynchronous mining. The first approach is based on the FDM algorithm. The second approach allows dynamic candidate set generation so that sites can work asynchronously without waiting. The third approach is to incorporate the inequality constraint into the candidate set generation steps. Unlike the constrained mining algorithm in Srikant, Vu, and Agrawal (1997), we would not only handle the existence of items but also their quantitative values. The major idea is to exploit the size information in the given inequality IN. The values of m and n can help us to predetermine the size of L_k that we are interested, and allow us to skip the generations of unnecessary candidate itemsets.

7.5.1 The FDM Approach

The first algorithm is based on the FDM algorithm, and is called the *Incremental algorithm.* It follows the steps in the FDM algorithm except at iteration k when $k = m + n$. At that step, we modify it to verify the given inequality IN. That is, at site S_i, while we count the support of an itemset in $C_{i(k)}$, we also evaluate if the values from the itemset in the transactions in DB_i satisfying IN (see figure 7.1). Suppose a candidate itemset {ADE} is contained in a transaction {ABCDE}, and we need to find associations which satisfy the inequality: "*Any three items whose total value is greater than \$100.*" At the kth-iteration, we evaluate the sum of the values of {ADE}. If it is less than \$100, its support count is not increased. Therefore, if IN is supposed to have k items, then the procedure in generating $L_{i(k)}$ is the same as in the FDM algorithm. Under this approach, $L_{i(k)}$ is found from L_{k-1}, L_{k-1} is from L_{k-2}, and so on. Hence, we are finding out $L_1, L_2, \ldots L_k$ incrementally even though we are only interest in itemsets of size k.

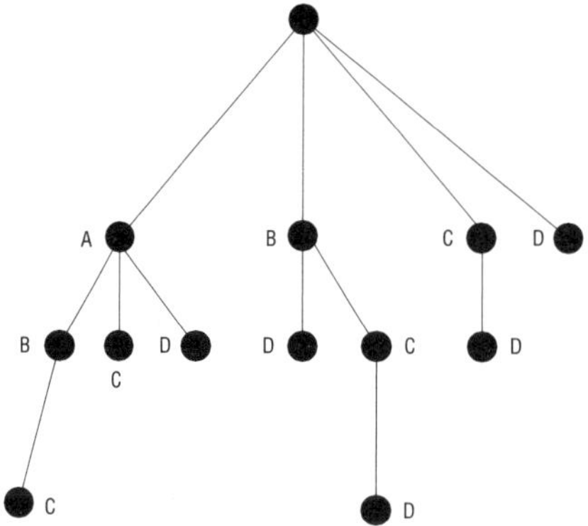

Figure 7.2: A trie.

7.5.2 The APM Approach

Dynamic candidate generation is proposed by Brin, Motawani, Ullman, and Tsur (1997) to reduce the scannings induced in the level-wise approach of mining association rules. The idea is to divide the database into equal size intervals, each containing the same number of transactions. The first interval is scanned to generate the size-1 itemsets. They are then used to generate the size-2 itemsets. After the second interval is scanned, support counts of all size-1 and size-2 itemsets are obtained. At the end of each interval scan, new candidate sets are formed and to be counted in the next interval. This candidate set generation and counting process is repeated until the termination condition becomes true.

The adaptive parallel mining (APM) algorithm (Cheung, Hu, and Xia 1998) adopted the above idea to generate the common candidates asynchronously for different nodes (sites) on a SMP machine. Every node (site) S_i will perform its counting on its own partition DB_i. In order to store candidates of different sizes, a trie instead of a hash tree is used to store the support counts in shared-memory. Figure 7.2 is a trie in APM. Every node on the trie is associated with a candidate itemset. For example, in the first branch of the trie, the nodes represent the candidates A, AB, ABC, AC and AD.

However, the APM algorithm cannot be directly applied to our problem because adaptive inter-partition interval configuration cannot be done. That is, in a distributed environment, databases may not freely copied from one site to the other. Therefore, the partitions $DB_1, DB_2, \ldots, DB_N$ are not of uniform sizes nor homogeneous in data distribution. Each partition represents an autonomous data source and may have different data distributions between different sites.

/* Preprocessing

1. all sites scan their partitions to compute local support counts of size-1 itemsets in their intervals
2. compute L_1 and generate C_2 by using *Apriori_gen*
3. initialize the trie in the polling site, S^p
4. perform the re-ordering of the intervals within each site

*/

- while (some site has not finished counting of all the itemsets on the trie on its partition)
  - while (S_i has not finished the counting of all the itemsets on the trie on DB_i)
    * Scan one more interval on DB_i and count the supports of the itemsets on the trie
    * Find out the locally large itemsets among the itemsets on the trie for the interval scanned
    * Generate new candidates from these locally large itemsets
    * Send the new candidate sets and its counts to site S^p
    * In S^p, it will
      · Perform pruning on these candidates and insert the survivors into the trie
      · Remove globally small itemsets on the trie
    * Receive the updated trie from S^p

Figure 7.3: The DCDM algorithm.

In adopting the idea of Brin, Motawani, Ullman, and Tsur (1997) and Cheung, Hu, and Xia (1998), we have developed the dynamic candidate distributed mining (DCDM) algorithm. Before any mining step, each site will perform an intra-partition interval configuration to approximate a homogeneous data distribution. In site S_i, its partition DB_i will be divided into a number of intervals of size q. Initially, we compute the local support counts of size-1 itemsets in the intervals. One possibility then is to re-distribute the transactions into different intervals so that the evenness factor (Cheung, Hu, and Xia 1998) is as close to zero as possible. However, this may involve a lot of shuffling among the transactions and create a large overhead. We decide to rearrange the intervals according to their distances (defined below) to the large itemsets for the whole partition.

Definition 1 Given two sets of large itemsets L^i and L for interval i and the complete partition respectively, the *distance* between them is defined as $dist(L^i, L) = 1 - \frac{|L^i \cap L|}{|L^i \cup L|}$

The outline of the DCDM algorithm for each site S_i to run on its partition DB_i is shown in figure 7.3. A polling station S^p is used to send and receive messages about the global itemsets which are stored in a trie. The trie is replicated at each site and synchronize with that in S^p at the end of each interval scan. For itemsets of size-k, the polling site will request all sites to verify the inequality constraint before coming out with the final set of rules.

7.5.3 The DMI Approach

In a typical distributed system, say a pool of workstations in a local-area network, machines would have different computational capabilities. In performing the FDM algorithm at the ith-iteration, some sites will finish quicker because of better processor speed or smaller local database sizes. These sites will have to wait for their peers to complete the same iteration. The delay can be significant if the configurations of the workstations are very different. By allowing dynamic candidate set generation, such as in the DCDM algorithm, we can allow faster workstations to continue their work without stopping and slower workstations to prune their local itemsets by using the results of the faster ones. However, in the DCDM algorithm, the constraint information has not been exploited and the overhead of storing the tries can be significant if data are not homogeneous.

As our ultimate interest is the L_k (not any intermediate itemsets), we are not interested in the intermediate itemsets. In the next section, we will discuss how we can use the inequality information to create a sequence which will help us in speeding up the candidate set generation steps while maintaining the asynchronous mining ability.

7.6 The DMI Algorithm

In the distributed mining under inequality (DMI) algorithm, we want to utilize the size information given by the input inequality, IN, in speeding up the pruning process. The main idea is to use a sequence to guide the generation of candidate sets.

There are two phases in this algorithm. The first step in phase 1 is to generate a sequence from the given inequality IN. Each site will then be given the sequence and use it to guide the mining steps on it own. Similar to the Incremental algorithm, each iteration done by site S_i will scan its partition DB_i entirely. There will not be any interval subdivisions. At iteration j, site S_i will generate its next set of candidate itemsets as shown in figure 7.4. Note that, in the procedure, there can be two pruning possibilities as discussed in section 7.6.2.

In phase 2, the $LL_{i(m+n)}$'s from the N sites will be collected and broadcasted to verify the given inequality IN. The local support counts returned from the sites will determine the final set of itemset of size-k. The candidate set generation procedures of the FDM algorithm is then used afterwards.

Next, we will describe how to create the sequence and the candidate set generation procedures.

7.6.1 Creating the Sequence

For a given inequality IN of size k, any found L_i when $i < k$ will not satisfy IN. In the previous algorithms, we have to generate many unnecessary candidate itemsets in order to find L_k. One possible idea is to generate C_k from $L_{k/2}$ if ever possible. With this method, there would only be $log_2 k$ steps in finding L_k instead of k steps. When k is not a multiple of 2, we first find out the L's up to L_w where $2^w < k < 2^{w+1}$. We then find L_k by utilizing L_w, $L_{w/2}$, $L_{w/4}$, ..., etc. For example, if k is 31, we find out L_1, L_2, L_4, L_8 and L_{16} first. We can then use the found L's to find L_{31} in an iterative fashion. As a result, instead of taking 31 steps to find out L_{31}, we will only take 9 steps as illustrated below.

$L_1 \rightarrow L_2 \rightarrow L_4 \rightarrow L_8 \rightarrow L_{16}$	5 steps
$L_{16} + L_8 \rightarrow L_{24}$	1 step
$L_{24} + L_4 \rightarrow L_{28}$	1 step
$L_{28} + L_2 \rightarrow L_{30}$	1 step
$L_{30} + L_1 \rightarrow L_{31}$	1 step

This method saves much computational effort when compared with the other algorithms. However, we would need to store many previously calculated L's. For example, in finding L_{31}, we stored L_1, L_2, L_4, L_8 and L_{16}. If the size of IN is large, there will be a large memory requirement. Therefore, we suggest a second method to store only a few L's and skip the unnecessary steps. Suppose L_k is a result of combining L_n and L_m where n and m are as specified in IN. Two integer sequences, W_n and W_m, are calculated for n and m respectively. For a given integer value n, the sequence W_n $(w_1, w_2, \ldots)$ is obtained by the following formula

$$w_{n-1} = \begin{cases} w_n/2 & \text{if } w_n \text{ is even} \\ w_n - 1 & otherwise \end{cases} \tag{6.1}$$

where w_1 equals to 1 initially. After finding the sequences W_n and W_m, we find out sequence W_{m+n} which equals to $W_n \cup W_m$ (see example 2). The resultant sequence is then used to guide the generation of the candidate itemsets.

Example 2. Suppose $n = 16$ and $m = 15$. The corresponding W_m will then be a sequence of integers as $15 \rightarrow 14 \rightarrow 7 \rightarrow 6 \rightarrow 3 \rightarrow 2 \rightarrow 1$, and W_n will be $16 \rightarrow 8 \rightarrow 4 \rightarrow 2 \rightarrow 1$. The two sequences are merged to form the W_{m+n}

which is 31 $\rightarrow$ 16 $\rightarrow$ 15 $\rightarrow$ 14 $\rightarrow$ 8 $\rightarrow$ 7 $\rightarrow$ 6 $\rightarrow$ 4 $\rightarrow$ 3 $\rightarrow$ 2 $\rightarrow$ 1. By finding out W_m and W_n first, we can, in many situations, filter out unwanted candidate itemsets before generating the desired L_k. If we are looking for "sum of L_{16} minus sum of L_{15} is greater than 100," we can filter out those L_{16} with the sum is less than 100. Q.E.D.

In example 2, it only take 11 steps to find out L_{31}. The number of steps in this algorithm will always be much smaller than that of the other two algorithms, which is 31 in the example. Moreover, it only requires the storage of two or three previous L's to generate the next candidate itemsets.

7.6.2 Generating Candidate Itemsets

Suppose in a distributed system, there are only two workstations, S_1 and S_2. S_1 has completed the ith-iteration while S_2 is still working on it. In the original FDM algorithm, S_1 will wait until S_2 completes the current iteration. If S_1 does not wait, it can proceed to the $(i + 1)^{th}$-iteration with the chance of having some extra candidate itemsets. If the situation is allowed, at some time point, S_1 may be working at the $(j + l + 1)^{th}$-iteration while S_2 is at the jth-iteration. Assuming that after each iteration, the workstations will send their results to the polling site, S^p, then the result representing $LL_{1(j+l)}$ from S_1 will be available for S_2 later. Before S_2 starts its $(j + 1)^{th}$-iteration, it can obtain $LL_{1(j+l)}$ to determine its next set of candidate itemsets. There are three possibilities.

1. Any itemset in $LL_{2(j)}$ can be found as a subset of one of the itemsets in $LL_{1(j+l)}$
2. All items in $LL_{1(j+l)}$ can be found in $LL_{2(j)}$, but some itemsets in $LL_{2(j)}$ cannot be found as a subset of any itemsets in $LL_{1(j+l)}$
3. Some items in $LL_{1(j+l)}$ cannot be found in $LL_{2(j)}$.

Case (1) is trivial because S_2 can now take $LL_{1(j+l)}$ as the next set of candidate itemsets and skipping possibly l iterations. In case (2), there will be 2 groups of candidate itemsets, one is of size $(j+1)$ and the other is $(j+l)$. In this case, any subsets in the itemsets of $LL_{2(j)}$ that can be found in $LL_{1(j+l)}$ can be removed from the candidate set generation for the size $(j+1)$ itemsets. Case (3) is the worst scenario where $LL_{1(j+l)}$ would not be utilized and $LL_{2(j)}$ is used to generate the next set of candidate itemsets.

The discussion above can be generalized for multiple sites. The polling site, S^p, then will store all the locally large itemsets in a trie and is responsible to coordinate the candidate set generations. One disadvantage is when there many iterations and sites, then the storage requirement for the trie can be large.

Given the sequence W_{n+m} as $\{s_1, s_2, \ldots\}$. Let $LL_{i(s_j)}$ be the current large itemset at site S_i and S^p be the polling site.

1. GL := get_pollsite_itemset(S^p) /* large itemsets from S^p */
2. Let G be the items in GL and LI be the items in $LL_{i(s_j)}$.
3. /* CASE 3 */
   if $((G \cup LI) \neq LI)$ then
   - if $((s_j - s_{j-1}) \neq 1)$ then /* section A */
     - for any two itemsets $X, Y \in LL_{i(s_j)}$
       * if $((X \cap Y) = \phi)$ then
         { $c := X \cup Y$
         Insert c into $C_{i(s_{j+1})}$ }

     else
     - for any two itemsets $X, Y \in LL_{i(s_j)}$ where $X = X_1X_2 \ldots X_j$ and $Y = Y_1Y_2 \ldots Y_j$
       * if ($X_1 = Y_1$ and $X_2 = Y_2$ and ... X_{j-1}=Y_{j-1}) then
         { $c := X_1X_2 \ldots X_j\ Y_j$
         Insert c into $C_{i(s_{j+1})}$ }

     /* end of section A */

   else
   - case2 := *false*
   - for_all $X \in LL_{i(s_j)}$ do
     - if X is not a subset of any itemset in GL then case2 := *true*
   - if (case2 = *false*) then /* CASE 1 */
     - C := { $X \epsilon GL$: there exists $Y \epsilon L_{i(s_j)}$ and $X \cup Y \neq \phi$ }
     - $C_{i(s_{j+1})} := C$
     - Update the current sequence number to the size of GL

     else /* CASE 2 */
     - for_all $X \in LL_{i(s_j)}$ do
       * if there exists an itemset in GL that contains X then
         $LL_{i(s_j)} := LL_{i(s_j)}$ - X
     - Generate $C_{i(s_{j+1})}$ as in *section A* above
     - $C_{i(s_{j+1})} := GL \cup C_{i(s_{j+1})}$

Figure 7.4: Generating candidate itemsets $C_{i(s_{j+1})}$ at S_i during the (j+1)th-iteration.

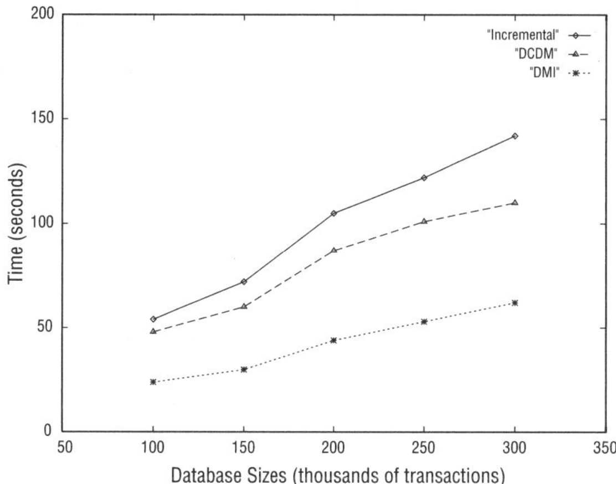

Figure 7.5: Discovery time for different database sizes.

7.7 Performance Studies

In order to assess the performance of the mining algorithms, we have implemented the three algorithms described in the previous section. We follow the methodology proposed by Agrawal and Srikant (1994) to develop synthetic databases for the experiments, which are run on a local-area network with 20 Sun workstations.

There are two sets of experiments. The first set is to test the effect of asynchronous mining and dynamic candidate set generations. This is done by varying the database sizes. Ten fast workstations (Sun Ultra-5) and ten slow ones (Sun Sparc4) are used in this set of experiments. They are all connected to a 100 mb/s local area network and running on the Solaris 2.6 operating system. The database size for each fast workstation will vary from 50,000 to 350,000 number of transactions. For slow workstations, their database sizes will be double of the fast ones. This set up will make a wider range of variations amongst the workstations with respect to the processing times spent in each mining iteration. The parameters for the inequality is (4,4,+,-,$\geq$,1000) and the support level is set to 1%. We are interested in measuring the times to discover the constrainted association rules for the different databases.

The results are shown in figure 7.5. From the results, it is a bit surprise at the beginning to notice that the DCDM algorithm only has a slightly better performance than the Incremental algorithm. After some analysis, we believe this is due to the randomness of the data. In our distributed environment, we cannot merge nor shuffle data between sites. Therefore, the heuristics used in the adaptive interval configuration (Cheung, Hu, and Xia 1998) cannot be

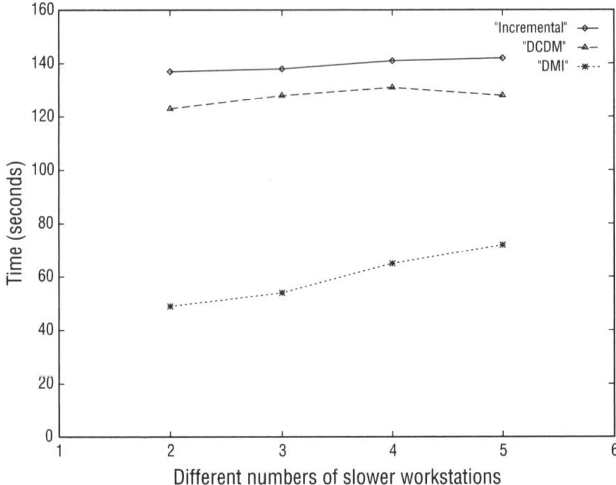

Figure 7.6: Discovery time with different numbers of slow workstations.

applied. Overall, the DMI algorithm has the best performance. This is particularly obvious when the size of the database is getting larger.

A second set of experiments is to test the effect of the number of slower sites (workstations) on the mining algorithms. In these experiments, we fixed the database size for all workstations as to have 300,000 transactions but varied the number of the slow workstations. The results are shown in figure 7.6. It is interesting to note that the performance of the Incremental algorithm and the DCDM algorithm do not have large variations. That is, the mining times seem to be independent on the number of slow workstations. On the other hand, the DMI algorithm has approximately a 20% speed up when there are two more fast workstations put into the workstation pool (i.e. from 5 slow workstations to 3 slow workstations.).

7.8 Conclusions

In this chapter, we have presented three distributed mining algorithms to discover constrained association rules of quantitative items. The *Incremental algorithm* is a simple extension of the FDM algorithm. The *DCDM algorithm* is a variant of the APM algorithm which allows asynchronous mining amongst the different sites. Besides the support of asynchronous mining, the *DMI algorithm* utilizes a sequence to guide the generation of candidate itemsets so as to reduce the database scanning and computational effort. The preliminary experimental results showed that the DMI algorithm out-performed the other two algorithms.

Part III

Architectural, Security, and Data Issues in Distributed Data Mining

Chapter 8

Facilitating Datamining on a Network of Workstations

Srinivasan Parthasarathy and Ramesh Subramonian

8.1 Introduction

As our ability to collect, store, and distribute huge amounts of data increases with advancing technology, discovering the knowledge hidden in these ever-growing databases has become a pressing problem. This problem is referred to as data-mining, an effort to derive interesting conclusions from large bodies of data automatically. Extracting knowledge from these massive databases is a computationally expensive process, which is amenable to and can benefit from being parallelized. This has prompted work in parallelizing data mining algorithms (Shafer, Agrawal, and Mehta 1996; Zaki, Parthasarathy, Ogihara, and Li 1997; Cheung, Han, Ng, Fu, and Fu 1996).

Modern-day enterprises usually contain a cluster of shared memory workstations connected by some (intra-enterprise)network. Such a cluster of shared-memory symmetric multi-processors (SMPs) is a cost effective computational resource. It is particularly attractive as it is a zero-cost resource that if properly harnessed can provide a powerful computational platform. Leveraging this enterprise wide resources for data mining poses several problems.

First, the programming model in cluster computing is based on message passing. In terms of programmability this model is more complicated than the intra-workstation shared memory model. Furthermore, parallel programming primitives like *doall* constructs that exist on a shared memory system are not available on a cluster platform. Corresponding primitives for parallelization on an SMP cluster can alleviate this problem.

Second, due to the large datasets involved, distributing the data across a limited bandwidth interconnection network is expensive. Techniques that can reduce the communications costs, by reducing the input data size, are essential for distributed data mining. Ideally, such techniques should compromise on result quality and comprehensiveness as little as possible.

Third, the very nature of the knowledge-discovery process requires the user to be tightly integrated into it. Providing interactivity in the form of monitoring, computational steering and fast response times in an asynchronous, distributed environment is difficult, but useful. In order for this to happen algorithms have to be re-architected in a fashion that permits such desirable features.

8.1.1 Contributions

In this chapter we present a programmable data parallel primitive D-DOALL that addresses each of the above problems in the following way.

Usability. Our solution takes the form of the traditional *doall* primitive, a popular way to express data parallelism in shared memory multiprocessors. The runtime system handles executing it across a network of workstations.

Limited Bandwidth and Large Datasets. The regularity of many data mining algorithms means that one can reason about the resource (input data) requirements of individual independent tasks. A good scheduling algorithm can take advantage of this information to minimize communication. Our runtime system incorporates a global affine scheduler which does this.

Interactivity. Our primitive supports partial (incremental) result reporting in a timely fashion and also permits clients to terminate execution at any point in the computation.

We evaluate the primitive on two commonly used data mining applications: discretization and clustering.

8.1.2 Organization

In section 8.2, we describe the architecture of the distributed data mining system we have implemented to set our primitive in context. In section 8.3, we describe the distributed doall (D-DOALL) primitive. In section 8.4 we highlight alternative scheduling policies for the D-DOALL primitive. In section 8.5, we evaluate the relative merits of these policies using a simulation of a template application. In section 8.6, we present actual speedups on a NOW for our applications. Finally, in section 8.7, we present our conclusions and outline directions for future work.

8.2 Architecture

In this section we sketch the architecture of a distributed data mining system we have implemented. The design of our system took into account the interactivity and large datasets involved in mining applications. In addition it is often possible to provide succinct descriptions of the input e.g."partition dataset X into 4 clusters" or "discretize the continuous attributes in dataset Y." This permitted us to decouple task description from the actual data required by the task and is reflected in our decoupled architecture. This decoupling is important as it potentially enables different tasks to obtain data from multiple sources simultaneously.

Our architecture consists of the following logical components:

Client, consisting of the GUI, a task manager that directs the mining process, and a local cache of data/results of prior computations. It is responsible for the interacting with the data mining engine in terms of invoking, guiding and monitoring computations as well as visualization of the results.

Compute server(s), each consisting of a task manager, a compute module, which is the core data mining engine, and a local data cache. All compute servers are indistinguishable in terms of structure and code base.

Data server, consisting of a data distiller and the source database. The data distiller reads data from the database and performs appropriate data compaction transformations before passing it to the compute servers.

The physical layout of these logical components depends on available resources. In a fully distributed mode the components, i.e. the client, each compute server and the data server are physically separated. When the data sets are relatively small and the client is relatively powerful, all components could be resident on the client. Figure 8.1 depicts the overall architecture with arrows indicating communication patterns.

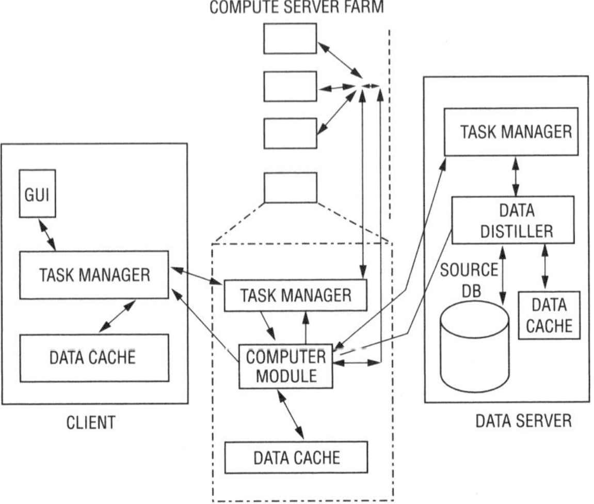

Figure 8.1: IntelliMiner architecture.

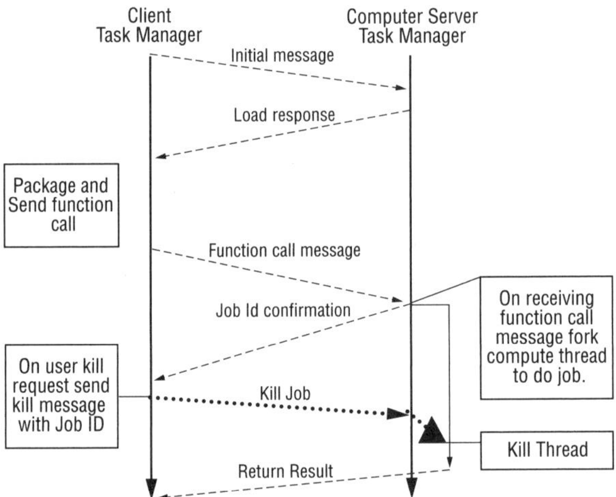

Figure 8.2: Communication protocol.

8.2.1 Communication Protocol

In this section, we describe the basic protocol for communicating across any two tiers in our architecture. For exposition, we describe with an example how the communication between a client and compute server transpires.

Figure 8.2 depicts a typical communication between a client and a compute server. The client task manager (caller), that needs to execute the remote service first pings the task manager on the compute server to see if it is overloaded. If the server is not overloaded, then the client packages the function call and transmits it to the compute server. On receiving the packed function call, the task manager forks a thread to execute the job, and returns a job identifier to the caller. This permits the caller to stop/kill the compute server job (callee) if and when required. The compute module thread that executes the job unmarshals the function call, invokes the appropriate function, and generates the results. When the function has completed its execution the results are packaged by the callee and returned to the caller.

The communication protocol is implemented on top of C++ sockets. We evaluated using distributed object technology like COM/CORBA but found sockets to be the cheapest (performance wise). We are investigating alternative message passing primitives to improve communication overheads[1] and to permit portability across different architectures.

8.3 Distributed DOALL Primitive

A *doall loop* is one in which the loop iterations are independent (Wolfe 1996), i.e. , where there are no conflicts between iterations. In other words where an element that is assigned is used on that iteration only then the loop is referred to as a *doall loop.* In such a case , executing the iterations sequentially or in parallel in any order is legal, since the result does not depend on the order. It is a simple mechanism that is often adequate to express parallelism. Loops that are not strictly doall loops (such as a loop that sums the elements of an array) can often be cast as doall loops by performing partial summations in parallel and then sequentially combining the results of the partial sums. A sample doall loop is shown below.

```
for ( i = 0; i ¡ N; i++ ) { A[i] = B[i];}
```

The doall primitive we adopt is loosely based on on the *parallel for* defined in OpenMP (www.openmp.org), an industry-wide initiative to unify parallel programming constructs on SMPs, and is similar in flavor to the *forall* construct in High Performance Fortran (although *forall* is more of a compile-time construct, whereas the doall in figure 8.3 is a pure runtime construct). Despite the restrictiveness of doall, its adherence to an industry standard, ease of use and portability make it an attractive choice on the SMP platform. Most existing implementations of doall have struck a balance between support from compilers (Fortran-90, HPF) and runtime systems and SMP platforms (SGI,

[1] www.via.org

```
doall((void (*)(void))body, iters,...,N, A, B); /* do in parallel */
void body1(int *start, int *iters, int A[], int B[])
{
      int i;
      for ( i = *start; i < start + *iters; i++ ) {
            A[i] = B[i];
      }
}
```

Figure 8.3: Sample parallelization using doall.

DEC). Secondly most of these implementations use a simple static or dynamic scheduler and have no support for interactive applications. In this work we present a purely runtime doall primitive for a network of NT stations, that uses a smart dynamic scheduler, and has support for basic interactivity. We present our primitive and its interactive support in this section. The next section is devoted to the development of our smart scheduler.

Figure 8.3 presents the invocation of the doall construct on our sample doall loop.

The run time system is responsible for scheduling different iterations of the loop body on different processors by assigning appropriate values to start and iters (a variable to chunk several consecutive iterations on the same processor) and invoking the function body.

Providing a variant of the doall mechanism on a cluster of SMPs would reduce the complexity of distributed programming. However the implicit assumption of shared memory in the doall primitive is an obstacle to a direct transformation into the distributed, memory model. To overcome this, we designed the distributed doall primitive, the D-DOALL. The D-DOALL is invoked as follows. The application specifies a set of tasks to be executed in parallel. For each task it marshalls the function to be executed and the input arguments to the function as a linear array of bytes. The result of each task is a linear array of bytes, the interpretation of which is the responsibility of the calling routine. Figure 8.4 specifies the calling mechanism. Note that the input/output semantics of the D-DOALL prevent passing of parameters by value.

The main thread that invokes the D-DOALL first identifies the available compute servers. This is identical to the first part of the communication protocol described in section 8.2.1. It then spawns a *local doall thread* for each available remote compute server. The main thread then blocks until all tasks

```
Distributed-DOALL(
    int T; /* number of independent tasks */
    void **inputsList; /* [T][] */
    void **outputsList; /* [T][] */
    FuncPtr body;/* body of doall loop */
);
```

Figure 8.4: Basic distributed DOALL interface.

```
typedef void ( *FuncPtr )( void *, int);
DistributedDOALL(
    int T; /* number of independent tasks */
    void **inputsList; /* [T][] */
    void **outputsList; /* [T][] */
    FuncPtr body;/* body of doall loop */
    int &interrupt_flag; /* global interrupt flag */
    FuncPtr fp /* functional processing */ );
```

Figure 8.5: Interactive resource-aware D-DOALL.

are done. Each *local doall thread* selects a task from the task queue and sends that task to its associated compute server and blocks until it receives the output. On receiving the result (output) it selects another task and repeats the process. When all tasks are done the local doall threads terminate and the main thread that invoked the D-DOALL is resumed.

Figure 8.4 shows the basic structure of the D-DOALL interface. We now describe how additional features such scheduling and support for interactivity can be added to this basis.

8.3.1 Supporting Interactivity

We extend the D-DOALL mechanism to support interactivity in two ways (figure 8.5). One is by providing a *terminate* mechanism. The other is by providing a mechanism which allows the calling thread to be made aware of the completion of a particular task.

Termination is handled as follows. We permit the application developer to pass as a parameter a location in global memory (interrupt_flag) that initially contains the boolean False. If the D-DOALL is to be terminated by the client the interrupt_flag is set to the value true. The main thread spins on this flag while waiting for all its tasks to complete. When this flag is set to "true," the main thread simply cancels all tasks which have not been scheduled and waits for any outstanding scheduled tasks to complete. Once these outstanding tasks complete, the main thread exits from the D-DOALL call.

We permit the application developer to pass as a parameter to the D-DOALL, a function pointer *fp* that takes as its argument a void* pointer. Essentially we modified the way each local doall thread behaves on receiving the output from a compute server. After scheduling the next job it executes the function pointed to by *fp* with the result output as the parameter. Within this function the local doall thread can notify the GUI of incremental progress made in an application specific manner.

8.4 Scheduling

In section 8.4.1, we describe prior work in the scheduling literature. In section 8.4.2, we indicate what aspects of scheduling need to be adequately modeled for data mining applications to be effectively parallelized on a network of workstations (NOW). In section 8.4.3, we discuss the application programming interface (API) to the D-DOALL primitive that we propose as a solution to the scheduling problem. In section 8.4.4, we describe several algorithms which could be used to implement the D-DOALL primitive and highlight the strengths and weaknesses of each.

8.4.1 Previous Work

Given a set of $\hat{T}$ tasks and a set of $\hat{S}$ servers or processors, the scheduling problem can be informally stated as deciding which server/processor executes which task when. One solution is to statically partition the work among the processors (Static Scheduling) at compile time (Wolfe 1996; Polychronopoulos 1988; (Li and Pingali 1993). Such schemes have been implemented on NOWs (Cierniak, Li, and Zaki 1995; Cheung and Reeves 1992; Grimshaw 1994). Another solution is to hand out tasks one at a time to a free processor requesting work (Simple (Dynamic) Scheduling) (Polychronopoulos 1988; Markatos and Leblanc 1994). More complicated dynamic strategies have also been proposed (in some cases application specific) (Lin and Keller 1987; Nishikawa and Steenkiste 1993; Berman 1996).

The scheduling policy for the D-DOALL specified in figure 8.4 is the simple, dynamic policy. Tasks are scheduled in the order specified, thus allowing the user to have limited control on the order in which partial results will be reported. The reason we qualify this control as "limited" is that processors, in our model, operate asynchronously. Hence, the fact that a task has started before another task, does not guarantee that it will also finish earlier. This feature is used in section 8.6.2.

8.4.2 Desired Scheduling Properties

A good scheduling algorithm should be able to satisfy certain basic requirements such as fault tolerance and load balancing. In addition, a desirable property is resource-aware scheduling, also called *affinity-scheduling* (Markatos and Leblanc 1994). A *resource-aware* scheduling algorithm takes into account the resources (in terms of data or partial results) that a processor possesses in its local cache when it determines what task to assign to that processor. Using matrix-multiply ($C \leftarrow A \times B$) as an example, the task of evaluating $C_{i,j}$ is ideally assigned to the processor that possesses row i of A and column j of B.

This feature is especially desirable in data-intensive applications such as data mining. In such applications, it is often the case that the format in which data is stored for report generation is not the most appropriate format for mining the data. In such cases the data has to be transformed into a form which is acceptable to the application. Furthermore, several applications like discretization (Fayyad and Irani 1993; Subramonian, Venkata, and Chen 1997), clustering (Smyth, Ghil, Ide, and Fraser 1997), and similarity analysis (Agrawal, Faloutsos, and Swarni 1993), may accept a distilled/compressed form of the output. Reduction of the output data prior to transmission reduces the bandwidth requirement of the interconnection network and storage requirements at the compute server. The need to minimize communication is especially important in a distributed environment where communication bandwidth is relatively small and one seeks to reduce demands on the database server.

We define a *resource* as an input to a computation. It may be a column in a relational table, a multi-dimensional histogram computed over a few columns, etc.

A good scheduling algorithm, which analyzes resource requirements and schedules tasks in resource-aware manner, can prove to be beneficial to such applications. Clearly this analysis will take time. However, if the time spent scheduling is small when compared with cost of obtaining such resources, then resource-aware scheduling should outperform traditional schedulers for such applications. In the ensuing sections we present such resource-aware algorithms and examine the performance of the scheduling algorithms both qualitatively and quantitatively.

8.4.3 Application Programming Interface

In this section, we describe how the D-DOALL API changes from that of figure 8.5 to that of figure 8.6 in order to become resource-aware. The application

```
Distributed-DOALL(
        int T; /* number of independent tasks */
        void **inputsList; /* [T][] */
        void **outputsList; /* [T][] */
        FuncPtr body /* loop body */
        int &interrupt_flag; /* global interrupt flag */
        FuncPtr fp /* functional processing */
        int R; /* number of resources */
        int *num_resources_per_task; /* [T] */
        int **resources_per_task; /* [T][] */
);
```

Figure 8.6: API for resource-aware D-DOALL.

needs to inform the scheduling algorithm about the resource requirements of each task as follows. The user specifies (i) a list of R resources, numbered $1 \ldots R$, (ii) a list of T tasks, numbered $1 \ldots T$, and (iii) for each task, a list of resources needed to perform that task.

We explain the above specification using matrix multiply as an example. Consider $C[m][p] \leftarrow A[m][n] \times B[n][p]$. There are $m + p$ resources, the m rows of A and the p columns of B. There are $m \times p$ tasks corresponding to the creation of each element of C. Task $(i \times m) + p$ is the creation of $C_{i,j}$ and requires resources i and $m + j$ where resource i is the ith row of A and resource $m + j$ is the jth column of B.

In section 8.4.4, we will show how specifying the resource requirements of each task, enables the scheduler to make educated guesses as to the resources possessed by a processor and hence, the suitability of assigning a specific task to a specific processor. We seek to answer the question: "can we do a better job of scheduling than the algorithms of section 8.4.1 without imposing an onerous burden either on the programmer or on the scheduler ?"

8.4.4 Algorithms

In sections 8.4.4 and 8.4.4, we present two different resource-aware scheduling algorithms, and a discussion of their respective advantages and disadvantages. Section 8.4.5 presents a relaxation of an assumption made in sections 8.4.4 and 8.4.4. In section 8.5, we present an empirical evaluation of their performance.

The fundamental idea behind resource-aware scheduling is to use the knowledge of the resources possessed by a processor to determine which task should be assigned to it. We hope to be able to have an approximate idea of the resources that a processor possesses based on tasks executed by it in the past. Knowing the resources a processor possesses allows us to define a metric to evaluate the relative suitability of different tasks. In section 8.4.4 and 8.4.4, we will make the assumption that each processor has an infinite cache. Hence, at any point in time, it possesses all resources for all tasks performed by that time. We will relax this assumption in section 8.4.5.

We introduce some useful notation. Let $\bar{S}$ be the set of processors (also called servers, to keep notation consistent). Let $\bar{R}$ be the set of resources. Let $\bar{T}$ be the set of tasks. When there is no possibility of confusion, we shall also use $\bar{T}$ to refer to the set of *incomplete* tasks at any point in time. For simplicity, we differentiate between sets (e.g., $\bar{X}$) and scalars (e.g., y) using an overhead bar.

Notation 8.4.1 $\bar{R}(t) \subseteq \bar{R}$ *is the set of resources required to execute task* t.

Notation 8.4.2 $\bar{R}(s) \subseteq \bar{R}$ *is the set of resources possessed by server* s.

Notation 8.4.3 $R(r, s) = 1$ *if* $r \in \bar{R}(s)$ *(i.e., server* s *possesses resource* r*); else, 0.*

We define the *cost*, $C_{t,s}$ (equation 8.1), of executing task, t, on server, s, as the sum of resources that need to be obtained before the task can be executed (equation 8.1). For instance, if a server s already has resources x and y and task t requires resources w, x, y, z the cost of evaluating t on s is 2, corresponding to obtaining resources w and z. Note that we are making the implicit assumption that all resources are equally expensive to obtain for all servers. Note that by *cost* we mean *only* the cost of acquisition of resources, not the computational time.

$$C_{t,s} = \sum_{r \in \bar{R}(t)} (1 - R(r, s)). \tag{8.1}$$

For complexity analysis, we assume that each task requires a constant number of resources i.e., $\forall t : |R(t)| = O(1)$.

Local Algorithm

In this section, we describe a scheduling algorithm which operates under the infinite-cache assumption. The algorithm is *local* i.e., each server assesses the cost of a task without consideration of other servers. While it is simple, it suffers, in performance (section 8.5), a limitation we address in section 8.4.4.

The local scheduler, under the infinite cache assumption, works as follows. Assume server s requests a task. From the set of uncompleted tasks, $\bar{T}$, assign task t' to processor s such that $C_{t',s}$ is minimum over all $t \in \bar{T}$.

Theorem 8.4.1 *The local algorithm requires $O(|T|)$ time per scheduling decision.*

Proof: Every time a server requests a task, there are $O(|T|)$ tasks to be evaluated. Each evaluation requires $O(1)$ work since, by assumption, $\forall t : |\bar{R}(t)| = O(1)$. The proof follows.

Global Algorithm

In this section, we show how one can make scheduling decisions from a global viewpoint, as opposed to a purely local viewpoint (section 8.4.4). In this algorithm, if server, s', requests a task and there exists a task, t', of zero cost for it, ($C_{t',s'} = 0$), we assign t' to s'. When no such task exists, the scheduling decision becomes more complex. Let the smallest cost (over all servers) to perform task t be C_t^{min} (equation 8.2).

$$C_t^{min} = min_{s \in \bar{S}}(C_{t,s}) \tag{8.2}$$

At a given point in time, let OC^{old} (equation 8.3), be the sum of the smallest cost to perform all *remaining* tasks. We use OC for *outstanding cost.*

$$OC^{old} = \sum_{t \in \bar{T}} C_t \tag{8.3}$$

Consider a tentative assignment of t' to s'. The cost or *investment* involved in making this assignment is $C_{t',s'}$. Based on this assignment, let the new outstanding cost (similar to equation 8.3) be $OC^{new}(t', s')$. Therefore, the gain or *return on investment* of this assignment is the difference between the old oust anding cost and the new oust anding cost (equation 8.4).

$$G(t', s') = OC^{old} - OC^{new}(t', s') \tag{8.4}$$

We choose t' so as to maximize the profit, $P'_{t',s'}$ (equation 8.5) which is the difference between the investment and the return on investment.

$$P'_{t',s'} = G(t', s') - C_{t',s'} \tag{8.5}$$

However, equation 8.5 does not capture the reality that the ability of s' to perform t' at a small, or zero, cost, does not guarantee that it will in fact be assigned t'. This is because of load balancing requirements. It might be preferable to assign t' to a different server, s'', rather than have s'' stay idle, even if the cost for server s'' to perform t' is greater than the cost for server s' to perform t'. Hence, we need to temper our estimate of the return on investment.

We do so by using a factor $\beta(0 < \beta < 1)$. Determining the optimal value of β remains an open problem. We now replace equation 8.5 with equation 8.6.

$$P_{t',s'} = \beta(C^{old} - C^{new}(t', s')) - C_{t',s'} \tag{8.6}$$

Note that when $\beta = 0$, maximizing $P_{t',s'}$ is the same as minimizing $C_{t',s'}$, which is precisely the local algorithm (section 8.4.4). We now discuss a tie-breaking mechanism invoked when more than one task has the same gain (equation 8.4) for a given server. The intuition behind this approach is to reduce the overlap between the resources possessed by different servers. N_r (equation 8.7) is the number of servers that possess r. Let $\bar{AR}(s', t')$ (equation 8.8) be the set of *additional* resources that s' must acquire to perform t'. We choose t' so as to minimize $RO(t', s')$ (equation 8.9), which measures the increase in Resource Overlap when s' acquires $\bar{AR}(t', s')$.

$$N_r = \sum_{s \in S} R(r, s) \tag{8.7}$$

$$\bar{AR}(s', t') = \bar{R}(t') - \bar{R}(s') \tag{8.8}$$

$$RO(t', s') = \sum_{r \in \bar{AR}(s', t')} N_r \tag{8.9}$$

The global scheduler under the infinite cache assumption works as follows. When a server s' requests a task, assign it task t' if $\exists t' : C_{t',s'} = 0$. Else, assign task t' such that equation 8.6 is maximized. In either case, if more than one task qualifies, assign the task, t, for which $RO(t, s')$ is minimum.

Lemma 8.4.1 *Neither $C_{t,s}$ nor C_t increase with time.*

Proof : Follows from fact that $R(r, s)$ does not change once it becomes 0 and from equation 8.4.3.

Theorem 8.4.2 *The global algorithm requires $O(|T|^2)$ time per scheduling decision.*

Proof : Let $C_{t,s}$, C_t^{min} and OC^{old} be constructed initially at a one-time cost of $O(|S| \times |T|)$. We have $|T|$ requests to the scheduler, one for each task. At each request, we have to evaluate $O(|T|)$ tasks to determine the best task for this server. We now need to establish that the cost of evaluating the goodness of task t' for server s' is $O(1)$.

Calculation of $OC^{new}(t', s')$ is an $O(1)$ cost. This is because it needs the calculation of a tentative C_t^{min}. However, since $C_{t,s}$ does not change for any of the other servers except when a scheduling decision for that server is being made, we need concern ourselves *only* with this server. This is where Lemma 8.4.1 is useful. We will see in a later section that $C_{t,s}$ might change at times other than when a scheduling decision is being made for s. This increases the scheduling complexity. Since the tentative assignment of a task to a server needs to deal with the acquisition of only a constant number of resources, this is an $O(1)$ cost. Note that the other calculations of gain and profit (Equations 8.4 and 8.6) are clearly $O(1)$.

Note that once the choice of t' is decided upon, it requires $O(1)$ additional time to update $C_{t,s'}$, C_t^{min} and OC^{old} appropriately. The time complexity of $O(|T|^2)$ follows.

8.4.5 Removing the Infinite Cache Assumption

In sections 8.4.4 and 8.4.4, we made the arguably unreasonable assumption that a server has an infinite cache i.e., once it acquires a resource, it possesses it for all subsequent time. In this section, we seek to relax that assumption. This requires reasoning about what resources a server is likely to relinquish. While this reasoning is rife with approximation, we show (section 8.5.3) that it can improve performance.

Assume the requests by server s to the scheduler to occur at times 0, 1, 2 ... where 0 refers to the most recent request. The scheduler can keep track of the last time, $V(r, s)$, at which resource r was acquired by server s. Initially, $\forall r \forall s : V(r, s) = \infty$. Assume that server s has just been assigned task t. This means that $\forall r \in \bar{R}(t),\ V(r, s) = 0$. Assume that s had been assigned t' at the previous point in time. This means that $\forall r \in (\bar{R}(t') - \bar{R}(t)),\ V(r, s) = 1$.

In sections 8.4.4 and 8.4.4, $R(s, r) = 1$ if s had been assigned a task that required r at some previous time and 0 otherwise. Now, we make a probabilistic estimate of $R(s, r)$ as $\alpha^{V(r,s)}$, where $0 < \alpha < 1$ is an aging parameter. To understand the role of α, consider the limiting cases. $\alpha = 0$ degenerates to the "no-cache" case i.e., no affinity scheduling possible. $\alpha = 1$ reverts to the infinite cache assumption of sections 8.4.4 and 8.4.4. A drawback of our current approach is that the value of α is set somewhat arbitrarily.

Both the local and global algorithms can be modified to remove the infinite cache assumption by simply changing the way $R(r, s)$ is calculated as shown above. Unfortunately, since Lemma 8.4.1 does not apply, this introduces a factor of $O(|S| \times |T|)$ with each scheduling decision.

In the next section we qualitatively compare the three policies on a simple template application and show why we believe resource-aware scheduling is so important for minimizing communication.

8.5 Scheduling Policy Analysis

In this section, we evaluate the pros and cons of the various scheduling policies. To do so, we first define a template application that closely mirrors, in its computational and data access patterns, several data mining applications. The experiments and discussions are in the context of this template application.

In section 8.5.1, we describe the template application. In section 8.5.2, we compare the global and local scheduling algorithms (sections 8.4.4 and 8.4.4) and a simple dynamic scheduler. Later in section 8.5.4, we discuss the primary limitation of the resource aware strategies, scheduling time complexity, and outline two ways in which this limitation can be alleviated.

8.5.1 Template Application

The template application is an upper diagonal matrix multiply. The tasks are: $\forall i, \forall j < i$, compute $C_{i,j} \leftarrow \sum_k A_{i,k} \times B_{k,j}$. The resources are the rows of A and the columns of B. The resource requirements of task $C_{i,j}$ is row i of A and column j of B. The cost to a server of performing $C_{i,j}$ is 2 if it possesses neither row i of A nor column j of B; 1, if it possesses either one and 0 if it possesses both.

We now motivate our choice of this particular template application by showing that it mirrors the computational and data access patterns of many commonly used data mining algorithms. We list a few examples below.

Feature selection: The goal of feature selection (Dougherty, Kohavi, and Sahami 1995) is to select the smallest subset of features, $\{X_1, \ldots X_n\}$, that best determines the class label, Y. Let $f(X_i, X_j)$ be the ability of features X_i and X_j to jointly predict Y. For expository simplicity, limit the number of features selected to 2. Feature selection can be rephrased as evaluating $\forall i \forall j < i : f(X_i, X_j)$, which is identical to the template application.

Diff: The diff primitive (Subramonian 1998) provides a high-level view of the differences between two databases that share the same set of attributes, $\{X_1, \ldots X_n\}$. Again for expository simplicity, assume that we are interested only in pair-wise differences. Let $f(X_i, X_j)$ be the difference between the data sets when each is projected onto attributes X_i and X_j. The diff problem is to rank $\forall i \forall j < i : f(X_i, X_j)$.

Decision trees: In the process of growing a decision tree (Quinlan 1993), the problem is to determine which leaf node to split and for each leaf node, which attribute to use for the decision at that node. Consider the computation at a node. While typically, a single attribute is used as the decision variable, one can well consider extensions to more than one attribute (e.g., $X > 5 \wedge Y < 6$) as long as the decisions remain simple (Parthasarathy, Subramonian, and Venkata 1998). We (Parthasarathy, Subramonian, and Venkata

1998) clearly demonstrate that this approach is comparable to, and in some instances better than, the state of the art work in discretization, at a fraction of the computational cost. Limiting oneself to selecting attributes pair-wise, the problem is to determine $f(X_i, X_j)$ for all pairs X_i, X_j, where $\{X_i, X_j\}$ are the attributes and $f(X_i, X_j)$ measures the goodness of X_i, X_j as a decision attribute. Another important problem in this domain is in visualizing the results of discretization (also clustering). Since current limitations in graphics pretty much restrict you to 2 or 3D (two base attributes and one goal attribute) visualizations, an important task of the discretizer is to decide what to display to the user, i.e, identify which of several base attribute pairs best display separations between discrete regions. In order to do this it has been suggested in past work that entropy (Subramonian, Venkata, and Chen 1997) could be used to pick the pair of attributes that best meet the desired objective. Once again the formulated problem (computing and comparing the entropy for all base attribute pairs) resembles our template application.

We note that while we are limiting our analysis, and thereby our examples from the data mining world, to datacubes (resources per task) of size two for expository simplicity, our scheduling algorithm is capable of handling larger datacube problems. Furthermore, while the examples we outlined above are such that can take advantage of our resource-aware scheduling algorithms, our primitive is capable of addressing other data mining applications as well. Many distributed data mining tasks like association mining (ECLAT [Zaki, Parthasarathy, Ogihara, and Li 1997]), sequence mining (SPADE [Zaki 1998]), and clustering (Smyth, Ghil, Ide, and Fraser 1997), take an approach of dividing or replicating the data set (or the dataset is predivided) and selectively broadcasting the data at the beginning of the process, thus eliminating the need for communication of the data set during the learning process. Our architecture and primitive allows us to handle these scenarios as well. By separating the data acquisition from the task acquisition, in our architecture, and having distributed data servers we actually permit multiple compute servers to obtain their data simultaneously, as opposed to the traditional centralized broadcast approach. If on the other hand the application requires a central broadcast of data, then our D-DOALL primitive supports this as well via the *inputsList* parameter (see figure 8.6).

8.5.2 Comparison of Scheduling Strategies

To compare the scheduling policies, we used our template application, upper-triangular matrix multiply where A, B, C are 8×8 matrices and 4 servers, so that

$$|R| = 16, |T| = \binom{8}{2} = 28, |S| = 4.$$

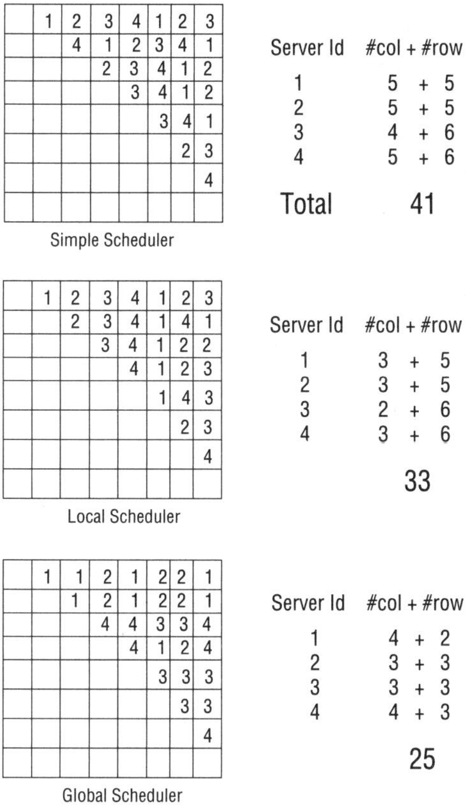

	1	2	3	4	1	2	3
		4	1	2	3	4	1
			2	3	4	1	2
				3	4	1	2
					3	4	1
						2	3
							4

Simple Scheduler

Server Id	#col + #row
1	5 + 5
2	5 + 5
3	4 + 6
4	5 + 6
Total	41

	1	2	3	4	1	2	3
		2	3	4	1	4	1
			3	4	1	2	2
				4	1	2	3
					1	4	3
						2	3
							4

Local Scheduler

Server Id	#col + #row
1	3 + 5
2	3 + 5
3	2 + 6
4	3 + 6
	33

	1	1	2	1	2	2	1
		1	2	1	2	2	1
			4	4	3	3	4
				4	1	2	4
					3	3	3
						3	3
							4

Global Scheduler

Server Id	#col + #row
1	4 + 2
2	3 + 3
3	3 + 3
4	4 + 3
	25

Figure 8.7: Comparison of different scheduling policies.

(The small numbers are merely to simplify presentation of results.) . The assumptions under which the scheduling strategies are evaluated are: (1) Servers request for new tasks in a fixed order. Without any loss of generality we assume that servers 1, 2, 3, and 4 request for tasks in that order. (2) All servers are equally fast and equally loaded. (3) Time to make a scheduling decision is the same for all policies.

The three 8×8 boxes in figure 8.7 depicts the schedule generated by simple, local resource aware, and the global resource aware scheduling policies. Consider a single 8×8 box. Numeric values in the corresponding task box indicate which server executed that particular task. Below each schedule, we indicate how many resources (broken down into rows of A and columns of B) each server acquired and the total resources acquired by all servers. For example from the analysis we see that under simple scheduling, server 4 obtained 5 columns and 6 rows.

The fewer the total number of resources acquired, the better the overall performance. The global scheduling policy (section 8.4.4) outperforms the local scheduling policy (section 8.4.4) which in turn outperforms the simple, dynamic scheduling policy. Interestingly enough, for this example, the schedule generated by the global policy is optimal.

8.5.3 Finite Cache Case

To study the effect of the cache being finite on the effectiveness of scheduling, we conducted the following experiment. We used the template application (section 8.5.1) with

$$n = 32, |S| = 2, |T| = \binom{n}{2} = 120, |R| = 2n = 64.$$

We used the global scheduling algorithm under the finite cache assumption (section 8.4.5) to make scheduling decisions. We varied the cache that each processor possessed from 2 to $n = 32$. Notice the assumption of an infinite cache would lead to inaccurate cost calculations. The better one can reason about the resources a processor possesses, the more accurate the cost calculations. We compared how scheduling effectiveness changed when one tried to reason about the likelihood of a resource having been purged from a processor's cache. The results, in figure 8.8, indicate that such a reasoning is beneficial. It also indicates that the choice of α is critical to the success.

In the next section we discuss the primary limitation of the resource aware strategies, scheduling time complexity, and outline two ways in which this limitation can be alleviated.

8.5.4 Reducing Scheduling Time Complexity

We have paid a price, in terms of scheduling complexity, to achieve better scheduling. We believe this is justified and beneficial because (1) the embarrassingly data-parallel nature of many data mining tasks allows us to create sufficiently large tasks without unduly limiting parallelism; and (2) the acquisition of a resource is often a costly process requiring both access to the database server and subsequent transformations e.g., a resource could be a precomputed multi-dimensional aggregate.

Nevertheless, we would like to reduce the time complexity of the scheduling operation without sacrificing performance. In this section, we propose two approaches (sections 8.5.4 and 8.5.4) to reduce the time complexity of scheduling.

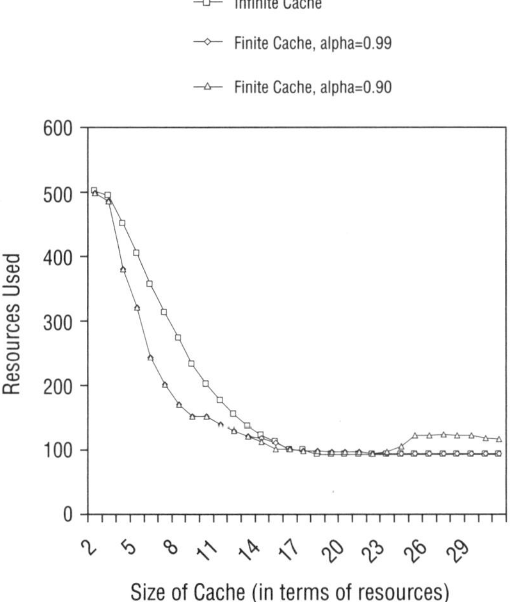

Figure 8.8: Effect of finite cache on scheduling effectiveness.

Reducing the Number of Tasks

Merging tasks into a smaller number of mega-tasks can reduce the time complexity. While we want $|T| > |S|$ for load-balancing purposes, having $|T| >> |S|$ makes scheduling harder without substantially improving load-balancing. The intuition underlying the merging is to aggregate those tasks into mega-tasks that have as much commonality in their resource requirements as possible. We now provide a graph-theoretic formalization of the problem.

Let $G = (T \cup R, E)$ be a bipartite graph with vertices $T \cup R$ and edges E. An edge $e = (x, y) \in E \Leftrightarrow x \in T \wedge y \in R$. Nodes in T represent tasks, nodes in R represent resources and an edge from t to r indicates that task t requires resource r. Let $n < |T|$ be the desired number of mega-tasks. Let T' be an exhaustive and mutually exclusive set of subsets of T i.e., $T' \subset 2^T$ such that $t'_i, t'_j \in T' \Rightarrow t'_i \cap t'_j = \phi \wedge \cup_i t'_i = T$ and 2^T is the power set of T. Let $r(t) \subseteq R$ be the set of resources required by task t i.e., $r \in r(t) \Rightarrow (t, r) \in E$. Ideally,there would be a high degree of overlap between the resources required by the tasks in a mega-task. This is formalized in Problem 8.5.1.

Problem Definition 8.5.1 *Given $G = (T \cup R, E)$, n, and r, find $T' \subset 2^T$ such that $|T'| = n$ and $\sum_{t' \in T'} |\cup_{t \in t'} r(t)|$ is minimum*

Algorithm for Problem 8.5.1 We have been unable to find an efficient solution to Problem Definition 8.5.1. Our heuristic approach is a simple, extension to the algorithm we used for resource-aware scheduling. We create as many "dummy servers" as the number of mega-tasks required. We make these dummy servers requests tasks in order. On completion, the set of tasks assigned to a given dummy server constitutes a mega-task. While expensive, this processing step can be done off-line and needs to be done only once for a given instantiation of $\bar{R}$, $\bar{T}$ and $\bar{S}$ and the resource dependency $\bar{R}(t)$.

Overlapping Scheduling with Task Execution

The scheduler could determine the next task to execute for *each* processor while waiting for a task request. Alternatively, it could order the processors in the likelihood of their being the next processor to make a request (based on when the processor last requested a task) and select the best task for the processors in that order.

8.6 Experimental Analysis

In this section, we examine the performance of D-DOALL scheduler on 2-dimensional Discretization and Clustering. We also provide a glimpse of why support for interactivity and specifying task order is essential for applications like clustering.

All experiments were performed on a client and upto four compute servers each a dual 200 MHz Intel Pentium Pro system running Windows NT 4.0 with 256 MB RAM. For every experiment, numbers reported were averaged over 16 runs at different times of the day.

8.6.1 2-D Discretization

In the process of growing a decision tree (Quinlan 1993), the problem is to determine which leaf node to split and for each leaf node, which attribute to use for the decision at that node. Consider the computation at a node. While typically, a single attribute is used as the decision variable, one can well consider extensions to more than one base attribute (e.g., $X > 5 \wedge Y < 6$) as long as the decisions remain simple (Parthasarathy, Subramonian, and Venkata 1998). Limiting oneself to selecting base attributes pair-wise, the problem is to determine $f(X_i, X_j)$ for all X_i and for all pairs X_i, X_j, where $\{X_i\}$ are the attributes and $f(X_i, X_j)$ measures the goodness of X_i, X_j as a decision attribute. This problem is referred to as 2-Dimensional Discretization. We evaluate our scheduling algorithms on a single node split using 2-Dimensional (all pairs X_i, X_j) Discretization where the evaluation function $f(X_i, X_j)$ used

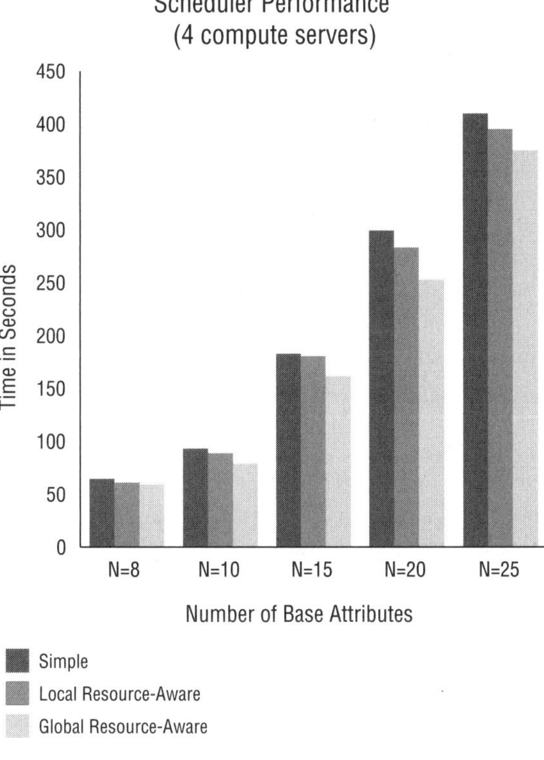

Figure 8.9: Locality based scheduling performance.

is Entropy. Evaluating any pair of attributes involves 3 steps, obtaining the data involving the two attributes, computing the probability density (pdf) estimate, searching for the optimal (determined by goodness function; Entropy) cut-point.

Effect of Locality Based Scheduling

In this experiment we evaluated the effect of our scheduling strategies on a synthetic dataset XOR (Parthasarathy, Subramonian, and Venkata 1998)[2] with N (base) +1 (goal) attributes, where N was varied from 8 to 25, and 100000 instances. Each pair-wise evaluation of the N base attributes is independent from the other and is executed as a D-DOALL loop. Resources (data) for any evaluation required the corresponding base attribute columns and the goal

[2]details of dataset generation can be found from the cited article

attribute column which were obtained from the dataserver. The corresponding task-resource matrix was encoded and passed to the D-DOALL primitive for the locality based scheduling algorithms.

Once a task (evaluating a base pair) is assigned to a compute server, that compute server determines if the resources required are present locally. If not, it goes and fetches the resources from a central data server. On receiving a request, the data server (refer section 8.2) generates the resource (row/column) on the fly and ships it to the corresponding compute server.Once the resources are acquired, the compute server places it on a local data cache and executes the task.

Results are presented (refer figure 8.9)for 3 scheduling algorithms, i.e., simple scheduling, local resource aware scheduling and global resource-aware scheduling. From the results we see that local resource scheduling outperforms simple scheduling by 5-10%. Global resource aware scheduling outperforms local resource aware scheduling anywhere from 5-15% and outperforms simple scheduling by as much as 20%. The speedups obtained by the global scheduling algorithm in spite of the increase in scheduling time underline the importance of global affinity scheduling for such applications. Note that these results reflect total running time without the optimizations for reducing scheduling time presented in section 8.5.4.

In terms of raw speedup global resource scheduling generates a speedup of 3 resulting in an efficiency of 75%. This lower efficiency is due to two reasons. First, there is contention at the data server. Second, with more number of processors the total number of resources acquired is more (attribute columns are replicated).

8.6.2 Clustering

Clustering is a commonly used data mining technique which partitions the attribute space, from which the data is drawn, into regions of similarity (Fayyad, Piatetsky-Shapiro, and Smyth 1999). The assignment of instances to classes (or clusters) could be deterministic (all instances in a region belong entirely to that class) or probabilistic (every instance belongs to every class to an extent determined by its location in the attribute space). Determining how similar two instances can be done either by defining a metric in the attribute space or by postulating the existence of probability density models. Search techniques are often used to find the best clustering, since efficient algorithms do not exist in most cases. These search algorithms are in general, computationally expensive. Searching for the best number of clusters to describe the data is one of the more expensive aspects of the search process. In this chapter, we use the cross-validated likelihood strategy of (Smyth, Ghil, Ide, and Fraser 1997) with $M = 40$, $\beta_c = 0.5$. M is the number of searches over which the

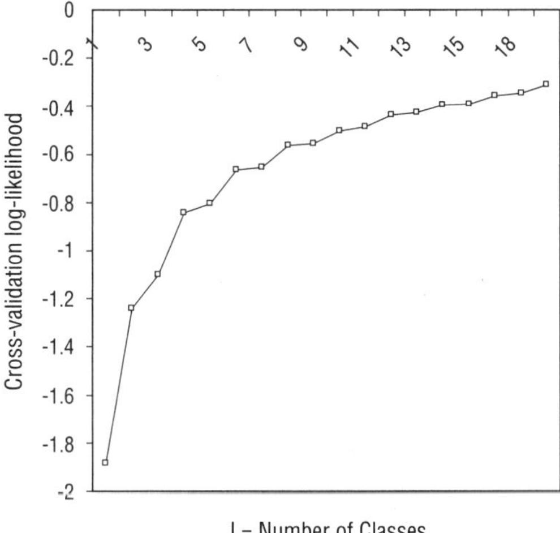

Figure 8.10: Improvement in cross-validated likelihood as J increases.

cross-validated likelihood is averaged. β_c is the fraction of the data used to estimate the model and $1 - \beta_c$ is the fraction used to evaluate the cross-validated likelihood.

The Need for Incremental Reporting and Task Ordering

The motivation for making data mining algorithms report their results incrementally and having parallelization primitives that provide this feature is evident from the following study. The search for the most appropriate number of classes is parallelized over different workstations using the interactive D-DOALL primitive (section 8.3). We generated a synthetic data set with $I = 2^{16}$ instances. Each of $K = 3$ independent attributes was modeled independently as a mixture of $J = 8$ Gaussians. We searched for the best J in [1..32]. None of the searches for $J > 19$ converged. Given that the tasks are handed out in order of increasing J, we can see that the marginal improvement in the ability to describe the data set begins to fall off around $J = 8$. Providing feedback to the user in the form of figure 8.10 allows the user to terminate searches for higher J when he/she feels that the incremental improvement is not worth the additional complexity. In figure 8.10, the x-axis represents the number of classes/clusters. The y-axis represents the likelihood that a particular number of classes is indeed the best representation of the underlying distribution.

Being able to specify the desired order of task execution is important since

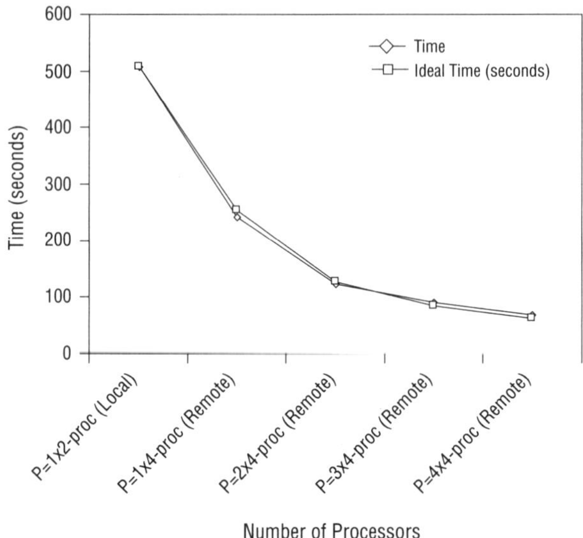

Figure 8.11: Speedup in clustering using D-DOALL.

one is often biased towards choosing simpler clusters (small J). This is an important scheduling characteristic of many data mining algorithms. Namely, that while there may be a large number of hypotheses to be explained, one often desires to impose an ordering in the exploration of those hypotheses.

Speedup Obtained Using D-DOALL

In this section, we present our results on the use of D-DOALL to parallelize the search for the best number of classes. The experimental setup is as follows. We searched for the best number of classes in $[2 \ldots 8]$ using the cross-validated likelihood strategy with $M = 20$, $\beta_c = 0.5$ (Smyth, Ghil, Ide, and Fraser 1997). The data set used was the *adult* data set with $I = 32561$ instances.[3] The client was a 2×200 MHz Pentium Pro machine running Windows NT 4.0. The remote compute servers were 4×200 MHz Pentium Pro machine running Windows NT 4.0. Our results are in figure 8.11. The ideal time line in the figure uses the time when the entire computation happens on the client ($1 \times 2-$proc (Local)) as the baseline and then computes the ideal time (assuming linear speedup) for the other configurations. We see from from the figure that the overhead of D-DOALL is small and that speedup is almost linear.

[3]Available at the University of California, Irvine, Repository of Learning Databases, http://www.ics.uci.edu/mlearn/MLRepository.html.

8.7 Conclusions and Future Work

Many data mining algorithms are computationally expensive and time consuming and can benefit from parallelization. Parallelizing these algorithms presents some unique problems because of the nature of the data mining and knowledge discovery (DMKD) process. Some of the distinguishing characteristics of DMKD applications are

1. There is often a loose ordering among the set of tasks to be performed i.e., the user would prefer some tasks to be completed before others

2. User interactivity is necessary because the DMKD process is best done with the human in the loop. The implications of this for the parallelization is that the results of tasks that have been completed should be made available to the user before all tasks have been completed. Further, the user should be allowed to terminate a computation, whose initial results indicate that further work is unlikely to be useful.

3. Since data mining applications tend to be data intensive, care must be taken to minimize the amount of data communication. This is the case even when some reduction of the data has been performed at one processor e.g., creating a histogram.

We designed the D-DOALL primitive with these specific needs in mind. Our experience with programming it and with the efficiency of the ensuing parallelizations has been very positive. We have used networks of workstations (NOWs) as our testbed since they represent easily available and cheap resources, although communication bandwidth is severely limited. Nevertheless, the results generalize to other parallel architectures as well.

There are several areas of promising future work. In section 8.4.4 and section 8.4.5, we introduced scheduling parameters α and β, the values of which were set somewhat arbitrarily. It would be interesting to see if the scheduler could *learn* the optimal values of α and β based on the actual scheduling decisions it makes and the quality of those decisions. The algorithms of sections 8.4.4, 8.4.5 and 8.4.5 could be improved and their analysis tightened. An exact solution to Problem Definition 8.5.1 would also be useful.

As part of ongoing work we are evaluating the primitive proposed on Feature Selection, and Diff Discovery and hope to have results for a later version of this chapter. We also plan to evaluate the effectiveness of this primitive on applications from other domains (such as interactive vision).

We would like to thank Ramana Venkata for many useful discussions on this work.

Chapter 9

The Preliminary Design of Papyrus: A System for High Performance, Distributed Data Mining over Clusters

Robert Grossman, Stuart Bailey, Ashok Ramu, Balinder Malhi, and Andrei Turinsky

9.1 Introduction

For many problems, clusters of workstations connected with specialized switching fabrics or high performance networks provide a competitive alternative to specialized high performance computers, including MPP computers.

Clusters of workstations have proved themselves to be very effective for a variety of data mining applications (Grossman, Bailey, and Hanley 1997). The data mining process involves both compute intensive and data intensive steps. Clusters serve two fundamental roles: Data-clusters provide the storage and data management services for the data sets being mined. Compute-clusters provide the compute services required by the data cleaning, data preparation and data mining tasks.

It is natural therefore to use distributed clusters as the infrastructure for distributed data mining. Our interest in this article is to focus on the special, but important case in which globally distributed high performance clusters of workstations are connected with networks supporting different levels of service.

Network quality of service (QoS) is measured along several dimensions: *rate guarantees* concerning the amount of data that an application requires, *delay and jitter guarantees* concerning the timeliness of delivery, and *loss guarantees* concerning the quality of delivery (Guerin and Schulzrinne 1999). A network with QoS provides some type of guarantee along one or more of these dimensions; in contrast, today's commodity internet uses a best effort model.

Today a network with high performance links may offer links which are 100x (or more) faster than commodity links. For example, the NFS vBNS network supports OC-3 links (155 MB/s), which in practice provides performance about 100x faster than the commodity internet. This provides a model for emerging premium services or differentiated services (Guerin and Schulzrinne 1999), which allow applications, for example, to request services with bandwidth guarantees. We call clusters (or clusters of clusters) connected with commodity services *metaclusters* and clusters (or clusters of clusters) connected with premium services *superclusters*.

The testbed used for the experimental studies described below consisted of five workstation clusters (in Chicago, Philadelphia, College Park, Davis, and Toronto) forming a supercluster connected to two clusters (in London and Canberra) to form a metacluster. More specifically, the clusters in Chicago and Toronto were connected by a 155 Mbs network; the clusters in Chicago, Davis and Philadelphia were connected by 45 Mbs network; and the remaining clusters were connected by the commodity internet.

We expect metaclusters and superclusters to grow more common with the emergence of the next generation internet. For example, a large company with distributed operations employing a virtual private network may have operational data in several cities connected with a high performance network employing premium services, while marketing related data may be accessible through a commodity network. As the amount of data grows, replacing servers with data and compute clusters provides a cost effective means of supplying the appropriate data management and processing capabilities required by data mining.

Concretely, data mining may be viewed as extracting a learning set from one or more (distributed) data warehouses and applying a data mining algorithm to produce a predictive model or rule set (Grossman, Bailey, Ramu,

Malhi, Hallstrom, Pulleyn, and Qin 1999). Different strategies are possible, depending upon the data, its distribution, the resources available, and the accuracy required:

Move results (MR): Today's commodity networks can be used to move the results of local data mining computations to a central site.

Move models (MM): Commodity networks can also be used to move predictive models from site to site.

Move data (MD): Next generation broadband networks also create the possibility of moving large amounts of data.

The majority of the work in distributed data mining has focused on the first two strategies MR and MM (Chan and Kargupta 1999). In this chapter, we introduce Papyrus, a distributed data mining system supporting all three strategies, as well as mixtures of the strategies. We also describe experimental studies for strategies MD and MM.

In this chapter, we are interested in distributed data mining problems with the following characteristics: data is available on data clusters, the fundamental task is to correlate data between two or more different data clusters, different strategies are available depending upon whether the clusters form a supercluster or metacluster, and the appropriate compute services are provided by compute clusters.

Section 9.2 provides background material and describes related work. The key concepts underlying the system are reviewed in section 9.3. Strategies are discussed in section 9.4. The design of the system is described in section 9.5 The implementation is described in section 9.6. Experimental studies are described in section 9.7. Section 9.8 contains the conclusion and future work.

9.2 Background and Related Work

Several systems have been developed for distributed data mining. Perhaps the most mature are: the JAM system developed by (Stolfo, Prodromidis, and Chan (1997), the Kensington system developed by Guo, Rueger, Sutiwaraphy, and Forbes-Millott (1997), and BODHI developed by Kargupta, Hamzaoglu, and Stafford (1997). These systems differ in several ways:

Data strategy. Distributed data mining can choose to move data, to move intermediate results, to move predictive models or to move the final results of a data mining algorithm. Distributed data mining systems which employ *local learning* build models at each site and move the models to a central location. Systems which employ *centralized learning* move the data to a central location for model building. Systems can also employ *hybrid learning*, that is strategies which combine local and centralized learning. JAM, Kensington and BODHI all employ local learning.

Task strategy. Distributed data mining systems can choose to coordinate a data mining algorithm over several sites or to apply data mining algorithms independently at each site. With *independent learning*, data mining algorithms are applied to each site independently. With *coordinated learning,* one or more sites coordinate the tasks within a data mining algorithm across several sites.

Model strategy. Several different methods have been employed for combining predictive models built at different sites. The simplest most common method is to use *voting* and combine the outputs of the various methods with a majority vote (Dietterich 1997). *Meta-learning* combines several models by building a separate metamodel whose inputs are the outputs of the various models and whose output is the desired outcome (Stolfo, Prodromidis, and Chan 1997). *Knowledge probing* considers learning from a black box viewpoint and creates an overall model by examining the input and the outputs to the various models, as well as the desired output (Guo, Rueger, Sutiwaraphy, and Forbes-Millott 1997). Multiple models, or what are often called ensembles or committees of models, have been used for quite a while in (centralized) data mining. A variety of methods have been studied for combining models in an ensemble, including Bayesian model averaging and model selection (Raftery, Madigan, and Hoeting 1996), stacking (Wolpert 1992), partition learning (Grossman, Bodek, Northcutt, and Poor 1996), and other statistical methods, such as mixture of experts (Xu and Jordan 1993). JAM employs metalearning, while Kensington employs knowledge probing.

Papyrus is designed to support different data, task and model strategies. For example, in contrast to JAM and Kensington, Papyrus can not only move models from node to node, but can also move data from node to node when that strategy is desired. In contrast to BODHI, Papyrus is built over a data warehousing layer which can move data over both commodity and high performance networks. Also, Papyrus is a specialized system which is designed for clusters, metaclusters, and superclusters, while JAM, Kensington and BODHI are designed for mining data distributed over the internet.

All four systems make use of Java. JAM employs Java applets to move machine learning algorithms to distributed data. Kensington uses Java JDBC to mine distributed data. Papyrus uses Java aglets (Lange and Oshima 1998).

The distributed data mining system developed in 1998 by Subramonian and Parthasarathy is designed to work with clusters of SMP workstations and, like Papyrus, is designed to exploit clusters of workstations. Both this system and Papyrus are designed around data clusters and compute clusters. Papyrus also explicitly supports clusters of clusters and clusters connected with different types of networks.

Distributed clusters of workstations are an example of what is becoming known as computational grids. A *computational grid* according to Foster and Kesselman (1999) is a "hardware and software infrastructure that provides

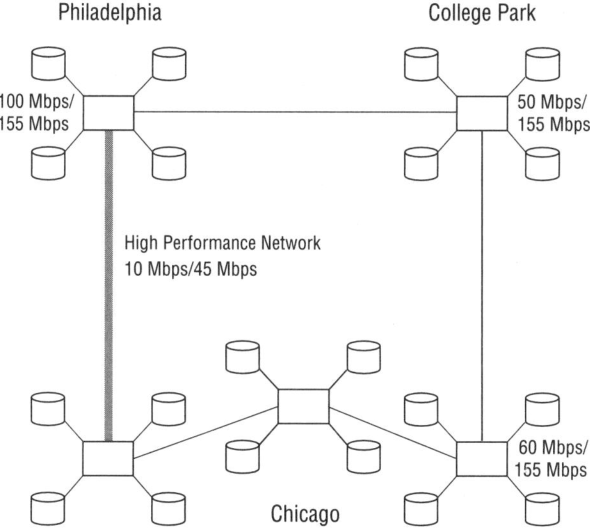

Figure 9.1: Clusters in Chicago and Philadelphia are connected with a high performance network to form a supercluster. The supercluster is connected with a cluster in College Park to form a metacluster. Clusters are of two types: data clusters providing data or compute cluster providing cycles. Papyrus applications have transparent access to any of the data or compute clusters in the metacluster.

dependable, consistent, pervasive, and inexpensive access to high-end computational capabilities." In Foster and Kesselman (1999), grid applications are divided into five classes: (1) distributed supercomputing applications requiring lots of cpu and memory, (2) high-throughput computing applications which use otherwise idle resources to tackle large problems, (3) on demand computing applications which integrate remote resources with local computation, (4) data intensive computing applications requiring the analysis of large data sets, and (5) collaborative computing applications which enhance human to human interactions.

Data mining cuts across each of these classes: data mining applications can be both cpu and i/o intensive (classes 1 and 4); data mining algorithms such as genetic algorithms which require searching a space of hypotheses can exploit high-throughput techniques (class 2); data mining has been applied to data from remote instrumentation (class 3); finally, the interactive exploration and visualizaton of large data sets is becoming more common (class 5).

There are several projects underway developing a computing infrastructure for grid applications, including Globus (Foster and Kesselman 1997), Legion

(Grimshaw and Wulf 1997, Gannon and Grimshaw 1999), and NOW (Anderson, Culler, and Patterson 1995). In contrast to these systems which are broadly concerned with providing general grid services to distributed applications, Papyrus is focused on just those services required for distributed data mining over grids built from clusters and clusters of clusters. The philosophy of Papyrus is to use general grid and cluster services whenever possible. As grid services such as Globus and Legion mature, we expect that future versions of Papyrus will be based, in part, upon them.

Similar to grid services such as Globus (Foster and Kesselman 1997), Papyrus provides a shared (wide area) persistent data space, transparent remote execution (of data mining processes), wide area parallel processing (of data mining processes), and scheduling (of data mining processes). Of course, Globus provides this for general grid applications, while Papyrus provides specialized vertically integrated versions of these services in a framework suitable for distributed data mining. Both Papyrus and Globus take an "hour glass" layered approach to system design in which a few protocols and services (the neck of the hour glass) are used to connect adjacent layers in the system.

Legion (Gannon and Grimshaw 1999) advocates an object and component view toward grid services. Objects have well defined interfaces, communicate with data and control paths and respond to events broadcast by other objects. Papyrus exploits data paths between clusters. Clusters communicate by using agents, and data access is via specialized servers designed for high performance and distributed data mining rather than through general object services or databases.

The Berkeley NOW Project (Anderson, Culler, and Patterson 1995) provides infrastructure for high performance distributed computing using workstation clusters, including scheduling middleware, a high performance messaging system, and a scalable parallel file system. Papyrus uses a high performance, light weight object manager (Grossman, Bailey, and Hanley 1997) instead of a parallel file system and is designing a scheduler specifically targeted towards data intensive computations over wide area networks with different levels of services instead of using a more general purpose scheduler for distributed applications.

9.3 Key Concepts

In this section, we describe some of the key concepts underlying Papyrus following the 1999 work of Turinsky and Grossman.

Data ensembles. In this chapter, we restrict our attention to data mining problems in which we are given 1) a mechanism for partitioning a data set and 2) a mechanism for combining partitioned data into a single data set. In this case, we speak of a *data partition* or *data ensemble*. For example, when building a fraud model for credit card accounts, the data may be partitioned by customer, and separate models built from different sets of customers. As another example, a delinquency model for credit card accounts may be built from two data sets – a set of credit card transactions and a set summarizing account level data, such as when payments were received and for how much. The first example illustrates what is sometimes called horizontal partitioning – the domain is partitioned, while the second example illustrates what is sometimes called vertical partitioning — the range is partitioned (Kargupta, Johnson, Sanseverino, Park, Silvestre, and Hershberger 1999).

Data mining. Data mining can be viewed quite broadly as the semi-automated extraction of knowledge from data (Fayyad, Piatetsky-Shapiro, and Smyth 1996). We take a much narrower point of view, regarding data mining as the process of extracting a learning set from a data warehouse and applying a data mining algorithm to produce a predictive model or rule set (Grossman, Bailey, Ramu, Malhi, Hallstrom, Pulleyn, and Qin 1999). Continuing, the model can be applied to data to obtain a numerical result, which we view as a vector.

Model ensembles. In this chapter, we also restrict attention to collections or *ensembles* of predictive models which may be combined to produce a single model. A basic example is provided by predictive models built from partitioned data and then combined by voting (Dietterich 1997). As another example consider a cluster model, in which a data set is summarized by specifying the centroids of k clusters. The model may be partitioned by creating two collections of centroids containing k_1 and k_2 centroids, where $k_1 + k_2 = k$ and two cluster models may be combined by simply concatenating their centroids.

The fundamental trade-off. Large data files may be several orders of magnitude larger than a file describing a model, while a model file may be several orders of magnitude larger than a result vector. In a distributed data mining system, different strategies are possible depending upon whether data files, model files, or result vectors are moved from node to node.

In general the most accurate result is obtained by moving all the data to a single node. This is usually also the most expensive. In this chapter, we measure the expense using a cost function which includes both computation and communication costs. At the other extreme, we can process all the data locally obtaining local results, and combine the local results to obtain the final result. In general, this approach is less expensive, but also less accurate. To summarize, in distributed data mining, there is a fundamental trade-off between the accuracy desired for the predictive model and the cost one is willing to bear for the computation.

Configurations. We assume that there are n different sites connected by a network. A *configuration* is given by specifying the following data:

1. A graph with nodes i, $i = 1, \ldots, n$ describing the network. One of the nodes, say the Kth, is the network *root* where the overall result will be computed.

2. A vector $\{D_i\}_{i=1}^n$ describing the initial distribution of the data.

3. The cost c_{ij} (measured in dollars per Gigabyte) to move data from the ith to the jth node, via the least expensive path.

4. The cost c_i (measured in dollars per Gigabyte) to process data at the ith node into a predictive model.

5. A constant α describing the amount of compression when the data on a node is processed to compute a predictive model.

9.4 Strategies

Fix a configuration as defined above. A node can employ one of three different strategies: (1) *Move data* (MD): Ship raw data across the network to another node for processing. (2) *Move models* (MM): Process the data locally to produce a predictive model and ship the predictive model to another node for further processing. (3) *Move results* (MR): Process the data locally until a result is obtained and ship the result to another node for further processing.

In general, as we progress from MD, to MM, to MR strategies, there is a loss of accuracy, but a decrease in the cost of the computation. A complete strategy moves data, models, and results from node to node until the root produces a final result.

For some problems, sufficient accuracy is required so that all the data must be moved to a central root. For other problems, sufficient speed is desired so that all the computation is done locally. Recall that it takes approximately 24 hours to move a terabyte of data over a OC-3 network. Given terabytes of data distributed over a metacluster of clusters and superclusters, the correct strategy can mean the difference between waiting minutes instead of hours.

To simplify the discussion, we only consider mixed strategies involving MD and MM; the general case can be handled similarly. A *strategy* X as a matrix of numbers $X = [x_{ij}]_{i,j=1}^n$

where x_{ij} is the amount of data D_i that is moved from the ith node to the jth node for processing by the strategy. After the move, the amount of data at the jth node becomes $\tilde{D}_j$. The *cost function* for a strategy X is easily computed as

$$C(X) = \sum_{ij} \left(c_{ij} x_{ij} + c_j x_{ij} + c_{jK} \alpha x_{ij} \right).$$

The sum is over nodes i which are the sources of data and over nodes j which are the targets of data.

A critical observation is that in many cases the cost function is convex. In such cases, the least possible error ϵ_0 occurs when all data is moved to a single node and the largest possible error $\epsilon_{\max}$ occurs when the data is evenly distributed among all nodes. Note that the vector $\tilde{D}(X) = \left(\tilde{D}_1, \ldots, \tilde{D}_n\right)$ defines the relevant data distribution, where each $\tilde{D}_j = \sum_i x_{ij}$.

We use the following form of the *error function* for a strategy X:

$$\epsilon(X) = \epsilon_0 + \rho_D \left(1 - \frac{\|\tilde{D}(X)\|}{|D|}\right), \qquad \rho_D = \frac{\epsilon_{\max} - \epsilon_0}{1 - \frac{1}{\sqrt{n}}}$$

where $|D| = \sum_j \tilde{D}_j$ is the overall amount of data in the network, $\|\tilde{D}\|$ is the usual Euclidean norm of a vector $\tilde{D}(X)$, and ρ_D is a scaling coefficient.

Suppose we are given an error tolerance threshold ϵ_{tol}. We can now find an optimal strategy by solving the optimization problem:

$\mathrm{Min}_X\ C(X)$

$\epsilon(X) \leq \epsilon_{tol}$.

It is easy to find examples in which there are intermediate strategies that are more cost effective than the naive ones of either leaving all the data in place or moving all the data to a single fixed node. Because of this, it makes sense to design distributed systems with the flexibility of moving data, moving predictive models, or moving the results of local computations. This is one of the key ideas behind the Papyrus system. Papyrus, as far as we know, is the first distributed data mining system to be designed with this level of flexibility.

9.5 Architectural Design

Recall that we are interested in distributed data mining systems in which the data is accessed through data clusters, analyzed using compute clusters, and where the data and compute clusters are combined using commodity networks to form metaclusters and using high performance networks to form superclusters.

For simplicity, we view a single node as a cluster of size one. In Papyrus, clusters interact in two ways: (1) Metadata is moved between clusters using agents. Each cluster has a single node with is designated as the *cluster access point* (CAP). Agents can move queries, predictive models, result vectors, and other metadata between the CAPs of different clusters. (2) Data is moved between clusters using a distributed data warehouse. In practice, even with only moderate amounts of data, this is only practical if the two clusters are connected with a high performance network.

Given the viewpoint described above, in which data mining is viewed as the process of applying data mining algorithms to learning sets extracted from data warehouses to produce predictive models, it is natural to design Papyrus as a layered system, consisting of the following four main layers (Grossman 1998):

Data warehouse layer. The lowest layer consists of a data warehouse which is designed for local and distributed clusters of workstations. Training sets are extracted from the data warehouse. In practice, small amounts of data can be moved between clusters in general, and larger amounts of data can be moved when the clusters are connected with high performance networks.

Data mining layer. The role of the data mining layer is to apply one or more data mining algorithms to training sets extracted from the data warehouse to produce predictive models, rule sets, or results. More precisely, we assume that the input to the data mining layer is a data set—the learning set—and the output is a model or ensemble of models. By a model, we mean both predictive rules and rule sets.

Predictive modeling layer. This layer manages predictive models and ensembles of predictive models. We have contributed to the development of an XML[1] mark up language called the Predictive Model Markup Language (PMML)[2] for predictive models and rule sets. PMML supports predictive models, ensembles of predictive models, and all the metadata required to describe them and use them effectively (Grossman, Bailey, Ramu, Malhi, Hallstrom, Pulleyn, and Qin 1999). A description of the current draft of PMML can be found at www.dmg.org. The predictive modeling layer handles models in PMML. Concretely, the data mining layer extracts learning sets from the data warehouse and produces models or rules in PMML, which are managed by the predictive modeling layer.

Agent layer. The agent layer moves queries, predictive models, metadata, and the results of local computations between the cluster access points. We have developed an XML markup language which we call the Data Discovery Markup Language (DDML) which is used to describe the queries and metadata associated with a distributed data mining computation. Agents move DDML metadata and PMML models between cluster access points. Separately, through control expressed in DDML files, data can be moved directly between two distributed data clusters.

As described above, a query to Papyrus can be processed using three different strategies (MR, MM, and MD).

Selecting a Query

1. A Papyrus application dispatches agents to gather DDML files from the

[1] see http://www.w3c.org

[2] The Data Mining Group, http://www.dmg.org

various registered CAPs.

2. The DDML files returned by the agents are analyzed by the application and the user chooses or specifies a query.

Move Results (MR)

3. The DDML query is carried by agents to the appropriate CAPs, where the query is executed to produce results.

4. The agents return the results in DDML using a commodity network to the Papyrus application, where they are processed to produce a final result.

Move Models (MM)

3. The query in DDML is carried by agents to the appropriate CAPs, where the query is executed to produce predictive models.

4. The agents return the predictive models in PMML using a commodity network to the Papyrus application, where they are processed to produce a final result.

Move Data (MD)

3. The query and the request to move data in DDML is carried by agents to the various CAPs. To process the query, data is moved by the data warehousing layer using a high performance network to a root cluster, where the query is processed.

4. Agents return the results in DDML from the root cluster to the Papyrus application, where they are processed to produce a final result.

9.6 Preliminary Implementation

We have developed two versions of Papyrus following the general design and ideas sketched above. Papyrus version 0.8 was developed and tested during 1997 and demonstrated at the Supercomputing 97 Conference in San Jose, California in November, 1997. Papyrus version 0.9 was developed and tested during 1998 and demonstrated at the Supercomputing 98 Conference in Orlando in November, 1998. We are currently developing version 1.0 of Papyrus.

The data management layer of version 0.8 of Papyrus used a high performance, light weight persistent object manager we developed called PTool (Grossman, Bailey, and Hanley 1997). Papyrus version 0.9 used a version of PTool we developed that provided some support for wide area clusters. In

Layer	Name	Version 0.8	Version 0.9
Agent	Bast	Agent-TCL moving PMML	Aglets moving DDML & PMML
Predictive Model	Anubis	unimplemented	unimplemented
Data Mining	Thoth	C4.5 producing PMML	C4.5 producing PMML
Data Warehouse	Osiris	PTool suppporting local clusters	PTool supporting local & wide area clusters

Table 9.1: Summary of implementation of version 0.8 and 0.9 of Papyrus. C4.5 was modified to produce SGML for v0.8 and PMML for version v0.9.

particular, we were able to stripe data over wide area data clusters. The data management layer of Papyrus version 1.0 will use a different design, with explicit support for data mining primitives, specialized protocols for moving data over high performance networks, and explicit support for multiple network protocols.

Since our main interest was in the system design of a high performance, distributed data mining system, and not in work related to high performance data mining algorithms per se, we chose to use standard algorithms for the data mining layer. We chose the popular C4.5 implementation of decision trees as the main tool in the data mining layer (Quinlan 1993).

We modified C4.5 to work with data clusters and to emit PMML. Papyrus version 0.8 used SGML as the basis for PMML. Papyrus version 0.9 used XML, as will Papyrus version 1.0. The general design for Papyrus calls for a layer to manage predictive models in PMML called Anubis. In versions 0.8 and 0.9 of Papyrus, we did not use a separate layer for this, but rather implemented the necessary code in the Papyrus applications themselves. For example, some of the applications combined several PMML models into a single metamodel using a simple voting strategy.

We built an agent layer called *bast* to move queries, predictive models, results and metadata between the various data clusters. Bast version 0.8 used Agent-TCL (Gray, Rus, and Kotz 1996) to move SGML data describing queries and the other associated data and metadata managed by Bast. Bast version 0.9 uses aglets (Lange and Oshima 1998) to move XML data and metadata in a language we designed for this purpose called the Data Discovery Markup Language (DMML).

For simplicity, we used the following strategy for moving data and metadata: (1) For data distributed across a supercluster, we used PTool to move the data and mine it as if it were locally resident. (2) For data distributed across a metacluster, we built predictive models locally on each data cluster or supercluster and merged the results with a voting scheme.

9.7 Experimental Results

In this section, we describe a series of five experiments which used Papyrus version 0.9. We performed two of the experiments in November, 1998 at the Supercomputing 98 Conference in Orlando. The other three experiments were conducted afterwards to explore some of the issues that arose in the first two experiments. We also describe how these experiments influenced the design of Papyrus 1.0, which is currently under development.

The goal of the first two experiments was to gain information about the overall suitability of the Papyrus system architecture and design, especially the design of the data warehouse and agent layers. We emphasize that our goal was not to test distributed data mining algorithms per se but rather to improve our understanding of some of the critical factors effecting a distributed data mining system operating over networks with different levels of services.

In the first experiment at Supercomputing 98, we analyzed high energy physics data with a 30 node supercluster distributed between Chicago, Philadelphia, College Park, Davis, Orlando, and Toronto. In the second experiment, we analyzed health care outcome data with a 6 node metacluster in Chicago, Philadelphia, College Park, Orlando, London and Canberra.

In the first experiment, the supercluster had access to approximately 480 Gigabytes of high energy physics data, organized into approximately 79 million "events," representing putative particle collisions. We adopted standard physics analysis code to run on the supercluster and created an application benchmark called Event1. The goal with Event1 is to maximize the number of events analyzed per second. As an example, the Event1 benchmark on a subset of approximately 6 million events, spanning approximately 38.4 Gigabytes distributed over 14 nodes, took between 18,000 and 54,000 seconds depending upon the node.

The US data clusters were connected by the NSFs very high speed backbone network server (vBNS), which consists of a 622 Mb/sec, fully switched, Asynchronous Transfer Mode (ATM) internal backbone and 45 Mb/sec – 155 Mb/sec edge ATM links to each site. The Toronto cluster was connected to the vBNS via a 45 Mb/sec link. The limit for the data analysis on the supercluster was essentially the speed with which data could be managed and moved across the network, which was the responsibility of Papyrus' data warehouse layer. Roughly speaking, each network interface of the Papyrus system could move data at approximately 4 Mb/sec per process, providing an upper bound per node of approximately 20-30 Mb/sec, and an upper bound per site of approximately 60-90 Mb/sec.

In version 0.9 of Papyrus, we used custom code which connected the various nodes in the supercluster with an appropriate number of sockets. Without taking this approach, the performance of the Event1 benchmark was rather

Number of Sockets	TT in seconds	AATR in Mb/sec
1 socket	96	8.3
2 sockets	57	14.0
3 sockets	34	23.5
4 sockets	30	26.7
5 sockets	26	30.8
6 sockets	26	30.8
7 sockets	26	30.8

Table 9.2: This table shows the result of using more than one socket with multiplexing to move data between nodes in a supercluster. The practical limit of thc 45 Mb/s DS-3 link appcars to bc about 35 Mb/s. TT – transfcr timc for 100 MBytes, AATR – application apparent transfer rate.

disappointing, despite the presence of the high performance links. In a follow up experiment described in table 9.2, we examined this issue more carefully, varying the number of sockets connecting two nodes in a supercluster from 1 to 7. On the basis of these two experiments, we made the decision to develop a library for moving data between two nodes in a supercluster which multiplexes several sockets to maximize the amount of data transfered per second. This library will be used in Papyrus version 1.0.

In the second follow up experiment described in table 9.3, the same event data was arranged two ways: by event and by attribute. For the Event1 benchmark, although more data was moved with the horizontal layout by event, more events could be analyzed with the vertical layout by attribute. The difference was over 6x, and could be larger depending upon the query. Of course, other queries would see the same speed up for exactly the opposite layout. For this reason, we are investigating supporting both vertical and horizontal layouts in Papyrus version 1.

For the second series of experiments at Supercomputing 98, the metacluster analyzed approximately 600,000 health care outcome records comprising less than a Gigabyte of data, but distributed over three continents. In this case, the analysis was essentially limited by the congestion of the commodity internet, which was especially pronounced for the international links. The agent based communication utilized by the Papyrus cluster layer worked effectively for the metacluster queries we tested.

In these experiments, we combined C4.5 trees (Quinlan 1993) built at each local site into a single classifier using the Papyrus cluster layer Bast. The Papyrus application combined the trees using a majority vote, which is a standard technique when working with ensembles of classifiers (Dietterich 1997). Our interest was understanding whether Papyrus would work over globally distributed metaclusters, in which there were wide variations in latency and

Horizontal Store: Store Size = 4 GB, Total Data Moved = 4GB				
Comp. Servers	Processes	Events/second	Mb/seconds	Seconds
1	1	92	4.67	7388
1	2	153	7.7	4466
1	4	242	12.2	2825
1	8	315	15.84	2168
4	4	320	16.12	2140
4	16	448	22.4	1526
8	32	503	25.6	1359
Vertical Store: Store Size = 6.85 GB, Total Data Moved = 0.47GB				
Comp. Servers	Processes	Events/second	Mb/seconds	Seconds
1	1	392	1.42	2833
1	2	664	2.42	1673
1	4	911	3.17	1218
1	8	951	3.31	1166
4	4	1555	5.64	714
4	8	2498	9.12	444
4	16	3044	10.53	365
4	32	3272	11.32	339

Table 9.3: Data may be placed on the disk by record (horizontally) or by attribute (vertically). The optimal choice depends upon the query. This table analyzes the performance of the Osiris data server for both of these choices for a particular benchmark query of high energy physics data called event1. The events processed per second, the amount of data moved per second, and the total time in seconds to complete the query are given.

bandwidths between the various sites. We concluded that this approach could work effectively. Since some queries were not able to complete due to network congestion, we are considering putting explicit support in Papyrus version 1.0 for more gracefully handling nodes which cannot respond in a timely fashion.

In the third follow up experiment, we empirically examined the trade-offs when moving models (MM) built on distributed data versus moving the data (MD) and building a centralized model for the health care outcome data. This experiment used a supercluster and a particular application benchmark called HCOD1. See tables 9.4 and 9.5. For this particular benchmark, essentially the same accuracy could be obtained by building local trees and merging them (MM). Moving models was approximately 2.5x faster than moving data. Notice that with a supercluster moving data (MD) takes essentially the same length of time whether the supercluster is local or geographically distributed. Of course, with other queries and other data sets, the loss suffered when employing the MM strategy might not be acceptable. These observations lead to the cost based approach to selecting strategies described in section 9.4. We plan to implement this for Papyrus version 1.0

Data Transfer vs. Model Transfer (5 locations)							
Strategy				Data Transfer		Model Transfer	
# Records	LAN DT	WAN DT	C45	LAN Total	WAN Total	LAN Total	WAN Total
5000	0.6	1.661	9.25	9.85	10.911	17.6	21.1
10000	0.96	2.885	18.62	19.58	21.505	20.91	27.28
50000	3	11.96	156.81	159.81	168.77	86.78	79.56
100000	4.3	21.75	424.14	428.44	445.89	114.03	161.24

Table 9.4: Query time using different strategies for local (LAN) and wide area (WAN) clusters connected with high performance links. Columns 2-8 indicates time in seconds for the health care application benchmark HCOD1. Total refers to the time required for both the execution time of C4.5 and the time required to move either the data (DT) or the model (MT) as indicated. DT – data transfer, MT – model transfer

# Records	Number of Models						
	1	3	5	7	9	15	21
1000	14.4	14.0	13.6	13.6	15.2	14.8	14.0
5000	14.9	14.96	15.36	15.36	15.12	15.6	15.2
10000	12.7	13.44	12.92	14.32	13.92	14.24	14.16
50000	13.8	11.984	13	12.912	13.072	13.072	13.126
100000	12.8	12.812	12.912	12.844	12.852	12.972	13.128
200000		12.37	12.16	12.284	12.226	12.228	12.198

Table 9.5: The prediction error in percent as the number of records and the number of models varies for the HCOD1 application benchmark.

9.8 Conclusions and Future Work

As workstation clusters and high performance networks grow more common, clusters, metaclusters (clusters linked by commodity networks), and superclusters (clusters linked by high performance networks) should prove a popular infrastructure for mining large and distributed data sets. Papyrus uses a simple layered architecture and is flexible enough to employ strategies which can either move data, move predictive models or move the numerical results of computations over distributed clusters of workstations linked by high performance and commodity connections.

As described in section 9.7, the Papyrus architecture and implementation has demonstrated the practicality of mining distributed Gigabyte size data sets over high performance DS-3 and OC-3 networks. With queries taking hundreds to thousands of seconds, it is important to develop systems which are intelligent enough and flexible enough to move only the smallest amount of data consistent with achieving results of acceptable accuracy. This is one of the goals of Papyrus version 1.0

Based upon the experiments performed to date using versions 0.8 and 0.9 of Papyrus, we are currently developing version 1.0:

(1) Effectively using high performance links in version 0.9 of Papyrus required that Papyrus applications explicitly make use of multiple sockets to deal with the well known latency problems of TCP ACKs. A library (PSocket) is provided in Papyrus 1.0 so that Papyrus applications can transparently use high performance links.

(2) Version 0.9 of Papyrus supports strategies where data is moved, where models are moved, and where numerical results are moved, but does not support mixed strategies where this choice varies from node to node. Papyrus version 1.0 will remedy this by supporting optimal strategies as described in section 9.4.

(3) Version 0.9 of Papyrus supports clusters of workstations linked by high performance networks and by commodity networks, but cannot effectively support mixed networks, where nodes may have several connections, each with a different quality of service. Papyrus version 1.0 will remedy this by supporting servers which can effectively schedule requests incorporating different qualities of service.

Chapter 10

Secure Distributed Database Mining: Principles of Design

Chris Jones, John Hall and John Hale

10.1 Introduction

Data mining is a useful tool for gathering, examining, and extracting knowledge from raw data. It has many applications in marketing, advertising, management and research. Product placement and advertising strategies can be based on correlations and trends mined from consumer data. Phone companies use data mining to derive customer calling patterns for determining optimal calling plans. Government agencies employ data mining to analyze social and economic behavior patterns. Medical researchers can use data mining to scan volumes of patient data distributed across the globe to look for telling patterns associated with particular conditions.

Distributed data mining commonly employs agent technology to synthesize knowledge from networked and potentially heterogeneous information resources (Aronis, Kolluri, Provost, and Buchanan 1997; Kargupta, Park, Hershberger, and Johnson 1999; Lee and Stolfo 1988). Mining often spans several enterprises. Databases are the primary sources for miners, but prose and other forms of partially structured and quasi-integrated data also can be mined. Regardless of the nature of the information sources, security and privacy issues are brought to the forefront when employing data mining services that operate across trust boundaries. This chapter identifies risks of distributed data mining, discusses security features and shortcomings of supporting software technologies, and presents guidelines for crafting a secure distributed data mining architecture.

10.2 Risks

Risks in distributed data mining exist for both mining agencies and information resource enterprises. In general, we consider risks that compromise the confidentiality, integrity and availability of a system. Loss of privacy is synonymous with a breach of system confidentiality. The following section describes in fuller details these principles of system security and explores their relationship to the fundamental elements of distributed data mining operations.

10.2.1 Security Principles

The three goals of security are confidentiality, integrity, and availibility. Confidentiality ensures that only authorized subjects can read or know sensitive information. Integrity preserves the accuracy and reliability of information. Availibility is timely accessibility of information. These goals are orthogonal in nature but common technology (such as encryption) often is used to achieve each.

A guiding design principle for secure systems is least privilege. *Least privilege* promotes the philosophy of endowing subjects with only enough permissions to discharge their duties. With respect to distributed data mining, least privilege is supported by enabling the extraction of nonsensitive knowledge needed by miners without sharing potentially sensitive raw data. Moreover, least privilege is an essential concept for data mining systems that collect information from potentially competitive enterprises.

Consider an example in which an investigator of credit card fraud initiates data mining on a variety of credit card transaction databases in competing financial institutions. The transaction records held by each institution are sensitive. They identify customers and credit card numbers, and associate this information with the amount, location and time of individual purchases. Banks and credit unions certainly wish to keep such records out the hands of their competitors, crooks, and the general public. However, a distributed data mining service can discover useful trends indicative of fraud without compromising the confidentiality and privacy of credit card holders. (The JAM –Java Agent Meta-learning– system from Columbia University has been used to discover credit card fraud [Stolfo, Prodromidis, Tselepis, Lee, Fan, and Chan 1997].)

A mining operation lacking a sound security architecture could be subject to eavesdropping, data tampering, or denial of service attacks. Depending upon the criticality and sensitivity of the mined knowledge, each of these compromises could prove devastating to an enterprise. On the database side, a failure to implement least privilege could give mining agents access to sensitive data.

10.2.2 Databases

Distributed data mining systems must interact with remote databases to glean knowledge from raw data. Data mining systems often sample databases or filter queries through database interfaces. Such interoperability must be controlled to protect the confidentiality, integrity and availability of sensitive and vital data in these databases. Recalling the earlier example, a security breach in any of these areas could itself manifest credit card fraud.

Database administrators must take steps to guarantee that data mining services cannot read sensitive data and leak it to competitors or unauthorized subjects. For instance, credit card holders will not want their credit card numbers distributed indiscriminately, nor will they want their purchase habits revealed. Either of these events constitutes a breach of confidentiality.

Administrators must safeguard the integrity of database information from rogue data mining agents attempting illicit updates to database systems. Potential integrity violations in the credit card fraud example could include modifying, adding to, or subtracting from, recorded purchases, and altering personal card holder data such as name and mailing address. Databases must audit accesses to ensure that subjects are held accountable for their actions.

Waves of mining agents trying to access the same database can effectively cripple an entire system. The effect of such an attack need not be localized to the database involved. Rather, an effective denial of service attack aimed at a database could crash its host and flood a network with unwanted traffic. Database administrators must take every reasonable precaution against this type of threat to preserve the availability of their systems. Unfortunately, denial of service attacks are among the easiest to mount and the most difficult to prevent.

10.2.3 Agents

Distributed data mining typically relies on software agent technology to gather and coalesce information from remote databases. Agents can collect information from databases, send and receive messages, move from host to host, spawn new agents, and terminate. The popularity of software agents in distributed data mining systems stems in part from the array of languages and toolkits available that make it easy to create and coordinate armies of information gatherers systematically mining a wide network of databases. However, agents that carry or transmit sensitive data have risks associated with them. Even those that do not work directly with sensitive data can pose some threat to the systems on which they are deployed.

Agents handling sensitive information must protect the secrecy of such information through prudent use of encryption technology. Agents sending cleartext messages across an open network run the risk of eavesdropping. Mobile agents carrying unencrypted state information are at similar risk in transit and are also exposed to various kinds of illicit memory inspection attacks upon arriving at their destination.

Agent code and data integrity is also a critical security issue. The mere potential for modifying or forging information held or sent by data mining agents raises serious concerns about the accuracy and authenticity of such information. Once again, the hazards associated with this risk depend upon the nature of the information being mined. For the credit card fraud example, forged agent data might lead investigators to false conclusions regarding an individual case. Code integrity is critical to the secure operation of distributed data mining agent software. Subverting or hijacking a distributed data mining agent places a trusted piece of mobile software under the control of an intruder. Such a co-opted agent could report false information, pass along confidential information to the intruder, serve as a trojan horse for various attacks, or could spawn waves of data mining agents with the intent of overloading a system or flooding a network.

Agent availability is primarily a concern where data mining is a mission critical activity for an enterprise. Unfortunately, there is no way to prevent malicious hosts from destroying resident agents. This threat can be partially addressed through selective replication in a fault tolerant agent architicture.

10.3 Elements of Distributed Data Mining

Distributed data mining integrates database and software agent technology. Databases and agent systems have their own security challenges. Security issues unique to distributed data mining exist at the seams of their interconnection.

10.3.1 Database Technology

Databases offer unique advantages and challenges to administrators. Databases facilitate shared access, minimal redundancy, data integrity, data consistency, and controlled access. As multiuser systems, database management systems (DBMSs) face the same basic issues of confidentiality, integrity, and availability as operating systems and networks. Some database security services, such as authentication, are implemented in much the same way as they are in operating systems. However, database security research has led to innovative access control models that are beginning to make their way into other kinds of computer systems and applications. In addition, database systems introduce unique concerns when it comes to data confidentiality.

Database authorization models regard granularity as a primary consideration. Access can be granted to an entire database, a subset of tables and records, or even for a collection of attributes. Moreover, the basis of authorization in access control models is widely varied. Access to an object can be based on a subject's identity, role, clearance or task. Distributed data mining enterprises face a serious challenge of negotiating access to federated databases employing a variety of authorization schemes.

Data integration also introduces concern regarding inference attacks as a potential security threat. The inference problem is exacerbated when database administrators are unable to determine the scope of the threat. This situation is most common when database access ranges across trust boundaries, where users are able to integrate knowledge from widely distributed information sources.

Access Control

Authorization schemes satisfy security policies that define legitimate bounds of access for a collection of subjects on a set of objects. Access control models take many shapes; discretionary access control (DAC), role-based access control (RBAC), mandatory access control (MAC), and task-based access control (TBAC). The proliferation of object-oriented systems has even led to the development of method-based access control (MBAC), which is a complementary scheme that identifies methods as a suitable granularity of protection.

Access in DAC systems, which is the most pervasive authorization model, is based on the identity of the subject. Most commercial and academic operating systems and databases employ some form of DAC. RBAC is based on user roles (Sandhu, Coyne, Feinstein, and Youman 1994). RBAC schemes associate a role name with a set of privileges. A user logs in under a certain role in a role hierarchy and assumes the permissions of that role. In MAC users and data items are associated with a classification in a partial ordering and a category in a discrete ordering. The classification is a rank of sensitivity (for example, confidential, secret or top secret). A category is a group name (for example, navy, air force or marines). Typical constraints in this military model stipulate that (1) read access is given to subjects for object their clearance *dominates* (where domination implies superior classification and identical category) and (2) write access is given at the level of the user and the clearance of the object to be written must dominate the clearance of the user, preventing declassification of sensitive data (Bell and LaPadula 1976). TBAC addresses the principle of least privilege by associating permissions with subjects engaged in particular tasks. TBAC excels at modeling situations of temporary trust.

Regardless of the policy, an agent will have to map itself to the access controls of the database in order to be given the access it requires. Agents behave as proxies for users and therefore must be regarded as subjects. If an agent is to interoperate within a system that employs DAC, it must be given an identity somehow tethered to its owner and manufacturer. If it is to gather information from an RBAC-centric database, the agent must be assigned a role. For MAC systems, agents need a clearance and for TBAC systems agents should specify precisely which tasks they are engaged in.

Inference

Functional relationships between attributes in databases enable inference attacks. In an inference attack, an intruder attempts to use accessible data to infer sensitive information in a database. Dealing with the potential for inference attacks within databases is one of the more challenging aspects of database security management (Buczkowski 1990; Garvey, Lunt, Qian, and Stickel 1992; Hinke 1998; Morgenstern 1988; Su and Ozsoyoglu 1991). To guard against inference attacks, administrators must engage in a dual process of analysis and control. Inference analysis involves checking a database to determine if an inference channel from accessible data to sensitive information exists. Inference control entails altering the security policy for selected tables so that the channel is broken.

Most administrators and researchers employ the closed world assumption when it comes to implementing schemes for protection against database inference attacks. The closed world assumption says that intruders only have knowledge legitimately accessible to them through the database. In practice, this assumption is far from accurate. Attackers can collect information from other databases, from public records, and even from commonly held rules of thumb (Hale and Shenoi 1997).

Consider the example in figure 10.1 where an attacker is trying to infer the salary of an employee. For a successful attack, it is not necessary to infer the exact annual salary of the victim. Let us assume that inferring a salary to within $5,000 is probably good enough for our villain. Suppose the attacker

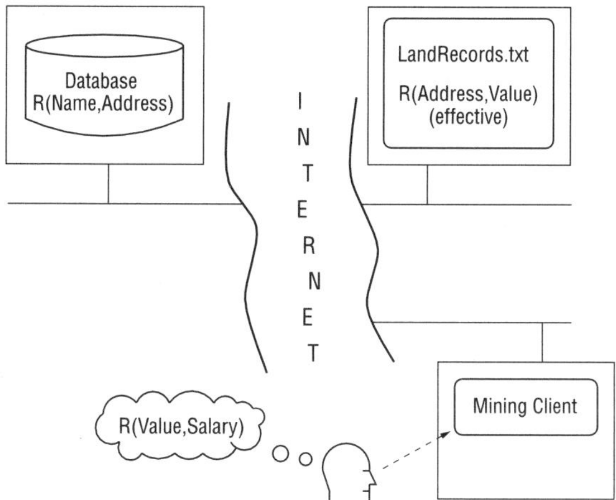

Figure 10.1: Inference in open environments.

is given access to the company database, which maintains a table listing the addresses of each employee, $R(Name, Address)$. The attacker can then use public records to pinpoint the approximate value and mortgage associated with the house at that address. That is, the attacker essentially has access to table $R(Address, Value)$. Finally, a rule of thumb can be used to link home value with salary, as mortgages are on the order of twice the amount of the annual household income, $R(Value, Salary)$. Combining database tables with public records and a rule of thumb has given the attacker the (albeit imprecise) inference channel $Name \rightarrow Address \rightarrow Value \rightarrow Salary$. This admittedly contrived example is much closer to the true nature of inference attacks than any model embracing the closed world assumption.

Distributed data mining combines elements of widely distributed information resources, agent-based software and machine learning that make inference attacks viable on a scale never before possible. With deception, money and persistence, the Internet can be used to retrieve individual credit reports, social security numbers, passwords and other sensitive types of information. Increasingly, enterprises are placing their operations online. Independently, a collection of databases can be safe from inference attack, but this may not be true when information from each is aggregated. Agents are tireless software servants that can roam the web gathering data for the purpose of inferring sensitive information.

Guarding against inference attacks in an open environment is a difficult if not impossible task. Administrators must coordinate with others managing related enterprises to conduct inference analysis on a much larger scale. Determinations must also be made regarding other kinds of information that are publicly available or commonly known. Enterprises might also employ distributed data mining agents to conduct cooperative inference analysis over the Internet.

10.3.2 Agent Technology

The characteristic feature of agent software is its ability to communicate with other software. Mobile agents can move from host to host carrying code to execute, accumulating state information. Agent systems can operate within a centralized architecture, in which they report to a central authority, or in a decentralized architecture with no single point of control. The popularity of agent models has led to the construction of several languages, toolkits and architectures for agent-based system development.

For agent-based enterprises where security is a concern, communication and mobility are focal points for agent security models (Chess 1998; Farmer, Guttag, and Swarup 1996; Vitek, Serrano, and Thanos 1997). Messages and agents in transport will demand integrity and may require confidentiality. For agent systems that play an integral role in an enterprise's mission critical service, availability is an added challenge.

Agent Communication Languages

Agent communication languages facilitate the transmission of data and commands between agents, allowing them to share knowledge and work together on a common problem. These languages are designed with consideration for the nature of their data content and the agent environment (which is often distributed and heterogeneous). They must be extensible to address the constantly changing needs of agent systems, and at the same time standardized for interoperability.

The knowledge query and manipulation language (KQML), developed by ARPA's knowledge sharing effort, is the most popular agent communication language (Finin, Fritzon, McKay, and McEntire 1994). KQML is divided into three layers; content, message and communication. The content layer of KQML currently accepts ASCII data but is easily extended to incorporate data in other formats. Performatives (agent commands) are issued in the message layer. The communication layer consists of header information such as the identities of the sender and recipient as well as a unique identifier for each message.

The extensibility of KQML has been exploited to introduce primitive security policy syntax in the communication layer (Thirunavukkarasu, Finin, and Mayfield 1995). The syntactic extensions integrate cryptographic mechanisms to authenticate messages, message originators, and to provide message confidentiality. The proposed extensions are divided into basic and enhanced security services. Basic services address message integrity, privacy, and authentication. The enhanced services incorporate mechanisms for nonrepudiation of message origination, protection from replay attacks, and protection from cipher attacks. The extensions adopts the inclusion of new security specific KQML parameters message digests, identifiers and keys. New performatives are also added for authentication requests and challenges, and for confidential communications. These extensions make good use of existing security technology to enable the specification of low level secure agent communication policies.

Agent Development Languages and Toolkits

Agent development languages and toolkits give agent system designers a specialized foundation on which to build. Agent systems written in general purpose computing languages such as C, C++, and Java, inherit the security vulnerabilities of those languages. Many of these vulnerabilities focus on weaknesses in type systems and bounds checking (McGraw and Felten 1997, Volpano and Smith 1998). However, programmers can mitigate these vulnerabilities with sound programming practices. Agent systems designers must take special care in constructing an implementation that is robust enough to overcome language weaknesses as there is a higher probability that roaming agents will interact with malicious software. More typically, general purpose programming languages can be used to build special purpose Application Programming Interfaces (APIs) and toolkits for agent development.

Java is one of the more popular general purpose programming languages embraced by agent designers. The popularity of this language is due in part to its portable remote evaluation system that permits code to be downloaded and executed over the web on virtually any platform. It also offers a simple, yet powerful, object-oriented model with a clean type system and novel security model. Another attraction that has fueled the momentum Java is the wide array of APIs and packages available for code serialization, remote method invocation, database connectivity, and secure communication.

Java's security model is based on a virtual sandbox from which untrusted code cannot escape (Dean, Felten, and Wallach 1996). Java also performs bytecode verification on downloaded bytecode to guard against stack overflows, illegal bytecode, improper use of registers, and other potential violations. Many attacks focus on circumventing the classloader, which is responsible for bytecode validation (McGraw and Felten 1997). Others try to foil aspects of the applet trust model within the Java security manager, which allows signed, and therefore trusted, applets extra privilege and constrains the abilities of untrusted applets

Java's security model has been enhanced in JDK 1.2 to include policy-based access control (Gong 1998). Access control in previous versions permitted either full access to a local environment or a sandbox with restricted access. The new fine-grained access control architecture allows users to restrict any code, local or downloaded, to specified resources. This new architecture provides security policies that are defined by a set of permissions available for code from any location and that can be easily configured by a user or system administrator. The permissions can give access to specific files, directories, or ports on hosts. The runtime system organizes code into domains. Domains are designated by a set of permissions and contain classes granted the same access.

JDK 1.2 also extends Java's cryptographic services. The previous JDK versions provided digital signature, message digest, and key-generation algorithms. Java 1.2 extends these with five new services; keystore creation and management, algorithm parameter management, algorithm parameter generation, key representation conversion, and factory support for certification generation and certification revocation lists (CGLs/CRLs).

IBM's Tokyo Research Laboratory has used Java to build IBM Tokyo's Aglets Software Development Kit, a toolkit for mobile agent development (Lange and Chang 1996). The toolkit encompasses an API and classes for Aglets, a mobile agent visual manager (Tahiti), and the agent transfer protocol (ATP), which can make distributed applications Aglet-aware.

Aglet security relies primarily on the security features of Java (Karjoth, Lange, and Oshima 1998). The Aglets framework extends the security for Java-based mobile agents with a layer between the underlying Java security model and the high level Java security APIs. This middle layer houses a special security manager, so that Aglet developers can implement their own security mechanisms and policies. Tahiti, the visual agent manager, implements a configurable security manager that limits access to local system resources. The flexible APIs and security architecture makes Aglets a popular choice for agent development in distributed data mining enterprises.

One general purpose language well-suited to agent system development is Tcl (Ousterhout 1990; Ousterhout 1993). Tcl is an embeddable interpreted scripting language. Extensions to Tcl can be built in other languages, principally C and C++. Four attributes of Tcl contribute to the safe execution of untrusted scripts: (1) Every action is mediated by the interpreter. (2) It has no pointers and array references are bounds-checked. (3) Scripts are encapsulated by their own execution stacks, variables, and commands, allowing different security attributes to be issued to isolated scripts. (4) interpreters can contain different command sets with different security properties.

Safe-Tcl adds two features to Tcl; safe interpreters and aliases (Ousterhout,

Levy, and Welch 1998). Each Tcl applet is given a separate "safe interpreter" in which to run that is isolated from other applets. Safe interpreters are coordinated by a single master interpreter. Applets may use aliases to request services from the master interpreter in a controlled manner. The alias mechanism is an association between a command in the safe interpreter, called the source command for the alias, and a command in the master interpreter, called the target. The master interpreter creates aliases for the safe interpreter choosing the source and target commands. An important point to this scheme is that a safe interpreter cannot create its own aliases. Otherwise a malicious script could make the safe interpreter generate an alias and issue a procedure call bypassing the master interpreter. Safe-Tcl also supports the implementation of security policies and can be extended to consider applet authentication services.

D'Agents (formerly named Agent Tcl) is a mobile-agent system under development at Dartmouth (Gray 1998). It is based on Safe-Tcl and provides a security model that supports authentication and access control for agents. Agent authentication is based on PGP. Migration requests are signed by the private key of the site hosting the agent and encrypted with the destination site's public key. It is assumed that all public keys are already known to all sites. Authorization is determined by access control lists internal to agents and by Safe-Tcl resource managers. Dangerous commands, such as opening and writing to a file, are closely monitored by trusted interpreters.

10.4 Secure Architectures for Distributed Data Mining

Distributed data mining has become a popular method for collecting knowledge in federated environments where trust between enterprises is not always complete or mutual. Miners can extract useful knowledge across trust boundaries from information resources containing sensitive data without compromise to confidentiality or integrity. The success of a distributed data mining venture in open and competitive environments relies upon a practical and coordinated integration of security functionality into each of the cooperating database and mining software architectures. This section presents general guidelines for integrating security into distributed enterprises and discusses how these relate in particular to data mining operations. A generic distributed data mining architecture that integrates security for agents, clients and hosts is also described. The architecture does not address the inference problem. However, sharing metadata and schema information to approximate a global intension seems to be a necessary first step in conducting inference analysis in open data mining environments.

10.4.1 Guidelines

When deciding on how best to integrate security into the operation of any enterprise, there are a number of guidelines that should be followed. The first objective is to *understand which risks are acceptable.* The second section of this chapter discussed the potential risks associated with distributed data mining from the perspective of both clients and information hosts. Before implementing a highly restrictive security model, a software architect should take into account the sensitivity and mission criticality of the knowledge extracted and data from which it will be mined. Identifying architectural components and interactions where confidentiality or integrity is not an issue will greatly simplify the task of seamless security integration. For instance, if mined knowledge is to enter the public domain, then there is little point in encrypting it in agent communications and migrations.

In assessing risks, designers must also identify and prioritize potential vulnerabilities in their software architectures. Thus, the second guideline is to *be paranoid.* Designers should assume that every element outside their immediate trust domain is potentially malicious. Clients dispatching agents to remote mining hosts must regard the network and the remote hosts as hostile environments. A related guideline is to *be explicit.* This refers to explicitly listing assumptions about trust, protocols, and any other factors relied upon for maintaining the security of a system. If a distributed data mining operation relies on the underlying operating system security of remote hosts then this assumption must be made explicit by the designers. Assumptions not made explicit tend to be ignored in the evaluation process and, far worse, not supported in implementations.

It is also important to know *which security measures are practical and which are not.* This requires an understanding of system performance requirements and the algorithmic complexity needed to solve particular problems. For example, a strict timely delivery requirement might sway designers to use shared key over public key encryption in authentication and secure communication service implementations.

These guidelines will help designers decide where to focus security integration efforts and also where not to focus them. Furthermore, designers should *rely on established security tools and technologies.* Security tools that have been in existence for several years benefit from inspection and testing by experts in the security and software design communities.

10.4.2 Integrated Security Technologies

Distributed data mining enterprises rely on interaction between several entities in open environments. The process is driven by a *client* that controls several *agents* engaged in knowledge gathering. These agents must traverse an open network to a *remote computational environment* where they typically communicate with *information resources* through a constrained interface. Security challenges and opportunities exist with each point of interaction between entities.

The most distinctive features of a newly created agent are: (1) the behavior it inherits from its manufacturer and (2) the mining objectives it is given by its owner. Agents should also inherit credentials from owners and manufacturers for the purposes of agent authentication, authorization and nonrepudiation. Most credentials will attest to the identity of agent owners and manufacturers, but this is not always appropriate, particularly where anonymity is desirable in the mining process. In this case, a trusted intermediary could give an agent relevant credentials (possibly based on roles or clearance levels) without revealing an owner's or manufacturer's identity.

Clients and remote hosts must communicate to dispatch mining agents and deliver agent management commands and information. Clients and remote hosts should engage in mutual authentication as part of the process of establishing a secure communication channel for mining agent migration and messaging. Without mutual authentication intruders can pose as legitimate clients or hosts. Kerberos or some other popular authentication service should be employed to offer a level of trust between clients and remote information resource sites (Kohl and Neuman 1993; Steiner, Neuman, and Schiller 1988).

Kerberos uses a centralized authentication server architecture to create secure communication channels between subjects. Data confidentiality and integrity is addressed by authenticating the parties involved and safely distributing session keys for encrypted network communications. Once authenticated locally by a "kerberized" workstation, the subject receives a ticket granting ticket from the authentication server. This ticket can be used by the subject to request other tickets for specific network services. One of the principal benefits of Kerberos is that passwords are never sent over the network. Kerberos tickets sent over the network are resistant to forgery and replay. This enables clients and remote hosts to exchange messages and migrate agents with a high level of confidence that intruders cannot forge, alter or replay distributed data mining network traffic. Figure 10.2 illustrates the role of a centralized authentication service in a distributed data mining enterprise.

Drawbacks to the centralized server architecture of Kerberos are that (1) the server must be available at all times, (2) the server is a potential bottleneck, and (3) each cooperating site must be kerberized. Alternatively, public key cryptography could be used in which each entity has its own public/private key pair. This is the approach adopted by the BODHI system under development at Washington State University (Kargupta, Park, Hershberger, and Johnson 1999). However, key distribution is always a challenge in a dynamic network

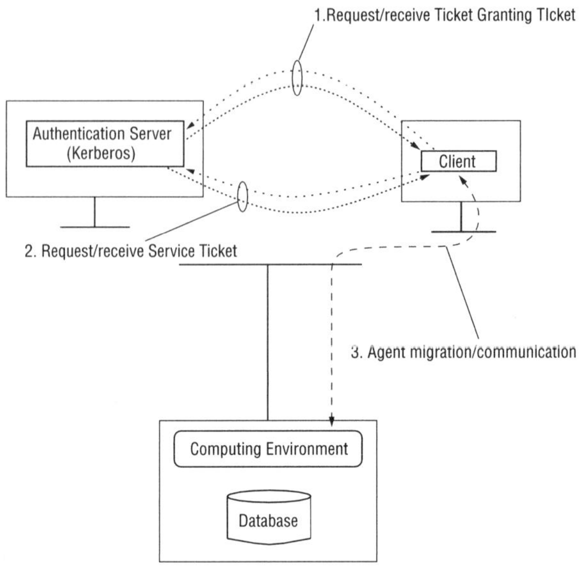

Figure 10.2: Client/host authentication for distributed data mining.

setting. Public key cryptography is notorious for its exorbitant computational overhead, but can be used effectively for digital signatures and secure key exchange.

Authenticated clients and remote hosts behave (or have their behavior limited) in accordance with a prevailing global authorization policy. The authorization policy states which activities are permitted by which entities. For example, a given client might not be granted access to the information resources at a particular site. Likewise, a remote host may not be trusted to communicate with certain clients. In a federated system the prevailing global authorization policy is determined by local policies established by administrators in each federation for resources under their locus of control.

Logging interactions between clients and remote computing environments is essential to delivering nonrepudiation. Intruders may focus attacks on underlying client or remote host operating systems, in which case such information will be invaluable in the forensic process. Failed connection attempts and other anomalous behavior should always be logged. The key to successful auditing is, in some sense, knowing what not to log. Careful selection of auditable activity will make logfiles manageable and tractable for analysis. Some types of communication may warrant less attention than others. For example, communications that involve the transmission of code should be more closely watched than those that consist of passive data. (However, this is not to suggest that untrusted passive data cannot be dangerous!)

Cooperative enterprises in a distributed data mining operation may choose to share information from audit trails to corroborate evidence of coordinated network intrusions. Of course, sharing such information in a federated network raises another set of security issues. A compromised organization may worry they are sharing audit trail data with competitors possibly responsible for the intrusions in the first place!

An agent that migrates to a remote computing environment must be authenticated and authorized upon arrival. The client, while an owner of the migrating agent, is not necessarily its manufacturer. Agent authentication requires information about both owners and manufacturers. Hosts accepting mobile agents must be certain that agent code has not been tampered with. Both owners and manufacturers can lend authenticity to mobile agents by signing agent code using message digest and digital signature technology, such as, MD5 and RSA, as used in PGP (Garfinkel 1995; Rivest 1992; Rivest, Shamir, and Adleman 1978).

Agents contain state information as well as code. The origins of agent code can be validated by code signing. However, since state information held by a mobile agent changes from site to site, it is more difficult to authenticate the origins of agent state information. Having each site sign its contribution to the state information held by resident agents is unlikely to be practical. Research presented by Vigna (1998) indicates that applying public key cryptography and digital signatures to agent execution tracing might offer a partial solution to this problem.

In mobile agent systems, hosts have complete access to agent environments. Since hosts can alter an agent's environment or the agent code itself, it is conventional wisdom that protecting mobile agents from hosts is impossible. However, work in the area of mobile cryptography (Sander and Tschudin 1998) promises to deliver mobile agent confidentiality/integrity. The idea is that an agent can be encrypted in such a way that: (1) the executing host cannot determine its function, (2) its environment cannot be predictably modified, and (3) it may carry and use secret information. An agent encrypted at its point of origin would be delivered to a remote host for evaluation. The result of the computation is itself encrypted, and can only be decrypted by the agent originator.

The field of mobile cryptography is still in its infancy, but a number of approaches have already yielded preliminary successes. One approach allows for the secure evaluation of Boolean circuits (Abadi and Feigenbaum 1990); Abadi, Feigenbaum, and Kilian 1990). This approach requires an undesirable level of interactivity and has other characteristics that make it less suitable for mobile code. However, the use of Boolean circuits illustrates the potential for a general solution to encrypting functions. Sander and Tschudin (1998),

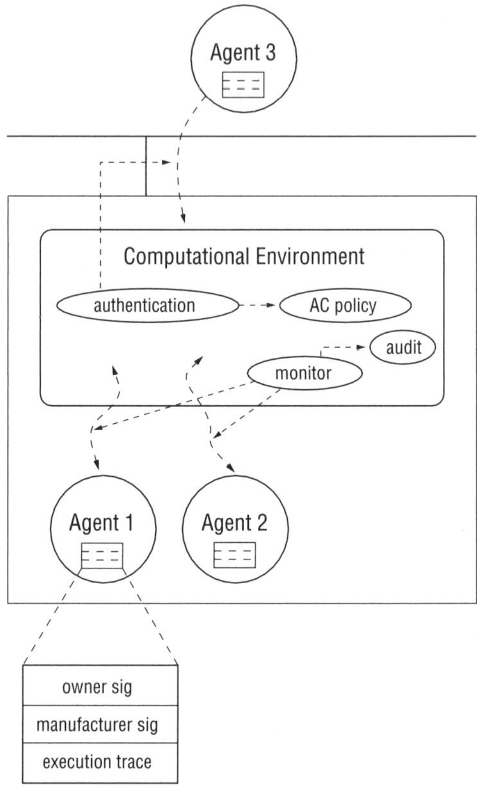

Figure 10.3: Agent/environment protection.

adapted the above approach for the noninteractive evaluation of a special class of encrypted polynomial functions. While no practical, general mobile agent encryption scheme is yet known, these results are far more promising than the initial conclusions drawn regarding mobile code protection.

On the other hand, standard techniques exist for protecting hosts from malicious agents. Agent computing environments commonly engage a monitor to watch the execution of the agent and guard against potential compromises. While preventing an environment from violating the integrity of an agent is not possible, code signing and cryptographic execution tracing can make such violations readily apparent. Figure 10.3 depicts security mechanisms for agent environment protection.

An authenticated agent is given access to resources by the remote computing environment according to its local policy. Establishing and enforcing an access control policy for executing agents constrains agent behavior. An es-

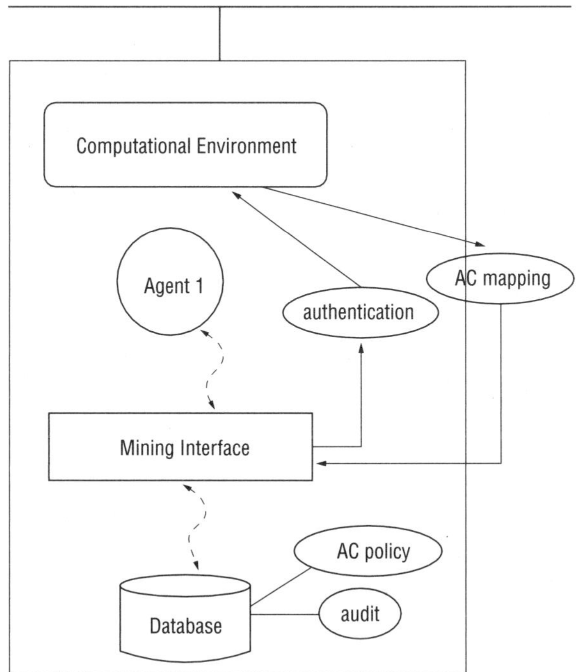

Figure 10.4: Agent mining interface.

tablished access control policy can be implemented effectively with an access control list and a monitor that checks all agent activities. Access control lists typically contain triples of the form *<subject,object,permission>*, where the *subject* maps to the agent, *object* maps to the resource, and *permission* refers to the type of access permitted. Monitors confer with access control lists to authorize or deny intercepted access attempts. Agents entering remote computing environments must be regarded as both subjects and objects. Where agent to agent communications are possible, the remote computing environment should adopt a policy that addresses inter-agent accesses. Auditing failed access attempts and other selected events can provide a measure of nonrepudiation at the agent level.

Agents mine databases through constrained interfaces (figure 10.4). These interfaces can perform authentication by checking an agent's identity and code signature against that registered with the computational environment. The database itself can provide authorization and audit services at this level of interaction. The database's authorization model actually affects authentication and authorization at the computational environment level. For example, if a database uses role-based access control (RBAC), then an agent should be authenticated and authorized within the computational environment as fulfilling a certain role. Computational environments must make the appropriate mappings to database authorization policies.

10.5 Conclusion

Distributed data mining poses new security and privacy issues to miners and managers of information resources. Agents roaming the web to gather information from databases spread across an open and potentially hostile environment must preserve data integrity and often have confidentiality and availability requirements. Distributed data mining can also present grave threats to personal privacy if used to mount global inference attacks. A secure architecture for distributed data mining integrates proven authentication and secure communication technology, with appropriate authorization policies to mitigate established risks. A total solution requires cooperation between data mining enterprises and online information resource managers.

Chapter 11

Data Quality in Distributed Environments

Beat Wüthrich, Vincent Cho, Joshua Pun, and Jian Zhang

11.1 Data Quality

Data quality or information quality is a topic which is of high importance to various research communities. Researchers from library science, information systems and databases are all studying this topic with different motivations and different perspectives. The importance of data quality is increasing because more and more data sources using a variety of data formats (e.g., structured, semi-structured or unstructured) are now available. This makes the judgement of the quality of a data source ever more difficult and hence important.

The rapid development of technology such as bar-code, credit card payment, e-commerce, OCR reading etc. enables a lot of organizations to produce and collect large amounts of data. In addition, the lowering of cost of storage media further encourages organizations to keep as much data as possible. We are now data rich but still starving for knowledge. The huge amount of data captures knowledge about many aspects of the corporation keeping this data. All organizations keep their data spread out over many different databases or data sources, hence they are operating in a *distributed environment*. Recently, organizations began to realize that hidden within this mass of data was a resource that has been ignored so far. Distributed mining is therefore a rapidly emerging field.

Real world data is never perfect. It is noisy, typically containing a lot of missing values, often containing residual variation (i.e. incomplete data in the sense of missing attributes), staled (i.e. out of date), distributed and heterogeneous, stored in legacy systems, constantly being updated and enormous, both in the number of tuples as well as in dimensionality. As such, the *quality of data* in the databases varies from one and other. Studying data quality is therefore needed because it helps identifying good sources to be integrated into the data warehous and it helps selecting the sources on which to perform preferably the mining.

In the rest of this section, related work on data quality is reviewed. Section 11.1.1 takes the view of library science. Section 11.1.2 is from the perspective of information systems. Section 11.1.3 is from the view of database research. Finally, as our research in section 11.2 is on data quality in the largest distributed environment built ever, the world wide web, a description of the current trends and research on web mining is contained in section 11.1.4.

11.1.1 Data Quality in Library Science

Criteria for evaluating information resources, particularly those on the Internet, are useful to librarians and others who select sites to be included in an information resource guide. Therefore, both Wilkinson (Bennett, Wilkinson, and Oliver 1997) and Janicke (1996) concentrate their studies of data quality on Internet resources. Wilkinson stated that unlike professional journals and commercial publishers, who employ a system of editorial review and external referees to ensure the caliber of materials distributed, information can be spread over the Internet by anyone without regard to accuracy, validity, or bias. This means that a great deal of information is posted on the world every day, but unfortunately very little is of high quality. As such, he developes a set of criteria and procedures that will assist students, teachers, and other users in evaluating the quality of Internet information and for standards to guide the design of web resources. On the other hand, Janicke addresses three questions on resource selection and information evaluation: Is the resource or information likely to be found on the Internet? Where is the resource or information located on the Internet? Is the resource or information that exists accurate and reliable?

11.1.2 Data Quality in Information Systems

In the context of information systems, data quality problems are increasingly evident, particularly in organizational databases. The social and economic impact of poor-quality data costs billions of dollars. Usually, many managers think that data quality problems occur while entering the data. However, a deeper analysis reveals that data quality problems occur at all stages of projects, in any part of a business process and for a variety of reasons. Hence, their data quality problems continue to occur because there is no systematic process to measure, analyze and correct the problems.

Poor information quality can create chaos. Unless its root cause is diagnosed, efforts to address it are simply patching potholes. Strong, Lee, and Wang (1997b) describes ten key causes and their warning signs. With this knowledge, organizations can identify and address these problems before they face financial and legal consequences.

Storey, Wang, and Firth (1995) present a comprehensive survey of the recent advances in the field of data quality. This survey evaluates the current research related to various aspects of the data quality problem. A framework for analyzing data quality research is developed using an analogy between product manufacturing and data manufacturing. It consists of seven elements: management responsibilities, operation and assurance costs, research and development, production, distribution, personnel management, and legal function. This framework can overcome the unaddressed problems from the traditional approach of data quality management in database literatures. Usually, those traditional approaches only ensured *syntactic correctness*. Though syntactic correctness is critical to data quality, these techniques fail to address many issues that are important to users.

Fox, Levitin, and Redman (1994) lays a foundation for the study of data quality. They discuss five different approaches to define data and propose data quality dimensions. The most important dimensions of data quality are: accuracy, completeness, consistency, and currentness.

Redman (1996) continues the study on the dimensions of data quality. He defines data consisting of two abstract parts: a conceptual model and data values. If the data are to be stored and/or used, an extra part of data representation is necessary. In other words, the dimension of data quality is associated with these three aspects of data. He explores 27 quality aspects and links them with corresponding activities in a data life-cycle model.

Strong, Lee, and Wang (1997a) define high-quality data as data that is fit for use by data consumers. This means that usefulness and usability are important aspect of quality. Using this definition, the characteristics of high-quality data consists of four categories: intrinsic, accessibility, contextual and representational aspects. Each data quality (DQ) category may have different data quality dimensions. For example, *Intrinsic DQ* has accuracy, objectivity, believability and reputation. *Accessibility DQ* has accessibility and access security. *Contextual DQ* has relevance, value-added, timeliness, completeness and amount of data. *Representational DQ* has interpretability, ease of understanding, concise representation and consistent representation. These all give a broader conceptualization of DQ than the conventional intrinsic view. Strong and colleagues also claim that the conventional DQ approaches alone focus on intrinsic aspects of DQ only. They fail to address the broader DQ concerns of data consumers. Conventional DQ approaches employ control techniques (like edit checks, database integrity constraints and program control of database updates) to ensure data quality and these approaches can improve intrinsic DQ substantially, especially the accuracy dimension. However, the control of data storage is not sufficient. As such, IS professionals need to apply process-oriented techniques, like IS auditing, to the processes that produce data.

Aebithi and Perrochon (1993) propose a framework to improve data quality of an information system. They define the notion of data quality as the sum of three context dependent aspects: correctness, completeness and minimality. Even a well designed and implemented information system cannot guarantee correct data in all circumstances. Data quality in a system tends to decrease gradually and therefore some data correction procedures should be applied from time to time. Their framework increases data quality by correcting data values. It is an iterative process and is composed of two parts: selection part and correction part. The selection part identifies and extracts problem data values for which at a later time, one must decide whether these data values have to be corrected, unchanged, used or thrown away. This part can be done without human interaction. However, in the correction part, the selected data values will be corrected or deleted, which is assisted by a human expert. In order to reduce the number of decisions a human expert has to be made to correct data as far as possible, some kind of sampling and learning from the corrections made by expert is needed.

11.1.3 Data Quality in Databases

Though database research has not focused on data quality management itself, many tools developed are related to data quality. For example, research on how to prevent data inconsistencies (integrity constraints and normalization theory) and how to prevent data corruption (transaction management). However, data in real world is imperfect. Data may not be timely and valid. In general, data may be of poor quality because of not reflecting the real world conditions, or not easily being used and understood by the data users. Even if you have accurate data, it is of little value if the data are not interpretable and accessible by users.

Data accuracy is one of the constituencies of the broader term—data quality. Studying the estimation of data accuracy is the first step of studying the data quality problem in databases. Reddy and Wang (1995) present a framework for estimating the accuracy of derived data in a relational database environment, which involve multiple base relations or multiple heterogeneous database systems in a federated environment. They propose a method to estimate the overall data accuracy in terms of the accuracy of relevant base relations and the actual database query. The query is examined in terms of its underlying set of base operators. The accuracy estimates are based on the assumption of uniform distribution of incorrect values across tuples and attributes.

Different users have different criteria for determining the quality of data. Tagging data at the cell level with quality indicators, which are objective characteristics of the data and its manufacturing process, is one of the approaches (Wang, Kon, and Madnick 1993; Wang, Reddy, and Kon 1995). Following a step-by-step procedure for defining and documenting data quality parameters important to users, quality indicators to be tagged to data items are derived from these parameters. Based on these indicators, the user may assess the data's quality for the intended application. This method attaches a label to every attribute value specifying the time when the value was recorded and a source from which it was obtained. Thus, the users can judge about the creditability of the data. As such, this technique addressed the timeliness and accuracy aspect of the data. Nevertheless, it seems that tagging all these data into the database would impose too much demand on data storage. The feasibility of applying this technique to a very large database would be questionable.

Motro's studies (Motro and Rakov 1996; Motro and Rakov 1997; Motro and Rakov 1998) are focused on the information sources, which are structured relational databases. Unlike most other approaches, their study is quantitative. They propose a standard for rating information resources with respect to their quality. This standard, based on the concepts of *soundness* and *completeness*, attemptes to gauge the distance of the information in a database from the truth. They combine manual verification with statistical methods to arrive at estimates of the quality of databases. They consider the variance in quality by isolating areas of databases that are homogeneous with respect to quality, and then estimate the quality of each separate area. These composite estimates may be regarded as *quality specifications* that are affixed to each database. Finally, they show how to derive quality estimates for individual queries from such quality specifications. They argue that the annotation of answers with their quality provides valuable information for users.

11.1.4 Data Quality, Data Mining and the Web

Semistructured data is data that contains some clearly identifiable features, but also some blocks of "unstructured" text (Buneman 1997). One of the motivations for studying semistructured data is from the popularity and widespread use of the world wide web (web for short). The web is considered to be semistructured because it contains some clearly identifiable features, e.g. web addresses, and also includes blocks of text that are considered unstructured components of documents. The web itself is the largest distributed and semistructured database built ever.

Traditionally, data mining problems and solutions are usually focused on well structured data sets (e.g. relational databases). Promising research results and real-world applications are reported. Indeed, structured data is only a tip of an iceberg in the data world. Much data resides on those ill-structured legacy systems or partially structured textual document systems. Therefore, web mining is getting more and more attention by researchers.

The term *web mining,* however, has been used in three distinct ways. The first, which is referred to as *web content mining*, is mainly describing the process of information or knowledge discovery from millions of sources across the world wide web. The second one is *Web usage mining*. This is the process of mining Web access logs or other user information such as browsing and access patterns on one or more Web localities. An overview of the various research issues, techniques, and development in web content mining and web usage mining can be found in Cooley, Mobasher, and Srivastava (1997). The third is *search oriented web mining* (Gudivada, Raghavan, Grosky, and Kasanagottu 1997). It emphasizes the search and indexing of the web, the classical information retrival topics. Two kinds of search tools are available. The first ones launch a web robot, also called worm, walker, spider or knowbot. Upon a user query, the web is systematically explored and documents are ranked according to their relevance and the most relevant ones returned to the user. Alternatively, search tools precompile an index (meta data kept in a local database) and periodically update it. Queries are executed on the locally kept index. There is a growing amount of work directed at exploiting textual content and link information for the purpose of search (Carriere and Kazman 1997; Golovchinsky 1997; Spertus 1997).

In the field of content mining, Feldman and Hirsh first propose a solution to text mining in Feldman and Dagan (1995). Later, they develop a FACT (Finding Associations in Collections of Text) system (Feldman and Hirsh 1997) for knowledge discovery from text to solve the web content mining problem. By labeling each document with a set of keywords that represent some of the topics discussed in the documents, FACT discovers correlations, associations, between the occurrence of various keywords labeling the documents. Thus, one can ask for interesting patterns of co-occurrence amongst the keywords of each article.

The goal of WebKB project[1] is to develop a probabilistic symbolic knowledge base that mirrors the content of the web.

Another project designs techniques to deal with information overload and to help users reading only relevant and authoritative matters. Various techniques based on machine learning and graph algorithms are employed to mine documents in large hypertext databases for relevance and quality [2].

In the area of search oriented web mining, a variety of techniques are available to categorize text (Nigram, McCallum, Thrum, and Mitchell 1998). Charabarti, Dom, Agrawal, and Raghavan (1998) explores how to organize large text databases hierarchically by topic to aid better searching, browsing and filtering.

Singh, Scheuermann, and Chen (1997) present a way to generate association rules from semistructured documents using an extended concept hierarchy (ECH). By using a pregenerated EECH to identify and relate concept that appear in the unstructure components of the documents, it relates the information from the structured and unstructured portions of a document databases. They further use the ECH to maintain parent, child and sibling relationships between concepts. This structure can generate rules that relate a given concept in the ECH and a given structured attribute value to the neighbours of the given concept in the ECH.

Extracting useful information within a web site and across web sites is one the goals in data mining (web mining). Essentially, a web site can be seen as a document database. Mining across numerous web sites would incur an exponential time. It is as if we were mining rules across many databases. Therefore, studies have been done on identifying relevant databases for mining rules (Yao and Liu 1997; Liu, Lu, and Yao 1998). By using a relevance measure, it identifies relevant databases for mining association rules.

The problem we investigate in the next section is the data source selection problem using a quantitative notion of data quality. In particular, the data sources we are interested in are web sources. The selection of data sources for mining is a preprocessing step in the whole KDD process and can be considered as the first part of web content mining.

First, relevant data sources have to be found (this belongs to search oriented web mining). This problem has been well investigated and excellent solutions in terms of powerful search engines are readily available.

[1] www.almaden.ibm.com/cs/kr53/ir.html

[2] www.cs.smu/edu/afs/project/thoe-11/www/wwkb, www.software.ibm.com/data/iminer/fortext/

Second, high quality data sources have to be selected from the relevant data (web content mining).

Finally, the high quality sources are mined using any of the techniques available (web content mining).

Surely, the definition of what high quality data is also depends on the mining goal, the phases are not totally independent from each other. Note also that when there is only a single data source available (nondistributed case) then there is no need to select from a manifold of various data sources.

Section 11.2 discusses the second problem by providing a definition of information source quality. A framework is presented in which the notion of quality becomes quantifiable. We show some intuitive properties of data quality and experimentally verify on an outstandingly difficult classification problem that from high quality information sources better prediction results should be expected than from low quality information sources - though this correlation is of course not perfect.

11.2 Measuring the Quality of Data Sources

The rich variety of on-line information and news available on the world wide web (web for short) make it an attractive resource from which to mine knowledge from multiple textual information sources. For example, in increasingly global and interconnected financial markets, the globalization and availability of on-line financial information and news drive the more-and-more urgent need for transforming the hyper-textual content into useful information and knowledge. On-line financial news sources describe and analyze the standings of major stock and financial markets around the world, present investment reports and advice, and track stock, bond and currency prices.[3] The richest textual financial information has always been used as the basis of financial market analysis, prediction and decision-making. Using multiple information sources is advisable since they provide different view points on the same object or event. This enhances the knowledge of the object or event. The combination and coordination of information from multiple information sources may lead to much deeper understanding of the object or event than when only taking a single information source into account. Effective data mining from multiple and distributed textual information sources is therefore a promising and fast emerging field (Han, Chen, and Yu 1998; Lander and Lesser 1997; Pregibon, Ymour, and Smyth 1997).

The first step in mining relevant and possibly useful knowledge on the web is finding *high quality information sources*. This allows the mining of

[3] Among many others, such sources include individual web pages from www.bloomberg.com, www.ft.com, www.iht.com, www.wsj.com, and www.asianupdate.com.

uncorrupted knowledge and information, as well as discarding misleading and conflicting information. Selecting high quality data sources is therefore of tremendous importance. This section discusses problems and aspects of finding high quality data or information sources.

Mining knowledge from different sources of formatted or unformatted, textual or hyper-textual sources poses new challenges to data mining. Distributed data mining from multiple textual information sources (from the web) is different from the more traditional data mining. (1) It is very difficult to establish a systematic theory for analyzing sources with unstructured textual content (from the web). (2) It is very difficult to establish flexible techniques for integrating the content from different information sources.

In order to support effective data mining from distributed information sources, quality assessment and reliability measurement of distributed information sources are recognized as key issues. Finding high quality information sources, which is regarded as an important component for distributed data mining, means designing reliable and effective metrics to evaluate the quality of information sources. Based on the metrics, high quality information sources are selected to conduct data mining. The overall goal of this study is to discuss the selection of high quality information sources and to provide an actual means to do this selection.

Note that the goodness of a data source could also be talked about in the context of a particular classifier with a very specific setting of its parameters. However, if one determines the quality in such a way, then there is no guarantee at all that the same quality is still valid if even the parameters are changed. It is rather likely that the quality notion is then overfit with respect to a particular classifier and its settings. What we hope to achieve is a way around this problem and find a metrics that is pretty much classifier independent and nevertheless still meaningful.

The rest of the section is structured as follows. Section 11.2.1 introduces the general framework and some notation. It also states the assumptions about how the content of a data source is represented (as a weighted feature or attribute set) and how the content of data sources is going to be used (to solve a k-classification problem). Section 11.2.2 shows that selecting high quality data sources is equivalent to estimating a conditional probability density function. Section 11.2.3 provides the definition of data quality and shows how to compute it from training examples. Section 11.2.4 empirically evaluates this definition. Given 42 data sources, each represented by 790 features or attributes, the task is to find the best feature subset and data sources so as to solve a k-classification problem. It is shown that preselecting high quality data sources and attribute subsets based on our definition of high quality data indeed leads to better classification performance. Section 11.2.5 concludes this research.

11.2.1 Data Sources

Suppose a *structured* data source such as a large relational table. Each tuple or training example of that table is represented by a set of values for a set of given attributes. Alternatively, for an *unstructured* data source, such as a web page, the content is represented by a set of features (Jain and Zongker 1997; Salton 1989). For the structured and unstructured case, we adopt the usual pattern recognition, machine learning and information retrieval terminology and talk about a *feature set.* The method to get the values of features is called *feature extraction method.* As usual, each feature value is a real number between zero and one (Croft 1981).

Suppose a feature set $f = \{f_1, f_2, ..., f_m\}$ that is used to describe an object, tuple or event. There is a set of information sources $s = \{s_1, s_2, ..., s_n\}$ each describing the same objects, tuples or events. We assume that each source describes the objects in terms of the same feature set. As a result, for each object or tuple t, there are n information sources containing m features describing it. Therefore, the complete information about an object t is described by a $m \times n$ dimensional feature matrix:

$$\begin{pmatrix} & s_1 & s_2 & \cdots & s_n \\ f_1: & w_{11}(t) & w_{12}(t) & \cdots & w_{1n}(t) \\ f_2: & w_{21}(t) & w_{22}(t) & \cdots & w_{2n}(t) \\ & & & \cdots & \\ f_m: & w_{m1}(t) & w_{m2}(t) & \cdots & w_{mn}(t) \end{pmatrix}$$

where $w_{ij}(t)$ denotes the weight or value of feature f_i of an information source s_j for object or time point t.

In addition, we assume that objects are classified into one of several mutually exclusive outcomes. That is, each object is classified into one of k exclusive classes $C_1, C_2, \cdots, C_k$. For example, suppose there are web pages containing financial and economic news as well as stock market analysis. The object of interest is the Hang Seng Index (Hong Kong's major stock market index). At each time point (each day), there is one of three possible outcomes: either the Hang Seng Index (Hong Kong's major stock index) went up, it remained steady, or it went down. Hence, at each time point, there are three mutually exclusive outcomes: up, steady or down. The basic assumptions about data sources are summarized as follows.

(1) Each data source contains information about the same objects or events. For example, there are many information sources describing the Hong Kong stock market.

(2) Each object or time point is associated with one of several mutually exclusive outcomes $C_1, C_2, \cdots, C_k$. For example, the possible outcomes are up, steady and down.

(3) The content of an information source is described by a set of weighted features. A feature may represent a keyword tuple such as "stocks rise." A weight attached to this feature can for instance express how frequently this keyword tuple occurs.

(4) The weighted features can be used to distinguish the outcomes C_1, $C_2, \cdots, C_k$ from each other. That is, from the weighting of the features of an information source, we can compute the outcome that is either one of $C_1, C_2, \cdots, C_k$.

The aim of data mining from web pages (or any other distributed data source) is to identify the relevant features (Domingos 1997a) and sources, to discard the irrelevant features and low quality sources, and finally to determine the classification of the object.

For the convenience of the following discussion, we introduce some notation about the feature information matrix.

For any $j (1 \leq j \leq n)$,

$$w_j(t) = (w_{1j}(t), w_{2j}(t), \cdots, w_{mj}(t))^T$$

This is the *feature vector* of information source s_j, where

$$(w_{1j}(t), w_{2j}(t), \cdots, w_{mj}(t))^T$$

means the transpose of matrix $(w_{1j}(t), w_{2j}(t), \cdots, w_{mj}(t))$. The feature vector represents the information about object t in source s_j.

For any $i (1 \leq i \leq m)$,

$$f_i(t) = (w_{i1}(t), w_{i2}(t), \cdots, w_{in}(t))$$

This is the *source vector,* which represents the information about feature f_i of an object t.

In this way, the *feature information matrix* for a distributed information source or repository is expressed as

$$w(t) = (w_1(t), w_2(t), \cdots, w_n(t))$$

In order to discuss the feature and source ranking principle, we need a few notions about k-dimensional Euclidean vectors. For any $P = (P_1, P_2, \cdots, P_k) \in \mathbf{R^k}$,

$$P \uparrow = (P_{[1]}, P_{[2]}, \cdots, P_{[k]})$$

where $P_{[1]} \geq P_{[2]} \geq \cdots \geq P_{[k]}$, $([1], [2], \cdots, [k])$ is a permutation on $(1, 2, \cdots, k)$ given by a permutation matrix

$$\begin{pmatrix} 1 & 2 & \cdots & k \\ [1] & [2] & \cdots & [k] \end{pmatrix}$$

In the sequel, P_i will represent a probability. We denote by $C_i(t)$ that the outcome of object t is class C_i. When the context is clear we sometimes write w, w_i and C_j instead of $w(t)$, $w_i(t)$ and $C_j(t)$ respectively.

11.2.2 Formal Description Based on Conditional Probability

Our aim is to select the optimal set of features and information sources to obtain the complete and most meaningful description of the objects or events. The object outcome must be determined by the feature information matrix. With this in mind, the formal model of mining knowledge from distributed information sources is based on the relationship between an object and the feature information matrix. The modeling task is to establish the relevant relationship between the object outcome and the feature information matrix.

The feature information matrix $w(t)$ describes the object t whose outcome is $C(t)$. Suppose training examples $\{(w(t), C(t))\}_{t=1}^{T}$ where T is a period of time (or a set of objects). We use the training set to determine the relationship between the object outcome and the feature information matrix.

The relationship between the object outcome $C_i(t)$ and the feature information matrix $w(t)$ is stochastically represented by a conditional probability

$$P(C_i(t)|w(t))$$

where P is a probability density function on the feature information matrix. It is the conditional probability of C_i occurring given the feature information matrix w.

A probabilistic model therefore calculates the k conditional probabilities

$$(P(C_1|w), P(C_2|w), \cdots, P(C_k|w)) \tag{11.1}$$

It represents the relevance measure between outcome C_i and feature matrix w. It follows immediately that the conditional probabilities sum up to 1, i.e.,

$$\sum_{i=1}^{k} P(C_i|w) = 1$$

Our classification model computes the conditional probabilities $P(C_i|w)$. This classification model then outputs the *most probable class* as the final outcome:

$$P(C_{[1]}|w) = max_{i=1,2,\cdots,k} P(C_i|w) \tag{11.2}$$

The quality of information sources depends on the correctness and the certainty of this final classification.

To actually compute the conditional probabilities we need to make some assumptions about how the classification is actually done. There are various theories and algorithms from different fields that are used to classify objects. In the addendum we show how to compute the conditional probability vector based on the popular k-center cluster model. Rule based systems (Agrawal and Srikant 1994; Wüthrich 1997), Bayesian Net (Heckerman 1997) and decision tree classifiers (Quinlan 1987a, 1987b) can be considered as sophisticated cluster models. Another option would have been to calculate the conditional probabilities using Naive Bayes (NB) method. However, though NB is a successful classifier, it has drawbacks for our purposes. NB is not good at estimating the actual probabilities, it is good at determining which class C_j has the highest probability $P(C_j|w)$. This is different from accurately estimating this probability.

11.2.3 Quality of Distributed Information Sources

The first fundamental question is what constitutes a good feature matrix. From there we are able to derive what a good feature and source subset is. Suppose there is a feature information matrix w and assume that the object outcomes C_i, C_j have the same conditional probabilities: $P(C_i|w) = P(C_j|w)$. This essentially means that w contains the same information about object outcomes C_i and C_j. This feature matrix cannot thus be used to distinguish between C_i and C_j. That said, this feature information matrix provides little information to solve the classification problem.

High quality distributed information sources are such that the feature information matrix can be used to distinguish the object outcomes from each other. In other words, high quality information sources can be used to reduce the uncertainty of the k-classification problem. A measurement of uncertainty of discriminating between two object classes can be obtained from measuring the distance of the conditional probabilities $(P(C_1|w), P(C_2|w), \cdots, P(C_k|w))$. The larger the distance measure, the more certain the discrimination of two object cases by the feature information matrix.

In general, high quality distributed information sources satisfy the following conditions.

1. Its feature information matrix distinguishes the object outcomes from each other most effectively and accurately. That is, the distance measure between two conditional probabilities $P(C_i|w)$ and $P(C_j|w)$ is expected to be as large as possible.

2. Whenever its feature information matrix chooses the most probable class according to equation (11.2), the classification should be correct.

For a feature information matrix $w(t)$ of an object t, the conditional probability vector is represented by

$$P = (P(C_1(t)|w(t)), P(C_2(t)|w(t)), \cdots, P(C_k(t)|w(t)))$$

We rank these conditional probabilities in descending order.

$$P \uparrow = (P_{[1]}(w(t)), P_{[2]}(w(t)), \cdots, P_{[k]}(w(t)))$$

The distance measure of two adjacent conditional probabilities is $d(P_{[i]}, P_{[i+1]})$, where d is some distance function. Ranking the conditional probabilities is equivalent to ranking the object outcomes given the feature information matrix. A high quality information source is given when there is maximal distance between adjacent probabilities. The sum of distance measures between the adjacent conditional probabilities provides a quantitative measure of the certainty of the classification:

$$\sum_{i=1}^{k-1} d(P_{[i]}, P_{[i+1]})$$

The feature ranking principle states that the larger the sum of distance measures between adjacent conditional probabilities, the higher quality the distributed information sources is. Finding high quality distributed information sources therefore means maximizing the distance measure of adjacent conditional probabilities. The feature ranking principle incorporates condition 1 stated before.

According to the feature ranking principle, we rank the conditional probabilities as

$$(P_{[1]}(w(t)), P_{[2]}(w(t)), \cdots, P_{[k]}(w(t)))$$

We use Euclidean distance measure to represent the distance between adjacent conditional probabilities.

$$[\sum_{i=1}^{k-1} (P_{[i]}(w(t)) - P_{[i+1]}(w(t)))^2]^{\frac{1}{2}}$$

The quality of the information feature matrix $w(t)$ is defined as follows.

$$quality(w(t)) = \delta_{C_{[1]}}(C(t))[\sum_{i=1}^{k-1} (P_{[i]}(w(t)) - P_{[i+1]}(w(t)))^2]^{\frac{1}{2}} \quad (11.3)$$

where $\delta_{C_{[1]}}(C(t))$ is the Delta function, which follows

$$\delta_{C_{[1]}}(C(t)) = \begin{cases} 1 & \text{when } C_{[1]} = C(t) \\ 0 & \text{otherwise} \end{cases}$$

Note that the Delta function realizes condition 2 which high quality distributed information sources should satisfy. We only add to the quality of the source if the actual classification (the most probable class) is correct.

Given a set of training examples, the quality of the distributed information source $s = \{s_1, s_2, ..., s_n\}$ with feature set $f = \{f_1, f_2, ..., f_m\}$ is therefore defined as follows.

$$quality(s, f) = \frac{1}{T} \sum_{t=1}^{T} quality(w(t)) \tag{11.4}$$

Some consequences are the following. Firstly, the quality is maximal if the classification is correct and done with one hundred percent certainty. Secondly, the quality is a real number between zero and one. Finally, if there are infinitely many training examples, then the quality is constant.

11.2.4 Empirical Evaluation

In this subsection, we discuss and evaluate data sources, features and classification, source and feature selection.

The Data Sources

We experiment with financial predictions about stock markets. These days, financial information networks such as the *Wall Street Journal* (www.wsj.com), *Financial Times* (www.ft.com), CNN (www.cnnfn.com), *International Herald Tribune* (www.iht.com), and Bloomberg (www.bloomberg.com) provide financial data twenty-four hours a day.

There are thousands of pages of information updated each day. Each page contains valuable information about stock markets. The address of each source is usually fixed[4] contains the news about Hong Kong's stock market. This page will be considered as one data source on the internet. However, some news page addresses change from time to time; usually these pages are under a content page.[5] is the content page for various regional financial news pages. But the individual news pages under this content page have changing URL addresses. The fixed content page together with its underlying news pages is considered as one identifiable information source.

Among numerous financial news web sites on the Internet, we restricted ourselves to five financial information networks - the ones named above. These networks provide fast and accurate information. From those networks we selected forty-two web sources that we consider - using our common sense and

[4]For example, www.wsj.com/edition/current/articles/HongKong.htm

[5]For example, www.ft.com/hippocampus/ftstats.htm

understanding of stock markets - to be already relevant to the task of predicting Hong Kong's stock market index, the Hang Seng Index. We collected these data in the period 14 Feb. 1997 to 8 Aug. 1997. This provides a total of 120 stock trading days, i.e., 120 objects.

The aim is to generate probabilistic rules (Wüthrich 1997, 1995) that then can predict the movement of the stock markets such as Hong Kong's Hang Seng Index (we developed a system predicting daily closing values of all major stock markets from financial news downloaded from the web.[6] The major challenge here is actually to get best possible input. That is, to select the highest quality sources among those 42 sources. Each tuple in each source is characterized by 790 features. The full feature information matrix is over 50 Mega Bytes large.

Initially, it may look natural to take all 42 sources as input as they have anyway been considered relevant using common sense. However, as will be shown, taking all sources yields much worse results than when considering only high quality sources.

The Features and the Classification

The features actually represent keyword sequences such as "dollar stalls," "US treasuries rally," "Dow slides," etc. There are 790 such keywords provided by domain experts. The following feature extraction method is used (Wüthrich, Leung, Peramunetilleke, and Chon 1998). Suppose one source, let's say s_j. Keyword or feature f_i occurs x times on day t in this source. The maximum number of occurrences in a day of feature f_i in source s_j in the training data is x'. Then the weight $w_{ij}(t)$ is equal to x/x'. Suppose a set of sources $s = \{s_1, s_2, ..., s_n\}$. Then the occurrence of keyword f_i is the sum of its occurrences in the individual sources. The weight is then computed as in the single source case. Wüthrich, Leung, Peramunetilleke, and Chon (1998) show that this feature extraction method is superior to other feature extraction methods (Aha, Wettschereck, and Mohr 1997).

The classification of an object is as follows. Whenever, the Hang Seng Index appreciates at least 0.5 percent then we classify it as *up*. If it remains between plus and minus 0.5 percent then it is *steady*. Finally, if it slides more than half a percentage point, it is going *down*. The majority class generated this way is *up*, occurring in 35.8% of all cases. In 35% of the cases the outcome is steady and in 29.2% of the cases the Hang Seng Index fell. So one benchmark is to achieve at least 35.8% prediction accuracy on the test data. The prediction itself is done using a generalization of if then rules that are

[6]The system's predictions and historical performance is available via www.cs.ust.hk/~beat/Predict.

also able to handle weighted features and not only Boolean features (Wüthrich 1997, 1995).

Source and Feature Selection

Given are a set of sources $s = \{s_1, s_2, ..., s_n\}$ and a set of features $f = \{f_1, f_2, ..., f_m\}$. The following greedy algorithm first selects a good source subset when keeping all features. Then a good feature subset is chosen when keeping all sources. Finally, only the good feature subset and the good source subset are kept. The computation of a high quality source subset is as follows.

1. s' = a random set of some sources;
2. Select that source s_j that for which $quality(s' + s_j, f)$ (or $quality(s' - s_j, f)$ resp.) is maximal;
3. If the new maximal quality is lower than $quality(s', f)$ then output s'; otherwise, $s' = s' + s_j$ ($s' = s' - s_j$ resp.) and go back to 2;

The computation of the high quality feature subset is done analogously. The output is then the source and the feature subset.

The above algorithm selects a good feature and source subset based on our definition of source quality. It computes the conditional probabilities according to appendix A. Its running time is polynomial in the number of possible features, sources and number of training examples. The algorithm is not guaranteed to find the optimal features and sources since this would require exponential time complexity. Exhaustive search is needed to get the optimal combination. This would involve computing the quality for each feature and source combination and finally selecting the optimal one. Once this algorithm selected a high quality distributed information source, a rule-based system solves the actual classification problem.

The tuples are split into a training and a test set. In a preliminary phase, we tried different sizes of training data and it turned out that about one hundred tuples are enough to obtain stable and good prediction results. When not stated otherwise, in all experiments five-fold cross validation with 96 tuples as training data is employed.

Evaluation

There is an equal number of cases in class up, steady and down respectively. Suppose that we randomly guess the outcome. On average, when guessing n times randomly, the mean of the accuracy is $n * p$ and the variance is $n * p * (1 - p)$ where p is the probability of guessing correctly (about 33% in our case). If n is rather large then this binomial distribution is approximately a normal

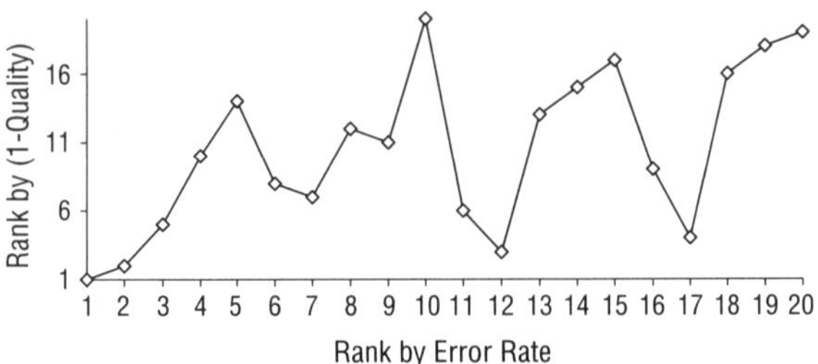

Figure 11.1: Accuracy achieved from each source individually.

distribution. There are 120 test cases. The probability that random guessing yields fourty one point eight percent accuracy on 120 cases is below ninty five percent probability. Figure 11.1 shows the accuracy of the rule-based system when taking as input only a single data source and all features. As can be seen from figure 11.1, only three data sources (those below the bar) are such that the predictions are better than random guessing with high probability. The best performing single source can be found at www.cnnfn.com/markets/bridge.

We next show that the prediction accuracy of the rule-based system is positively correlated to the data quality. Ideally, if the quality of the input is higher, then the prediction accuracy is also higher. It is, however, not necessarily the case that if the data input is of higher quality then the accuracy of the system is higher. This may be the case but it does not need to be the case. This is partly also because if the rule-based system is fed with a subset of all features $f' \subset f$, then the rule-based system in turn will only select a small subset $f'' \subset f'$ from which to predict. On the other hand, if the prediction system would make use of all provided features f' (as the method discussedby Cost and Salzberg [1997]) does) then a stricter correlation between quality and accuracy is expected. However, our rule-based approach proved superior to other forecasting techniques when predicting stock and foreign exchange markets.

In order to have a further benchmark for the selection of high quality data sources we use our rule-based system to do forward source selection. Using our rule-based system, we test each source individually and then choose the best one. Let's say s_j has the highest prediction accuracy on the test data. Then we test all pairs of sources $\{s_1, s_j\}$, $\{s_2, s_j\}$, ...$\{s_n, s_j\}$ and choose the best performing source pair, and so on. The results of these experiments are shown in figure 11.2. The best performing source pair is a combination of www.iht.com and www.cnnfn.com/markets/bridge. The accuracy from the best single source is lower than the accuracy achieved from the source pair, triple, etc. as shown in figure 11.2. Forward source selection, however, cannot guarantee that we find the optimal source combination. Only an exhaustive search can do this,

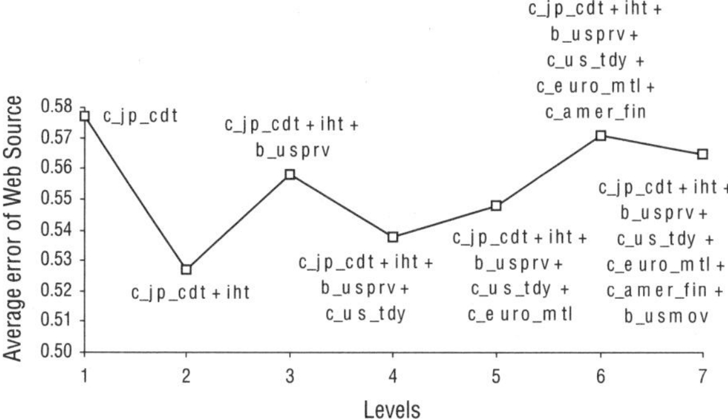

Figure 11.2: Forward selection of best source combination using a specific system.

but an exhaustive search is too expensive, even for source selection alone as there are 2^{42} combinations that need to be tested. Despite the fact that our prediction techniques are much faster than other forecasting techniques such as neural nets and Bayesian classifiers, the testing of one such source combination already takes several hours on a Sun Sparc machine.

One may now argue that this direct forward source selection would be the best way to select high quality data sources. However, it has a severe drawback, because it is system specific. Using forward selection strategy with a specific system does not guarantee that the best source combination for one prediction system is also the best source combination when using another prediction system. Even slight modifications in the way the forecasting is done can change the situation dramatically.

We use the algorithm in the Source and Feature Selection subsection to determine thirteen combinations of sources and features that are of relatively high quality. These combinations are ranked by quality. The combination with highest quality gets rank number thirteen. We also give these thirteen combinations as input to our prediction system. The accuracy results are now ranked by error. The best combination, that with the fewest errors is ranked number thirteen. figure 11.3 shows the correlation between the two rankings. Though the correlation is not perfect, for the reasons explained above, it is rather strong. In particular, the two combinations with highest quality yield the highest prediction accuracy as well.

In another experiment we first select the twenty-five individual sources with the highest quality. From those twenty-five sources we build twenty source subsets consisting of five sources: $\{s_1, ..., s_5\}$, $\{s_2, ..., s_6\}$, ..., $\{s_{20}, ..., s_{25}\}$. As before, we determine the quality of those sources by taking all

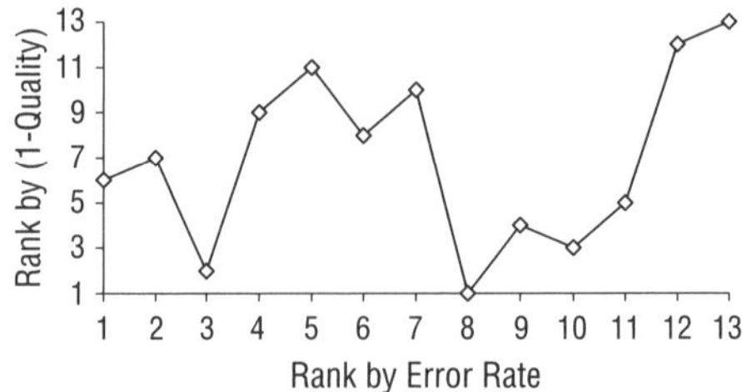

Figure 11.3: Correlation between data quality and prediction accuracy for relatively high quality source and feature subsets.

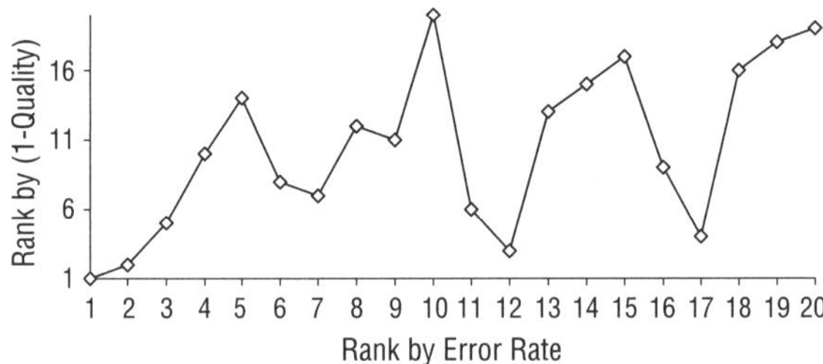

Figure 11.4: Correlation between data quality and prediction accuracy for relatively low quality source and feature subsets.

features into account and we also measure the prediction accuracy achieved from these source combinations. The source combinations are again ranked by quality and also ranked by accuracy. The correlation between the two rankings is shown in figure 11.4. Though the correlation is still strong, this time the highest accuracy is not achieved from the source combination having the highest quality. Again, this is due to the fact that our prediction system does not make use of all features but selects only the most suitable ones. Furthermore, this time the correlation is weaker the quality of those combinations in figure 11.4 is around ten times lower than the quality of the combinations shown in figure 11.3.

11.2.5 Conclusions

When trying to make use of the rapidly growing amount of information on the world wide web, users are confronted with two fundamental problems. First they must find relevant information sources. This problem is well investigated and excellent solutions in terms of powerful search engines are readily available. The second issue is, once relevant sources are provided, how do we determine which ones are of "high quality?" This section investigates the second problem. We assume that the information is used to solve a classification problem and that the content of an information source is available in the form of a feature vector.

We introduce a definition of quality of information source that is independent from a specific system solving the classification problem. Our notion of quality only takes into account the data. We prove that the notion of quality fulfills certain desirable properties. For example, the quality of any combination of sources and features is a real number between zero and one.

We then use a 50 MB data set to evaluate the notion of quality experimentally. The actual prediction is done by a rule-based system that is able to deal with weighted information. Though this rule-based system is independent from our notion of quality, it has been shown that there is a strong correlation between the classification accuracy achieved by the rule-based system and the quality of the data. The higher the quality, the higher the prediction accuracy achieved.

An open issue is the design of heuristics finding efficiently the optimal combinations of sources and features.

Addendum: Cluster Classification

The cluster classification model usually involves calculating the classes cluster center from the given training examples. The cluster center of an object class is identified by the average weighted feature vectors of training examples being in that class. Given the new feature vector, the mechanism of classifying the new feature vector is based on a similarity distance function between the new feature vector and the cluster centers. The cluster center closest to the new feature vector gets the highest probability.

In order to compute $quality(s, f)$ as defined via equations (11.3) and (11.4) we first show how to compute the conditional probabilities $P_j(w_i) = P(C_j|w_i)$ when having only one source s_i from its feature vector w_i. Then we show how to compute the conditional probabilities $P_j(w) = P(C_j|w)$ when there are multiple sources and w is a feature information matrix.

For information source s_i, suppose the training examples $D = \{w_i(t), C(t)\}_{t=1}^{T}$. Assume we partition the training example set D into k subsets $D_1, D_2, \cdots, D_k$, where $D_r (r = 1, 2, \cdots, k)$ contains all those cases that have the object outcome C_r.

$$D_r = \{(w_i(t), C(t))|C(t) = C_r, t = 1, 2, \cdots, T\}$$

Let $T_1, T_2, \cdots, T_k$ be the corresponding time point (or object) subsets of $D_1, D_2, \cdots, D_k$ respectively. The cluster center $\bar{w}_i(C_r)$ of class C_r and source

s_i is computed as follows.

$$\bar{w}_i(C_r) = \frac{\sum_{t \in T_r} w_i(t)}{|D_r|}$$

The cluster center of class r represents the average feature vector whenever the outcome is actually C_r.

The cluster classification scheme is based on the similarity distance metrics between the new feature vector and the cluster center. We define the similarity metrics of a feature vector $w_i(t) = (w_{1i}(t), w_{2i}(t), ..., w_{mi}(t))$ and the class center $\bar{w}_i(C_r)$ as follows.

$$sim(w_i(t), \bar{w}_i(C_r)) = [(w_i(t) - \bar{w}_i(C_r))(w_i(t) - \bar{w}_i(C_r))^T] \tag{11.5}$$

The above distance metrics is used to compare the similarity between a new feature vector and class C_r. A new feature vector is classified according to the probability of nearest cluster center. For any feature vector w_i, a k-center cluster classifier will compute the conditional probability $P(C_j|w_i)$ according to the posterior probabilistic distribution

$$\mathbf{P(C_j|w_i)} = \frac{\mathbf{K(sim(w_i, \bar{w}_i(C_j))}}{\sum_{\mathbf{r=1}}^{\mathbf{k}} \mathbf{K(sim(w_i, \bar{w}_i(C_r))}} \tag{11.6}$$

where $K()$ is a kernel function defined as

$$K(sim(w_i, \bar{w}_i(C_r)) = \frac{1}{sim(w_i, \bar{w}_i(C_r))} \tag{11.7}$$

From equation (11.5), (11.6) and (11.7) the conditional probability of $P(C_j|w_i)$ can be computed for each class r and each source s_i.

We show how to compute the conditional probability $P(C_j|w)$ in case of having more than one source from the individual conditional probabilities $P(C_j|w_i)$. In fact, $P(C_j|w)$ can be calculate from the Bayesian formula with the assumption that each class C_j occurs with same probability and assuming independence of the feature vectors given the class, i.e. $P(w|C_j) = P(w_1|C_j) * ... * P(w_n|C_j)$

$$\mathbf{P(C_j|w)} = \frac{\prod_{\mathbf{i=1}}^{\mathbf{n}} \mathbf{P(w_i|C_j)}}{\sum_{\mathbf{r=1}}^{\mathbf{k}} \prod_{\mathbf{i=1}}^{\mathbf{n}} \mathbf{P(w_i|C_r)}} \tag{11.8}$$

It remains to be shown the calculation of $P(w_i|C_j)$. From the definition of conditional probability, we get $P(w_i|C_j) = P(C_j|w_i) * \frac{P(w_i)}{P(C_j)}$. We assumed $P(C_j)$ to be the same for all j and it is assumed that all feature vectors occur equally likely, hence $\frac{P(w_i)}{P(C_j)}$ is actually a constant. It follows that in equation (11.8), $P(w_i|C_j)$ can simply be replaced by $P(C_j|w_i)$.

Part IV

Parallel Data Mining

Chapter 12

Parallel Out-of-Core Decision Tree Classifiers

Mahesh K. Sreenivas, Khaled AlSabti and Sanjay Ranka

12.1 Introduction

One of the important problems in the field of knowledge discovery and data mining is classification. It may be defined as the process of generating a description or a model for each class of a given data set. The data set consists of a number of example records, or examples in short, each consisting of one or more fields called *attributes* or *features*. An attribute is *numeric* (*continuous*), if it has an ordered domain. On the other hand, a *categorical* attribute comes from an unordered domain. Each record belongs to one of the given classes. The set of records available for developing classification methods may in general be decomposed into two disjoint subsets named *training set* and *test set*. The former is used for deriving the classifier while the latter is used for measuring the accuracy and generalization capabilities of the classifier. The accuracy of the classifier obtained is determined by the percentage of the test data set that are correctly classified (Weiss and Kulikowski 1991). Another measure of goodness of a classifier is the size of the model generated; compact models are preferred as they generalize better.

Classification has applications in a wide variety of disciplines including medicine, science, engineering, business and the internet. Grouping of vehicles by govermental agencies for licensing and other administrative purposes, classification of web pages based on their contents, categorization of credit card customers by financial institutions, classification of sky objects etc. are just a few of the several interesting examples.

A decision tree is a class discriminator that recursively partitions the training set until each partition consists entirely or dominantly of examples from one class (Shafer, Agrawal, and Mehta 1996). Each nonleaf node of the tree contains a *splitter point,* which is a test on one or more attributes and determines how the data is partitioned. Divide-and-conquer paradigm can be used to efficiently construct decision trees (Breiman, Friedman, Olshen, and Stone 1984; Quinlan 1993; Shafer, Agrawal, and Mehta 1996; AlSabti, Ranka, and Singh 1998).

Decision trees are particularly suited for data mining compared to other classification models like neural networks, genetic models, linear/quadratic discriminants, and so forth for a variety of reasons. The foremost among them is the fact that decision trees are simple and easy to understand. They can be constructed relatively fast compared to other methods of classification. Moreover, trees can easily be converted into SQL statements that may be used for efficient access to databases (Agrawal, Ghosh, Imielinski, Iyer, and Swami 1992).

Figure 12.1b shows a sample decision tree classifier for the training set given in figure 12.1b. The splitting criteria $(Age \leq 35)$ and $(Profession = Clerk)$ partition the records into the classes C1 and C2. Note that *Age* is a numeric attribute whereas *Profession* is an example for a categorical attribute.

The divide-and-conquer paradigm can be used for finding efficient solutions to a class of practical problems. These problems are recursive in nature. The divide-and-conquer paradigm involves three steps at each level of recursion. The first step is the *divide* step where the problem is divided into two or more subproblems. We *conquer* the subproblems by solving them recursively in the next step. If the subproblem sizes are small enough, then they may be solved in a straightforward manner. The final step involves *combining* the solutions of the subproblems to create a solution to the original problem. The execution of a problem instance is represented by a divide-and-conquer tree where each node represents a task or subtask. Divide-and-conquer paradigm has been effectively used for the construction of decision trees, regression trees, quad trees and multi-dimensional binary search trees (Breiman, Friedman, Olshen,

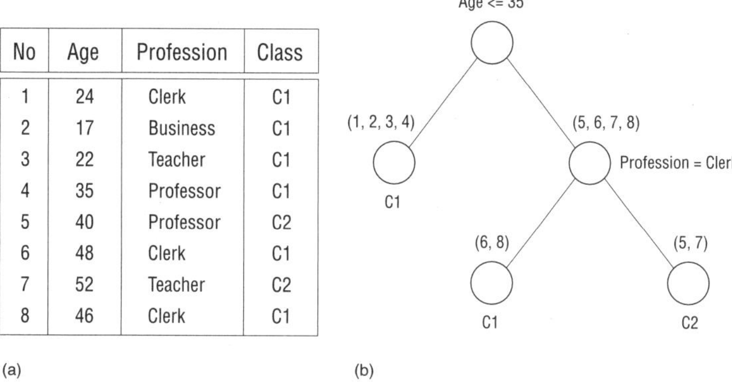

No	Age	Profession	Class
1	24	Clerk	C1
2	17	Business	C1
3	22	Teacher	C1
4	35	Professor	C1
5	40	Professor	C2
6	48	Clerk	C1
7	52	Teacher	C2
8	46	Clerk	C1

Figure 12.1: Example of a decision tree classifier. a. Training Data set. b. Decision tree.

and Stone 1984; Quinlan 1993; Shafer, Agrawal, and Mehta 1996; Srivastava, Han, Kumar, and Singh 1998; Aluru, Goil, and Ranka 1996). Examples of other algorithms that use the divide-and-conquer paradigm are quick sort, merge sort, quick hull and selection (Aluru, Goil, and Ranka 1996). Note that there is no merging step involved in the construction of a decision tree classifier.

Parallelization is inevitable for achieving substantial reduction in the overall response time while dealing with problems of large magnitude. *Task parallelism* and *data parallelism* are two basic techniques that may be used for the parallel construction of a divide-and-conquer tree. *Concatenated parallelism* is a variant of data parallelism, where multiple tasks are solved together using all the processors. Aluru, Goil, and Ranka (1996) present several applications of concatenated parallelism and show that this technique yields better results compared to data parallelism irrespective of the nature of the divide-and-conquer tree. However, the study does not address performance degradation due to I/O, normally associated with large out-of-core applications.

Srivastava, Han, Kumar, and Singh (1998) present two approaches to parallel construction of trees: *synchronized tree construction* and *partitioned tree construction*. The former is based on the concept of concatenated parallelism and the latter employs task parallelism (Aluru, Goil, and Ranka 1996). The synchronized tree construction gives good performance at upper levels of the tree unlike the partitioned tree construction approach, which performs well at lower levels of the tree. Thus a hybrid approach is suggested by the authors for achieving better performance. The chapter does not discuss the demanding I/O requirements of large out-of-core applications.

Parallel I/O is an expensive operation and can significantly affect the overall performance of parallel out-of-core algorithms (Vitter 1998). This is especially true for dynamic and recursive problems where data needs to be fetched from the disk multiple number of times. A large body of work has been done in the literature to study and design efficient parallel I/O algorithms (Kotz 1994; Vitter 1998). Kotz (1994) advocates collective I/O for parallel file systems to realize high performance for I/O intensive applications. The study presents three implementation alternatives for collective I/O: traditional caching, two-phase I/O, and disk-directed I/O. The disk-directed model allows disk servers to control the order and timing of the flow of data for maximum performance. The data flow is thus controlled by the file system rather than by the application. Several useful paradigms for the design and implementation of efficient external memory algorithms (these algorithms are also known as out-of-core algorithms or I/O algorithms) can be found in Vitter (1998). This extensive survey concentrates on the I/O communication between the random access internal memory and the magnetic disk.

In this chapter we present the parallel construction of an efficient and scalable decision tree classifier (pCLOUDS) used for mining large disk-resident data. pCLOUDS is the parallel version of a sequential decision tree classifier called CLOUDS (AlSabti 1998; AlSabti, Ranka, and Singh 1998). Before introducing pCLOUDS algorithm, we present a detailed discussion of various techniques for parallel divide-and-conquer paradigm. Further, these basic techniques are extended to include parallel I/O for efficient out-of-core parallel divide-and-conquer. We argue that data parallelism may be a better technique compared to concatenated parallelism for parallel external memory divide-and-conquer applications. Also, a generic technique for parallelizing out-of-core divide-and-conquer problems is suggested.

The rest of the chapter is organized as follows. In section 12.2 we present a brief discussion on coarse-grained parallel machines. We give a short discussion on various decision tree classifiers in section 12.3. Techniques for efficient parallel divide-and-conquer are presented in section 12.4. The parallel formulation of the classifier (pCLOUDS) is presented in section 12.5. In section 12.6, we present a performance evaluation of the pCLOUDS algorithm, and conclude with a summary in section 12.7.

12.2 Coarse Grained Parallel Machines

Coarse grained machines (CGMs) consist of a set of processors (tens to a few thousands) connected through an interconnection network. The main memory is physically distributed across the processors. Interaction between processors is either through message passing or through a shared address space.

In dealing with large out-of-core data sets, efficient management of disk-

Primitive	Time complexity
All-to-all Broadcast	$O(\tau \log p + \mu m(p-1))$
Gather	$O(\mu \log p + \tau mp)$
Global Combine	$O(\tau \log p + \mu m)$
Prefix Sum	$O(\tau \log p + \mu m)$

Table 12.1: Time complexity of primitives on a hypercube interconnection network.

resident data is critical for minimizing performance degradation due to I/O. There are two main alternatives for handling the I/O subsystem: sequential and parallel. Sequential I/O gives poor performance for large I/O intensive applications and hence we focus only on parallel I/O in this chapter. Further, we assume a shared-nothing type of architecture where each processor has its own disk that can be controlled independently. CGMs with cut-through routed networks is used for modeling the communication cost of various algorithms discussed in this chapter.

Parallelization of applications requires distributing some or all of the data structures among the processors. Each processor needs to access all the non-local data required for its local computation. This generates aggregate or collective communication structures. Several algorithms have been described in the literature for these primitives and are part of standard textbooks (Kumar, Grama, Gupta, and Karypis 1994).

The complexity analysis of the algorithms is presented for a p-processor hypercube interconnection architecture with cut-through routing. The analysis for permutation networks (e.g. IBM SP Series) and hypercubes is the same in most cases.

Table 12.1 describes the collective communication primitives, that may be used quite frequently in the discussions to follow, and their communication time requirements on cut-through routed hypercubes. Note that p refers to the number of processors. We model the cost of sending a message from one node to another as $O(\tau + \mu m)$, where m is the size of the message, τ represents the handshaking costs, and μ is the inverse bandwidth of the communication network. For more details see AlSabti, Ranka, and Shankar (1995), Kumar, Grama, Gupta, and Karypis (1994), and Sreenivas (1998).

12.3 Decision Tree Classifiers for Data Mining

As mentioned earlier, the aim of classification is to generate a description or a model for each class of a given data set. Derivation of a decision tree classifier typically consists of a *construction* phase and a *pruning* phase. In construction phase we build the initial decision tree using the training data set. Pruning improves the generalization capabilities of the classifier by removing any over fitting to the training data set. We use an algorithm based on the *minimum description length* (MDL) principle to prune the decision tree (Sreenivas 1998). The pruning phase can generally be executed in-memory and its cost is very small compared to that of the construction phase. We therefore focus only on parallelizing the construction phase.

The well-known decision tree classifiers CART (Breiman, Friedman, Olshen, and Stone 1984) and C4.5 (Quinlan 1993) build trees in a depth-first manner. The data is sorted repeatedly at every node of the tree to determine the best splits for numeric attributes. SLIQ (Mehta, Agrawal, Rissanen 1996) replaces this repeated sorting with one-time sorting by maintaining separate lists for each attribute. However, SLIQ uses a memory-resident data structure called *class list,* which limits the number of input records it can handle. Another popular decision tree classifier that achieves good accuracy, compactness and efficiency for very large data sets is SPRINT (Shafer, Agrawal, and Mehta 1996).

In order to derive the splitting criterion at every internal node of the decision tree, classifiers like CART, SLIQ, and SPRINT, use the *gini* index. The use of gini index to derive the splitting criterion is computationally challenging. SPRINT uses a presorting technique to calculate gini index for numeric attributes. However, the use of memory-resident hash tables to split the sorted attribute lists limits its scalability. ScalParC (Joshi, Karypis, and Kumar 1998) is a more scalable parallel implementation of SPRINT algorithm.

CLOUDS (CLOUDS stands for classification of large out of core data sets) algorithm also uses the gini index to derive the splitting criterion (AlSabti 1998; AlSabti, Ranka, and Singh 1998). *Gini* index of diversity gives a measure of *node impurity* (Breiman, Friedman, Olshen, and Stone 1984). The idea is to find a splitter point having minimum gini so that we get purer descendant nodes. Node impurity, which is a function of the relative class frequencies, is the largest when all classes are equally mixed together in it, and smallest when the node contains only one class. Consider a data set S consisting of n records, each belonging to one of the c classes. Formula (12.1) gives the definition for the gini index of the entire data set where p_j is the relative frequency of class j in S.

$$gini(S) = 1 - \sum_{j=1}^{c} {p_j}^2 \tag{12.1}$$

Let the set S be partitioned into two disjoint subsets S_1 and S_2 such that S_1 contains n_1 examples. Then formula (12.2) gives the gini index of the partitioned data where, a denotes the splitting criterion.

$$gini^D(S, a) = \frac{n_1}{n} gini(S_1) + \frac{n - n_1}{n} gini(S_2) \tag{12.2}$$

CLOUDS mainly differs from SPRINT in the way it handles the numeric attributes. It presents two new methods for deriving the splitting point: *sampling the splitting points* (SS) and *sampling the splitting points with estimation* (SSE). Both methods evaluate only a subset of the entire splitting points along each numeric attribute. CLOUDS has substantially lower I/O and computational requirements compared to any other state-of-the-art classifiers. Moreover, the accuracy and compactness of the decision trees generated by CLOUDS remain the same or comparable to those of SPRINT.

12.3.1 Deriving the Splitting Point

CLOUDS evaluates categorical and numeric attributes differently. Categorical attributes are evaluated in the same way as in SPRINT. Therefore, we describe only the processing of numeric attributes.

Evaluation of Numeric Attributes

CLOUDS uses either the SS method or the SSE method to derive the splitter at each node of the tree. In the SS method the range of each numeric attribute is divided into q intervals such that each interval contains approximately the same number of points. These intervals are generated using a predrawn random sample set S. Gini indices are evaluated at the interval boundaries. These gini values, together with those computed for categorical attributes, are used to determine the minimum gini ($gini_{min}$). The splitting point with $gini_{min}$ is used as the splitter for the node under consideration. Note that this requires only one pass over the data set to derive the splitting point.

The SSE method goes beyond the SS method further as it estimates a lower bound for the gini value ($gini^{est}$) of each interval. The subset of intervals satisfying the inequality $gini^{est} < gini_{min}$ form a list of candidate intervals and are called *alive* intervals. For an alive interval we evaluate gini index at every distinct point in the interval to determine the best splitter. This may require another traversal through the entire data set. The SSE method effectively reduces the search space for the best splitting criterion. For more details on CLOUDS algorithm, see AlSabti (1998), AlSabti, Ranka, and Singh (1998), and Sreenivas (1998). SSE method is more scalable and robust than SS method and hence we focus on the SSE method for the design of the parallel algorithm.

```
function decisionTreeClassifier(Level l)
{
  for each node node in level l do
    if the stopping criteria is not met then
      Step 1:
            for each categorical attribute a do
              for each value v in attribute list do
                Update the count matrix
              Find subset of a that gives the best split
      Step 2:
            for each numeric attribute a do
              Divide the range of attribute a into q intervals
              for each interval [v_l..v_r] do
                Compute gini^D for interval boundary v_l
      Step 3:
            Find the minimum gini (gini_min) across all the categorical attributes
            and at the interval boundaries for numeric attributes
      Step 4:
            for each numeric attribute a do
              for each interval do
                Estimate a lower bound of the gini index gini^est for this interval
                if gini^est >= gini_min then prune this interval
      Step 5:
            for each numeric attribute a do
              for each alive interval I do
                Update class histogram
                for each value v ∈ I do
                  Compute gini^D(a <= v)
              Find the value v of a that results in the best split
      Step 6:
            if there is at least one split then
              Partition the records between the child nodes using the best split
            partition node into its child nodes

  if at least one node at level l is partitioned then decisionTreeClassifier(l+1)
}
```

Figure 12.2: A high level description of CLOUDS algorithm.

12.3.2 Partitioning the Data Set

The splitting criterion is applied to each record in the data and sample sets to determine their partition (left or right). The number of records read and written is equal to the number of records represented by the internal node. During the partitioning of the data set, the count matrices for categorical attributes, and the class frequencies at the interval boundaries for numeric attributes are also updated. This avoids a separate additional pass over the entire data to evaluate these frequencies. A high level description of CLOUDS algorithm is presented in figure 12.2.

12.4 Parallel Out of Core Divide and Conquer Techniques

Problem statement: Execution of a problem instance is represented by a divide-and-conquer tree. The root node contains the entire data set. Each internal node in the tree represents a task. The task is split into two subtasks[1] that correspond to the children of the node. The subtasks are solved recursively and the solution may have to be combined to find the solution for the parent task. For some problems, it may not be necessary to solve every subtask that is created at any given level in the tree. The cost of processing a subtask can be any function in the size of the subtask. For a problem instance of size n on p processors, we assume that the data is initially distributed at random among the p processors. Let the task of size n be divided into two subtasks of sizes n_l and n_r. We consider only those problems where $n_l + n_r \leq n$. The objective is to efficiently build the divide-and-conquer tree in parallel for the given problem. We assume that the entire data set cannot fully reside in the aggregate main memory of the parallel machine.

The initial distribution of the data points can affect the overall performance of different techniques for parallel divide-and-conquer. We use the theorem of Angluin and Valiant (1979) for studying and designing the techniques and algorithms presented in this chapter.

Theorem 1 *For a random distribution of n elements into b buckets, where $n \gg b$, the maximum number of elements in a bucket is less than $\frac{n}{b} + O(c\sqrt{n/b}\ \log n)$ with high probability of $1 - n^{-c/2}$, where c is a positive constant.*

As a result of theorem 1, the maximum number of elements assigned to each processor is less than $\frac{n}{p} + O(c\sqrt{n/p}\ \log n)$ with high probability of $1 - n^{-c/2}$. For large applications, it is expected that each processor has almost n/p elements. Furthermore, we use theorem 1 to prove the following lemma.

Lemma 2 *Let n elements be randomly distributed into b buckets, where $n \gg b$. Then, for any subset of size m elements, where $m \gg b$, the maximum number of elements in a bucket from the m elements is less than $\frac{m}{b} + O(c\sqrt{m/b}\ \log m)$ with high probability of $1 - m^{-c/2}$, where c is a positive constant.*

Proof: We prove Lemma 2 by a contradiction. Assume that there exists a subset of size m, where $m \gg b$, such that the the maximum number of elements in a bucket, from the m elements, is greater than $\frac{m}{b} + O(c\sqrt{m/b}\ \log m)$

[1] In this chapter, we consider only binary trees since the extension of different techniques to n-ary trees is straightforward.

with probability of greater than $m^{-c/2}$, where c is a positive constant. Since the n elements are distributed at random into the b buckets, the same is true for the m elements, where $m \leq n$. Therefore, by theorem 1, the maximum number of elements in a bucket from the m elements is less than $\frac{m}{b} + O(c\sqrt{m/b}\ \log m)$ with high probability of $1 - m^{-c/2}$, where c is a positive constant. This contradicts the initial assumption. Q.E.D.

Several techniques for parallel in-core divide-and-conquer have been proposed in the literature. The popular ones are task parallelism, data parallelism, concatenated parallelism and mixed parallelism. We describe and compare each of these techniques and extend them for large out-of-core applications.

12.4.1 Task Parallelism

In task parallelism processors are divided into subgroups and subtasks are assigned to processor subgroups based on the cost of processing each subtask. Subtasks belonging to different processor groups are solved concurrently.

There are two main approaches to handle the disk-resident data corresponding to the subtasks while applying task parallelism. In the first approach, when a subtask is assigned to a processor group, its data is also moved to that processor group. We call this I/O subsystem strategy as *compute dependent parallel I/O*. The data movement may be required for every internal node of the tree. This redistribution of data can be a very expensive operation; it requires the reading of data at source processors, communication to a destination processor group, followed by a writing step. For divide-and-conquer problems with linear (or near-linear) cost for computation, the redistribution cost may dominate the overall cost. At upper levels of the tree, the size of data to be processed at each node is relatively large and hence redistribution of data involves significant communication overhead in addition to the I/O. However, task parallelism involves no further communication overhead once the number of subtasks becomes equal to or greater than the number of processors. Task parallelism with compute dependent parallel I/O can provide very good performance when used at lower levels of the tree where the task grain size is small enough for in-core processing. The load balance can be improved with the presence of large number of such nodes.

When subtasks are assigned to processor subgroups it is not necessary to move the data to the destination processor subgroup. In this alternative approach we continue with the initial random distribution of data among the processors. Since data is not moved during processor regrouping we name this strategy as *compute independent parallel I/O*. For more details see Sreenivas (1998).

12.4.2 Data Parallelism

Tasks are solved in parallel using all the processors in data parallelism. This requires no movement of disk-resident data. Note that tasks are solved one after another in data parallelism. Solving a task using all the processors may require additional communication overhead.

Data parallelism may suffer from severe load imbalance because the data for subtasks may not be uniformly spread across the processors, even if we ensure a uniform distribution of data for the parent task. Expensive redistribution of data may be needed to restore load balance in such a case. However, by Lemma 2, it is expected that each processor has approximately n/p of elements for a node of size n, where $n \gg p$. Thus, data parallelism is expected to achieve a good load balance for such cases. Data parallelism is very attractive for large out-of-core applications since it does not require any I/O overhead for data redistribution and the amount of I/O performed is balanced among the processors. For tasks (nodes) with large data, the cost of the synchronization and and message startups is small compared to the overall cost.

12.4.3 Concatenated Parallelism

Concatenated parallelism is a variant of data parallelism where multiple tasks are solved collectively using all the processors (Aluru, Goil, and Ranka 1996). Communication for all the subtasks can now be spooled together to save message startup costs for individual communication. Concatenated parallelism achieves good load balance even if the data for individual subtasks are not distributed uniformly across the processors but their aggregate distribution is uniform.

In concatenated parallelism the available memory has to be shared by the many tasks that are solved together. This may lead to substantial I/O overhead for large out-of-core applications. With data distributed randomly across all the processors, data parallelism and concatenated parallelism are expected to provide similar load balance. Therefore, data parallelism seems to be a better alternative than concatenated parallelism for large external memory algorithms.

12.4.4 Mixed Parallelism

For parallel out-of-core divide-and-conquer, better performance can be achieved by the use of mixed parallelism, since it allows us to combine the good aspects of basic techniques. There are different variants of mixed parallelism, choice of each one depends on the nature of the problem (Sreenivas 1998). We primarily focus on an approach where data parallelism is used at upper levels of the tree. At lower levels of the tree we switch to task parallelism with compute dependent parallel I/O for managing disk-resident data.

In mixed parallelism, a criterion is needed for switching from one technique to another. For example, when the cost of task subdivision exceeds the cost of task redistribution we may stop using data parallelism and do redistribution for task parallelism. This switching criteria is generally problem dependent. The dynamic nature of the underlying I/O and computational pattern of divide-and-conquer problems makes the derivation of an optimal switching criteria very challenging.

For the problem studied in this chapter, we use mixed parallelism in the following way. Nodes whose sizes are larger than a specified threshold are called *large* nodes and those that fall below the threshold are named *small* nodes. We use data parallelism for processing large nodes. It is recommended that the size of the large nodes be significantly larger than the number of processors. As the tree grows the number of examples at each node may decrease and as a consequence, computation time also decreases. However, there may not be a similar decrease in communication time since the message startup time is independent of the volume of communication. Hence communication time is expected to dominate the overall processing time when the node size becomes small. To overcome this, we switch to task parallelism for small nodes. Each small node is assigned to only one processor. The task-processor assignment is based on the task costs. The data of each task is redistributed to its destination processor by which building the subtree is performed locally within the processor. The assigning and processing of small nodes are delayed until all the large nodes have been processed to reduce the number of message start-ups. In this form of mixed parallelism data parallelism is followed by *delayed* task parallelism. Thus, the tree can be built in an arbitrary order. We will use the above technique for efficiently building decision tree classifiers.

12.5 Parallel Formulation of CLOUDS

In this section we present the design and implementation of the pCLOUDS algorithm. As mentioned earlier, the decision tree is built using mixed parallelism, with data parallelism for constructing the large nodes. For the small nodes, we use task parallelism, with compute dependent parallel I/O, where each small node is entirely assigned to one processor (cf. section 3). The size of a small node is generally a few percent of the total data size.

For large applications, the cost of parallel I/O for divide-and-conquer problems can dominate the overall cost. In designing pCLOUDS, we gave special attention for the I/O. pCLOUDS maintains very good load balance for the performed I/O while keeping the associated overhead low for the overall process.

For small nodes, we use a direct method to arrive at the best split. In the direct method we sort the points along every numeric attribute and compute the gini index at each point. Further, these small nodes are processed in-memory. Large nodes are processed using data parallelism. For each large node of the tree, pCLOUDS performs the following steps:

1. Preprocessing
2. Deriving the splitting point
3. Partitioning of data and sample points

For a detailed description of each of the above steps see Sreenivas (1998). We discuss only those steps that are the most important. Note that all of the above steps, except portions of the preprocessing step, have to be performed at each large node of the tree and hence they collectively represent a task/subtask in the divide-and-conquer paradigm. In what follows, n denotes the total number of examples or records at some node of the decision tree. Therefore, at the root of the tree n denotes the total number of examples/records in the training set. Also, q denotes the number of intervals at some node. It should be noted that the value of q decreases as the node size decreases (as in CLOUDS).

12.5.1 Deriving the Splitting Point

pCLOUDS derives the splitting point by finding the point with the minimum (or near-minimum, as in CLOUDS) gini value. This is achieved by finding the minimum gini across all the categorical and numeric attributes. For details regarding the evaluation of categorical attributes see Sreenivas (1998). In the following subsections we briefly describe the sub-steps in evaluating the numeric attributes.

Evaluation of Interval Boundaries for Numeric Attributes

In this step the global frequency vectors of all the interval boundaries are generated, followed by evaluating the gini index at the boundary points to find the minimum gini among them. This step does not require any I/O. We consider two approaches for the implementation of this step. In the first method (the replication method), all the statistics of the interval boundaries are replicated across all the processors. The second method (the distributed method) approximately distributes these statistics among the processors.

The Replication Method: This method replicates the class frequency vectors for all boundary points at each processor for every numeric attribute. This requires $O(q\ c\ f)$ amount of storage at each processor, where c is the number of classes and f is the number of numeric attributes. The local vectors are combined to form the global vectors, followed by finding the minimum gini among the interval boundaries. This step can be performed using one of the following three approaches.

Attribute-based approach: In this approach, all the global frequency vectors of each numeric attribute are assigned to only one processor. This requires $\delta\, O(q\, c) + O\,(\tau\ \log\ p\ +\ \mu\, q\, c)$ time for each numeric attribute. One of the main advantages of this option is that no further communication is needed for the calculation of gini index in the next step. However, during gini computation it is possible for some processors to idle and hence can lead to poor load balancing.

In order to compute the gini index, we perform a prefix sum to update the frequency vectors at the boundary points. The prefix sum operation is completely local to the processor; it takes $\delta\ O(q\, c)$ time. Gini indices can now be calculated at all interval boundary points in $\delta\ O(q\, c)$ time. This approach has a total time complexity of $\delta\ O\ (q\, c)\ +\ O(\tau \log\ p\ +\ \mu\, q\, c)$ for each numeric attribute.

Interval-based approach: In this approach the global frequency vector of each interval is assigned to only one processor. In other words, the global frequency vectors for a numeric attribute are distributed across more than one processor. For more details see Sreenivas (1998).

Hybrid approach: The third approach combines the above approaches to generate better load balancing. Details of this approach can be found in Sreenivas (1998).

The global minimum gini (among the interval boundaries) is calculated by using a min-reduction primitive on the local minimum gini indices among the processors. $gini_{min}$ is thus the minimum value among the gini indices of categorical attributes and those at the interval boundary points of numeric attributes. We choose the attribute-based method to implement the replication method (Sreenivas 1998).

Distributed method: Unlike in the replication method, the global frequency vectors are approximately distributed among the processors. This method can be implemented using efficient algorithms for *random access write* (RAW). For more details, see Bae (1997) and Sreenivas (1998).

The replication method is relatively simple to implement compared to the distributed method. Also, for large external memory applications, replication method incurs relatively less communication overhead compared to distributed method. For the above reasons, we choose the replication method for our implementation. A detailed comparison of these two methods was presented by Sreenivas (1998).

Determination of Alive Intervals

In this step, each processor determines the alive intervals (among the local intervals) using the sequential algorithm. This step does not require any I/O. An estimate ($gini^{est}$) for the minimum gini for each interval is computed (as in CLOUDS). The ratio of the number of examples in the alive intervals to the total number of examples is called *survival ratio.* The status of the intervals (alive or not) is broadcasted to all the processors for further evaluation of alive intervals. The communication cost of this step is proportional to $q\ c$.

Evaluation of Alive Intervals

For each alive interval, the gini index is calculated at all the potential splitting. During this process, each processor keeps track of the local minimum gini. The global minimum gini is found by using min-reduction on these local values. The corresponding splitting point is broadcasted to all the processors. This point is needed for partitioning the data. Evaluating the gini index for all the points in the alive intervals can be performed in several ways (Sreenivas 1998). We briefly describe the single-assignment approach, which is used for our implementation. The communication cost of these approaches is proportional to the size of the alive intervals (we assume that the size of each alive interval is small enough to fit in the main memory).

Single-assignment approach: In this case we assign each interval to only one (single) processor. One advantage of this approach is that no further communication is required after assigning the intervals to processors. The entire process can be performed locally. Assuming that the size of each alive interval is $O(n/q)$, it takes $\mu\ O(n/q)$ time to transfer the elements of each alive interval. The computation requirement for sorting the points in an alive intervals takes $\delta\, O\left(\frac{n}{q}\ \log\ \frac{n}{q}\right)$ time. Calculation of gini indices for an alive interval can be carried out in $\delta\ O(n\,c/q)$ time. Thus the total time complexity associated with this option for processing each alive interval is $\delta\ O\left(\frac{n\,c}{q} + \frac{n}{q}\ \log\ \frac{n}{q}\right) + \mu\ O\left(\frac{n}{q}\right)$. The assignment of intervals to processors is done based on the cost of processing each alive interval, i.e. the sorting cost.

12.5.2 Partitioning the Data and Sample Points

As in the sequential case, once the splitting attribute and the splitting point are determined, the data and the sample points may be split accordingly. The cost of the I/O read and write, for each attribute, is proportional to $2n/p$. During partitioning, the local frequency vectors along all the numeric attributes as well as the count matrix for each categorical attribute for the left and right partitions are updated to avoid an additional pass over the entire data. The cost of the I/O, read and write, and computations across all the processors are (near) uniform. Further, this step does not require any communication, and gives almost perfect load balance.

pCLOUDS is expected to achieve a high degree of load balance for processing the large nodes. Further, the overall overhead for achieving load balance is small compared to the overall processing cost. This is due to keeping the I/O local to each processor as well as keeping the amount of I/O performed at each processor to be uniform (Sreenivas 1998).

12.6 Results and Discussions

pCLOUDS is implemented using standard MPI[2] communication primitives and is relatively portable to different parallel architectures. Experiments were conducted on a 16-node IBM-SP2 shared nothing parallel processing supercomputer (Sreenivas 1998).

We use the data generator proposed by Mehta, Agrawal, Rissanen (1996) to generate large synthetic data sets required for our experiments. A record in the data set consists of three categorical and six numeric attributes and a field describing the class label for the record. Each synthetic data set contains two classes and the records are generated by using the second classification function (Mehta, Agrawal, Rissanen 1996). In the rest of the section we present the speedup, sizeup and scaleup characteristics of pCLOUDS.

We have measured the performance of pCLOUDS using training data sets varying in size from 3.6 to 8.4 million tuples. The data is distributed equally to all the processors at random, prior to the beginning of computation. Also, the pages of the training data set in the operating system's file buffer pool are invalidated before the start of decision tree construction. We used a value of 10,000 for the number of intervals at the root. For descendant nodes in the tree the value is scaled down based on the size of each node. Note that the actual number of intervals (q) can be lesser than the specified value and this depends on the number of distinct interval boundary points selected at random from the sample set. Large nodes are processed out-of-core if the size of those nodes exceed a prespecified memory limit. We have used a memory limit of 1 MB for 6.0 million tuples. The value of memory limit is linearly scaled based on the size for other data sets. For switching from data parallelism to task parallelism we used a value of ten (in terms of the number of intervals) for the threshold. In the absence of any numeric attribute in a given training data set, the threshold can be specified in terms of the size of the node. The above value is found acceptable, after conducting a series of experiments with

[2] http://www.mpi-forum.org/

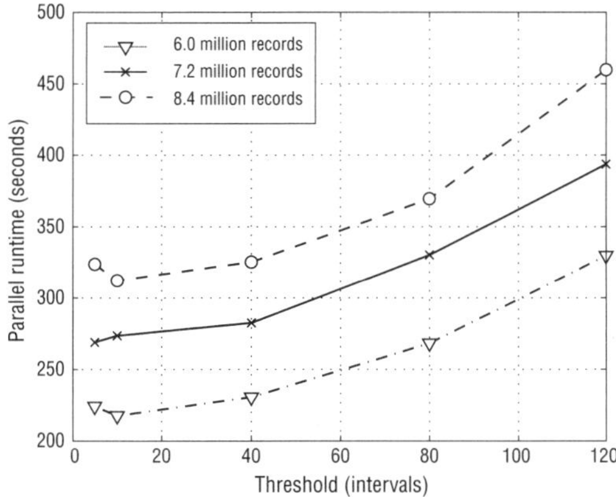

Figure 12.3: Parallel runtime for different values of threshold.

Records (million)	**File size** (MB)	**Maximum read/write I/O at a processor (MB)**			
		1 processor	4 processors	8 processors	16 processors
3.6	137.3	1446.3/593.3	362.2/148.7	129.7/74.4	76.9/37.2
4.8	183.1	1926.1/789.9	408.8/197.5	202.2/98.8	102.2/49.4
6.0	228.9	2403.4/985.3	592.6/246.9	257.8/123.5	124.2/61.8
7.2	274.7	2888.6/1184.6	623.7/296.0	356.2/148.5	147.8/74.2

Table 12.2: Maximum read/write I/O performed at any processor.

different data sets, with varying values for the threshold (figure 12.3). Parallel run time depicted in figure 12.3 is given for sixteen processors on the IBM-SP2. Analytical characterization of the switching criteria is currently under investigation.

Experiments show a very good load balance for the I/O performed at each processor. Table 12.2 gives the maximum I/O (read/write) performed at any processor for the experimental configuration described above. Note that the total I/O performed by individual processors may not add up to that performed for the single processor case. This is because the sample points, selected at random at each processor, vary for different cases. For this reason the trees generated for the single processor case may not exactly be the same as (but similar to) those built in parallel. The value given in table 12.2 is calculated by taking the maximum of the amount of I/O performed among all the processors, after the tree is fully constructed. Hence, these values correspond to actual performed I/O by one or possibly more processors.

Table 12.3 gives the maximum I/O that *may be* performed at any processor for the experimental configuration we have discussed. The values in this

Records	**File size**	**Maximum read/write I/O at a processor (MB)**			
(million)	(MB)	1 processor	4 processors	8 processors	16 processors
3.6	137.3	1446.3/593.3	360.4/151.9	134.6/77.6	82.6/40.7
4.8	183.1	1926.1/789.9	415.2/201.8	207.3/103.2	107.5/54.1
6.0	228.9	2403.4/985.3	603.3/252.2	265.8/128.8	130.5/67.3
7.2	274.7	2888.6/1184.6	633.2/302.3	371.5/154.8	158.7/81.3

Table 12.3: Maximum read/write I/O at any processor.

table are computed by adding up the step-wise maximum, with each internal node representing a step. Therefore, the total I/O actually performed at any processor can be less than or equal to the maximum shown in the table. The differences between the values in tables 12.2 and 12.3 are marginal and this shows that there is indeed a good load balance for the I/O performed.

One of the dominant factors in the parallel runtime is the time to process alive intervals. Alive intervals were distributed to processors using two different cost functions to study the influence on load balance (results not reported). In the first case we estimate the cost of processing an alive interval to be its size. Let $[v_l, v_r]$ be an alive interval. Then the size (n_a) of the alive interval is the number of points in the open interval (v_l, v_r). From the algorithm given in the previous section, we know that it requires $O(n_a \log n_a)$ time to process the alive interval since it involves a sorting step. Therefore, in the second case we estimate the cost of processing the alive interval to be $n_a \log n_a$. As expected, the latter case gives much better load balance for all the data sets.

Figure 12.4 depicts the parallel runtime of pCLOUDS. The parallel runtime does not include the time for pruning the trees. Speedup characteristics of pCLOUDS is presented in figure 12.4. As can be seen from figure 12.4, speedup performance improves with increase in the data size. Superlinear speedup is observed in some cases on four processors. This is because of the cache effects, and the gain in I/O bandwidth with data being distributed across multiple disks. The speedup curve shows the presence of a glitch for 6.0 million records on four processors. Noticeable load imbalance is observed for this particular case in processing the alive intervals, possibly due to the presence of highly skewed (in size) alive intervals.

Sizeup characteristic is a measure of algorithm's performance with increase in data size. Figure 12.5 presents the performance of pCLOUDS for various data sizes. The gain in performance is marginal with increase in data size for the cases of four processors and eight processors. This is because the speedup is already close to the maximum even for 3.6 million tuples. However, for sixteen processors there is appreciable increase in speedup with increasing data size. As the data size increases the computation time also increases. On the contrary, the communication time required for exchanging count matrices

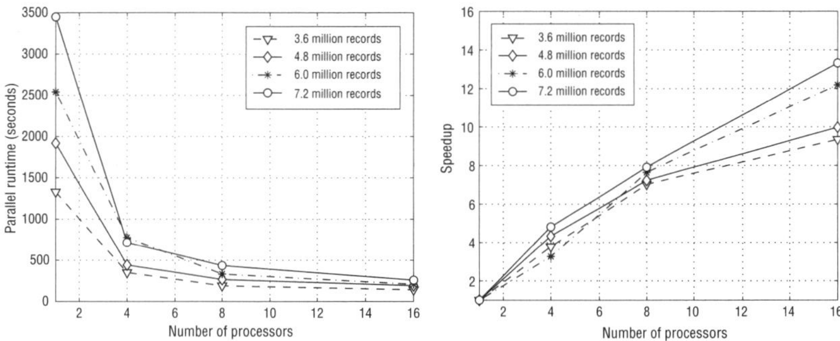

Figure 12.4: Speedup characteristics of pCLOUDS on IBM-SP2. Parallel runtime (left). Speedup of pCLOUDS (right).

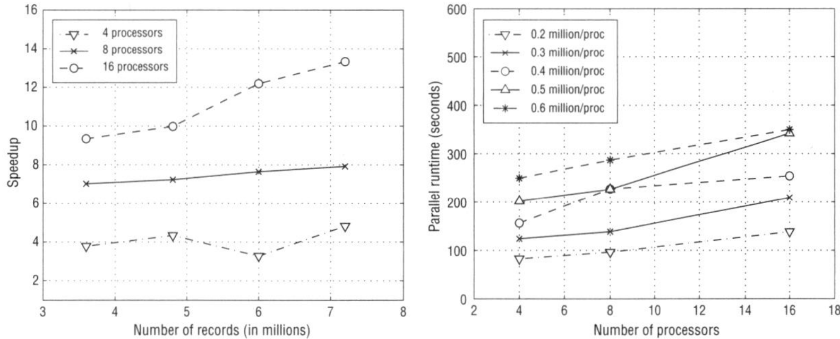

Figure 12.5: Sizeup (left) and scaleup (right) characteristics of pCLOUDS on IBM-SP2.

and split points does not change much. This accounts for the superior sizeup performance of pCLOUDS.

An algorithm is *scalable* if it is able to maintain its performance at a fixed value while the the data size (problem size) and the number of processors are increased simultaneously. In scaleup experiment we assign to each processor a fixed (equal) number of tuples and then vary the number of processors. The scaleup performance of pCLOUDS is presented in figure 12.5. With each processor having the same amount of data, parallel runtime should ideally remain constant as the number of processors is increased. The experimental results show that pCLOUDS has excellent scaleup characteristics. The graphs show a near linear relationship between parallel runtime and the number of processors for different data densities. However, there is an increase in parallel runtime as the number of processors is increased. This is mainly due to load imbalance in our current implementation of task parallelism. In this phase, we do not regroup the processors as they become idle.

12.7 Conclusions

In this chapter we have presented various techniques for the parallel construction of a generic divide-and-conquer tree. The basic techniques for parallelization are extended to efficiently handle I/O subsystem.

We have presented pCLOUDS, a parallel decision tree classifier for data mining. pCLOUDS is an application of out-of-core parallel divide-and-conquer paradigm. It uses the mixed approach involving data parallelism and delayed task parallelism. The performance evaluation and the complexity analysis show that pCLOUDS exhibits excellent speedup, scaleup and sizeup characteristics and is hence an efficient tool for developing fast and accurate decision tree classifiers for data mining applications.

The mixed approach, with data parallelism for large nodes, followed by delayed task parallelism for small nodes, is a very efficient technique for building divide-and-conquer trees for large applications. Data partitioning and shared nothing architecture are fundamentally important for achieving scalability while dealing with large data sets. The initial distribution of the data points can affect the overall performance of different techniques for parallel divide-and-conquer.

We have not presented any concrete criteria for switching from data parallelism to task parallelism. This analytical characterization is currently under investigation.

Acknowledgments

We thank Prof. V. Kumar, P. Dokas, and the Department of Computer Science and Engineering, University of Minnesota, for extending their parallel computing facility to conduct our experiments. We acknowledge the many fruitful discussions we had with H. Yoon. This research was supported in part by ARO under DAAG 55-97-1-0368, and Q000302 (subcontract from NMSU), and by NSF under CDA 96344470, and ASC 9318151 (subcontract 98031207 from Cornell University).

Chapter 13

Hierarchical Parallel Algorithms for Association Mining

Mohammed J. Zaki

13.1 Introduction

The association mining task is to discover a set of attributes shared among a large number of objects in a given database. For example, consider the sales database of a bookstore, where the objects represent customers and the attributes represent books. The discovered patterns are the set of books most frequently bought together by the customers. An example could be that, "40% of the people who buy Jane Austen's *Pride and Prejudice* also buy *Sense and Sensibility.*" The store can use this knowledge for promotions, shelf placement, etc. There are many potential application areas for association rule technology, which include catalog design, store layout, customer segmentation, telecommunication alarm diagnosis, and so on.

The task of discovering all frequent associations in very large databases is quite challenging. The search space is exponential in the number of database attributes, and with millions of database objects the problem of I/O minimization becomes paramount. However, most current approaches are iterative in nature, requiring multiple database scans, which is clearly very expensive. Some of the methods, especially those using some form of sampling, can be sensitive to the data-skew, which can adversely affect performance. Furthermore, most approaches use very complicated internal data structures which have poor locality and add additional space and computation overheads. Our goal is to overcome all of these limitations.

Since the discovery of association rules is a very computational and I/O intensive task, it is crucial to leverage the combined computational power of multiple processors for fast response and scalability. In this chapter I present new parallel algorithms for discovering the set of frequent attributes (also called itemsets). The key features of my approach are as follows: (1) I use a *vertical tid-list* database format, where I associate with each itemset a list of transactions in which it occurs. I show that all frequent itemsets can be enumerated via simple tid-list intersections. (2) I use a lattice-theoretic approach to decompose the original search space (lattice) into smaller pieces (sublattices), which can be processed independently in main-memory. I propose two techniques for achieving the decomposition: prefix-based and maximal-clique-based partition. (3) I decouple the problem decomposition from the pattern search. I propose three new search strategies for enumerating the frequent itemsets within each sublattice: bottom-up, top-down and hybrid search. (4) My approach roughly requires only a few database scans (with some preprocessed information), minimizing the I/O costs.

I present four new algorithms combining the features listed above, depending on the database format, the decomposition technique, and the search procedure used. These include *Par-Eclat, Par-MaxEclat, Par-Clique,* and *Par-MaxClique.* The parallel work is distributed among the processors in such a way that each processor can compute the frequent itemsets independently, using simple intersection operations. These techniques eliminate the need for synchronization after the initial set-up phase, and enable us to scan the database only two times, drastically cutting down the I/O overhead. The tid-list based approach is also insensitive to data-skew. Furthermore, the use of simple intersection operations makes the new algorithms an attractive option for direct implementation in database systems, using SQL.

The experimental testbed is a 32-processor DEC Alpha SMP cluster (8 hosts, 4 processors/host) inter-connected by the Memory Channel (Gillett 1996) network. The new parallel algorithms are also novel in that they are hierarchical in nature, i.e., they assume a distributed-memory model across the 8 cluster hosts, but assume a shared-memory model for the 4 processors on each host.

With the help of an extensive set of experiments, I show that the best new algorithm improves over current methods by over an order of magnitude. At the same time, the proposed techniques retain linear scalability in the number of transactions in the database.

The rest of this chapter is organized as follows: In section 13.2 I describe the association discovery problem. I look at related work in section 13.3. In section 13.4 I develop our lattice-based approach for problem decomposition and pattern search. Section 13.5 describes the sequential algorithm, and section 13.6 presents our new parallel algorithms. An experimental study is presented in section 13.7, and I conclude in section 13.8.

13.2 Problem Statement

The association mining task, first introduced in Agrawal, Imielinski, and Swami (1993b), can be stated as follows: Let $\mathcal{I}$ be a set of items, and $\mathcal{D}$ a database of transactions, where each transaction has a unique identifier (*tid*) and contains a set of items. A set of items is also called an *itemset*. An itemset with k items is called a k-itemset. The *support* of an itemset X, denoted $\sigma(X)$, is the number of transactions in which it occurs as a subset. A k length subset of an itemset is called a k-subset. An itemset is maximal if it is not a subset of any other itemset. An itemset is *frequent* if its support is more than a user-specified *minimum support (min_sup)* value. The set of frequent k-itemsets is denoted $\mathcal{F}_k$.

An *association rule* is an expression $A \Rightarrow B$, where A and B are itemsets. The support of the rule is given as $\sigma(A \cup B)$, and the *confidence* as $\sigma(A \cup B)/\sigma(A)$ (i.e., the conditional probability that a transaction contains B, given that it contains A). A rule is *strong* if its confidence is more than a user-specified *minimum confidence (min_conf)*.

The data mining task is to generate all association rules in the database, which have a support greater than *min_sup*, i.e., the rules are frequent. The rules must also have confidence greater than *min_conf*, i.e., the rules are strong. This task can be broken into two steps (Agrawal, Mannila, Srikant, Toivonen, and Verkamo 1996):

Find all frequent itemsets. This step is computationally and I/O intensive. Given m items, there can be potentially 2^m frequent itemsets. Efficient methods are needed to traverse this exponential itemset search space to enumerate all the frequent itemsets. Thus frequent itemset discovery is the main focus of this chapter.

Generate strong rules. This step is relatively straightforward; rules of the form $X \backslash Y \Rightarrow Y$, where $Y \subset X$, are generated for all frequent itemsets X, provided the rules have at least minimum confidence.

ITEMS

Jane Austen	A
Agatha Christie	C
Sir Arthur Conan Doyle	D
Mark Twain	T
P. G. Wodehouse	W

DATABASE

Transaction	Items
1	A C T W
2	C D W
3	A C T W
4	A C D W
5	A C D T W
6	C D T

FREQUENT ITEMSETS (min_sup = 50%)

Support	Itemsets
100% (6)	C
83% (5)	W, CW
67% (4)	A, D, T, AC, AW CD, CT, ACW
50% (3)	AT, DW, TW, ACT, ATW *CDW*, CTW, *ACTW*

Maximal Frequent Itemsets: *CDW*, *ACTW*

ASSOCIATION RULES (min_conf = 100%)

A → C (4/4)	AC → W (4/4)	TW → C (3/3)
A → W (4/4)	AT → C (3/3)	AT → CW (3/3)
A → CW (4/4)	AT → W (3/3)	TW → AC (3/3)
D → C (4/4)	AW → C (4/4)	ACT → W (3/3)
T → C (4/4)	DW → C (3/3)	ATW → C (3/3)
W → C (5/5)	TW → A (3/3)	CTW → A (3/3)

Figure 13.1: (a) Bookstore database, (b) frequent itemsets and strong rules.

Consider an example bookstore sales database shown in figure 13.1. There are five different items (names of authors the bookstore carries), i.e., $\mathcal{I} = \{A, C, D, T, W\}$, and the database consists of six customers who bought books by these authors. Figure 13.1 shows all the frequent itemsets that are contained in at least three customer transactions, i.e., $min\_sup = 50\%$. It also shows the set of all association rules with *min_conf* = 100%. The itemsets $ACTW$ and CDW are the maximal frequent itemsets. Since all other frequent itemsets are subsets of one of these two maximal itemsets, we can reduce the frequent itemset search problem to the task of enumerating only the maximal frequent itemsets. On the other hand, for generating all the strong rules, we need the support of all frequent itemsets. This can be easily accomplished once the maximal elements have been identified, by making an additional database pass, and gathering the support of all uncounted subsets.

13.2.1 Computational Complexity

The search space for enumeration of all frequent itemsets is 2^m, which is exponential in m, the number of items. One can prove that the problem of finding a frequent set of a certain size is NP-Complete, by reducing it to the balanced bipartite clique problem, which is known to be NP-complete (Zaki and Ogihara 1998). However, if we assume that there is a bound on the transaction length, we can prove that frequent itemset enumeration is essentially linear in the database size (Zaki and Ogihara 1998).

Once the frequent itemsets are known, they can be used to obtain rules that describe the relationship between different itemsets. We generate and test the confidence of all rules of the form $X \backslash Y \Rightarrow Y$, where $Y \subset X$, and X is frequent. For example, the itemset CDW generates the following rules $\{CD \Rightarrow W, CW \Rightarrow D, DW \Rightarrow C, C \Rightarrow DW, D \Rightarrow CW, W \Rightarrow CD\}$. For an itemset of size k there are $2^k - 2$ potentially strong rules that can be generated. This follows from the fact that we must consider each subset of the itemset as an antecedent, except for the empty and the full itemset. The complexity of the rule generation step is thus $O(r \cdot 2^l)$, where r is the number of frequent itemsets, and l is the longest frequent itemset.

13.3 Related Work

In this section I describe prior work on association mining. I begin with uniprocessor or sequential algorithms, and then consider the extant parallel algortithms. I next describe Apriori and count distribution algorithms in more detail, since I use them as base cases for comparison with the new algorithms.

13.3.1 Sequential Algorithms

Several algorithms for mining associations have been proposed in the literature (Agrawal, Imielinski, and Swami 1993b; Agrawal, Mannila, Srikant, Toivonen, and Verkamo 1996; Brin, Motwani, Ullman, and Tsur 1997; Houtsma and Swami 1995; Lin and Kedem 1998; Lin and Dunham 1998; Mueller 1995; Park, Chen, and Yu 1995a; Savasere, Omiecinski, and Navathe 1995; Toivonen 1996). The Apriori algorithm (Agrawal, Mannila, Srikant, Toivonen, and Verkamo 1996) is the best known previous algorithm, and it uses an efficient candidate generation procedure, such that only the frequent itemsets at a level are used to construct candidates at the next level. However, it requires multiple database scans. The DHP algorithm (Park, Chen, and Yu 1995a) tries to reduce the number of candidates by collecting approximate counts in the previous level. Like Apriori, it requires as many database passes as the longest itemset. The partition algorithm (Savasere, Omiecinski, and Navathe 1995) minimizes I/O by scanning the database only twice. It partitions the database into small chunks which can be handled in memory. In the first pass it generates the set of all potentially frequent itemsets, and in the second pass it counts their global support. The DLG (Yen and Chen 1996) algorithm uses a bit-vector per item, noting the tids where the item occurred. It generates frequent itemsets via logical AND operations on the bit-vectors. However, DLG assumes that the bit vectors fit in memory, and thus scalability could be a problem for databases with millions of transactions. The DIC algorithm (Brin, Motwani, Ullman, and Tsur 1997) dynamically counts candidates of varying length as the database scan progresses, and thus is able to reduce the number of scans. Another way to minimize the I/O overhead is to work with only a small sample of the database. An analysis of the effectiveness of sampling for association mining, presented by Zaki, Parthasarathy, Li, and Ogihara (1997), and Toivonen (1996), presents an exact algorithm that finds all rules using sampling. The AS-CPA algorithm and its sampling versions (Lin and Dunham 1998) build on top of *Partition* and produce a much smaller set of potentially frequent candidates. It requires at most two database scans. Also, sampling may be used to eliminate the second pass altogether. Approaches using only general-purpose DBMS systems and relational algebra operations have also been studied (Holsheimer, Kersten, Mannila, and Toivonen 1995; Houtsma and Swami 1995). New algorithms were proposed (Zaki, Parthasarathy, Ogihara, and Li 1997b; Zaki, Parthasarathy, Ogihara, and Li 1997c) that were shown to outperform previous approaches.

All the above algorithms generate all possible frequent itemsets. Methods for finding the maximal elements include *All-MFS* (Gunopulos, Mannila, and Saluja 1997), which is a randomized algorithm to discover maximal frequent itemsets. The pincer-search algorithm (Lin and Kedem 1998) not only constructs the candidates in a bottom-up manner like Apriori, but also starts a top-down search at the same time. This can help in reducing the number of database scans. MaxMiner (Bayardo 1998) is another algorithm for finding the maximal elements. It uses efficient pruning techniques to quickly narrow the search space.

13.3.2 Parallel Algorithms

Distributed-memory machines: Three different parallelizations of Apriori on IBM-SP2, a distributed memory machine, were presented by Agrawal and Shafer (1996). The count distribution algorithm is a straight-forward parallelization of Apriori. Each processor generates the partial support of all candidate itemsets from its local database partition. At the end of each iteration the global supports are generated by exchanging the partial supports among all the processors. The data distribution algorithm partitions the candidates into disjoint sets, which are assigned to different processors. However to generate the global support each processor must scan the entire database (its local partition, and all the remote partitions) in all iterations. It thus suffers from huge communication overhead. The candidate distribution algorithm also partitions the candidates, but it selectively replicates the database, so that each processor proceeds independently. The local database portion is still scanned in every iteration. Count distribution was shown to have superior performance among these three algorithms (Agrawal and Shafer 1996). Other parallel algorithms improving upon these ideas in terms of communication efficiency, or aggregate memory utilization have also been proposed (Cheung, Ng, Fu, and Fu 1996; Cheung, Han, Ng, Fu, and Fu 1996; Han, Karypis, and Kumar 1997). The PDM algorithm (Park, Chen, and Yu 1995b) presents a parallelization of the DHP algorithm (Park, Chen, and Yu 1995a). The hash based parallel algorithms NPA, SPA, HPA, and HPA-ELD, proposed by Shintani and Kitsuregawa (1996) are similar to those by Agrawal and Shafer (1996). Essentially NPA corresponds to Count Distribution, SPA to Data Distribution, and HPA to Candidate Distribution. The HPA-ELD algorithm is the best among NPA, SPA, and HPA, since it eliminates the effect of data skew, and reduces communication by replicating candidates with high support on all processors. A new parallel algorithm Eclat (Zaki, Parthasarathy, and Li 1997c; Zaki, Parthasarathy, Ogihara, and Li 1997c) was also presented on a DEC Alpha Cluster. Eclat uses the equivalence class decomposition scheme along with a bottom-up lattice traversal. It was shown to outperform *Count Distribution* by more than an order of magnitude.

Shared-memory machines: In recent work I presented the CCPD parallel algorithm for shared-memory machines (Zaki, Ogihara, Parthasarathy, and Li 1996). It is similar in spirit to *Count Distribution.* The candidate itemsets are generated in parallel and are stored in a hash tree which is shared among all the processors. Each processor then scans its logical partition of the database and atomically updates the counts of candidates in the shared hash tree. CCPD uses additional optimization such as candidate balancing, hash-tree balancing and short-circuited subset counting to speed up performance (Zaki, Ogihara, Parthasarathy, and Li 1996). APM (Cheung, Hu, and Xia 1998) is an asynchronous parallel algorithm for shared-memory machines based on the DIC algorithm (Brin, Motwani, Ullman, and Tsur 1997).

13.3.3 The Apriori and Count Distribution Algorithms

I now describe the apriori algorithm (Agrawal, Mannila, Srikant, Toivonen, and Verkamo 1996) in more detail, since it forms the basis of almost all parallel algorithms proposed to-date. For comparison with the methods I will describe in this chapter, I also look at the Count distribution algorithm (Agrawal and Shafer 1996) which is one of the current best parallel methods.

Apriori algorithm: (Agrawal, Mannila, Srikant, Toivonen, and Verkamo 1996) The apriori algorithm is an iterative algorithm that counts itemsets of a specific length in a given database pass. The process starts by scanning all transactions in the database and computing the frequent items. Next, a set of potentially frequent *candidate* 2-itemsets is formed from the frequent items. Another database scan is made to obtain their supports. The frequent

$\mathcal{F}_1$ = {frequent 1-itemsets };
for ($k = 2$; $\mathcal{F}_{k-1} \neq \emptyset$; $k++$)
  C_k = Set of New Candidates;
  for all transactions $t \in \mathcal{D}$
    for all k-subsets s of t
      if ($s \in C_k$) $s.count++$;
  $\mathcal{F}_k = \{c \in C_k | c.count \geq min\_sup\}$;
Set of all frequent itemsets = $\bigcup_k \mathcal{F}_k$;

Figure 13.2: The apriori algorithm.

2-itemsets are retained for the next pass, and the process is repeated until all frequent itemsets have been enumerated. The complete algorithm is shown in figure 13.2. I refer the reader to Agrawal, Mannila, Srikant, Toivonen, and Verkamo (1996) for additional details. There are three main steps in the algorithm: (1) Generate candidates of length k from the frequent ($k - 1$) length itemsets, by a self join on $\mathcal{F}_{k-1}$. For example, if $\mathcal{F}_2 = \{AB, AC, AD, AE, BC, BD, BE\}$. Then $C_3 = \{ABC, ABD, ABE, ACD, ACE, ADE,$ - $BCD, BCE, BDE\}$. (2) Prune any candidate with at least one infrequent subset. As an example, ACD will be pruned since CD is not frequent. After pruning we get a new set $C_3 = \{ABC, ABD, ABE\}$. 3) Scan all transactions to obtain candidate supports. The candidates are stored in a hash tree for fast support counting.

The count distribution algorithm: The count distribution algorithm (Agrawal and Shafer 1996) is a simple but effective parallelization of *Apriori*. All processors generate the entire candidate hash tree from $\mathcal{F}_{k-1}$. Each processor can thus independently get partial supports of the candidates from its local database partition. This is followed by a sum-reduction to obtain the global counts. Note that only the partial counts need to be communicated, rather than merging different hash trees, since each processor has a copy of the entire tree. Once the global $\mathcal{F}_k$ has been determined each processor builds C_{k+1} in parallel, and repeats the process until all frequent itemsets are found. This simple algorithm minimizes communication since only the counts are exchanged among the processors. However, since the entire hash tree is replicated on each processor, it doesn't utilize the aggregate memory efficiently.

13.4 Itemset Enumeration: Lattice-Based Approach

Before embarking on the algorithm description, I will briefly review some terminology from lattice theory (see Davey and Priestley [1990] for a good introduction).

Definition 1 *Let P be a set. A* partial order *on P is a binary relation $\leq$, such that for all $X, Y, Z \in P$, the relation is: 1) Reflexive: $X \leq X$. 2) Anti-Symmetric: $X \leq Y$ and $Y \leq X$, implies $X = Y$. 3) Transitive: $X \leq Y$ and $Y \leq Z$, implies $X \leq Z$. The set P with the relation $\leq$ is called an* ordered set.

Definition 2 *Let $X, Z, Y \in P$. We say X is* covered by Y, *denoted $X \sqsubset Y$, if $X < Y$ and $X \leq Z < Y$, implies $Z = X$, i.e., if there is no element Z of P with $X < Z < Y$.*

Definition 3 *Let P be an ordered set, and let $S \subseteq P$. An element $X \in P$ is an* upper bound *(*lower bound*) of S if $s \leq X$ ($s \geq X$) for all $s \in S$. The least upper bound, also called* join, *of S is denoted as $\bigvee S$, and the greatest lower bound, also called* meet, *of S is denoted as $\bigwedge S$. The greatest element of P, denoted $\top$, is called the* top element, *and the least element of P, denoted $\bot$, is called the* bottom element.

Definition 4 *Let L be an ordered set. L is called a* join (meet) semilattice *if $X \vee Y$ ($X \wedge Y$) exists for all $X, Y \in L$. L is called a* lattice *if it is a join and meet semilattice, i.e., if $X \vee Y$ and $X \wedge Y$ exist of all $X, Y \in L$. L is a* complete lattice *if $\bigvee S$ and $\bigwedge S$ exist for all $S \subseteq L$. A ordered set $M \subset L$ is a* sublattice *of L if $X, Y \in M$ implies $X \vee Y \in M$ and $X \wedge Y \in M$.*

For set S, the ordered set $\mathcal{P}(S)$, the power set of S, is a complete lattice in which join and meet are given by union and intersection, respectively:

$$\bigvee\{A_i \mid i \in I\} = \bigcup_{i \in I} A_i \qquad \bigwedge\{A_i \mid i \in I\} = \bigcap_{i \in I} A_i$$

The top element of $\mathcal{P}(S)$ is $\top = S$, and the bottom element of $\mathcal{P}(S)$ is $\bot = \{\}$. For any $L \subseteq \mathcal{P}(S)$, L is called a *lattice of sets* if it is closed under finite unions and intersections, i.e., $(L; \subseteq)$ is a lattice with the partial order specified by the subset relation $\subseteq$, $X \vee Y = X \cup Y$, and $X \wedge Y = X \cap Y$.

Figure 13.3 shows the powerset lattice $\mathcal{P}(\mathcal{I})$ of the set of items in the example database $\mathcal{I} = \{A, C, D, T, W\}$. Also shown are the frequent (grey circles) and maximal frequent itemsets (black circles). It can be observed that the set of all frequent itemsets forms a meet semilattice since it is closed under the meet operation, i.e., for any frequent itemsets X, and Y, $X \cap Y$ is also frequent. On the other hand, it doesn't form a join semilattice, since X and Y frequent, doesn't imply $X \cup Y$ is frequent. It can be mentioned that the infrequent itemsets form a join semilattice.

Lemma 1 *All subsets of a frequent itemsets are frequent.*

The above lemma is a consequence of the closure under meet operation for the set of frequent itemsets. As a corollary, it can be seen that all supersets of an infrequent itemset are infrequent. This observation forms the

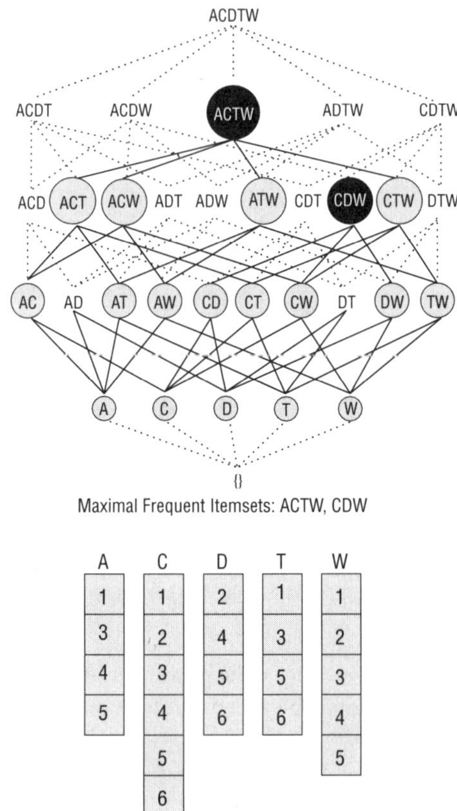

Figure 13.3: (a) The complete powerset lattice $\mathcal{P}(\mathcal{I})$, (b) tid-list for the atoms.

basis of a very powerful pruning strategy in a bottom-up search procedure for frequent itemsets, which has been leveraged in many association mining algorithms (Agrawal, Mannila, Srikant, Toivonen, and Verkamo 1996; Park, Chen, and Yu 1995a; Savasere, Omiecinski, and Navathe 1995). Namely, only the itemsets found to be frequent at the previous level need to be extended as candidates for the current level. However, the lattice formulation makes it apparent that we need not restrict ourselves to a purely bottom-up search, i.e., if we view the lattice as a collection of (multiple) paths leading to the maximal frequent itemsets, then one can formulate alternate ways of reaching the maximal elements. We need not look at all intermediate levels as in a bottom-up approach. For example, in a depth-first search, once can reach $ACTW$ in just four steps using the path A, AC, ACT, and $ACTW$. Later, I will describe practical implementations of such alternate enumeration schemes.

Lemma 2 *The maximal frequent itemsets uniquely determine all frequent itemsets.*

This observation tells us that our goal should be to devise a search procedure that quickly identifies the maximal frequent itemsets. In the following sections I will see how to do this efficiently.

13.4.1 Support Counting

Definition 5 *A lattice L is said to be* distributive *if for all $X, Y, Z \in L$, $X \wedge (Y \vee Z) = (X \wedge Y) \vee (X \wedge Z)$.*

Definition 6 *Let L be a lattice with bottom element $\bot$. Then $X \in L$ is called an* atom *if $\bot \sqsubset X$, i.e., X covers $\bot$. The set of atoms of L is denoted by $\mathcal{A}(L)$.*

Definition 7 *A lattice L is called a* Boolean lattice *if (1) It is distributive. (2) It has $\top$ and $\bot$ elements. (3) Each member X of the lattice has a complement.*

Note that the powerset lattice $\mathcal{P}(\mathcal{I})$ on the set of database items $\mathcal{I}$ is a *Boolean* lattice, with the complement of $X \in L$ given as $\mathcal{I} \backslash X$. The set of atoms of the powerset lattice corresponds to the set of items, i.e., $\mathcal{A}(\mathcal{P}(\mathcal{I})) = \mathcal{I}$. I associate with each atom (database item) X its *tid-list*, denoted $\mathcal{L}(X)$, which is a list of all transaction identifiers containing the atom. Figure 13.3 shows the tid-lists for the atoms in our example database. For example consider atom A. Looking at the database in figure 13.1, we see that A occurs in transactions 1, 3, 4, and 5. This forms the tid-list for atom A.

Lemma 3 *(Davey and Priestley 1990) For a finite Boolean lattice L, with $X \in L$, $X = \bigvee\{Y \in \mathcal{A}(L) \mid Y \leq X\}$.*

In other words every element of a Boolean lattice is given as a join of a subset of the set of atoms. Since the powerset lattice $\mathcal{P}(\mathcal{I})$ is a Boolean lattice, with the join operation corresponding to set union, we get

Lemma 4 *For any $X \in \mathcal{P}(\mathcal{I})$, let $J = \{Y \in \mathcal{A}(\mathcal{P}(\mathcal{I})) \mid Y \leq X\}$. Then $X = \bigcup_{Y \in J} Y$, and $\sigma(X) = \mid \bigcap_{Y \in J} \mathcal{L}(Y) \mid$.*

The above lemma states that any itemset can be obtained as a join of some atoms of the lattice, and the support of the itemset can be obtained by intersecting the tid-list of the atoms. We can generalize this lemma to a set of itemsets:

Lemma 5 *For any $X \in \mathcal{P}(\mathcal{I})$, let $X = \bigcup_{Y \in J} J$. Then $\sigma(X) = \mid \bigcap_{Y \in J} \mathcal{L}(Y) \mid$.*

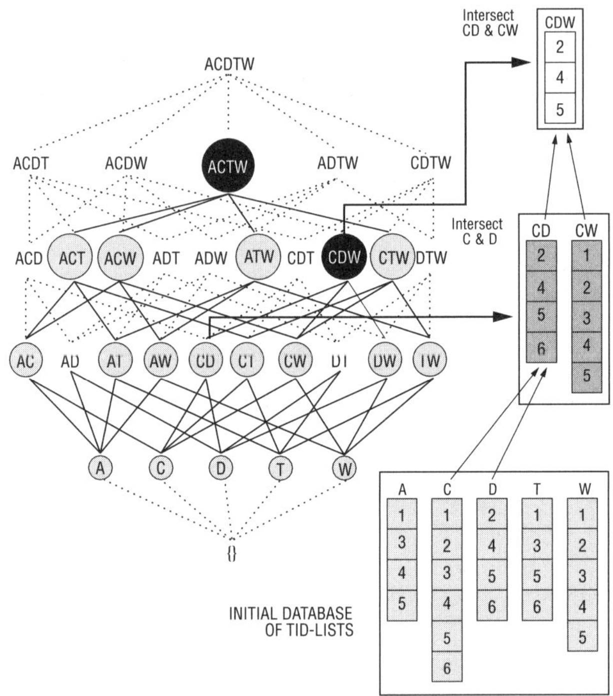

Figure 13.4: Computing support of itemsets via tid-list intersections.

This lemma says that if an itemset is given as a union of a set of itemsets in J, then its support is given as the intersection of tid-lists of elements in J. In particular we can determine the support of any k-itemset by simply intersecting the tid-lists of any two of its $(k-1)$ length subsets. A simple check on the cardinality of the resulting tid-list tells us whether the new itemset is frequent or not. Figure 13.4 shows this process pictorially. It shows the initial database with the tid-list for each item (i.e., the atoms). The intermediate tid-list for CD is obtained by intersecting the lists of C and D, i.e., $\mathcal{L}(CD) = \mathcal{L}(C) \cap \mathcal{L}(D)$. Similarly, $\mathcal{L}(CDW) = \mathcal{L}(CD) \cap \mathcal{L}(CW)$, and so on. Thus, only the lexicographically first two subsets at the previous level are required to compute the support of an itemset at any level.

Lemma 6 *Let X and Y be two itemsets, with $X \subseteq Y$. Then $\mathcal{L}(X) \supseteq \mathcal{L}(Y)$.*

Proof: Follows from the definition of support. Q.E.D.

This lemma states that if X is a subset of Y, then the cardinality of the tid-list of Y (i.e., its support) must be less than or equal to the cardinality of the tid-list of X. A practical and important consequence of the above lemma is that the cardinalities of intermediate tid-lists shrink as we move up the lattice. This results in very fast intersection and support counting.

13.4.2 Lattice Decomposition: Prefix-Based Classes

If we had enough main-memory we could enumerate all the frequent itemsets by traversing the powerset lattice, and performing intersections to obtain itemset supports. In practice, however, we have only a limited amount of main-memory, and all the intermediate tid-lists will not fit in memory. This brings up a natural question: can we decompose the original lattice into smaller pieces such that each portion can be solved independently in main-memory. I address this question below.

Definition 8 *Let P be a set. An* equivalence relation *on P is a binary relation $\equiv$ such that for all $X, Y, Z \in P$, the relation is: 1) Reflexive: $X \equiv X$. 2) Symmetric: $X \equiv Y$ implies $Y \equiv X$. 3) Transitive: $X \equiv Y$ and $Y \equiv Z$, implies $X \equiv Z$. The equivalence relation partitions the set P into disjoint subsets called* equivalence classes. *The equivalence class of an element $X \in P$ is given as $[X] = \{Y \in P \mid X \equiv Y\}$.*

Define a function $p : \mathcal{P}(\mathcal{I}) \times N \mapsto \mathcal{P}(\mathcal{I})$ where N is the set of nonnegative integers and $p(X, k) = X[1 : k]$, the k length prefix of X. Define an equivalence relation θ_k on the lattice $\mathcal{P}(\mathcal{I})$ as follows: $\forall X, Y \in \mathcal{P}(\mathcal{I}),\ X \equiv_{\theta_k} Y \Leftrightarrow p(X, k) = p(Y, k)$. That is, two itemsets are in the same class if they share a common k length prefix. I therefore call θ_k a *prefix-based* equivalence relation.

Figure 13.5a shows the lattice induced by the equivalence relation θ_1 on $\mathcal{P}(\mathcal{I})$, where we collapse all itemsets with a common 1 length prefix into an equivalence class. The resulting set or lattice of equivalence classes is $\{[A], [C], [D], [T], [W]\}$.

Lemma 7 *Each equivalence class $[X]_{\theta_k}$ induced by the relation θ_k is a sublattice of $\mathcal{P}(\mathcal{I})$.*

Proof: Let U and V be any two elements in the class $[X]$, i.e., U, V share the common prefix X. $U \vee V = U \cup V \supseteq X$ implies that $U \vee V \in [X]$, and $U \wedge V = U \cap V \supseteq X$ implies that $U \wedge V \in [X]$. Therefore $[X]_{\theta_k}$ is a sublattice of $\mathcal{P}(\mathcal{I})$. Q.E.D.

Each $[X]_{\theta_1}$ is itself a Boolean lattice with its own set of atoms. For example, the atoms of $[A]_{\theta_1}$ are $\{AC, AD, AT, AW\}$, and the top and bottom elements are $\top = ACDTW$, and $\bot = A$. By the application of lemmas 4,

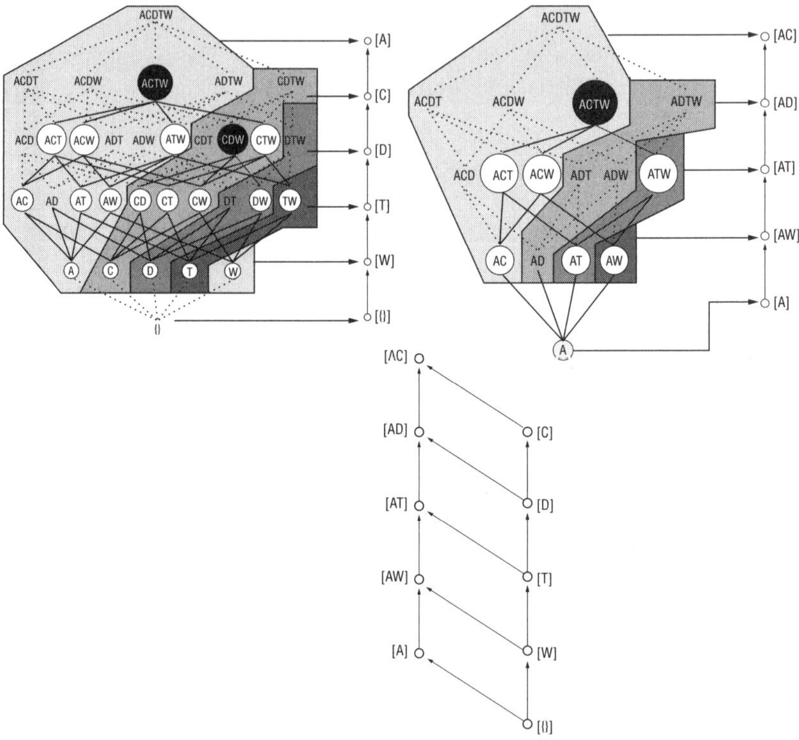

Figure 13.5: Equivalence classes of (a) $\mathcal{P}(\mathcal{I})$ induced by θ_1, and (b) $[A]_{\theta_1}$ induced by θ_2; (c) final lattice of independent classes.

and 5, we can generate all the supports of the itemsets in each class (sublattice) by intersecting the tid-list of atoms or any two subsets at the previous level. If there is enough main-memory to hold temporary tid-lists for each class, then we can solve each $[X]_{\theta_1}$ independently. Another interesting feature of the equivalence classes is that the links between classes denote dependencies. That is to say, if we want to prune an itemset if there exists at least one infrequent subset (see lemma 1), then we have to process the classes in a specific order. In particular we have to solve the classes from bottom to top, which corresponds to a reverse lexicographic order, i.e., we process $[W]$, then $[T]$, followed by $[D]$, then $[C]$, and finally $[A]$. This guarantees that all subset information is available for pruning. For example, assume that we have already enumerated all frequent itemsets of $[W]$, $[T]$, $[D]$, and $[C]$. When we are processing $[A]$, we have full pruning information for itemsets that do not belong to $[A]$. For example we know that CTW is frequent, thus $ACTW$ is a possible candidate. If we further label classes in decreasing order of their size (number of atoms), then we solve small classes first, and the large ones later, allowing us to fully use all pruning information.

In practice we have found that the one level decomposition induced by θ_1 is sufficient. However, in some cases, a class may still be too large to be solved in main-memory. In this scenario, we apply recursive class decomposition. Let's assume that $[A]$ is too large to fit in main-memory. Since $[A]$ is itself a Boolean lattice, it can be decomposed using θ_2. Figure 13.5b shows the equivalence class lattice induced by applying θ_2 on $[A]$, where we collapse all itemsets with a common 2 length prefix into an equivalence class. The resulting set of classes are $\{[AC], [AD], [AT], [AW]\}$. Like before, each class can be solved independently, and we can solve them in reverse lexicographic order to enable subset pruning. The final set of independent classes obtained by applying θ_1 on $\mathcal{P}(\mathcal{I})$ and θ_2 on $[A]$ is shown in figure 13.5c. As before, the links show the pruning dependencies that exist among the classes. Depending on the amount of main-memory available we can recursively partition large classes into smaller ones, until each class is small enough to be solved independently in main-memory.

13.4.3 Search for Frequent Itemsets

In this section I discuss efficient search strategies for enumerating the frequent itemsets within each class.

Bottom-Up Search

The bottom-up search is based on a recursive decomposition of each class into smaller classes induced by the equivalence relation θ_k. Figure 13.6 shows the decomposition of $[A]_{\theta_1}$ into smaller classes, and the resulting lattice of equivalence classes. Also shown are the atoms within each class, from which all other elements of a class can be determined. The equivalence class lattice can be traversed in either depth-first or breadth-first manner. In this chapter I will only show results for a breadth-first traversal, i.e., I first process the classes $\{[AC], [AT], [AW]\}$, followed by the classes $\{[ACT], [ACW], [ATW]\}$, and finally $[ACTW]$. For computing the support of any itemset, I simply intersect the tid-lists of two of its subsets at the previous level. Since the search is breadth-first, this technique enumerates all frequent itemsets.

Top-Down Search

The top-down approach starts with the top element of the lattice. Its support is determined by intersecting the tid-lists of the atoms. This requires a k-way

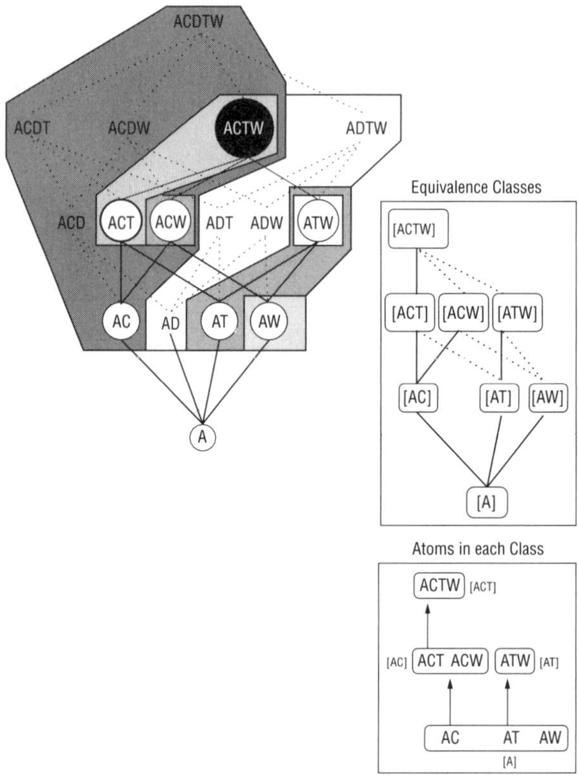

Figure 13.6: Bottom-up search.

intersection if the top element is a k-itemset. The advantage of this approach is that if the maximal element is fairly large then one can quickly identify it, and one can avoid finding the support of all its subsets. The search starts with the top element. If it is frequent we are done. Otherwise, we check each subset at the next level. This process is repeated until we have identified all minimal infrequent itemsets. Figure 13.7 depicts the top-down search. We start with a 5-way tid-list intersection to obtain the support for $ACDTW$, which turns out to be infrequent. We next have to try its subsets at the next level. Out of the 4 subsets, only $ACTW$ is frequent. This means we don't check any of its subsets, since they all must be frequent. For the other three itemsets $ACDT$, $ACDW$, and $ADTW$, we check their subsets that are not known to be frequent, i.e., we check ACD, ADT and ADW, all of which are infrequent. Finally, at the next level, we find the minimal infrequent itemset AD, and the process stops. As it turns out, we had to perform 9 intersections here, the same

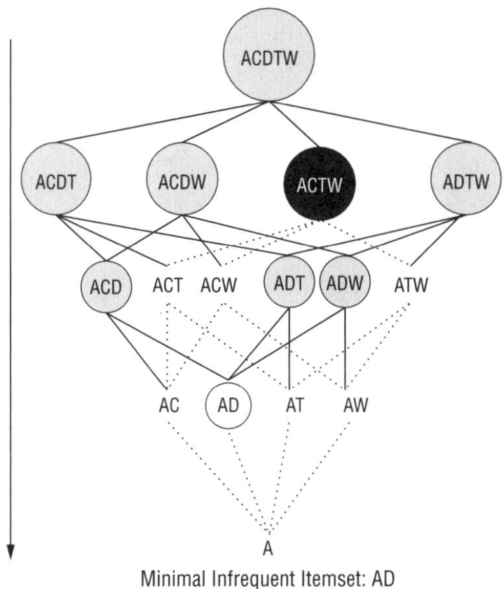

Figure 13.7: Top-down search.

as in bottom-up search. But if $ACDTW$ had been frequent, we would have saved a lot of computation.

This scheme enumerates only the maximal frequent itemsets within each sublattice. However, the maximal elements of a sublattice may not be globally maximal. It can thus generate some nonmaximal itemsets.

Hybrid Search

The hybrid scheme is based on the intuition that the greater the support of an frequent itemset the more likely it is to be a part of a longer frequent itemset. There are two main steps in this approach. We begin with the set of atoms of the class sorted in descending order based on their support. The first, hybrid phase starts by intersecting the atoms one at a time, beginning with the atom with the highest support, generating longer and longer frequent itemsets. The process stops when an extension becomes infrequent. We then enter the second, bottom-up phase. The remaining atoms are combined with the atoms in the first set in a breadth-first fashion described above to generate all other frequent itemsets. Figure 13.8 illustrates this approach (just for this case, to better show the bottom-up phase, I have assumed that AD and ADW are also frequent). Initially, we have four 2-itemsets (or atoms) in the sublattice. We sort them in decreasing order of support to obtain the atom list AC, AW, AT,

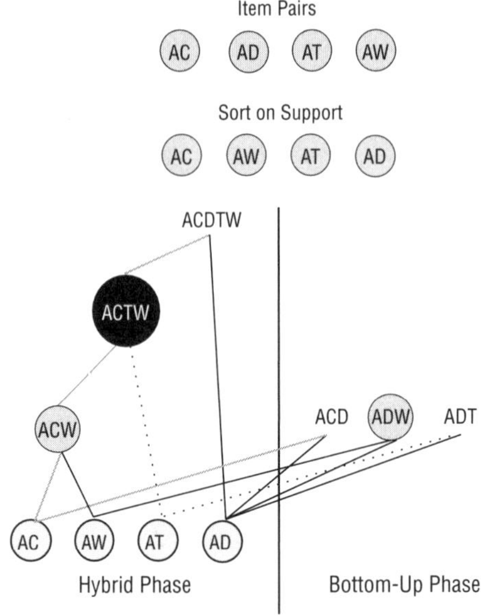

Figure 13.8: Hybrid search.

and AD. We now start the hybrid phase. Starting with AC we try to join it with AW, getting ACW which is frequent. We next join ACW with the next atom AT, to get $ACTW$ which is also frequent. Finally we try $ACTW$ with the last atom AD, but $ACDTW$ is infrequent. Note, that if $ACDTW$ were frequent, we would stop the computation at this stage, having found the maximal frequent itemset. The algorithm now shifts into the bottom-up phase. AD is the atom which could not be combined with $ACTW$. With AD as the bottom element, we generate a new sublattice, whose atoms are the join of AD with itemsets that precede it in the sorted initial ordering, i.e., the new atoms are ACD, ADW, and ADT. This sublattice can be solved using the bottom-up approach. In fact, if there are many atoms like AD which could not be combined with $ACTW$, then one can even re-apply hybrid search on the newly generated sublattice.

Like the bottom-up approach this scheme only requires 2-way intersections. This scheme enumerates the "long" maximal frequent itemsets discovered in the hybrid phase, and also the nonmaximal ones found in the bottom-up phase. Another modification of this scheme is to recursively substitute the second bottom-up phase with the hybrid phase. This approach will enumerate some maximal elements (hybrid phase) and the remaining frequent itemset (bottom-phase).

Frequent 2-Itemsets
{12, 13, 14, 15, 16, 17, 18, 23, 25, 27, 28, 34, 35, 36, 45, 46, 56, 58, 68, 78}

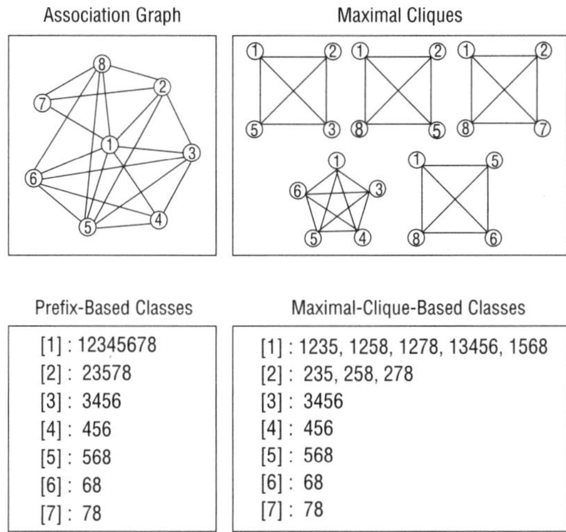

Figure 13.9: Maximal cliques of the association graph; prefix-based and maximal-clique-based classes.

13.4.4 Generating Smaller Classes: Maximal Clique Approach

In this section I show how to produce smaller sublattices or equivalence classes compared to the pure prefix-based approach, by using additional information. As we shall see later in this section, smaller sublattices have fewer atoms and can save unnecessary intersections. For example, if there are k atoms, then we have to perform $\binom{k}{2}$ intersections for the next level in the bottom-up approach. Fewer atoms thus lead to fewer intersections in the bottom-up search. Fewer atoms also reduce the number of intersections in the hybrid scheme, and lead to smaller maximum element size in the top-down search.

Definition 9 *Let P be a set. A* pseudo-equivalence relation *on P is a binary relation $\equiv$ such that for all $X, Y \in P$, the relation is: (1) Reflexive: $X \equiv X$. (2) Symmetric: $X \equiv Y$ implies $Y \equiv X$. The pseudo-equivalence relation partitions the set P into possibly overlapping subsets called* pseudo-equivalence classes.

Let $\mathcal{F}_k$ denote the set of frequent k-itemsets. Define an *k-association graph*, given as $G_k = (V, E)$, with the vertex set $V = \{X \mid X \in \mathcal{F}_1\}$, and edge set $E = \{(X, Y) \mid X, Y \in V \text{ and } \exists\ Z \in \mathcal{F}_{(k+1)}$, such that - $X, Y \subset Z\}$. Let M_k denote the set of maximal cliques in G_k. Figure 13.9 shows the association graph G_1 for the example $\mathcal{F}_2$ shown. Its maximal clique set $M_1 = \{1235, 1258, 1287, 13456, 1568\}$.

Define a pseudo-equivalence relation ϕ_k on the lattice $\mathcal{P}(\mathcal{I})$ as follows: $\forall X, Y \in \mathcal{P}(\mathcal{I}),\ X \equiv_{\phi_k} Y \Leftrightarrow \exists\ C \in M_k$ such that $X, Y \subseteq C$ and $p(X, k) = p(Y, k)$. That is, two itemsets are related, i.e, they are in the same *pseudo-class*, if they are subsets of the same maximal clique and they share a common prefix of length k. We therefore call ϕ_k a *maximal-clique-based* pseudo-equivalence relation.

Lemma 8 *Each pseudo-class* $\lfloor X \rfloor_{\phi_k}$ *induced by the relation* ϕ_k *is a sublattice of* $\mathcal{P}(\mathcal{I})$.

Proof: Let U and V be any two elements in the class $[X]$, i.e., U, V share the common prefix X and there exists a maximal clique $C \in M_k$ such that $U, V \subseteq C$. Clearly, $U \cup V \subseteq C$, and $U \cap V \subseteq C$. Furthermore, $U \vee V = U \cup V \supseteq X$ implies that $U \vee V \in [X]$, and $U \wedge V = U \cap V \supseteq X$ implies that $U \wedge V \in [X]$. Q.E.D.

Thus, each pseudo-class $[X]_{\phi_1}$ is a Boolean lattice, and the supports of all elements of the lattice can be generated by applying lemmas 4, and 5 on the atoms, and using any of the three search strategies described above.

Lemma 9 *Let* $\aleph_k$ *denote the set of pseudo-classes of the maximal-clique-based relation* ϕ_k. *Each pseudo-class* $[Y]_{\phi_k}$ *induced by the prefix-based relation* ϕ_k *is a subset of some class* $[X]_{\theta_k}$ *induced by* θ_k. *Conversely, each* $[X]_{\theta_k}$, *is the union of a set of pseudo-classes* Ψ, *given as* $[X]_{\theta_k} = \bigcup\{[Z]_{\phi_k} \mid Z \in \Psi \subseteq \aleph_k\}$.

Proof: Let $\Gamma(X)$ denote the neighbors of X in the graph G_k. Then $[X]_{\theta_k} = \{Z \mid X \subseteq Z \subseteq \{X, \Gamma(X)\}\}$. In other words, $[X]$ consists of elements with the prefix X and extended by all possible subsets of the neighbors of X in the graph G_k. Since any clique Y is a subset of $\{Y, \Gamma(Y)\}$, we have that $[Y]_{\phi_k} \subseteq [X]_{\theta_k}$, where Y is a prefix of X. On the other hand it is easy to show that $[X]_{\theta_k} = \bigcup\{[Y]_{\phi_k} \mid Y \text{ is a prefix of } X\}$. Q.E.D.

This lemma states that each pseudo-class of ϕ_k is a refinement of (i.e., is smaller than) some class of θ_k. By using the relation ϕ_k instead of θ_k, we can therefore generate smaller sublattices. These sublattices require less memory, and can be processed independently using any of the three search strategies described above. Figure 13.9 contrasts the classes (sublattices) generated by ϕ_1 and θ_1. It is apparent that ϕ_1 generates smaller classes. For example, the prefix class $[1] = 12345678$ is one big class containing all the elements, while the maximal-clique classes for $[1] = \{1235, 1258, 1278, 13456, 1568\}$. Each

```
1: for (i = N; i >= 1; i − −) do
2:    [i].CliqList = ∅;
3:    for all x ∈ [i].CoveringSet do
4:       for all cliq ∈ [x].CliqList do
5:          M = cliq ∩ [i];
6:          if M ≠ ∅ then
7:             insert ({i} ∪ M) in [i].CliqList such that
8:             ∄XorY ∈ [i].CliqList, X ⊆ Y, orY ⊆ X;
```

Figure 13.10: The maximal clique generation algorithm.

of these classes is much smaller than the prefix-based class. The increased refinement of ϕ_k comes at a cost, since the enumeration of maximal cliques can be computationally expensive. For general graphs the maximal clique decision problem is NP-complete (Garey and Johnson 1979). However, the k-association graph is usually sparse and the maximal cliques can be enumerated efficiently. As the edge density of the association graph increases the clique based approaches may suffer. ϕ_k should thus be used only when G_k is not too dense. Some of the factors affecting the edge density include decreasing support and increasing transaction size. The lower the support and the longer the transaction size, the greater the edge density of the k-association graph.

Maximal Clique Generation

U used a modified version of the Bierstone's algorithm (Mulligan and Corneil 1972) for generating maximal cliques in the k-association graph. For a class $[x]$, and $y \in [x]$, y is said to *cover* the subset of $[x]$, given by $cov(y) = [y] \cap [x]$. For each class $\mathcal{C}$, we first identify its *covering set*, given as $\{y \in \mathcal{C} | cov(y) \neq \emptyset$, and $cov(y) \not\subseteq cov(z)$, for any $z \in \mathcal{C}, z < y\}$. For example, consider the class $[1]$, shown in figure 13.9. $cov(2) - \{3, 5, 7, 8\} = [2]$. Similarly, for our example, $cov(y) = [y]$, for all $y \in [1]$, since each $[y] \subseteq [1]$. The covering set of $[1]$ is given by the set $\{2, 3, 5\}$. The item 4 is not in the covering set since, $cov(4) = \{5, 6\}$ is a subset of $cov(3) = \{4, 5, 6\}$. Figure 13.10 shows the complete clique generation algorithm. Only the elements in the covering set need to be considered while generating maximal cliques for the current class (step 3). We recursively generate the maximal cliques for elements in the covering set for each class. Each maximal clique from the covering set is prefixed with the class identifier to obtain the maximal cliques for the current class (step 7). Before inserting the new clique, all duplicates or subsets are eliminated. If the new clique is a subset of any clique already in the maximal list, then it is not inserted. The conditions for the above test are shown in line 8.

Weak Maximal Cliques: For some database parameters, the edge density of the k-association graph may be too high, resulting in large cliques with significant overlap among them. In these cases, not only the clique generation takes more time, but redundant frequent itemsets may also be discovered within each sublattice. To solve this problem we introduce the notion of weak maximality of cliques. Given any two cliques X, and Y, we say that they are *α-related*, if $\alpha \leq \frac{|X \cap Y|}{|X \cup Y|}$, i.e., the ratio of the common elements to the distinct elements of the cliques is at least α. A *weak maximal* clique, $Z = \{X \cup Y\}$, is generated by collapsing the two cliques into one, provided that they are α-related. During clique generation only weak maximal cliques are generated for some user specified value of α. Note that for $\alpha = 1$, we obtain regular maximal cliques, while for $\alpha = 0$, we obtain a single clique. Preliminary experiments indicate that using an appropriate value of α, most of the overhead of redundant cliques can be avoided. We found $\alpha = 0.5$ to work well in practice.

13.5 Sequential Algorithm

In this section I describe the sequential algorithm for efficient enumeration of frequent itemsets. The first step involves the computation of the frequent items and 2-itemsets. The next step generates the sublattices (classes) by applying either the prefix-based equivalence relation θ_1, or the maximal-clique-based pseudo-equivalence relation ϕ_1 on the set of frequent 2-itemsets $\mathcal{F}_2$. The sublattices are then processed one at a time in reverse lexicographic order in main-memory using either bottom-up, top-down or hybrid search. I will now describe these steps in some more detail.

13.5.1 Computing Frequent 1-Itemsets and 2-Itemsets

Most of the current association algorithms (Agrawal, Mannila, Srikant, Toivonen, and Verkamo 1996; Brin, Motwani, Ullman, and Tsur 1997; Lin and Dunham 1998; Park, Chen, and Yu 1995a; Savasere, Omiecinski, and Navathe 1995; Toivonen 1996) assume a *horizontal* database layout, such as the one shown in figure 13.1, consisting of a list of transactions, where each transaction has an identifier followed by a list of items in that transaction. In contrast our algorithms use the *vertical* database format, such as the one shown in figure 13.3, where we maintain a disk-based tid-list for each item. This enables us to check support via simple tid-list intersections.

Computing $\mathcal{F}_1$: Given the vertical tid-list database, all frequent items can be found in a few database scans. For each item, we simply read its tid-list from disk into memory. We then scan the tid-list, incrementing the item's support for each entry.

Computing $\mathcal{F}_2$: Let $N = |\mathcal{I}|$ be the number of frequent items, and A the average tid-list size in bytes. A naive implementation for computing the frequent 2-itemsets requires $\binom{N}{2}$ tid-list intersections for all pairs of items. The amount of data read is $A \cdot N \cdot (N-1)/2$, which corresponds to around $N/2$ data scans. This is clearly inefficient. Instead of the naive method I propose two alternate solutions: 1) Use a preprocessing step to gather the counts of all 2-sequences above a user specified lower bound. Since this information is invariant, it has to be computed once, and the cost can be amortized over the number of times the data is mined. 2) Perform a vertical to horizontal transformation on-the-fly. This can be done quite easily. For each item i, we scan its tid-list into memory. We insert i in an array indexed by tid for each $t \in \mathcal{L}(i)$. This approach can be implemented with little overhead. For example, *Partition* performs the opposite inversion from horizontal to vertical tid-list format on-the-fly, with very little cost. I plan to implement on-the-fly inversion in the future. However, the current implementation uses the first approach due to its simplicity.

13.5.2 Search Implementation

Bottom-Up Search: Figure 13.11 shows the pseudo-code for the bottom-up search. The input to the procedure is a set of atoms of a sublattice S. Frequent itemsets are generated by intersecting the tid-lists of all distinct pairs of atoms and checking the cardinality of the resulting tid-list. A recursive procedure call is made with those itemsets found to be frequent at the current level. This process is repeated until all frequent itemsets have been enumerated. In terms of memory management it is easy to see that we need memory to store intermediate tid-lists for at most two consecutive levels. Once all the frequent itemsets for the next level have been generated, the itemsets at the current level can be deleted.

One practical implementation note for the bottom-up search using tid-list intersections is that the candidate pruning was found to be of little or no benefit. Recall that in *Apriori*, whenever we generate a new candidate a check is made to see if all its subsets are frequent. If there is any infrequent subset then we can prune the candidate. We can implement a similar step in our approach, since each sublattice is processed in reverse lexicographic order, and thus all subset information is available for itemset pruning. Furthermore, for fast subset checking the frequent itemsets can be stored in a hash table. However, in the experiments on synthetic data pruning was found to be of no help. This is mainly because of lemma 6, which says that the tid-list intersection is especially efficient for large itemsets. Nevertheless, there may be databases where pruning is crucial for performance, and pruning can be supported for those datasets.

```
Bottom-Up(S):
for all atoms A_i ∈ S do
   T_i = ∅;
   for all atoms A_j ∈ S, with j > i do
      R = A_i ∪ A_j;
      L(R) = L(A_i) ∩ L(A_j);
      if σ(R) ≥ min_sup then
         T_i = T_i ∪ {R}; F_|R| = F_|R| ∪ {R};
   end
end
delete S; //reclaim memory
for all T_i ≠ ∅ do Bottom-Up(T_i);
```

Figure 13.11: Pseudo-code for bottom-up search.

```
Top-Down(S):
R = ⋃{A_i ∈ S};
if R ∉ F_|R| then
   L(R) = ⋂{L(A_i) | A_i ∈ S};
   if σ(R) ≥ min_sup then
      F_|R| = F_|R| ∪ {R};
   else
      for all Y ⊂ R, with |Y| = |R| − 1
         if Y ∉ HT then
            Top-Down({A_j | A_j ∈ Y});
            if σ(Y) < min_sup then HT = HT ∪{Y};
      end
```

Figure 13.12: Pseudo-code for top-down search.

Top-Down Search: The code for top-down search is given in figure 13.12. The search begins with the maximum element R of the sublattice S. A check is made to see if the element is already known to be frequent. If not we perform a k-way intersection to determine its support. If it is frequent then we are done. Otherwise, we recursively check the support of each of its $(k-1)$-subsets. A hash table HT of itemsets known to be infrequent from previous recursive calls is also maintained to avoid processing sublattices that have already been examined. In terms of memory management the top-down approach requires that only the tid-lists of the atoms of a class be in memory.

Hybrid Search: Figure 13.13 shows the pseudo-code for the hybrid search. The input consists of the atom set S sorted in descending order of support. The maximal phase begins by intersecting atoms one at a time until no frequent extension is possible. All the atoms involved in this phase are stored in the set S_1. The remaining atoms $S_2 = S \backslash S_1$ enter the bottom-up phase. For each atom in S_2, we intersect it with each atom in S_1. The frequent itemsets form

```
Hybrid(S sorted on support):
R = A_1; S_1 = {A_1};
for all A_i ∈ S, i > 1 do /* Maximal Phase */
   R = R ∪ A_i; L(R) = L(R) ∩ L(A_i);
   if σ(R) ≥ min_sup then
      S_1 = S_1 ∪ {A_i}; F_|R| = F_|R| ∪ {R};
   else break;
end
S_2 = S − S_1;
for all B_i ∈ S_2 do /* Bottom-Up Phase */
   T_i = {X_j | σ(X_j) ≥ min_sup, L(X_j) = L(B_i) ∩ L(A_j), ∀A_j ∈ S_1};
   S_1 = S_1 ∪ {B_i};
   if T_i ≠ ∅ then Bottom-Up(T_i);
end
```

Figure 13.13: Pseudo-code for hybrid search.

the atoms of a new sublattice and are solved using the bottom-up search. This process is then repeated for the other atoms of S_2. The maximal phase requires main-memory only for the atoms, while the bottom-up phase requires memory for at most two consecutive levels.

13.5.3 Number of Database Scans

Before processing each sublattice from the initial decomposition all the relevant item tid-lists are scanned into memory. The tid-lists for the atoms (frequent 2-itemsets) of each initial sublattice are constructed by intersecting the item tid-lists. All the other frequent itemsets are enumerated by intersecting the tid-lists of the atoms using the different search procedures. If all the initial classes have disjoint set of items, then each item's tid-list is scanned from disk only once during the entire frequent itemset enumeration process over all sublattices. In the general case there will be some degree of overlap of items among the different sub-lattices. However only the database portion corresponding to the frequent items will need to be scanned, which can be a lot smaller than the entire database. Furthermore, sublattices sharing many common items can be processed in a batch mode to minimize disk access. Thus the algorithms will usually require a few database scans after computing $\mathcal{F}_2$, in contrast to the current approaches which require as many scan as the longest frequent itemset.

There are cases where more concern has to be paid to minimize database scans. For example if there is a large degree of overlap among the atoms of different classes, then it is best to adopt a mixed approach where we simply apply *Apriori* for the initial levels, and then switch to our methods when the overlap is manageable. What this means is that we need to go beyond a simple one level partitioning based on θ_1, instead we might have to use θ_2 or θ_3.

13.6 Parallel Algorithm Design and Implementation

In this section I will discuss the design and implementation of new parallel algorithms for mining frequent itemsets. I present four new parallel algorithms, depending on the decomposition relation used to generate independent classes, and the lattice search scheme used. (1) *Par-Eclat:* It uses prefix-based equivalence relation θ_1 along with bottom-up search. It enumerates all frequent itemsets. (2) *Par-MaxEclat:* It uses prefix-based equivalence relation θ_1 along with hybrid search. It enumerates the "long" maximal frequent itemsets, and some nonmaximal ones. (3) *Par-Clique:* It uses maximal-clique-based pseudo-equivalence relation ϕ_1 along with bottom-up search. It enumerates all frequent itemsets. (4) *Par-MaxClique:* It uses maximal-clique-based pseudo-equivalence relation ϕ_1 along with hybrid search. It enumerates the "long" maximal frequent itemsets, and some nonmaximal ones.

I next present the parallel design and implementation issues, which are applicable to all four algorithms.

13.6.1 Initial Database Partitioning

I assume that the database is in the vertical format, and that I have the support counts of all 2-itemsets available locally on each host. I further assume that the database of tid-lists is initially partitioned among all the hosts. This partitioning is done off-line, similar to the assumption made in count distribution (Agrawal and Shafer 1996). The tid-lists are partitioned so that the total length of all tid-lists in the local portions on each host are roughly equal. This is achieved using a greedy algorithm. The items are sorted on their support, and the next item is assigned to the least loaded host. Note that the entire tid-list for an item resides on a host. Figure 13.15 shows the original database, and the resultant initial partition on two processors.

13.6.2 Parallel Design and Implementation

The new algorithms overcome the shortcomings of the count and candidate distribution algorithms. They utilize the aggregate memory of the system by partitioning the itemsets into disjoint sets, which are assigned to different processors. The dependence among the processors is decoupled right in the beginning so that the redistribution cost can be amortized by the later iterations.

```
Begin ParAssociation:
  /* Initialization Phase*/
  F2 = { Set of Frequent 2-Itemsets }
  Generate Independent Classes from F2 using:
    Prefix-Based or Maximal-Clique-Based Partitioning
  Schedule Classes among the processors P
  Scan local database partition
  Transmit relevant tid-lists to other processors
  Receive tid-lists from other processors

  /* Asynchronous Phase */
  for each assigned Class, C2
    Compute Frequent Itemsets: Bottom-Up(C2) or Hybrid(C2)

  /* Final Reduction Phase*/
  Aggregate Results and Output Associations
End ParAssociation
```

Figure 13.14: Pseudo-code for the new parallel algorithms.

Since each processor can proceed independently, there is no costly synchronization at the end of each iteration. Furthermore the new algorithms use the vertical database layout which clusters all relevant information in an itemset's tid-list. Each processor computes all the frequent itemsets from one class before proceeding to the next. The local database partition is scanned only once. In contrast candidate distribution must scan it once in each iteration. The new algorithms don't pay the extra computation overhead of building or searching complex data structures, nor do they have to generate all the subsets of each transaction. As the intersection is performed an itemset can immediately be inserted in $\mathcal{F}_k$. Notice that the tid-lists also automatically prune irrelevant transactions. As the itemset size increases, the size of the tid-list decreases, resulting in very fast intersections. There are two distinct phases in the algorithms. The initialization phase, responsible for communicating the tid-lists among the processors, and the asynchronous phase, which generates frequent itemsets. The pseudo-code for the new algorithms is shown in figure 13.14, and a pictorial representation of the different phases is shown in figure 13.15.

Initialization Phase

The initialization step consists of three substeps. First, the support counts for 2-itemsets from the preprocessing step are read, and the frequent ones are inserted into $\mathcal{F}_2$. Second, applying one of the two decomposition schemes to $\mathcal{F}_2$ – prefix-based or maximal-clique-based – the set of independent classes is generated. These classes are then scheduled among all the processors so that a suitable level of load-balancing can be achieved. Third, the database

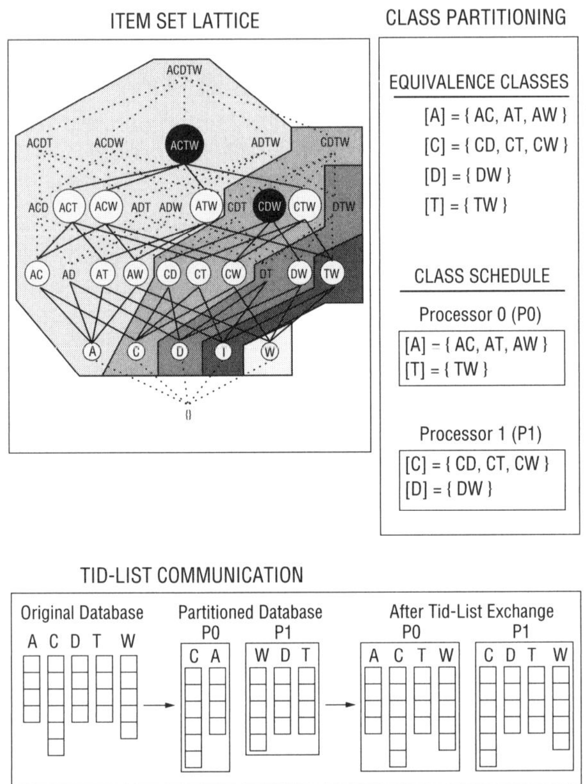

Figure 13.15: Database partitioning and class scheduling.

is repartitioned so that each processor has on its local disk the tid-lists of all 1-itemsets in any class assigned to it.

Class Scheduling: We first partition $\mathcal{F}_2$ into equivalence classes using prefix-based or maximal-clique-based partitioning. We next generate a schedule of the equivalence classes on the different processors in a manner minimizing the load imbalance and minimizing the inter-process communication required in partially replicating the tid-lists. Note that it may be necessary to sacrifice some amount of load balancing for a better communication efficiency. For this reason, whole equivalence classes are assigned to the same processor. Load balancing is achieved by assigning a weight to each equivalence class based on the number of elements in the class. Since we have to consider all pairs of atoms for the next iteration, we assign the weight $\binom{s}{2}$ to a class with s atoms. Once the weights are assigned we generate a schedule using a greedy heuristic. We sort the classes on the weights, and assign each class in turn to

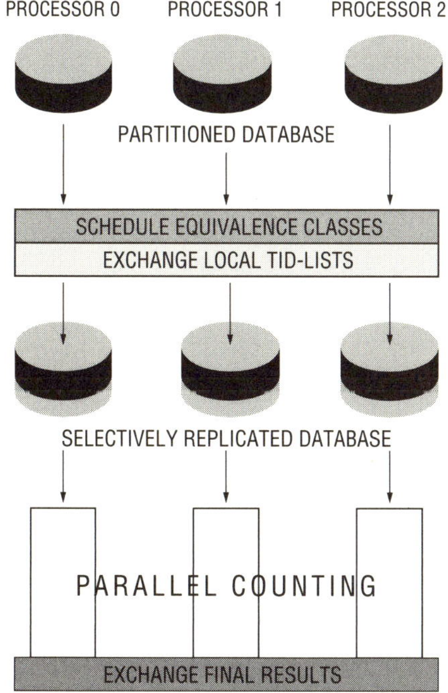

Figure 13.16: The par-eclat algorithm.

the least loaded processor, i.e., one having the least total weight at that point. Ties are broken by selecting the processor with the smaller identifier. These steps are done concurrently on all the processors since all of them have access to the global $\mathcal{F}_2$. Figure 13.15 shows how the prefix-based classes of our example database (from figure 13.1) are scheduled on two processors. Notice how an entire class is assigned to a single processor. Although the number of atoms of a class gives a good indication of the amount of work that needs to be done for that class, better heuristics for generating the weights are possible. For example, if we could better estimate the number of frequent itemsets that would be enumerated from a class we could use that as our weight.

Tid-list Communication: Once the classes have been scheduled among the processors, each processor has to exchange information with every other processor to read the nonlocal tid-lists over the memory channel network. To minimize communication, and being aware of the fact that in our configuration there is only one local disk per host (recall that our cluster has 8 hosts, with 4 processors per host), only the hosts take part in the tid-list exchange. Additional processes on each of the 8 hosts are spawned only in the asynchronous phase. To accomplish the inter-process tid-list communication, each processor scans the item tid-lists in its local database partition and writes it to a transmit region which is mapped for receive on other processors. The other processors extract the tid-list from the receive region if it belongs to any class assigned to them. For example, figure 13.15 shows the initial local database on two hosts, and the final local database after the tid-list communication.

Asynchronous Phase

At the end of the initialization step, the relevant tid-lists are available locally on each host, thus each processor can independently generate the frequent itemsets from its assigned classes eliminating the need for synchronization with other processors. Each class is processed in its entirety before moving on to the next class in the schedule. This step involves scanning the local database partition only once (depending on the amount of overlap among the classes). We can thus benefit from huge I/O savings. Since each class induces a sublattice, depending on the algorithm, we either use a bottom-up traversal to generate all frequent itemsets, or we use the hybrid traversal to generate only the "long" maximal and other frequent itemsets. The pseudo-code and implementation of the two lattice search schemes was presented in the last section (see figure 13.11 and figure 13.12). As an illustration of the various steps, the par-eclat algorithm is shown in figure 13.16. At the end of the asynchronous phase we accumulate all the results from each processor and print them out.

13.6.3 Salient Features of the New Algorithms

In this section I will recapitulate the salient features of the proposed algorithms, contrasting them against count distribution. The algorithms differ in the following respects: (1) They utilize the aggregate memory of the parallel system by partitioning the candidate itemsets among the processors using the prefix-based and maximal-clique-based decomposition schemes. (2) They decouple the processors right in the beginning by repartitioning the database, so that each processor can compute the frequent itemsets independently. This eliminates the need for communicating the frequent itemsets at the end of each iteration. (3) They use the vertical database layout which clusters the transactions containing an itemset into tid-lists. Using this layout enables the algorithms to scan the local database partition only a few times on each processor. It usually takes two scans, the first for communicating the tid-lists, and the second for obtaining the frequent itemsets. In contrast, count distribution scans the database multiple times – once during each iteration. (4) To compute frequent itemsets, they perform simple intersections on two tid-lists. There is no extra overhead associated with building and searching complex hash tree data structures. Such complicated hash structures also suffer from poor cache locality (Pathasarathy, Zaki, and Li 1998). In thealgorithms, all the available memory is utilized to keep tid-lists in memory which results in good locality. As larger itemsets are generated the size of tid-lists decreases, resulting in very fast intersections. (5) The algorithms avoid the overhead of generating all the subsets of a transaction and checking them against the candidate hash tree during support counting.

13.7 Experimental Results

All the experiments were performed on a 32-processor (8 hosts, 4 processors/host) Digital Alpha cluster inter-connected via the memory channel network (Gillett 1996). Each Alpha processor runs at 233MHz. There's a total of 256MB of main memory per host (shared among the 4 processors on that host). Each host also has a 2GB local disk, out of which less than 500MB was available to us.

The Digital memory channel: Digital's memory channel network provides applications with a global address space using memory mapped regions. A region can be mapped into a process' address space for transmit, receive, or both. Virtual addresses for transmit regions map into physical addresses located in I/O space on the memory channel's PCI adapter. Virtual addresses for receive regions map into physical RAM. Writes into transmit regions are collected by the source memory channel adapter, forwarded to destination memory channel adapters through a hub, and transferred via DMA to receive regions with the same global identifier. Figure 13.17 shows the memory channel space (The lined region is mapped for both transmit and receive on node 1 and for receive on node 2; The gray region is mapped for receive on node 1 and for transmit on node 2). Regions within a node can be shared across different processors on that node. Writes originating on a given node will be sent to receive regions on that same node only if *loop-back* has been enabled for the region. I do not use the loop-back feature. I use *write-doubling* instead, where each processor writes to its receive region and then to its transmit region, so that processes on a host can see modification made by other processes on the same host. Though we pay the cost of double writing, we reduce the amount of messages to the hub.

In the system unicast and multicast process-to-process writes have a latency of 5.2 μs, with per-link transfer bandwidths of 30 MB/s. Memory chan-

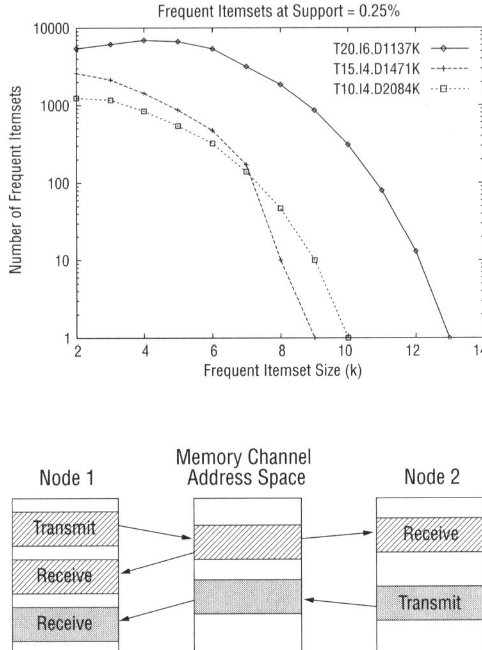

Figure 13.17: (a) number of frequent itemsets (top), (b) The memory channel space (bottom).

nel peak aggregate bandwidth is also about 32 MB/s. Memory channel guarantees write ordering and local cache coherence. Two writes issued to the same transmit region (even on different nodes) will appear in the same order in every receive region. When a write appears in a receive region it invalidates any locally cached copies of its line.

Synthetic databases: All the partitioned databases reside on the local disks of each processor. I used different synthetic databases that have been used as benchmark databases for many association rules algorithms (Agrawal, Imielinski, and Swami 1993b; Agrawal, Mannila, Srikant, Toivonen, and Verkamo 1996; Brin, Motwani, Ullman, and Tsur 1997; Houtsma and Swami 1995; Lin and Kedem 1998; Lin and Dunham 1998; Park, Chen, and Yu 1995a; Savasere, Omiecinski, and Navathe 1995; Zaki, Parthasarathy, Ogihara, and Li 1997a). The dataset generation procedure is described by Agrawal, Mannila, Srikant, Toivonen, and Verkamo (1996), and the code is publicly available from IBM[1].

[1] Quest Data Mining Project, IBM Almaden Research Center, San Jose, California USA 95120 (www.almaden.ibm.com/cs/quest/syndata.html)

Database	T	I	$\mathcal{D}_1$	$\mathcal{D}_1$ Size	$\mathcal{D}_4$	$\mathcal{D}_4$ Size	$\mathcal{D}_6$ Size
T10.I4.D2084K	10	4	2,084,000	91 MB	8,336,000	364MB	546MB
T15.I4.D1471K	15	4	1,471,000	93 MB	5,884,000	372MB	558MB
T20.I6.D1137K	20	6	1,137,000	92 MB	4,548,000	368MB	552MB

Table 13.1: Database properties.

These datasets mimic the transactions in a retailing environment, where people tend to buy sets of items together, the so called potential maximal frequent set. The size of the maximal elements is clustered around a mean, with a few long itemsets. A transaction may contain one or more of such frequent sets. The transaction size is also clustered around a mean, but a few of them may contain many items.

Let D denote the number of transactions, T the average transaction size, I the size of a maximal potentially frequent itemset, L the number of maximal potentially frequent itemsets, and N the number of items. The data is generated using the following procedure. I first generate L maximal itemsets of average size I, by choosing from the N items. I next generate D transactions of average size T by choosing from the L maximal itemsets. I refer the reader to Agrawal and Srikant (1994) for more detail on the database generation.

Table 13.1 shows the databases used and their properties. The number of transactions is denoted as $\mathcal{D}_r$, where r is the replication factor. Using a replication factor allows us to keep the number of frequent itemsets the same for a given minimum support, but it allows us to study larger databases. For $r = 1$, all the databases are roughly 90MB in size. Except for the sizeup experiments, all results shown are on databases with a replication factor of $r = 4$ ($\approx$360MB). I could not go beyond a replication factor of 6 ($\approx$540MB; used in sizeup experiments) since the repartitioned database would become too large to fit on disk. The average transaction size is denoted as T, and the average maximal potentially frequent itemset size as I. The number of maximal potentially frequent itemsets was $L = 2000$, and the number of items was $N = 1000$. All the experiments were performed with a minimum support value of 0.25%. The number of large itemsets discovered are shown in figure 13.17. For a fair comparison, all algorithms discover frequent k-itemsets for $k \geq 3$, using the supports for the 2-itemsets from the preprocessing step.

13.7.1 Performance Comparison

In this section I will compare the performance of the new algorithms with count distribution (henceforth referred to as CD), which was shown to be superior to both Data and candidate distribution (Agrawal and Shafer 1996). In all the figures the different parallel configurations are represented as $Hx.Py$.

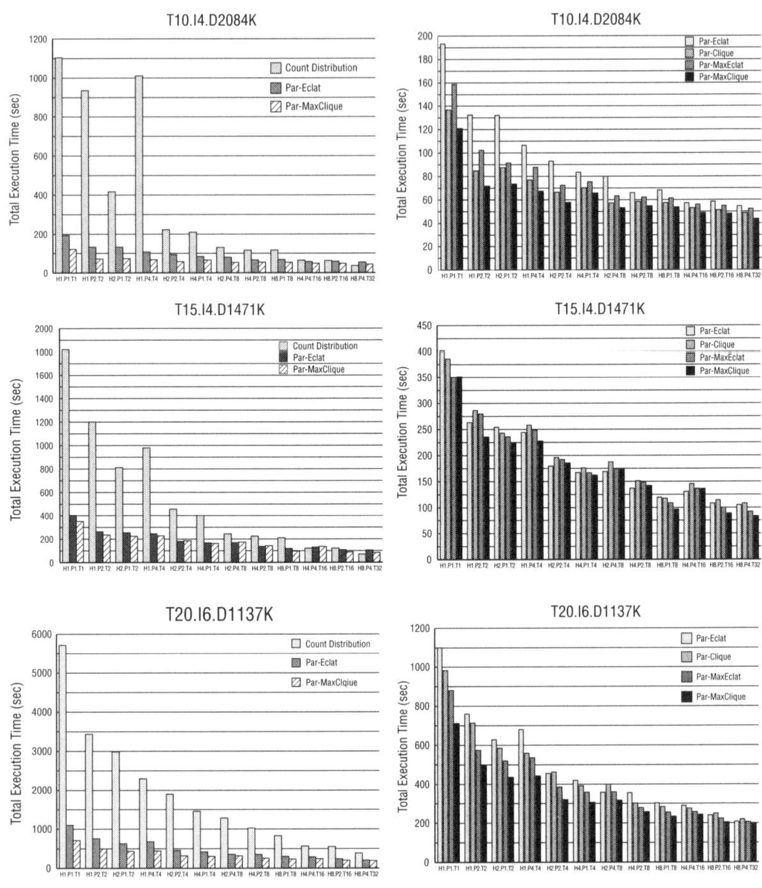

Figure 13.18: Parallel performance.

Tz, where $H = x$ denotes the number of hosts, $P = y$ the number of processors per host, and $T = H \cdot P = z$, the total number of processors used in the experiments. Figure 13.18 shows the total execution time for the different databases and on different parallel configurations. The configurations have been arranged in increasing order of T. Configurations with the same T are arranged in increasing order of H. The left column compares par-MaxClique, the best new algorithm, with par-Eclat and CD, while the right column compares only the new algorithms, so that the differences among them become more apparent. It can be clearly seen that par-Eclat out-performs CD for almost all configurations on all the databases, with improvements as high as a factor of 5. If we compare with the best new algorithm par-MaxClique, we

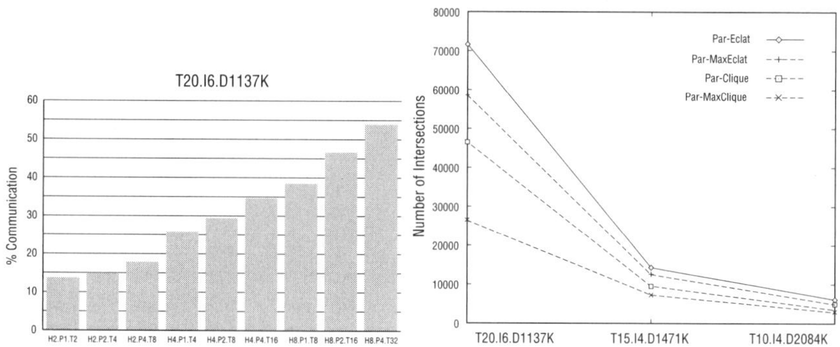

Figure 13.19: (a) Communication cost, (b) number of intersections.

see an improvement of upto an order of magnitude over CD. Even more dramatic improvements are possible for lower values of minimum support (Zaki, Parthasarathy, and Li 1997c). An interesting trend in the figures is that the performance gap seems to decrease at larger configurations, with CD actually performing better on the 32 processor configuration H8.P4.T32 for the databases T10.I4.D2084K and T15.I4.D1471K. To see why, consider figure 13.17, which shows the total number of frequent itemsets of different sizes for the different databases. Also from figure 13.19, which shows the initial database repartitioning and tid-list communication cost as a percentage of the total execution time of *par-Eclat*, it becomes clear that there is not enough work for these two databases to sufficiently offset the communication cost, consequently more than 70% of the time is spent in the initialization phase. For T20.I6.D1137K, which has more work, par-Eclat is still about twice as fast as CD on 32 processors. The basic argument falls on the computation versus communication trade-off in parallel computing. Whenever this ratio is high I would expect par Eclat to out perform CD. I would also expect the relative improvements of par-Eclat over CD to be better for larger databases. Unfortunately due to disk space constraints I was not able to test the algorithms on larger databases. In all except the $H = 1$ configurations, the local database partition is less than available memory. Thus for CD the entire database is cached after the first scan. The performance of CD is thus a best case scenario for it since the results do not include the "real" hit CD would have taken from multiple disk scans. As mentioned in section 13.6, par-Eclat was designed to scan the database only once during frequent itemset computation, and would thus benefit more with larger database size.

Figure 13.18 (right column) shows the differences among the new algorithms for different databases and parallel configurations. There are several parameters affecting their performance. It can be seen that in general par-

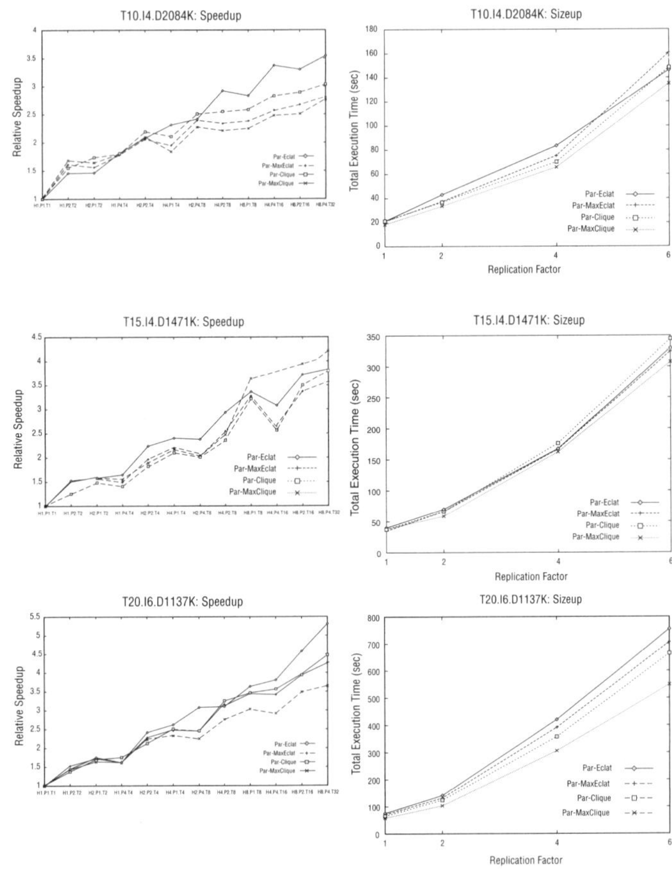

Figure 13.20: Parallel speedup and sizeup (H4.P1.T4).

Clique and par-MaxClique perform better than par-Eclat and par-MaxEclat, respectively. This is because they use the maximal-clique-based decomposition, which generates more precise classes. On the other axis, in general par-MaxClique and par-MaxEclat, out-perform par-Clique and par-Eclat, respectively. This is because the hybrid lattice search scheme quickly generates the long maximal frequent itemsets, saving on the number of intersections. The results are also dependent on the number of frequent itemsets. The larger the number of frequent itemsets, the more the opportunity for the hybrid approach to save on the joins. For example, consider figure 13.19, which shows the total number of tid-list intersections performed for the four algorithms on the three databases. For T20.I6.D1137K, which has the largest number of frequent itemsets (see figure 13.17), par-MaxClique cuts down the number of intersections by more than 60% over par-Eclat. The reduction was about 20% for par-MaxEclat, and 35% for par-Clique. These factors are responsible for the trends indicated above. The winner in terms of the total execution time is clearly par-MaxClique, with improvements over par-Eclat as high as 40%.

13.7.2 Sensitivity Analysis

Speedup: The goal of the speedup experiments is to see how the new algorithms perform as the number of processors is increased while keeping the data size constant. Figure 13.20, shows the speedup on the different databases and parallel configurations. Due to disk constraints I used a replication factor of 4, for database sizes of approximately 360MB. The speedup numbers are not as impressive at first glance. However, this is not surprising. For example, on the largest configuration H8.P4.T32, there is only about 11MB of data per processor. Combined with the fact that the amount of computation is quite small (see figure 13.17), and that about 50% to 70% of the time is spent in tid-list communication (see figure 13.19), we see a maximum speedup of about 5. Another reason is that the communication involves only the 8 hosts. Additional processes on a host are only spawned after the initialization phase, which thus represents a partially-parallel phase, limiting the speedups. If we take out the communication costs we see a maximum speedup of 12 to 16. An interesting trend is the step-effect seen in the speedup graphs. For the configurations which have the same number of total processors, the ones with more hosts perform better. Also, for configurations with more total processors, with $P = 4$, the configurations immediate preceding it, with only 1 processor per host, performs better. In both cases, the reason is that increasing the number of processors on a given host, causes increased memory contention (bus traffic), and increased disk contention, as each processor tries to access the database from the local disk at the same time.

Sizeup: The goal of the sizeup experiments is to see how the new algorithms perform as we increase the size of the database while keeping the number of processors constant. For the sizeup experiments I fixed the parallel configuration to H4.P1.T4, and varied the database replication factor from 1 to 6, with the total database size ranging from about 90MB to 540MB. Figure 13.20 shows the sizeup for the four algorithms on the different databases. The figures indicate an almost linear sizeup. The slightly upward bend is due to the relative computation versus communication cost. The larger the database the more the time spent in communication, while the tid-list intersection cost doesn't increase at the same pace. Moreover, the number of frequent itemsets remains constant (since we use percentages for minimum support, as opposed to absolute counts) for all replication factors.

13.8 Conclusions

In this chapter I presented new parallel algorithms for efficient enumeration of frequent itemsets. I presented a lattice-theoretic approach to partition the frequent itemset search space into small, independent subspaces using either prefix-based or maximal-clique-based methods. Each subproblem can be solved in main-memory using bottom-up, top-down, or a hybrid search procedure, and the entire process usually takes only a few database scans.

The set of independent classes is scheduled among the processors, and the database is also selectively replicated so that the portion of the database needed for the computation of associations is local to each processor. After the initial set-up phase the algorithms do not need any further communication or synchronization. The algorithms minimize I/O overheads by scanning the local database portion only two times. Once in the set-up phase, and once when processing all the itemset classes. I implemented the algorithms on a 32 processor Digital cluster interconnected with the memory channel network, and compared them against a well known parallel algorithm count distribution (Agrawal and Shafer 1996). Experimental results indicate that our best parallel algorithm *Par-MaxClique* outperformed *Count Distribution* by upto an order of magnitude.

Chapter 14

Parallel Classification on Shared-Memory Systems

Mohammed J. Zaki, Ching-Tien Ho, and Rakesh Agrawal

14.1 Introduction

An important task of data mining can be thought of as the process of assigning things to predefined categories or classes—a process called *classification*. Since the classes are predefined this is also known as *supervised induction*. The input for the classification system consists of a set of example records, called a *training set*, where each record consists of several fields or *attributes*. Attributes are either *continuous*, coming from an ordered domain, or *categorical*, coming from an unordered domain. One of the attributes, called the *classifying* attribute, indicates the *class* or label to which each example belongs. The induced model consists of patterns that are useful in class discrimination. Once induced, the model can help in the automatic prediction of new unclassified data. Classification has been identified as an important problem in the emerging field of data mining (Agrawal, Imielinski, and Swami 1993a). It has important applications in diverse domains like retail target marketing, customer retention, fraud detection and medical diagnosis (Michie, Spiegelhalter, and Taylor 1994).

Classification is a well-studied problem (see Weiss and Kulikowski [1991] and Michie, Spiegelhalter, and Taylor [1994] for excellent overviews) and several models have been proposed over the years, including neural networks (Lippmann 1987), statistical models like linear/quadratic discriminants (James 1985), decision trees (Breiman, Friedman, Olshen, and Stone 1984; Quinlan 1993) and genetic algorithms (Goldberg 1989). Among these models, decision trees are particularly suited for data mining (Agrawal, Imielinski, and Swami 1993a; Mehta, Agrawal, and Rissanen 1996). Decision trees can be constructed relatively fast compared to other methods. Another advantage is that decision tree models are simple and easy to understand (Quinlan 1993). Moreover, trees can be easily converted into SQL statements that can be used to access databases efficiently (Agrawal, Ghosh, Imielinski, Lyer, and Swami 1992). Finally, decision tree classifiers obtain similar, and sometimes better, accuracy when compared with other classification methods (Michie, Spiegelhalter, and Taylor 1994). We have therefore focused on building scalable and parallel decision-tree classifiers.

While there has been a lot of research in classification in the past, the focus had been on memory-resident data, thus limiting their suitability for mining over large databases. Recent work has targeted the massive databases usual in data mining. Classifying larger datasets can enable the development of higher accuracy models. Various studies have confirmed this hypothesis (Catlett 1991; Chan and Stolfo 1993). Examples of fast scalable classification systems include SLIQ (Mehta, Agrawal, and Rissanen 1996), which for the first time was successful in handling disk-resident data. However, it did require some hashing information to be maintained in memory, restricting its scalability. The SPRINT (Shafer, Agrawal, and Mehta 1996) classifier was able to remove all such restrictions. It was also parallelized on the IBM SP2 distributed-memory machine (Shafer, Agrawal, and Mehta 1996).

A continuing trend in data mining is the rapid and inexorable growth in the data that is being collected. The development of high-performance scalable data mining tools must necessarily rely on parallel computing techniques. Past work on parallel classification has utilized distributed-memory parallel machines. In such a machine, each processor has private memory and local disks, and communicates with other processors only via passing messages. Parallel distributed-memory machines are essential for scalable massive parallelism. However, shared-memory multiprocessor systems (SMPs), often called shared-everything systems, are also capable of delivering high performance for low to medium degree of parallelism at an economically attractive price. SMP machines are the dominant types of parallel machines currently used in industry. Individual nodes of parallel distributed-memory machines are also increasingly being designed to be SMP nodes. For example, an IBM SP2 parallel system may consist of up to 64 *high nodes*, where each high node is an 8-way SMP system with PowerPC 604e processors[1]. A shared-memory system offers a single memory address space that all processors can access. Processors communicate through shared variables in memory and are capable of accessing any memory location. Synchronization is used to co-ordinate processes. Any processor can also access any disk attached to the system.

This chapter presents fast scalable decision-tree-based classification algorithms targeting shared-memory systems, the first such study. The algorithms are based on the sequential SPRINT classifier, and span the gamut of data and task parallelism. The data parallelism is based on attribute scheduling among processors. This is extended with task pipelining and dynamic load balancing to yield more complex schemes. The task parallel approach uses dynamic subtree partitioning among processors. These algorithms are evaluated on two SMP configurations: one in which data is too large to fit in memory and must be paged from a local disk as needed and the other in which memory is sufficiently large to hold the whole input data and all temporary files. For the local disk configuration, the speedup ranged from 2.97 to 3.86 for the build phase and from 2.20 to 3.67 for the total time on a 4-processor SMP. For the large memory configuration, the range of speedup was from 5.36 to 6.67 for the build phase and from 3.07 to 5.98 for the total time on an 8-processor SMP.

The rest of the chapter is organized as follows. We review related work in section 14.2. In section 14.3 we describe the sequential SPRINT decision-tree classifier, which forms the backbone of the new algorithms. This section is adapted from Shafer, Agrawal, and Mehta (1996). Section 14.4 describes our new SMP algorithms based on various data and task parallelization schemes. We give experimental results in section 14.5 and conclude with a summary in section 14.6.

14.2 Related Work

Random sampling is often used to handle large datasets when building a classifier. Previous work on building tree-classifiers from large datasets includes Catlett's study of two methods (Catlett 1991; Wirth and Catlett 1988) for improving the time taken to develop a classifier. The first method used data sampling at each node of the decision tree, and the second discretized continuous attributes. However, Catlett only considered datasets that could fit in memory; the largest training data had only 32,000 examples. Chan and Stolfo (1993)

[1] See www.rs6000.ibm.com/hardware/largescale/index.html

considered partitioning the data into subsets that fit in memory and then developing a classifier on each subset in parallel. The output of multiple classifiers is combined using various algorithms to reach the final classification. Their studies showed that although this approach reduces running time significantly, the multiple classifiers did not achieve the accuracy of a single classifier built using all the data. Incremental learning methods, where the data is classified in batches, have also been studied (Quinlan 1979; Wirth and Catlett 1988). However, the cumulative cost of classifying data incrementally can sometimes exceed the cost of classifying the entire training set once. In Agrawal, Ghosh, Imielinski, Lyer, and Swami (1992), a classifier built with database considerations, the size of the training set was overlooked. Instead, the focus was on building a classifier that could use database indices to improve the retrieval efficiency while classifying test data.

Work by Fifield (1992) examined parallelizing the ID3 (Quinlan 1986) decision-tree classifier, but it assumes that the entire dataset can fit in memory and does not address issues such as disk I/O. The algorithms presented there also require processor communication to evaluate any given split point, limiting the number of possible partitioning schemes the algorithms can efficiently consider for each leaf. The Darwin toolkit from Thinking Machines also contained a parallel implementation of the decision-tree classifier CART (Breiman, Friedman, Olshen, and Stone 1984); however, details of this parallelization are not available in published literature.

The recently proposed SLIQ classification algorithm (Mehta, Agrawal, and Rissanen 1996) addressed several issues in building a fast scalable classifier. SLIQ gracefully handles disk-resident data that is too large to fit in memory. It does not use small memory-sized datasets obtained via sampling or partitioning, but builds a single decision tree using the *entire* training set. However, SLIQ does require that some data per record stay memory-resident all the time. Since the size of this in-memory data structure grows in direct proportion to the number of input records, this limits the amount of data that can be classified by SLIQ. Its successor, the SPRINT classifier (Shafer, Agrawal, and Mehta 1996) removed all memory restrictions and was fast and scalable. It was also parallelized on the IBM SP2 distributed-memory system. ScalParC (Joshi, Karypis, and Kumar 1998) is also a parallel classifier for the Cray T3D distributed-memory machine. Other recent work on scalable classification includes CLOUDS (Alsabti, Ranka, and Singh 1998) and its distributed-memory parallelization pCLOUDS (Sreenivas, Alsabti, and Ranka 1999), PUBLIC (Rastogi and Shim 1998), and Rainforest (Gehrke, Ramakrishnan, and Ganti 1998).

As noted earlier, our goal in this chapter is to study the efficient implementation of SPRINT on shared-memory systems. These machines represent a popular parallel programming architecture and paradigm, and have very dif-

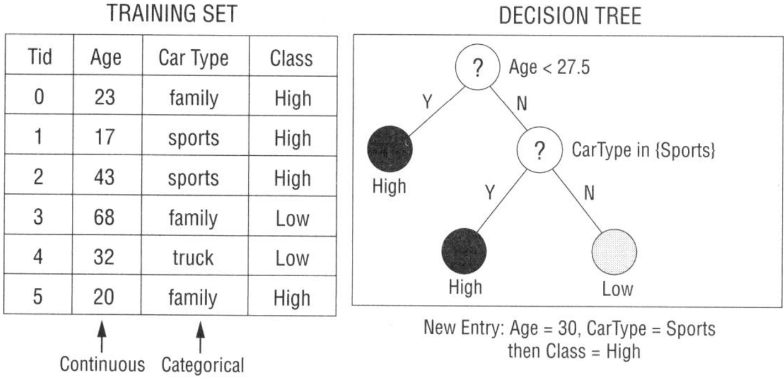
TRAINING SET

Tid	Age	Car Type	Class
0	23	family	High
1	17	sports	High
2	43	sports	High
3	68	family	Low
4	32	truck	Low
5	20	family	High

Figure 14.1: Car insurance example.

ferent characteristics. A shorter version of this chapter appears in Zaki, Ho, and Agrawal (1999a).

14.3 Serial Classification

A decision tree contains tree-structured nodes. Each node is either a *leaf*, indicating a class, or a *decision node*, specifying some test on one or more attributes, with one branch or subtree for each of the possible outcomes of the split test. Decision trees successively divide the set of training examples until all the subsets consist of data belonging entirely, or predominantly, to a single class. Figure 14.1 shows a decision-tree classifier developed from the example training set. $(Age < 27.5)$ and $(CarType \in \{sports\})$ are two split points that partition the records into *high* and *low* risk classes. The decision tree can be used to screen future insurance applicants by classifying them into the high or low risk categories.

A decision tree classifier is usually built in two phases (Breiman, Friedman, Olshen, and Stone 1984; Quinlan 1993): a growth phase and a prune phase. The tree is grown using an elegantly simple divide and conquer approach. It takes as input a set of training examples S. There are basically two cases to be considered. If all examples in S entirely or predominantly (a user specified parameter) belong to a single class, then S becomes a leaf in the tree. If on the other hand it contains a mixture of examples from different classes, we need to further partition the input into subsets that tend towards a single class. The data is partitioned based on a test on the attributes, and can take the form of a binary or k-ary split. We will consider only binary splits because they usually lead to more accurate trees; however, our techniques can be extended to handle multi-way splits. Based on the outcomes, the data is

```
Partition(Data S)
  if (all points in S are of the same class) then
    return;
  for each attribute A do
    evaluate splits on attribute A;
  Use best split found to partition S into S1 and S2;
  Partition(S1);
  Partition(S2);

Initial call: Partition(TrainingData)
```

Figure 14.2: General tree-growth algorithm.

partitioned into two subsets S_1 and S_2, which in turn serve as inputs to the recursive process. This tree growth phase is shown in figure 14.2.

The tree built using the recursive partitioning approach can become very complex, and as such can be thought of as being an "overfit" of the data. Remember that the goal of classification is to predict new unseen cases. The tree pruning phase tries to generalize the tree by removing dependence on statistical noise or variation that may be particular only to the training set. This step requires access only to the fully grown tree, while the tree growth phase usually requires multiple passes over the training data, and as such is much more expensive. Previous studies from SLIQ suggest that usually less than 1% of the total time needed to build a classifier was spent in the pruning phase. In this chapter we will therefore only concentrate on the computation and I/O intensive tree growth phase. We use a minimum description length (Rissanen 1989) based algorithm for the tree pruning phase. (see Mehta, Agrawal, and Rissanen [1996] for additional details). There are two major issues that have critical performance implications in the tree-growth phase. (1) How to find split points that define node tests. (2) Having chosen a split point, how to partition the data. We will first look at the data structures used in SPRINT, and then describe how it handles the two steps above.

14.3.1 Data Structures

The SPRINT classifier was designed to be disk-based. It builds the tree breadth-first and uses a one-time pre-sorting technique to reduce the cost of continuous attribute evaluation. In contrast to this, the well-known CART (Breiman, Friedman, Olshen, and Stone 1984) and C4.5 (Quinlan 1993) classifiers, grow trees depth-first and repeatedly sort the data at every node of the tree to arrive at the best splits for continuous attributes.

Training Set

Tid	Age	Car Type	Class
0	23	family	High
1	17	sports	High
2	43	sports	High
3	68	family	Low
4	32	truck	Low
5	20	family	High

Attribute lists

Age	Class	Tid
17	High	1
20	High	5
23	High	0
32	Low	4
43	High	2
68	Low	3

continuous (sorted)

Car Type	Class	Tid
family	High	0
sports	High	1
sports	High	2
family	Low	3
truck	Low	4
family	High	5

categorical (original order)

Figure 14.3: Attribute lists.

Attribute lists: SPRINT initially creates an disk-based *attribute list* for each attribute in the data. Each entry in the list is called an *attribute record*, and consists of an attribute value, a class label, and a record identifier or *tid*. Initial lists for continuous attributes are sorted by attribute value when first created. The lists for categorical attributes remain in unsorted order. Figure 14.3 shows the initial attribute lists for our example training set. The initial lists created from the training set are associated with the root of the classification tree. As the tree is grown and is split into two subtrees, the attribute lists are also split at the same time. By simply preserving the order of records in the partitioned lists, they don't require resorting. Figure 14.5 shows an example of the initial sorted attribute lists associated with the root of the tree and also the resulting partitioned lists for the two children.

Histograms: SPRINT uses histograms tabulating the class distributions of the input records. For continuous attributes, two histograms are maintained—C_{below} keeps the counts for examples that have already been processed, and C_{above} for those that have not been seen yet. For categorical attributes one histogram, called the *count matrix*, is sufficient for the class distribution of a given attribute. There is one set of histograms for each node in the tree. However, since the attribute lists are processed one after the other, only one set of histograms need be kept in memory at any given time. Example histograms are shown in figure 14.4.

14.3.2 Finding Good Split Points

The form of the split used to partition the data depends on the type of the attribute used in the split. Splits for a continuous attribute A are of the form $value(A) < x$ where x is a value in the domain of A. Splits for a categorical attribute A are of the form $value(A) \in X$ where $X \subset domain(A)$.

To build compact trees modeling the training set, one approach would be

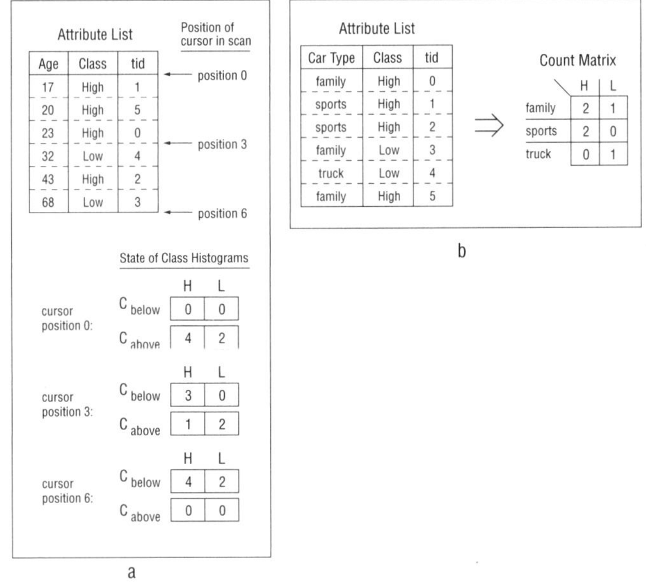

Figure 14.4: Evaluating (a) continuous and (b) categorical split points.

to explore the space of all possible trees and select the best one. This process is unfortunately NP-Complete. Most tree construction methods therefore use a *greedy* approach, the idea being to determine the split point that "best" divides the training records belonging to that leaf. The "goodness" of the split obviously depends on how well it separates the classes. Several splitting indices have been proposed in the past to evaluate the goodness of the split. SPRINT uses the *gini* index (Breiman, Friedman, Olshen, and Stone 1984) for this task. For a data set S containing examples from n classes, $gini(S)$ is defined as

$$gini(S) = 1 - \sum p_j^2$$

where p_j is the relative frequency of class j in S. If a split divides S into two subsets S_1 and S_2, with n_1 and n_2 classes, respectively, the index of the divided data $gini_{split}(S)$ is given by

$$gini_{split}(S) = \frac{n_1}{n} gini(S_1) + \frac{n_2}{n} gini(S_2)$$

The computation of the gini index only requires the class distributions on each side of a candidate partition point. This information is kept in the class histograms described above. Once this information is known, the best split can be found using a simple approach. Each node's attribute lists are scanned, the histograms are updated, and the gini value for different split points is calculated. The attribute with the minimum gini value and the associated split point is used to partition the data.

Continuous attributes: For continuous attributes, the candidate split points are mid-points between every two consecutive attribute values in the training data. Initially C_{below} has all zeros, while C_{above} has the class distributions of the current node under consideration. For each attribute record, the histograms are updated and the gini index is calculated. The current minimum gini value, also called the *winning* split point is saved during this process. Since all the continuous values are sorted one scan over the attribute lists is sufficient. Figure 14.4a illustrates the histogram update for continuous attributes.

Categorical attributes: For categorical attributes, all possible subsets of the attribute values are considered as potential split points. If the cardinality is too large a greedy subsetting algorithm (initially used in IND [NASA Ames Research Center 1992]) is used. The histogram updation is shown in figure 14.4b.

14.3.3 Splitting the Data

Once the winning split point has been found for a node, the node is split into two children, along with the division of the node's attribute lists into two. Figure 14.5 shows this process. The attribute list splitting for the winning attribute (Age in our example) is quite straightforward. We simply scan the attribute records, and apply the split test. Those records satisfying the test go to the left child, and those that fail the test go to the right child. For the remaining "losing" attributes ($CarType$ in our example) more work is needed. While dividing the winning attribute SPRINT also constructs a probe structure (bit mask or hash table) on the *tids*, noting the child where a particular record belongs. To split the other attributes now only requires a scan of each record and a probe to determine the child where this record should be placed. This probe structure need not be memory-resident. If it occupies too much memory the splitting takes multiple steps. In each step only a portion of the attribute lists are partitioned. At the same time the split happens, SPRINT also collects the new class distribution histograms for the children nodes.

Avoiding multiple attribute lists: Recall that the attribute lists of each attribute are stored in disk files. As the tree is split, we would need to create new files for the children, and delete the parent's files. File creation is usually an expensive operation, and this process can add significant overhead. For example, figure 14.6 shows that if we create new files at each level, then if the tree has N levels, we would potentially require 2^N files. Rather than creating a separate attribute list for each attribute for each node, SPRINT actually uses only four physical files per attribute. Since we are dealing with binary splits,

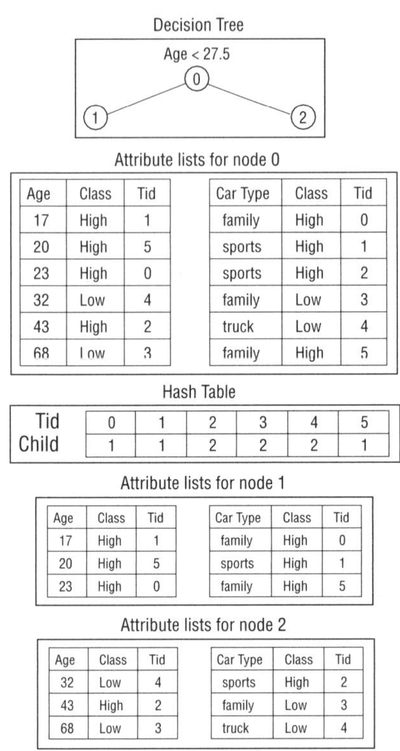

Figure 14.5: Splitting a node's attribute lists.

we have one attribute file for all leaves that are "left" children (file $L0$) and one file for all leaves that are "right" children (file $R0$). We also have two more list files per attribute that serve as alternates (files $L1$ and $R1$). All the attribute records for a node are kept in a contiguous section within one of the two primary files (files $L0$ and $R0$). When reading records for a particular node, we read the corresponding portion of the attribute's left or right file. When splitting a node's attribute records, we append the left and right child's records to the end of the alternate left and right files (files $L1$ and $R1$).

After splitting each node, all the training data will reside in the alternate files. These become the primary files for the next level. The old primary lists are cleared and they become new alternate files. Thus, we never have to pay the penalty of creating new attribute lists for new leaves; we can simply reuse the ones we already have. By processing tree nodes in the order they appear in the attribute files, this approach also avoids any random seeks within a file to find a node's records — reading and writing remain sequential operations.

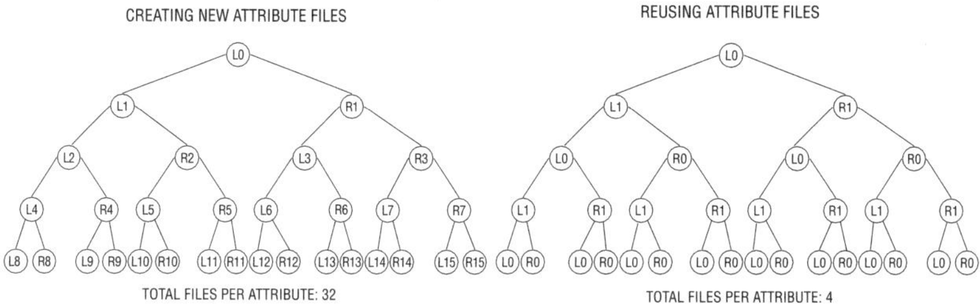

Figure 14.6: Avoiding multiple attribute files.

This optimization can be done with virtually no overhead and with no modifications to the SPRINT algorithm. It also has important implications for the parallelization strategies presented below.

14.4 Parallel Classification on Shared-Memory Systems

We now turn our attention to the problem of building classification trees in parallel on SMP systems. We will only discuss the tree growth phase due to its compute and data-intensive nature. Tree pruning is relatively inexpensive (Mehta, Agrawal, and Rissanen 1996), as it requires access to only the decision-tree grown in the training phase.

14.4.1 SMP Schemes

While building a decision-tree, there are three main steps that must be performed for each node at each level of the tree: (1) Evaluate split points for each attribute (denoted as step $\mathcal{E}$). (2) Find the winning split-point and construct a probe structure using the attribute list of the winning attribute (denoted as step $\mathcal{W}$). (3) Split all the attribute lists into two parts, one for each child, using the probe structure (denoted as step $\mathcal{S}$). Our parallel schemes will be described in terms of these steps. Our prototype implementation of these schemes uses the POSIX threads (pthread) standard (Lewis and Berg 1996). A thread is a light weight process. It is a *schedulable* entity that has only those properties that are required to ensure its independent flow of control, including the stack, scheduling properties, set of pending and blocking signals, and some thread-specific data. To keep the exposition simple, we will not differentiate between threads and processes and pretend as if there is only one process per processor. We propose two approaches to building a tree classifier in parallel: a *data parallel* approach and a *task parallel* approach.

Data parallel: In data parallelism the P processors work on distinct portions of the datasets and synchronously construct the global decision tree. It essentially exploits the intra-node parallelism, i.e. that available within a decision tree node. There are two kinds of data parallelism possible in classification. In the first case, called *attribute parallelism*, the attributes are divided equally among the different processors so that each element is responsible for $1/P$ attributes. In the second case, called *record parallelism*, we split the attribute lists evenly among all the processors. Each processor is responsible for $1/P$ records from each attribute list. The implementation of this scheme on the IBM SP2 was presented by Shafer, Agrawal, and Mehta (1996).

The record parallelism approach doesn't look very promising on an SMP system. Some of the reason are: First, for each continuous attribute, SPRINT sorts the attribute list then partitions the sorted list into P "continuous" sublists of the same size so that each processor has the same amount of work. As the tree grows, different sublists with varying numbers of records are split into a left or right child. When some of these nodes become pure (i.e., contain records belonging to the same class), the work associated with that node disappears. This creates load imbalance, especially when the data distribution is skewed and the tree is large. Performing dynamic load balancing with record data parallelism is quite complex and likely to introduce extra overhead.

Second, for each categorical attribute, its class histogram will have to be replicated on all processors, so that they can independently process their local attribute lists. If there are many categorical attributes or if they have a large domain of possible values, the incurred space overhead can be significant. Without such replication, the synchronization (say, of acquiring and releasing a lock) will have to be done at the record level.

Finally, the entire hash probe will have to be replicated on all processes. Furthermore, at every tree level, the information stored in each bit probe needs to be copied to all other bit probes. Thus, there are associated space and time overheads. Alternatively, if the bit probe is not replicated, then either a single global bit probe has to be lock-protected (due to concurrent writes at the record level) which is unattractive performance-wise, or a complicated scheduling, of when to write to bit probe and by which process, has to be devised to avoid sequential bottleneck. Having said this, we will implement the record parallel approach in the future, to experimentally confirm these points.

In summary, we see that one of the main reasons why record parallelism or a horizontal data partitioning is not good on a SMP, has to do with the fact that we don't want to allow more than one processor to access the same attribute file. Doing so will play havoc with the common bus and will result in disk contention, as more than one process tries to read/write to a different file location at the same time. A vertical partitioning using attribute partitioning eliminates this problem, since each attribute file can be the sole responsibility of a single processor. The other main reason is the replication of data structures needed to implement the record parallelism. On a distributed memory machine each processor gets a local copy of the data structures anyway, but on a SMP all the copies must reside on the same machine, which consumes precious memory resources. This is undesirable. Thus, in this chapter we only deal with the attribute parallelism approach.

Task parallelism: The other major kind of parallelism is provided by the task parallel approach. It exploits the inter-node parallelism, i.e. different portions of the decision tree can be built in parallel among the processors.

14.4.2 Attribute Data Parallelism

We first describe the Moving-Window-K algorithm (MWK) based on attribute data parallelism. For pedagogical reasons, we will introduce two intermediate schemes called BASIC and Fixed-Window-K (FWK) and then evolve them to the more sophisticated MWK algorithm. MWK and the two intermediate schemes utilize dynamic attribute scheduling. In a static attribute scheduling, each process gets d/P attributes where d denotes the number of attributes. However, this static partitioning is not particularly suited for classification. Different attributes may have different processing costs because of two reasons. First, there are two kinds of attributes—continuous and categorical, and they use different techniques to arrive at split tests. Second, even for attributes of the same type, the computation depends on the distribution of the record values. For example, the cardinality of the value set of a categorical attribute determines the cost of gini index evaluation. These factors warrant a dynamic attribute scheduling approach.

The Basic Scheme (BASIC)

Figure 14.7 shows the pseudo-code for the BASIC scheme. A barrier represents a point of synchronization. At each level a processor evaluates the assigned attributes, which is followed by a barrier.

Attribute scheduling: Attributes are scheduled dynamically by using an attribute counter and locking. A processor acquires the lock, grabs an attribute, increments the counter, and releases the lock. This method achieves the same effect as self-scheduling (Tang and Yew 1986), i.e., there is lock synchronization per attribute. For typical classification problems with up to a few hundred attributes, this approach works fine. For thousands of attributes self-scheduling can generate too much unnecessary synchronization. The latter can be addressed by using guided self-scheduling (Polychronopoulos and Kuck 1987) or its extensions, where a processor grabs a dynamically shrinking

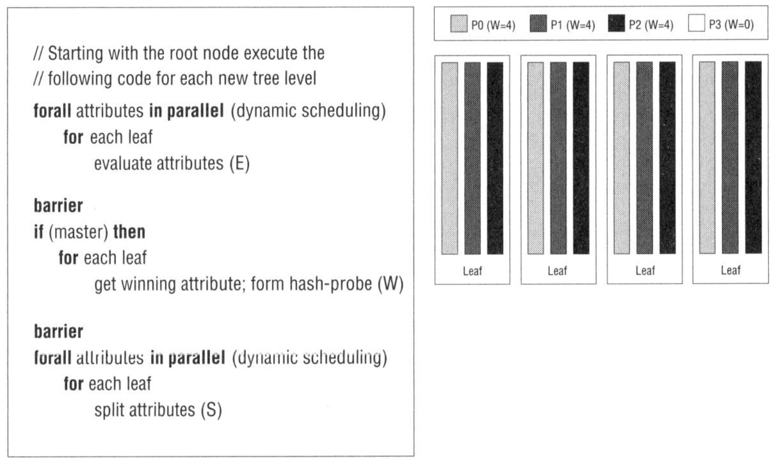

Figure 14.7: The BASIC algorithm (4 processors, 3 attributes).

chunk of remaining attributes, thus minimizing the synchronization. Another possibility would be to use affinity scheduling (Markatos and LeBlanc 1994), where attention is paid to the location of the attribute lists so that accesses to local attribute lists are maximized.

Finding split points ($\mathcal{E}$): Since each attribute has its own set of four reusable attribute files, as long as no two processors work on the same attribute at the same time, there is no need for file access synchronization. To minimize barrier synchronization the tree is built in a breadth-first manner. The advantage is that once a processor has been assigned an attribute, it can evaluate the split points for that attribute for all the leaves in the current level. This way, each attribute list is accessed only once sequentially during the evaluation for a level. Once all attributes have been processed in this fashion, a single barrier ensures that all processors have reached the end of the attribute evaluation phase. In contrast, depth-first tree growth would require a barrier synchronization once per leaf, which could become a significant source of overhead in large trees. As each processor works independently on the entire attribute list, it can independently carry out gini index evaluation to determine the best split point for each attribute assigned to it.

Hash probe construction ($\mathcal{W}$): Once all the attributes of a leaf have been processed, each processor will have what it considers to be the best split for that leaf. We now need to find the best split point from among each processor's locally best split. We can then proceed to scan the winning attribute's records and form the hash probe.

The breadth-first tree construction imposes some constraints on the hash probe construction. We could keep separate hash tables for each leaf. If there is insufficient memory to hold these hash tables in memory, they would have to be written to disk. The size of each leaf's hash table can be reduced by keeping only the smaller child's *tids*, since the other records must necessarily belong to the other child. Another option is to maintain a global bit probe for all the current leaves. It has as many bits as there are tuples in the training set. As the records for each leaf's winning attribute are processed, the corresponding bit is set to reflect whether the record should be written to a *left* or *right* file. A third approach is to maintain an index of valid *tids* of a leaf, and relabel them starting from zero. Then each leaf can keep a separate bit probe.

BASIC uses the second approach, that maintains a global bit vector, due to its simplicity. Both the tasks of finding the minimum split value and bit probe construction are performed serially by a pre-designated master processor. This step thus represents a potential bottleneck in this BASIC scheme, which we will eliminate later in MWK. During the time the master computes the hash probe, the other processors enter a barrier and go to sleep. Once the master finishes, it also enters the barrier and wakes up the sleeping processors, setting the stage for the splitting phase.

Attribute list splitting ($\mathcal{S}$): The attribute list splitting phase proceeds in the same manner as the evaluation. A processor dynamically grabs an attribute, scans its records, hashes on the *tid* for the child node, and performs the split. Since the files for each attribute are distinct there is no read/write conflict among the different processors.

Figure 14.7 shows a small example of how BASIC works. In the example there are four processors and three attributes per leaf. There are four leaves in the current level. Assuming equal work for all attributes, there is always one processor that is idle at each leaf. The figure shows one worst case where the first three processors get $W = 4$ units of work each counting a leaf as one unit, while the last processor has no work to do. This example illustrates the limitation of the BASIC scheme.

The Fixed-Window-K Scheme (FWK)

We noted above that the winning attribute hash probe construction phase $\mathcal{W}$ in BASIC is a potential sequential bottleneck. The Fixed-Window-K (FWK) scheme shown in figure 14.8 addresses this problem. The basic idea is to overlap the $\mathcal{W}$-phase with the $\mathcal{E}$-phase of the next leaf at the current level, a technique called *task pipelining*. The degree of overlap can be controlled by a parameter K denoting the window of current overlapped leaves. Let $\mathcal{E}_i$, $\mathcal{W}_i$, and $\mathcal{S}_i$ denote the evaluation, winning hash construction, and partition steps for leaf i at a given level. Then for $K = 2$, we get the overlap of $\mathcal{W}_0$ with $\mathcal{E}_1$. For $K = 3$, we get an overlap of $\mathcal{W}_0$ with $\{\mathcal{E}_1, \mathcal{E}_2\}$, and an overlap of $\mathcal{W}_1$ with

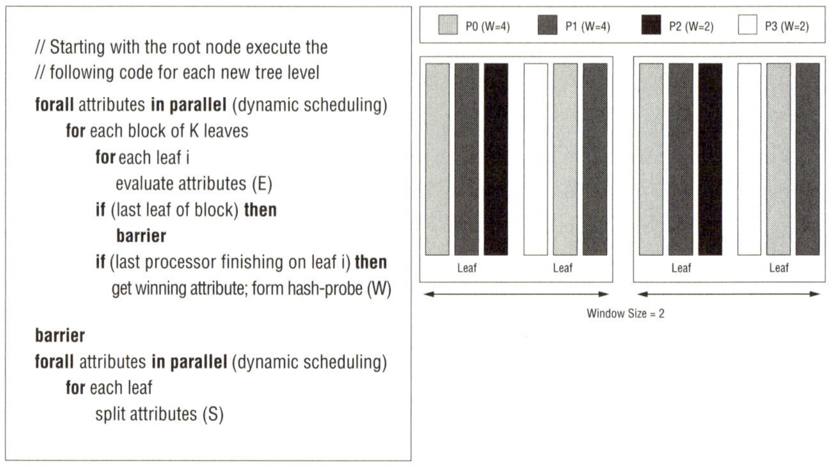

Figure 14.8: The FWK algorithm (4 processors, 3 attributes).

$\mathcal{E}_2$. For a general K, we get an overlap of $\mathcal{W}_i$ with $\{\mathcal{E}_{i+1}, \cdots, \mathcal{E}_{K-1}\}$, for all $1 \leq i \leq K - 1$.

The attribute scheduling, split finding, and partitioning remain the same. The difference is that depending on the window size K, we group K leaves together. For each leaf within the K-block (i.e., K leaves of the same group), we first evaluate all attributes. At the last leaf in each block we perform a barrier synchronization to ensure that all evaluations for the current block have completed. The hash probe for a leaf is constructed by the last processor to exit the evaluation for that leaf. This ensures that no two processors access the hash probe at the same time.

Managing attribute files: There are four reusable files per attribute in the BASIC scheme. However, if we are to allow overlapping of the hash probe construction step with the evaluation step, which uses dynamic attribute scheduling within each leaf, we would require K distinct files for the current level, and K files for the parent's attribute lists, that is $2K$ files per attribute. This way all K leaves in a group have separate files for each attribute and there is no read/write conflict. Another complication arises from the fact that some children may turn out to be pure (i.e., all records belong to the same class) at the next level. Since these children will not be processed after the next stage, we have to be careful in the file assignment for these children. A simple file assignment, without considering the child purity, where children are assigned files from $0, \cdots, K - 1$, will not work well, as it may introduce "holes" in the schedule (see figure 14.9). However, if we knew the pure children of the next level, we can do better.

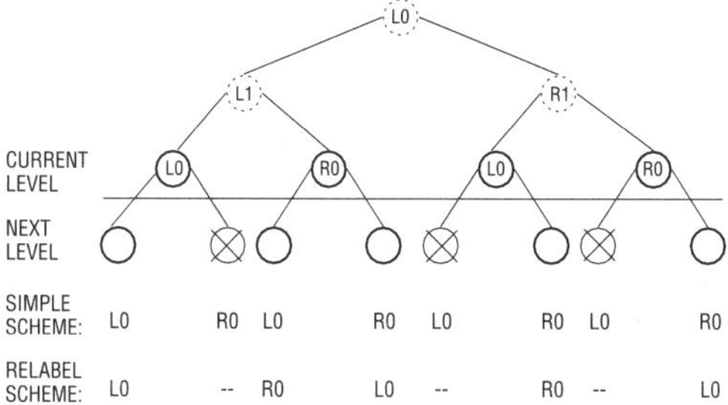

Figure 14.9: Scheduling attribute files.

The class histograms gathered while splitting the children are adequate to determine purity. We add a pre-test for child purity at this stage. If the child will become pure at the next level, it is removed from the list of valid children, and the files are assigned consecutively among the remaining children. This insures that there are no holes in the K block, and we get perfect scheduling. The two approaches are contrasted in figure 14.9. The bold circles show the valid children for the current and next level. With the simple labeling scheme the file labels for the valid children are $L0$, $L0$, $R0$, $R0$, $R0$. With a window of size $K = 2$, there is only one instance where work can overlap, i.e., when going from $L0$ to $R0$. However, if we relabel the valid children's files then we obtain the perfectly schedulable sequence $L0$, $R0$, $L0$, $R0$, $L0$.

Note that the overlapping of work is achieved at the cost of increased barrier synchronization, one per each K-block. A large window size not only increases the overlap but also minimizes the number of synchronizations. However, a larger window size requires more temporary files, which incurs greater file creation overhead and tends to have less locality. The ideal window size is a trade-off between the above conflicting goals.

Figurc 14.8 shows an illustration of thc algorithm. With a window size of two we count the attributes in two leaves as a single block. The example shows a possible assignment of work with round-robin scheduling (i.e., assuming all leaves have equal work) of attributes within a block. FWK is clearly an improvement over BASIC. We have two processors that have 4 units of work and two that have 2 units of work. No processor is completely idle as in BASIC.

The Moving-Window-K Algorithm (MWK)

We now describe the Moving-Window-K (MWK) algorithm which eliminates the serial bottleneck of BASIC and exploits greater parallelism than FWK. Figures 14.10 shows the pseudo-code for MWK.

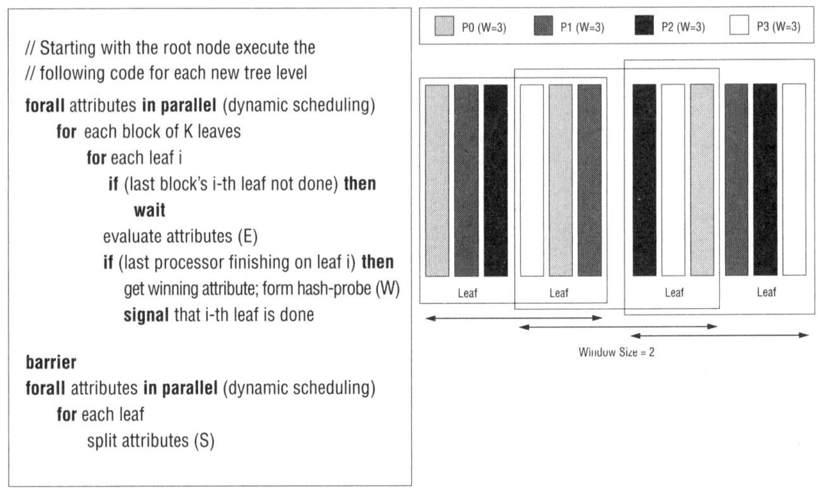

Figure 14.10: The MWK algorithm (4 processors, 3 attributes).

Consider a current leaf frontier: $\{L0_1, R0_1, L0_2, R0_2\}$. With a window size of $K = 2$, not only is there parallelism available for fixed blocks $\{L0_1, R0_1\}$ and $\{L0_2, R0_2\}$ (used in FWK), but also between these two blocks, $\{R0_1, L0_2\}$. The MWK algorithm makes use of this additional parallelism.

This scheme is implemented by replacing the barrier per block of K leaves with a wait on a *conditional variable*. Before evaluating leaf i, a check is made whether the i-th leaf of the previous block has been processed. If not, the processor goes to sleep on the conditional variable. Otherwise, it proceeds with the current leaf. The last processor to finish the evaluation of leaf i from the previous block constructs the hash probe, and then signals the conditional variable, so that any sleeping processors are woken up.

It should be observed that the gain in available parallelism comes at the cost of increased lock synchronization per leaf (however, there is no barrier anymore). As in the FWK approach, the files are relabeled by eliminating the pure children. A larger K value would increase parallelism, and while the number of synchronizations remain about the same, it will reduce the average waiting time on the conditional variable. Like FWK, this scheme requires $2K$ files per attribute, so that each of the K leaves has separate files for each attribute and there is no read/write conflict.

Figure 14.10 shows an illustration of MWK. With a window size of 2, any two consecutive leaves are treated as a single block of schedulable attributes. The block shifts one leaf to the right each time ultimately encompassing all the leaves. The net effect is that all attributes in that level form one logical block.

With this moving window scheme we see that all processors get equal (three units) amount of work, showing the benefit of MWK over BASIC and FWK.

14.4.3 Task Parallelism— The Subtree Algorithm (SUBTREE)

The data parallel approaches target the parallelism available among the different attributes. On the other hand the task parallel approach is based on the parallelism that exists in different sub-trees. Once the attribute lists are partitioned, each child can be processed in parallel. One implementation of this idea would be to initially assign all the processors to the tree root, and recursively partition the processor sets along with the attribute lists. Once a processor gains control of a subtree, it will work only on that portion of the tree. This approach would work fine if we have a full tree. In general, the decision trees are imbalanced and this static partitioning scheme can suffer from large load imbalances. We therefore use a dynamic subtree task parallelism scheme.

The pseudo-code and illustration for the dynamic SUBTREE algorithm is shown in figure 14.11. To implement dynamic processor assignment to different subtrees, we maintain a queue of currently idle processors, called the *FREE* queue. Initially this queue is empty, and all processors are assigned to the root of the decision tree, and belong to a single group. One processor within the group is made the master (we chose the processor with the smallest identifier as the master). The master is responsible for partitioning the processor set.

At any given point in the algorithm, there may be multiple processor groups working on distinct subtrees. Each group independently executes the following steps once the BASIC algorithm has been applied to the current subtree level. First, the new subtree leaf frontier is constructed. If there are no children remaining, then each processor inserts itself in the *FREE* queue, ensuring mutually exclusive access via locking. If there is more work to be done, then all processors except the master go to sleep on a conditional variable. The group master checks if there are any new arrivals in the *FREE* queue and grabs all free processors in the queue. This forms the new processor set.

There are three possible cases at this juncture. If there is only one leaf remaining, then all processors are assigned to that leaf. If there is only one processor in the previous group and there is no processor in the *FREE* queue, then it forms a group on its own and works on the current leaf frontier. Lastly, if there are multiple leaves and multiple processors, the group master splits the processor set and the leaves into two parts. The two newly formed processor sets become the new groups, and work on the corresponding leaf sets.

Finally, the master wakes up the all the relevant processors—those in the original group and those acquired from the *FREE* queue. Since there are *P*

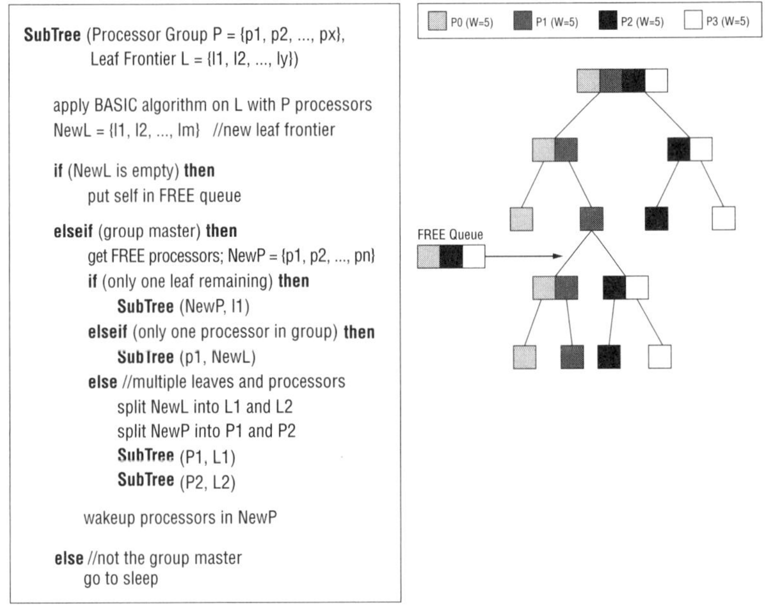

Figure 14.11: The SUBTREE algorithm (4 processors).

processors, there can be at most P groups, and since the attribute files for all of these must be distinct, this scheme requires up to $4P$ files per attribute.

Figure 14.11 shows how the algorithm works. We have four processors all of which are initially assigned to the root node. At the next level $P0$ and $P1$ work on the left child and the other two on the right. At the subsequent level each processor works independently on one portion of the emerging dynamic decision tree. In our example only $P1$'s subtree survives, and the remaining subtrees (actually leaves) turn out to be pure. Thus $P0$, $P2$, and $P3$ insert themselves into the *FREE* queue. When $P1$ expands the leaf to the next level there are two children. $P1$ checks the queue and grabs all idle processors. Thus there are now four available processors and two new leaves. $P0$ and $P1$ work on the left child and $P2$ and $P3$ work on the right. Finally at the next level all leaves turn out to be pure and the computation ends. This example illustrates how we achieve dynamic processor group assignments of good load-balance. As we can see each processor ends up working on an equal number of leaves ($W = 5$).

14.4.4 Discussion

We now qualitatively discuss the relative merits of each of the proposed algorithms. The MWK scheme eliminates the hash-probe construction bottleneck of BASIC via task pipelining. Furthermore, it fully exploits the available parallelism via the moving window mechanism, instead of using the fixed window approach of FWK. It also eliminates barrier synchronization completely. However, it introduces a lock synchronization per leaf per level. If the tree is bushy, then the increased synchronization could nullify the other benefits. A feature of MWK and FWK is that they exploit parallelism at a finer grain. The attributes in a K-block may be scheduled dynamically on any processor. This can have the effect of better load balancing compared to the coarser grained BASIC approach where a processor works on all the leaves for a given attribute. While MWK is essentially a data parallel approach, it utilizes some elements of task parallelism in the pipelining of the evaluation and hash probe construction stages.

The SUBTREE approach is also a hybrid approach in that it uses the BASIC scheme within each group. In fact we can also use FWK or MWK as the subroutine. The pros of SUBTREE are that it has only one barrier synchronization per level within each group and it has good processor utilization. As soon as a processor becomes idle it is likely to be grabbed by some active group. Some of the cons are that it is sensitive to the tree structure and may lead to excessive synchronization for the *FREE* queue, due to rapidly changing groups. Another disadvantage is that it requires more memory, because we need a separate hash probe per group.

As described above, our SMP algorithms ostensibly can create a large number of temporary files ($2Kd$ for MWK and $4dP$ for SUBTREE). However, it is possible to have a little more complex design so that lists for different attributes are combined into the same physical file. Such a design will reduce the number of temporary files to $2K$ for MWK and $4P$ for SUBTREE. The essential idea is to associate physical files for writing attribute lists with a processor (rather than with an attribute). In the split phase, a processor now writes all attribute lists to the same two physical files (for the left and right children). Additional bookkeeping data structures keep track of the start and end of different attribute lists in the file. These data structures are shared at the next tree level by all processors to locate the input attribute list for each dynamically assigned attribute. Note that this scheme does not incur additional synchronization overhead because a processor starts processing a new attribute list only after completely processing the one on hand.

Machine Name	Number Processors	Main Memory	Disk Space Available	Access Type	Operating System
Machine A	4	128 MB	300 MB	local disk	AIX 4.1.4
Machine B	8	1 GB	2 GB	main-memory(cached)	AIX 4.1.5

Table 14.1: Machine configurations.

14.5 Experimental Results

The primary metric for evaluating classifier performance is *classification accuracy* — the percentage of *test* examples (different from training examples used for building the classifier) that are correctly classified. The other important metrics are time to build the classifier and the *size* of the decision tree. The ideal goal for a decision tree classifier is to produce compact, accurate trees in a short time.

The accuracy and tree size characteristics of our SMP classifier are identical to SLIQ and SPRINT since they consider the same splits and use the same pruning algorithm. SLIQ's accuracy, execution time, and tree size have been compared with other classifiers such as CART (Breiman, Friedman, Olshen, and Stone 1984) and C4 (a predecessor of C4.5 [Quinlan 1993]). This performance evaluation, presented by Mehta, Agrawal, and Rissanen (1996), shows that compared to other classifiers SLIQ achieves comparable or better classification accuracy, but produces small decision trees and has small execution times. We, therefore, focus only on the classifier build time in our performance evaluation.

14.5.1 Experimental Setup

Machine configuration: Experiments were performed on two SMP machines with different configurations shown in table 14.1. On both machines, each processor is a PowerPC-604 processor running at 112 MHz with a 16 KB instruction cache, a 16 KB data cache, and a 1 MB L2-Cache. These two machines represent two possible scenarios. With Machine A, the amount of memory is insufficient for training data, temporary files, and data structures to fit in memory. Therefore, the data will have to be read from and written to the disk for almost every new level of the tree. Machine B has a large memory relative to the size of the data. Therefore, all the temporary files created during the run are cached in memory. The first case is of greater interest to the database community and we present a detailed set of experiments for this configuration. However, due to the decreasing cost of RAM, the second configuration is also increasingly realizable in practice. We present this case to study the impact of large memories on the performance of our algorithms.

Function 2 (F2) - Group A:
$((age < 40) \wedge (50K \leq salary \leq 100K)) \vee$
$((40 \leq age < 60) \wedge (75K \leq salary \geq 125K)) \vee$
$((age \geq 60) \wedge (25K \leq salary \leq 75K))$

Function 7 (F7) - Group A:
$disposable > 0$
$where\ disposable = (0.67 \times (salary + commission)) - (0.2 \times loan - 20K)$

Figure 14.12: Classification functions for synthetic data.

Datasets: An often used classification benchmark is STATLOG (Michie, Spiegelhalter, and Taylor 1994). Its largest dataset contains about 57,000 records. In our performance study we are interested in evaluating the SMP algorithms on large out-of-core data. We therefore use the synthetic benchmark proposed by Agrawal, Ghosh, Imielinski, Lyer, and Swami (1992) and used in several past studies. Example tuples in this benchmark have both continuous and categorical attributes. The benchmark gives several classification functions of varying complexity to generate synthetic databases. We present results for two of these functions, which are at the two ends of the complexity spectrum. Function 2 is a simple function to learn and results in fairly small decision trees, while Function 7 is the most complex function and produces large trees (see table 14.2). Both these functions divide the database into two classes: group A and group B. Figure 14.12 shows the predicates for group A for each function. For each of Functions 2 and 7, we try 3 different databases: 8 attributes with 1 million records, 32 attributes with 250K records, and 64 attributes with 125K records. The database parameters are shown in table 14.2. The notation Fx-Ay-DzK is used to denote the dataset with function x, y attributes and $z \cdot 1000$ example records. The above choices allow us to investigate the effect of different data characteristics such as number of tuples and number of attributes. Also note that while the initial input size of the ASCII databases is around 60MB, the final input size after the creation of attribute lists is roughly 4 times more, i.e., around 240MB. Since machine A has only 128MB main memory, the databases will be disk resident.

Algorithms: Our initial experiments confirmed that MWK was indeed better than BASIC as expected, and that it performs as well or better than FWK. Thus, we will only present the performance of MWK and SUBTREE.

We experimented with window sizes of 2, 4 and 8 for MWK. A larger window size implies more overhead on the file creation and managing related data structures. On the other head, a smaller window size may not have enough parallelism, especially when there are many processors and relatively few attributes. We found for our experiments a window size of 4 to be a good overall

Dataset						Corresponding Tree	
Dataset Notation	Func.	No. Attr.	No. Tuple	Initial Size	Final Size	No. Levels	Max. No. Leaves/Level
F2-A8-D1000K	F2	8	1000K	61 MB	240MB	4	2
F2-A32-D250K	F2	32	250K	57.3 MB	225MB	4	2
F2-A64-D125K	F2	64	125K	56.6 MB	225MB	4	2
F2-A128-D64K	F2	128	64K	55.6 MB	225MB	4	2
F7-A8-D1000K	F7	8	1000K	61 MB	240MB	60	4662
F7-A32-D250K	F7	32	250K	57.3 MB	225MB	59	802
F7-A64-D125K	F7	64	125K	56.6 MB	225MB	55	384
F7-A128-D64K	F7	128	64K	55.6 MB	225MB	73	194

Table 14.2: Dataset characteristics.

Dataset	Setup Time (seconds)	Sort Time (seconds)	Total Time (seconds)	Setup %	Sort %
F2-A8-D1000K	721	633	3597	20.0%	17.6%
F2-A32-D250K	685	598	3584	19.1%	16.6%
F2-A64-D125K	705	626	3665	19.2%	17.1%
F2-A128-D64K	706	624	3802	18.6%	16.4%
F7-A8-D1000K	989	817	23360	4.2%	3.5%
F7-A32-D250K	838	780	24706	3.4%	3.2%
F7-A64-D125K	672	636	22664	3.0%	2.8%
F7-A128-D64K	707	719	25021	2.8%	2.9%

Table 14.3: Sequential setup and sorting times.

choice unless the ratio of the number of attributes to the number of processors is small (less than 2) and in that case we use a window size of 8 (which performs better than a window size of 4 by as much as 9%). In general, a simple rule of thumb for the window size is that if the number of attributes is at least twice the number of processors (which is typically the case for a real world run), a window size of 4 should be chosen. In the rare case when $d/P < 2$, we choose the smallest W such that $W * d/P \geq 8$.

14.5.2 Initial Setup and Sort Time

Table 14.3 shows the uniprocessor time spent in the initial attribute list creation phase (*setup* phase), as wells as the time spent in one-time sort of the attribute lists for the continuous attributes (*sort* phase). The time spent in these two phases as a fraction of total time to build a classifier tree depends on the complexity of the input data for which we are building the classification model. For simple datasets such as F2, it can be significant, whereas it is negligible for complex datasets such as F7.

We have not focussed on parallelizing these phases, concentrating instead on the more challenging build phase. There is much existing research in par-

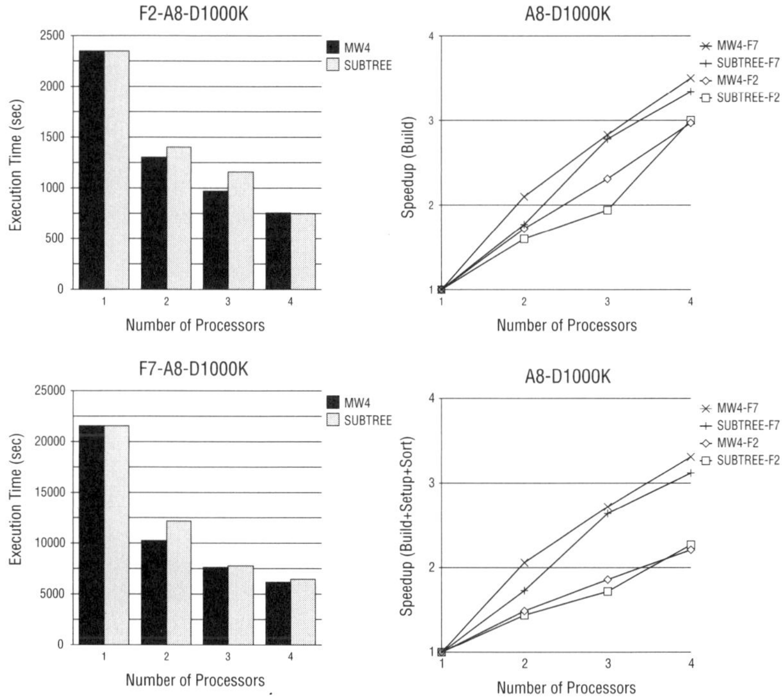

Figure 14.13: Local disk access: functions 2 and 7; 8 attributes; 1000K records.

allel sorting on SMP machines (Bitton, DeWitt, Hsiao, and Menon 1984). The creation of attribute lists can be speeded up by essentially using multiple input streams and merging this phase with the sort phase. In our implementation, the data scan to create attribute lists is sequential, although we write attribute lists in parallel. Attribute lists are sorted in parallel by assigning them to different processors. When we present the speedup graphs in the next section, we will show the speedups separately for the build phase as well as for the total time (including initial setup and sort times). There is obvious scope for improving the speedups for the total time.

14.5.3 Parallel Build Performance: Local Disk Access

We consider four main parameters for performance comparison: 1) number of processors, 2) number of attributes, 3) number of example tuples, and 4) classification function (function 2 or function 7). We first study the effect of varying these parameters on the MWK and SUBTREE algorithms on machine

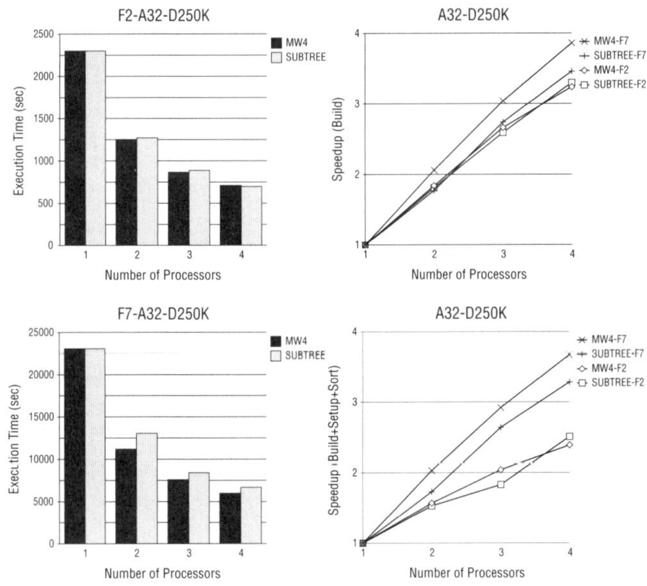

Figure 14.14: Local disk access: functions 2 and 7; 32 attributes; 250K records.

A, which has less main memory than the database size, so that disk I/O is required at each level while building the tree.

Figure 14.13 shows the parallel performance and speedup of the two algorithms as we vary the number of processors for the two classification functions F2 and F7, and using the dataset with eight attributes and one million records (*A8-D1000K*). Figures 14.14, 14.15 and 14.16 show similar results for datasets A32-D250K, A64-D125K, and A128-D64K respectively. The SUBTREE times for 4 processors are missing in A128-D64K since we exceeded the number of open files limit in Unix. The speedup chart in the bottom right part of each figure shows the speedup of the total time (including setup and sort time), while the speedup chart on top of it and the two bar charts show only the build time (excluding setup and sort time).

Considering the build time only, the speedups for both algorithms on 4 processors range from 2.97 to 3.32 for function F2 and from 3.25 to 3.86 for function F7. For function F7, the speedups of total time for both algorithms on 4 processors range from 3.12 to 3.67. The important observation from these figures is that both algorithms perform quite well for various datasets. Even the overall speedups are good for complex datasets generated with function F7. As expected, the overall speedups for simple datasets generated by function F2,

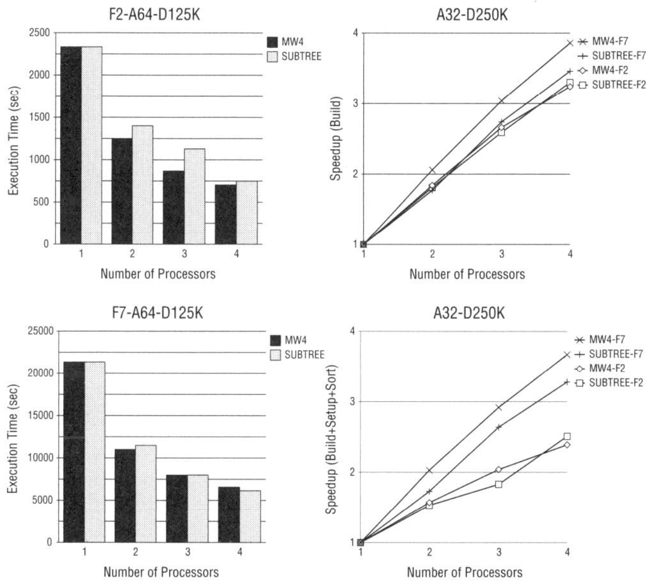

Figure 14.15: Local disk access: functions 2 and 7; 64 attributes; 125K records.

in which build time is a smaller fraction of total time, are relatively not as good (around 2.2 to 2.5 on 4 processors). These speedups can be improved by parallelizing the setup phase more aggressively.

MWK's performance is mostly comparable or better than SUBTREE. The difference ranges from 8% worse than SUBTREE to 22% better than SUBTREE. Most of the MWK times are within 10% better than SUBTREE.

An observable trend is that having greater number of processors tends to favor SUBTREE. In other words, the advantage of MWK over SUBTREE tends to decrease as the number of processors increases. This is can be seen from figures for both $F2$ and $F7$ by comparing the build times for the two algorithms first with 2 processors, then with 4 processors. This is because after about $\log P$ levels of the tree growth, the only synchronization overhead for SUBTREE, before any processor becomes free, is that each processor checks the FREE queue once per level. On the other hand, for MWK, there will be relatively more processor synchronization overhead, as the number of processors increases, which includes acquiring attributes, checking on conditional variables, and waiting on barriers. As part of future work we plan to compare these algorithms on larger SMP configurations.

We next compare the parallel performance and speedups of the algorithms

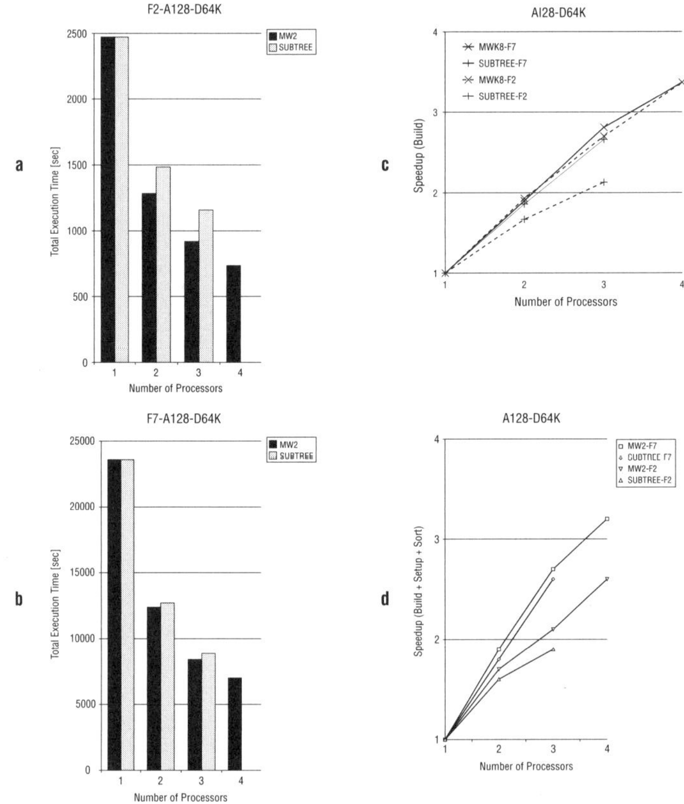

Figure 14.16: Local disk access: functions 2 and 7; 128 attributes; 64K records.

on Machine B. This configuration has 1 GB of main-memory available. Thus after the very first access the data will be cached in main-memory, leading to fast access times. Machine B has 8 processors. Figures 14.17, 14.18, and 14.19 show three sets of timing and speedup charts for the *A8-D1000K*, *A32-D250K* and *A64-D125K* datasets, on Functions 2 and 7, and on 1, 2, 4 and 8 processors.

14.5.4 Parallel Build Performance: Main-Memory (Cached) Access

Considering the build time only, the speedups for both algorithms on 8 processors range from 5.46 to 6.37 for function F2 and from 5.36 to 6.67 (and at least

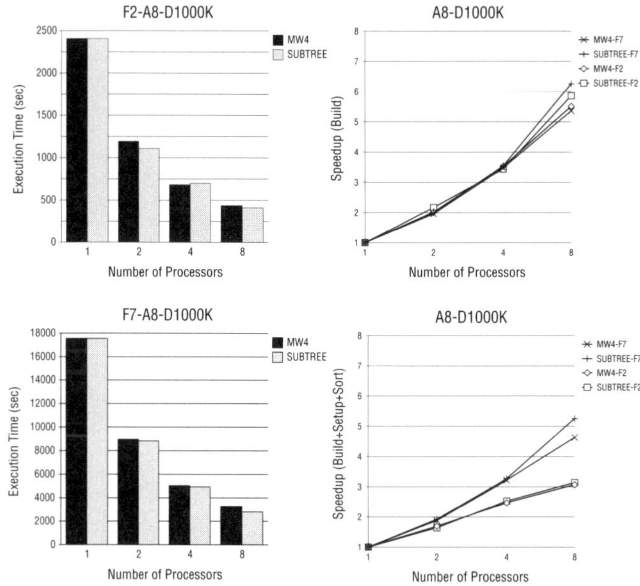

Figure 14.17: Main-memory access: functions 2 and 7; 8 attributes; 1000K records.

6.22 with 32 or 64 attribute) for function F7. For function F7, the speedups of total time for both algorithms on 8 processors range from 4.63 to 5.77 (and at least 5.25 for 32 or 64 attributes). Again, the important observation from these figures is that both algorithms perform very well for various datasets even up to 8 processors. The advantage of MWK over SUBTREE is more visible for the simple function F2. The reason is that F2 generates very small trees with 4 levels and a maximum of 2 leaves in any new leaf frontier. Around 40% of the total time is spent in the root node, where SUBTREE has only one process group. Thus on this dataset SUBTREE is unable to fully exploit the inter-node parallelism successfully. MWK is the winner because it not only overlaps the $\mathcal{E}$ and $\mathcal{W}$ phases, but also manages to reduce the load imbalance.

The overall trends observable from these figures are similar to those for the disk configuration. First, shallow trees (e.g., generated by F2) tend to hurt SUBTREE, 2) Greater number of processors tends to favor SUBTREE more, 3) Having a small number of attributes tends to hurt MWK.

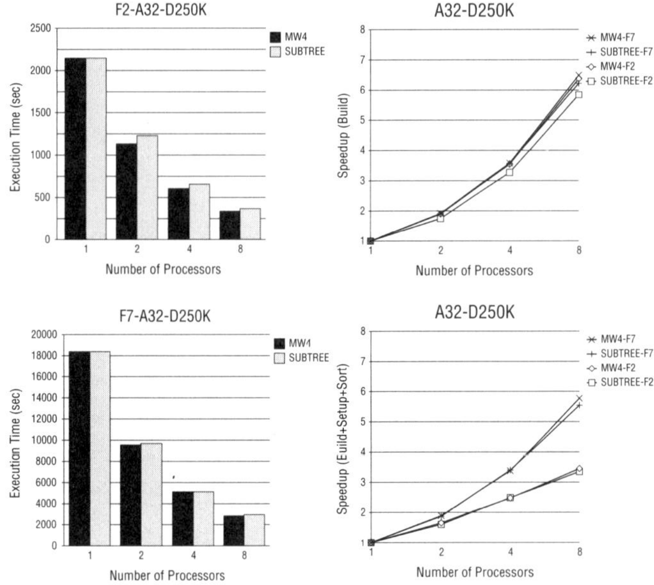

Figure 14.18: Main-memory access: functions 2 and 7; 32 attributes; 250K records.

14.6 Conclusions

We presented parallel algorithms for building decision-tree classifiers on SMP systems. The proposed algorithms span the gamut of data and task parallelism. The MWK algorithm uses data parallelism from multiple attributes, but also uses task pipelining to overlap different computing phases within a tree node, thus avoiding potential a sequential bottleneck for the hash-probe construction in the split phase. The MWK algorithm employs a conditional variable, instead of a barrier, among leaf nodes to avoid unnecessary processor blocking time. It also exploits dynamic assignment of attribute files to a fixed set of physical files, which maximizes the number of concurrent accesses to disk without file interference. The SUBTREE algorithm uses recursive divide-and-conquer to minimize processor interaction, and assigns free processors dynamically to busy groups to achieve load balancing.

Experiments show that both algorithms achieve good speedups in building the classifier on a 4-processor SMP with disk configuration and on an 8-processor SMP with memory configuration, for various numbers of attributes, various numbers of example tuples of input databases, and various complexities of data models. The performance of both algorithms are comparable, but

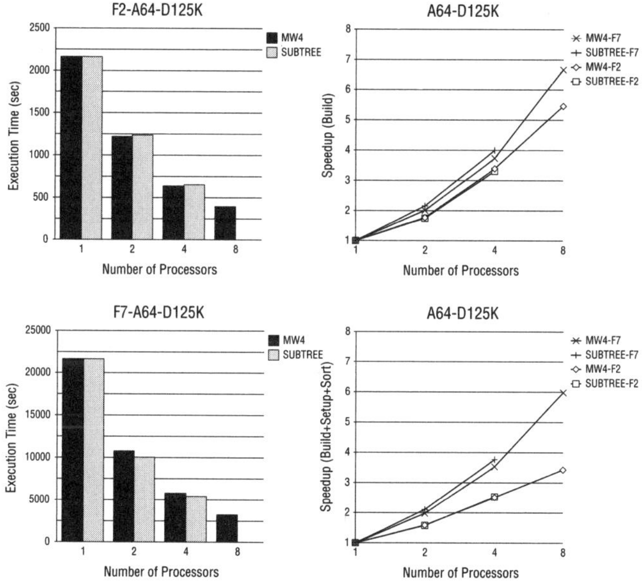

Figure 14.19: Main-memory access: functions 2 and 7; 64 attributes; 125K records.

MWK has a slight edge on the SMP configurations we looked at. These experiments demonstrate that the important data mining task of classification can be effectively parallelized on SMP machines.

Chapter 15

Distributed and Parallel Data Mining: Emergence, Growth, and Future Directions

Hillol Kargupta, Chandrika Kamath, and Philip Chan

15.1 Introduction

Distributed resources of data have become a practical issue since the emergence of network-based distributed computing environments. The fast growth of interest on distributed data mining (DDM) has created a natural demand for a book that provides a comprehensive exposure to the state-of-the-art in DDM technology. This book serves that purpose. In addition it exposes the readers to some of the recent advances in parallel data mining (PDM).

Although parallel data mining is just as important as DDM, this book focuses on the DDM issues since several books on parallel data mining are already available (Freitas and Lavington 1998, Zaki and Ho 2000). The book starts with general overviews and walks the readers through different mining algorithms, architectures, data preprocessing techniques, and human-computer interaction issues in distributed and parallel data mining. It should help both beginners and mature readers to advance their knowledge in these two areas.

In this epilogue, we take a closer look at the roots and the developments of the distributed and parallel data mining technology. We note the growing interest in these areas and sketch some of the exciting applications that we may see in the near future. At the end, we also provide a list of web sites that may be useful for the readers.

15.2 Distributed and Parallel Data Mining: Emerging Disciplines

Distributed data mining shares the same motivation and philosophy behind fields like distributed control (Larson 1982), distributed artificial intelligence (Durfee, Lesser, and Corkill 1989; Holland 1975; Nii 1986), and the relatively new field of multi-agent systems (Sen 1997). They all deal with distributed environments. However, DDM deals with several unique issues that distinguish it from other fields related to distributed computing. The main distinction is its focus on scalable distributed data analysis. Although data analysis is a classical problem, doing the analysis in a distributed fashion is a new development. For example, consider statistics; it is an important tool for data analysis. Although it is a well developed field, most of the popular statistical algorithms are designed for centralized data. Analyzing data in a distributed fashion with minimal communication of raw data requires the development of distributed statistical algorithms. Clearly, this is a new territory that awaits extensive exploration. DDM deals with problems like this that are new, challenging, and have immediate practical applications.

The development and practice of algorithms, systems, and architectures for distributed data analysis are the main objectives of the field of DDM. Moreover, scalability with respect to large databases, number of data sites, and other aspects of the application environment are also important and unique aspects of DDM.

Although DDM is a unique new field, it is likely to benefit from many other related fields. For example, the distributed control and the multi-agent systems communities have contributed a large volume of literature investigating different architectures and communication protocols for large, decentralized, problem solving environments. The development of information and data management technology (e.g. XML) in the world-wide-web should also be quite useful for developing DDM applications for the web. The learning algorithms for multi-learner systems (Heath, Kasif, and Salzberg 1996; Selfridge 1958; Sharkey 1998) are useful for homogeneous DDM. Similarly, the literature on distributed decision making (Kumar, Singhai, and Liu 1987) should help the evaluation of data patterns in a DDM application. DDM is clearly an inter-disciplinary field and it should continue to benefit from the different techniques developed in many fields such as the ones listed above. The participation of DDM researchers from different disciplines like Computer Science, Statistics, Business, Electrical Engineering, and others also reflects this growing inter-disciplinary nature of the field.

In contrast with the recent emergence of DDM as a field, the importance of exploiting parallelism in data analysis and knowledge discovery was recognized ever since high performance computers and storage devices became readily available. Although terms like parallel data mining and parallel knowledge discovery were coined relatively recently, early efforts in scalable parallel data analysis using machine learning techniques can be found in the literature for parallel artificial intelligence architectures (Uhr 1987) and connectionist systems (Rumelhart and McCLelland 1986).

As parallel computers have moved from experimental systems to mainstream production machines, and parallel architectures have converged, the software to support parallelism has also evolved into standards that enable parallel programs to be efficient and portable. These developments allow efficient analysis of large amounts of data that are generated and collected from our increasingly digital and wired world.

As with distributed data mining, parallel data mining is a multi-disciplinary field, borrowing ideas from machine learning, statistics, image processing, mathematical optimization, business, high performance computing, linear algebra, to name only a few. In some of these fields, parallel processing has had a long and illustrious history, enabling parallel data mining to benefit from algorithms and software that have been extensively used in practice. However, this does not imply that much of what needs to be done in parallel data mining has already been done in other fields. To the contrary, it is a field ripe with technical challenges as we attempt to analyze data sets measured in Terabytes and Petabytes on parallel machines with thousands of processors.

The focus in parallel data mining is on fine-grained parallelism, where the data to be mined is typically at a single site and the processors are tightly coupled by a high bandwidth interconnection network. Technical challenges include scaling algorithms to massive data sets without losing accuracy, parallel implementations that scale to thousands of processors, and, most importantly, finding ways of making the end-to-end data mining process scalable. While many data mining researchers in academia and industry focus on parallelizing the pattern recognition step, they tend to overlook the data preprocessing steps, which are frequently very time consuming and could definitely benefit from parallelism. Further, as new applications try to take advantage of these techniques, new challenges must be addressed. For example, in remote sensing, we may want to mine multiple data sets obtained from different sensors with different resolutions. Or, in domains such as astrophysics or network intrusion detection, we may want near-real-time turnaround while analyzing vast amounts of data as they are being collected. In the following section we note some of the events that have facilitated the fast growth of the two areas of distributed and parallel data mining.

15.3 Growing Level of Interest

Both distributed and parallel data mining are enjoying an increasing amount of professional activity. The first workshop on Distributed Data Mining, held at the Fourth International Conference on Knowledge Discovery and Data Mining (1998), brought together interested researchers and practitioners and facilitated further development of this area. The workshop had thirteen presentations, including three invited talks. It was sponsored by the Intel Corporation and Magnify Inc. Further details about the (1998) workshop can be found at http://www.eecs.wsu.edu/˜hillol/ddm.html. This book contains extended versions of several papers from that workshop. Today, after barely two years, the field has gained a large momentum. The number of researchers and practitioners working in this area has nearly tripled. More research issues have been introduced and the field is starting to crystallize its shape. The KDD 2000 Conference will host the second workshop on Distributed and Parallel Knowledge Discovery.

A series of related workshops on high performance parallel data mining were also held during the last few years, including The 1999 Workshop on High Performance Data Mining,[1] The Workshop on Mining Scientific Datasets,[2] and The 1999 ACM SIGKDD Workshop on Large-Scale Parallel KDD Systems.[3]

At least two parallel data mining books (Freitas and Lavington 1998)[4] and (Zaki and Ho 2000)[5] on parallel data mining are currently available.

---

[1] www.cise.ufl.edu/˜ranka/hpdm99.html

[2] www.arc.umn.edu/˜conferences/MSD/poster.html

[3] /www.cs.rpi.edu/˜zaki/WKDD99

[4] www.wkap.nl/book.htm/0-7923-8048-7

[5] www.springer.de/cgi–bin/search_book.pl?isbn=3-540-67194-3

15.4 Some Exciting Possibilities

Both distributed and parallel data mining technology are finding increasing number of real-life applications. Automobile maintenance transaction data mining, network-intrusion detection, credit card fraud detection, insurance data mining are only a few examples of many successful DDM applications that have been already reported in the literature.

However, we believe that some of the most exciting applications of DDM are yet to come. Applications of DDM technology in the world-wide-web is one example. The web is a source of a lot of valuable information; an increasing number of databases are getting connected to the web every day. Therefore, mining the information available in the web can be very useful. This possibility is already recognized and web mining is emerging as a new area in itself. Although the web is an inherently distributed environment, most of the web mining applications are done in a centralized fashion. As the standards for storing and retrieving data on the web start to emerge, DDM may be effectively used for developing a highly scalable distributed architecture for web mining. In future, we may see web servers that post partial data analysis models that are ready to be downloaded and integrated with other models generated from different sites. The development of data-oriented languages like the extensible markup language (XML) should significantly advance the practice of DDM tools by facilitating the management and representation of data on the web. Distributed mining of multi-media data in the world-wide-web is another interesting possibility.

Another exciting application area is the mobile computing field. Typically mobile environments have very limited bandwidth, and often, the bandwidth is asymmetric. We believe that in the future, mobile computing is going to play a very important role in our everyday life; accessing and analyzing data will certainly be an integral part of that. Regardless of the increase in the bandwidth capacity, the ratio of the bandwidth and the quantity of available data is always likely to be low. Therefore, downloading large amounts of raw data may not be a practical option for mobile data mining applications. Since DDM often requires as little communication of raw data as possible, it is likely to play a significant role in mobile environments.

Data security is one of the primary concerns of information management systems. Data mining systems certainly have to abide by the security protocols controlling the access of information. Exchange of raw data over a network is typically susceptible to a breach of security protocols. However, exchanging the data analysis models like classifiers, clusters, and other structures may be acceptable since they typically do not expose the sensitive data. Since DDM mainly requires exchange of data analysis models with minimal exchange of raw data, the vulnerability of these systems is relatively lower compared to that of the centralized data mining systems. More DDM applications are likely to show up because of this sensitive aspect of information exchange.

On the other hand, distributed data mining can enhance current intrusion detection systems to provide stronger protection from coordinated malicious attacks. The recent distributed denial of service (DOS) attacks to various major web sites caused substantial interruption to regular activities at those sites. Detecting distributed attacks requires correlation of distributed events on the network. Data mining systems can be applied to network and host audit data to identify patterns for known attacks as well as features for normal activities. These mined patterns can then be used to monitor the network and hosts for detecting known attacks and abnormal activities. Correlation among alarms at distributed sites could indicate a wide-spread attack. Also, coordinated attacks might only cause "weak" alarms at individual sites, but, collectively, strong correlation among them could trigger a more severe alarm.

On a more personal front, distributed data mining techniques can be utilized to enhance our lives at home. With the advent of networked appliances at homes, data stored in these distributed devices can be used to mine user profiles for the inhabitants. For example, a person might frequently perform the following tasks within a short period of time: starting a movie in the VCR, turning on the TV, switching on the theater sound system, and dimming the lights. A data mining algorithm can correlate these tasks as a frequently occurring cluster of events. The correlation can then be used to build a user profile that recommends the tasks in the cluster to be performed automatically whenever a movie is started on the VCR. A distributed architecture for analyzing data in such a wired environment is likely to scale up better than a centralized approach.

Parallel data mining, despite its longer history, also offers the potential of exciting new applications in areas such as astrophysics, medical imaging, climate modeling, computer simulations, and remote sensing. Some of these applications have long used techniques similar to those in data mining, albeit on much smaller data sets which do not require parallel processors for their analysis. However, as these data sets have grown, it is becoming clear that using parallel processing to mine massive datasets, whether commercial or scientific, is an idea which is here to stay. Several vendors already provide tools that perform the pattern recognition step in parallel using algorithms such as classification, clustering, and association rules. Such software has been used extensively in commercial applications such as market basket analysis, customer churn, and credit card fraud detection. In many of these cases, the data preprocessing has already been done, and cleaned data is available in a data warehouse.

There are two broad application areas which offer rather exciting possibilities in the future - scientific data sets from observations and simulations.

Examples of the former includes data from astronomical observations, remote sensing, medical image analysis, target detection and identification, as well as robotics and other computer vision applications. Sometimes, an object or a scene might be viewed with different types of sensors. This may result in multi-spectral images with different resolutions and different types of noise, where an object may appear different in each image (or not appear at all) depending on the sensor used. In such cases, removing noise from the images and registering them are challenging problems that must be addressed before we can even attempt data mining.

In some applications, such as a satellite or a spacecraft collecting data, a limited bandwidth between the sensor and the data collecting station may make it impractical to download large amounts of data. In such cases, on-board ability to do data analysis, using perhaps limited parallel processing capabilities within the sensor, could be vital. An interesting possibility arises when the data is collected simultaneously by many sensors, and each sensor is coordinating with the other sensors in the collection of the data. This situation could benefit from both parallel data mining within a single sensor, and distributed data mining across the sensors in a manner similar to mobile computing.

Mining data from computer simulations also presents several interesting opportunities. As scientists gain access to parallel systems with many hundreds, if not thousands of processors, they are simulating increasingly complex phenomena in three dimensions, involving several variables. These simulations could be in fields as diverse as computational physics, chemistry, climate modeling, structural mechanics, or fluid dynamics. They could produce Terabytes of data at each time step, making the traditional visual means of data analysis infeasible. For such problems, semi-automated techniques, such as those from data mining, may be necessary. For example, these techniques can help identify interesting areas to the scientist which can then be analyzed further via visualization. Since many of these simulations run for several days, it might also be possible to use data mining to analyze the output during the simulation, and steer the simulation accordingly. One can also use these tech niques to compare the output from different computer models, or compare models with real data, for example in climate simulations.

Parallel data mining has the potential of solving a problem that has many scientists concerned, namely, the massive size of their datasets has led to the lack of serendipitous discoveries that used to be so vital to progress in the past. However, with the current advances in parallel data mining, such discoveries might not only be possible, but be possible in time for scientists to observe the phenomena of interest, or control and understand a simulation. The following section presents a partial list of web sites that provide useful information for the distributed and parallel data mining communities.

15.5 Resources on the World-Wide-Web

There exist several web sites that host distributed and parallel data mining related resources. A few of them are listed in the following subsections.

15.5.1 Distributed Data Mining

1. **Distributed KDD Site**
   Web site: www.distributed-kdd.com
   This site contains general information about the field of distributed KDD, conference announcements, links to other related sites, links to several papers, and other useful information for practitioners and researchers of distributed KDD.

2. **National Center for Data Mining Site**
   Web site: www.ncdm.uic.edu/m3d2.html
   This site contains general information about the M3D2 project on distributed KDD at University of Illinois at Chicago, information regarding upcoming conferences/workshops, and other useful information for parallel and distributed data mining researchers.

15.5.2 Parallel Data Mining

1. **1999 ACM SIGKDD Workshop on Parallel KDD Site**
   Web site: www.cs.rpi.edu/~zaki/WKDD99/
   This site contains electronic versions of papers from the 1999 ACM SIGKDD Workshop on Large-Scale Parallel KDD Systems.

2. **1998 IEEE IPPS Workshop Site**
   Web site: www.cise.ufl.edu/~ranka/hpdm98p.html
   This site contains electronic versions of papers from the 1998 IEEE IPPS Workshop on High Performance Data Mining.

15.5.3 General Data Mining

1. **ACM Special Interests Group on Knowledge Discovery and Data Mining (SIGKDD) Site**
   Web site: www.acm.org/sigkdd/

2. **AAAI KDD Electronic Library Site**
   Web site: www.aaai.org/Library/Conferences/KDD/ This site contains electronic versions of papers from the first four knowledge discovery and data mining conferences, as well as KDD papers published in the

AAAI *National Conference Proceedings,* the *FLAIRS Conference Proceedings,* and selected AAAI workshops.

3. **Knowledge Discovery Nuggets Site**
   Web site: www.kdnuggets.com
   This site contains general information about the data mining field, conference announcements, links to other related sites, and other useful information for data mining practitioners and researchers.

Acknowledgements

The work of Chandrika Kamath was performed under the auspices of the U.S. Department of Energy by University of California Lawrence Livermore National Laboratory under contract No. W-7405-Eng-48, UCRL-JC-138954.

Bibliography

Abadi, M., and Feigenbaum, J. 1990. Secure Circuit Evaluation. *Journal of Cryptography* 2(1): 1–12.

Abadi, M.; Feigenbaum, J.; and Kilian, J. 1989. On Hiding Information from an Oracle. *Journal of Computer System Science* 39(1): 21–50.

Aebi, D., and Perrochon, L. 1993. Toward Improving Data Quality. In Paper presented at the Fourth International Conference on Information Systems and Management of Data (CISMOD'93), 6–8 October, New Delhi, India.

Aggarwal, J. K.; Ghosh, J.; Nair, D.; and Taha, I. 1996. A Comparative Study of Three Paradigms for Object Recognition—Bayesian Statistics, Neural Networks, and Expert Systems. In Advances In Image Understanding: A Festschrift for Azriel Rosenfeld, eds. K. Boyer and N. Ahuja, 241–262. Washington, D.C.: IEEE Computer Society.

Agrawal, R., and Schafer, J. C. 1996. Parallel Mining of Association Rules. *IEEE Transactions on Knowledge and Data Engineering* 8(6): 962–969.

Agrawal, R., and Shim, K. 1995. Developing Tightly Coupled Applications on IBM DB2/CS Relational Database System: Methodology and Experience. Research Report RJ 10005 (89094), IBM Corporation, San Jose, California.

Agrawal, R., and Shim, K. 1996. Developing Tightly Coupled Data-Mining Applications on a Relational Database System. In *Proceedings of the Second International Conference on Knowledge Discovery and Data Mining,* 287–290. Menlo Park, Calif.: American Association for Artificial Intelligence.

Agrawal, R., and Srikant, R. 1994. Fast Algorithms for Mining Association Rules in Large Databases. In *Proceedings of the International Conference on Very Large Data Bases,* 487–499. San Francisco, Calif.: Morgan Kaufmann.

Agrawal, R., and Srikant, R. 1995. Mining Sequential Patterns. In Proceedings of the International Conference on Data Engineering, 3–14. Washington, D.C.: IEEE Computer Society.

Agrawal, R.; Faloutsos, C.; and Swami, A. 1993. Efficient Similarity Search in Sequence Databases. In *Foundations of Data Organization and Algorithms*, 69–84. Berlin: Springer Verlag.

Agrawal, R.; Ghosh, S.; Imielinski, T.; Iyer, B.; and Swami, A. 1992. An Interval Classifier for Database-Mining Applications. Paper presented at the Eighteenth Very Large Databases Conference, 23–27 August, Vancouver, Canada.

Agrawal, R.; Imielinski, T.; and Swami, A. 1993a. Database Mining: A Performance Perspective. *IEEE Transactions on Knowledge and Data Engineering* (Special Issue on Learning and Discovery in Knowledge-Based Databases) 5(6): 914–925.

Agrawal, R.; Imielinski, T.; and Swami, A. 1993b. Mining Association Rules between Sets of Items in Large Databases. In Proceedings of the ACM-SIGMOD International Conference on Management of Data, 207–216. New York: Association of Computing Machinery.

Agrawal, R.; Mannila, H.; Srikant, R.; Toivonen, H.; and Verkamo, A. I. 1996. Fast Discovery of Association Rules. In *Advances in Knowledge Discovery and Data Mining*, eds. U. Fayyad, G. Piatetsky-Shapiro, P. Smyth, and R. Uthurusamy, 307–328. Menlo Park, Calif.: AAAI Press.

Agrawal, R.; Mehta, M.; and Rissanen, J. 1995. MDL-Based Decision Tree Pruning. Paper presented at the International Conference on Knowledge Discovery in Databases and Data Mining, 20–21 August, Montreal, Canada.

Aha, D.; Wettschereck, D.; and Mohr, T. 1997. A Review and Empirical Evaluation of Feature-Weighting Methods for a Class of Lazy Learning Algorithms. *Artificial Intelligence Review* 11(1–5): 273–314.

Ali, K. 1996. Learning Probabilistic Relationship Concept Descriptions. Ph.D. dissertation, Information and Computer Science, University of California at Irvine.

Ali, K., and Pazzani, M. 1995. Classification Using Bayes Averaging of Multiple Relational Rule-Based Models. In *Learning from Data: Artificial Intelligence and Statistics, Volume 5*, eds. D. Fisher and H. Lenz, 207-217. Berlin: Springer-Verlag.

Ali, K., and Pazzani, M. 1996a. Error Reduction through Learning Multiple Descriptions. *Machine Learning* 24(3): 173–202.

Ali, K., and Pazzani, M. 1996b. HYDRA-MM: Learning Multiple Descriptions to Improve Classification Accuracy. *International Journal on Artificial Intelligence Tools* 4(1): 115–133.

AlSabti, K. 1998. Efficient Algorithms for Data Mining. Ph.D. dissertation, Department of Computer Science, Syracuse University.

AlSabti, K.; Ranka, S.; and Shankar, R. 1995. Many-to-Many Personalized Communication with Bounded Traffic. Paper presented at the Fifth Symposium on the Frontiers of Massively Parallel Computation, 6–9 February, McLean, Virginia.

AlSabti, K.; Ranka, S.; and Singh, V. 1997. A One-Pass Algorithm for Accuratly Estimating Quantiles for Disk-Resident Data. Paper presented at the Twenty-Third International Conference on Very Large Databases (VLDB97), 26–29 August, Athens, Greece.

AlSabti, K.; Ranka, S.; and Singh, V. 1998. CLOUDS: A Decision Tree Classifier for Large Datasets. In *Proceedings of the Fourth International Conference on Knowledge Discovery in Databases and Data Mining,* 27–31. Menlo Park, Calif.: AAAI Press.

Aluru, S.; Goil, S.; and Ranka, S. 1996. Concatenated Parallelism: A Technique for Efficient Parallel Divide and Conquer. In Proceedings of the IEEE Symposium on Parallel and Distributed Processing, 488–495. Washington, D.C.: IEEE Computer Society.

Anderberg, M. R. 1973. *Cluster Analysis for Applications*. San Diego, Calif.: Academic.

Anderson, E.; Bai, Z.; Bischof, C.; Blackford, S.; Demmel, J.; Dongarra, J.; Du Croz, J.; Greenbaum, A.; Hammarling, S.; McKenney, A.; and Sorensen, D. 1995. LAPACK User's Guide. 3d ed. Philadelphia, Pa.: Society for Industrial and Applied Mathematics.

Anderson, J. M., and Lam, M. 1993. Global Optimizations for Parallelism and Locality on Scable Parallel Machines. In Proceedings of the ACM Conference on Programming Language Design and Implementation, 112–125. New York: Association of Computing Machinery.

Anderson, T.; Culler, D.; and Patterson, D. 1995. A Case for NOW (Networks of Workstations). *IEEE Micro* 15(1): 54–64.

Angluin, D., and Valiant, L. 1979. Fast Probabilistic Algorithms for Hamiltonian Circuits and Matchings. *Journal of Computer Systems and Science* 18(2): 155–193.

Arnold, B.; Balakrishnan, N.; and Nagaraja, H. 1992. *A First Course in Order Statistics*. New York: Wiley.

Aronis, J. M., and Provost, F. M. 1997. Increasing the Efficiency of Data-Mining Algorithms with Breadth-First Marker Propagation. Paper presented at the Third International Conference on Knowledge Discovery and Data Mining, 14–17 August, Newport Beach, California.

Aronis, J. M.; Kolluri, V.; Provost, F. M.; and Buchanan, B. G. 1997. The WoRLD: Knowledge Discovery from Multiple Distributed Databases. Paper presented at the Florida Artificial Intelligence Research Symposium (FLAIRS-97), 11–14 May, Daytona Beach, Florida.

Atkeson, C. G.; Schaal, S. A.; and Moore, A. W. 2000. Locally Weighted Learning. *AI Review* (Special Issue on Lazy Learning) 11(1), February.

Bader, D. A., and Ja'Ja', J. 1995. Practical Parallel Algorithms for Dynamic Data Redistribution, Median Finding, and Selection. Technical Report, CS-TR-3449, UMIACS-TR-95-44, Department of Electrical Engineering, University of Maryland.

Bader, D. A.; Ja'Ja', J.; and Chellappa, R. 1993. Scalable Data Parallel Algorithms for Texture Synthesis and Compression using Gibbs Random Fields. Technical Report, CS-TR-3123, UMIACS-TR-93-80, Department of Electrical Engineering, University of Maryland.

Bader, D. A.; Ja'Ja', J.; Harwood, D.; and Davis, L. S. 1995a. Parallel Algorithms for Image Enhancement and Segmentation by Region Growing with an Experimental Study. Technical Report, CS-TR-3494, UMIACS-TR-95-74, Department of Electrical Engineering, University of Maryland.

Bader, D. A.; Ja'Ja', J.; Harwood, D.; and Davis, L. S. 1995b. Parallel Algorithms for Image Histogramming and Connected Components with an Experimental Study. Technical Report, CS-TR-3384, UMIACS-TR-95-133, Department of Electrical Engineering, University of Maryland.

Bae, S. 1997. Runtime Support for Unstructured Data Accesses on Coarse-Grained Distributed Memory Parallel Machines. Ph.D. dissertation, Department of Computer Science, Syracuse University.

Baldwin, C.; Kamath, C.; and Musick, R. 1999. An LLNL Perspective on ASCI Data Mining and Pattern-Recognition Requirements, UCRL-ID-132850, Center for Applied Scientific Computing, Lawrence Livermore National Laboratory, Livermore, California.

Barnett, J. 1981. Computational Methods for a Mathematical Theory of Evidence. In Proceedings of the Seventh International Joint Conference on Artificial Intelligence, 868–875. Menlo Park, Calif.: International Joint Conferences on Artificial Intelligence.

Bartlett, P., and Shawe-Taylor, J. 1998. Generalization Performance of Support Vector Machines and Other Pattern Classifiers. In *Advances in Kernel Methods—Support Vector Learning*, eds. B. Scholkopf and A. Smola. Cambridge, Mass.: MIT Press.

Bauer, E., and Kohavi, R. 1999. An Empirical Comparison of Voting Classification Algorithms: Bagging, Boosting, and Variants. *Machine Learning* 36(1–2): 105–139.

Bayardo, R. J. 1998. Efficiently Mining Long Patterns from Databases. In Proceedings of the ACM SIGMOD Conference on the Management of Data, 85–93. New York: Association of Computing Machinery.

Belford, M. 1998. Information Overload. *Computer Shopper*, July, 61–66.

Bell, D. E., and LaPadula, L. J. 1976. Secure Computer Systems: Unified Exposition and Multics Interpretation, MTR-2997 (ESD-TR-75-306) (available as NTIS AD-A023 588), MITRE Corporation, Bedford, Massachusetts.

Bell, G., and Van Ingen, C. 1999. DSM Perspective: Another Point of View. *Proceedings of the IEEE* (Special Issue on Distributed Shared Memory Systems) 87(3): 412–418.

Bennett, L. T.; Wilkinson, G. L.; and Oliver, K. 1997. Evaluation Criteria and Indicators of Quality for Internet Resources. *Educational Technology* 37(3): 52–59.

Berman, F.; Wolski, R.; Figueira, S.; Schopf, J.; and Shao, G. 1996. Application-Level Scheduling on dist. het. Networks. Paper presented at the International Conference on High-Performance Computing (Supercomputing '96), 17–22 November, Pittsburgh, Pennsylvania.

Bertsekas, D. P., and Tsitsiklis, J. N. 1989. *Parallel and Distributed Computation: Numerical Methods*. Englewood Cliffs, N.J.: Prentice Hall.

Bitton, D.; DeWitt, D.; Hsiao, D. K.; and Menon, J. 1984. A Taxonomy of Parallel Sorting. *ACM Computing Surveys* 16(3): 287–318.

Blackford, L. S.; Choi, J.; Cleary, A.; D'Azevedo, E.; Demmel, J.; Dhillon, I.; Dongarra, J.; Hammarling, S.; Henry, G.; Petitet, A.; Stanley, K.; Walker, D.; and Whaley, R. C. 1997. SCALAPACK User's Guide. Philadelphia, Pa.: Society for Industrial and Applied Mathematics.

Bradley, P. S., and Fayyad, U. M. 1998. Refining Initial Points for K-Means Clustering. In *Proceedings of the International Conference on Machine Learning (ICML-98)*, 91–99.

Bradley, P. S.; Fayyad, U. M.; and Mangasarian, O. L. 1998. Mathematical Programming for Data Mining: Formulations and Challenges. *INFORMS Journal on Computing* (Special Issue on Data Mining) 11:209–217.

Bradley, P. S.; Mangasarian, O. L.; and Street, W. N. 1998. Feature Selection via Mathematical Programming. *INFORMS Journal on Computing* 10:209–217.

Breiman, L. 1994. Heuristics of Instability in Model Selection. Technical Report, Department of Statistics, University of California at Berkeley.

Breiman, L. 1996a. Bagging Predictors. *Machine Learning* 26(2): 123–140.

Breiman, L. 1996b. Stacked Regressions. *Machine Learning* 24(1): 41–48.

Breiman, L. 1999. Combining Predictors. In *Combining Artificial Neural Nets*, eds. A. Sharkey, 31–50. Berlin: Springer-Verlag.

Breiman, L.; Friedman, J. H.; Olshen, R. A.; and Stone, C. J. 1984. *Classification and Regression Trees*. Belmont, Calif.: Wadsworth.

Bridges, C. L., and Goldberg, D. E. 1991. The Nonuniform Walsh-Schema Transform. In *Foundations of Genetic Algorithms*, ed. G. J. E. Rawlins, 13–22. San Francisco, Calif.: Morgan Kaufmann.

Brin, R.; Motwani, J.; Ullman, J.; and Tsur, S. 1997. Dynamic Itemset Counting and Implication Rules for Market Basket Data. In Proceedings of the 1997 ACM-SIGMOD International Conference on Management Data, 255–264. New York: Association of Computing Machinery.

Buchanan, B., and Mitchell, T. 1978. Model-Directed Learning of Production Rules. In *Pattern-Directed Inference Systems,* eds. D. Waterman and F. Hayes-Roth, 297–312. San Diego, Calif.: Academic.

Buczkowski, L. J. 1990. Database Inference Controller. In *Database Security III: Status and Prospects*, eds. D. L. Spooner and C. Landwehr, 311–322. New York: Elsevier Science.

Buneman, P. 1997. Semistructured Data. In Proceedings of PODS'97, 117–121. New York: Association of Computing Machinery.

Buntine, W. 1992. A Theory of Learning Classification Rules. Ph.D. dissertation, School of Computing Science, University of Technology, Sydney, Australia.

Burges, C. J. 1998. A Tutorial on Support Vector Machines for Pattern Recognition. *Data Mining and Knowledge Discovery: An International Journal* 2(2): 955-974.

Cantu-Paz, E. 1998. A Survey of Parallel Genetic Algorithms. *Calculateurs Paralleles, Reseaux et Systems Repartis* 10(2): 141–171.

Carriere, J., and Kazman, R. 1997. WEBWUERY: Searching and Visualizing the Web through Connectivity. In Proceedings of the International World Wide Web Conference, 7–11 April, Santa Clara, California.

Carson, E. R., and Fischer, U. 1990. Models and Computers in Diabetes Research and Diabetes Care. *Computer Methods and Programs in Biomedicine* 32(3–4).

Catlett, J. 1991. Megainduction: Machine Learning on Very Large Databases. Ph.D. dissertation, Computer Science Department, University of Technology, Sydney, Australia.

Censor, Y., and Zenios, S. A. 1997. *Parallel Optimization.* New York: Oxford University Press.

Chan P. K., and Kargupta, H., editors. 1999. Proceedings of the Workshop on Distributed Data Mining, The Fourth International Conference on Knowledge Discovery and Data Mining. Menlo Park, Calif.: American Association for Artificial Intelligence.

Chan P. K., and Stolfo, S. 1993a. Experiments on Multistrategy Learning by Meta-Learning. In Proceedings of the Second International Conference on Information and Knowledge Management, 314–323. New York: Association of Computing Machinery.

Chan P. K., and Stolfo, S. 1993b. MetaLearning for Multistrategy and Parallel Learning. In Proceedings of the Second International Workshop on Multistrategy Learning, 150–165. Fairfax, Va.: George Mason University.

Chan P. K., and Stolfo, S. 1993c. Toward Parallel and Distributed Learning by Meta-Learning. In Knowledge Discovery in Databases: Papers from the AAAI Workshop, 227–240. Technical Report WS-93-02. Menlo Park, Calif.: AAAI Press.

Chan P. K., and Stolfo, S. 1995. A Comparative Evaluation of Voting and Meta-Learning on Partitioned Data. In *Proceedings of the Twelfth International Conference on Machine Learning,* 90–98. San Francisco, Calif.: Morgan Kaufmann.

Chan P. K., and Stolfo, S. 1996. Sharing Learned Models among Remote Database Partitions by Local Meta-Learning. In *Proceedings of the Second International Conference on Knowledge Discovery and Data Mining,* eds. E. Simoudis, J. Han, and U. Fayyad, 2–7. Menlo Park, Calif.: AAAI Press.

Chan P. K., and Stolfo, S. 1997. On the Accuracy of Meta-Learning for Scalable Data Mining. *Journal of Intelligent Information Systems* 8(1): 5–28.

Chan P. K., and Stolfo, S. 1998a. Learning with Non-Uniform Class and Cost Distributions: Effects and a Distributed Multi-Classifier Approach. Paper presented at the Distributed Data Mining Workshop at the Fourth International Conference of Knowledge Discovery and Data Mining, 27–31 August, New York.

Chan P. K., and Stolfo, S. 1998b. Toward Scalable Learning with Non-Uniform Class and Cost Distribution: A Case Study in Credit Card Fraud Detection. In *Proceedings of the Fourth International Conference on Knowledge Discovery and Data Mining,* 164–168. Menlo Park, Calif.: AAAI Press.

Chan, P. K.; Stolfo, S.; and Wolpert, D. 1996. Workshop on Integrating Multiple Learned Models for Improving and Scaling Machine Learning Algorithms, Thirteenth National Conference on Artificial Intelligence, 4–8 August, Portland, Oregon.

Charabarti, S.; Dom, B.; Agrawal, R.; and Raghavan, R. 1998. Scalable Feature Selection, Classification, and Signature Generation for Organizing Large-Text Databases into Hierarchical Topic Taxonomies. *VLDB Journal* 7(3): 163–178.

Chattratichat, J.; Darlington, J.; Ghanem, M.; Guo, Y. K.; Huning, H.; Kohler, M.; Sutiwaraphun, J. J.; To, H. W.; and Yang, D. 1997. Large-Scale Data Mining: Challenges and Responses. Paper presented at the Third Conference on Knowledge Discovery and Data Mining, 14–17 August, Newport Beach, Rhode Island.

Cherkauer, K. J., and Shavlik, J. W. 1993. Selecting Salient Features for Machine Learning from Large Candidate Pools through Parallel Decision Tree Construction. In *Massively Parallel Artificial Intelligence*, ed. H. Kitano, 102–136. Menlo Park, Calif.: AAAI Press.

Chess, D. M. 1998. Security Issues in Mobile Code Systems. In *Mobile Agents and Security*, ed. G. Vigna, 1–14. Lecture Notes in Computer Science 1419. New York: Springer Verlag.

Chesseman, P.; Kelly, J.; Self, M.; Stutz, J.; Taylor, W.; and Freeman, D. 1988. AUTOCLASS: A Bayesian Classification System. In *Proceedings of the Fifth International Machine Learning Confernce*, 54–64. San Francisco, Calif.: Morgan Kaufmann.

Cheung, A. L., and Reeves, A. P. 1992. High-Performance Computing on a Cluster of Workstations. In Proceedings of the First IEEE International Symposium on High-Performance Distributed Computing, 152–160. Washington, D.C.: IEEE Computer Society.

Cheung, D. W., and Xiao, Y. 1998. Effect of Data Skewness in Parallel Mining of Association Rules. Paper presented at the Second Pacific-Asia Conference on Knowledge Discovery and Data Mining, 15–17 April, Melbourne, Australia, 1998.

Cheung, D. W.; Han, J.; Ng, V. T.; Fu, A. W.; and Fu, Y. 1996. A Fast Distributed Algorithm for Mining Association Rules. In Proceedings of the IEEE Fourth International Conference on Parallel and Distributed Information System, 31–42. Washington, D.C.: IEEE Computer Society.

Cheung, D. W.; Han, J.; Ng, V. T.; Wong, C. Y. 1996. Maintenance of Discovered Association Rules in Large Databases: An Incremental Updating Technique. In Proceedings of the International Conference on Data Engineering, 26 February–1 March, New Orleans, Louisiana.

Cheung, D. W.; Hu, K.; and Xia, S. 1998. Asynchronous Parallel Algorithm for Mining Association Rules on Shared-Memory Multi-Processors. Paper presented at the Tenth ACM Symposium on Parallel Algorithms and Architectures, 28 June–2 July, Puerto Vallarta, Mexico.

Cheung, D.; Han, J.; Ng, V.; Fu, A. W.; and Fu, Y. 1996. A Fast Distributed Algorithm for Mining Association Rules. Paper presented at the 1996 International Conference on Parallel and Distributed Information Systems (PDIS'96), 18–20 December, Miami Beach, Florida.

Cheung, D.; Hu, K.; and Xia, S. 1998. Asynchronous Parallel Algorithm for Mining Association Rules on Shared-Memory Multi-Processors. In Proceedings of the Tenth ACM Symposium on Parallel Algorithms and Architectures, 279–288. New York: Association of Computing Machinery.

Cheung, D.; Ng, V.; Fu, A.; and Fu, Y. 1996. Efficient Mining of Association Rules in Distributed Databases. In *IEEE Transactions on Knowledge and Data Engineering* 8(6): 911–922.

Chipperfield, A. J., and Fleming, P. J. 1995. Parallel Genetic Algorihms. In *Handbook of Parallel and Distributed Computing*, ed. A. Y. Zomaya, 1034–1059. New York: McGraw Hill.

Cho, V., and Wüthrich, B. 1998. Toward Real-Time Discovery from Distributed Information Sources. In *Research and Development in Knowledge Discovery and Data Mining*, eds. X. Wu, R. Kotagiri, and K. B. Korb, 376–377. Lecture Notes in Computer Science 1394. Berlin: Springer-Verlag.

Chung, Y., and Prasanna, V. K. 1998. Parallelizing Image Feature Extraction on Course-Grain Machines. *IEEE Transactions on Pattern Analysis and Machine Intelligence* 20(12): 1389–1394.

Cierniak, M.; Li, W.; and Zaki, M. J. 1995. Loop Scheduling for Heterogeneity. In Proceedings of the Fourth IEEE International Symposium on High-Performance Distributed Computing, 78–85. Washington, D.C.: IEEE Computer Society.

Clark P. and Niblett, T. 1989. The CN2 Induction Algorithm. *Machine Learning* 3(4): 261–285.

Clearwater, S. H.; Cheng, T. P.; Hirsh, H.; and Buchanan, B. G. 1989. Incremental Batch Learning. In *Proceedings of the Sixth International Workshop on Machine Learning*, 366–370. San Francisco, Calif.: Morgan Kaufmann.

Clearwater, S. H.; Huberman, B. A.; and Hogg, T. 1991. Cooperative Solution of Constraint-Satisfaction Problems. *Science* 254:1181–1183.

Clearwater, S. H.; Huberman, B. A.; and Hogg, T. 1992. Cooperative Problem Solving. In *Computation: The Micro and the Macro View*, ed. B. A. Huberman, 33–70. River Edge, N.J.: World Scientific.

Clearwater, S., and Provost, F. 1990. RL4: A Tool for Knowledge-Based Induction. In Proceedings of the Second International IEEE Conference on Tools for Artificial Intelligence, 24–30. Washington, D.C.: IEEE Computer Society.

Clearwater, S.; Cheng, T.; Hirsh, H.; and Buchanan, B. 1989. Incremental Batch Learning. In *Proceedings of the Sixth International Workshop on Machine Learning*, 366–370. San Francisco, Calif.: Morgan Kaufmann.

Cohen, W. 1995. Fast Effective Rule Induction. In *Proceedings of the Twelfth International Conference on Machine Learning*, 115–123. San Francisco, Calif.: Morgan Kaufmann.

Cook, D., and Holder, L. 1990. Accelerated Learning on the Connection Machine. In Proceedings of the Second International IEEE Conference on Tools for Artificial Intelligence, 366–370. Washington, D.C.: IEEE Computer Society.

Cooley, R.; Mobasher, B.; and Srivastava, J. 1997. Web Mining: Information and Pattern Discovery on the World Wide Web. In Proceedings of the Ninth IEEE International Conference on Tools with Artificial Intelligence (ICTAI'97), 558-567. Washington, D.C.: IEEE Computer Society.

Cooper, G. F., and Herskovits, E. 1992. A Bayesian Method for the Induction of Probabilistic Networks from Data. *Machine Learning* 9(4): 309–347.

Copty, N. 1995. Language and Run-Time Support for the Execution of Hierarchical Clustering Applications on Distributed Memory Machines, Technical Report, SCCS-751, School of Computer Science, Syracuse University.

Cost, S., and Salzberg, S. 1993. A Weighted Nearest-Neighbor Algorithm for Learning with Symbolic Features. *Machine Learning* 10(1): 57–78.

Cost, S., and Salzberg, S. 1997. A Weighted Nearest-Neighbor Algorithm for Learning with Symbolic Features. *Machine Learning* 10:57–78.

Craven, M. W. 1996. Extracting Comprehensible Models from Trained Neural Networks. Technical Report, 1326. Ph.D. dissertation, Department of Computer Science, University of Wisconson at Madison.

Crestana, V.; Soparkar, N. Mining Decentralized Data Repositories. Technical Report CSE-TR-385-99, Dept. of Computer Science, University of Michigan, Ann Arbor.

Croft, W. B. 1981. Document Representation in Probabilistic Models of Information Retrieval. *Journal of the American Society of Information Science* 32(6): 451–457.

Danyluk, A., and Provost, F. 1993. Small Disjuncts in Action: Learning to Diagnose Errors in the Telephone Network Local Loop. In *Machine Learning: Proceedings of the Tenth International Conference*, ed. P. Utgoff, 81–88. San Francisco, Calif.: Morgan Kaufmann.

Darlington, J.; Guo, Y. K.; Sutiwaraphun, J. J.; and To, H. W. 1997. Parallel Induction Algorithms for Data Mining. Paper presented at the Second International Symposium on Reasoning about Intelligent Data Analysis (IDA), 4–6 August, London, United Kingdom.

Dasarathy, B. 1994. *Decision Fusion*. Los Alamitos, Calif.: IEEE Computer Society Press.

Davey, B. A., and Priestley, H. A. 1990. *Introduction to Lattices and Order*. New York: Cambridge University Press.

David, H. A. 1970. *Order Statistics*. New York: Wiley.

Dean, D.; Felten, E.; and Wallach, D. 1996. JAVA Security: From HOTJAVA to NETSCAPE and Beyond. In Proceedings of the IEEE Symposium on Security and Privacy, 190–200. Washington, D.C.: IEEE Computer Society.

DeJong, K. A. 1988. Learning with Genetic Algorithms: An Overview. *Machine Learning* 3(1): 121–138.

DeJong, K. A.; Spears, W. M.; and Gordon, D. F. 1993. Using Genetic Algorithms for Concept Learning. *Machine Learning* 13:161–188.

Dempster, A.; Laird, N.; and Rubin, D. 1977. Maximum Likelihood from Incomplete Data via the EM Algorithm. *Journal of the Royal Statistical Society* 39(1): 1–38.

DesJardins, M., and Gordon, D. F. 1995. *Machine Learning* (Special Issue on Bias Evaluation and Sclcction) 20(1–2).

Detrano, R.; Janosi, A.; Steinbrunn, W.; Pfisterer, M.; Schmid, J.; Sandhu, S.; Guppy, K.; Lee, S.; and Froelicher, V. 1989. International Application of a New Probability Algorithm for the Diagnosis of Coronary Artery Disease. *American Journal of Cardiology* 64:304–310.

Dhillon, I., and Modha, D. 1999. A Data-Clustering Algorithm on Distributed Memory Multiprocessors. Paper presented at the KDD'99 Workshop on High-Performance Knowledge Discovery, 15 August, San Diego, California.

Dietterich, T. 2000. An Experimental Comparison of Three Methods for Constructing Ensembles of Decision Trees: Bagging, Boosting, and Randomization. *Machine Learning* 40(2): 139–157.

Dietterich, T. G. 1997. Machine Learning Research: Four Current Directions. *AI Magazine* 18(4): 97–136.

Domingos, P. 1996a. Efficient Specific-to-General Rule Induction. In *Proceedings of the Second International Conference on Knowledge Discovery and Data Mining,* 319–322. Menlo Park, Calif.: AAAI Press.

Domingos, P. 1996b. Using Partitioning to Speed Up Specific-to-General Rule Induction. Paper presented at the AAAI-96 Workshop on Integrating Multiple Learned Models, 4–9 August, Portland, Oregon.

Domingos, P. 1997a. Context-Sensitive Feature Selection for Lazy Learners. *Artificial Intelligence Review* 11(1-5): 227–253.

Domingos, P. 1997b. Knowledge Acquisition from Examples via Multiple Models. In *Proceedings of the Fourteenth International Conference on Machine Learning*, ed. D. Fisher, 98–106. San Francisco, Calif.: Morgan Kaufmann.

Dongarral, J. J.; Du Croz, J.; Duff, I. S.; and Hammarling, S. 1990. A Set of Level-3 Basic Linear Algebra Subprograms. *ACM Transactions on Mathematical Software* 16(1): 1–17.

Dongarral, J. J.; Du Croz, J.; Hammarling, S.; and Hanson, R. J. 1988. An Extended Set of FORTRAN Basic Linear Algebra Subroutines. *ACM Transactions on Mathematical Software* 14(1):1–32.

Dougherty, J.; Kohavi, R.; and Sahami, M. 1995. Supervised and Unsupervised Discretization of Continuous Features. In *Proceedings of the Twelfth International Conference on Machine Learning*, 194–202. San Francisco, Calif.: Morgan Kaufmann.

Dowd, K., and Severance, C. 1998. *High-Performance Computing*. 2d ed. Sebastopol, Calif.: O'Reilly and Associates.

Drucker, H.; Cortes, C.; Jackel, L. D.; LeCun, Y.; and Vapnik, V. 1994. Boosting and Other Ensemble Methods. *Neural Computation* 6(6): 1289–1301.

Duda, R., and Hart, P. 1973. *Pattern Classification and Scene Analysis*. New York: Wiley.

Duda, R.; Gaschnig, J.; and Hart, P. 1979. Model Design in the PROSPECTOR Consultant System for Mineral Exploration. In *Expert Systems in the Micro-Electronic Age*, ed. D. Michie, 153–167. Edinburgh, U.K.: Edinburgh University Press.

DuMouche, W.; Volinsky, C.; Johnson, T.; Cortes, C.; and Pregibon, D. 1999. Squashing Flat Files Flatter. In Proceedings of the Fifth ACM SIGKDD International Conference on Knowledge Discovery and Data Mining (KDD-99), eds. S. Chaudhuri and D. Madigan, 6–15. New York: Association of Computing Machinery.

Durfee, E.; Lesser, V. R.; and Corkill, D. D. 1989. Cooperative Distributed Problem Solving. In *The Handbook of Artificial Intelligence, Volume 4*, eds. A. Barr, P. R. Cohen, and E. A. Feigenbaum. Reading, Mass.: Addison Wesley.

Farmer, W. M.; Guttag, J. D.; and Swarup, V. 1996. Security for Mobile Agents: Authentification and State Appraisal. In *Proceedings of the Fourth European Symposium on Research in Computer Security*, eds. E. Bertino, H. Kurth, G. Martella, and E. Montolivo, 118–130. Lecture Notes in Computer Science. Berlin: Springer-Verlag.

Fayyad, U. 1997. Editorial. *Data Mining and Knowledge Discovery* 1(1): 5–10.

Fayyad, U. M., and Irani, K. B. 1993. Multi-Interval Discretization of Continuous-Valued Attributes for Classification Learning. In Proceedings of the Fourteenth International Joint Conference on Artificial Intelligence, 1022–1027. Menlo Park, Calif.: International Joint Conferences on Artificial Intelligence.

Fayyad, U. M., and Smyth, P. 1995. From Massive Data Sets to Science Catalogs: Applications and Challenges. In *Proceedings of the Workshop on Massive Data Sets*, eds. J. Kettenring and D. Pregibon, 105–114. Washington, D.C.: National Academy.

Fayyad, U. M., and Uthurusamy, R. 1996. *Communications of the ACM* (Special Issue on Data Mining) 39(11).

Fayyad, U. M.; Haussler, D.; and Stolorz, P. 1996. KDD for Science Data Analysis: Issues and Examples. In Proceedings of Conference on Knowledge Discovery and Data Mining (KDD96), 50–56. Menlo Park, Calif.: American Association for Artificial Intelligence.

Fayyad, U. M.; Piatesky-Shapiro, G.; and Smyth, P. 1996a. The KDD Process for Extracting Useful Knowledge from Volumes of Data. *Communications of the ACM* 39(11): 27–34.

Fayyad, U. M.; Piatetsky-Shapiro, G.; and Smyth, P. 1996b. From Data Mining to Knowledge Discovery: An Overview. In *Advances in Knowledge Discovery and Data Mining*, eds. U. M. Fayyad, G. Piatetsky-Shapiro, P. Smyth, and R. Uthurusamy, 1–34. Menlo Park, Calif.: AAAI Press.

Fayyad, U. M.; Piatetsky Shapiro, G.; Smyth, P.; and Uthurusamy, R. 1996. *Advances in Knowledge Discovery and Data Mining*. Menlo Park, Calif.: AAAI Press.

Fayyad, U. M.; Smyth, P.; Burl, M.; and Perona, P. 1996. Learning to Catalog Science Images. In *Early Visual Learning*, 237–268. New York: Oxford University Press.

Fayyad, U. M.; Weir, N.; and Djorgovski, S. 1993. SKICAT: A Machine-Learning System for Automated Cataloging of Large-Scale Sky Surveys. In *Proceedings of the Tenth International Conference on Machine Learning*, 112–119. San Francisco, Calif.: Morgan Kaufmann.

Feldman, R., and Dagan, I. 1995. Knowledge Discovery in Textual Databases. In Proceedings of the First International Conference on Knowledge Discovery in Databases, ed. U. M. Fayyad, 112–117. Menlo Park, Calif.: American Association for Artificial Intelligence.

Feldman, R., and Hirsh, H. 1997. Exploiting Background Information in Knowledge Discovery from Text. *Journal of Intelligent Information Systems* 9(1): 83–97.

Fifield, D. J. 1992. Distributed Tree Construction from Large Data-Sets. Bachelor's honors thesis, Computer Science Department, Australian National University.

Finin, T.; Fritzon, R.; McKay, D.; and McEntire, R. 1994. KQML—A Language and Protocol for Knowledge and Information Exchange. Paper presented at the Thirteenth International Workshop on Distributed Artificial Intelligence, 28–30 July, Seattle, Washington.

Finin, T.; Labrou, Y.; and Mayfield, J. 1997. KQML as an Agent Communication Language. In *Software Agents*, ed. J. Bradshaw, 291–316. Menlo Park, Calif.: AAAI Press.

Fisher, R. A. 1936. The Use of Multiple Measurements in Taxonomic Problems. *Anals of Eugenics* 7:179–188.

Flockhart, I. W., and Radcliffe, N. J. 1995. GA-MINER: Parallel Data Mining with Hierarchical Genetic Algorithms: Final Report, EPCC-AIKMS-GA-MINER-REPORT 1.0, Edinburgh Parallel Computing Center, University of Edinburgh.

Flockhart, I. W., and Radcliffe, N. J. 1996. A Genetic Algorithm–Based Approach to Data Mining. In Proceedings of Conference on Knowledge Discovery and Data Mining (KDD96). Menlo Park, Calif.: American Association for Artificial Intelligence.

Foster, I., and Kesselman, C. 1997. GLOBUS: A Metacomputing Infrastructure Toolkit. *International Journal Supercomputing Applications* 11(2): 115–128.

Foster, I., and Kesselman, C., editors. 1999. *The Grid: Blueprint for a New Computing Infrastructure*. San Francisco, Calif.: Morgan Kaufmann.

Fox, C.; Levitin, A.; and Redman, T. 1994. The Notion of Data and Its Quality Dimensions. *Information Processing and Management* 30(1): 9–19.

Fox, E. A.; Akscyn, R. M.; Furuta, R.; and Legsett, J. 1995. *Communications of the ACM* (Special Issue on Digital Libraries) 38(4).

Fox, G. C. 1988. *Solving Problems on Concurrent Processors, Volume 1*. Englewood Cliffs, N.J.: Prentice Hall.

Fox, G. C.; Williams, R. D.; and Messina, P. C. 1994. *Parallel Computing Works!* San Francisco, Calif.: Morgan Kaufmann.

Freitas, A. A. 1997. Toward Large-Scale Knowledge Discovery in Databases (KDD) by Exploiting Parallelism in Generic KDD Primitives. Paper presented at the Third International Workshop on Next-Generation Information Technologies and Systems, 1–5 July, Neve Ilan, Israel.

Freitas, A. A., and Lavington, S. 1996b. Using SQL Primitives and Parallel DB Servers to Speed Up Knowledge Discovery in Large Relational Databases. In Cybernetics and Systems'96: Proceedings of the Thirteenth European Meeting on Cybernetics and Systems Research, 955–960. Vienna, Austria: Austrian Society for Cybernetic Studies.

Freitas, A. A., and Lavington, S. H. 1996a. Parallel Data Mining for Very Large Relational Databases. Paper presented at the International Conference on High-Performance Computing and Networking (HPCN), 15–19 April, Brussels, Belgium.

Freitas, A. A., and Lavington, S. H. 1997. *Mining Very Large Databases with Parallel Processing*. Norwell, Mass.: Kluwer Academic.

Freitas, A. A., and Lavington, S. H. 1998. *Mining Very Large Databases with Parallel Processing*. New York: Kluwer Academic.

French, C. D. 1995. "One Size Fits All" Database Architectures Do Not Work for DSS. In Proceedings of the ACM SIGMOD International Conference on Management of Data, 449-450. New York: Association of Computing Machinery.

Freund, Y., and Schapire, R. 1995. A Decision-Theoretic Generalization of On-Line Learning and an Application to Boosting. In *Proceedings of the Second European Conference on Computational Learning Theory*, 23–37. Berlin: Springer-Verlag.

Freund, Y., and Schapire, R. 1996. Experiments with a New Boosting Algorithm. In *Proceedings of the Thirteenth Conference on Machine Learning*, 148–156. San Francisco, Calif.: Morgan Kaufmann.

Frey, L. J., and Fisher, D. H. 1999. Modeling Decision Tree Performance with the Power Law. In *Proceedings of the Seventh International Workshop on Artificial Intelligence and Statistics*, eds. D. Heckerman and J. Whittaker, 59–65. San Francisco, Calif.: Morgan Kaufmann.

Friedman, J. H. 1991. Multivariate Adaptive Regression Splines. *The Annals of Statistics* 19(1): 1–141.

Friedman, J. H. 1997. Data Mining and Statistics: What's the Connection? Paper presented at the Twenty-Ninth Symposium on the Interface between Computer Science and Statistics, 14–17 May, Houston, Texas.

Fürnkranz, J. 1998. Integrative Windowing. *Journal of Artificial Intelligence Research* 8:129–164.

Galal, G.; Cook, D. J.; and Holder, L. 1999. Exploiting Parallelism in a Scientific Discovery System to Improve Scalability. *Journal of the American Society for Information Science* 50(1): 65–73.

Gannon, D., and Grimshaw, A. 1999. Object-Based Approaches. In *The Grid: Blueprint for a New Computing Infrastructure*, eds. I. Foster and C. Kesselman, 205–236. San Francisco, Calif.: Morgan Kaufmann.

Garey, M. R., and Johnson, D. S. 1979. *Computers and Intractability: A Guide to the Theory of NP-Completeness*. New York: Freeman.

Garfinkel, S. 1995. PGP: Pretty Good Privacy. O'Reilly and Associates, Inc., Sebastopol, California.

Garvey, T. D.; Lunt, T. F.; Qian, X.; and Stickel, M. E. 1992. Toward a Tool to Detect and Eliminate Inference Problems in the Design of Multilevel Databases. In *Proceedings of the IFIP TC11/WG11.3 Sixth Working Conference on Database Security*, 159–177. London: Chapman and Hall.

Gehrke, J.; Ramakrishnan, R.; and Ganti, V. 1998. RAINFOREST—A Framework for Fast Decision Tree Construction of Large Datasets. Paper presented at the Twenty-Fourth International Conference on Very Large Databases, 24–27 August, New York.

Geist, G. A.; Kohl, J. A.; and Papadopoulos, P. M. 1996. PVM and MPI: A Comparison of Features. *Calculateurs Paralleles* 8(2): 137–150.

Geman, S.; Bienenstock, E.; and Doursat, R. 1992. Neural Networks and the Bias/Variance Dilemma. *Neural Computation* 4(1): 1–58.

Ghosh, J.; Deuser, L.; and Beck, S. 1992. A Neural Network–Based Hybrid System for Detection, Characterization, and Classification of Short-Duration Oceanic Signals. *IEEE Journal of Ocean Engineering* 17(4): 351–363.

Ghosh, J.; Tumer, K.; Beck, S.; and Deuser, L. 1992. Integration of Local and Global Neural Classifiers for Passive Sonar Signals. Paper presented at the International Simulation Technology Conference, 12–14 November, Houston, Texas.

Gillett, R. 1996. Memory Channel: An Optimized Cluster Interconnect. *IEEE Micro* 16(2): 12–18.

Goldberg, D. E. 1989. *Genetic Algorithms in Search, Optimization, and Machine Learning*. Reading, Mass.: Addison-Wesley.

Golovchinsky, G. 1997. What the Query Told the Link: The Integration of Hypertext and Information Retrieval. In Proceedings of the ACM Conference on Hypertext, 67–74. New York: Association of Computing Machinery.

Golub, G., and Van Loan, C. 1989. *Matrix Computations*. 2d ed. Baltimore, Md.: Johns Hopkins University Press.

Gong, L. 1998. *The* JAVA *Security Model: Cryptography, Architectures, APIs, and Implementations*. Reading, Mass.: Addison-Wesley.

Goodman, E. 1996. An Introduction to GALOPPS. Technical Report, 96-07-01, College of Engineering, Michigan State University.

Gordon, V. S., and Whitley, D. 1993. Serial and Parallel Genetic Algorithms as Function Optimizers. Paper presented at the International Conference on Genetic Algorithms, 17–21 July, Urbana-Champaign, Illinois.

Graefe, G.; Fayyad, U.; and Chaudhuri, S. 1998. On the Efficient Gathering of Sufficient Statistics for Classification of Large SQL Databases. In Proceedings of the Fourth International Conference on Knowledge Discovery and Data Mining, 204–208. Menlo Park, Calif.: American Association for Artificial Intelligence.

Granger, C. W. J. 1989. Combining Forecasts—Twenty Years Later. *Journal of Forecasting* 8(3): 167–173.

Gray, R. 1998. AGENT TCL: A Flexible and Secure Mobile-Agent System. Technical Report, PCS-TR98-327, Department of Computer Science, Dartmouth College.

Gray, R.; Rus, D.; and Kotz, D. 1996. Transportable Information Agents. Technical Report, PCS-TR96-278, Department of Computer Science, Dartmouth College.

Grefenstette, J. J. 1981. Parallel Adaptive Algorithms for Function Optimization. Technical Report, CS-81-19, Department of Computer Science, Vanderbilt University.

Grimshaw, A. S., and Wulf, W. 1997. The Legion Vision of a Worldwide Virtual Computer. *Communications of the ACM* 40(1): 39–45.

Grimshaw, A. S.; Weissman, J.; West, E.; and Lyot, E., Jr. 1994. Metasystems: An Approach Combining Parallel Processing and Heterogeneous Distributed Computing Systems. *Journal of Parallel and Distributed Computing* 21(3): 257–270.

Grossman, R. L. 1998. Supporting the Data-Mining Process with Next-Generation Data-Mining Systems. *Enterprise System Journal* (Special Issue), 52–56.

Grossman, R. L., and Bailey, S. 1998. A Tutorial Introduction to High- Performance Data Mining. Tutorial given at the Fourth International Conference on Knowledge Discovery and Data Mining (KDD-98), 15–18 August, San Diego, California.

Grossman, R. L.; Bailey, S.; and Hanley, D. 1997. Data Mining Using Light Weight Object Management in Clustered Computing Environments. In *Proceedings of the Seventh International Workshop on Persistent Object Stores*, 237–249. San Francisco, Calif.: Morgan Kaufmann.

Grossman, R. L.; Bailey, S.; Kasif, S.; Mon, D.; and Ramu, A. 1998. The Preliminary Design of PAPYRUS: A System for High Performance. Paper presented at the KDD-98 Workshop on Distributed Data Mining, 27–31 August, New York City.

Grossman, R. L.; Bailey, S.; Kasif, S.; Mon, D.; Ramu, A.; and Malhi, B. 1997. The Preliminary Design of PAPYRUS: A System for High-Performance, Distributed Data Mining over Clusters, Meta-Clusters and Super-Clusters. Paper presented at the KDD-97 Workshop on Distributed Data Mining, 14–17 August, Newport Beach, California.

Grossman, R. L.; Bailey, S.; Ramu, A.; Malhi, B.; Hallstrom, P.; Pulleyn, I.; and Qin, X. 1999. The Management and Mining of Multiple Predictive Models Using the Predictive Modeling Markup Language (PMML). *Information and Software Technology* 41(9): 589–595.

Grossman, R. L.; Bodek, H.; Northcutt, D.; and Poor, H. V. 1996. Data Mining and Tree-Based Optimization. In Proceedings of the Second International Conference on Knowledge Discovery and Data Mining, 323–326. Menlo Park, Calif.: American Association for Artificial Intelligence.

Gudivada, V. N.; Raghavan, V. V.; Grosky, W. I.; and Kasanagottu, R. 1997. Information Retrieval on the World Wide Web. *IEEE Internet Computing* 15:58–68.

Guerin, R., and Schulzrinne, H. 1999. Network Quality of Service. In *The Grid: Blueprint for a New Computing Infrastructure*, eds. I. Foster and C. Kesselman, 479–503. San Francisco, Calif.: Morgan Kaufmann.

Gunopulos, D.; Mannila, H.; and Saluja, S. 1997. Discovering All the Most Specific Sentences by Randomized Algorithms. Paper presented at the International Conference on Database Theory, 8–10 January, Delphi, Greece.

Guo, Y., and Sutiwaraphun, J. 1997. Knowledge Probing in Distributed Data Mining. Paper presented at the KDD-97 Workshop on Distributed Data Mining, 14–17 August, Newport Beach, California.

Guo, Y., and Sutiwaraphun, J. 1998. Knowledge Probing in Distributed Data Mining. Paper presented at the KDD-98 Workshop on Distributed Data Mining, 27–31 August, New York.

Guo, Y.; Rüeger, S.; Sutiwaraphun, J.; and Forbes-Millott, J. 1997. Meta-Learning for Parallel Data Mining. Paper presented at the Seventh Parallel Computing Workshop, 25–26 September, Australia National University, Canberra, Australia.

Hale, J., and Shenoi, S. 1997. Catalytic Inference, Knowledge Discovery, and Database Security. In Proceedings of the 1997 IEEE Symposium on Research in Security and Privacy, 188–201. Washington, D.C.: IEEE Computer Society.

Hall, L. O.; Chawla, N.; and Bowyer, K. W. 1998. Combining Decision Trees Learned in Parallel. Paper presented at the KDD-97 Workshop on Distributed Data Mining, 14–17 August, Newport Beach, California.

Han, E. H.; Karypis, G.; and Kumar, V. 2000. Scalable Parallel Data Mining for Association Rules. *IEEE Transactions on Knowledge and Data Engineering* 12(3). Forthcoming.

Han, E.-H.; Karypis, G.; and Kumar, V. 1997. Scalable Parallel Data Manufacturing and Management of Data. In Proceedings of the ACM SIGMOD International Conference on Management of Data, 277–288. New York: Association of Computing Machinery.

Han, J. 1998. Toward On-Line Analytic Data Mining in Large Databases. *SIGMOD Record* 27(1): 97-107.

Han J.; Chen, J. M.; and Yu, P. 1996. Data Mining: An Overview from a Database Perspective. *IEEE Transactions on Knowledge and Data Engineering* 8(6): 866–883.

Hansen, L., and Salamon, P. 1990. Neural Network Ensembles. *IEEE Transactions on Pattern Analysis and Machine Intelligence*, 12(10): 993–1001.

Harinarayan, V.; Rajaraman, A.; and Ullman, J. D. 1996. Implementing Data Cubes Efficiently. In Proceedings of the ACM SIGMOD International Conference on Management of Data, 205–216. New York: Association of Computing Machinery.

Harris-Jones, C., and Haines, T. L. 1997. Sample Size and Misclassification: Is More Always Better? Working Paper AMSCAT-WP-97-118, AMS Center for Advanced Technologies, Fairfax, Virginia.

Hashem, S., and Schmeiser, B. 1993. Approximating a Function and Its Derivatives Using MSE-Optimal Linear Combinations of Trained Feedforward Neural Networks. In *Proceedings of the Joint Conference on Neural Networks, Volume 87*, 617–620. Hillsdale, N.J.: Lawrence Erlbaum.

Haussler, D. 1988. Quantifiying Inductive Bias: AI Learning Algorithms and Valiant's Learning Framework. *Artificial Intelligence* 36(2): 177–221.

Havens, W. S., and Rehfuss, P. S. 1989. PLATYPUS: A Constraint-Based Reasoning System. In Proceedings of the Eleventh International Joint Conference on Artificial Intelligence, XX–XX. Menlo Park, Calif.: International Joint Conferences on Artificial Intelligence.

Haykin, S. 1999. *Neural Networks: A Comprehensive Foundation*. Upper Saddle River, N.J.: Prentice Hall.

Heath, D.; Kasif, S.; and Salzberg, S. 1996. Committees of Decision Trees. In *Cognitive Technology: In Search of a Humane Interface*, 305 317. Amsterdam, The Netherlands: Elsevier Science.

Heckerman, D. 1997. Bayesian Networks for Data Mining. In *Data Mining and Knowledge Discovery*, 79–119. New York: Kluwer Academic.

Hershberger, D., and Kargupta, H. 1999. Distributed Multivariate Regression Using Wavelet-Based Collective Data Mining. Technical Report, EECS-99-02, School of Electrical Engineering and Computer Science, Washington State University.

High-Performance Fortran Forum. 1993. High-Performance Fortran Language Specification. *Scientific Programming* 2(1–2): 1–170.

Hinke, T. H. 1988. Inference Aggregation Detection in Database Management Systems. In Proceedings of the 1988 IEEE Symposium on Research in Security and Privacy, 96–106. Washington, D.C.: IEEE Computer Society.

Holland, J. H. 1962. Outline for a Logical Theory of Adaptive Systems. *Journal of the Association of Computing Machinery* 9(3): 297–314.

Holland, J. H. 1975. *Adaptation in Natural and Artificial Systems.* Ann Arbor, Mich.: University of Michigan Press.

Holland, J. H. 1986. Escaping Brittleness: The Possibilities of General-Purpose Learning Algorithms Applied to Parallel Rule-Based Systems. In *Machine Learning: An Artificial Intelligence Approach, Volume 2*, eds. R. Michalski, J. Carbonell, and T. Mitchell, 593–623. San Francisco, Calif.: Morgan Kaufmann.

Holmstrom, L.; Koistinen, P.; Laaksonen, J.; and Oja, E. 1997. Neural and Statistical Classifiers—Taxonomy and Two Case Studies. *IEEE Transactions on Neural Networks* 8(1): 5–17.

Holsheimer, M. 1996. Data Surveyor: Searching the Nuggets in Parallel. In *Advances in Knowledge Discovery and Data Mining*, eds. U. M. Fayyad, G. Piatetsky-Shapiro, and P. Smyth, XX–XX. Menlo Park, Calif.: AAAI Press.

Holsheimer, M.; Kersten, M.; Mannila, H.; and Toivonen, H. 1995. A Perspective on Databases and Data Mining. Paper presented at the First International Conference on Knowledge Discovery and Data Mining, 20–21 August, Montreal, Quebec, Canada.

Holte, R.; Acker, L.; and Porter, B. 1989. Concept Learning and the Problem of Small Disjuncts. In Proceedings of the Eleventh International Joint Conference on Artificial Intelligence, 813–818. Menlo Park, Calif.: International Joint Conferences on Artificial Intelligence.

Houstma, M., and Swami, A. 1993. Set-Oriented Mining of Association Rules, Technical Report RJ 8567, IBM Almaden Research Laboratory, San Jose, California.

Houtsma, M., and Swami, A. 1995. Set-Oriented Mining of Association Rules in Relational Databases. Paper presented at the Eleventh International Conference on Data Engineering, 610 March, Taipei, Taiwan.

Hower, W. 1990. Constraint-Directed Reasoning with Partial Information. Presentation made at the Constraint-Directed Reasoning Workshop, the Eighth National Conference on Artificial Intelligence, 29 July–3 August, Boston, Massachusetts.

Hubbard, B. B. 1998. *The World accoring to Wavelets.* Wellesley, Mass.: A. K. Peters.

Huber, P. 1997. From Large to Huge: A Statistician's Reaction to KDD and DM. In *Proceedings of the Third International Conference on Knowledge Discovery and Data Mining*, 304–308. Menlo Park, Calif.: AAAI Press.

Informix. 1998. Informix Decision Support Indexing for the Enterprise Data Warehouse. White paper, Informix Corporation, Menlo Park, California.

Jackson, J. E. 1991. *A User's Guide to Principal Components.* New York: Wiley.

Jacobs, R. A.; Jordan, M. I.; Nowlan, S. J.; and Hinton, G. E. 1991. Adaptive Mixture of Local Experts. *Neural Computation* 3(1): 79–87.

Jahne, B. 1997. *Practical Handbook on Image Processing for Scientific Applications.* Boca Raton, Fla.: CRC.

Jain, A. K., and Dubes, R. C. 1988. *Algorithms for Clustering Data.* Upper Saddle River, N.J.: Prentice Hall.

Jain, A. K., and Zongker, D. 1997. Feature Selection: Evaluation, Application, and Small Sample Performance. *IEEE Transactions on Pattern Analysis and Machine Intelligence* 19(8): 153–158.

James, M. 1985. *Classificaton Algorithms*. New York: Wiley.

Janicke, L. 1996. Resource Selection and Information Evaluation. Technical Report, Dept. of Computer Science, University of Illinois at Urbana-Champaign. (alexia.lis.uiuc.edu/ janicke/Evaluate.html).

Jensen, D., and Cohen, P. R. 1999. Multiple Comparisons in Induction Algorithms. *Machine Learning* 38(3): 309–338.

John, G., and Langley, P. 1996. Static versus Dynamic Sampling for Data Mining. In Proceedings of the Second International Conference on Knowledge Discovery and Data Mining, 367–370. Menlo Park, Calif.: American Association for Artificial Intelligence.

John, G., and Lent, B. 1997. SIPping from the Data Firehose. In Proceedings of Third International Conference on Knowledge Discovery and Data Mining, 199–202. Menlo Park, Calif.: American Association for Artificial Intelligence.

Johnson, E., and Kargupta, H. 1999. *Collective, Hierarchical Clustering from Distributed, Heterogeneous Data.* Lecture Notes in Computer Science 1759. Berlin: Springer-Verlag.

Jordan, M. I., and Jacobs, R. A. 1994. Hierarchical Mixture of Experts and the EM Algorithm. *Neural Computation* 6(1):181–214.

Joshi, M. V.; Karypis, G.; and Kumar, V. 1998. SCALPARC: A New Scalable and Efficient Parallel Classification Algorithm for Mining Large Datasets. Paper presented at the International Parallel Processing Symposium, 30 March–3 April, Orlando, Florida.

Judd, D.; McKinley, P. K.; and Jain, A. K. 1998. Large-Scale Parallel Data Clustering. *IEEE Transactions on Pattern Analysis and Machine Intelligence* 20(8): 871–876.

Kanal, L. 1974. Patterns in Pattern Recognition. *IEEE Transactions on Information Theory* 20(11): 697–722.

Karagupta, H.; Johnson, E.; Sanseverino, E. R.; Park, B.-H.; Silvestre, L. D.; and Hershberger, D. 1999. Scalable Data Mining from Vertically Partitioned Feature Space Using Collective Mining and Gene Expression–Based Genetic Algorithms. Paper presented at the KDD-98 Workshop on Distributed Data Mining, 27–31 August, New York.

Kargupta, H., and Park, H. 1999a. Fast Construction of Distributed and Decomposed Evolutionary Representation. In *Late Breaking Papers of the Genetic and Evolutionary Computation Conference*, 139–148. Menlo Park, Calif.: AAAI Press.

Kargupta, H.; Huang, W.; Krishnamurthy, E.; and Johnson, E. 2000. Distributed Clustering Using Collective Principal Component Analysis. Paper presented at the ACM SIGKDD-2000 Workshop on Distributed and Parallel Knowledge Discovery, August 20, 2000. Boston, Mass.

Kargupta, H., and Sarkar, K. 1999. Function Induction, Gene Expression, and Evolutionary Representation Construction. In *Proceedings of the Genetic and Evolutionary Computation Conference*, 313–320. Menlo Park, Calif.: AAAI Press.

Kargupta, H.; Hamzaoglu, I.; and Stafford, B. 1997. Scalable, Distributed Data Mining Using an Agent-Based Architecture. In *Proceedings of Third International Conference on Knowledge Discovery and Data Mining*, eds. D. Heckerman, H. Mannila, D. Pregibon, and R. Uthurusamy, 211–214. Menlo Park, Calif.: AAAI Press.

Kargupta, H.; Hamzaoglu, I.; Stafford, B.; Hanagandi, V.; and Buescher, K. 1996. PADMA: Parallel Data-Mining Agent for Scalable Text Classification. In Proceedings of the Conference on High-Performance Computing '97, 290–295. San Diego, Calif.: The Society for Computer Simulation International.

Kargupta, H.; Huang, W.; Krishnamurthy, S.; Park, B.; and Wang, S. 2000. Collective PCA from Distributed and Heterogeneous Data. Paper presented at the Fourth European Conference on Principles and Practice of Knowledge Discovery in Databases, September 13-16, Lyon, France.

Kargupta, H.; Johnson, E.; Sanseverino, E. R.; Park, B.-H.; Silvestre, L. D.; and Hershberger, D. 1998. Scalable Data Mining from Distributed, Vertically Partitioned Feature Space Using Collective Mining and Gene Expression–Based Genetic Algorithms. Paper presented at the KDD-97 Workshop on Distributed Data Mining, 14–17 August, Newport Beach, California.

Kargupta, H.; Park, B.; Hershberger, D.; and Johnson, E. 1999. Collective Data Mining: A New Perspective toward Distributed Data Mining. Technical Report, EECS-99-01, Department of Electrical Engineering and Computer Science, Washington State University. (Chapter 5 is a revised version of this paper.)

Karjoth, G.; Lange, D. B.; and Oshimam, M. 1998. A Security Model for Aglets. In *Mobile Agents and Security*, ed. G. Vigna, 188–205. Lecture Notes in Computer Science 1419. Berlin: Springer-Verlag.

Kaski, S. 1997. Data Exploration Using Self-Organizing Maps, Technical Report, Acta Polytechnica Scandinavia, Mathematics, Computing, and Management in Engineering Series, 82, Laboratory for Computer and Information Science, Helsinki University of Technology.

Kearns, M., and Seung, S. 1995. Learning from a Population of Hypotheses. *Machine Learning* 18(2–3): 255–276.

Kennedy, R. L.; Lee, Y.; Van Roy, B.; Reed, C. D.; and Lippman, R. P. 1998. Solving Data-Mining Problems through Pattern Recognition. Upper Saddle River, N.J.: Prentice Hall.

Kleiman, S.; Shah, D.; and Smaalders, B. 1995. *Programming with Threads*. New York: Prentice Hall.

Klemettinen, M.; Mannila, H.; Ronkainen, P.; Toivonen, H.; and Verkamo, A. I. 1994. Finding Interesting Rules from Large Sets of Discovered Association Rules. In Proceedings of the Third International Conference on Information and Knowledge Management, 29 November–2 December, Gaithersburg, Maryland.

Knuth, D. 1968. *The Art of Computer Programming*. Reading, Mass.: Addison-Wesley.

Kohavi, R. 1996. Wrappers for Performance Enhancement and Oblivious Decision Graphs. Ph.D. thesis, Department of Computer Science, Stanford University.

Kohavi, R., and John, G. 1997. Wrappers for Feature Subset Selection. *Artificial Intelligence* 97(1–2): 273–324.

Kohavi, R., and John, G. 1998. The WRAPPER Approach. In *Feature Extraction, Construction, and Selection: A Data Mining Perspective,* eds. H. Liu and H. Motoda, 33–50. New York: Springer Verlag.

Kohavi, R., and Sommerfield, D. 1995. Feature Subset Selection Using the Wrapper Model: Overfitting and Dynamic Search Space Topology. In Proceedings of the First International Conference on Knowledge Discovery and Data Mining, 192–197. Menlo Park, Calif.: American Association for Artificial Intelligence.

Kohl, J., and Neuman, C. 1993. The Kerberos Network Authentication Service (V5). RFC 1510, Digital Equipment Corporation, ISI, Cambridge, Massachusetts.

Kohonen, T. 1997. *Self-Organizing Maps*. 2d ed. New York: Springer Verlag.

Kornfeld, W. A. 1982. Combinatorially Implosive Algorithms. *Communications of the ACM* 25(10): 155–171.

Kotz, D. 1994. Disk-Directed I/O for MIMD Multiprocessors. Paper presented at the Symposium on Operating Systems Design and Implementation, 14–17 November, Monterey, California.

Krogh, A., and Vedelsby, J. 1995. Neural Network Ensembles, Cross Validation, and Active Learning. In *Advances in Neural Information Processing Systems-7*, eds. G. Tesauro, D. S. Touretzky, and T. K. Leen, 231–238. Cambridge, Mass.: MIT Press.

Kuck, D. J.; Davidson, E. S.; Lawrie, D. H.; and Sameh, A. H. 1986. Parallel Supercomputing Today and the CEDAR Approach. *Science* 231(4741): 967.

Kufrin, R. 1995. Decision Trees on Parallel Processors. Paper presented at the Fourteenth IJCAI Workshop on Parallel Processing for Artificial Intelligence, 20–25 August, Montreal, Canada.

Kufrin, R. 1997. Generating C4.5 Production Rules in Parallel. In *Proceedings of the Fourteenth National Conference on Artificial Intelligence,* 565–570. Menlo Park, Calif.: AAAI Press.

Kumar, A.; Singhal, M.; and Liu, M. T. 1987. A Model for Distributed Decision Making: An Expert System for Load Balancing in Distributed Systems. In *IEEE Proceedings of COMPSAC*, 507–513. Washington, D.C.: IEEE Computer Society.

Kumar, V., and Rao, V. 1987. Parallel Depth-First Search, Part 2: Analysis. *International Journal of Parallel Programming* 16(6): 501–519.

Kumar, V.; Grama, A. Y.; and Rao, V. N. 1994. Scalable Load Balancing Techniques for Parallel Computers. *Journal of Parallel and Distributed Computing* 22(1): 60–79.

Kumar, V.; Grama, A.; Gupta, A.; and Karypis, G. 1994. *Introduction to Parallel Computing: Design and Analysis of Algorithms.* Wokingham, U.K.: Benjamin-Cummings.

Kumar, V.; Shekhar, S.; and Amin, M. B. 1994. A Highly Parallel Formulation of Backpropagation on Hypercubes. *IEEE Transactions on Parallel and Distributed Systems* 5(10): 1073–1091.

Kushilevitz, S., and Mansour, Y. 1991. Learning Decision Trees Using Fourier Spectrum. In Proceedings of the Twenty-Third Annual ACM Symposium on Theory of Computing, 455–464. New York: Association of Computing Machinery.

Kwok, S., and Carter, C. 1990. Multiple Decision Trees. In *Uncertainty in Artificial Intelligence, Volume 4*, 327–335. New York: Elsevier Science.

Labio, W. L.; Quass, D.; and Adelberg, B. 1997. Physical Database Design for Data Warehouses. Paper presented at the International Conference on Data Engineering, 7–11 April, Birmingham, United Kingdom.

Lam, W., and Segre, A. M. 1997. Distributed Data Mining of Probabilistic Knowledge. In Proceedings of the Seventeenth International Conference on Distributed Computer Systems (ICDCS), 178–185. Washington, D.C.: IEEE Computer Society.

Lander, E., and Lesser, R. 1997. Sharing Meta-Information to Guide Cooperative Search among Heterogeneous Reusable Agents. *IEEE Transactions on Knowledge and Data Engineering* 9(2): 193–208.

Lang, K. 1995. News Weeder: Learning to Filter Net News. In *Proceedings of the Twelfth International Conference on Machine Learning*, eds. A. Prieditis and S. Russel, 331–339. San Francisco, Calif.: Morgan Kaufmann.

Lange, D. B., and Chang, D. T. 1996. Programming Mobile Agents in JAVA—A White Paper. Technical report, IBM Corp., Tokyo, Japan.

Lange, D. B., and Oshima, M. 1998. *Programming and Deploying* JAVA*(tm) Mobile Agents with Aglets(tm).* Reading, Mass.: Addison-Wesley.

Larson, R. 1982. Tutorial : Distributed Control. 2d ed. Washington, D.C.: IEEE Computer Society.

Lathrop, R.; Webster, T.; Smith, T.; and Winston, P. 1990. ARIEL: A Massively Parallel Symbolic Learning Assistant for Protein Structure/Function. In *AI at MIT: Expanding Frontiers*, eds. P. Winston and S. Shellard. Cambridge, Mass.: MIT Press.

Lawrence, S., and Giles, C. L. 1999. Accessibility of Information on the Web. *Nature* 8: 107–109

Lawson, C. L.; Hanson, R. J.; Kincaid, D.; and Krogh, F. T. 1979. Basic Linear Algebra Subprograms for FORTRAN Usage. *ACM Transactions on Mathematical Software* 5(3): 308–323.

LeBlanc, M., and Tibshirani, R. 1993. Combining Estimates in Regression and Classification. Technical Report, 9318, Department of Statistics, University of Toronto.

Lee, J. S.; Ranka, S., and Shankar, R. V. 1995. Communication-Efficient and Memory-Bounded External Redistribution, Technical Report, Department of Computer Science, Syracuse University.

Lee, W., and Stolfo, S. 1988. Data-Mining Approaches for Intrusion Detection. Paper presented at the Seventh USENIX Security Symposium, 26–29 January, San Antonio, Texas.

Lee, W.; Stolfo, S.; and Mok, K. 1999. A Data-Mining Framework for Adaptive Intrusion Detection. In Proceedings of the 1999 IEEE Symposium on Security and Privacy, XXX–XXX. Washington, D.C.: IEEE Computer Society.

Levine, D. 1996. User Guide to the PGAPACK Parallel Genetic Algorithm Library. Technical Report ANL-95/18, Argonne National Laboratory, Chicago, Illinois.

Lewinson, L. 1994. Data Mining: Tapping into the Mother Lode. *Database Programming and Design* 7(2): 50–56.

Lewis, B., and Berg, D. J. 1995. *Threads Primer: A Guide to Multithreaded Programming*. Upper Saddle River, N.J.: Prentice Hall.

Li, W., and Pingali, K. 1993. Access Normalization: Loop Restructuring for NUMA Compilers. *ACM Transactions on Computer Systems* 11(4): 353–375.

Lin, D.-I., and Kedem, Z. M. 1998. PINCER-SEARCH: A New Algorithm for Discovering the Maximum Frequent Set. Paper presented at the Sixth International Conference on Extending Database Technology, 23–27 March, Valencia, Spain.

Lin, F., and Keller, R. 1987. The Gradient Model Load-Balancing Method. *IEEE Transactions on Software Engineering* 13(1): 32–38.

Lin, J.-L., and Dunham, M. H. 1998. Mining Association Rules: Anti-Skew Algorithms. Paper presented at the Fourteenth International Conference on Data Engineering, 23–27 February, Orlando, Florida.

Lippmann, R. 1987. An Introduction to Computing with Neural Nets. *IEEE Acoustics, Speech, and Signal Processing Magazine* 5(2): 4–22.

Liu, H.; Lu, H.; and Yao, J. 1998. Identifying Relevant Databases for Multidatabase Mining. In *Proceedings of the Second Pacific-Asia Conference on Knowledge Discovery and Data Mining (PAKDD'98)*, 210–221. Lecture Notes in Computer Science 1394. New York: Springer.

Maitan, J.; Ras, Z. W.; and Zemankova, M. 1989. Query Handling and Learning in a Distributed Intelligent System. In *Methodologies for Intelligent Systems, 4*, ed. Z. W. Ras, 118–127. New York: North Holland.

Malliaris, M., and Salchenberger, L. 1993. A Neural Network Model for Estimating Option Prices. *Applied Intelligence* 3(3): 193–206.

Manderick, B., and Spiessens, P. 1989. Fine-Grained Parallel Genetic Algorithms. In Proceedings of the International Conference on Genetic Algorithms, 428–433. San Francisco, Calif.: Morgan Kaufmann.

Mangasarian, O. L. 1993. Mathematical Programming in Neural Networks. *ORSA Journal on Computing* 5:349–360.

Margineantu, D., and Dietterich, T. 1997. Pruning Adaptive Boosting. In *Proceedings of the Fourteenth International Conference on Machine Learning*, 211–218. San Francisco, Calif.: Morgan Kaufmann.

Markatos, E. P., and LeBlanc, T. 1994. Using Processor Affinity in Loop Scheduling on Shared-Memory Multiprocessors. *IEEE Transactions on Parallel and Distributed Systems* 5(4): 379–400.

Maschhoff, K. J., and Sorensen, D. C. 1996. P_ARPACK: An Efficient Portable Large-Scale Eigenvalue Package for Distributed Memory Parallel Architectures. Paper presented at the Copper Mountain Conference on Iterative Methods, 9–13 April, Copper Mountain, Colorado.

McGraw, G., and Felten, E. 1997. JAVA *Security: Hostile Applets, Holes, and Antidotes*. New York: Wiley.

McQuitty, L. 1966. Similarity Analysis by Reciprocal Pairs for Discrete and Continuous Data. *Educational and Psychological Measurement* 26:825–831.

Mehta, M.; Agrawal, R.; and Rissanen, J. 1996. SLIQ: A Fast Scalable Classifier for Data Mining. Paper presented at the Fifth International Conference on Extending Database Technology (EDBT), 25–29 March, Avignon, France.

Merz, C. 1998. Using Correspondence Analysis to Combine Classifiers. *Machine Learning* 36(1): 33–58.

Merz, C., and Pazzani, M. 1997. Combining Neural Network Regression Estimates with Regularized Linear Weights. In *Advances in Neural Information Processing Systems-9*, eds. M. C. Mozer, M. I. Jordan, and T. Petsche, 564–570. Cambridge, Mass.: MIT Press.

Merz, C., and Pazzani, M. 1998. A Principal Components Approach to Combining Regression Estimates. *Machine Learning* 36(1): 932.

Michalski, R. 1983. A Theory and Methodology of Inductive Learning. In *Machine Learning: An Artificial Intelligence Approach*, eds. R. Michalski, J. Carbonell, and T. Mitchell, 83–134. San Francisco, Calif.: Morgan Kaufmann.

Michie, D.; Spiegelhalter, D. J.; and Taylor, C. C. 1994. *Machine Learning, Neural and Statistical Classification*. New York: Ellis Harwood.

Migdalas, A.; Pardalos, P. M.; and Storoy, S. 1997. *Parallel Computing in Optimization*. Dordrecht, The Netherlands: Kluwer Academic.

Miller, R. J., and Guo, Y. K. 1997. Parallelization of AUTOCLASS. Paper presented at the Parallel Computing Workshop, 25–26 September, Canberra, Australia.

Miller, R. J., and Yang, Y. 1997. Association Rules over Interval Data. In Proceedings of the 1997 ACM SIGMOD, 452–461. New York: Association of Computing Machinery.

Milutinovic, V., and Stenstr'om, P., editors. 1999. *IEEE Proceedings* (Special Issue on Distributed Shared Memory Systems) 87(3): 412–507.

Minsky, M. 1991. Logical Versus Analogical or Symbolic versus Connectionist or Neat versus Scruffy. *AI Magazine* 12(2): 34–51.

Minksy, M., and Papert, S. 1969 (1988, exp. ed.). *Perceptrons: An Introduction to Computation Geometry*. Cambridge, Mass.: MIT Press.

Misra, M. 1997. Parallel Environments for Implementing Neural Networks. *Neural Computing Surveys* 1:48–60.

Mitchell, T. M. 1982. Generalization as Search. *Artificial Intelligence* 18(2): 203–226.

Mitchell, T. M. 1997a. Does Machine Learning Really Work? *AI Magazine* 18(3): 11–20.

Mitchell, T. M. 1997b. *Machine Learning*. San Francisco, Calif.: Morgan Kaufmann.

Moga, A. N.; Cramariuc, B.; and Gabbouj, M. 1998. Practical Aspects of Parallel Watershed Transformation Algorithms for Image Segmentation. *Parallel Computing* 24(14): 1981–2001.

Mok K.; Lee, W.; Stolfo, S. 1998. Mining Audit Data to Build Intrusion Models. In Proceedings of the Fourth International Conference on Knowledge Discovery and Data Mining, eds. G. Piatetsky-Shapiro, R. Agrawal, and P. Stolorz, 66–72. Menlo Park, Calif.: American Association for Artificial Intelligence.

Moore, R. W.; Baru, C.; Marciano, R.; Rajasekar, A.; and Wan, M. 1999. Data-Intensive Computing. In *The Grid: Blueprint for a New Computing Infrastructure*, eds. I. Foster and C. Kesselman, 105–129. San Francisco, Calif.: Morgan Kaufmann.

Morgenstern, M. 1988. Controlling Logical Inference in Multilevel Database Systems. In Proceedings of the 1988 IEEE Symposium on Security and Privacy, 245–256. Washington, D.C.: IEEE Computer Society.

Mosteller, F., and Tukey, J. W. 1977. *Data Analysis and Regression*. Reading, Mass.: Addison-Wesley.

Motro, A., and Rakov, I. 1996. Estimating the Quality of Data in Relational Databases. Paper presented at the 1996 Conference on Information Quality, 25–26 October, Cambridge, Massachusetts.

Motro, A., and Rakov, I. 1997. Not All Answers Are Equally Good: Estimating the Quality of Database Answers. In *Flexible Query Answering Systems: Second International Conference, FQAS'97, Proceedings*, eds. H. Christiansen, T. Andreasen, and H. L. Larsen, 1–21. New York: Kluwer Academic.

Motro, A., and Rakov, I. 1998. Estimating the Quality of Databases. In *Flexible Query Answering Systems: Second International Conference, FQAS'97, Proceedings*, eds. H. Christiansen, T. Andreasen, and H. L. Larsen, 298–307. New York: Kluwer Academic.

Mueller, A. 1995. Fast Sequential and Parallel Algorithms for Association Rule Mining: A Comparison. Technical Report, CS-TR-3515, Department of Computer Science, University of Maryland at College Park.

Mukherjee, S. S.; Sharma, S. D.; Hill, M. D.; Larus, J. R.; Rogers, A.; and Saltz, J. 1985. Efficient Support for Irregular Applications on Distributed-Memory Machines. In Proceedings of the ACM SIGPLAN Symposium on Principles and Practice of Parallel Programming, 68–79. New York: Association of Computing Machinery.

Mulcahy, C. 1996. Plotting and Scheming with Wavelets. *Mathematics Magazine* 69(5): 323–343.

Mulcahy, C. 1997. Image Compression Using the Haar Wavelet Transform.*Spelman Science and Mathematics Journal* 1(1): 22–31.

Mulligan, G. D., and Corneil, D. G. 1972. Corrections to Bierstone's Algorithm for Generating Cliques. *Journal of the ACM* 19(2): 244–247.

Musick, R. 1998. Supporting Large-Scale Computational Science. Technical Report UCRL-ID-129903, Center for Applied Scientific Computing, Lawrence Livermore National Laboratory, Livermore, California.

Musick, R.; Catlett, J.; and Russell, S. 1993. Decision-Theoretic Subsampling for Induction on Large Databases. Paper presented at the Tenth International Conference on Machine Learning, 27–29 June, Amherst, Massachusetts.

Myers, R. H. 1986. *Classical and Modern Regression with Applications*. Boston, Mass.: Duxbury.

Narendra, K., and Balakrishnan, J. 1997. Adaptive Control Using Multiple Models. *IEEE Transactions on Automatic Control* 42(2): 171–187.

NASA. 1992. NAS92. Introduction to IND Version 2.1. Technical Report, GA23-2475-02, NASA Ames Research Center, Mountain View, California.

Nichols, B.; Buttlar, D.; and Farrell, J. P. 1996. PTHREADS Programming. O'Reilly and Associates, Sebastopol, California.

Nigram, K.; McCallum, A.; Thrum, S.; and Mitchell, T. 1998. Learning to Classify from La beled and Unlabled Documents. In *Proceedings of the Fifteenth National Conference on Artificial Intelligence (AAAI'98),* 792–799. Menlo Park, Calif.: AAAI Press.

Nii, P. 1986. Blackboard Systems: The Blackboard Model of Problem Solving and the Evolution of Blackboard Architectures. *AI Magazine* 7(2): 38–53.

Nishikawa, H., and Steenkiste, P. 1993. A General Architecture for Load Balancing in a Distributed-Memory Environment. In Proceedings of the Thirteenth IEEE International Conference on Distributed Computing, 47–54. Washington, D.C.: IEEE Computer Society.

Noordewier, M. O.; Towell, G. G.; and Shavlik, J. W. 1991. Training Knowledge-Based Neural Networks to Recognize Genes in DNA Sequences. In *Advances in Neural Information Processing Systems-3*, eds. R. Lippmann, J. Moody, and D. Touretzky, 530–536. San Francisco, Calif.: Morgan Kaufmann.

O'Neil, P., and Quass, D. 1997. Improved Query Performance with Variant Indexes. In Proceedings of the ACM SIGMOD International Conference on Management of Data, 38–49. New York: Association of Computing Machinery.

Oates, T., and Jensen, D. 1997. The Effects of Training Set Size on Decision Tree Complexity. In *Machine Learning: Proceedings of the Fourteenth International Conference*, ed. D. Fisher, 254–262. San Francisco, Calif.: Morgan Kaufmann.

Oates, T., and Jensen, D. 1998. Large Datasets Lead to Overly Complex Models: As Explanation and a Solution. Paper presented at KDD-98, 27–31 August, New York City.

Oates, T.; Schmill, M.; and Cohen, P. 1997. Parallel and Distributed Search for Structure in Multivariate Time Series. In *Proceedings of the Ninth European Conference on Machine Learning*, 191–198. Berlin: Springer-Verlag.

Olson, C. F. 1995. Parallel Algorithms for Hierarchical Clustering. *Parallel Computing* 21(8): 1313–1325.

Opitz, D. W., and Shavlik, J. J. W. 1996. Generating Accurate and Diverse Members of a Neural-Network Ensemble. In *Advances in Neural Information Processing Systems,* 535–541. Cambridge, Mass.: MIT Press.

Ou, C. W., and Ranka, S. 1996. SPRINT: Scalable Partitioning, Refinement, and Incremental Partitioning Techniques. Technical Report, NPAC SCCS-795, Northeast Parallel Architectures Center, Syracuse University.

Ousterhout, J. K. 1990. TCL: An Embeddable Command Language. In Proceedings of the USENIX Association Winter Conference, 133–146. Berkeley, Calif.: USENIX Association.

Ousterhout, J. K. 1993. *An Introduction to* TCL *and* TK. Reading, Mass.: Addison-Wesley.

Ousterhout, J.; Levy, J.; and Welch, B. 1998. The SAFE-TCL Security Model, 217–234. In Mobile Agent Security, 217–234. Lecture Notes in Computer Science 1419. Berlin: Springer-Verlag.

Parikh, S.; Ganesh, M.; and Srivastava, J. 1996. Data Mining for Functional Dependencies. Technical Report, TR 96-033, Department of Computer Science, University of Minnesota.

Park, J. S.; Chen, M. S.; and Yu, P. S. 1995a. An Effective Hash-Based Algorithm for Mining Association Rules. In Proceedings of the ACM SIGMOD, 175–186. New York: Association of Computing Machinery.

Park, J. S.; Chen, M. S.; and Yu, P. S. 1995b. Efficient Parallel Data Mining for Association Rules. Paper presented at International Conference on Information and Knowledge Management (CIKM95), 29 November–2 December, Baltimore, Maryland.

Park, H., Kargupta, H.; Johnson, E.; Sanseverino, R. E.; Silvestre, L. D.; and Hershberger, D. 2000. Distributed, Collaborative Data Analysis from Heterogeneous Sites Using a Scalable Evolutionary Technique. Technical Report, EECS98-001, School of Electrical Engineering and Computer Science, Washington State University.

Parthasarathy, S; Subramonian, R.; and Venkata, R. 1998. Generalized Discretization for Summarization and Classification. In Proceedings of the Second International Conference on Practical

Applications of Knowledge Discovery and Data Mining, 219–239. London: Practical Application Company.

Parthasarathy, S.; Zaki, M. J.; and Li, W. 1998. Memory Placement Techniques for Parallel Association Mining. In Proceedings of the Fourth International Conference on Knowledge Discovery and Data Mining, 304–308. New York: Association of Computing Machinery.

Pei, M.; Goodman, E. D.; and Punch, W. F. 1997. Pattern Discovery from Data Using Genetic Algorithms. Paper presented at the First Pacific Asia Conference on Knowledge Discovery and Data Mining, 23–24 February, Singapore.

Perrone, M. P. 1993. Improving Regression Estimation: Averaging Methods for Variance Reduction with Extensions to General Convex Measure Optimization. Ph.D. dissertation, Department of Computer Science, Brown University.

Perrone, M. P., and Cooper, L. N. 1993. When Networks Disagree: Ensemble Methods for Hydrid Neural Networks. In *Artificial Neural Networks for Speech and Vision*, 126–142. London: Chapman-Hall.

Petrowski, A.; Personnaz, L.; Dreyfus, G.; and Girault, C. 1989. Parallel Implementations of Neural Network Simulations. In Hypercube and Distributed Computers, eds. F. Andre and J. P. Verjus, 205–218. Amsterdam, The Netherlands: North Holland.

Piatetsky-Shapiro, G., and Frawley, W. J. 1991. *Knowledge Discovery in Databases*. Menlo Park, Calif.: AAAI Press.

Pit, L. J. 1995. Parallel Genetic Algorithms, Department of Computer Science, Leiden University.

Pokrajac, T.; Fiez, T.; Obradovic, D.; Kwek, S.; and Obradovic, Z. 1999. Distribution Comparison for Site-Specific Regression Modeling in Agriculture. Paper presented at the 1999 International Joint Conference on Neural Networks, 1016 July, Washington, D.C.

Polychronopoulos, C. D. 1988. *Parallel Programming and Compilers*. New York: Kluwer Academic.

Polychronopoulos, C. D., and Kuck, D. J. 1987. Guided Self-Scheduling: A Practical Scheduling Scheme for Parallel Supercomputers. *IEEE Transactions on Computers* C-36(12): 1425–1439.

Pomerleau, D. 1992. Neural Network Perception for Mobile Robot Guidance. Ph.D. dissertation, Technical Report, CMU-CS-92-115, School of Computer Science, Carnegie Mellon University.

Prechelt, L. 1994. PROBEN1—A Set of Benchmarks and Benchmarking Rules for Neural Network Training Algorithms. Technical Report 21/94, Fakultät für Informatik, Universität Karlsruhe.

Pregibon, D.; Ymour, C.; and Smyth, S. 1997. Statistical Themes and Lessons for Data Mining. In *Data Mining and Knowlege Discovery*, 11–28. New York: Kluwer Academic.

Prodromidis, A. L. 1999. Management of Intelligent Learning Agents in Distributed Data-Mining Systems. Ph.D. dissertation, Department of Computer Science, Columbia University.

Prodromidis, A. L., and Stolfo, S. J. 1998a. Mining Databases with Different Schemas: Integrating Incompatible Classifiers. In Proceedings of the Fourth International Conference on Knowledge Discovery and Data Mining, eds. G. Piatetsky-Shapiro, R. Agrawal, and P. Stolorz, 314–318. Menlo Park, Calif.: American Association for Artificial Intelligence.

Prodromidis, A. L., and Stolfo, S. J. 1998b. Pruning Meta-Classifiers in a Distributed Data-Mining System. Paper presented at the First National Conference on New Information Technologies, 8–10 October, Athens, Greece.

Prodromidis, A. L., and Stolfo, S. J. 1999. Agent-Based Distributed Learning Applied to Fraud Detection. Technical Report CUCS-014-99, Dept. of Computer Science, Columbia Univ., New York, New York.

Prodromidis, A. L.; Stolfo, S. J.; and Chan, P. K. 1999. Effective and Efficient Pruning of Meta-Classifiers in a Distributed Data-Mining System. Technical Report, CUCS-017-99, Department of Computer Science, Columbia University.

Provost, F. 1992. Policies for the Selection of Bias in Inductive Machine Learning. Ph.D. thesis, Department of Computer Science, University of Pittsburgh.

Provost, F., and Aronis, J. 1996. Scaling Up Inductive Learning with Massive Parallelism. *Machine Learning* 23(1): 33–46.

Provost, F., and Buchanan, B. 1995. Inductive Policy: The Pragmatics of Bias Selection. *Machine Learning* 20(1–2): 35–61.

Provost, F., and Fawcett, T. 1997. Analysis and Visualization of Classifier Performance: Comparison under Imprecise Class and Cost Distributions. In *Proceedings of the Third International Conference on Knowledge Discovery and Data Mining,* 43–48. Menlo Park, Calif.: AAAI Press.

Provost, F., and Fawcett, T. 1998. Robust Classification Systems for Imprecise Environments. In Proceedings of the Fifteenth National Conference on Artificial Intelligence, 706–713. Menlo Park, Calif.: American Association for Artificial Intelligence.

Provost, F., and Hennessy, D. 1994. Distributed Machine Learning: Scaling Up with Coarse-Grained Parallelism. in *Proceedings of the Second International Conference on Intelligent Systems for Molecular Biology (ISMB94)*, 340–348. Menlo Park, Calif.: AAAI Press.

Provost, F., and Hennessy, D. 1996. Scaling Up: Distributed Machine Learning with Cooperation. In *Proceedings of the Thirteenth National Conference on Artificial Intelligence,* 74–79. Menlo Park, Calif.: American Association for Artificial Intelligence.

Provost, F., and Kolluri, V. 1997. Scaling Up Inductive Algorithms: An Overview. In *Proceedings of the Third International Conference on Knowledge Discovery and Data Mining,* 239–242. Menlo Park, Calif.: AAAI Press.

Provost, F., and Kolluri, V. 1999. A Survey of Methods for Scaling Up Inductive Algorithms. *Data Mining and Knowledge Discovery: An International Journal* 3(2): 131–169.

Provost, F.; Fawcett, T.; and Kohavi, R. 1998. The Case against Accuracy Estimation for Comparing Induction Algorithms. Paper presented at the Fifteenth International Conference on Machine Learning, 23–27 July, Madison, Wisconsin.

Provost, F.; Jensen, D.; and Oates, T. 1999. Efficient Progressive Sampling. In Proceedings of the SIGKDD Fifth International Conference on Knowledge Discovery and Data Mining, 23–32. Washington, D.C.: IEEE Computer Society.

Punch, W.; Goodman, E. D.; Pei, M.; Lai, C.-S.; Hovland, P.; and Enbody, R. 1993. Further Research on Feature Selection and Classification Using Genetic Algorithms. Paper presented at the International Conference on Genetic Algorithms, 17–21 July, Urbana-Champaign, Illinois.

Quillian, R. 1968. Semantic Memory. In *Semantic Information Processing*, ed. M. Minsky, 216–270. Cambridge, Mass.: MIT Press.

Quinlan, J. R. 1979. Induction over Large Databases. Technical Report, STAN-CS-739, Computer Science Department, Stanford University.

Quinlan, J. R. 1983. Learning Efficient Classification Procedures and Their Application to Chess Endgames. In *Machine Learning: An AI Approach*, eds. R. Michalski, J. Carbonell, and T. Mitchell, 463–482. San Francisco, Calif.: Morgan Kaufmann.

Quinlan, J. R. 1986. Induction of Decision Trees. *Machine Learning* 1(1): 81–106.

Quinlan, J. R. 1987. Generating Production Rules from Decision Trees. In Proceedings of the Tenth International Joint Conference on Artificial Intelligence, 304–307. Menlo Park, Calif.: International Joint Conferences on Artificial Intelligence.

Quinlan, J. R. 1987. Simplifying Decision Trees. *International Journal of Man-Machine Studies* 27(3): 221–234.

Quinlan, J. R. 1993. *C4.5: Programs for Machine Learning.* San Francisco, Calif.: Morgan Kaufman.

Radcliffe, N. J. and Flockhart, I. W. 1996. Scalable Data Mining Systems. Tech. Rep., Quadstone Ltd., Edinburgh Scotland (ftp://ftp.quadstone.co.uk/pub/papers/).

Raftery, A. E.; Madigan, D.; and Hoeting, J. A. 1996. Bayesian Model Averaging for Linear Regression Models. Journal of the American Statistical Association 92(440): 179–191.

Ramamurti, V., and Ghosh, J. 1999. Structurally Adaptive Modular Networks for Non-Stationary Environments. *IEEE Transactions on Neural Networks* 10(1): 152–60.

Ranka, S., and Sahni, S. 1991. Clustering on a Hypercube Multicomputer. *IEEE Transactions on Parallel and Distributed Systems* 2(2): 129–137.

Rao, V., and Kumar, V. 1987. Parallel Depth-First Search, Part 1: Implementation. *International Journal of Parallel Programming* 16(6): 479–499.

Ras, Z. W. 1998. Answering Non-Standard Queries in Distributed Knowledge-Based Systems. In *Rough Sets in Knowledge Discovery, Studies in Fuzziness and Soft Computing, Volume 2*, eds. L. Polkowski and A. Skowron, 98–108. New York: Springer Verlag.

Rastogi, R., and Shim, K. 1998. PUBLIC: A Decision Tree Classifier That Integrates Building and Pruning. Paper presented at the Twenty-Fourth International Conference on Very Large Databases, 24–27 August, New York.

RedBrick. 1998. Star Schema Processing for Complex Queries. White Paper, RedBrick Systems, Inc., Los Gatos, California.

Reddy, M. P., and Wang, R. Y. 1995. Estimating Data Accuracy in a Federated Database Environment. In *Proceedings of the Sixth International Conference on Information Systems and Management of Data (CISMOD'95)*, 115–134. Lecture Notes in Computer Science 1006. New York: Springer.

Redman, T. C. 1996. Dimensions of Data Quality. In *Data Quality for the Information Age*, ed. T. C. Redman, 245–269. Norwood, Mass.: Artech.

Richard, M., and Lippmann, R. 1991. Neural Network Classifiers Estimate Bayesian a posteriori Probabilities. *Neural Computation* 3(4): 461–483.

Rissanen, J. 1989. *Stochastic Complexity in Statistical Inquiry*. River Edge, N.J.: World Scientific.

Rivera, F. F.; Ismail, M. A.; and Zapata, E. L. 1990. Parallel Squared Error Clustering on Hypercube Arrays. *Journal of Parallel and Distributed Computing* 8(3): 292–299.

Rivest, R. 1992. The MD5 Message-Digest Algorithm. RFC 1321, MIT, RSA Data Security, Bedford, Massachusetts.

Rivest, R.; Shamir, A.; and Adleman, L. 1978. A Method for Obtaining Digital Signatures and Public-Key Cryptosystems. *Communications of the ACM* 21(2): 120–126.

Ruck, D. W.; Rogers, S. K.; Kabrisky, M. E.; Oxley, M. E.; and Suter, B. W. 1990. The Multilayer Perceptron as an Approximation to a Bayes Optimal Discriminant Function. *IEEE Transactions on Neural Networks* 1(4): 296–298.

Rumelhart, D. E.; McClelland, J. L.; and the PDP Research Group. *Parallel Distributed Processing: Explorations in the Microstructure of Cognition, Volume 1: Foundations*. Cambridge, Mass.: MIT Press.

Saad, Y. 1992. *Numerical Methods for Large Eigenvalue Problems*. Manchester, U.K.: Manchester University Press.

Salton, G. 1989. *Automatic Text Processing: The Transformation, Analysis, and Retrieval of Information by Computer*. Reading, Mass.: Addison Wesley.

Sander, T., and Tschudin, C. 1998. Toward Mobile Cryptography. In Proceedings of the 1998 IEEE Symposium on Research in Security and Privacy. Washington, D.C.: IEEE Computer Society.

Sandhu, R. S.; Coyne, E. J.; Feinstein, H. L.; and Youman, C. E. 1994. Role-Based Access Control: A Multi-Dimensional View. Paper presented at the Tenth Annual Computer Security Applications Conference, 5–9 December, Orlando, Florida.

Sarawagi, S.; Thomas, S.; and Agrawal, R. 1998. Integrating Association Rule Mining with Relational Database Systems: Alternatives and Implications. In Proceedings of the ACM SIGMOD International Conference on Management of Data, 343–354. New York: Association of Computing Machinery.

Sarhan, A. E., and Greenberg, B. G. 1956. Estimation of Location and Scale Parameters by Order Statistics from Singly and Doubly Censored Samples. *Annals of Mathematical Statistics Science* 27:427–451.

Savasere, A.; Omiecinski, E.; and Navathe, S. 1995. An Efficient Algorithm for Mining Association Rules in Large Databases. In *Proceedings of the Twenty-First International Conference on Very Large Data Bases*, 432–444. San Francisco, Calif.: Morgan Kaufmann.

Schapire, R. 1990. The Strength of Weak Learnability. *Machine Learning* 5(2): 197–226.

Schapire, R.; Freund, Y.; Bartlett, P.; and Lee, S. W. 1997. Boosting the Margin: A New Explanation for the Effectiveness of Voting Methods. In *Proceedings of the Fourteenth International Conference on Machine Learning*, 322–330. San Francisco, Calif.: Morgan Kaufmann.

Schapire, R.; Freund, Y.; Bartlett, P.; and Lee, S. W. 1998. Boosting the Margin: A New Explanation for the Effectiveness of Voting Methods. *The Annals of Statistics* 26(5): 1651–1686.

Segal, R., and Etzioni, O. 1994. Learning Decision Lists Using Homogeneous Rules. In Proceedings of the Twelfth National Conference on Artificial Intelligence, 619–625. Menlo Park, Calif.: American Association for Artificial Intelligence.

Selfridge, O. G. 1958. PANDEMONIUM: A Paradigm for Learning. In *Mechanization of Thought Processes: Proceedings of Symposium Held at the National Physical Lab*, 513–526. London: HMSO.

Selfridge, O. G., and Neisser. U. 1960. Pattern Recognition by Machine. *Scientific American* 203:60–68.

Sen, S. 1997. Multiagent Systems: Milestones and New Horizons. *Trends in Cognitive Science* 1(9): 334–339.

Shafer, J. C., and Agrawal, R. 1997. Parallel Algorithms for High-Dimensional Proximity Joins. Paper presented at the 1997 Very Large Databases Conference (VLDB97), 25–29 August, Athens, Greece.

Shafer, J. C.; Agrawal, R.; and Mehta, M. 1996. SPRINT: A Scalable Parallel Classifier for Data Mining. In *Proceedings of the Twenty-Second International Conference on Very Large Data Bases*, 544–555. San Francisco, Calif.: Morgan Kaufmann.

Shankar, R. V., and Ranka, S. 1997. Random Data Accesses on a Coarse-Grained Parallel Machine. II. One-to-Many and Many-to-One Mappings. *Journal of Parallel and Distributed Computing* 44(1): 24–34.

Sharkey, A. 1996. On Combining Artificial Neural Nets. *Connection Science* (Special Issue on Combining Artificial Neural Networks: Ensemble Approaches) 8(3–4): 299–314.

Sharkey, A. 1998. *Combining Artificial Neural Nets*. Berlin: Springer-Verlag.

Shepherd, G. 1979. *The Synaptic Organization of the Brain*. 2d ed. Oxford, U.K.: Oxford University Press.

Shintani, T., and Kitsuregawa, M. 1995. Hash-Based Parallel Algorithms for Mining Association Rules. Paper presented at the Conference on Information and Knowledge Management, 29 November–2 December, Baltimore, Maryland.

Shintani, T., and Kitsuregawa, M. 1996. Hash-Based Parallel Algorithms for Mining Association Rules. Paper presented at the Fourth International Conference on Parallel and Distributed Information Systems, 18–20 December, Miami, Florida.

Shintani, T., and Kitsuregawa, M. 1998a. Mining Algorithms for Sequential Patterns in Parallel: Hash-Based Approach. Paper presented at the Pacific Asia Conference on Knowledge Discovery and Data Mining, 15–17 April, Melbourne, Australia.

Shintani, T., and Kitsuregawa, M. 1998b. Parallel Mining Algorithms for Generalized Association Rules with Classification Hierarchy. In Proceedings of the ACM SIGMOD. New York: Association of Computing Machinery.

Sikora, R., and Shaw, M. J. 1996. A Computational Study of Distributed Rule Learning. *Information Systems Research* 7(2): 189–197.

Singh, L.; Scheuermann, P.; and Chen, B. 1997. Generating Association Rules from Semi-Structured Documents Using an Extended Concept Hierarchy. In *Proceedings of the International Conference on Information and Knowledge Management (CIKM'97)*, 193–200. New York: Association of Computing Machinery.

Smith, S. F. 1980. A Learning System Based on Genetic Adaptive Algorithms. Technical Report, 8112638, Department of Computer Science, University of Pittsburgh.

Smyth, P., and Goodman, R. 1992. An Information-Theoretic Approach to Rule Induction from Databases. *IEEE Transactions on Knowledge and Data Engineering* 4(4): 301–316.

Smyth, P.; Ghil, M.; Ide, K.; and Fraser, A. 1997. Detecting Atmospheric Regions Using Cross-Validated Clustering. In Proceedings of the Third International Conference on Knowledge Discovery and Data Mining, 61–66. Menlo Park, Calif.: American Association for Artificial Intelligence.

Sollich, P., and Krogh, A. 1996. Learning with Ensembles: How Over-Fitting Can Be Useful. In *Advances in Neural Information Processing Systems, Volume 8*, eds. D. Touretzky; M. Mozer; and M. Hasselmo, 190–196. Cambridge, Mass.: MIT Press.

Spertus, E. 1997. PARASITE: Mining Structural Information on the Web. Paper presented at the International World Wide Web Conference, 7–11 April, Santa Clara, California.

Sreenivas, M. K. 1998. Parallel Out-of-Core Decision Tree Classifiers. Master's thesis, Department of Computer and Information Sciences, University of Florida.

Sreenivas, M. K.; Alsabti, K.; and Ranka, S. 1999. Parallel Out-of-Core Divide and Conquer Techniques with Application to Classification Trees. Paper presented at the Thirteenth International Parallel Processing Symposium.

Srikant, R., and Agrawal, R. 1995. Mining Generalized Association Rules. Paper presented at the 1995 Very Large Databases Conference (VLDB95), 11–15 September, Zurich, Switzerland.

Srikant, R., and Agrawal, R. 1996. Mining Quantitative Association Rules in Large Relational Tables. In Proceedings of the 1996 ACM-SIGMOD, 1–12. New York: Association of Computing Machinery.

Srikant, R.; Vu, Q.; and Agrawal, R. 1997. Mining Association Rules with Item Constraints. In *Proceedings of the Third International Conference on Knowledge Discovery and Data Mining*, 67–73. Menlo Park, Calif.: AAAI Press.

Srivastava, A. and Singh, V. and Han, E. H. and Kumar, V. 1997. An Efficient, Scalable, Parallel Classifier for Data Mining. Tech. Report., Dept. of Computer Science, University of Minnesota, Minneapolis, Minnesota (ftp://ftp.cs.umn.edu/dept/users/kumar/class-paper.ps)

Srivastava, A.; Han, E. H.; Kumar, V.; and Singh, V. 1998. Parallel Formulations of Decision-Tree Classification Algorithms. Paper presented at the International Conference on Parallel Processing, 10–15 August, Minneapolis, Minnesota.

Srivastava, A.; Han, E. H.; Kumar, V.; and Singh, V. 1999. Parallel Formulations of Decision-Tree Classification Algorithms. *Data Mining and Knowledge Discovery: An International Journal* 3(3): 237–261.

Stanfill, C., and Waltz, D. 1986. Toward Memory-Based Reasoning. *Communications of the ACM* 29(12): 1213–1228.

Starck, J. L.; Murtagh, F.; and Bijaoui, A. 1998. *Image Processing and Data Analysis: The Multiscale Approach.* Cambridge, U.K.: Cambridge University Press.

Steinberg, I., and Solomon, M. 1990. Searching Game Trees in Parallel. Paper presented at the International Conference on Parallel Processing, August, St. Charles, Illinois.

Steiner, J.; Neuman, C.; and Schiller, J. 1988. KERBEROS: An Authentication Service for Open Network Systems. In the Proceedings of the USENIX Conference Proceedings, 191–202. Berkeley, Calif.: USENIX Association.

Stolfo, S.; Fan, D.; Lee, W.; Prodromidis, A.; and Chan, P. 1997. Credit Card Fraud Detection Using Meta-Learning: Issues and Initial Results. In Proceedings of the AAAI-97 Workshop on AI Approaches to Fraud Detection and Risk Management, 83–90. AAAI Technical Report WS-97-07. Menlo Park, Calif.: AAAI Press.

Stolfo, S.; Prodromidis, A. L. ; Tselepis, S.; Lee, W.; Fan, D.; and Chan, P. K. 1997. JAM: JAVA Agents for Meta-Learning over Distributed Databases. In *Proceedings of the Third International Conference on Knowledge Discovery and Data Mining,* eds D. Heckerman, H. Mannila, D. Pregibon, and R. Uthurusamy, 74–81. Menlo Park, Calif.: AAAI Press.

Stollnitz, E.; DeRose, T. D.; and Salesin, D. H. 1995a. Wavelets for Computer Graphics: A Primer, Part 1. *IEEE Computer Graphics and Applications* 5(3): 76–84.

Stollnitz, E.; DeRose, T. D.; and Salesin, D. H. 1995b. Wavelets for Computer Graphics: A Primer, Part 2. *IEEE Computer Graphics and Applications* 5(4): 75–85.

Stollnitz, E. J.; Derose, T. D.; and Salesin, D. H. 1996. *Wavelets for Computer Graphics: Theory and Applications.* San Francisco, Calif.: Morgan Kaufmann.

Storey, V. C.; Wang, R. Y.; and Firth, C. P. 1995. A Framework for Analysis of Data Quality Research. *IEEE Transactions on Knowledge and Data Engineering* 7(4): 623–640.

Strong, D. M.; Lee, Y. W.; and Wang, R. W. 1997a. Data Quality in Context. *Communications of the ACM* 40(5): 103–110.

Strong, D. M.; Lee, Y. W.; and Wang, R. W. 1997b. Ten Potholes in the Road to Information Quality. *Computer* 30(8): 38–46.

Su, T. A., and Ozsoyoglu, G. 1991. Controlling FD and MVD Inferences in Multilevel Relational Database Systems. *IEEE Transactions on Knowledge and Data Engineering* 3(4): 474–485.

Subramonian, R. 1998. Defining *diff* as a Data-Mining Primitive. In Proceedings of the Fourth International Conference on Knowledge Discovery and Data Mining. Menlo Park, Calif.: American Association for Artificial Intelligence.

Subramonian, R.; Venkata, R.; and Chen, J. 1997. A Visual Interactive Framework for Attribute Discretization. In Proceedings of the Third International Conference on Knowledge Discovery and Data Mining, 82–88. Menlo Park, Calif.: American Association for Artificial Intelligence.

Sullivan, S. 1991. Vector and Parallel Implementations of the Wavelet Transform. Technical Report, CSRD-1093, Center for Supercomputing Research and Development, University of Illinois.

Sundararajan, N., and Saratchandran, P. 1998. *Parallel Architectures for Artificial Neural Networks: Paradigms and Implementations.* Los Alamitos, Calif.: IEEE Computer Society Press.

Sutiwaraphun, J. 1998. Investigating into Distributed Data Mining. Technical Report, TR-DMG-98-05, Department of Computing, Imperial College.

Taha, I., and Ghosh, J. 1997. Hybrid Intelligent Architecture and Its Application to Water Reservoir Control. *International Journal of Smart Engineering Systems* 1(1): 59–75.

Tang, P., and Yew, P.-C. 1986. Processor Self-Scheduling for Multiple Nested Parallel Loops. Paper presented at the International Conference on Parallel Processing.

Thirunavukkarasu, C.; Finin, T.; and Mayfield, J. 1995. Secret Agents–A Security Architecture for the KQML Agent Communication Language. Paper presented at the Intelligent Information Agents Workshop at the Fourth International Conference on Information and Knowledge Management (CIKM'95), 29 November–2 December, Baltimore, Maryland.

Ting, K. M., and Low, B. T. 1997. Model Combination in the Multiple-Data-Base Scenario. In *Machine Learning: ECML-97*, eds. M. van Someren and G. Widmer, 250–265. Lecture Notes in Computer Science 1224. Berlin: Springer-Verlag.

Toivonen, H. 1996. Sampling Large Databases for Association Rules. In *Proceedings of the Twenty-Second International Conference on Very Large Data Bases*, 134–145. San Francisco, Calif.: Morgan Kaufmann.

Tresp, V., and Taniguchi, M. 1995. Combining Estimators Using Non-Constant Weighting Functions. Paper presented at the Conference on Advances in Neural Information Processing Systems 7, 28 November–1 December, Denver, Colorado.

Tumer, K., and Ghosh, J. 1996a. Analysis of Decision Boundaries in Linearly Combined Neural Classifiers. *Pattern Recognition* 29(2): 341–348.

Tumer, K., and Ghosh, J. 1996b. Error Correlation and Error Reduction in Ensemble Classifiers. *Connection Science* Special Issue on Combining Artificial Neural Networks: Ensemble Approaches, 8(3–4): 385–404.

Tumer, K., and Ghosh, J. 1999. Linear and Order Statistics Combiners for Pattern Classification. In *Combining Artificial Neural Nets: Ensemble and Modular Multi-Net Systems*, ed. A. J. C. Sharkey, 127–162. London: Springer-Verlag.

Uhl, A. 1996. Wavelets: Adaptive and Parallel Methods in Image Coding and Signal Processing. Technical Report, University of Salzburg.

Uhr, L. 1987. *Multi-Computer Architecture for Artificial Intelligence: Toward Fast, Robust, Parallel Systems*. New York: Wiley.

Ullman, J. D. 1989. *Principles of Database and Knowledge-Base Systems, Volumes 1 and 2*. New York: Computer Science Press.

Utgoff, P. 1988. ID5: An Incremental ID3. In *Proceedings of the Fifth International Conference on Machine Learning*, 107–120. San Francisco, Calif.: Morgan Kaufmann.

Utgoff, P. 1989. Incremental Induction of Decision Trees. *Machine Learning* 4(1): 161–186.

Utgoff, P. 1994. An Improved Algorithm for Incremental Induction of Decision Trees. In *Proceedings of the Eleventh International Conference on Machine Learning*, 318–325. San Francisco, Calif.: Morgan Kaufmann.

Vafaie, H., and De Jong, K. 1998. Feature Space Tranformation Using Genetic Algorithms. *IEEE Expert* 13(2).

Valiant, L. G. 1984. A Theory of the Learnable. *Communications of the ACM* 27(11): 1134–1142.

Vigna, G. 1998. Cryptographic Traces for Mobile Agents. In *Mobile Agents and Security*, ed. G. Vigna, 137-153. Lecture Notes in Computer Science 1419. New York: Springer Verlag.

Vitek, J.; Serrano, M.; and Thanos, D. 1997. Security and Communication in Mobile Object Systems. In *Mobile Object Systems: Toward the Programmable Internet*, 177–199. Berlin: Springer-Verlag.

Vitter, J. S. 1998. External Memory Algorithms. Paper presented at the Seventeenth Annual ACM Symposium on Principles of Database Systems (PODS'98), 1–3 June, Seattle, Washington.

Volpano, D., and Smith, G. 1998. Language Issues in Mobile Program Security. In *Mobile Agents and Security*, ed. G. Vigna, 25–43. Lecture Notes in Computer Science 1419. New York: Springer Verlag.

Wang, R. Y.; Kon, H. B.; and Madnick, S. E. 1993. Data Quality Requirements Analysis and Modeling. In *Proceedings of the Ninth International Conference on Data Engineering*, 670–677. Washington, D.C.: IEEE Computer Society.

Wang, R. Y.; Reddy, M. P.; and Kon, H. B. 1995. Toward Quality Data: An Attribute-Based Approach. *Decision Support Systems* 13(3–4): 349–372.

Wang, W.; Yang, J.; and Muntz, R. 1997. STING: A Statistical Information Grid Approach to Spatial Data Mining. Paper presented at the 1997 Very Large Databases Conference (VLDB97), 25–29 August, Athens, Greece.

Way, J., and Smith, E. A. 1991. The Evolution of Synthetic Aperture Radar Systems and Their Progression to the eos sar. *IEEE Transactions on Geoscience and Remote Sensing* 29(6): 962–985.

Webb, G. 1995. OPUS: An Efficient Admissible Algorithm for Unordered Search. *Journal of Artificial Intelligence Research* 3: 383–417.

Weiss, S. M., and Kulikowski, C. A. 1991. *Computer Systems that Learn: Classification and Prediction Methods from Statistics, Neural Nets, Machine Learning, and Expert Systems*. San Francisco, Calif.: Morgan Kaufmann.

Whitley, D. 1995. Genetic Algorithms and Neural Networks. In *Genetic Algorithms in Engineering and Computer Science*, eds. G. Winter, J. Periaux, M. Galan, and P. Cuesta, 203–216. New York: Wiley.

Wickerhauser, M. V. 1994. *Adapted Wavelet Analysis from Theory to Software*. Natick, Mass.: A. K. Peters.

Williams, G. 1990. Inducing and Combining Multiple Decision Trees. Ph.D. thesis, Australian National University, Canberra, Australia.

Wirth, J., and Catlett, J. 1988. Experiments on the Costs and Benefits of Windowing in ID3. Paper presented at the Fifth International Conference on Machine Learning, 12–14 June, Ann Arbor, Michigan.

Wolfe, M. 1996. *High-Performance Compilers for Parallel Computing*. Reading, Mass.: Addison Wesley.

Wolpert, D. H. 1992. Stacked Generalization. *Neural Networks* 5(2): 241–259.

Wolpert, D., and Tumer, K. 2001. A Survey of Collective Intelligence. In *Handbook of Agent Technology*, ed. J. M. Bradshaw. Menlo Park, Calif.: AAAI Press. Forthcoming.

Wu, X., and Lo, W. H. 1998. Multi-Layer Incremental Induction. In *Proceedings of the Fifth Pacific Rim International Conference on Artificial Intelligence*, 24–32. Berlin: Springer-Verlag.

Wüthrich, B. 1995. Probabilistic Knowledge Bases. *IEEE Transactions on Knowledge and Data Engineering* 7(5): 691–698.

Wüthrich, B. 1997. Discovering Probabilistic Decision Rules. *International Journal of Intelligent Systems in Accounting, Finance, and Management* 6:269–277.

Wüthrich, B.; Leung, S.; Peramunetilleke, D.; Cho, V.; et al. 1998. Automatic Stock Market Predictions from World Wide Web Data. In Proceedings of the International Conference on Knowledge Discovery and Data Mining, 269–274. Menlo Park, Calif.: American Association for Artificial Intelligence.

Xu, L., and Jordan, M. I. EM Learning on A Generalized Finite Mixture Model for Combining Multiple Classifiers. In *Proceedings of the World Congress on Neural Networks*, PP–PP. Hillsdale, N.J.: Lawrence Erlbaum.

Yamanishi, K. 1997. Distributed Cooperative Bayesian Learning Strategies. In Proceedings of the Tenth Annual Conference on Computational Learning Theory, 250–262. New York: Association of Computing Machinery.

Yang, L., and Misra, M. 1998. Coarse-Grained Parallel Algorithms for Multi-Dimensional Wavelet Transforms. *The Journal of Supercomputing* 12(1–2): 99–118.

Yao, J., and Liu, H. 1997. Searching Multiple Databases for Interesting Complexes. In *Proceedings of the First Pacific-Asia Conference on Knowledge Discovery and Data Mining (PAKDD'97)*, 198–210. River Edge, N.J.: World Scientific.

Yen, S.-J., and Chen, A. L. P. 1996. An Efficient Approach to Discovering Knowledge from Large Databases. Paper presented at the Fouth International Conference on Parallel and Distributed Information Systems, 18–20 December, Miami, Florida.

Zaki, M. 1998a. Scalable Data Mining for Rules. Ph.D. dissertation, Department of Computer Science, University of Rochester.

Zaki, M. J. 1998b. Efficient Enumeration of Frequent Sequences. Paper presented at the Seventh International Conference on Information and Knowledge Management (CIKM), 3–7 November, Bethesda, Maryland.

Zaki, M. J., and Ogihara, M. 1998. Theoretical Foundations of Association Rules. In Proceedings of the Third ACM SIGMOD Workshop on Research Issues in Data Mining and Knowledge Discovery, 7:1–7:8. New York: Association of Computing Machinery.

Zaki, M. J.; Ho, C. T.; and Agrawal, R. 1998a. Parallel Classification on SMP Systems. Paper presented at the First Workshop on High-Performance Data Mining, 31 March, Orlando, Florida.

Zaki, M. J.; Ho, C. T.; and Agrawal, R. 1998b. Memory Placement Techniques for Parallel Association Mining. Paper presented at the KDD98 Conference, XX–XX MONTH, New York.

Zaki, M. J.; Ho, C.-T.; and Agrawal, R. 1999a. Parallel Classification for Data Mining on Shared-Memory Multiprocessors. Paper presented at the Fifteenth International Conference on Data Engineering, 23–26 March, Sydney, Australia.

Zaki, M. J.; Ho, C. T.; and Agrawal, R. 1999b. Scalable Parallel Classification for Data Mining on Shared-Memory Multiprocessors. In Proceedings of the IEEE International Conference on Data Engineering, 198–205. Washington, D.C.: IEEE Computer Society.

Zaki, M. J.; Ogihara, M.; Parthasarathy, S.; and Li, W. 1996. Parallel Data Mining for Association Rules on Shared-Memory Multi-Processors. Paper presented at Supercomputing '96, 17–22 November, Pittsburgh, Pennsylvania.

Zaki, M. J.; Parthasarathy, S.; and Li, W. 1997. A Localized Algorithm for Parallel Association Mining. In Proceedings of the Ninth ACM Symposium on Parallel Algorithms and Architectures, 321–330. New York: Association of Computing Machinery.

Zaki, M. J.; Parthasarathy, S.; Li, W.; and Ogihara, M. 1997. Evaluation of Sampling for Data Mining of Association Rules. In Proceedings of the Seventh International Workshop on Research Issues in Data Engineering, 42–50. Washington, D.C.: IEEE Computer Society.

Zaki, M. J.; Parthasarathy, S.; Ogihara, M.; and Li, W. 1997a. New Parallel Algorithms for Fast Discovery of Association Rules. In *Proceedings of the Third International Conference on Knowledge Discovery and Data Mining,* 283–286. Menlo Park, Calif.: AAAI Press.

Zaki, M. J.; Parthasarathy, S.; Ogihara, M.; and Li, W. 1997b. New Algorithms for Fast Discovery of Association Rules. Technical Report, URCS TR 651, Department of Computer Science, University of Rochester.

Zaki, M. J.; Parthasarathy, S.; Ogihara, M.; and Li, W. 1997c. Parallel Algorithms for Fast Discovery of Association Rules. *Data Mining and Knowledge Discovery: An International Journal* 1(4): 343–373.

Zaki, M. J.; Parthasarathy, S.; Ogihara, M.; and Li, Wei. 1998. Parallel Algorithms for Discovery of Association Rules. In *Scalable High-Performance Computing for Data Mining and Knowledge Discovery*, eds. P. Stolorz and R. Musick, 5–37. New York: Kluwer Academic.

Zaki, M., and Ho, C.-T. 2000. *Large-Scale Parallel Data Mining*. Berlin: Springer-Verlag.

Zhang, T.; Ramakrishnan, R.; and Livny, M. BIRCH: An Efficient Data-Clustering Method for Very Large Databases. In Proceedings of the 1996 ACM-SIGMOD, 103–114. New York: Association of Computing Machinery.

Zomaya, A. Y., and Olaiu, S. 1997. Introduction. *Journal of Parallel and Distributed Computing* (Special Issue on Parallel Evolutionary Computing) 47(1): 1-7.

Index